A PHOTOGRAPHIC HISTORY OF

THE ROLLING STONES

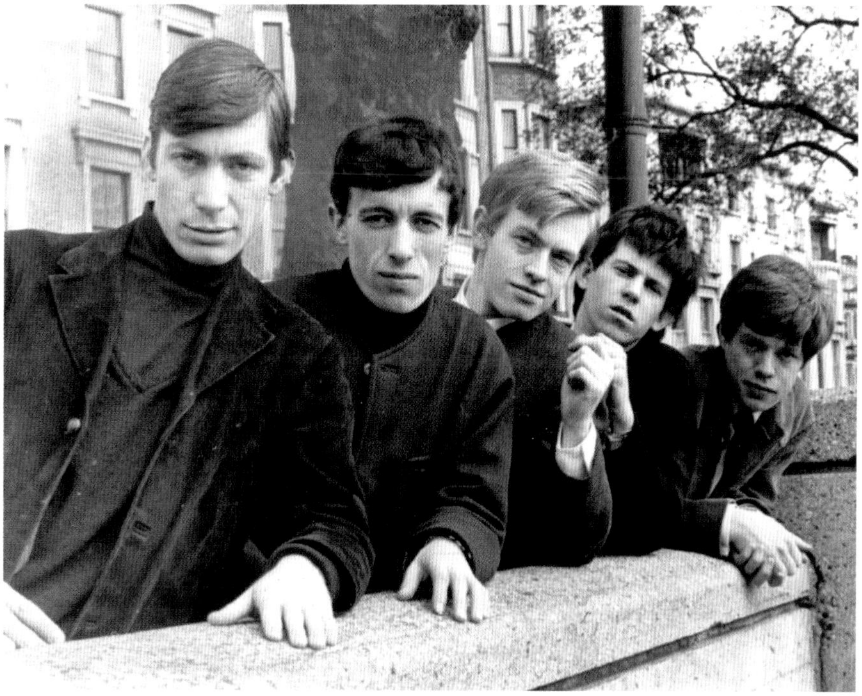

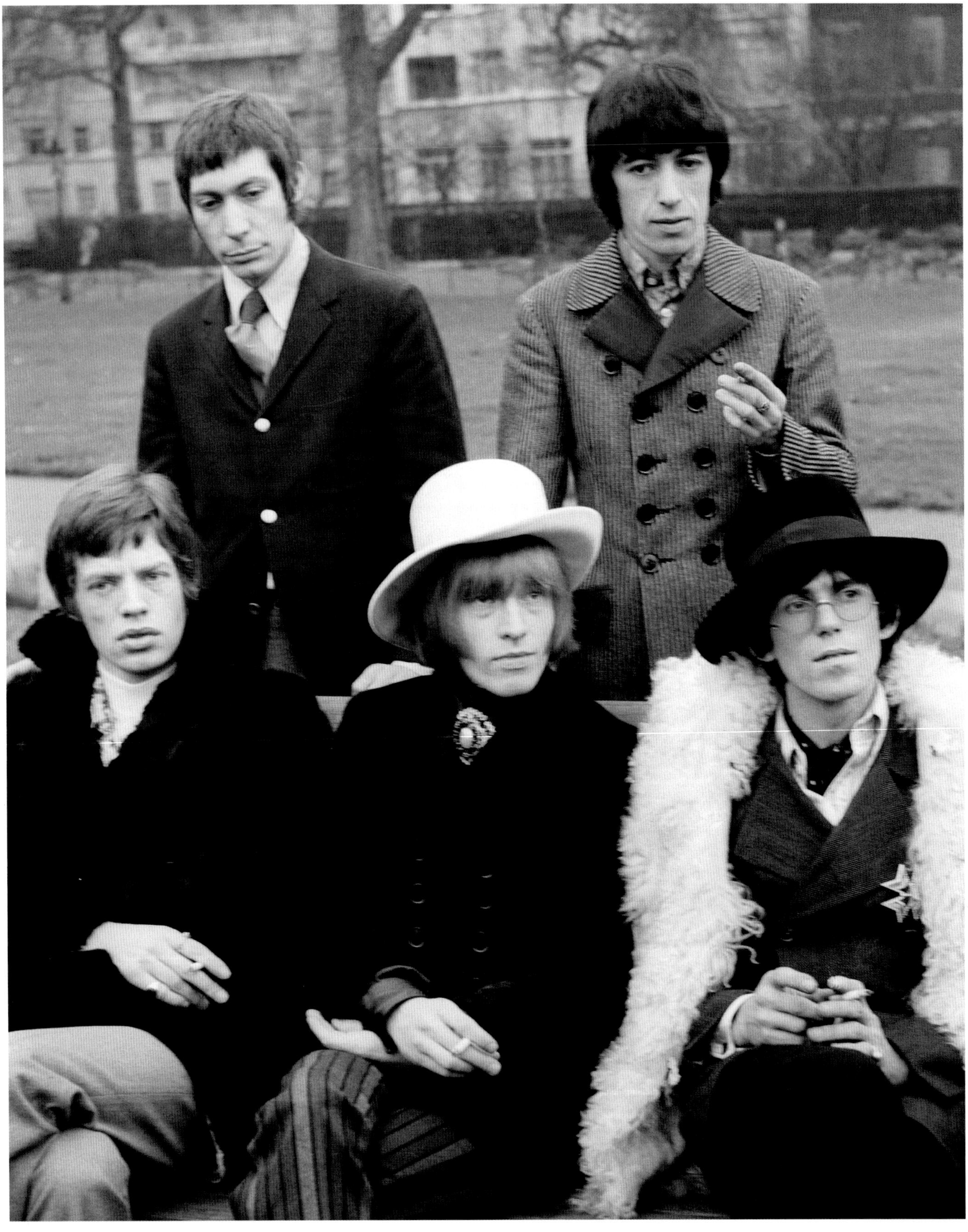

A PHOTOGRAPHIC HISTORY OF

THE ROLLING STONES

Susan Hill

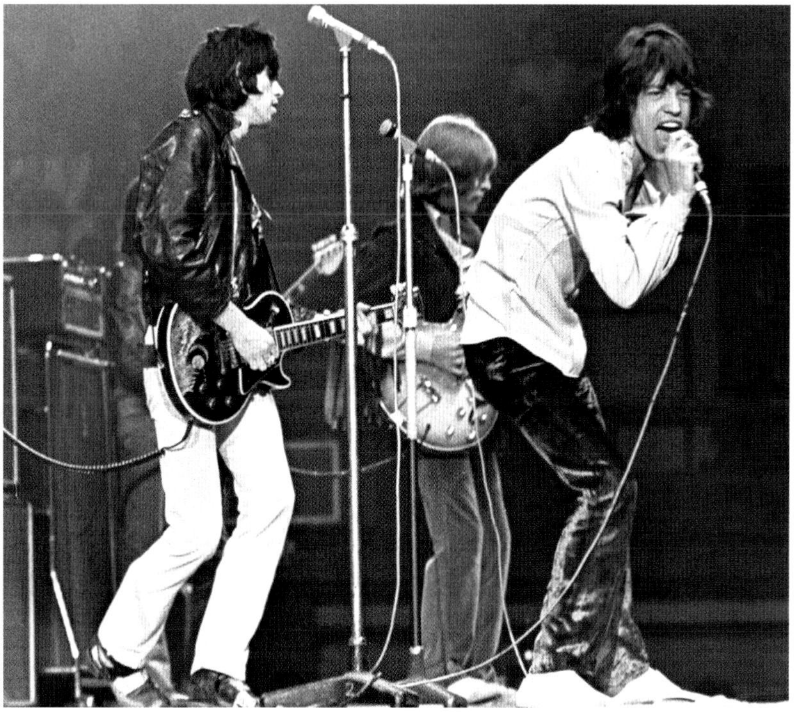

Parragon

Bath • New York • Singapore • Hong Kong • Cologne • Delhi
Melbourne • Amsterdam • Johannesburg • Shenzhen

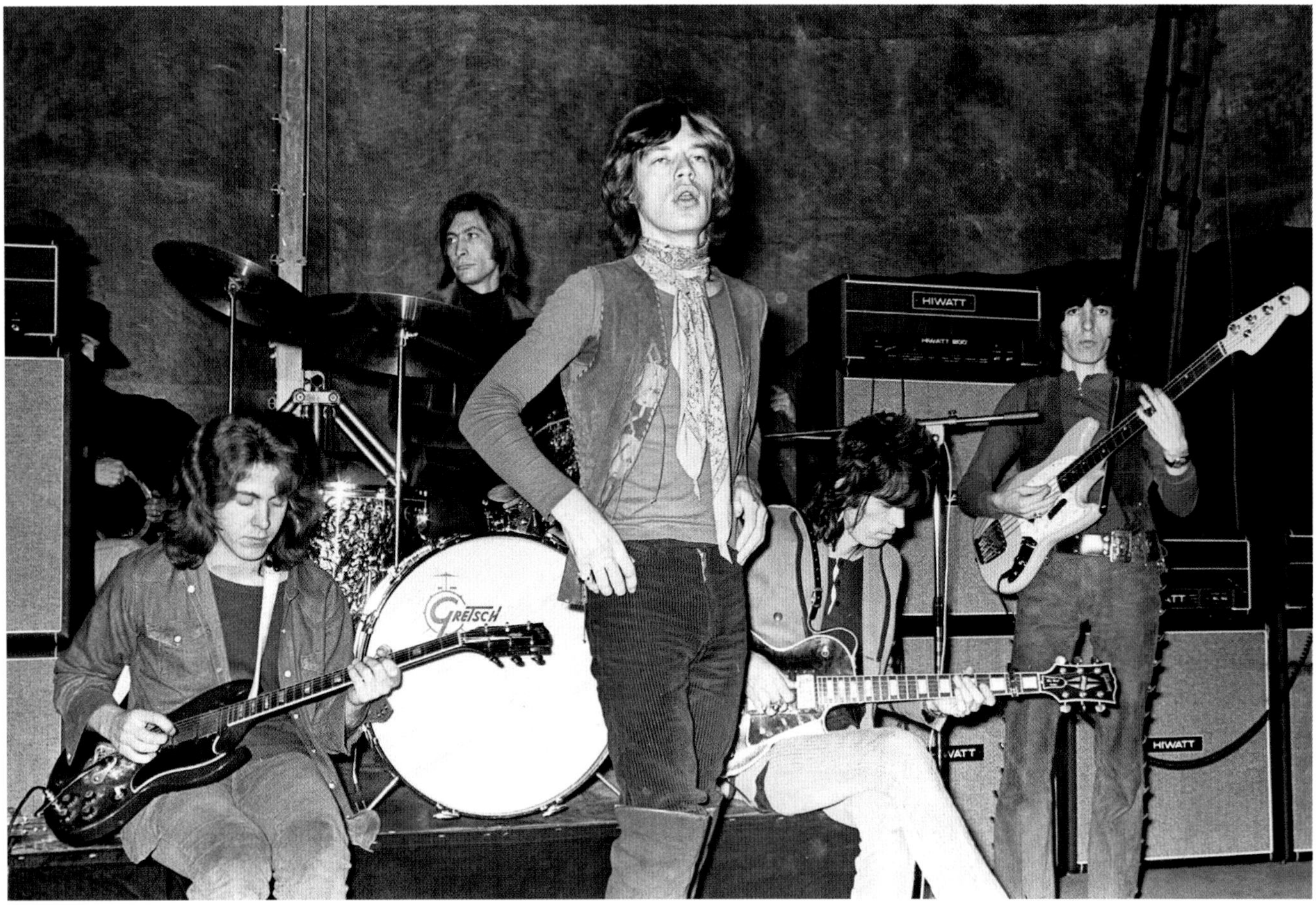

This edition published by Parragon in 2012

Parragon
Queen Street House
4 Queen Street
Bath BA1 1HE, UK
www.parragon.com

Produced by Atlantic Publishing

A catalogue record for this book is available from the British Library.

ISBN: 978–1–4454–9330–5

Printed in China

Contents

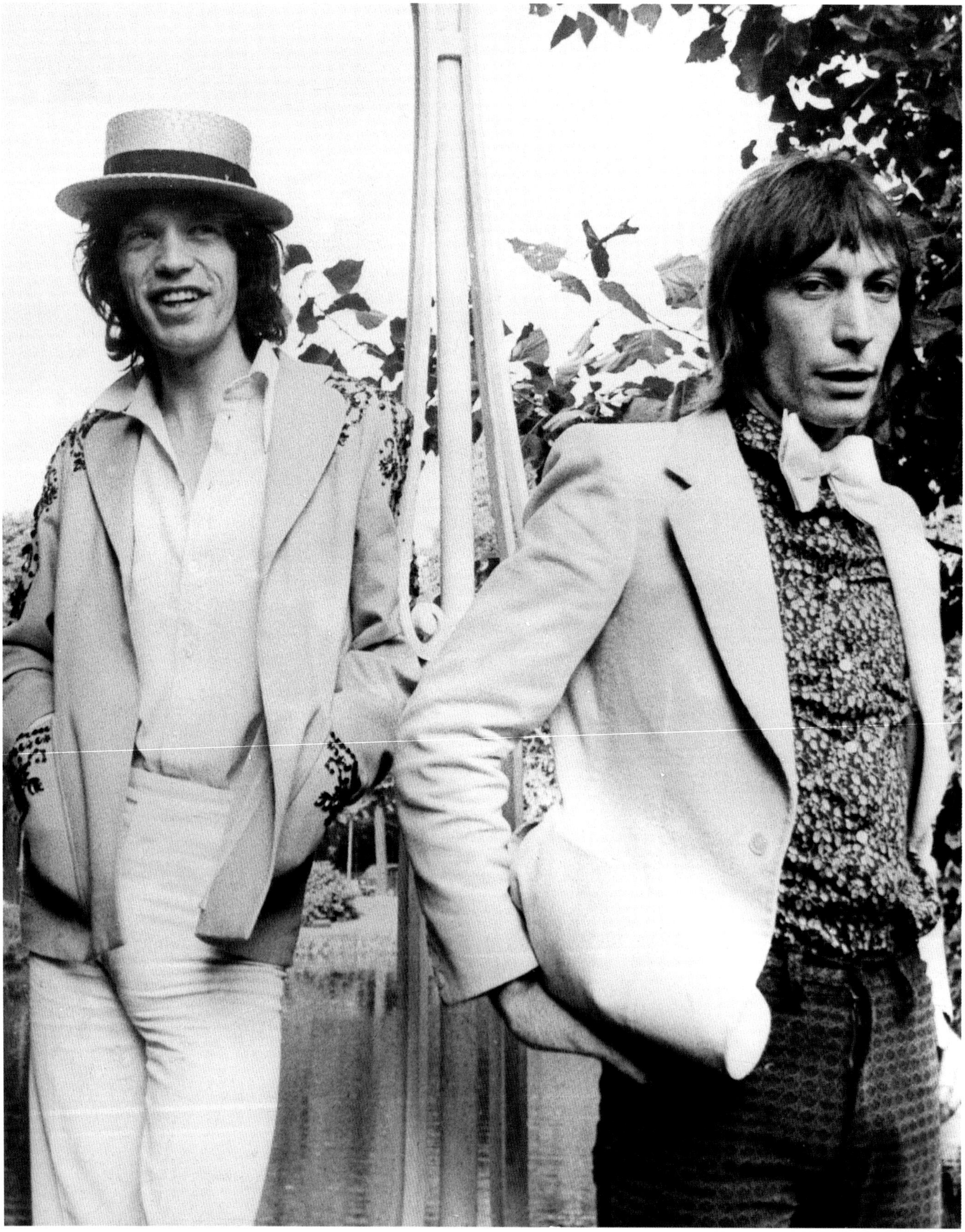

Introduction

Almost 50 years after they first strutted and glowered centre stage, The Rolling Stones still embody all that is bad, dirty, angry and sexy about rock 'n' roll. Some, whose reverence for jazz or blues musicians increases as the artist ages, still cling to the idea that it is undignified for rockers to keep on roaring. Yet the pulling power of The Rolling Stones continues to confound. Their audiences – by no means restricted to those who grew up with them – know how dangerously exciting a Stones concert can still be.

In the early 1960s the Stones seemed to stalk The Beatles, out-rousing the fans and out-shocking the parents. Just as there were Mods and Rockers, so there was often a divide between Beatles fans and Stones fans – before they realized it was possible to be both. But for a while The Rolling Stones made The Beatles seem tidy and safe. 'Let It Be', sang The Beatles sweetly. 'Let It Bleed', was the Stones' reply. Raw and bruised energy was ever their style.

To have survived, let alone triumphed, for so long in a notoriously fickle industry speaks of art, guile, musicianship and planning, as well as skill at expressing and rousing primal instincts. And the right looks, of course. Mick's sulky look redefined male beauty. The tragically doomed, blond Brian was always a fallen angel. Skeletal Keith with his black leather just looked so dirty, and Bill and Charlie so moody and cool. Later Mick Taylor and Ronnie Wood became Rolling Stones, and they helped the band grow old disgracefully and remain legendarily subversive.

This book charts the amazing career of The Rolling Stones, through a series of revealing photographs drawn from the *Daily Mail*'s comprehensive archive. The pictures are accompanied by perceptive captions which add context and depth to give a rounded and comprehensive portrait of the greatest rock 'n' roll band in the world.

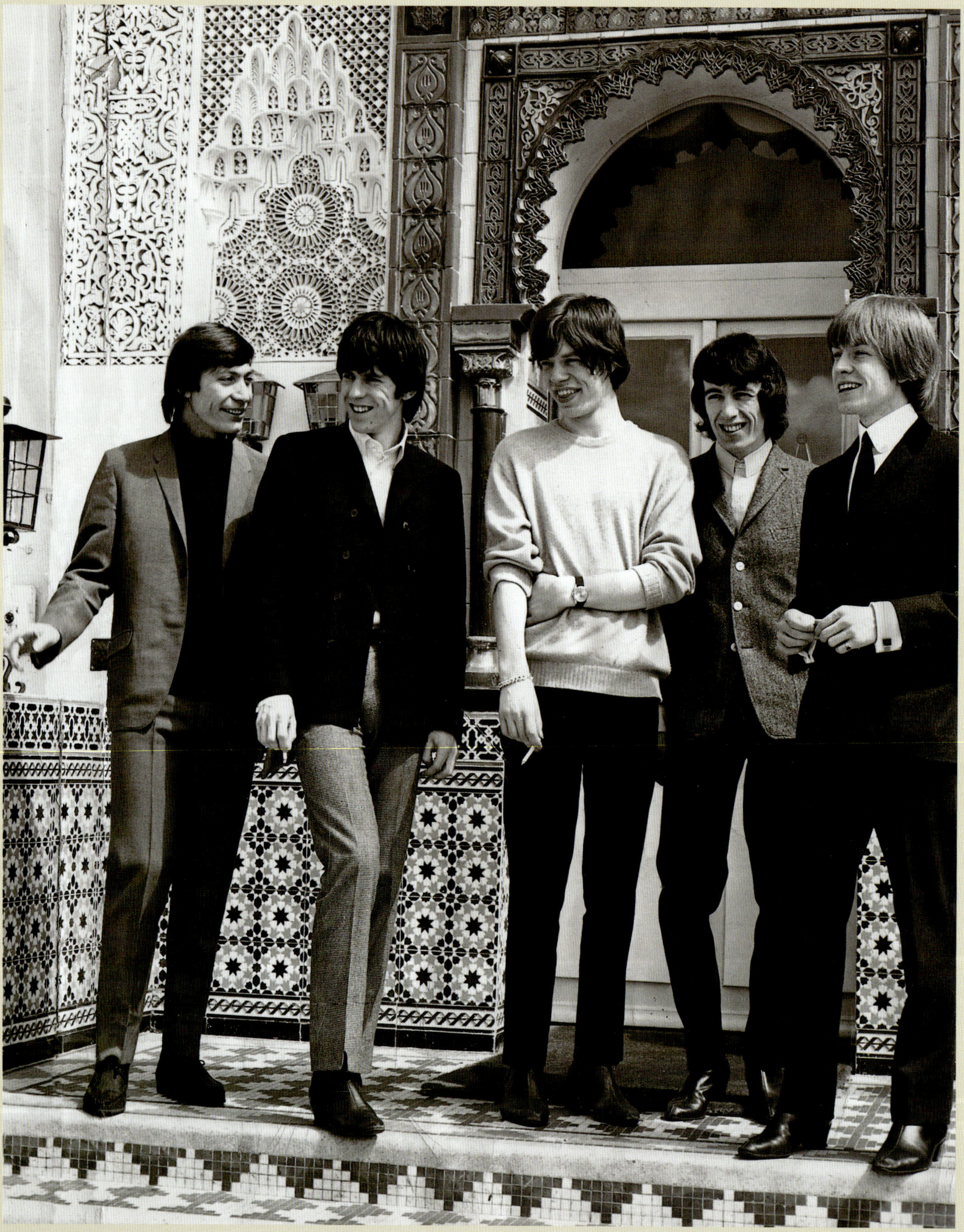

CHAPTER ONE

Come On

Rock 'n' roll came to Britain in the early 1960s, brought by merchant seamen from America, and the end of National Service led to a first glimmering of youth culture. However, youthful virtue was still widely perceived in a 'short-back-and-sides' and obedient order. Public houses had opening hours imposed during World War I and almost the only outlets for teenagers' energies were youth clubs – often Church run – or school hall hops. Elvis Presley was popular, perhaps because he had entered his post-GI ballad phase. But a few years earlier his music had been raunchy and had filtered across the country from the Soho coffee bars where British beatniks hung out and from whence the careers of Brit rock 'n' rollers such as Tommy Steele and Billy Fury had been launched.

Across this canvas five young men who became The Rolling Stones were inspired to make their mark. After the 1963 Liverpool beat explosion, from The Beatles and other groups in Brian Epstein's care, pop pundits attempted to generate a north/south pop war by declaring Dave Clark Five's 'London Sound' the new big thing. If there *was* a London Sound it was the blues and R & B-influenced music that flourished in small clubs south of the Thames – particularly near art schools. These were popular with many teenagers in further education; they often had a relaxed atmosphere and were great places to tune into music that was somehow more intelligent than pure pop. Students would carry imported blues albums almost as a fashion item, like expensively imported American denims. That's how Mick Jagger and Keith Richards, both still living with their parents, met early in 1962. An album sleeve was spotted during a train journey, as Keith headed towards art school and Mick to the London School of Economics, and cultural history was made. From that moment they became the two enduring constants of The Rolling Stones. In fact, the two had overlapped at Wentworth County Primary School but barely noticed each other. Mick was born in Dartford, Kent, into middle-class respectability on 26 July 1943. Keith, born nearby on 18 December 1943, came from a more working-class background. The two found they had a mutual friend in Dick Taylor, with whom Mick played in a group called Little Boy Blue And The Blue Boys. Keith also joined the band.

Brian Lewis Jones was born on 28 February 1941 and raised in the gracious spa town of Cheltenham, Gloucestershire. By the time he left school, aged 17, he had already fathered two children. He was also so widely proficient an instrumentalist in a local band (The Ramrods) that he was 'talent-spotted' by the legendary jazz musician Alexis Korner. Alexis invited Brian to stay at his flat during his escapes from Cheltenham to visit London clubs. Brian had already committed himself to a career in music and wanted to form a band.

In spring 1962, Korner's band, Blues Incorporated, played regularly at Ealing Jazz Club. The band's drummer was a long-faced, quiet young man, Charlie Watts (born 2 June 1941 in Islington). Mick, Keith and Dick Taylor made contact with Brian after hearing him play slide guitar. Soon Mick, Keith, Dick, Brian and Charlie began jamming together, and Mick joined Blues Incorporated as a singer. Mick, Keith and Brian took a small flat off Chelsea's King's Road, and the London boys ignited Brian's interest in R & B guitar and harmonica.

Meanwhile, Bill Wyman (born William Perks on 24 October 1936 in Lewisham) had completed National Service (during which he learned to play guitar), married and begun work in a shop in Streatham. By 1962 he was playing bass guitar semi-professionally, backing mid-rank pop singers. He auditioned for the as yet unnamed new band without great enthusiasm, but on hearing that the respected Charlie Watts was joining, Bill decided to commit. By June the band were named The Rollin' Stones – as suggested by Brian, inspired by a Muddy Waters song. When they played at London's Marquee Club for the first time in July 1962, they had become The Rolling Stones.

The three legendary managers in British pop history were Brian Epstein, Malcolm Maclaren and Andrew Loog Oldham. Arguably the least holy of this remarkable trinity was Loog Oldham. He worked by day as a runner for Mary Quant and by night as a waiter at Soho's Flamingo Club. Later he worked in pop PR and, briefly, for Brian Epstein. After seeing The Rolling Stones in Richmond in April 1963, Oldham was determined to manage the band. He was 19 years old, hip and cool; a month later he signed the band and kept them working hard in the clubs until they were good enough to get a recording deal. In a little over a year they had done it – The Rolling Stones' first single, 'Come On', was released on 7 June 1963. A cover of the old Chuck Berry song, it was a furious rant listing a series of teenage frustrations: wrong numbers, clapped-out cars and a lack of success with the opposite sex all made for dissatisfaction. 'Come On' made a brief appearance low in the June charts.

When the Stones performed on ABC-TV's *Thank Your Lucky Stars* wearing identical dark trousers, jackets and ties it was the first and last time the band dressed the same. In an era in which even The Beatles wore suits and all groups had a uniform of sorts, from then on the Stones wore a disparate selection of clothes that might have been picked randomly from charity shops – although occasionally each sported a daring black leather waistcoat.

By the end of 1963 it was a case of 'lock up your daughters' – the Stones had begun to roll! No one could have predicted that one minor hit record (on Decca, a record label still smarting at its folly at turning down The Beatles) would prove so significant. Pop acts were expected to fade fast. Even Ringo Starr, when questioned about his plans after The Beatles' third UK No.1 single, said he hoped to open a hairdressing salon soon. Mick Jagger had negotiated a mere 'gap year' from the London School of Economics as the Stones' first major British tour began in September 1963. A second tour opened in Harrow, near Charlie's former art school, early in January 1964. The band's first EP, featuring four songs, was released later that month, and between live gigs there were radio and TV appearances. Work on a debut album progressed, with musicians such as Graham Nash and Allan Clarke of Manchester's Hollies and American singer Gene Pitney sitting in on sessions. The album (known as *Rolling Stones*, but without any formal title on the cover) was released in April 1964. Meanwhile, the band searched for months for a follow-up to their first single.

Oldham had seen there was a division between fans who preferred the rough and raw approach of the Stones and those who followed The Beatles (whose melodies had even parents' toes tapping). The Stones had better be bad, dirty and dangerous enough to outrage parents and thrill daughters. News of Brian's early parenthood was great PR. So was an episode in March when members of the band urinated against a garage forecourt wall, having been refused entry to a lavatory. Oldham's masterstroke in publicizing the band may well have been the line 'Would you let your daughter go out with one?'

In November 1963, the Stones' second single, 'I Wanna Be Your Man', was released. The song was written by John Lennon and Paul McCartney, whose prodigious output enabled them to offer songs to rival bands, scuppering any idea of a war between The Beatles and the Stones. In fact they were the best of friends. 'I Wanna Be Your Man' stayed in the charts for 13 weeks. It possibly irritated Jagger and Richards (writing as Nanker and Phelge) that others were collecting writers' royalties; just a month later Gene Pitney released a Jagger/Richard song (Keith had been advised to drop the final 's' from his name), 'That Girl Belongs To Yesterday'. Thereafter, the Stones increasingly recorded their own material.

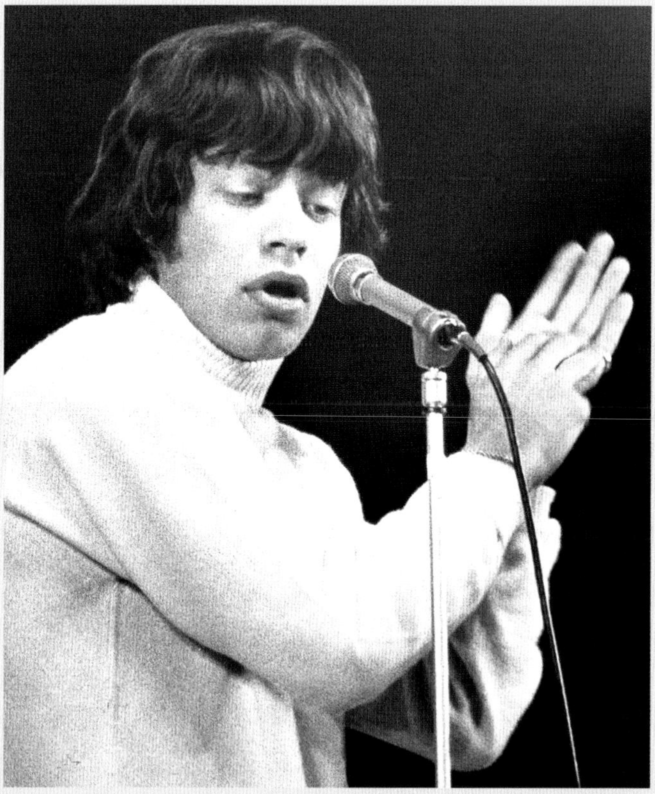

Previous page: No sign of tensions to come in this 1966 photograph.
Above: Mick Jagger on stage in 1965.

'Not Fade Away' was released in February 1964 and reached No.3 in the UK charts. Touring, including a restrained foray to New York to promote 'Not Fade Away' (which charted for a few weeks in the United States in May 1964), interviews, radio and TV secured their immediate future. Despite accounting that enabled their record company to retain earnings for many months, each Stone was now committed to rock 'n' roll independence. Mick and Keith found their own places, and could run to better meals than eggs and potatoes. Brian had a flat in west London with his girlfriend and second son (although he spent time elsewhere). Bill got a mortgage for his wife and family. In October 1964 Charlie added to this domestic harmony with new wife Shirley Ann Shephard.

On stage the band seemed more rebellious than ever. Longish hair for men was now accepted, so the Stones' hair had to be longer, lankier, dirtier. Accusations of incitement to civil insurrection did not seem to trouble them. There was no public contrition when 30 of 8,000 fans were arrested at Wembley in April 1964 for riotous behaviour. Riots in Scotland over bootleg tickets followed, just as the album went to No.1.

The pattern for the following three decades was set when yet another tour began in May 1964. There were more riots in Scotland, and Mick's maracas became a temporary symbol for shaking convention. When the Stones flew to New York in early June pundits predicted they would soon eclipse The Beatles. However, after two concerts at Carnegie Hall, Mick stated on 20 June that he gave the Stones another two years. Perhaps he was hedging his bets prior to the release of the band's new single 'It's All Over Now', but by 8 July it was the UK's No.1.

Throughout the rest of 1964 the band toured triumphantly and in August the EP, 'Five by Five', kept fans happy. In September they were voted most popular group in a *Melody Maker* poll and 'Not Fade Away' was declared best single of the year. On 13 September in Liverpool the Stones hired 24 rugby players to protect them at a concert, but some 5,000 fans stormed the stage and overcame the guards. Four days later police dogs had to control 4,000 fans in Carlisle. The year rolled on with recordings, dates in Europe and further US concerts. In their absence 'Little Red Rooster' was released in Britain in November 1964 and by the time the Stones were back in Britain for their *Ready, Steady, Go* TV slot the single was No.1. Just before Christmas 1964, Brian issued the first of many denials that he was leaving the band.

The year 1965 began with more touring, TV shows and the band's second album (*Rolling Stones No.2*) entering the charts at No.1 in late January. Once again, at Oldham's insistence, the sleeve showed just the band's faces with no title or mention of their name. The band's commitments early that year included recording in Los Angeles, then a series of concerts in Honolulu, Fiji, New Zealand and Australia. Before that, they had to meet UK obligations, some of which had been contracted cheaply before the band's current success. 'The Last Time', their fifth UK single, was released at the end of February 1965. Consolidating the band's success, it had topped the charts by the end of March. This coincided with the band's return from their overseas tour, which was followed by yet another British tour, then concerts all over Europe and North America.

In March 1965, on tour in Manchester, the Stones were ejected from their hotel for not observing the dress code. The band provoked further anger that April when they refused to stand and wave on the revolving stage at the traditional finale of *Sunday Night at the London Palladium*, Britain's top TV variety show. North America's equivalent, *The Ed Sullivan Show*, relaxed a veto on the band, and allowed them to perform in May, midway through the US tour. Towards the end of the tour, the Stones pipped The Beatles to come top for the first time in an American pop poll.

In Hollywood in May the band cut a Jagger/Richard song '(I Can't Get No) Satisfaction', based on a hard, fierce, daggered riff Bill had experimented with. At the time, the band thought the song would be a useful album filler; it would soon become their first US No.1 single, the intro becoming an all-time rock 'n' roll classic. But there was more trouble at home; in July summonses were issued against Mick, Brian and Bill for 'insulting' behaviour after the incident when they had urinated against a wall of a petrol station. They were later fined £5 apiece and costs.

The band's third album, *Out Of Our Heads*, was released in July 1965, around the time of their return from the United States and the start of another tour. A month later Oldham announced the birth of Immediate – a record label to enable the Stones to write and record their own material without restrictions and with increased royalty earnings. However, the Stones remained contracted to Decca for the release of the iconic '(I Can't Get No) Satisfaction' in August that year. It entered the UK charts in August at No.3 and held the No.1 slot for three weeks.

That summer a few faint rumblings threatened to challenge the stability of the band. Bill began producing records for other acts and Mick announced in New York that the entire British music scene had become boring. But then, with 'Satisfaction' topping the UK singles charts in August, a new agent (Tito Burns) and a new five-year recording deal with Decca, any fears that they were splitting up were dampened.

There were short breaks for individual band members, more gigs and further outrage. Hotels in Germany cancelled reservations in autumn for fear of insurrection. Brian had another son (by Linda Lawrence) to worry about. Each band member was worn out, but nothing could stem the onward and upward drive. In late October, they released the clangingly discordant single 'Get Off Of My Cloud' with the wistful and gently melancholic 'The Singer Not The Song' on the B side, establishing a pattern of contrast in their singles. The Stones had defied the odds in remaining true to their original image, but were confident enough to display tender lyricism too.

The band kicked into a new British tour in late September 1965, just before the release of 'Get Off Of My Cloud'. By November, the record was simultaneously No.1 in Britain and the United States. Their North American fan base demanded another tour before the year's end; The Rolling Stones have never forgotten those who made them, and they increasingly recorded and toured in the United States. Towards the end of the 1965 tour German actress Anita Pallenberg flew to join Brian in California, though rumours of an impending marriage were denied.

The defining year for the band was 1965, closing with 'Satisfaction' being voted best single in the United Kingdom and the United States, plus numerous other awards for being best group across a range of categories. A generation had anticipated or learned about teenage pleasures to the soundtrack of The Rolling Stones' first recordings, and for fans power escalated with every tour, TV appearance, chart single and album. By the end of 1965 The Rolling Stones were huge all over Europe and in the United States. They'd had three successful albums and a string of singles, which almost routinely topped the charts. There may have been the odd mutter of internal dissent, but the band was truly part of the rock establishment when another new year drew in.

There's no doubt that the behaviour of The Rolling Stones during their early years was responsible for an obsessive interest in their private lives. Little was known about Bill, except he was married to Diane. Charlie's 1964 marriage proved to be steady as a rock, and jazz has remained his spare-time passion. Little is known of Keith's early romances but eventually he developed a relationship with Anita Pallenberg.

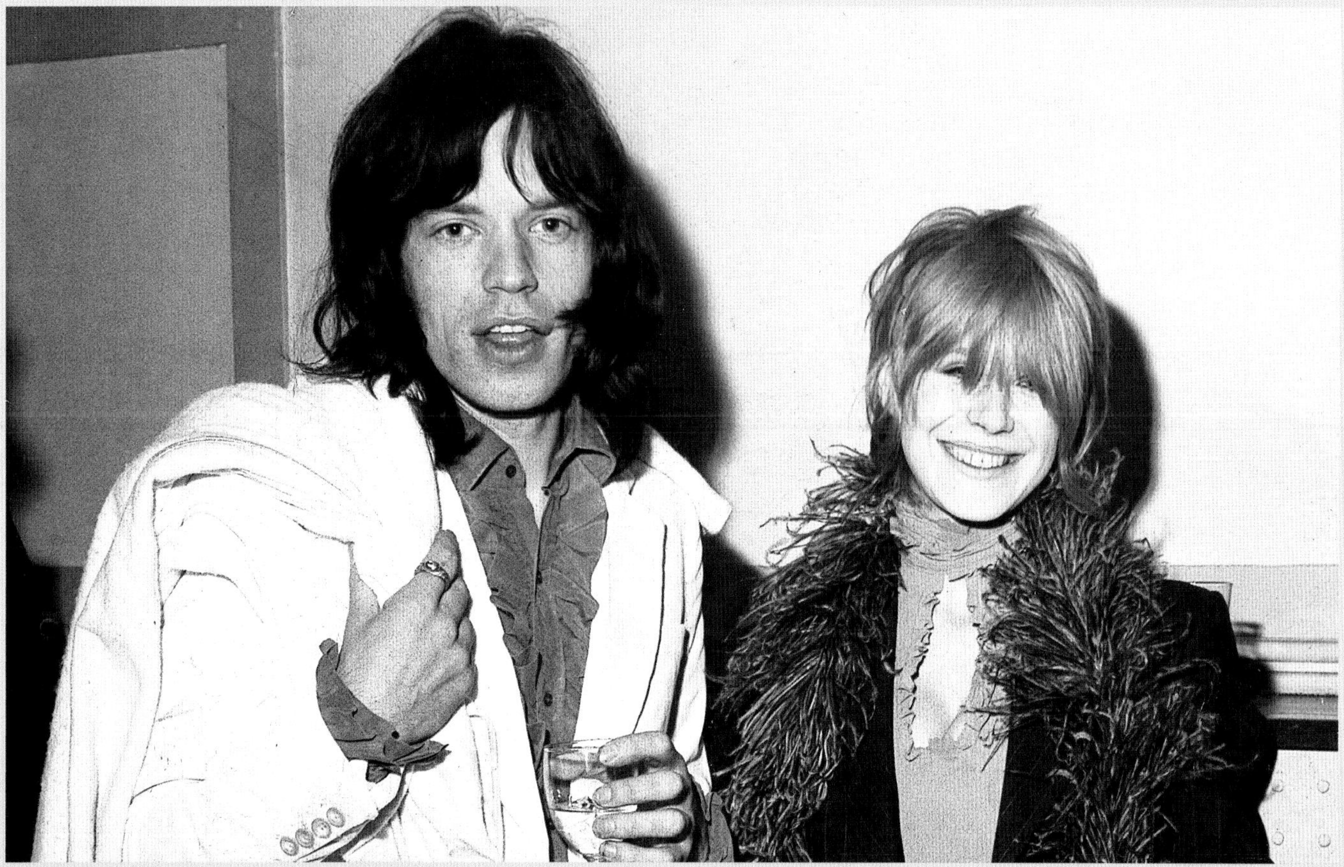

Above: Mick and Marianne Faithfull photographed in 1968.

Almost from the start, however, the affairs of Brian and Mick were played out in public. By spring 1963, Mick Jagger was stepping out with pretty brunette Chrissie Shrimpton, younger sister of iconic 1960s supermodel Jean. The connection with the middle-class Shrimpton family exemplified Mick's enduring penchant for lofty thoroughbred beauties even as he was class rebellion personified. The relationship with Chrissie lasted for more than two years and in June 1965 the pair were rumoured to be considering marriage. But the union was volatile, then doomed once Mick fell for the daughter of a baroness …

Marianne Faithfull may have lived in provincial Reading, but her ancestors had glittered at imperial courts and waltzed with Vienna's finest. Her mother, Eva, had been a ravishing, stateless beauty when Glyn Faithfull, a wartime officer in British Intelligence, rescued her. Marianne was born in 1947 and lived in Lancashire until her parents separated. The little house in Reading was a shrine to a noble past, and convent-educated Marianne grew up amid sophistication, culture and taste. At 17, Marianne was an astonishing beauty with a lovely, husky singing voice. Her potential was spotted by Oldham, who suggested Mick and Keith write her a song. By 1964 she was involved with Cambridge undergraduate and later art dealer John Dunbar, but soon after the sweetly melancholy 'As Tears Go By' charted for her that summer, she and Mick became an item. They reigned supreme as rock's defining couple for nearly six years. But while Mick seemed to thrive on life at the edge and on scandal, Marianne was fragile. Eventually, after a miscarriage in 1968, a botched suicide attempt the following year, the hurt of Mick's affair with the singer/actress Marsha Hunt in 1969 and a series of drug-related crises, Marianne found the strength to leave Mick.

The story of Keith and Anita overlaps that of Mick and Marianne – and begins with Brian. Even with the new birth control pill, somehow men were most liberated in the climate of sexual freedom. Jagger/Richard lyrics of the mid-1960s, from the wonderful 'Under My Thumb' and 'Stupid

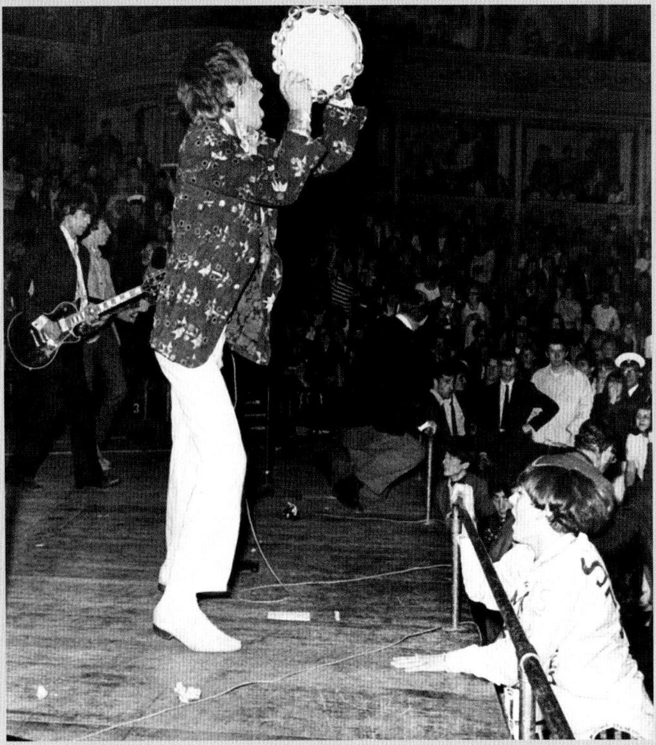

Opposite: Bill pictured during one of the Stone's many court appearances.
Above: Mick bangs a tambourine during an early gig.

Girl' on the *Aftermath* album to 'Out Of Time', also written in 1966 and bellowed by Chris Farlowe on a hit single later that year, expertly make the point – ironically expressing the old love 'em and leave 'em chauvinism.

Brian had luxuriant fair hair and a 'lost boy' aura that alternated with an equally appealing aloof glamour. It was understandable if he sometimes seemed almost sulky on stage, standing motionless with his guitar clamped across his chest. He had thought he was the leader of the band until he'd been eclipsed by Mick. But thousands of girls adored him. And at least three of them bore him sons; his first child was born to a 14-year-old girl when he was 16 and still at school. Three years later, he fathered another son, Julian Mark, after his jazz hero Julian 'Cannonball' Adderley. Soon after the Stones' first success, a third son was born to a young model. When Brian cited his hobbies as bus and train spotting, some girls might have begged to differ. Emotionally, he met his nemesis in 1965 with the formidable Anita Pallenberg. Their relationship was riven with upsets, but he never recovered when Anita left him, particularly since it was Keith to whom she fled three years later. It seems that other girlfriends, such as socialite Suki Poitier and Anna Wohlin, the young Swede who was with him at the end, never reached him in the same way.

The start of 1966 must have opened with a glow; polls on both sides of the Atlantic had named 'Satisfaction' best single of the previous year, and the Stones as best band. By February their ninth UK single, '19th Nervous Breakdown' was headed for No.1. However, they continued a punishing schedule of touring and fans continued to riot – with the band often held responsible. And they were still barred from some hotels due to security fears or concern for the peace of other guests.

One of the finest albums, *Aftermath*, was released in April 1966. In May plans for a film, *Only Lovers Left Alive*, were announced: the Stones would star as individual actors but record the soundtrack as a band. The film never progressed, but Mick's enduring interest in cinematic projects may have been ignited then. Indian-inspired "Paint It Black" was released the same month and the single made it to No.1 in both the United Kingdom and United States.

By September 1966 the band were ready to promote their new single, 'Have You Seen Your Mother Baby, Standing In The Shadow' – the sleeve of which showed the band in 1940s drag, with Bill, dressed in female army uniform, in a wheelchair. The accompanying promotional film was banned by the BBC. Brian managed to trump this in November, when he posed wearing Nazi SS uniform with a doll crushed beneath his jackbooted foot.

The band were busy recording in London as 1966 closed, the compilation album *Big Hits (High Tide And Green Grass)* set to storm the Christmas charts. It was not a happy Christmas for Mick and Chrissie, who broke up shortly beforehand. She was traumatized and attempted suicide; but Mick was in love with Marianne Faithfull.

'Let's Spend The Night Together', released in January 1967, proved nothing could stifle the Stones' bold exuberance, the uncompromising lyrics reinforcing their bad-boy image. The B side, 'Ruby Tuesday', was another gem, reminding everyone that The Beatles weren't the only band who never offered a weak B side. The album who never offered a weak B side. The album *Between The Buttons* was high in the charts by the end of the month.

If The Rolling Stones had a bad year, that 'year' spanned 1967 to 1969. The more flamboyant trio within the band were reduced to the indestructible partnership (song-writing and otherwise) of the Glimmer Twins (a nickname given to Mick and Keith). It would seem that three was a crowd and Brian was an accident waiting to happen.

With the dawning of the age of Aquarius in 1967, or the 'summer of love', there sometimes seemed no Stone unturned-on. A newspaper report in February said Mick had taken LSD and hash, which led to him taking out a libel action. The summer was blighted by a series of drug busts. The most celebrated – or notorious – took place at Keith's Sussex house in February. It resulted in a court case in which Keith was charged with allowing his premises to be used for the consumption of illegal substances and Mick for possession (even though only traces of an amphetamine legally purchased abroad the previous year were found). Although innocent of any offence, Marianne was effectively tried for the much-publicized 'crime' of being wrapped in a fur rug when the police raided. Before the trial various Rolling Stones and girlfriends visited Morocco. When Anita returned to London it was the end of her affair with Brian, the start of a new one with Keith and of tensions that eventually led to Brian leaving the band. Meanwhile Mick and Keith's drugs case was heard and both were given prison sentences, causing a public outcry. The sentences were quashed on appeal in July 1967 and the release of the single 'We Love You' in August was widely supposed to contain a message of ironic forgiveness to the Establishment. Throughout all this Brian had his own drugs-related court case pending. A prison sentence imposed in December was set aside on medical grounds and he was placed on probation instead.

In December 1967 the Stones – on their mettle – had released *Their Satanic Majesties Request* as an answer to The Beatles' album *Sergeant Pepper's Lonely Hearts Club Band.* Where The Beatles had dressed in satin tin-soldier outfits on their album sleeve, The Rolling Stones posed in wizards' outfits. But while *Sergeant Pepper* became a defining classic, few would argue that the Stones' album (mockingly titled after the command on the blue passport travelling Britons carried at the time) was their finest. Two songs ('She's A Rainbow' and 'Two Thousand Light Years From Home') were marvellous, but others were a little disappointing. Brian's heart may not have been in it; he had long resented Mick's apparent leadership of the band. He'd lost his girlfriend to Keith and he was increasingly drawn towards musical interests that weren't shared by the others. Other band members also developed outside interests. In particular, in May 1968 Mick announced his starring role in Nicolas Roeg's film *Performance*. This diversification didn't threaten the band, but an impression remains that Brian was allowed to go his own way.

For a while, 1968 seemed to be business as usual. 'Jumpin' Jack Flash' made No.1 in June, its success speeded by a short promotional film (an early version of a rock video). 'Street Fighting Man', their next US single, a track from the forthcoming *Beggars' Banquet* album, was banned in Chicago in September after recent riots at the Democratic Convention. Earlier that year, students manned the barricades in Paris and students rioted across the world in protest at America's involvement in Vietnam. Mick 'went

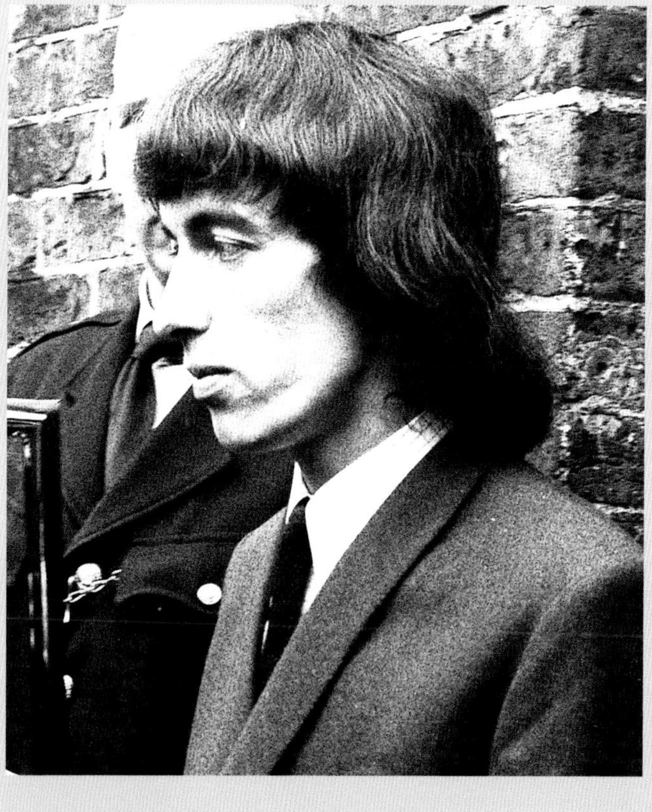

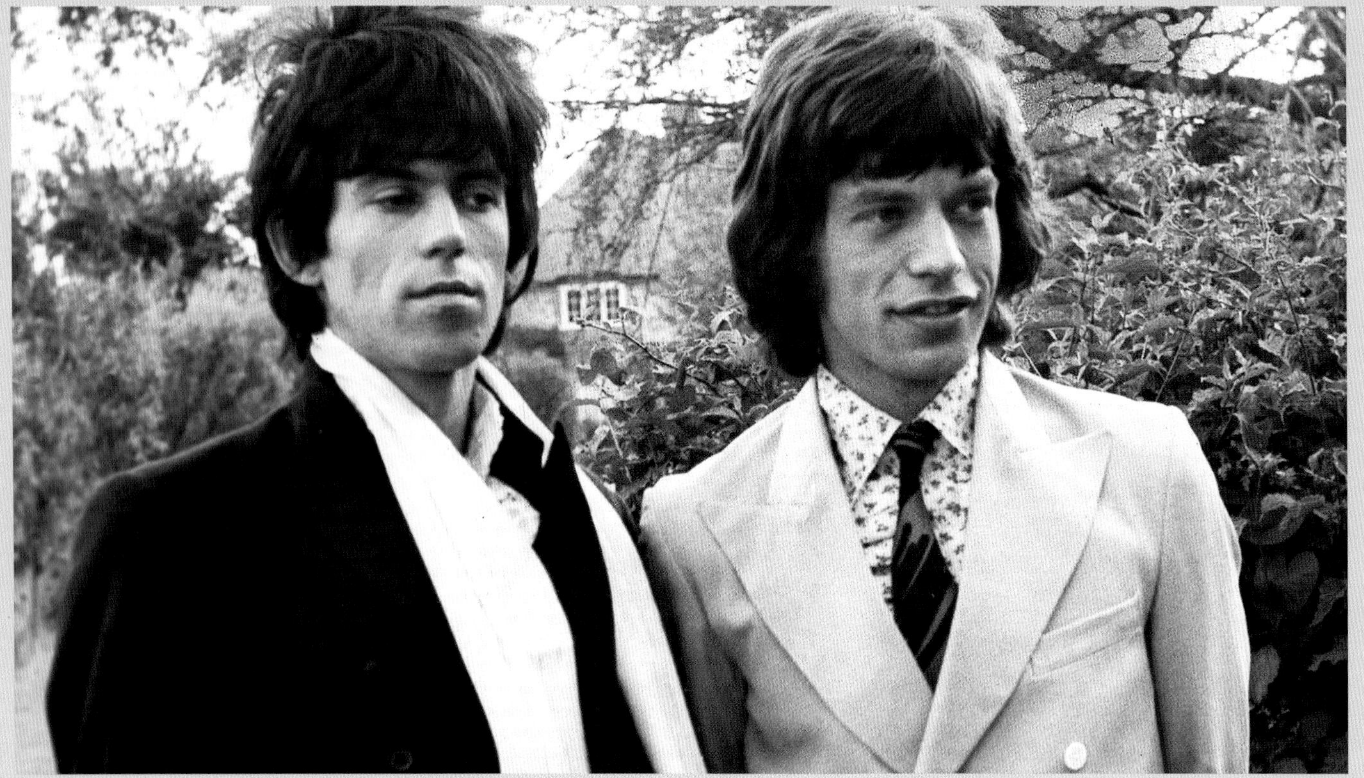

Above: Keith and Mick, known as the 'Glimmer Twins'.

down to the demonstration' (another lyric from 'You Can't Always Get What You Want') outside the US Embassy in Grosvenor Square, London. In less than a year the feeling of universal peace and harmony captured by The Beatles' single 'All You Need Is Love' (on which some Stones had sung in a studio performance) had evaporated.

In October 1968 a delighted Mick and Marianne announced her pregnancy; she lost the baby in November. Brian, meanwhile, purchased Cotchford Farm in Sussex. Throughout 1968, the inspired brilliance behind Brian's muffled xylophones that introduced 'Under My Thumb', his fierce lead guitar, and the percussion and brass undertows that shaped many other tracks, seemed increasingly absent. As The Beatles were finding last ways of papering over cracks that, after five sublime years, were beginning to widen, similar fault lines were forming in the foundations of The Rolling Stones. Early drafts of a plan to buy Brian out of The Rolling Stones for a sum of money that would ultimately cover half his debts (had he lived to receive it) were privately considered as the very fabric of The Rolling Stones corroded. By the end of 1968, Brian seemed very isolated. Keith and Anita had confounded sceptics by settling into something resembling steady domesticity. Charlie and Bill had their own peaceful places of marital escape. Heartbreak, despair, disappointment, jealousy, betrayal and a fresh series of drug busts all conspired to crush Brian as his dreadful destiny called. Depressed and in debt, he retreated to his house in Sussex.

In December 1968 *Beggars' Banquet* was released in the United States amid rumours that the band were splitting even though a new world tour was being planned. Controversy had also stalked *Beggars' Banquet* in Britain, but in a different way. Its release was delayed until December 1968 because the original sleeve – which depicted a graffiti-covered toilet – was banned, so it was replaced by a dignified parody of a formal invitation card.

By the end of 1968 the Stones had not merely nursed their notoriety but increased it. At the same time, Mick and Keith had become respected lyricists, and the musicianship of the entire band was much more complex, assured and professional. Mick was almost married to the ethereal Marianne and talking of a future in films. The others were also diversifying, and 'Time Is On My Side', a track from the album *Rolling Stones No.2*, seemed apt. However, by 1968 it was more the case of borrowing time than having it on their side.

Although 1968 had ended with the Stones voted best R & B band in the *New Musical Express* poll, the new year began dismally for Brian. Alone in Sri Lanka, he was declined admission to several hotels, mistaken for a penniless beatnik. Back in England, he was to spend ever more time at Cotchford Farm. It wasn't a large house but there was a lovely untamed garden and a swimming pool. Brian was a keen swimmer so the pool was a plus and the farm itself provided him with peace, space and calm.

Early in 1969, work began on a new Stones album, with recording in both London and Italy. Progress was slow as Mick was also committed to writing the soundtrack of the Kenneth Anger film *Invocation Of My Demon Brother*, and he and Marianne were discussing roles in a forthcoming Australian movie, *Ned Kelly*. Furthermore, in May 1969 the pair were arrested for possession of cannabis at home in Chelsea. A few days later, Keith and a heavily pregnant Anita were involved in a car crash in Sussex. Anita broke her collarbone but a son, Marlon, was safely born in London on 10 August. Meanwhile, Bill and Diane Wyman's marriage had been quietly disintegrating, and their divorce was announced early in July.

Amid this climate of stress and diversification it was agreed at Cotchford Farm in early June that Brian and the Stones should part company; 'musical differences' was the reason given. Two days later a tall, young, blond, vegetarian teetotaller called Mick Taylor was appointed as the band's new lead guitarist. On the night of 2 July 1969, exactly three weeks after leaving the band, Brian Jones' body was found at the bottom of his swimming pool. He had been drinking prior to a midnight swim and frequently resorting to his asthma inhaler. The coroner returned a verdict of death by drowning under the influence of drugs and alcohol. But wild rumours of more sinister events circulated almost at once and are still occasionally aired. He was just 27.

The Rolling Stones had planned a free concert in Hyde Park on 5 July 1969 to introduce Mick Taylor to fans and as a celebration of moving on. Despite Brian's death, the band insisted the show should go ahead. It was a hot day and the park heaved with about 300,000 kaftan-clad flower children. Towards the end of the concert Mick recited lines from Shelley's *Adonais*:

'Peace, peace! He is not dead, he doth not sleep –
He hath awakened from the dream of life …'

He then released thousands of white butterflies into the blazing blue skies. Four days later, in Australia, Marianne overdosed and sank into a five-day coma. Brian was buried on 10 July at the Cheltenham church where he had sung as a choirboy. The priest read from a telegram that Brian had recently sent to his parents. It said: 'Please don't judge me too harshly.' The Stones' single 'Honky Tonk Women' (which later won a BBC poll as best single of the year) hitting the charts may have been small compensation for a month of extraordinary strain and tragedy.

The new Rolling Stones may have hoped the rest of 1969 would quietly fade away. Mick had Marianne to look after and a film to make. Keith jammed with Eric Clapton and Ginger Baker on Billy Preston's 'That's The Way God Planned It', produced by George Harrison. In the absence of new material a greatest hits album, *Through The Past Darkly (Big Hits Vol. 2)* was released. But the worst was to come towards the end of the year. On the final date of an American tour, 6 December, some 500,000 fans amassed for a free concert at the Altamont Speedway Stadium in California. The event was policed by Hell's Angels, who were paid in beer and took their duties seriously. By the time the Stones made their usual late appearance the crowd was in uproar, the Angels beating teenagers with billiard cues. The show went on even when one Angel pulled a knife on a fan who jumped on stage. Two fans were killed when a car ploughed through the crowds; a third drowned in a ditch. There were hundreds of injuries. The horrible year closed with the release of *Let It Bleed* in early December (a huge success both sides of the Atlantic) – but also with Mick being fined for possession of cannabis, Marianne's acquittal and a holiday in Rome with an Italian film producer, and Home Office pressure on Anita to marry because of her alien immigrant status.

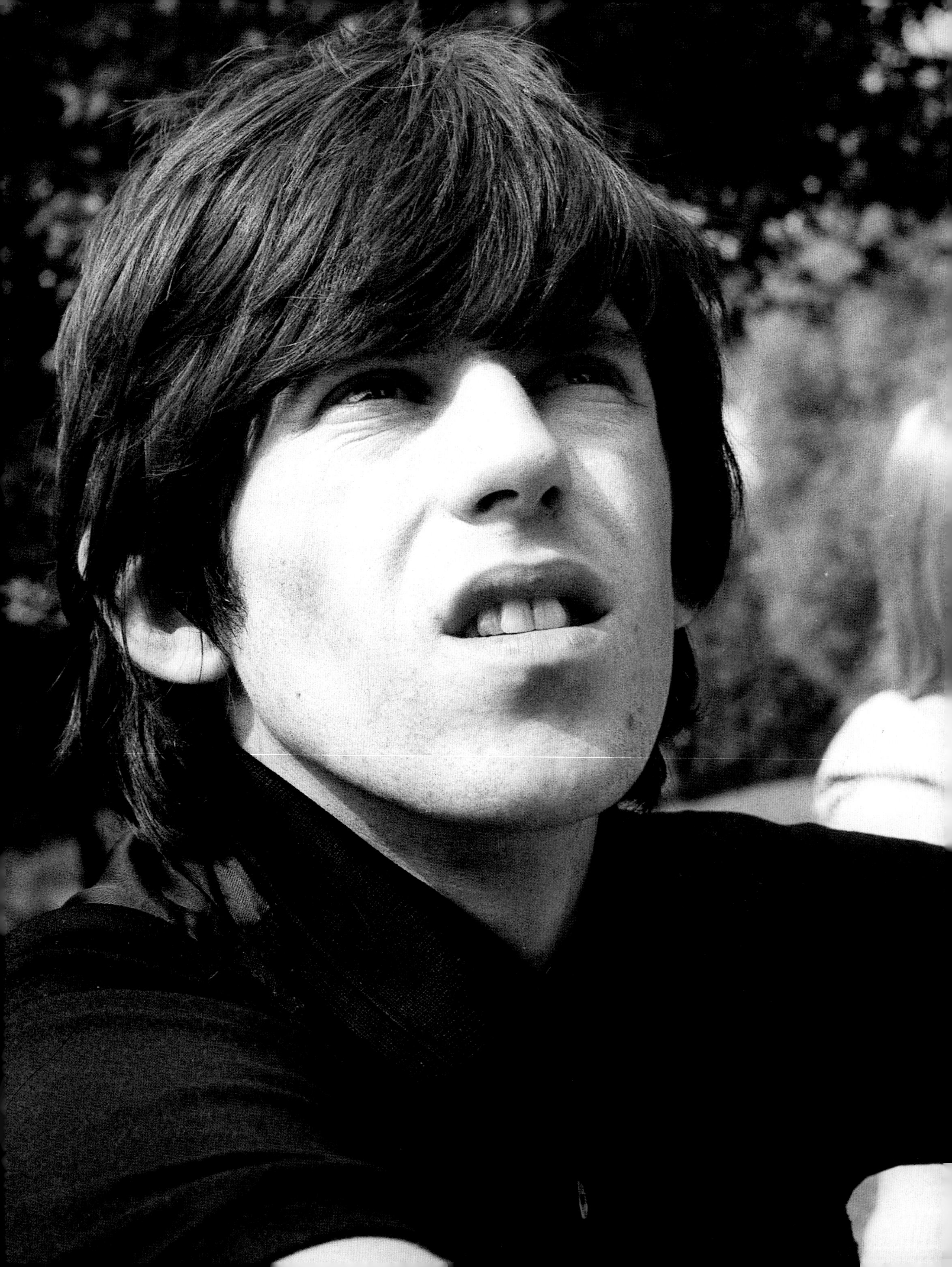

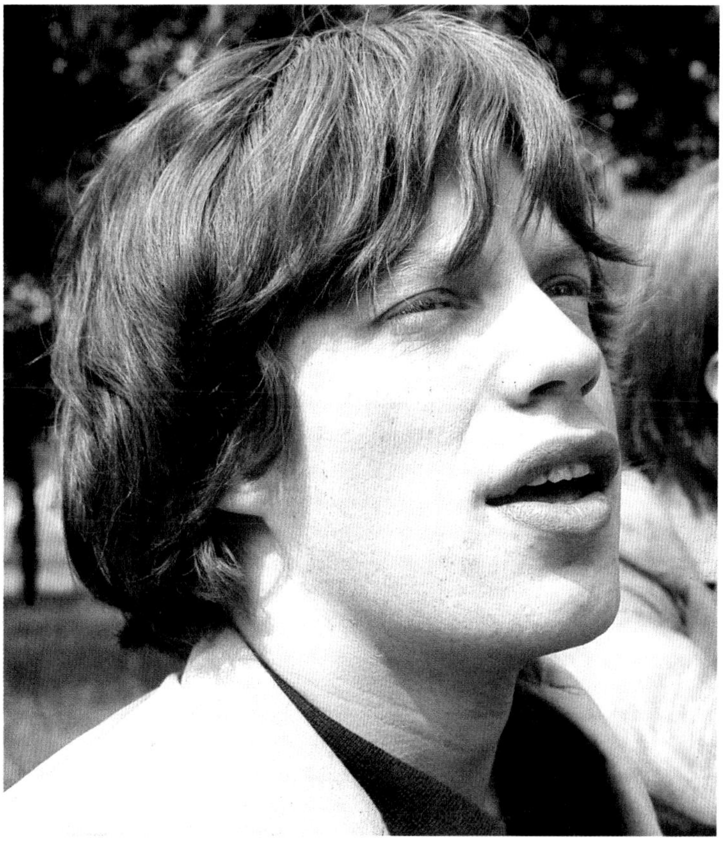

Mick, Charlie, Brian, Bill and Keith

In early 1962 Mick Jagger (*left*) and Keith Richards (*opposite*) meet by chance on a train and quickly become friends. Soon after, they hear Brian Jones play slide guitar at the Ealing Jazz Club, and a band is formed that will be the nucleus of The Rolling Stones. In July 1962 they play a gig at the Marquee in London, still under their previous name the Rollin' Stones.

Below: A rare early picture of the band.

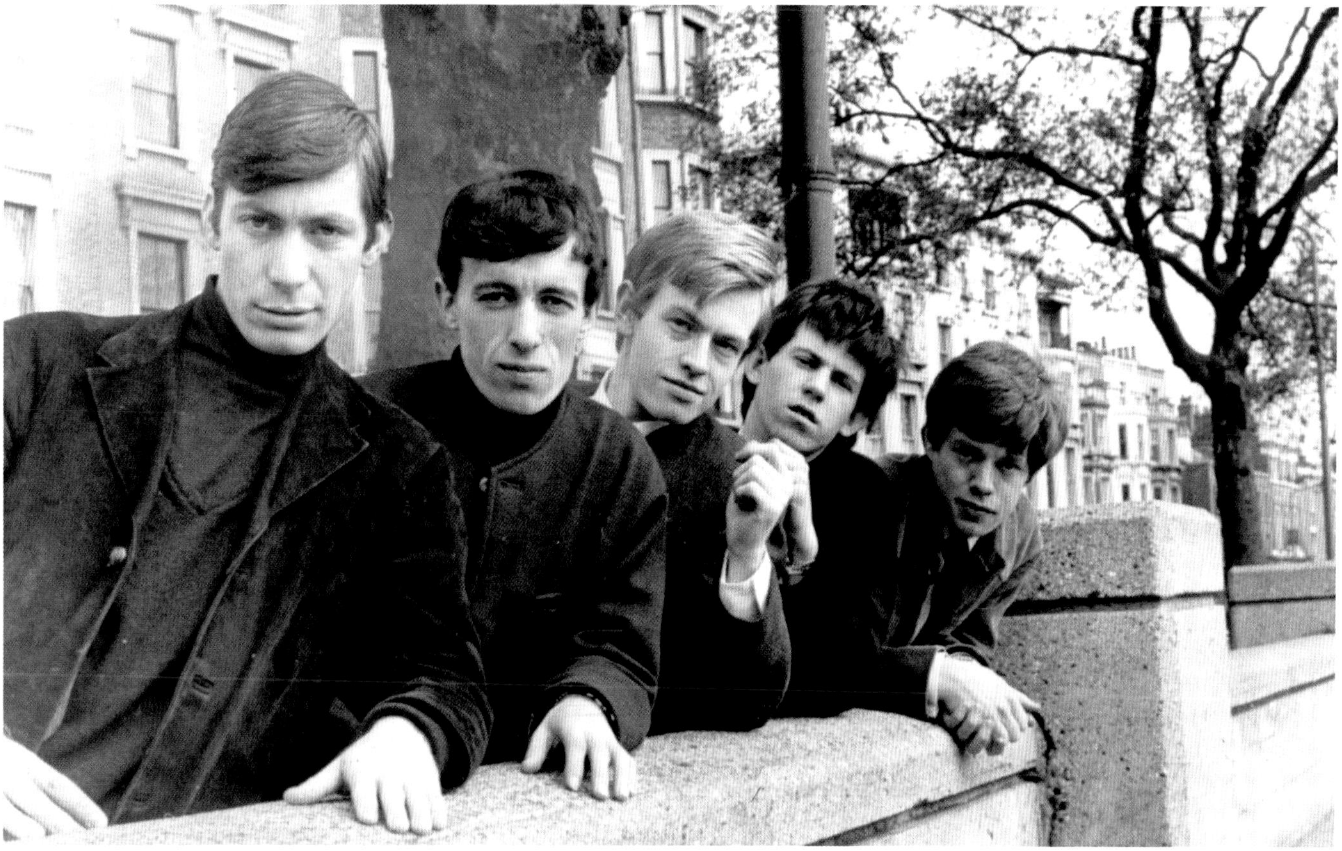

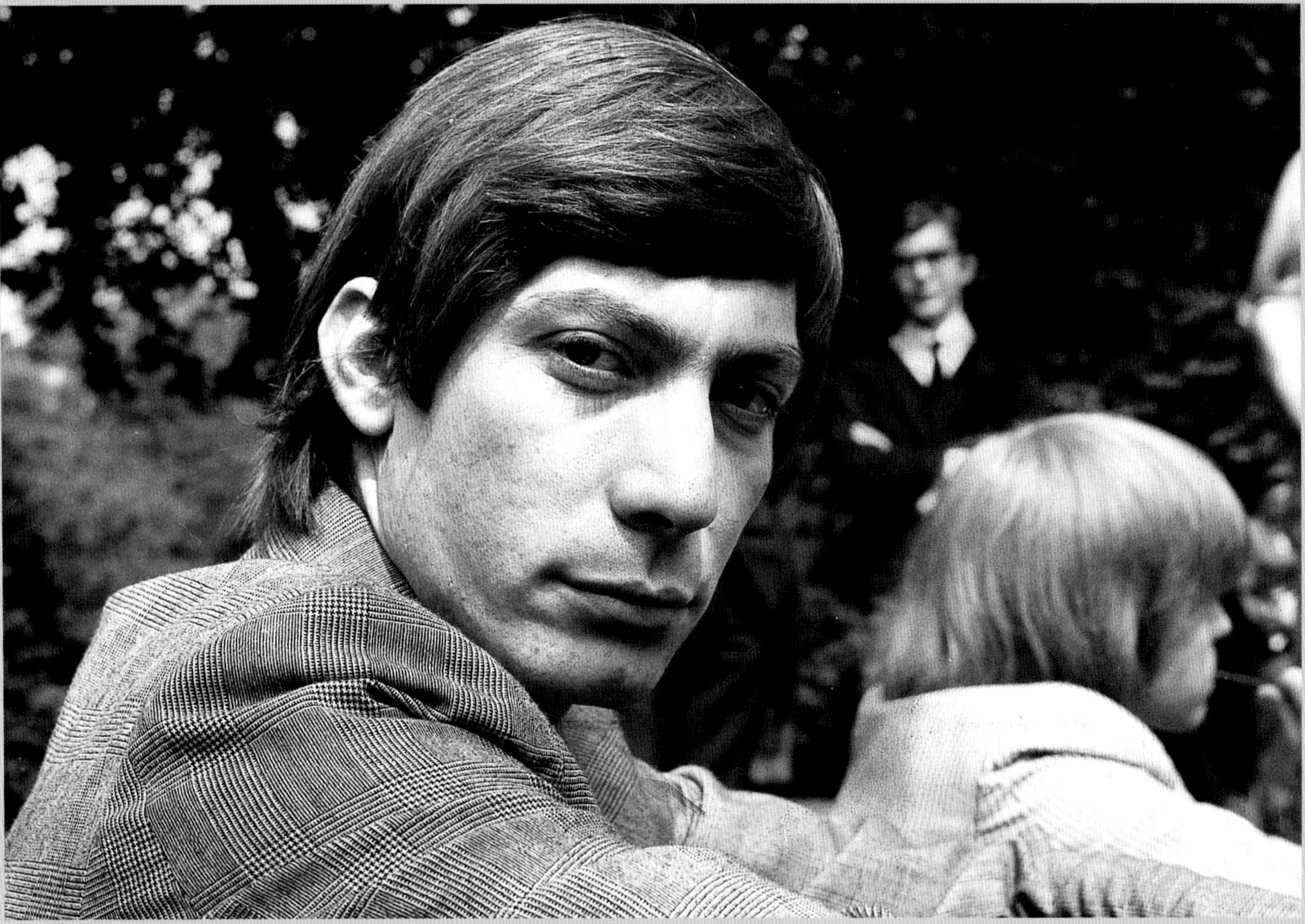

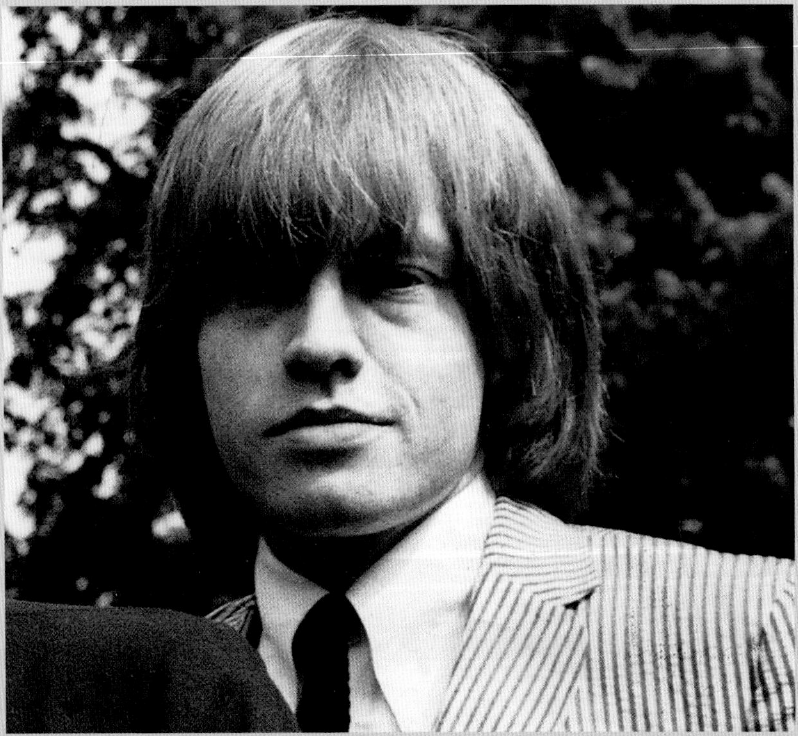

Announcing The Rolling Stones

By the beginning of the new year Charlie Watts (*above*) and Bill Wyman (*opposite below*) had joined Mick, Keith and Brian (*left*), and now the band were called The Rolling Stones. The band worked hard during 1963 under the direction of Andrew Loog Oldham, their newly acquired manager, playing in clubs and at parties until they were ready to cut their first single. 'Come On/I Wanna Be Loved' was released in June 1963, reaching No.20 in the charts.

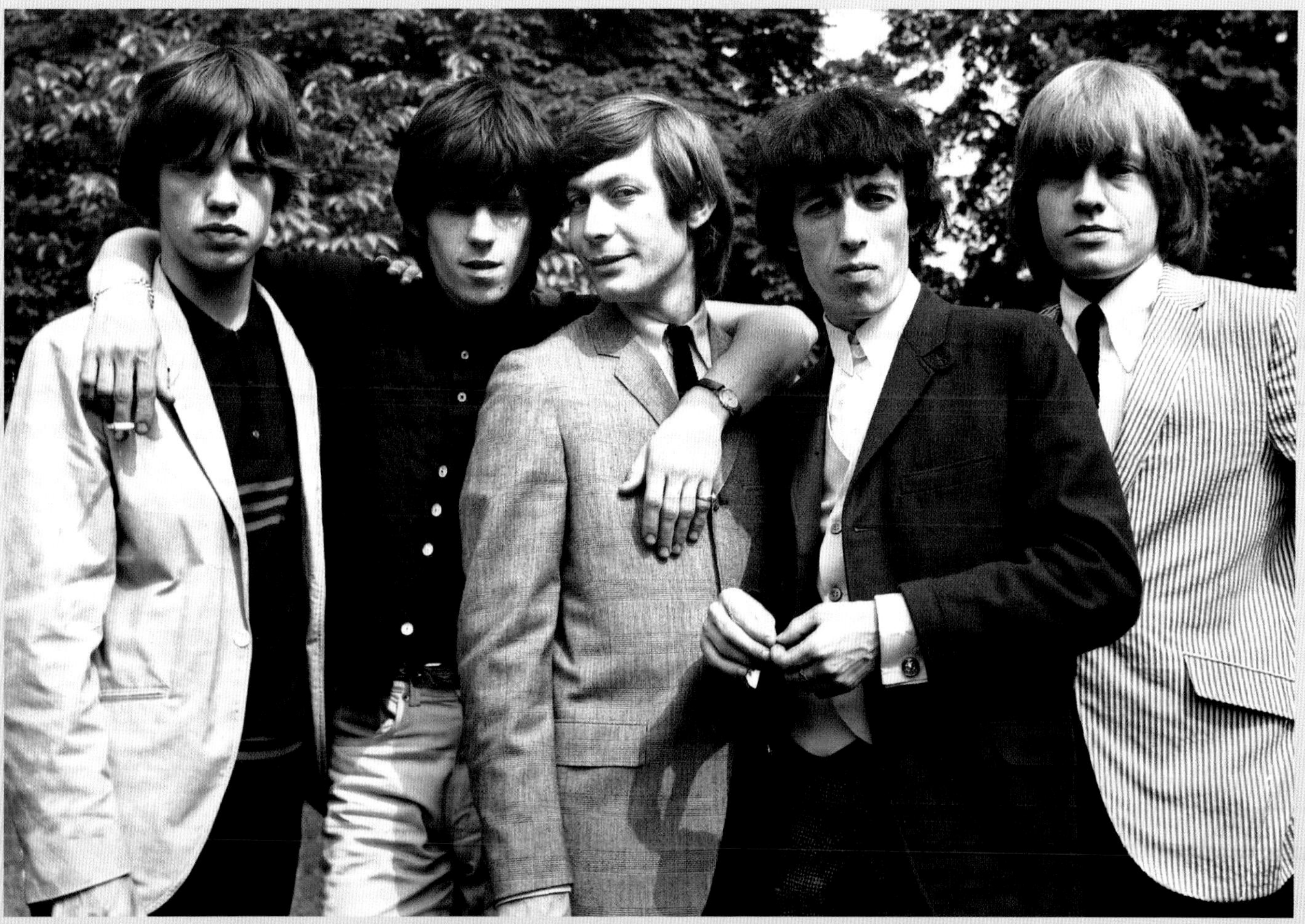

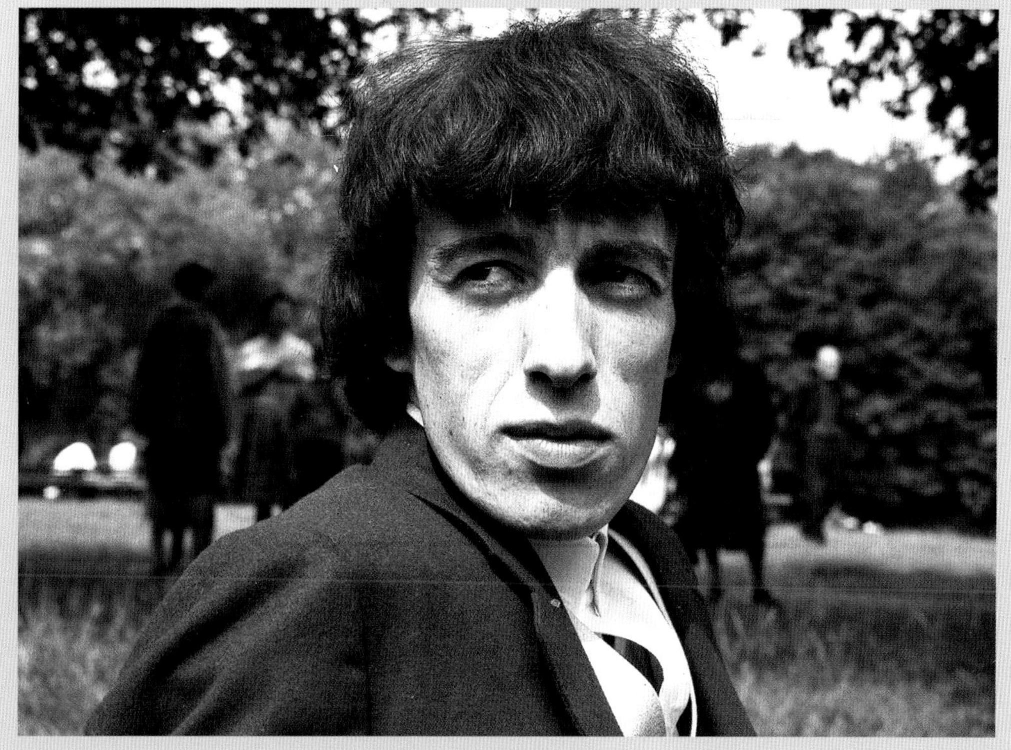

Second single

Above: Mick, Brian and Keith moved into a flat in Edith Grove, Chelsea, together, although it was a struggle to pay the rent. However, by November 1963 they had released a second single, 'I Wanna Be Your Man', which spent 13 weeks in the UK charts, and it was beginning to look like The Rolling Stones had a future.

Right: When Bill Wyman joined the Stones he was already playing semi-professionally, although by day he worked in a shop in south London.

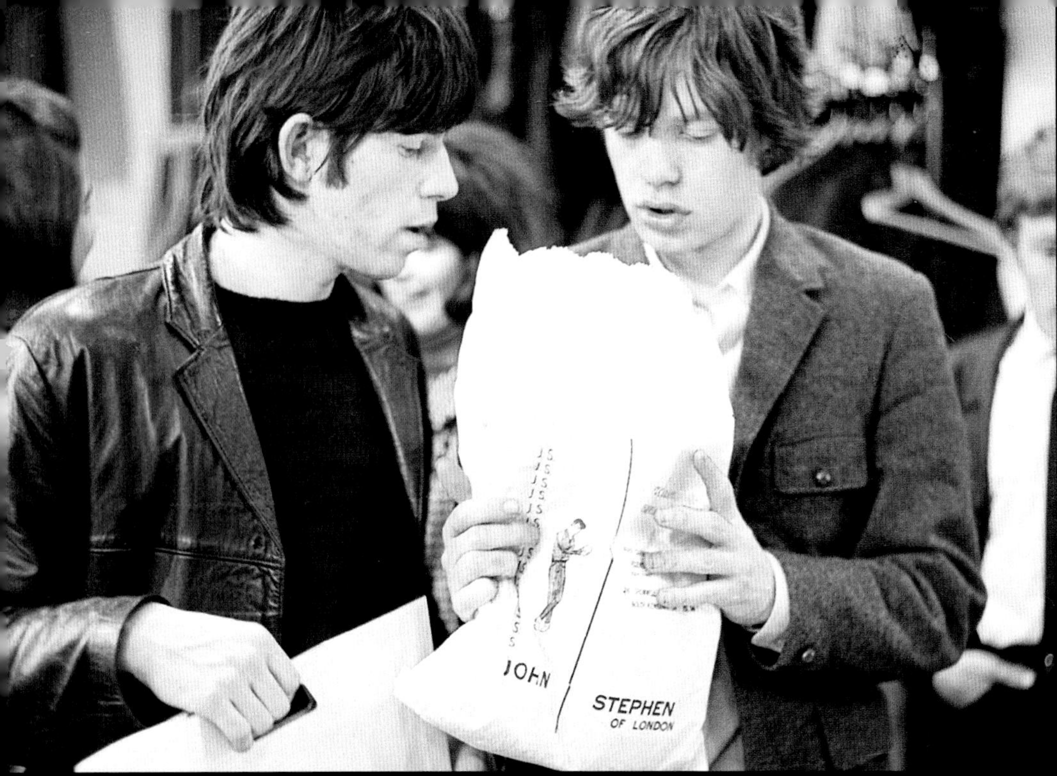

Taking off

Left: Mick and Keith in Carnaby Street in London. The band's first album, *The Rolling Stones,* was released and reached No.1 in the British album charts on 24 April.

Below: Mick and Keith on stage. In April 1964 the band went to the Montreux Television Festival in Switzerland. By now they were in high demand and they were invited to all kinds of media events.

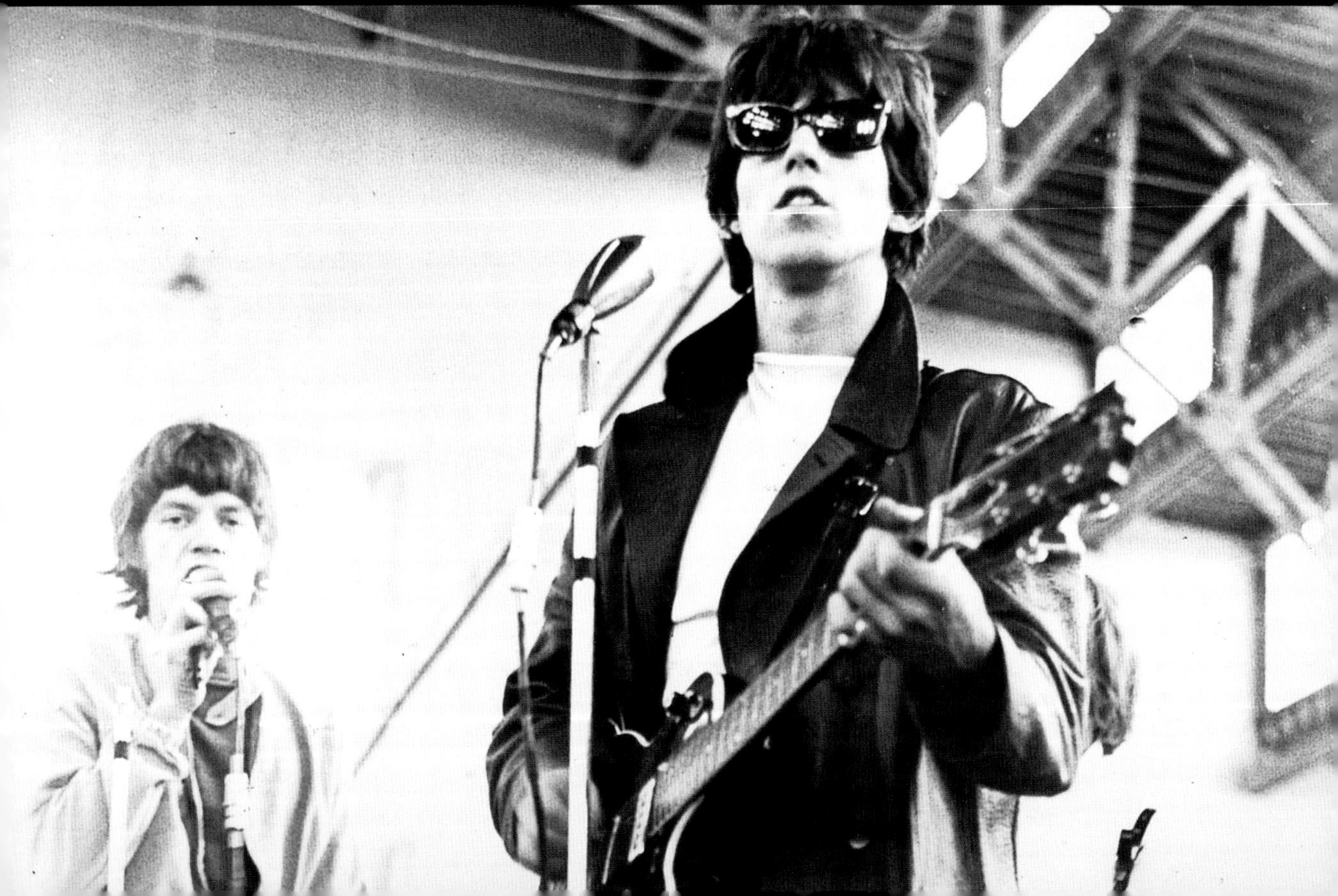

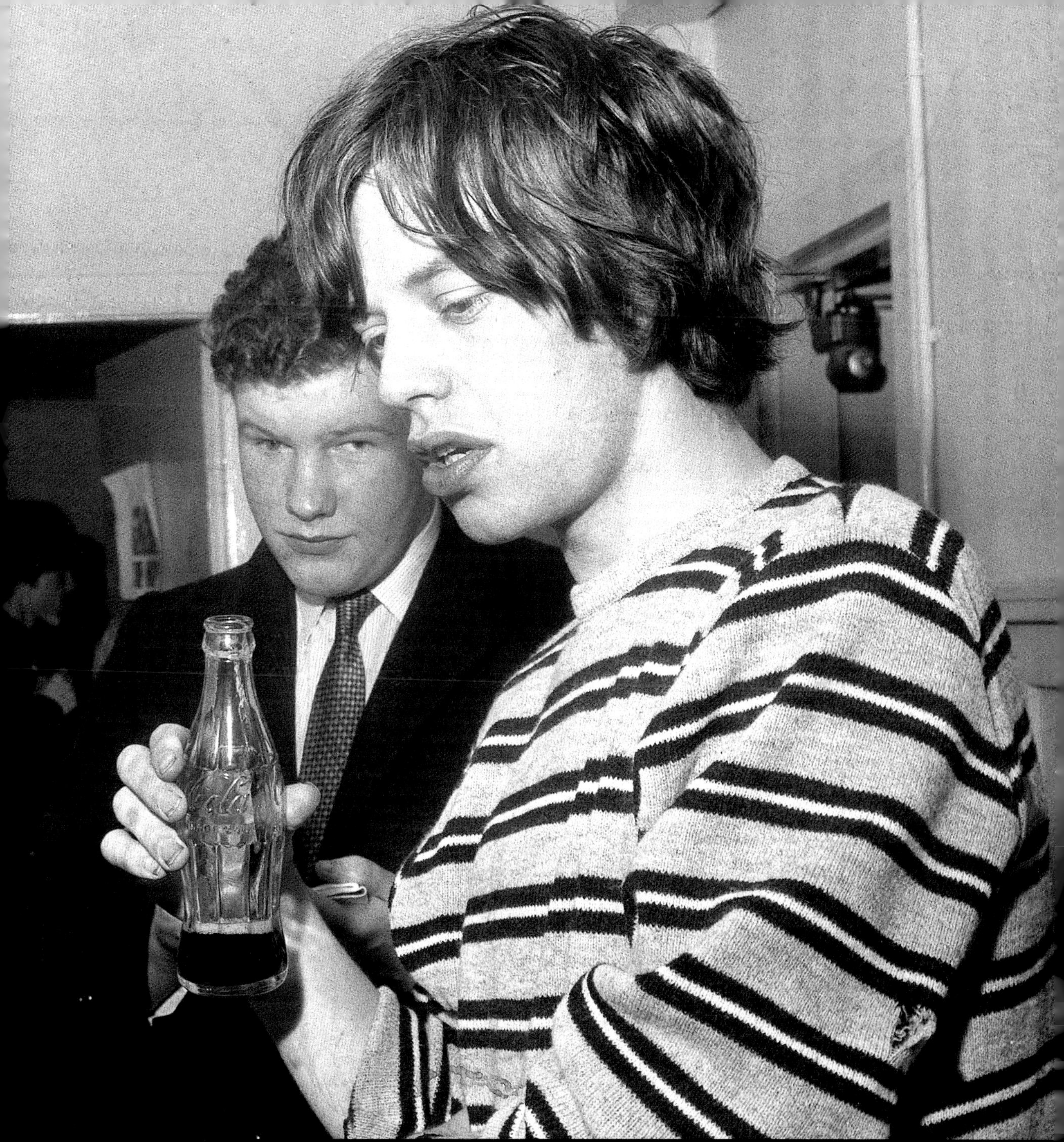

Hotel hell in UK tour

Above: A casually dressed Mick. By May of 1964 the band had embarked on their third UK tour. Failing to observe the dress code in a smart Bristol hotel, they were refused lunch. A few days later in Hamilton, Scotland, police had to restrain 4,000 fans who stormed a gig in a local hotel.

On 1 June 1964 the Stones headed off for their first US tour. Only their manager, Andrew Loog Oldham, was confident that the tour would be a success. Their recent first US single, 'Not Fade Away', had not sold particularly well. After an uncertain start, the final two concerts of the tour at Carnegie Hall were both instant sell-outs.

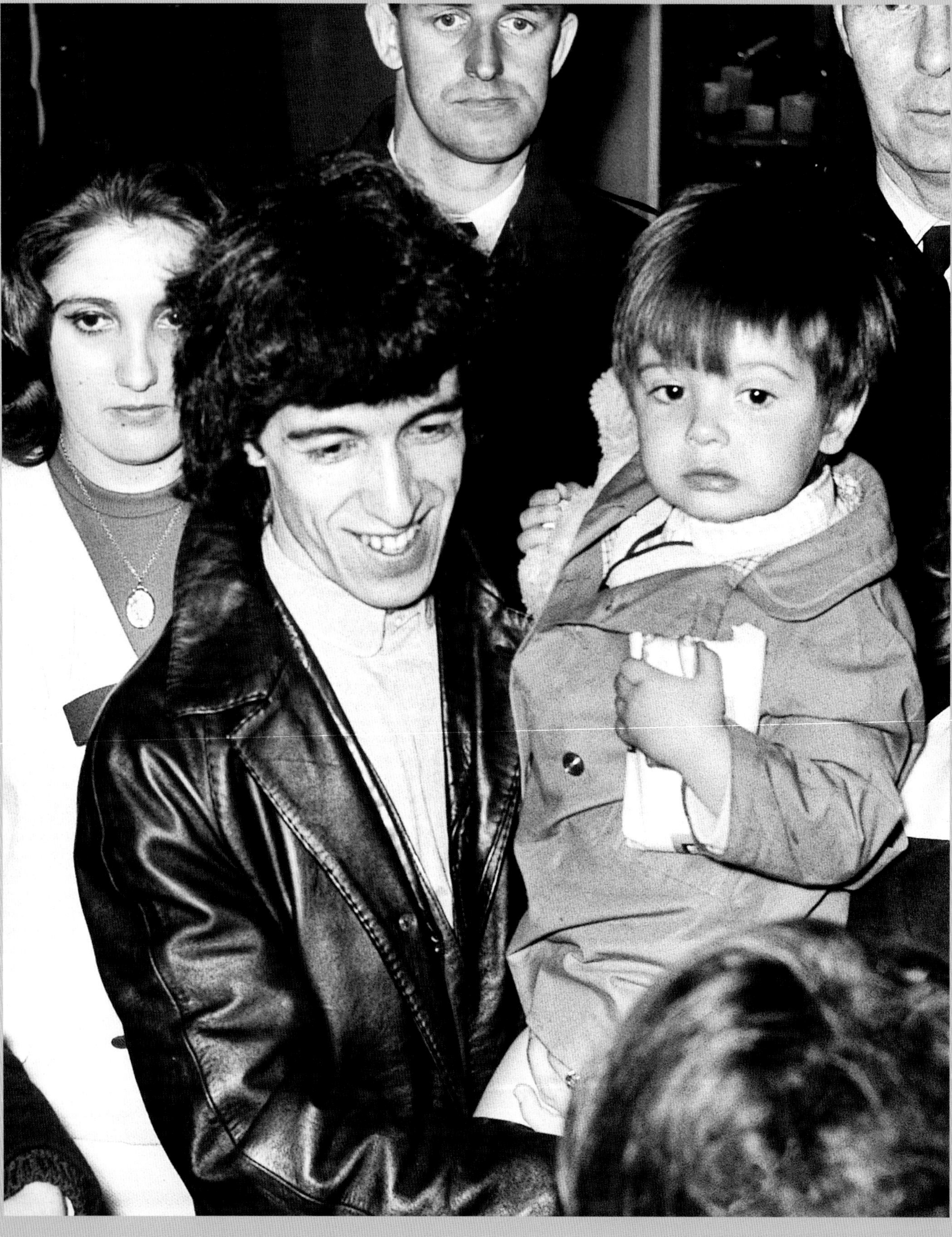

'Papa Was A Rolling Stone'

Opposite: Bill Wyman holds his two-year-old son Stephen before leaving for the three-week US tour. His wife Diane, as ever, is discreetly in the background.

Right: At a press conference on the band's return from the States on 23 June 1964, the police had to cope with rioting fans who tried to gain entry.

Below: The Stones, none of them particularly tall, helped to popularize footwear that became known as Chelsea boots. Brian Jones (*left*) and Keith Richard (*right*) share centre stage with Mick Jagger for a TV recording.

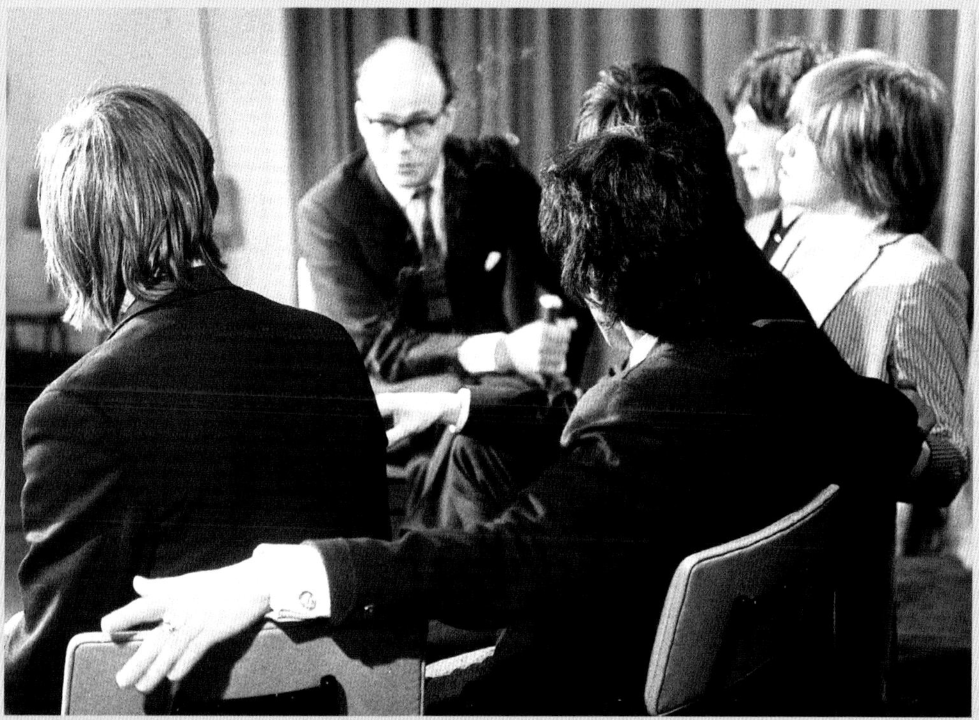

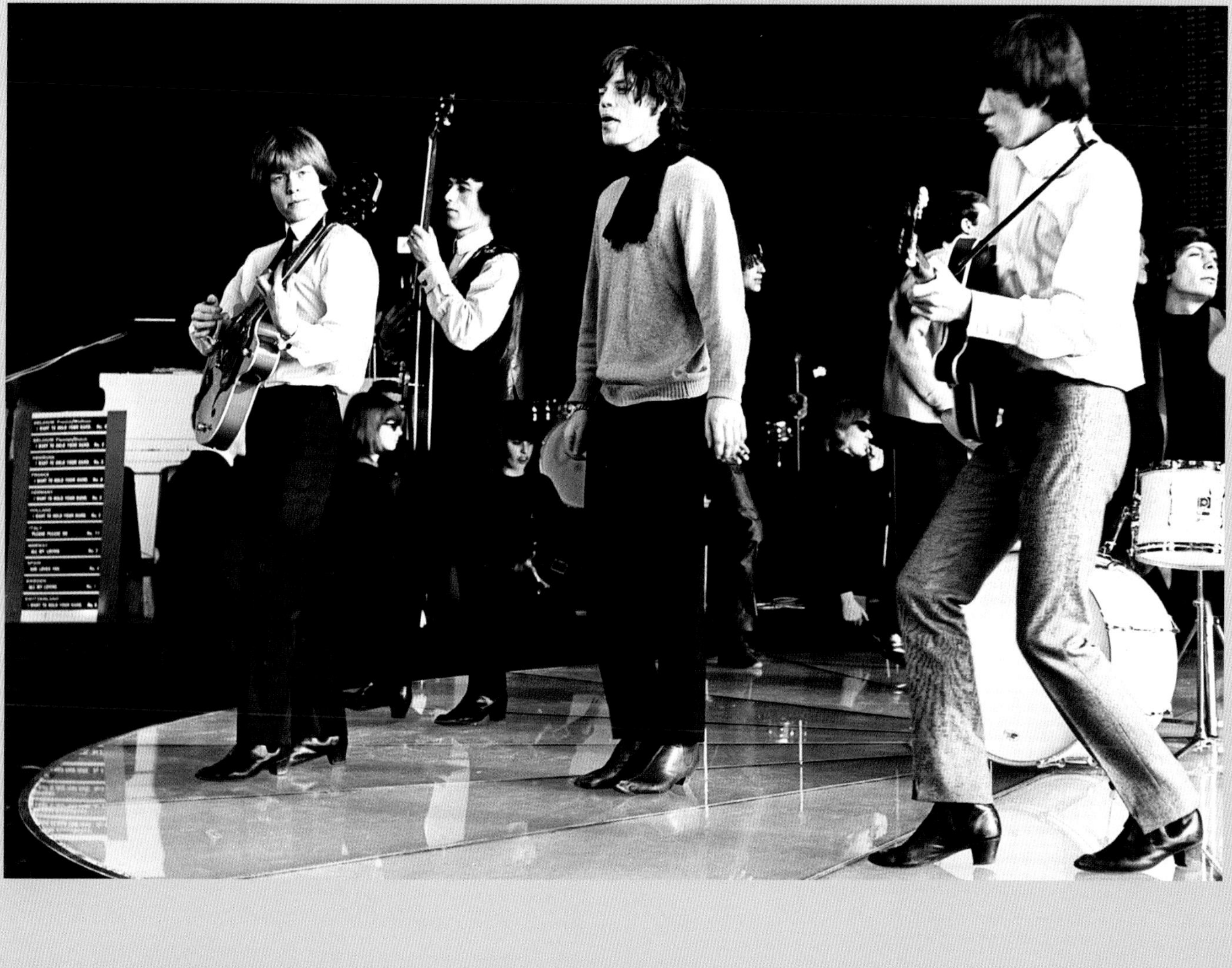

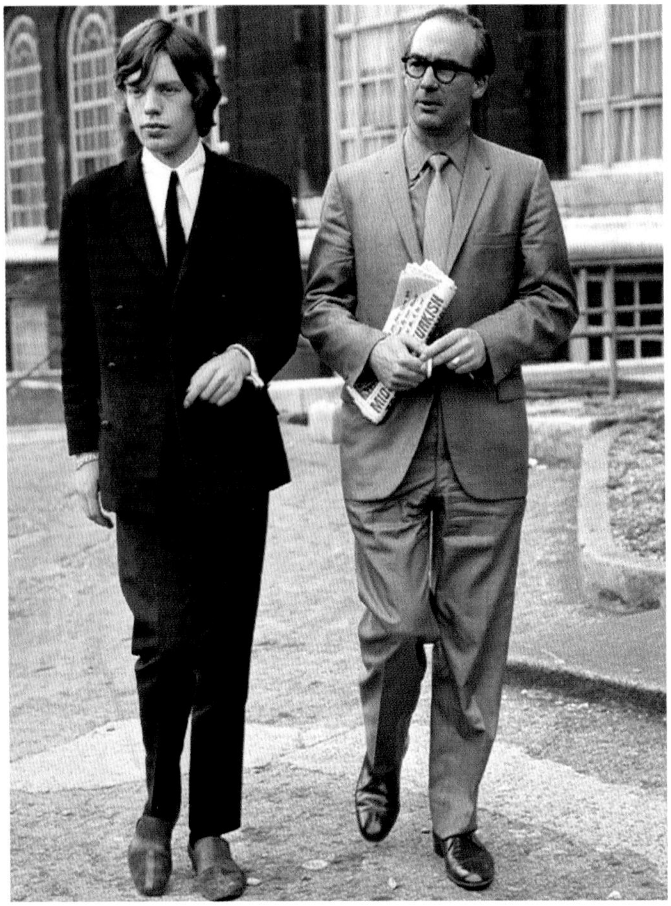

Jagger fined for speeding

Left: Mick Jagger leaving a Liverpool court with his manager Eric Easton after being fined £32 for speeding in August 1964. Things were to look up a few days later though, as the band's EP 'Five By Five' hit the British singles chart.

Andrew Loog Oldham, who had been employed briefly by Brian Epstein to publicize bands, had seen The Rolling Stones play in Richmond. After Epstein turned down Oldham's proposal that they both managed the group, Oldham asked Easton to come and watch them. Soon after, the band signed a management contract with Oldham and Easton.

Below: The Rolling Stones receive an award for being the most popular group at a Variety Club of Great Britain luncheon at London's Savoy Hotel in September 1964. Despite looking pensive, Brian Jones *(far right)* grinned when asked how they felt about pipping The Beatles for the accolade.

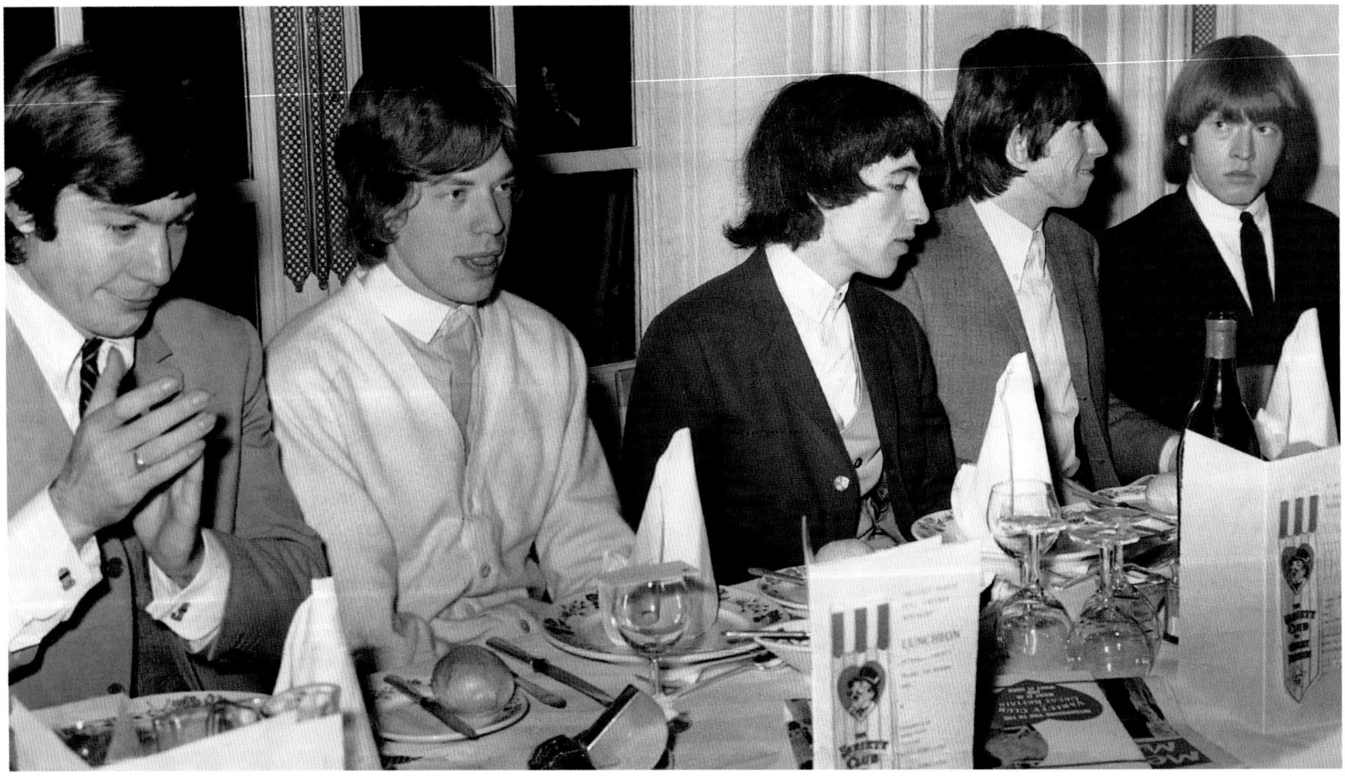

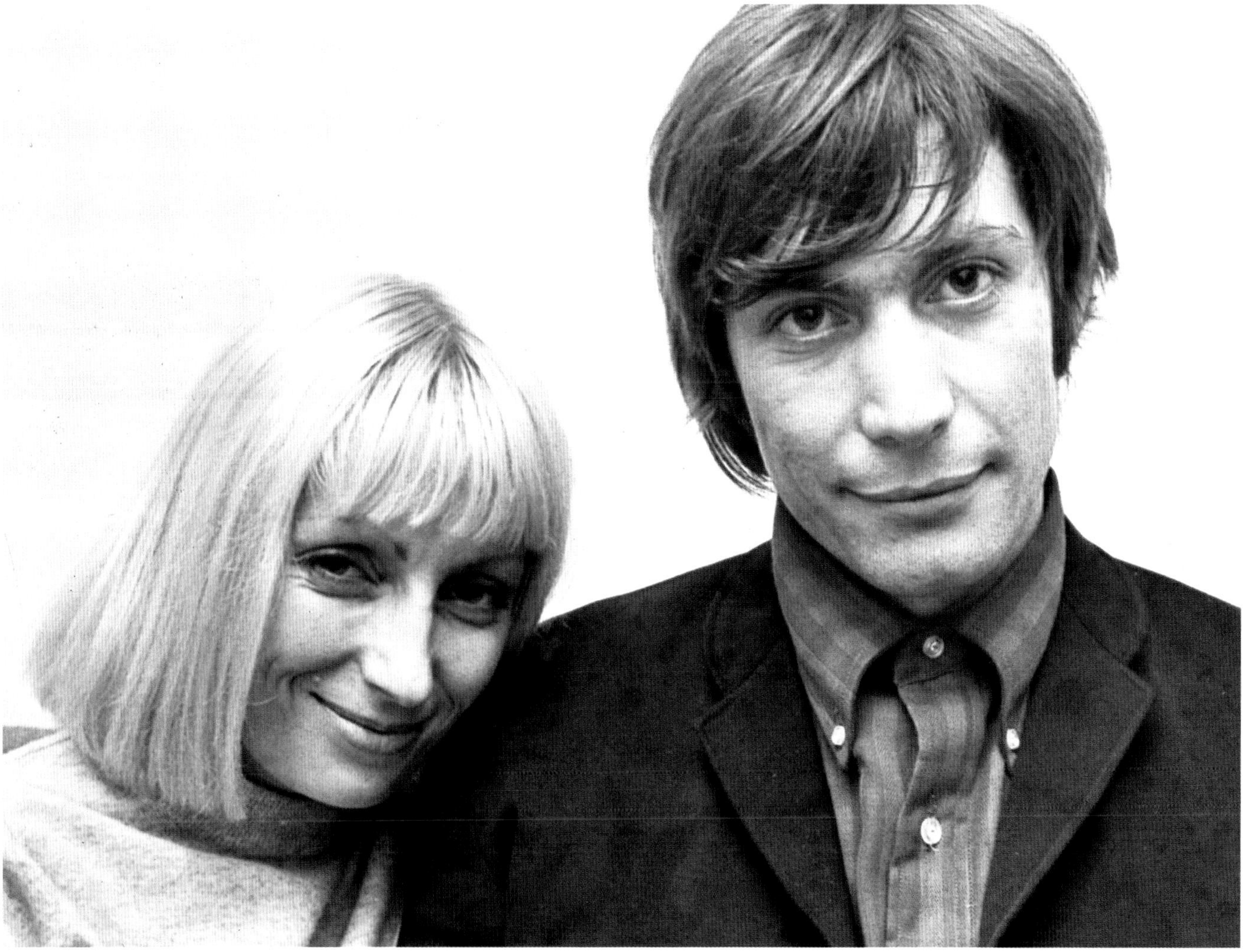

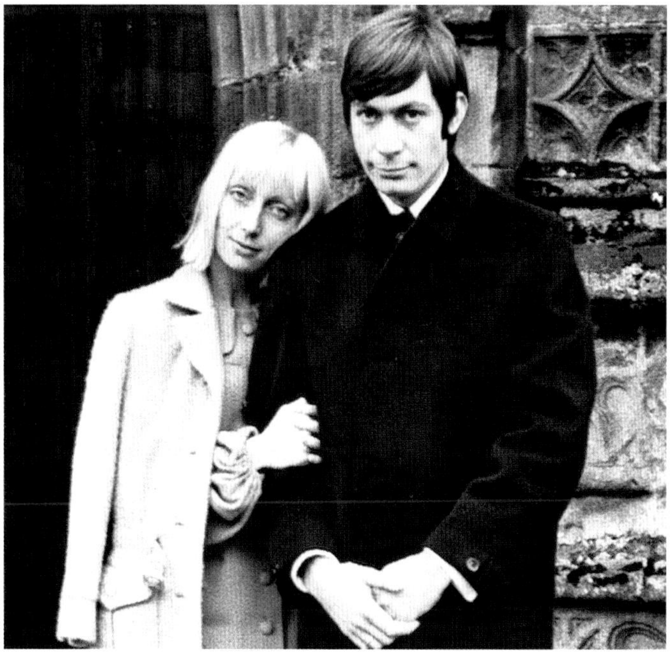

A quiet wedding

Above and right: When Charlie and Shirley married quietly in Yorkshire on 14 October 1964, not even the other Rolling Stones were told. The couple feared that their news would upset Charlie's fans.

Despite a very private ceremony, Shirley Watts epitomized the fashionable mid-1960s bride – blonde bob, bouclé coat, yellow dress and strappy low-heeled shoes. Shirley was an art student – as Charlie had once been. She intended to teach after her marriage, but more than 40 years later she hasn't yet started. After a brief honeymoon, Shirley had to wave farewell to Charlie as he left for the Stones' second US tour on 23 October.

On their return from the tour, Decca released 'Little Red Rooster', a blues song first recorded by Howlin' Wolf. Oldham had been reluctant to release it as a single, but the band, Charlie in particular, was keen. The record went straight to No.1 in the UK charts.

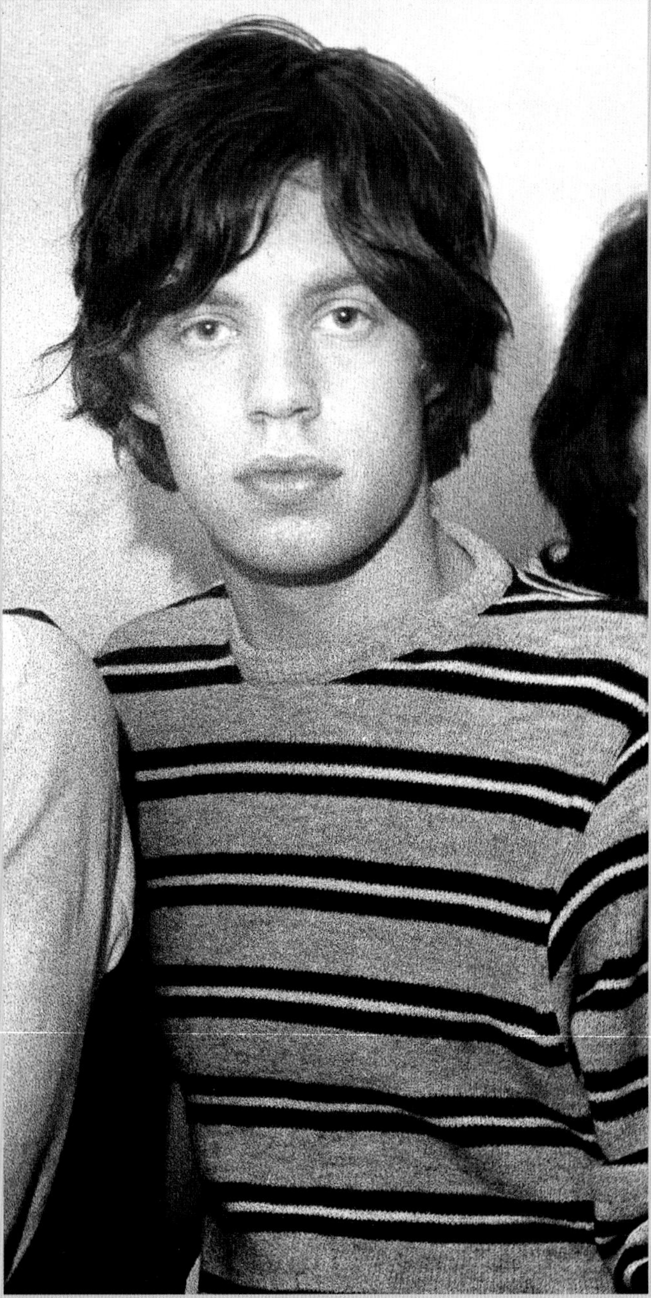

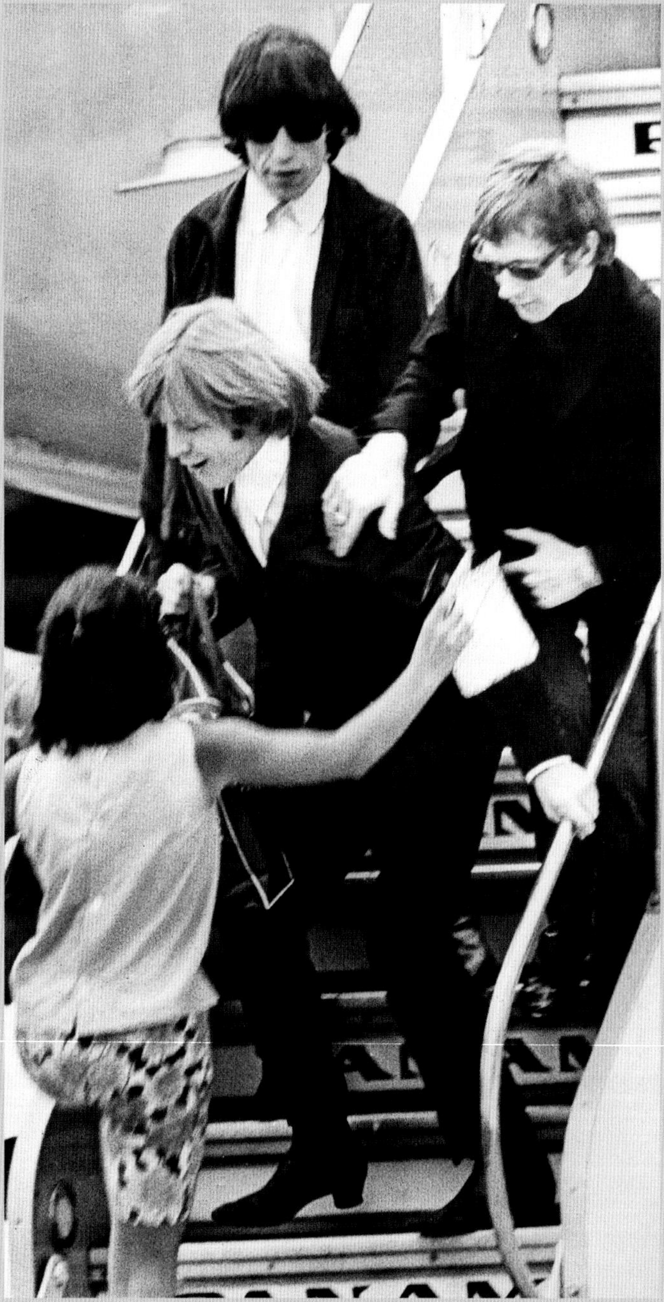

On tour

Above left: Mick, on the Stones' third tour of North America in May 1965. By then the writing was on the wall for Mick Jagger's long-term girlfriend Chrissie Shrimpton – he'd fallen for Marianne Faithfull, an aristocratic blonde teenager whose first hit record, 'As Tears Go By', was written by Jagger and Keith Richard.

Above right: The band arriving at Sydney for their first Australian tour on 21 January 1965. As they descended the steps of the plane, barricades broke and 3,000 fans burst through a police cordon. Here, manager Andrew Loog Oldham – in trademark shades – helps Brian Jones to ward off a particularly enthusiastic fan.

Opposite below: The band takes a moment while on a short tour of Scotland in June the same year. Rumours were rife that Brian and Mick didn't see eye to eye about who led the Stones.

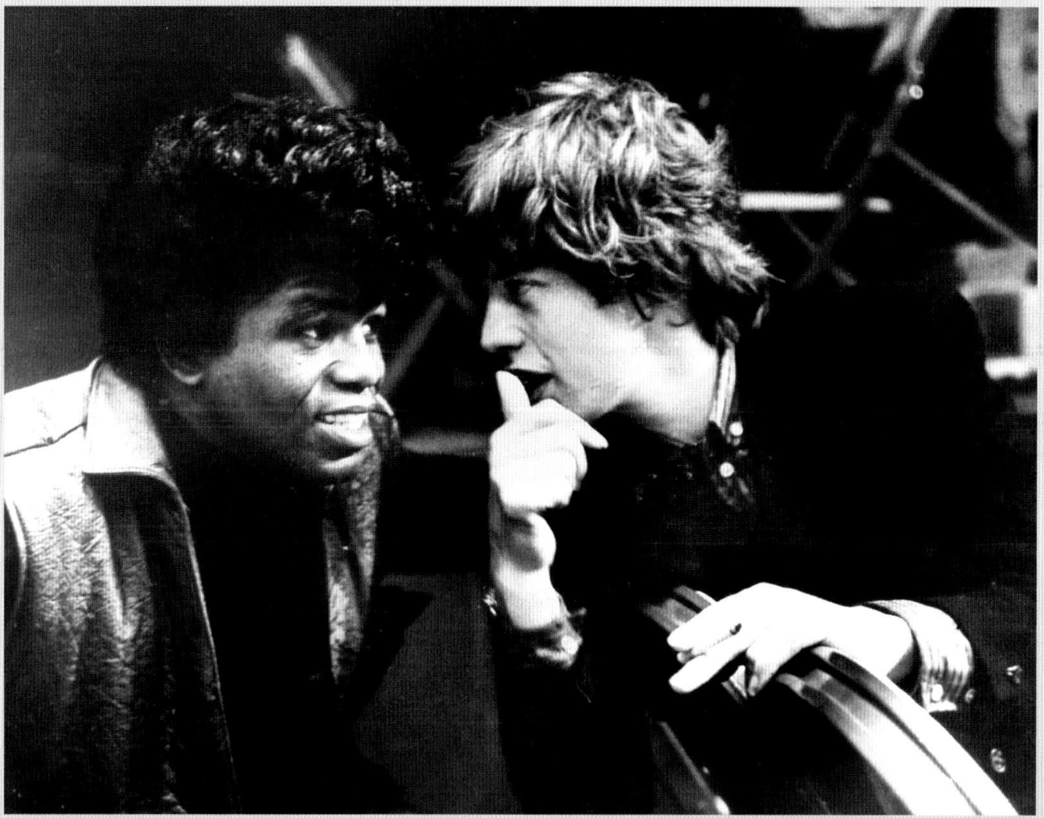

Right: Mick Jagger with rock legend James Brown. The Rolling Stones, most notably Keith Richard and Charlie Watts, have never forgotten their debt to black American blues and jazz musicians.

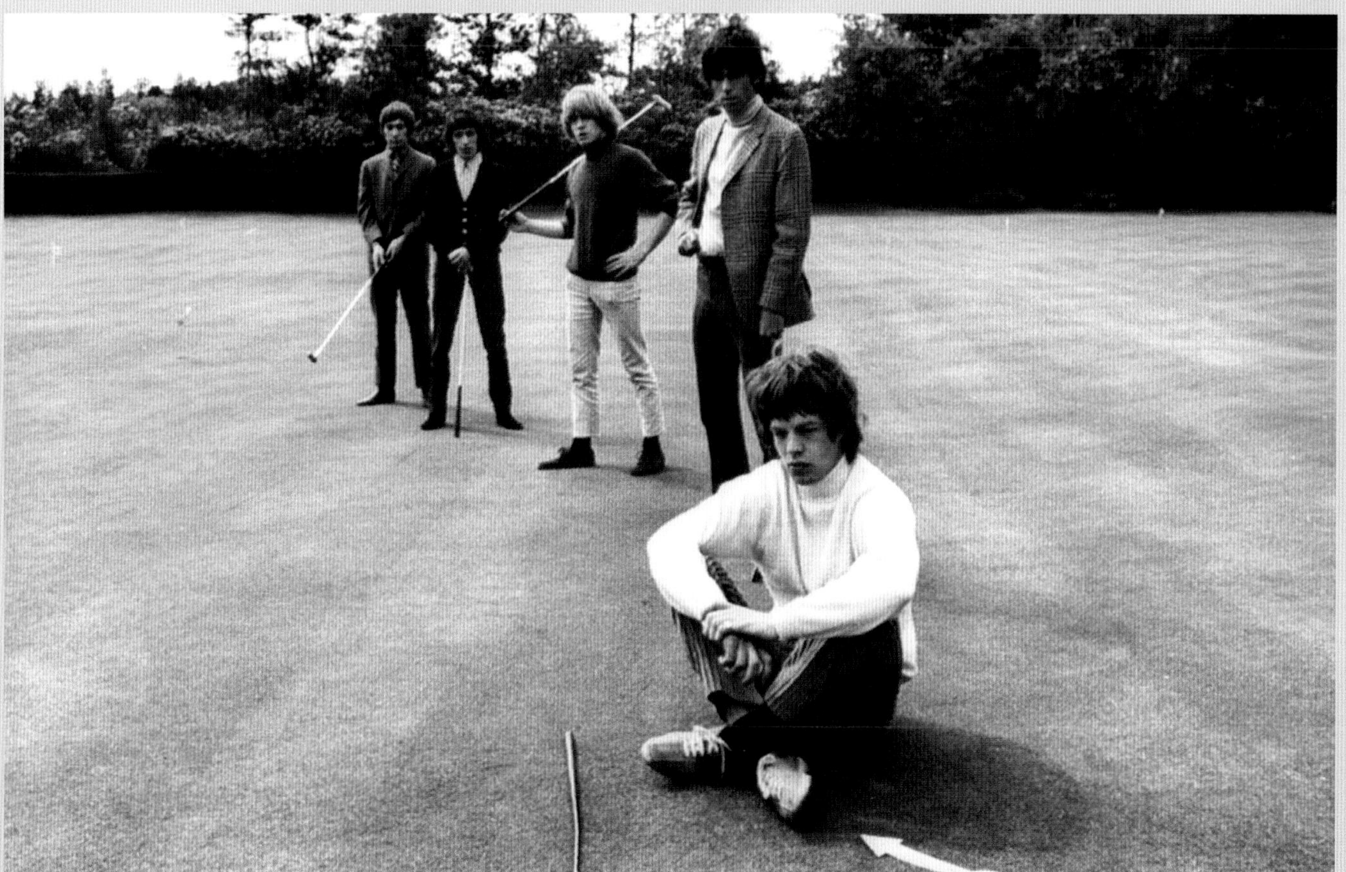

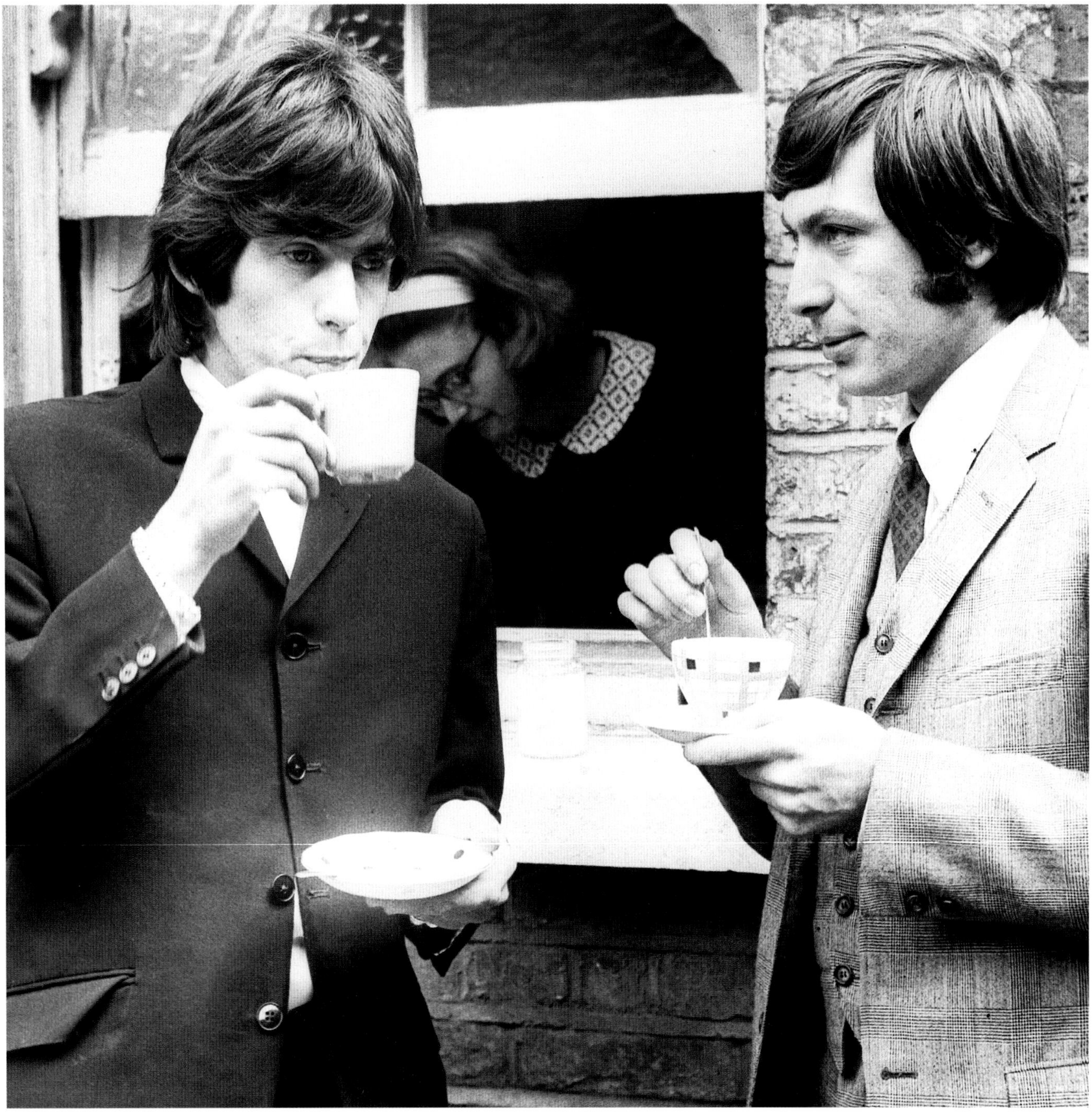

'Insulting behaviour'

Opposite above left: A sharp-suited Charlie Watts waiting outside a London magistrates' court in July 1965, where charges of 'insulting behaviour' relating to an incident in which they urinated on a garage forecourt are heard against the other three band members.

Opposite above right and opposite below: Bill Wyman and Mick Jagger (right), along with Brian Jones, were later fined £5.

Above: Messrs Richard and Watts appear to be unconcerned during a break in court proceedings. The case shocked parents and delighted Stones fans across the country. In contrast to their attitude towards The Beatles, who had just been awarded MBEs, much of the press and many ordinary people were hostile to the Stones. It was not the police that brought the case to court, but the garage owner and a member of the public.

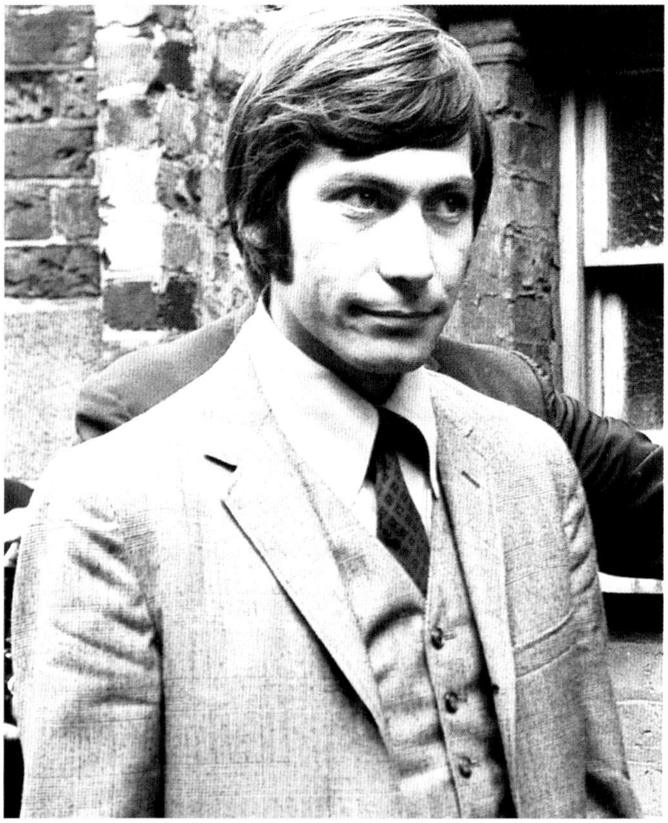

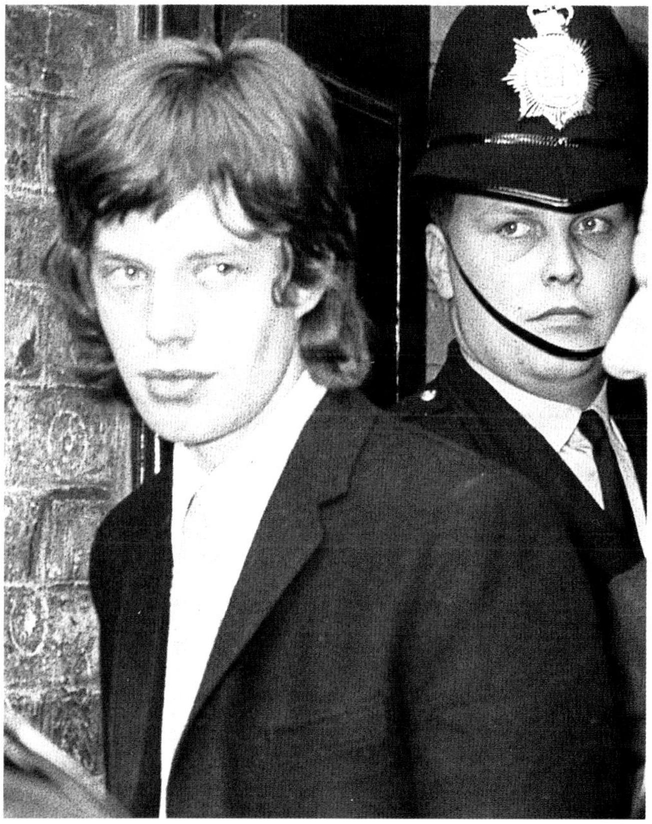

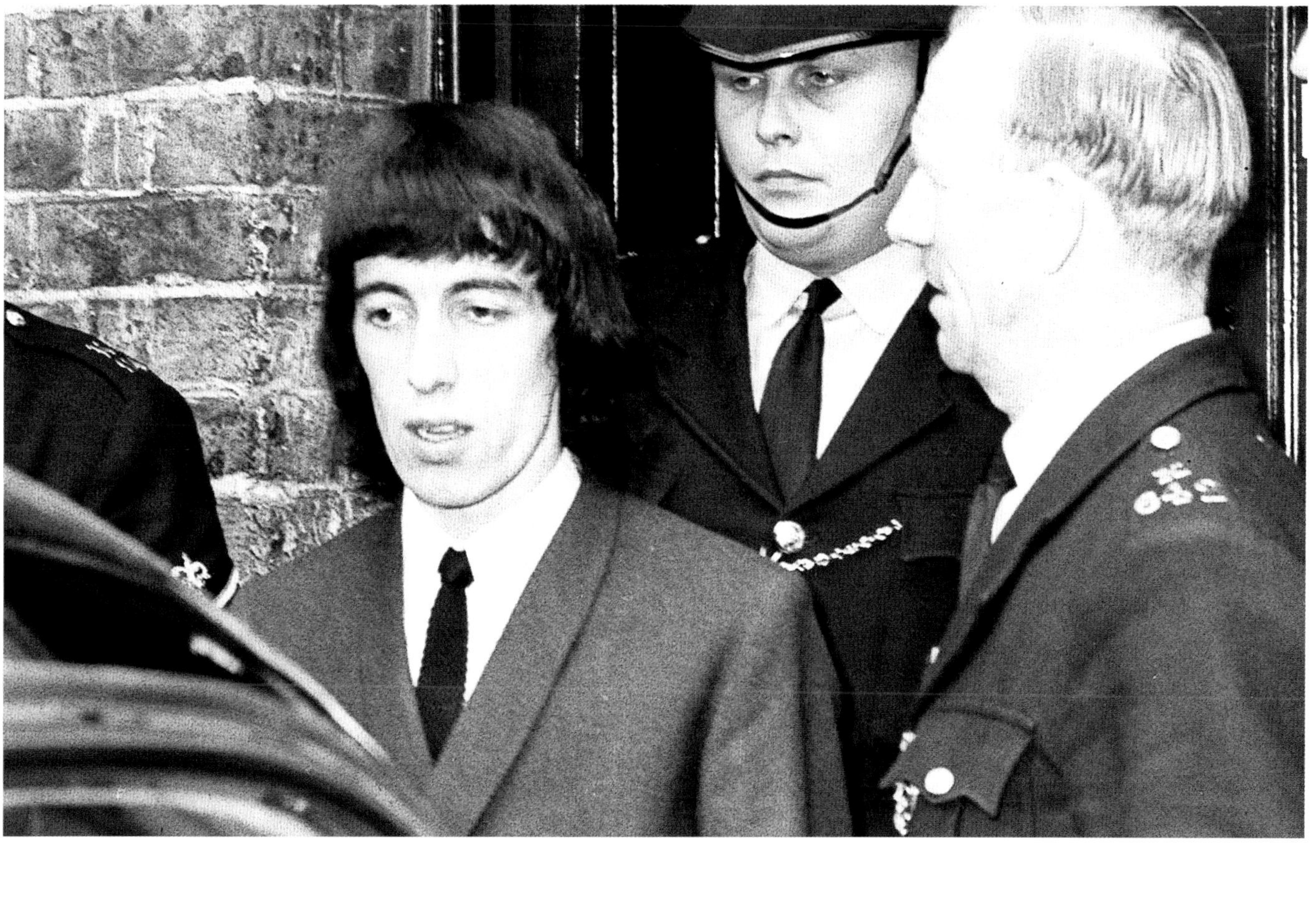

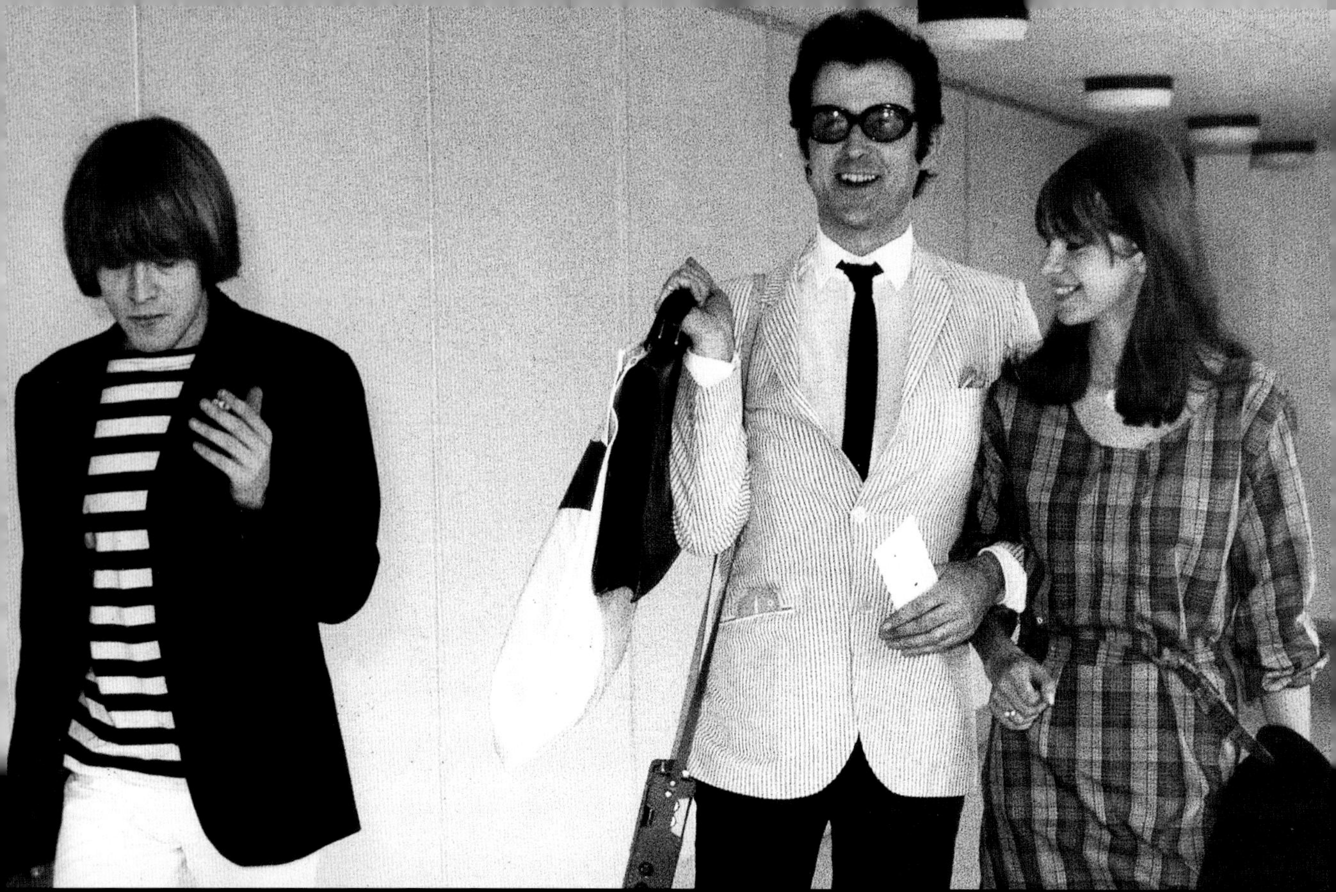

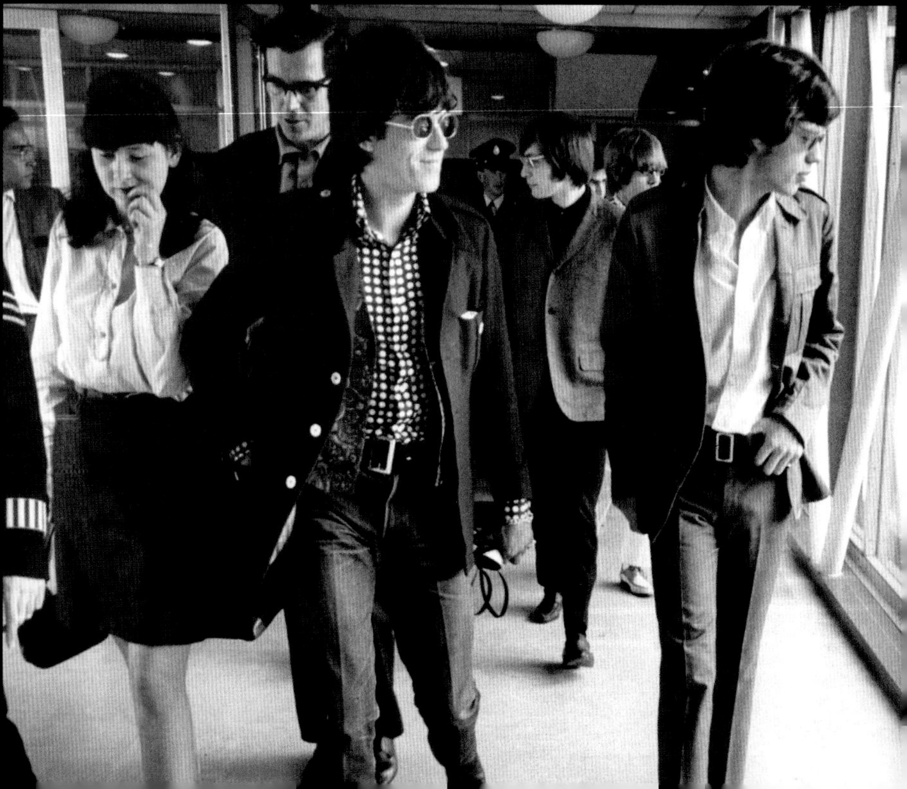

On tour

Above: Brian Jones at Tangier Airport in August 1965 with friend 'Betty', who is pretending to be with the other man in the picture. Brian was fascinated by the colours, clothes, music and spirituality of Morocco and Marrakesh. Soon he was to meet Anita Pallenberg and together they made several trips to north Africa.

Right: The Stones on their travels again. Rioting fans, injuries and police discipline marred a Rolling Stones concert in Berlin in September 1965. Fifty rows of seats were demolished, and a train was vandalized.

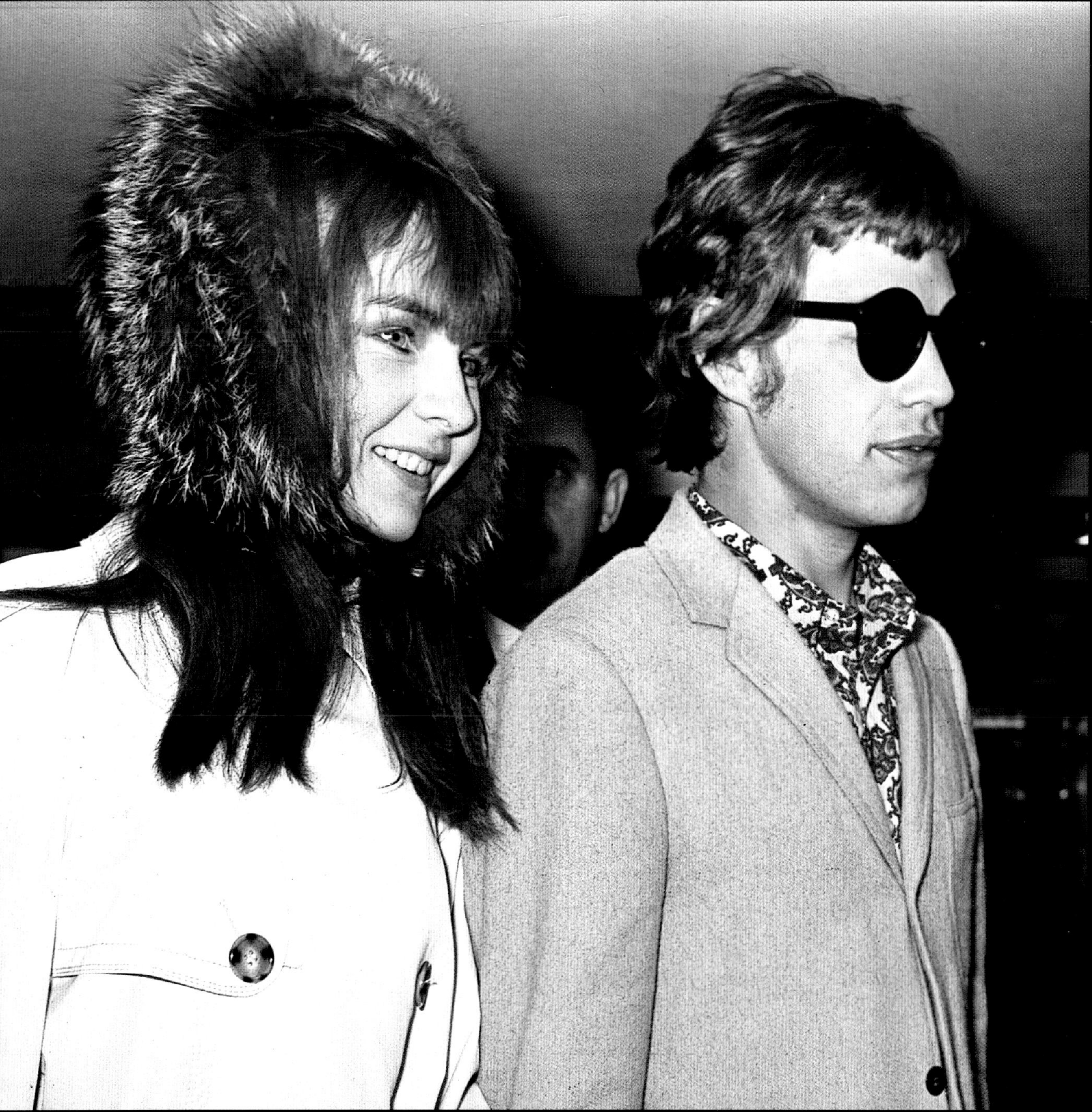

Dating Chrissie Shrimpton

Above: On Christmas Eve 1965 Mick Jagger and Chrissie Shrimpton return from a holiday in Jamaica. The previous August Mick had been best man at the London wedding of legendary French beauty and film star Catherine Deneuve and celebrated photographer David Bailey. Bailey used to step out with Jean Shrimpton, the first supermodel and sister to Chrissie.

Although the press had concentrated on their misdemeanours, the band had worked hard during 1965. The year began in Australia and the Far East, then there were various shorter tours of Britain and Europe. They also had spells in America in the spring and the autumn, and took time out to work in the recording studio. The chart-topping single 'Satisfaction' was originally recorded at the Chess Studios in Chicago and later reworked at the RCA studio where *Out Of Our Heads* was made. In November 1965 'Get Off Of My Cloud' was No.1 simultaneously in the United Kingdom and the United States.

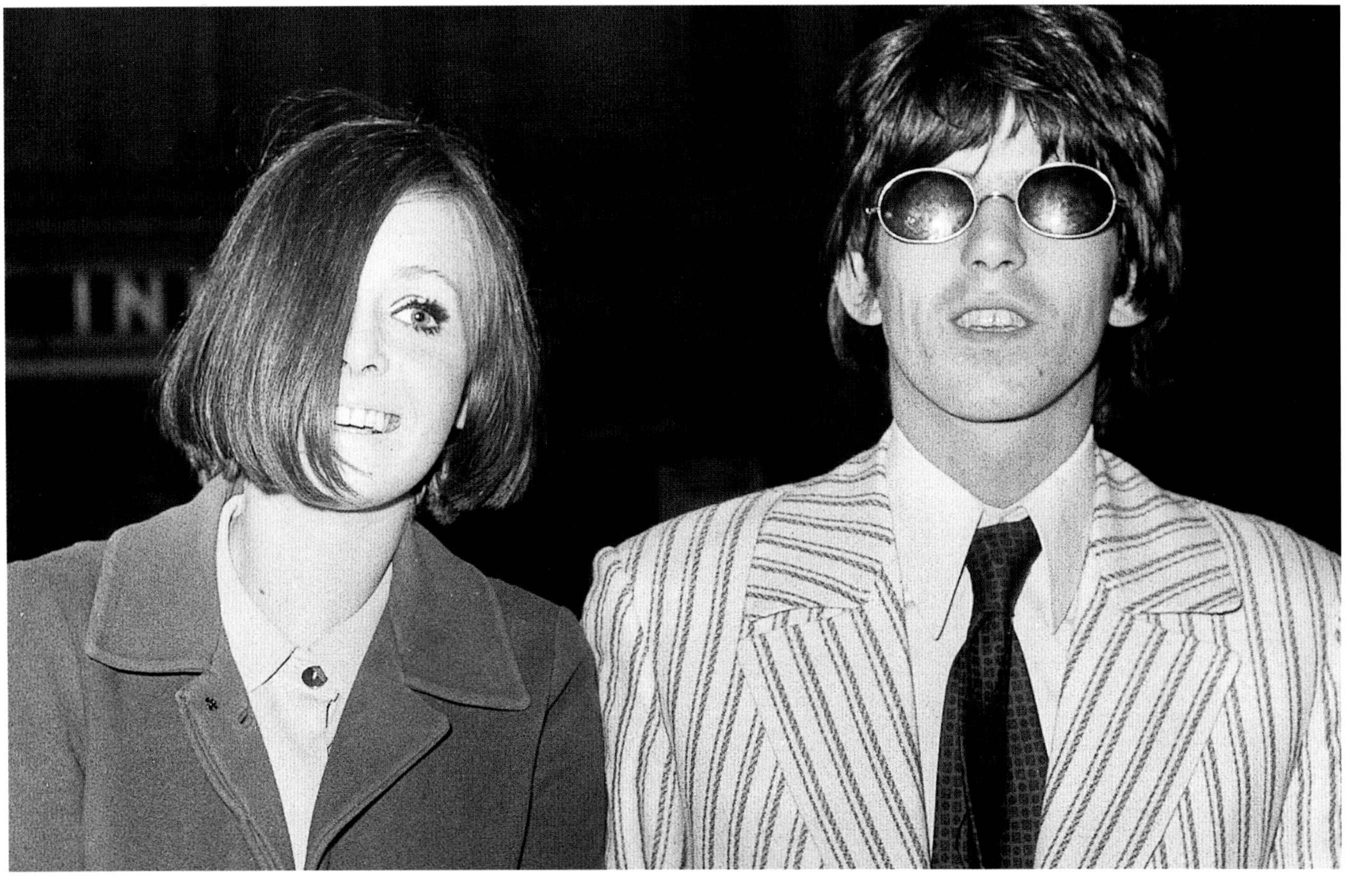

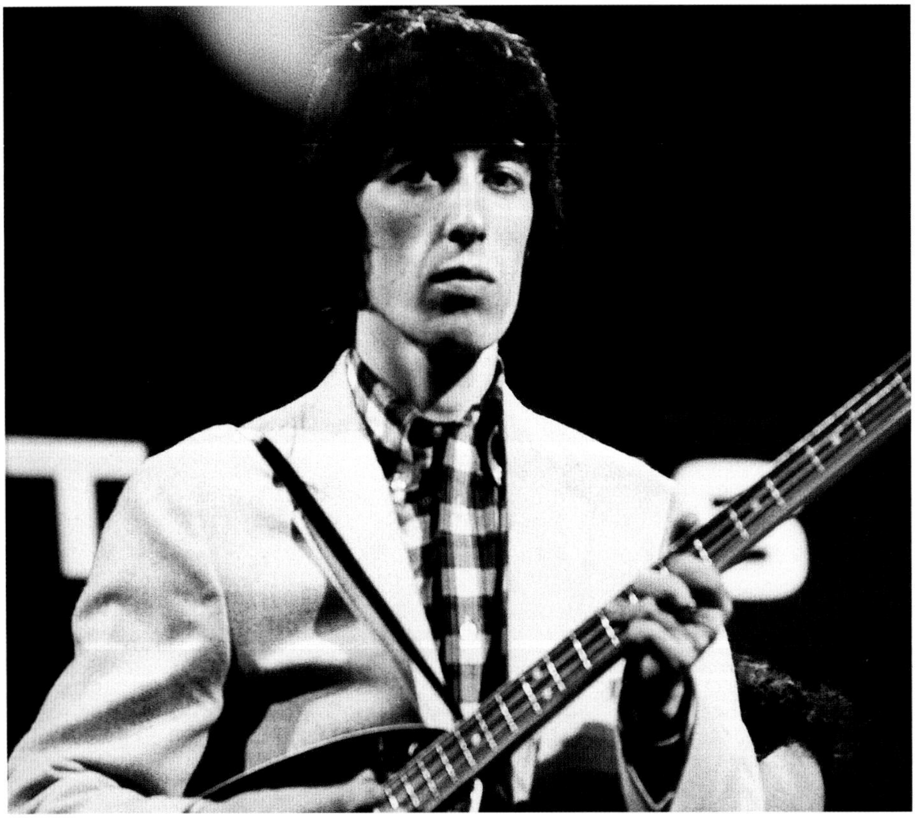

Seven weeks at No.1

Left: Bill Wyman – impassive, unsmiling and the corner Stone of a band now bathed in worldwide admiration. The classic album *Aftermath* was released in April 1966 and spent seven weeks at No.1 in the British charts.

While their previous album *Out Of Our Heads* only contained four Jagger and Richard compositions, all 14 of the tracks on *Aftermath* were their own. In 1966 Mick and Keith had also written Cliff Richard's single 'Blue Turns To Grey', and Chris Farlowe released 'Out Of Time', a track from *Aftermath*.

Above: Keith Richard at the London premiere of Roman Polanski's cult film *Cul de Sac*. His companion was Mari Ann Moller, but no deep romance ensued.

Opposite: By January 1967 Mick Jagger could sit, almost enthroned, knowing that his band had conquered the world. A new single, 'Let's Spend The Night Together', had just been released, shortly followed by an album, *Between The Buttons*.

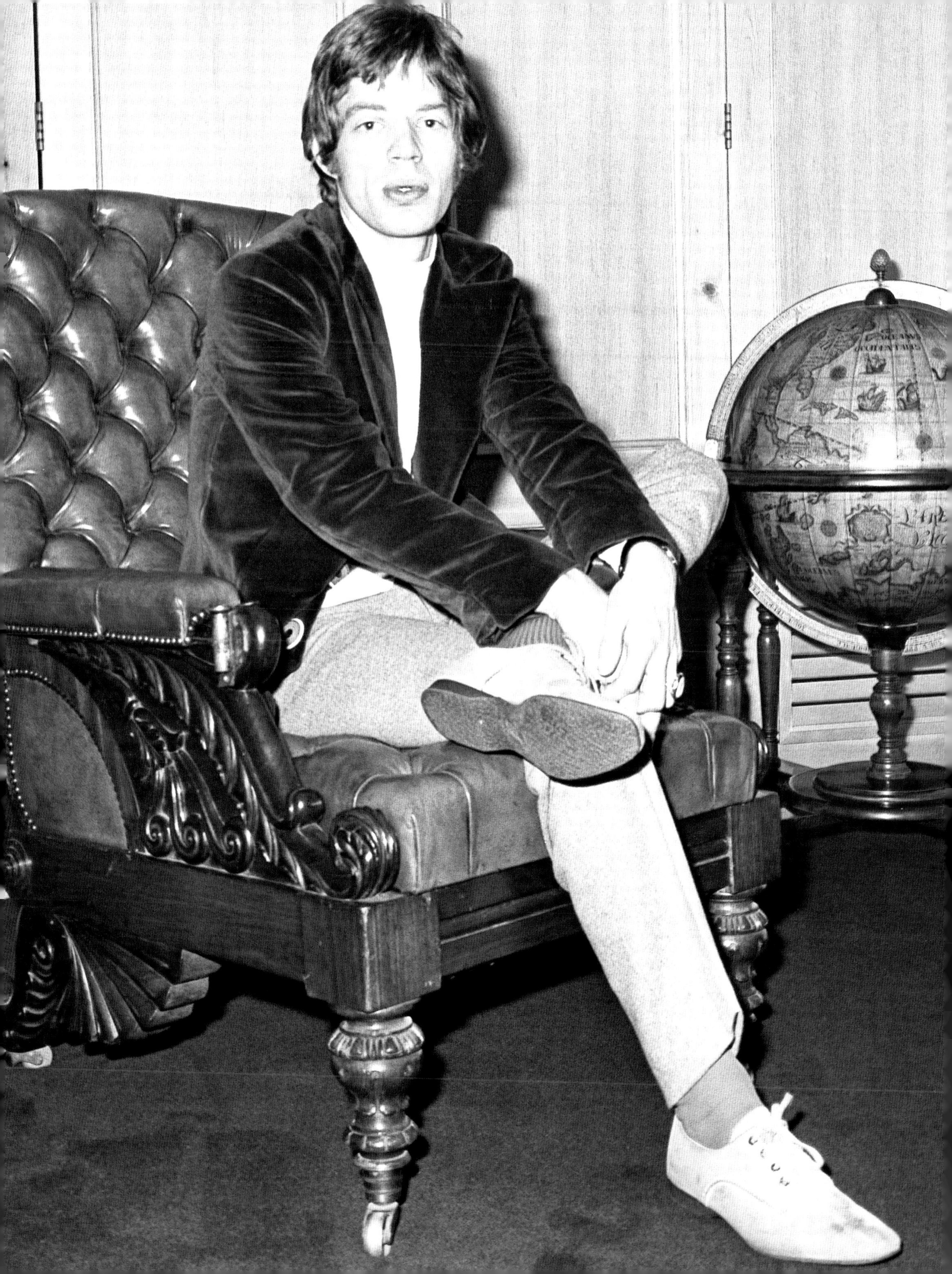

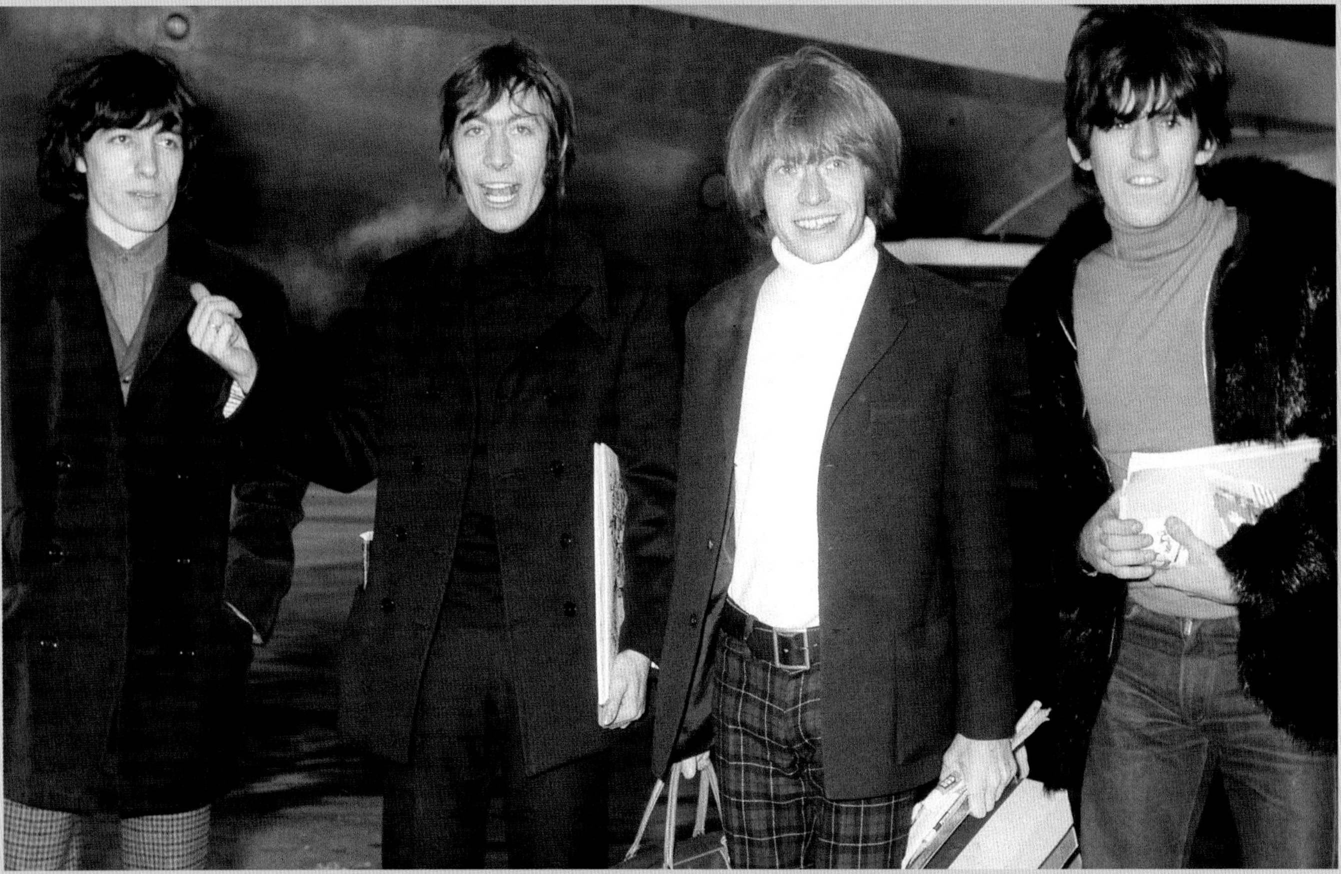

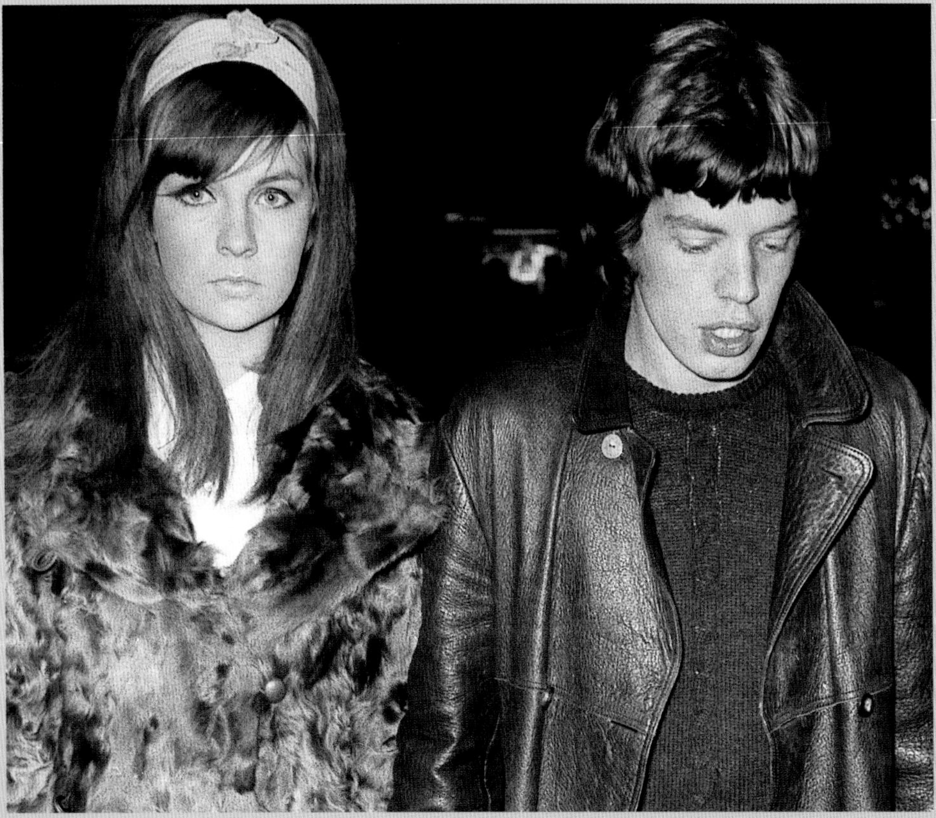

Mick and Chrissie split

Left: Chrissie and Mick in February 1966 – this time they are off to New York, where the group is doing some TV appearances. Chrissie's relationship with Mick ended in December 1966. Both their stricken faces in this photograph suggest that things were not going well. Soon Mick was to have Marianne Faithfull on his arm.

Above: A rarely seen glimpse of The Rolling Stones without Mick Jagger, and a smiling Brian and Charlie in New York, 1966. The band's fifth American tour began in June that year. So many hotels had refused to take their booking that on arrival in New York they stayed on a yacht moored in the harbour. After all the touring and recording it was a shame that Brian's summer holiday in Morocco was ruined by a broken hand, leading to fears that he wouldn't play for two months.

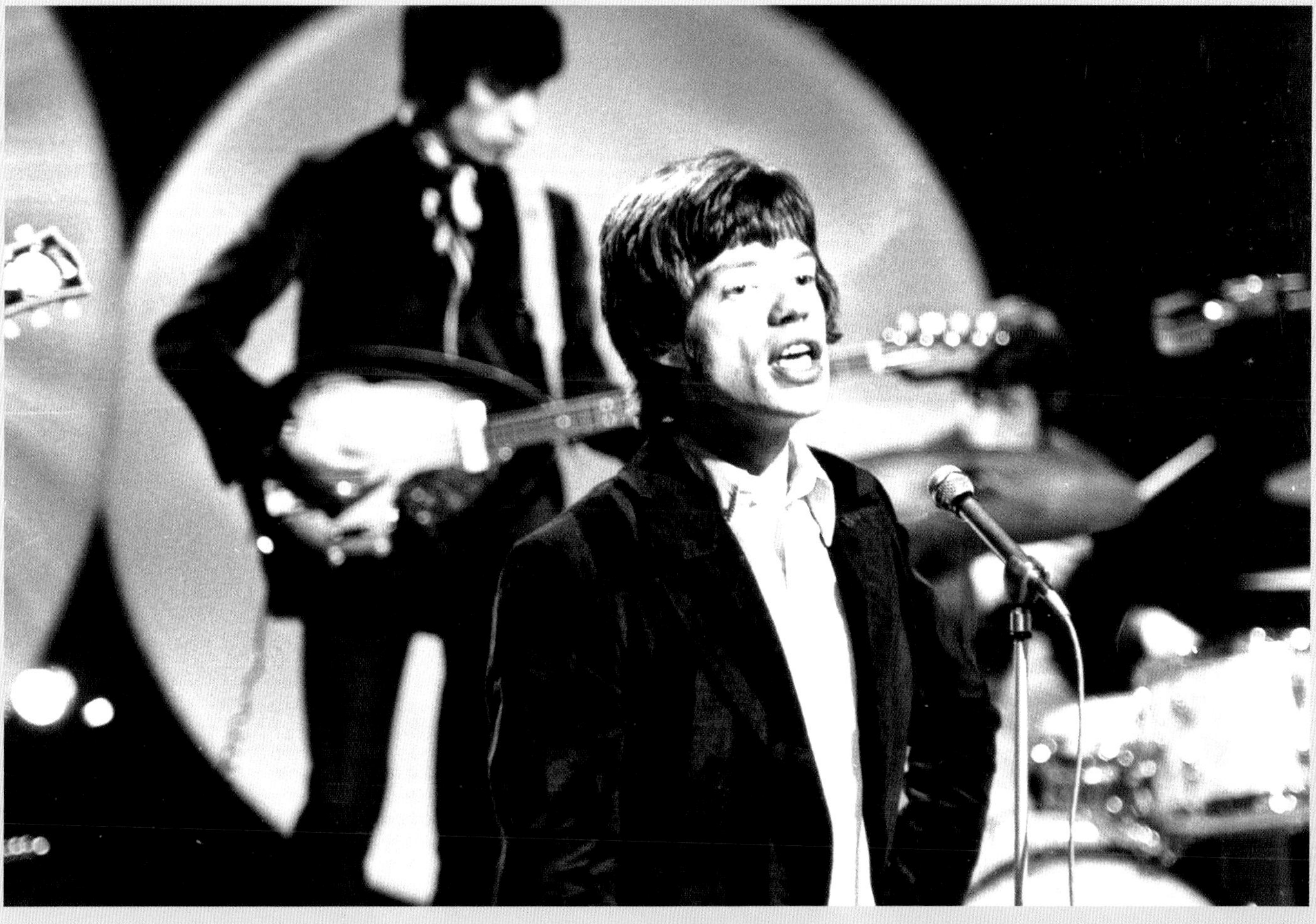

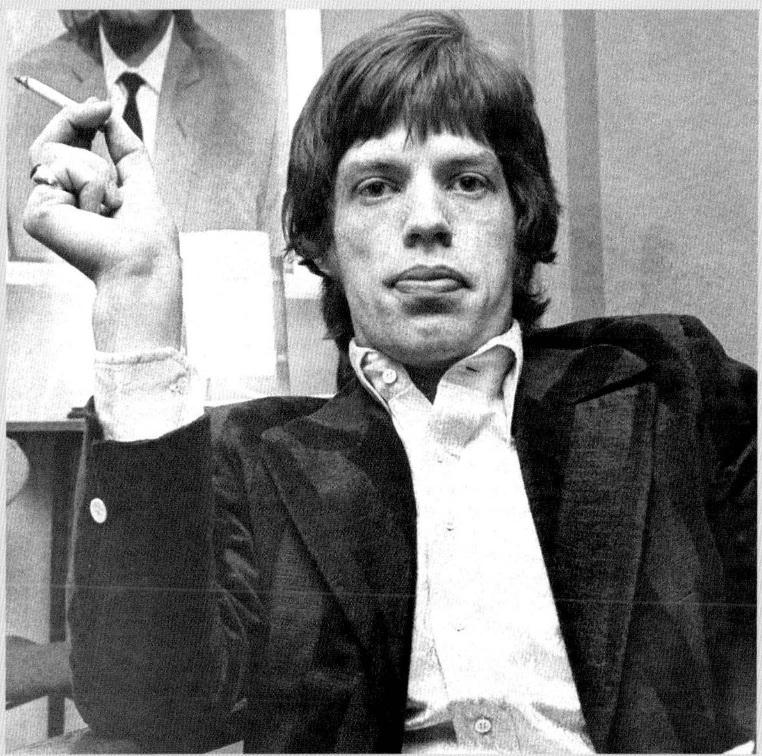

Causing controversy

Right: Mick Jagger shortly before being banned from appearing on Eamonn Andrews' TV show because the band planned to sing to a pre-recorded backing track. Soon it would become routine for pop stars to mime – even to hit songs that had been recorded by session musicians – but it caused controversy at the time.

Above: A compromise with the show's producers seemed to be reached when the band played 'She Smiled Sweetly' which they could do live, instead of their current smash, 'Let's Spend The Night Together'. When on *The Ed Sullivan Show* in America, the Stones were forced to change the title of the single to 'Let's Spend Some Time Together'.

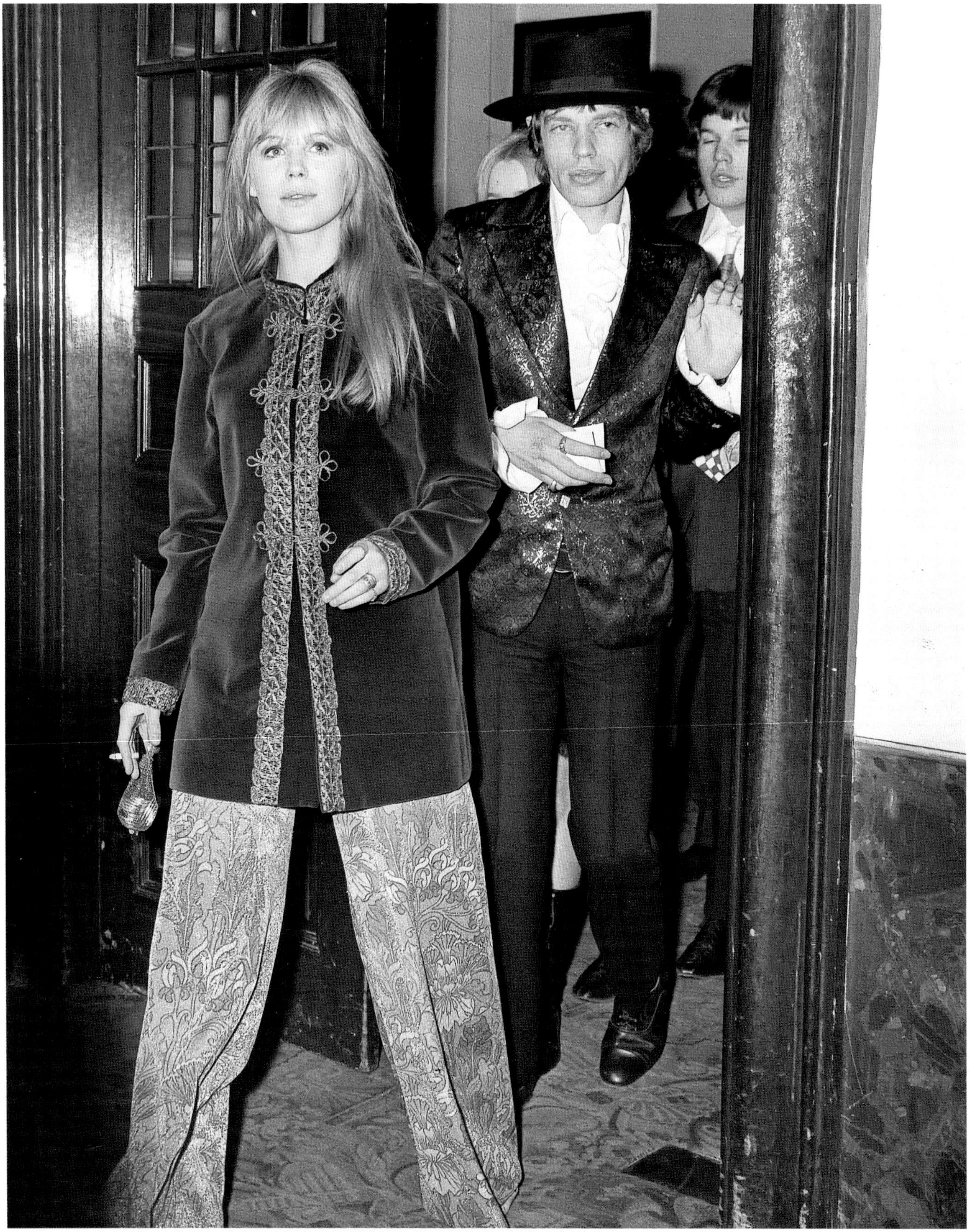

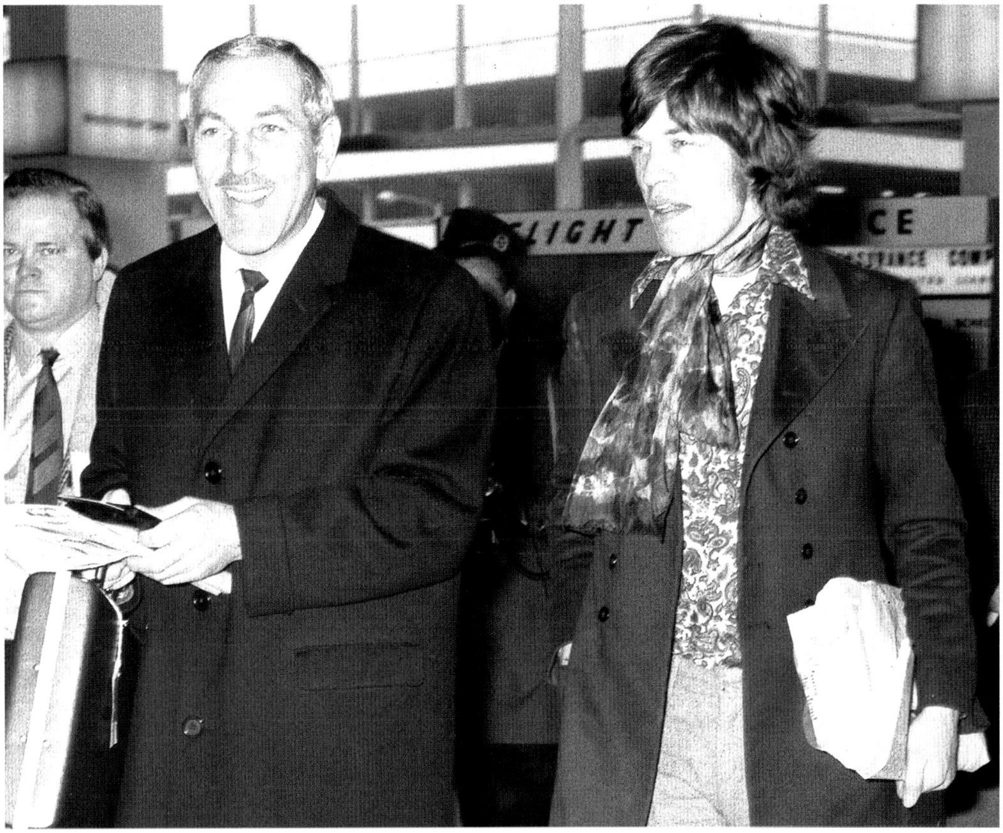

'Let's Spend The Night Together'

Opposite: 23 February 1967, and a luminously beautiful Marianne Faithfull and smartly dressed Mick Jagger upstage Covent Garden patron Princess Margaret by arriving at the Royal Opera House five minutes late. Sticklers for protocol were outraged.

Right and below: Work or pleasure? Mick leaves London for some of both in Paris in April 1967. The Stones' three-week European tour had just finished.

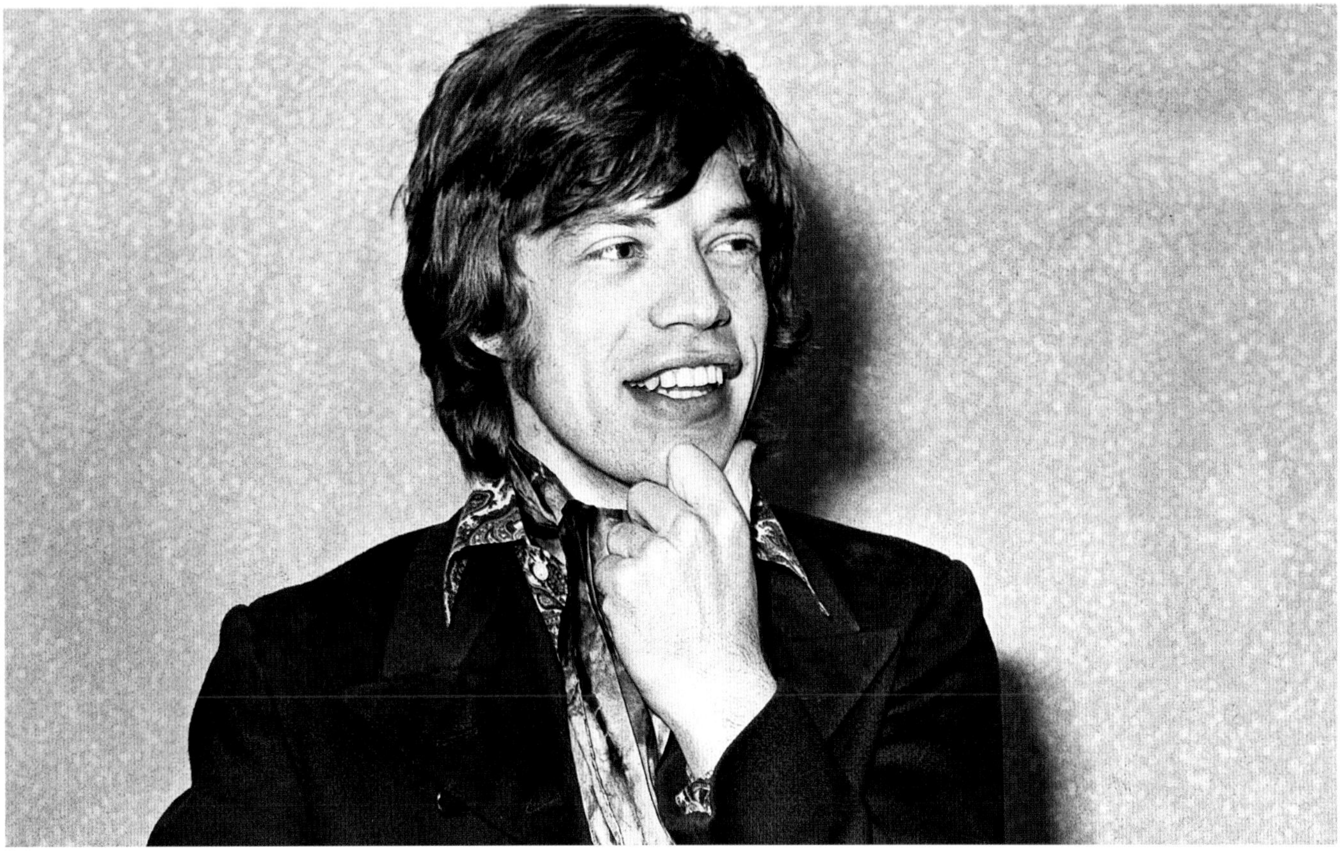

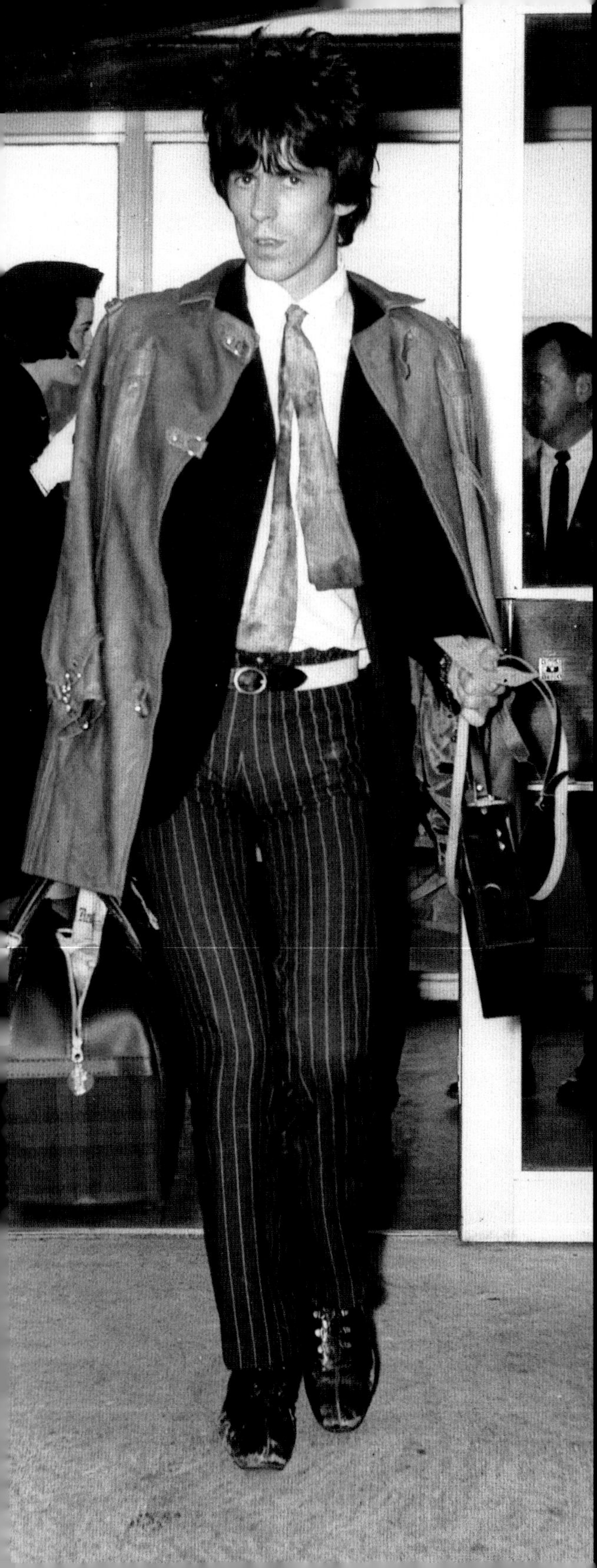

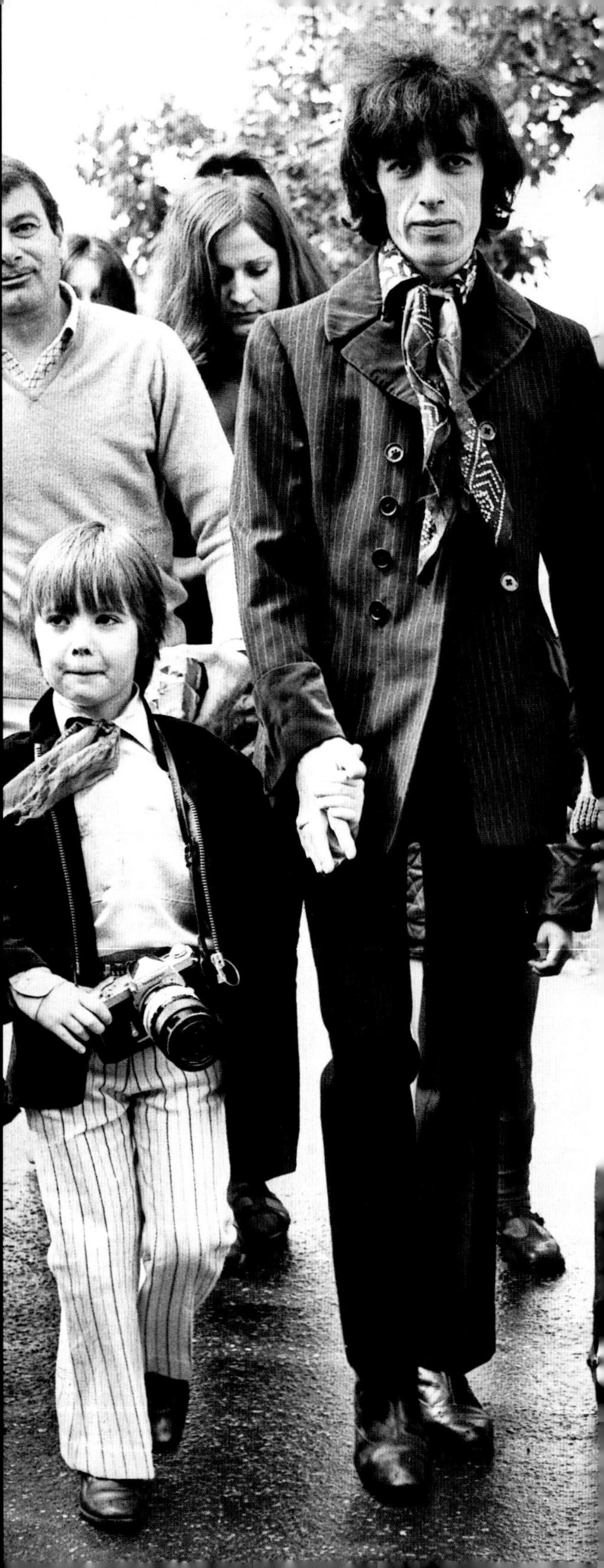

rugs charges

pposite left: Keith Richard travelling between London nd Paris. A series of drugs-related charges clouded his nd Mick Jagger's lives that summer. In February the olice raided Redlands, Richard's Sussex home. Among ther evidence, they took away amphetamines found in he pocket of a jacket belonging to Marianne Faithfull. lick claimed that the jacket and drugs were his.

pposite right: Bill Wyman's interest in charitable work egan early. Here he holds the hand of his five-year-old on Stephen as they attend the opening of a community ssociation retreat in Essex during May 1967.

ight: Mick Jagger in May 1967. The Stones had just ompleted a European tour, during which relations etween the band and the police and customs officials ad been tense, given the band's association with rowd violence and alleged drugs offences. On 10 May lick and Keith appeared in court following the raid on eith's home.

elow: A band on the brink. Some eyes meet the camera, thers don't. Only the two 'quiet men' at the back seem ble to meet the lens. Brian Jones had also been arrested or separate drugs-related offences the same day, and he, agger and Richard were all out on bail.

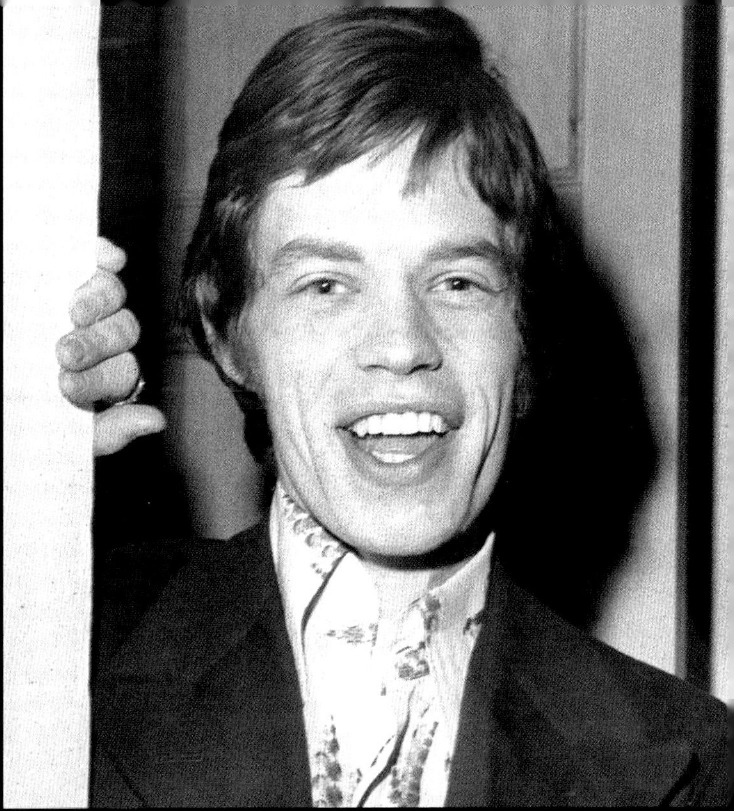

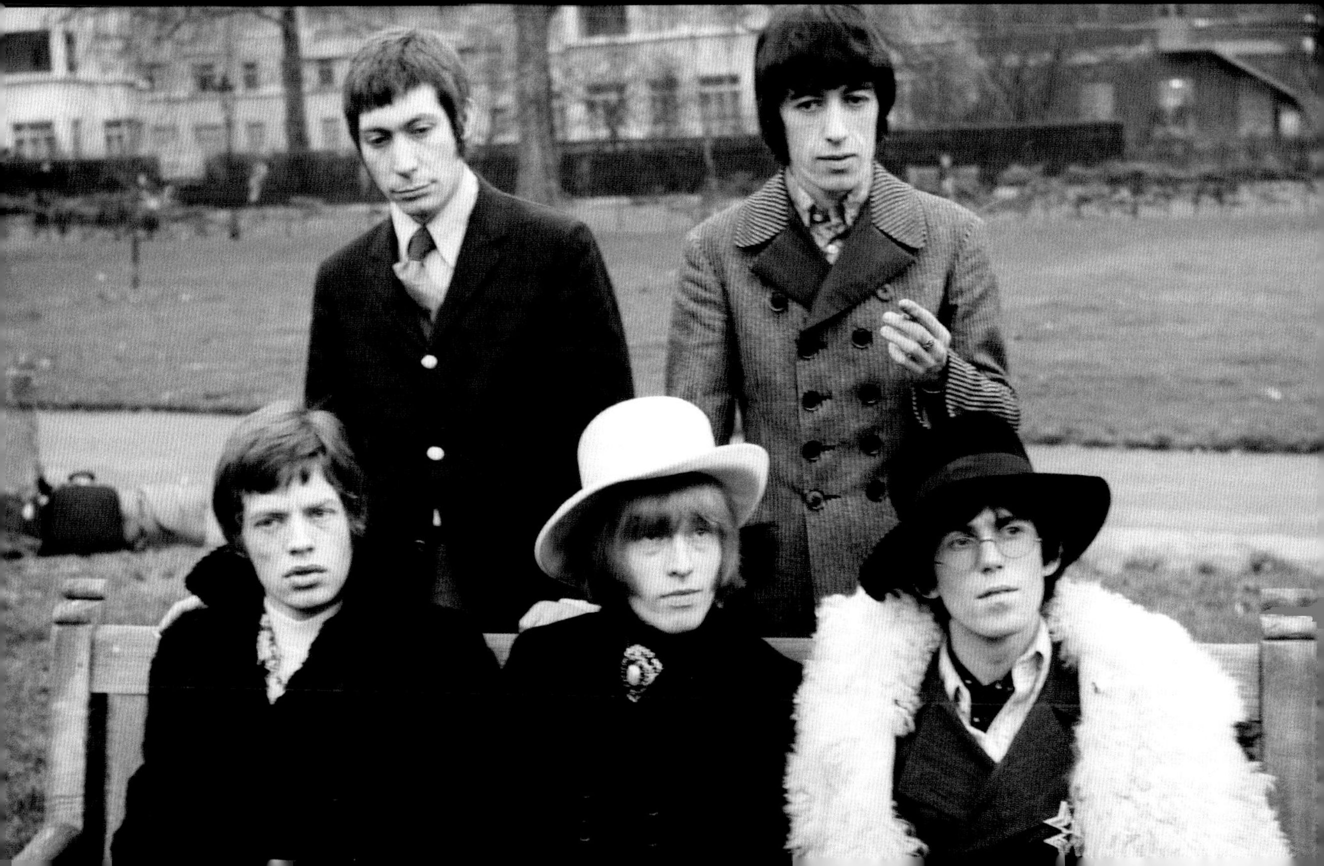

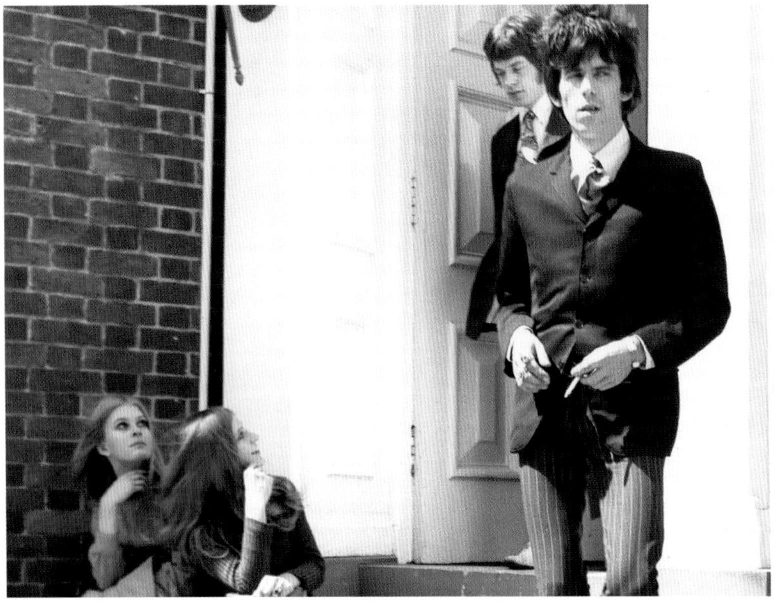

Trials and tribulations

Left: Adoring girl fans can't begin to lift Keith's mood as he faces the first stage of the court proceedings that followed the recent drug bust at his Sussex home. It was alleged that a cocktail of drugs including marijuana and heroin were found during a party. Jagger was charged with possession, while Richard was accused of allowing the premises to be used for the smoking of Indian hemp. A friend of theirs, Robert Fraser, was charged with possession of heroin and amphetamines.

Below: Mick's smile is as wide as his trendy tie, but Keith faced the more serious charge and looks understandably glum.

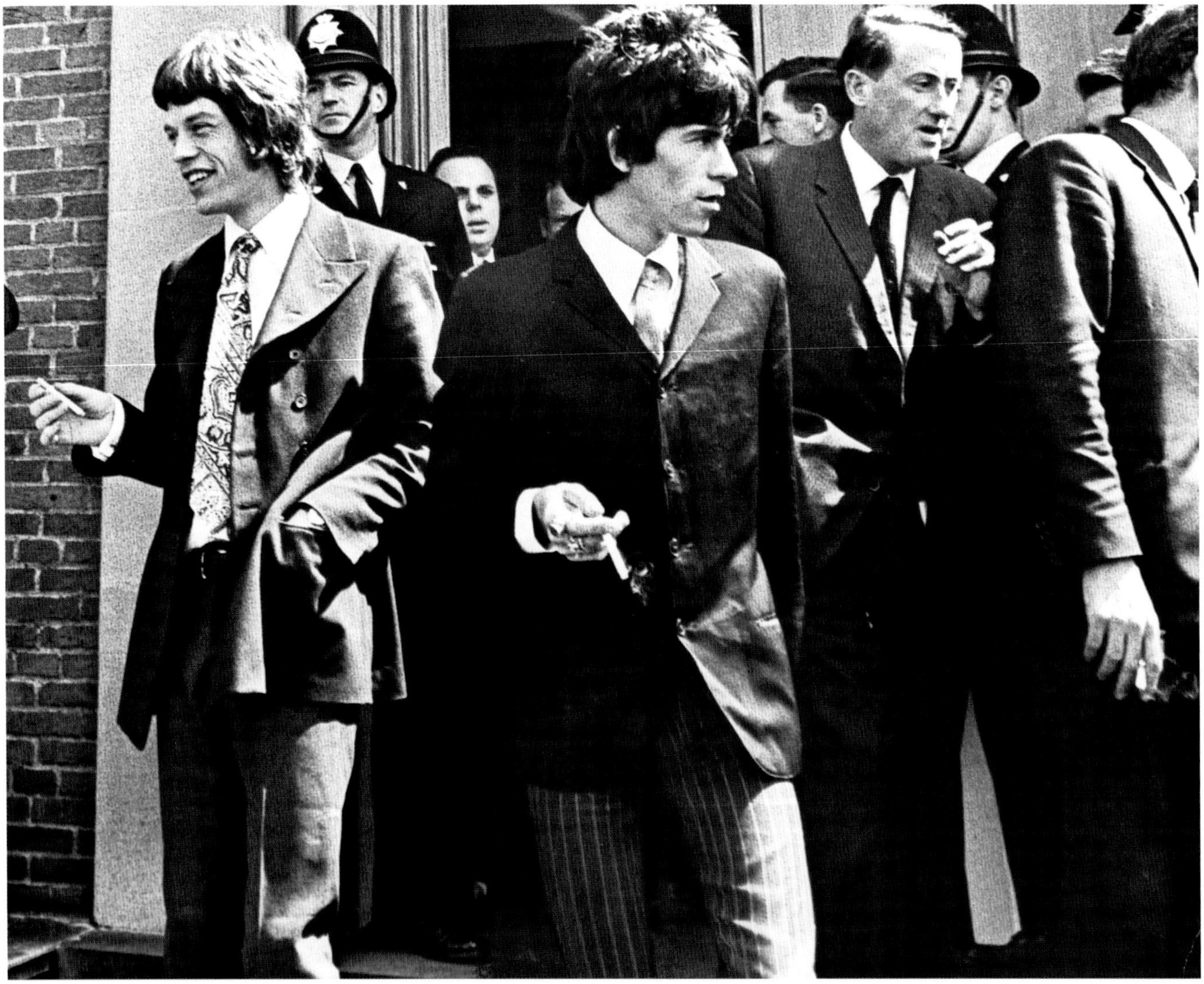

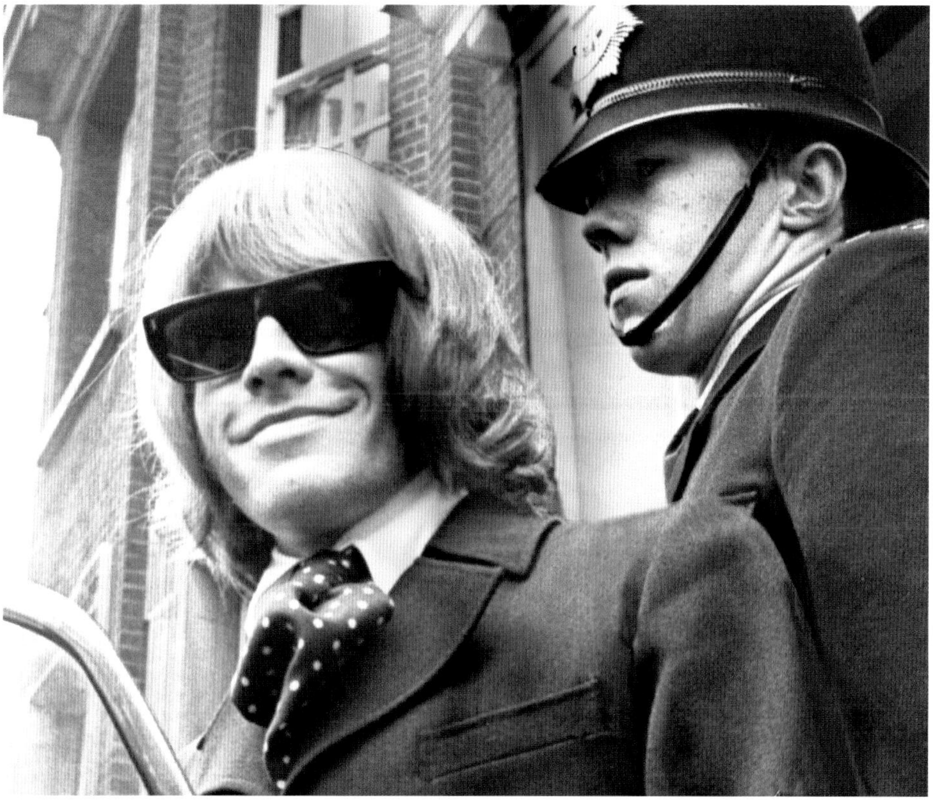

Jones convicted

Left: Brian Jones at his own court proceedings following his arrest at home in Kensington in May 1967 for possession. He was soon to face a jail sentence, but this was commuted on appeal on the grounds of his fragile health – he spent time in hospital because of nervous strain.

Below: Keith Richard outside the Chichester court. The court heard the cases against Mick Jagger and Robert Fraser first but did not sentence either of them until after Keith's case had been dealt with. As a result Jagger and Fraser spent time in Lewes prison until the court was ready to sentence all three.

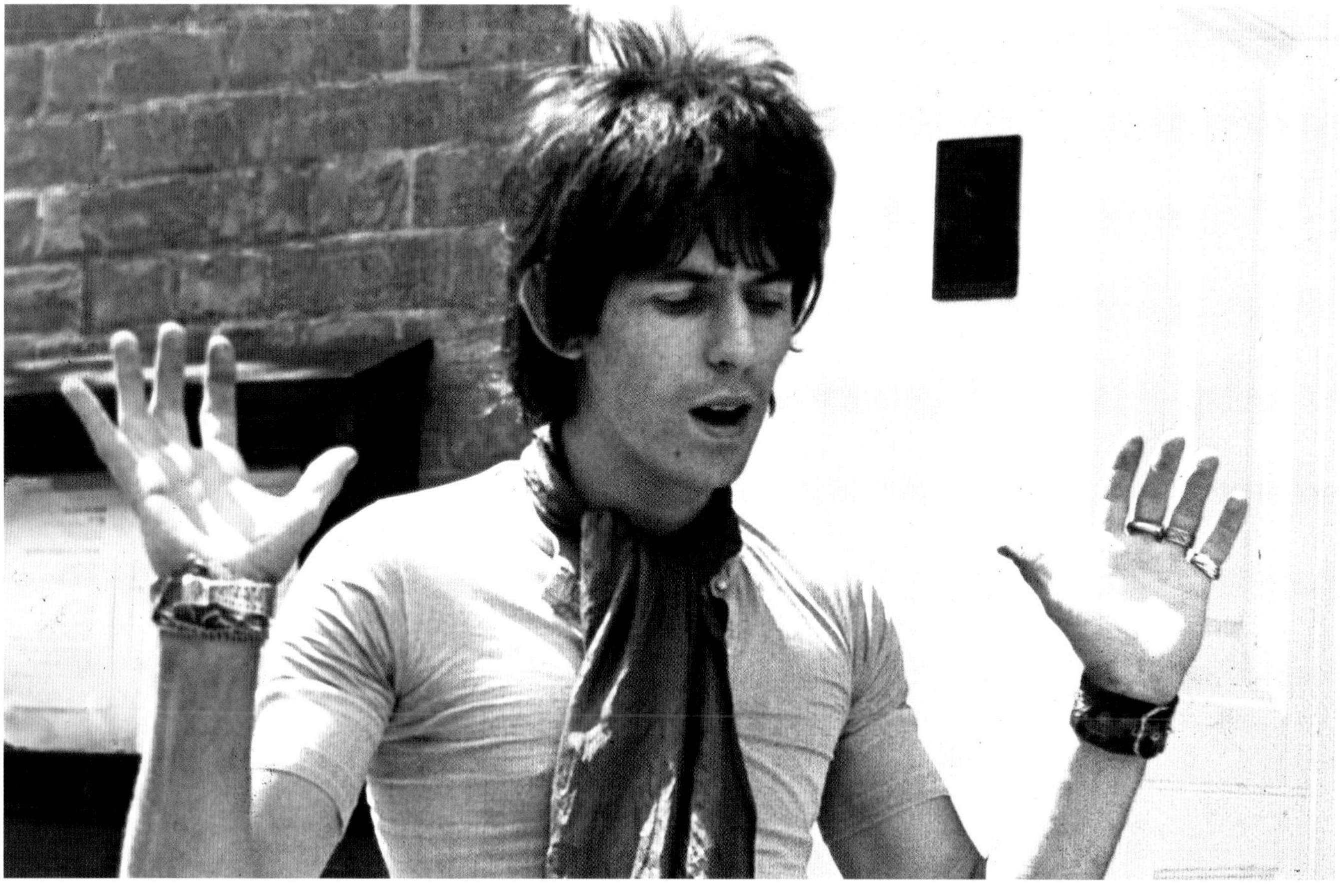

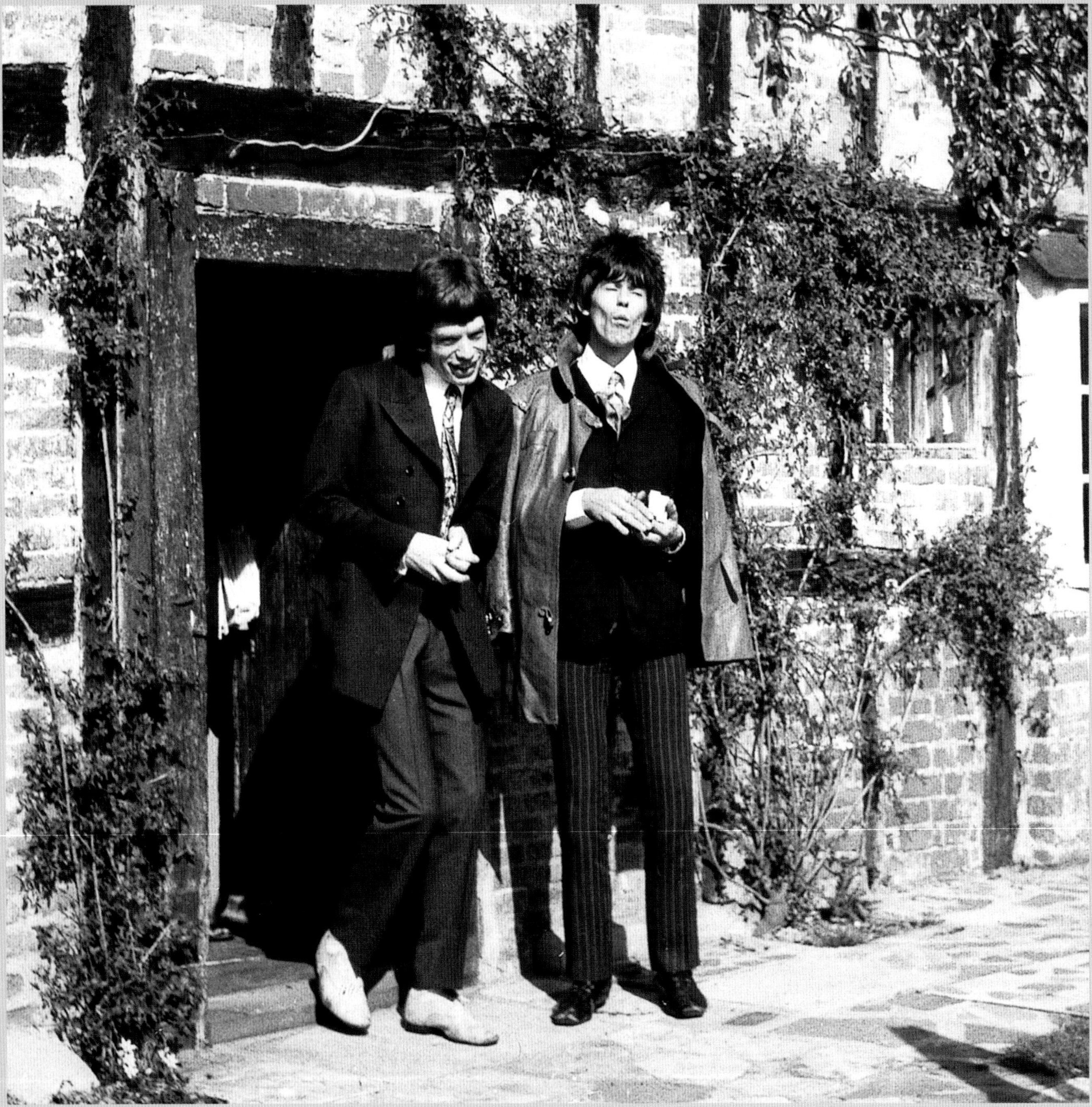

Chichester courthouse

Above: Mick and Keith at Keith's house Redlands, before their next appearance at Chichester court for their trial on 27 June 1967.

Opposite: Mick and Keith outside the courtroom. When they adjourned for lunch, police had to clear a way as they were mobbed by hundreds of screaming teenagers. If found guilty Keith could face a maximum sentence of ten years in prison. On his return to court he received a jail sentence of one year; Mick was sentenced to three months. Bill and Charlie were not involved in the court cases and began work on a new Stones album in response to The Beatles' *Sgt. Pepper's Lonely Hearts Club Band*. The album, which had been long awaited by fans, was eventually titled *Their Satanic Majesties Request*. Although advance orders were worth $2,000,000 in the United States, the album was not a critical success.

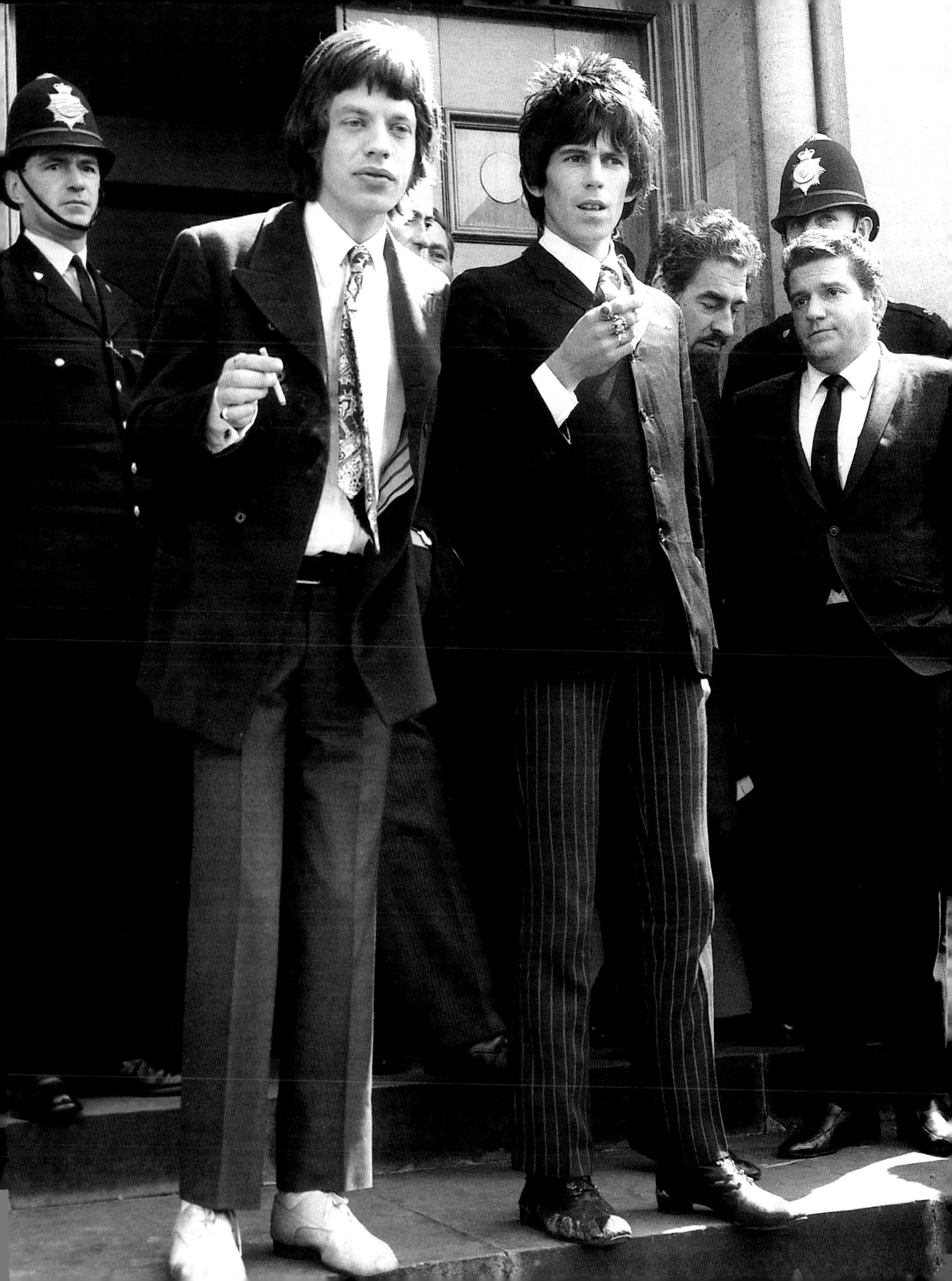

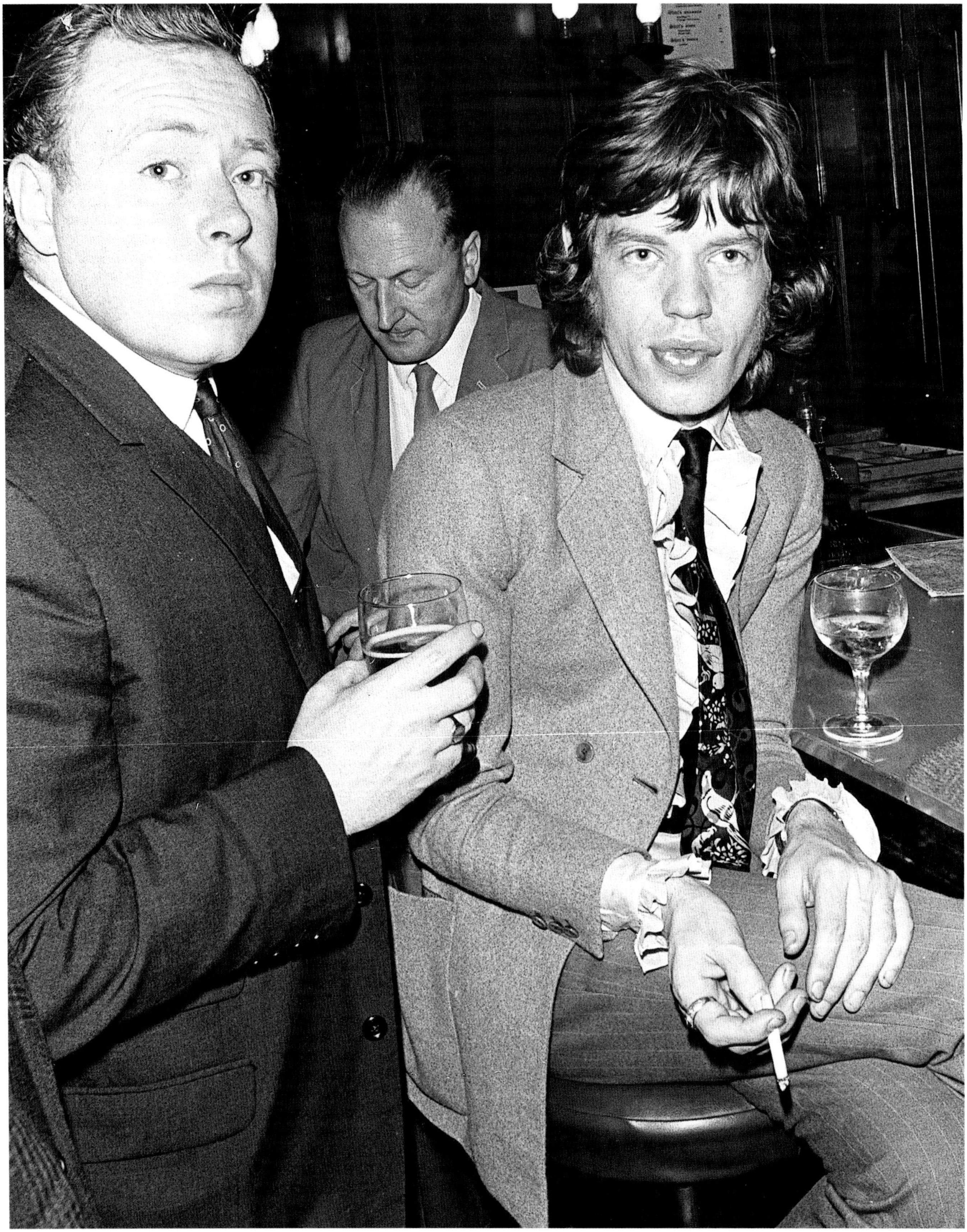

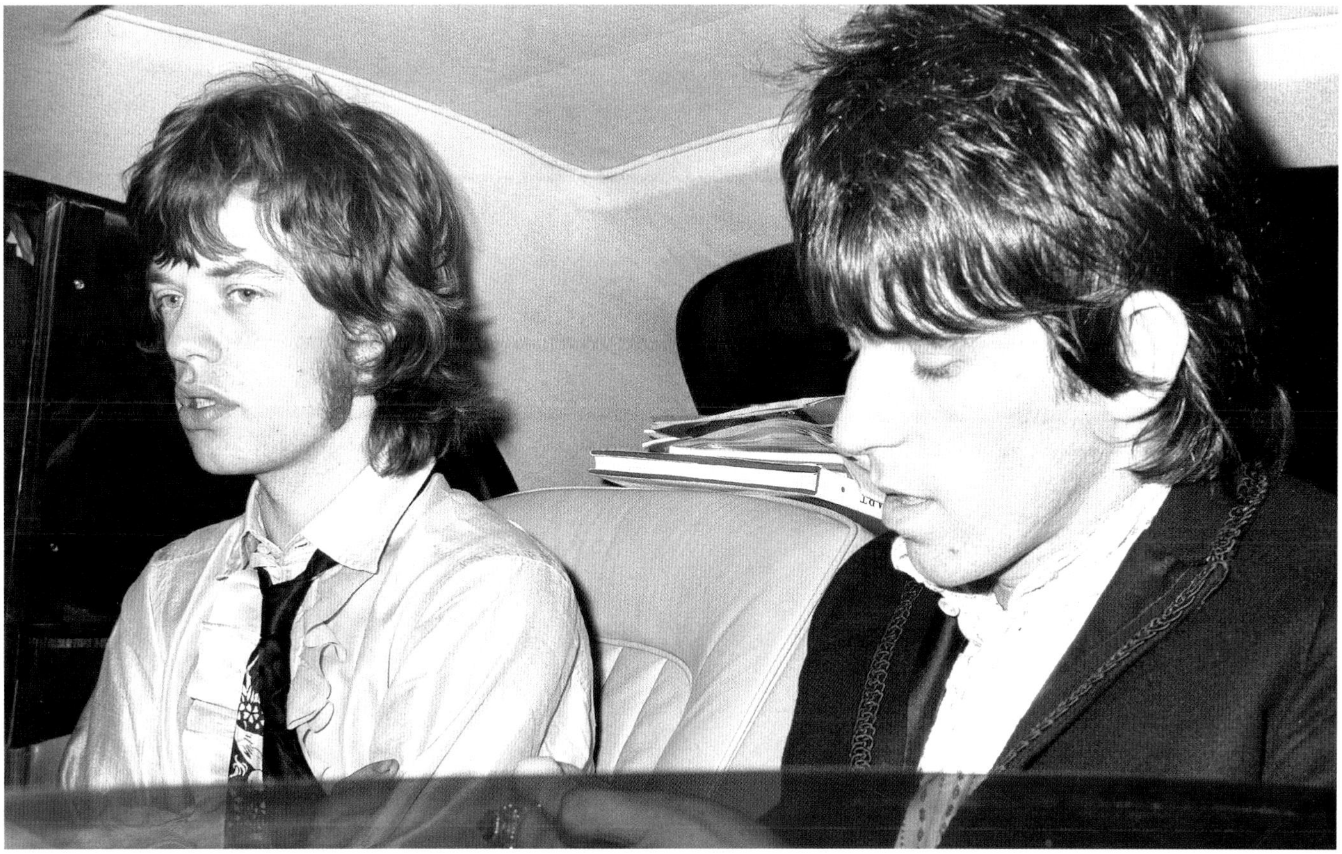

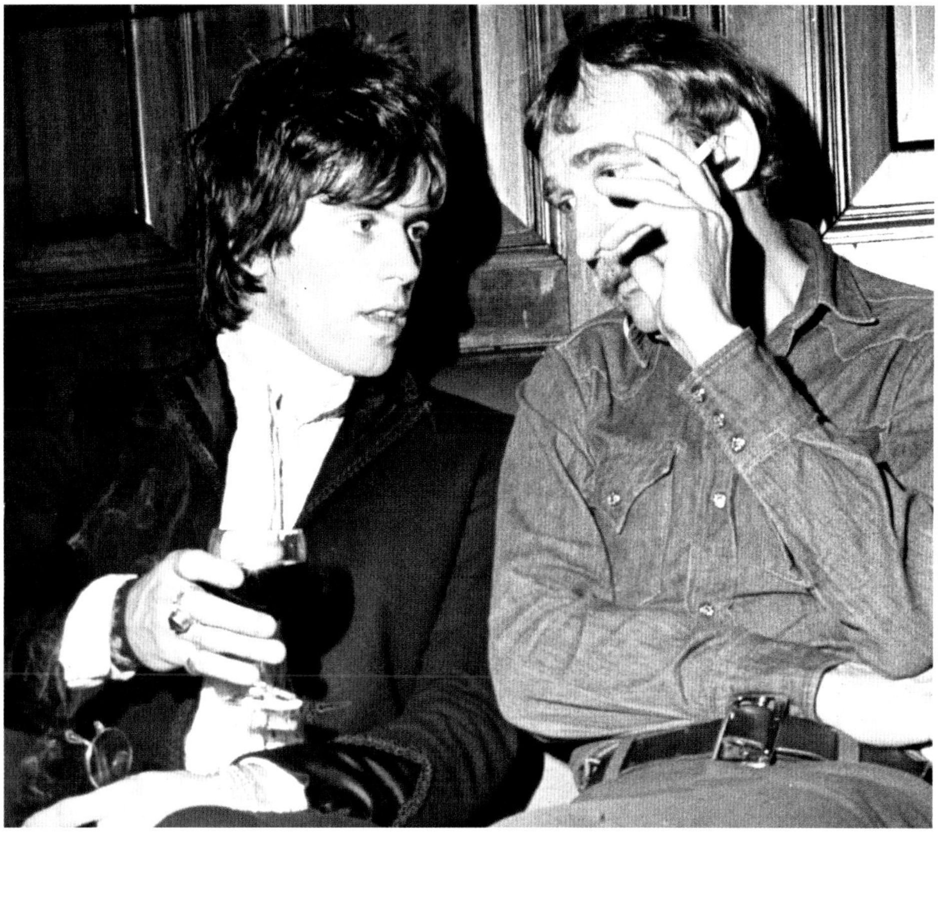

Free men

Above: The strain shows on the faces of Mick and Keith even as they are driven to London in a Bentley on 30 June 1967 following their release from prison on bail, pending appeals against their convictions. A broad public outcry had greeted the severity of their sentencing – even a *Times* editorial had criticized it.

Opposite and right: Mick and Keith enjoy a drink in a pub near Fleet Street, London, on the day of their release. Mick had written poetry in prison. Keith admitted to weeping. The pair would have to wait weeks for their appeals to be heard, and were not allowed to leave the country in the meantime.

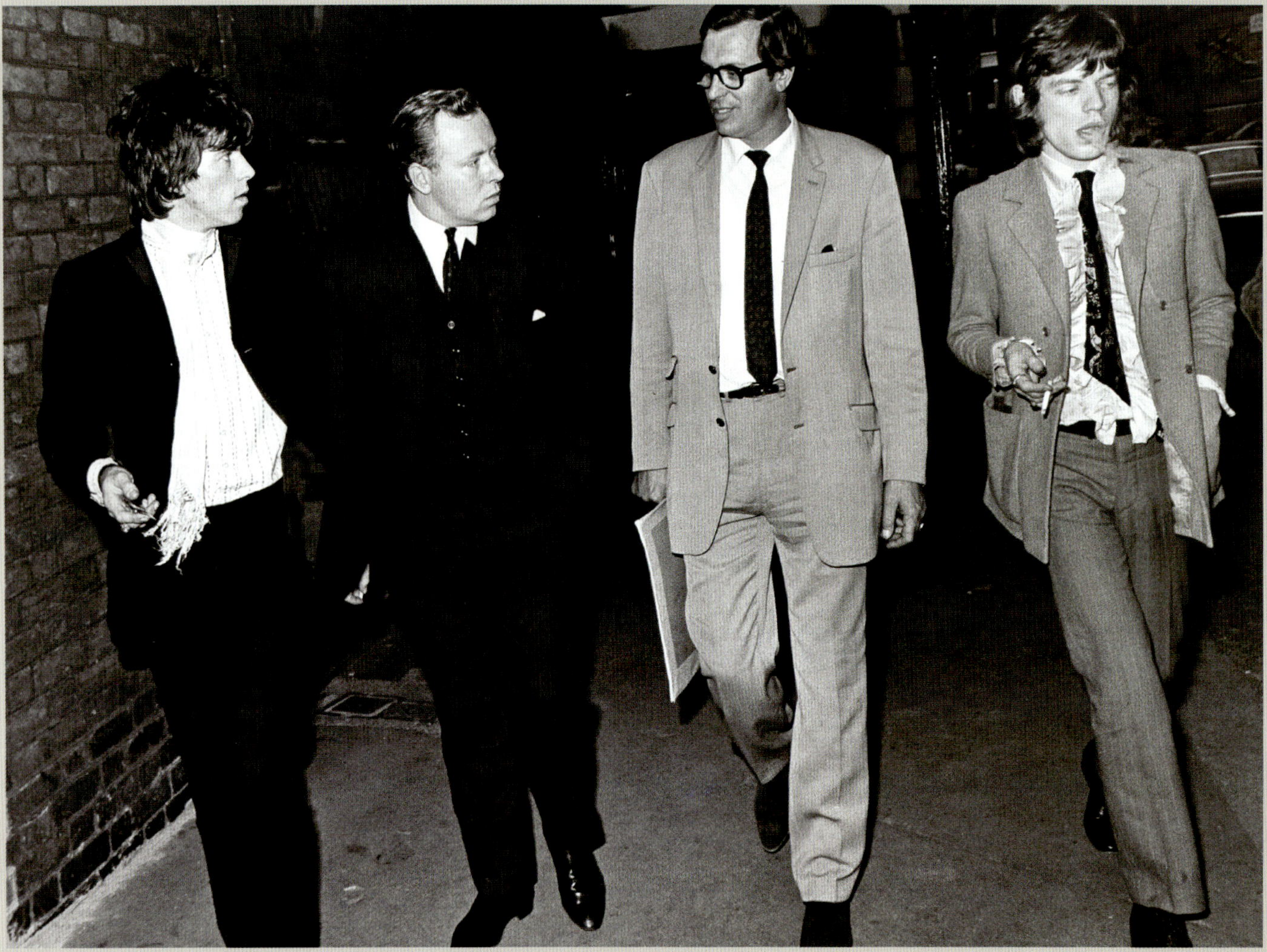

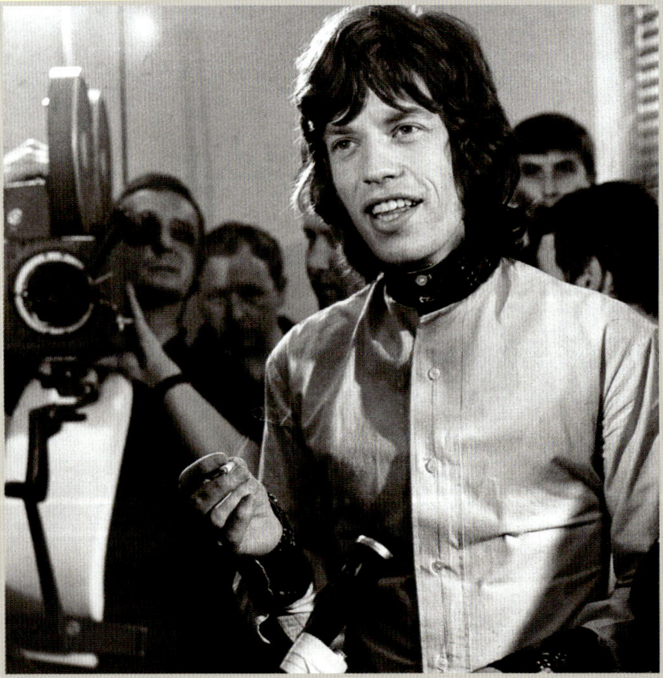

Mick's conditional discharge

Above: Keith reviews recent events with companions. Mick seems pensive following his release from prison.

The appeal was brought forward to 31 July. Keith had chickenpox and was not admitted to the courtroom for fear that the virus would be contagious. However, the news of the verdict, when it reached him, was good. Mick's sentence was altered to a one-year conditional discharge and Keith's conviction was quashed.

Left and opposite: Later that day, having changed from formal attire into purple trousers and an embroidered jacket, Mick left London in a chartered helicopter with girlfriend Marianne Faithfull.

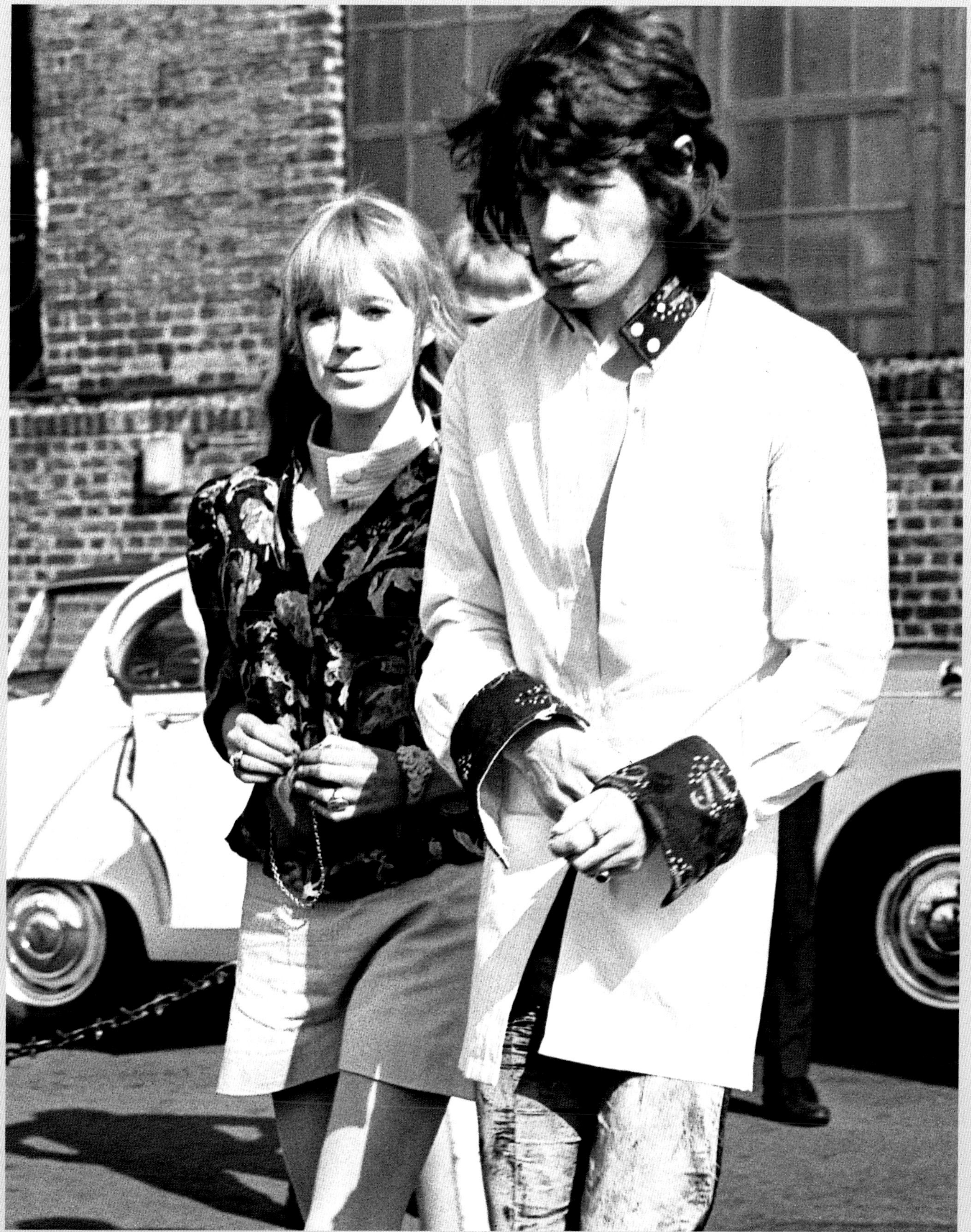

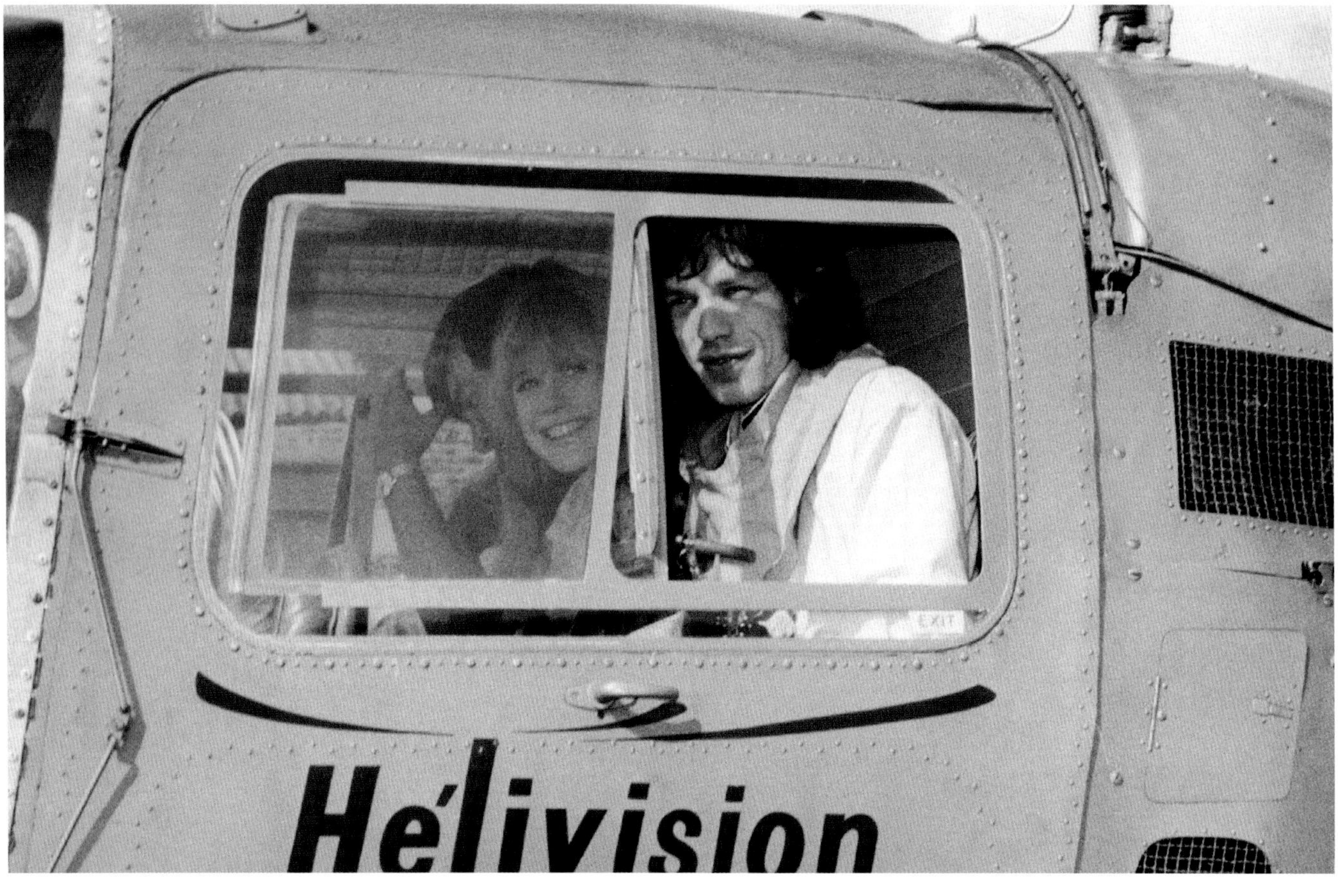

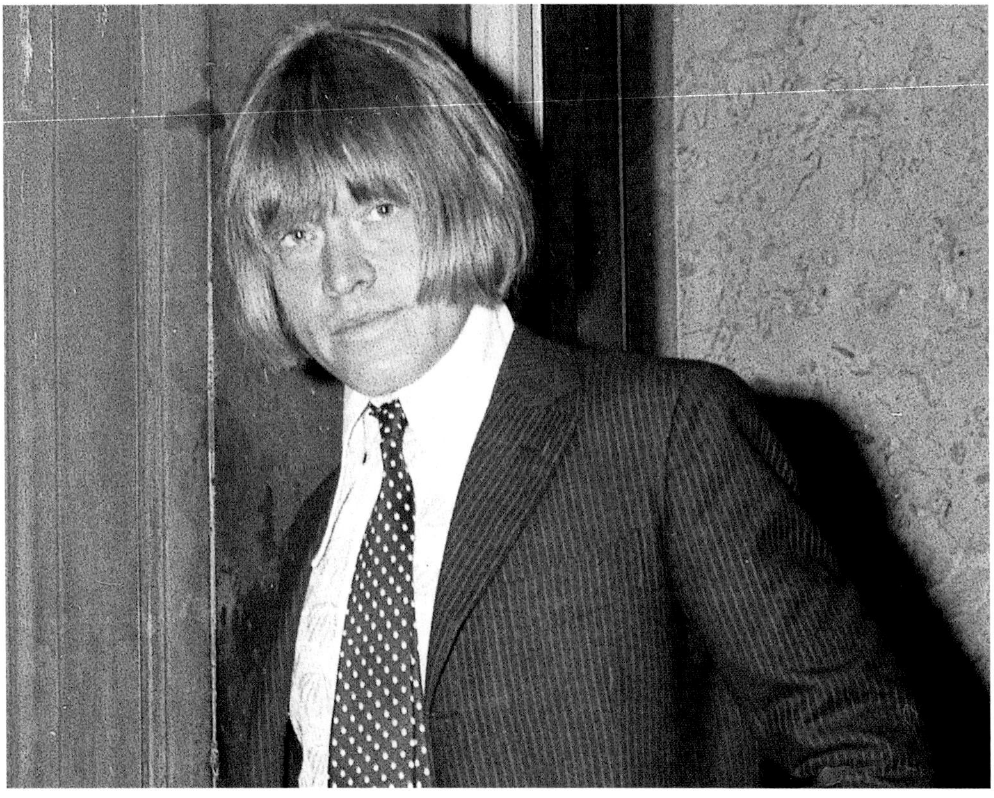

Destination unknown

Above and opposite: No one knew where Mick and Marianne were headed after the court case but two weeks later, on 14 August, they arrived back from Ireland. Such was their notoriety, several taxi drivers at Heathrow refused to take them before one cabbie took pity on them. After the court case Mick and Marianne moved into 48 Cheyne Walk with her son Nicholas.

Left: Brian Jones' case relating to drugs charges was finally heard. He was later sentenced to nine months in prison, commuted to three years' probation on appeal. Brian's mental state was fragile and one of the conditions of probation was that he should undergo psychiatric treatment.

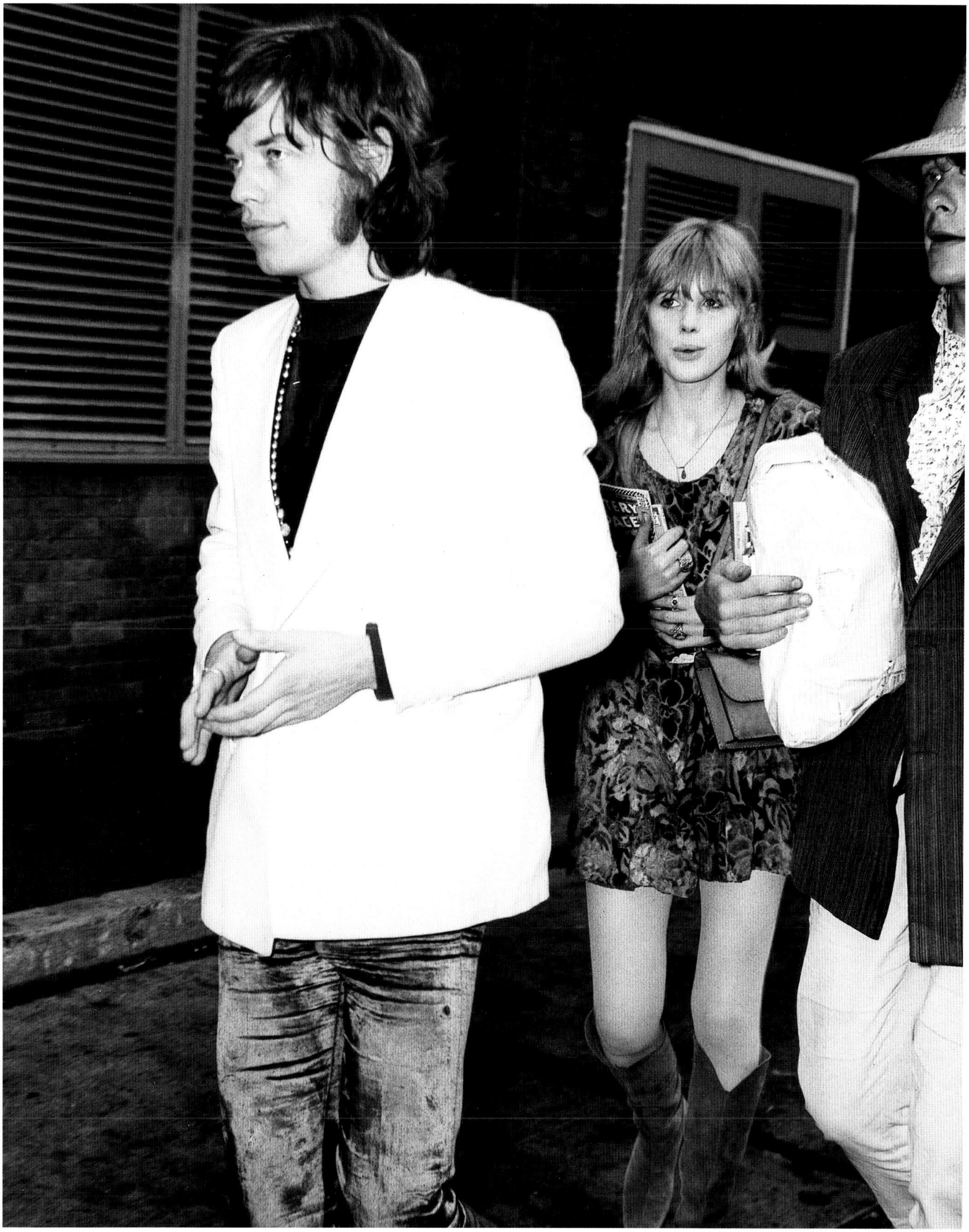

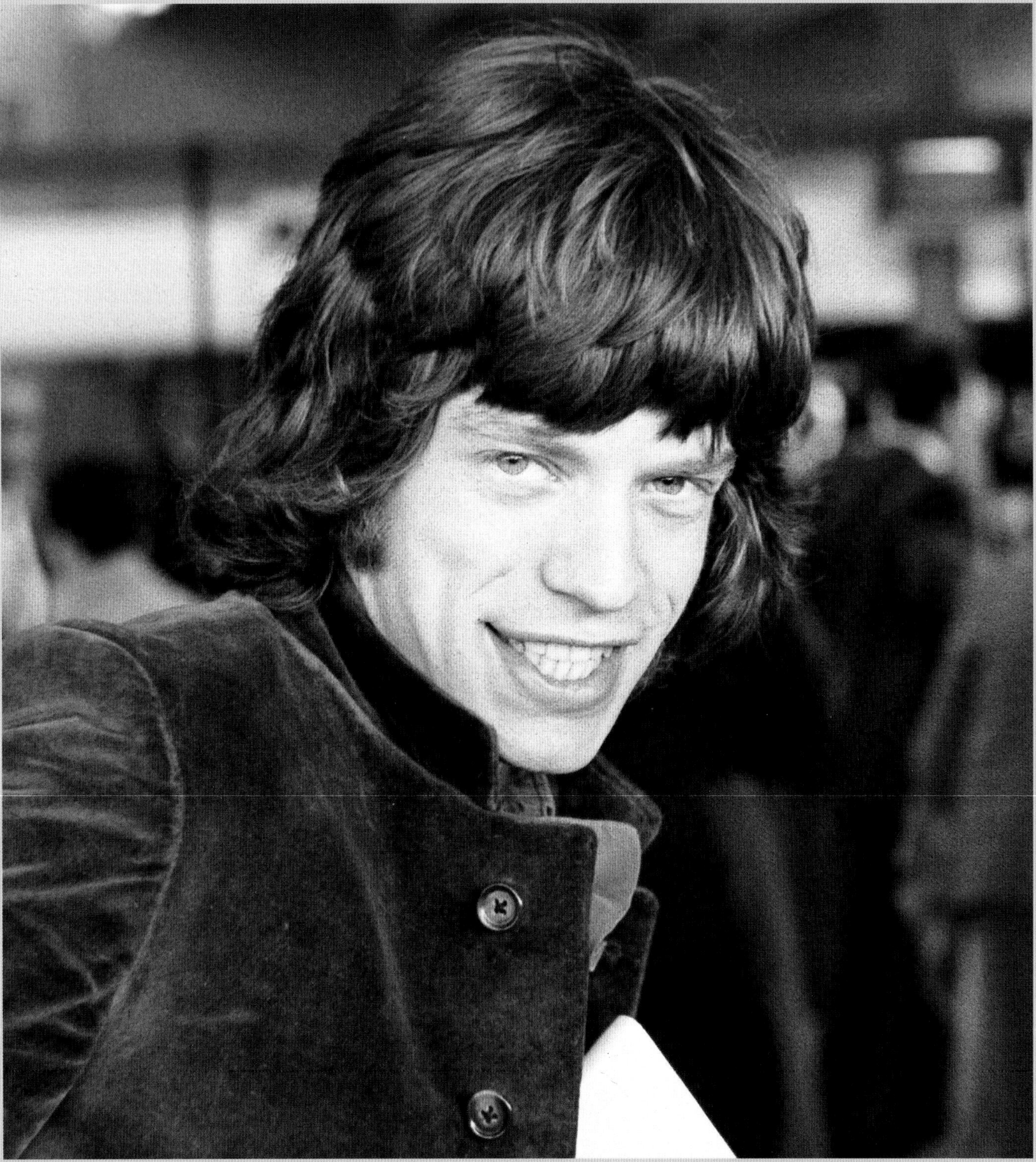

Off again

Above: September 1967 and Mick Jagger looks happy again as he makes his way to New York. When he and the other band members arrived they were questioned by immigration officials – there were fears that his earlier drugs conviction would prevent entry to the United States.

Opposite: Brian also heads off to New York on 13 September 1967. The pair embody his 'n' hers hippie chic.

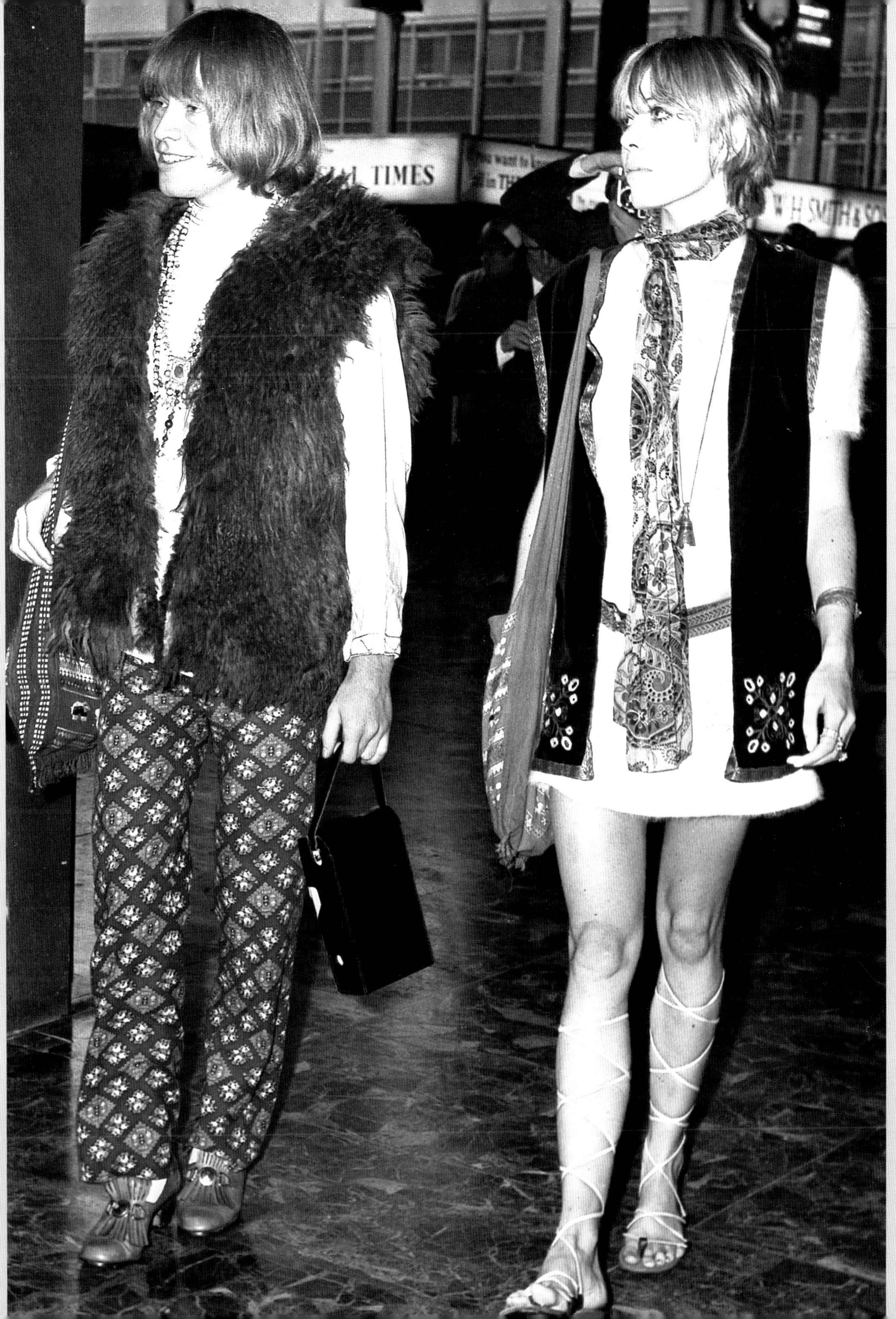
TIMES
W H SMITH

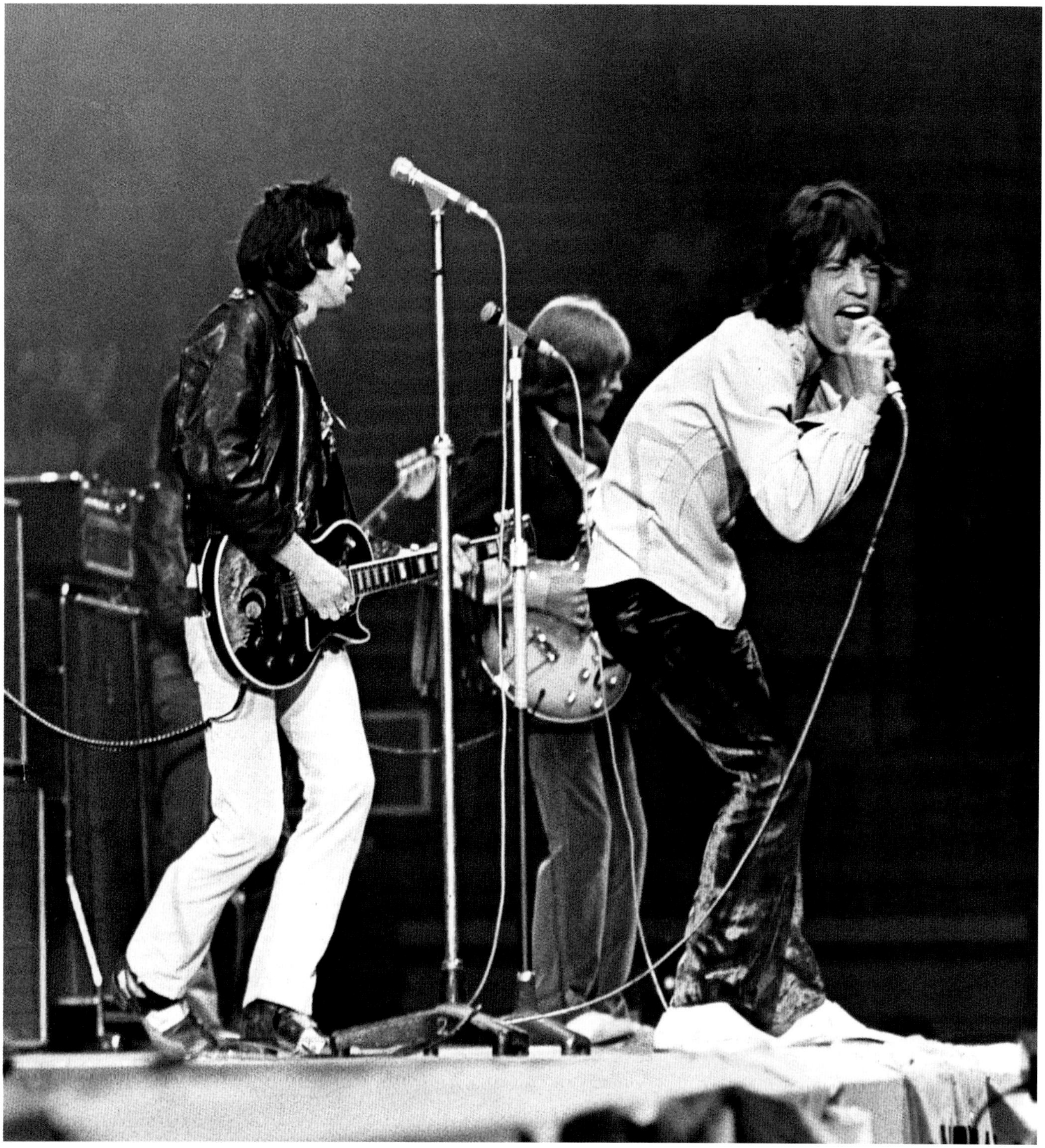

'Jumpin' Jack Flash'

Above and opposite: Wembley Arena, 12 May 1968, and the Stones are back in full cry with a surprise appearance at an annual concert sponsored by the *NME*. Brian Jones seems to have recovered from another spell in hospital for strain and exhaustion.

The band performed 'Jumpin' Jack Flash' for the first time – it was released as a single two weeks later and reached No.1 in the United Kingdom and the United States.

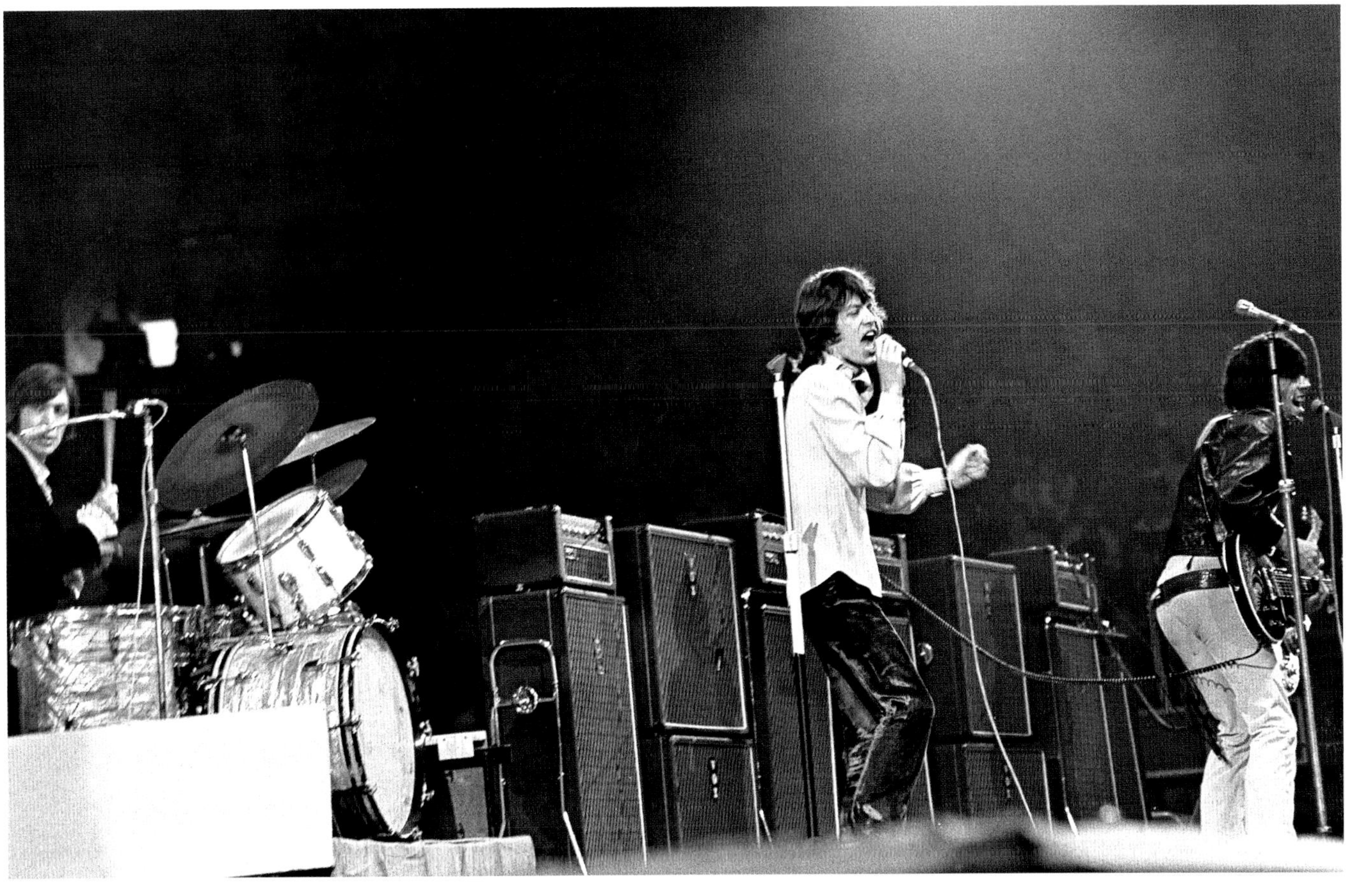

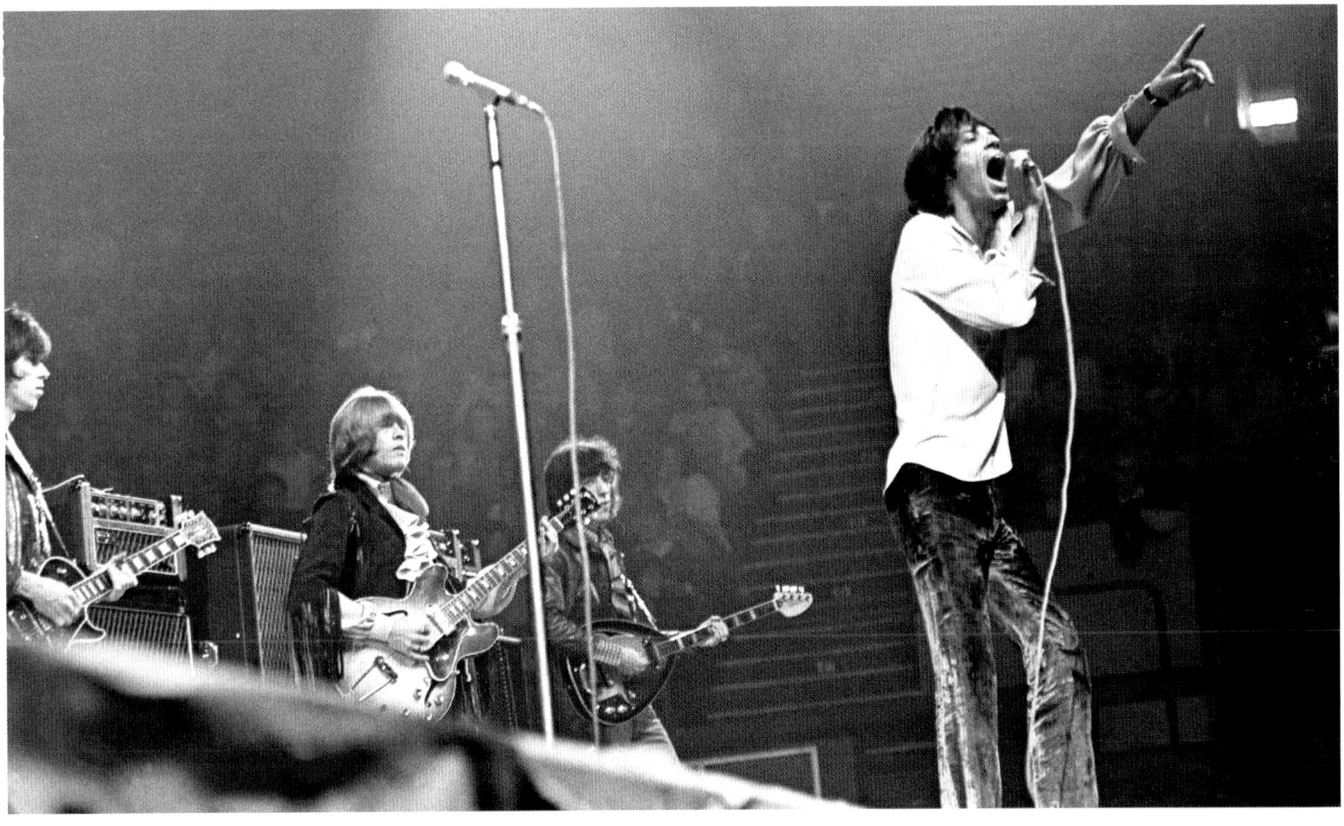

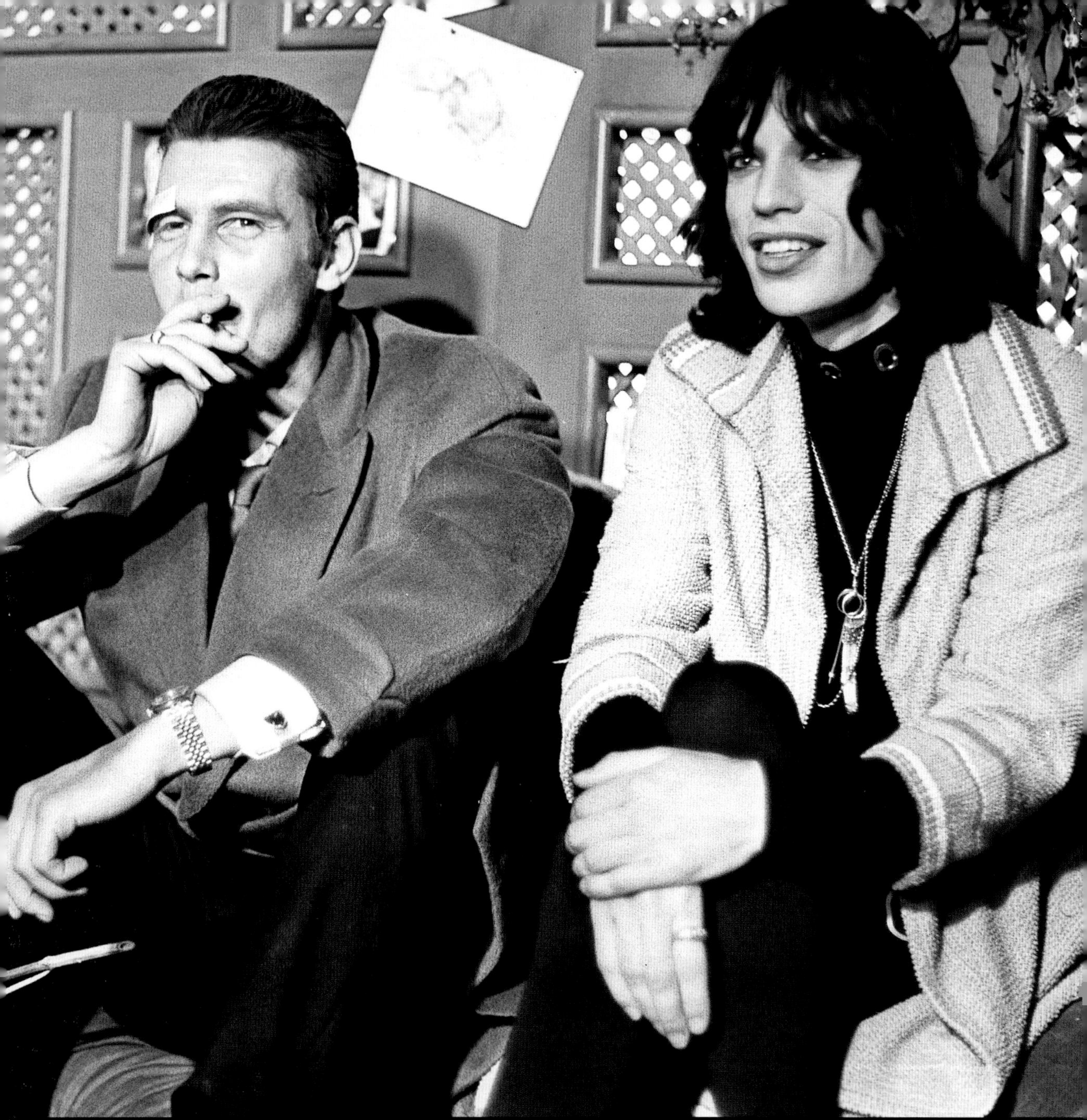

Performance

Above: Mick Jagger with actor James Fox on 17 September 1968, on the set of the cult movie *Performance* in which Jagger's character wore women's make-up.

Opposite above: Charlie and his wife Shirley assess the form. Shirley had given birth to a daughter, Serafina, on 18 March.

Opposite below: Keith Richard and Anita Pallenberg on 18 July 1968 at the premiere of The Beatles' animated film *Yellow Submarine*. Keith and Anita began seeing each other in March 1967 while her then boyfriend Brian Jones was in hospital in France with respiratory problems. Pallenberg played Mick's girlfriend in *Performance* and this led to tension between Keith and Mick.

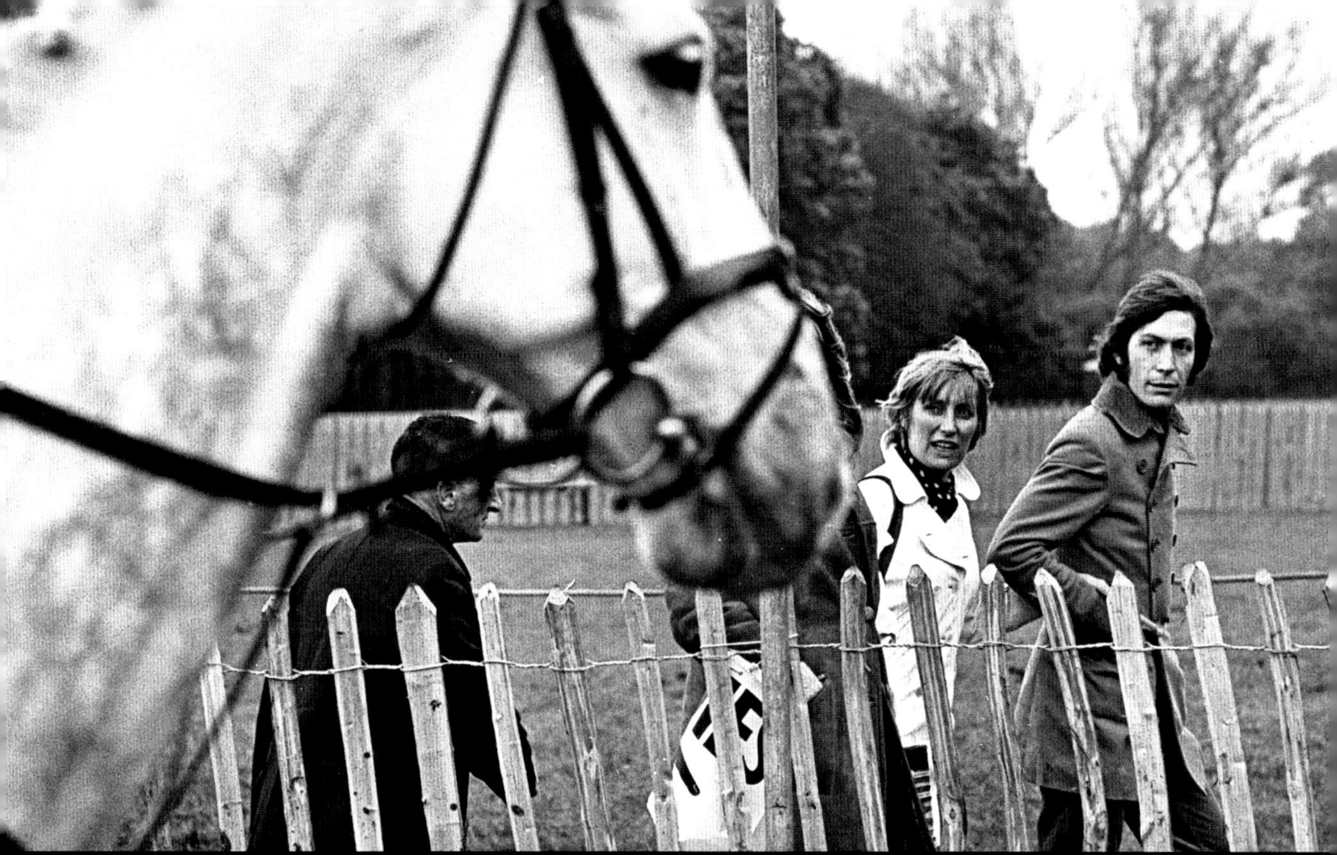

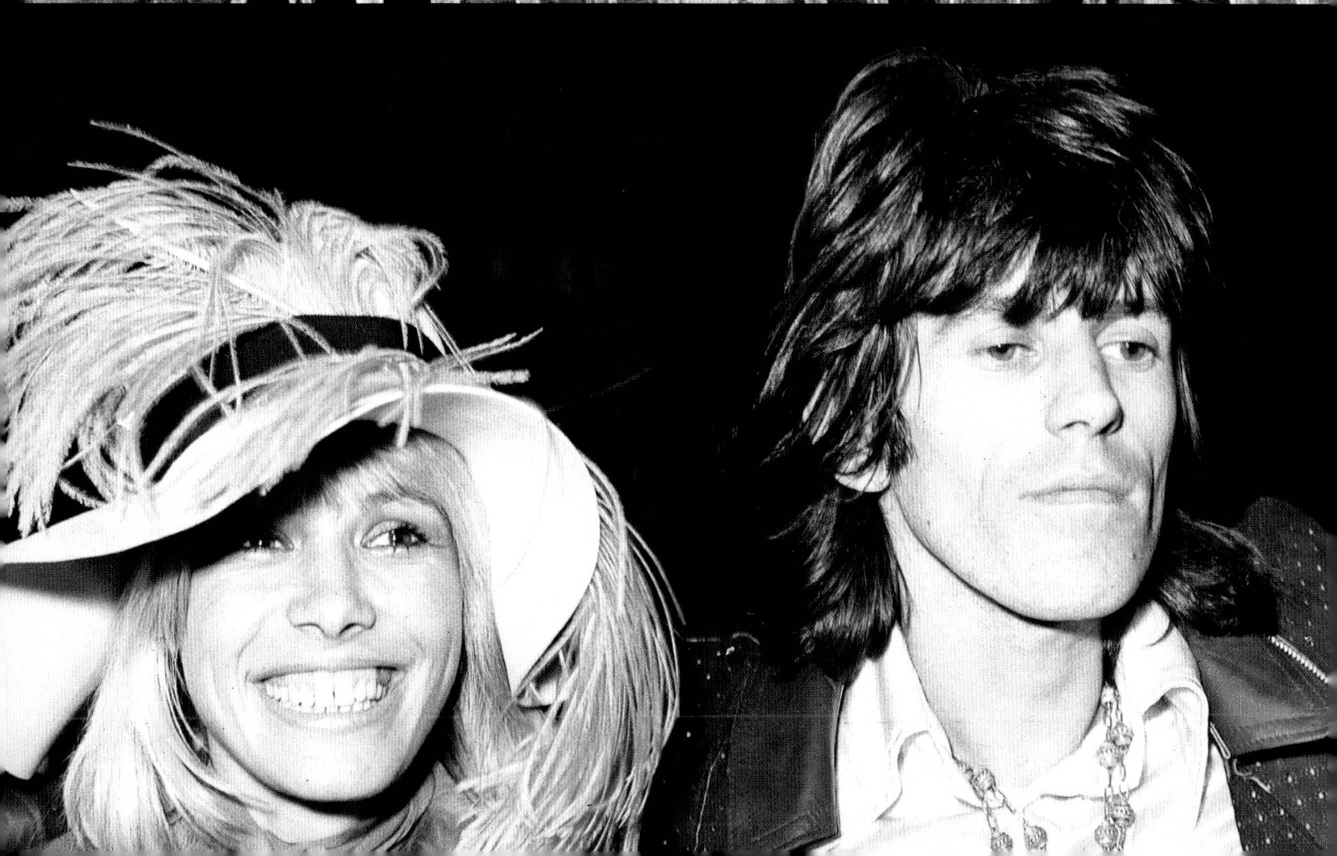

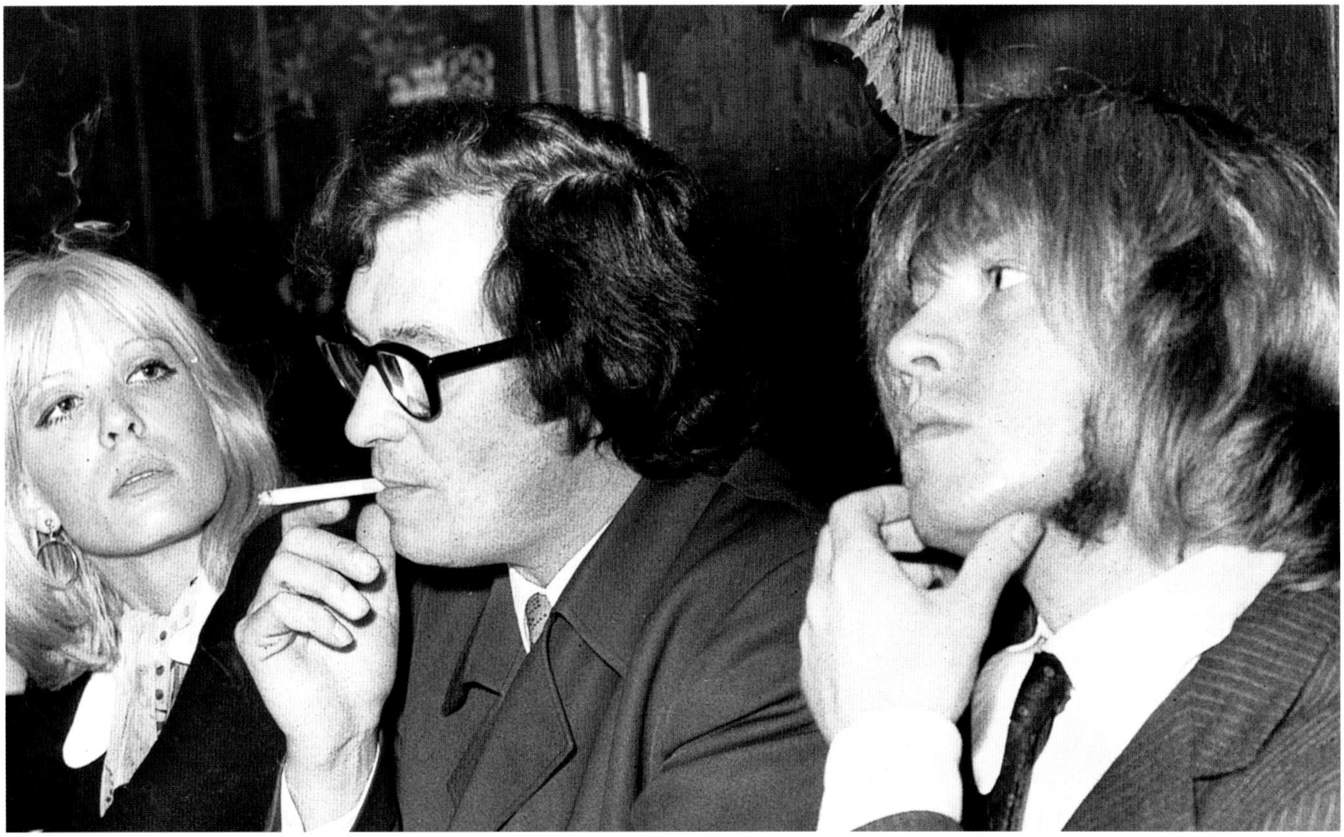

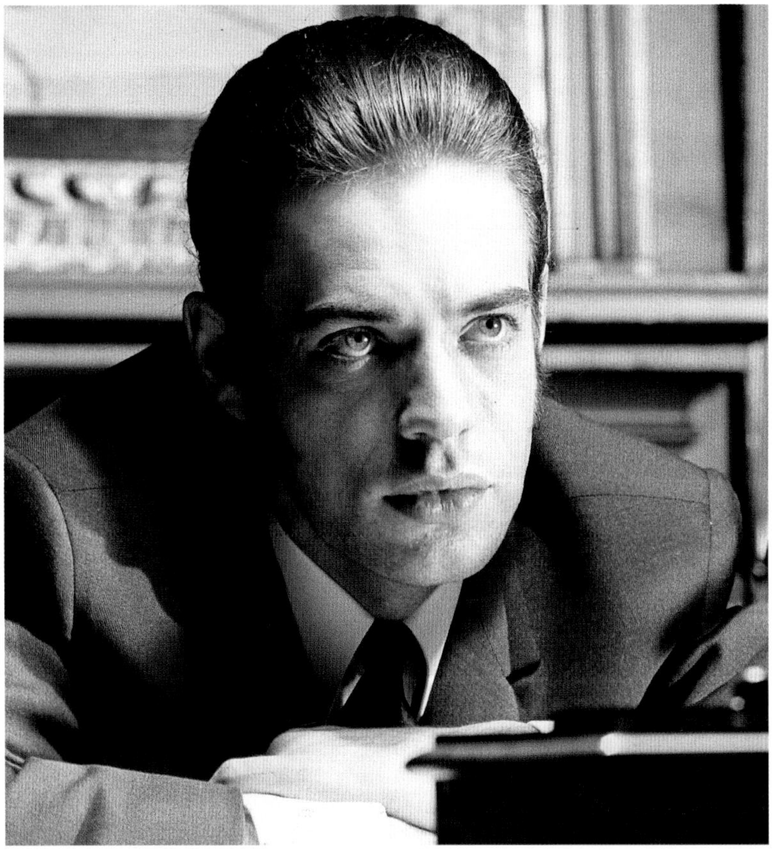

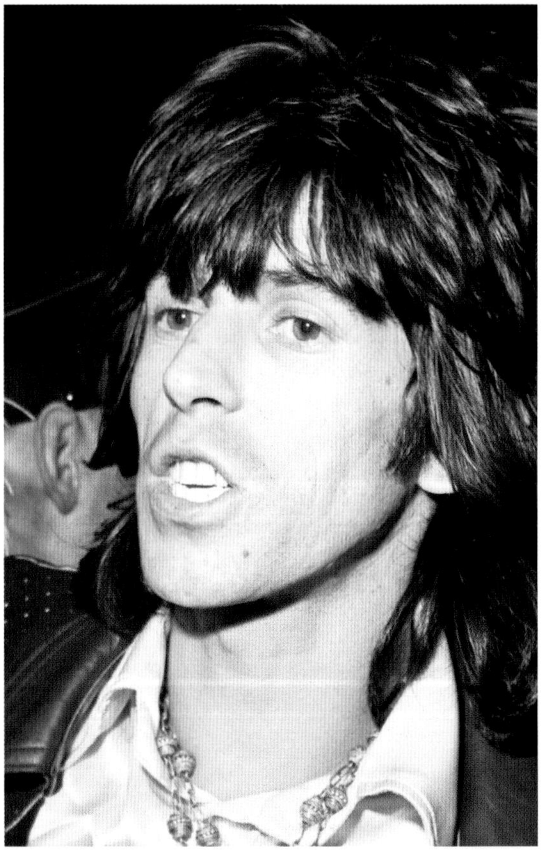

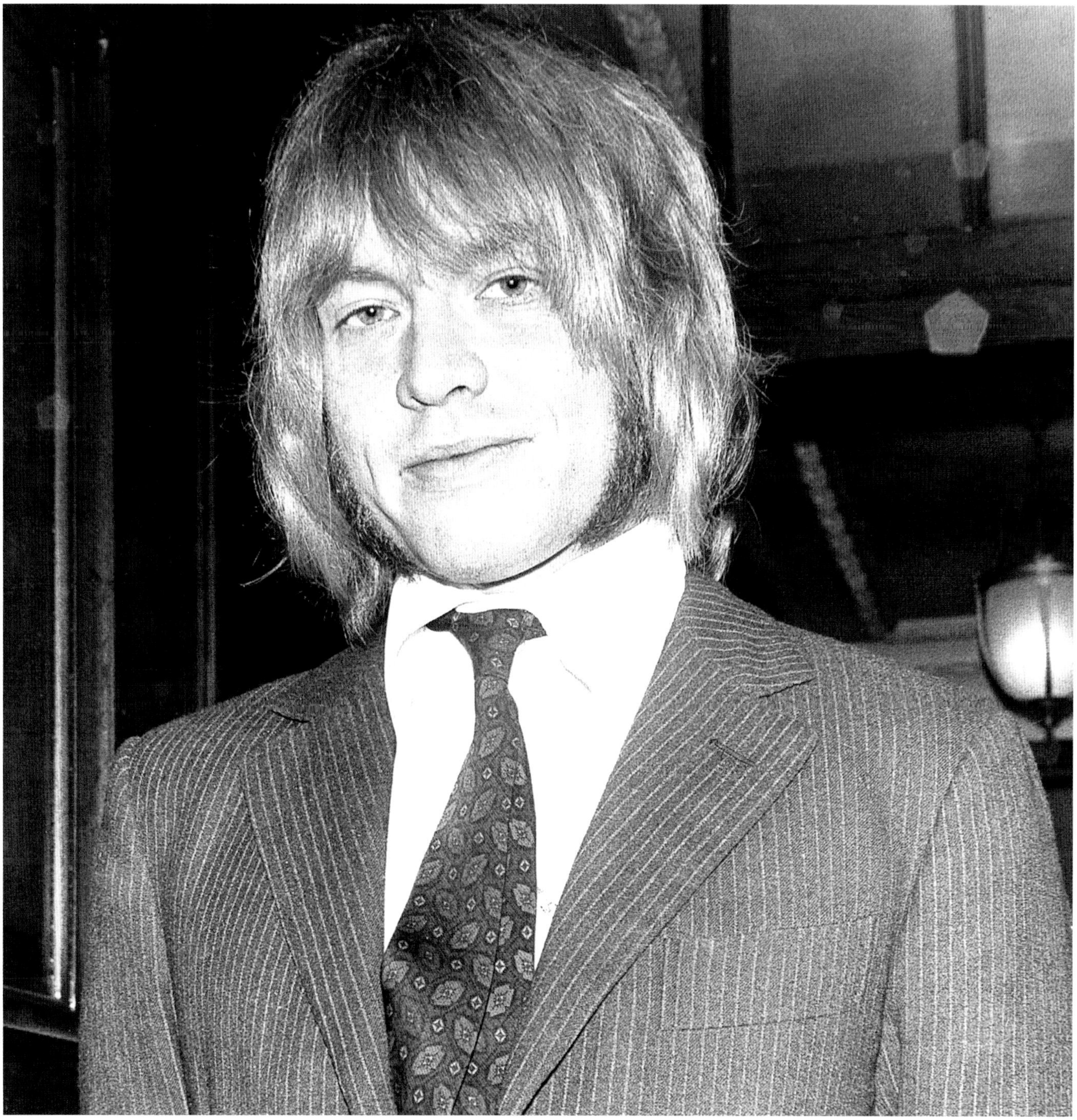

Jones back in court

Opposite above: Brian Jones, pictured here on 26 September 1968 with his girlfriend Suki Poitier and tour manager Tom Keylock, reflects on a narrow escape: he had just been fined £50 for his second drugs offence.

Above: Although smartly suited for his court appearance, his hair remains unrepentantly luxuriant. In an attempt to escape, Jones bought Cotchford Farm in Sussex two months later.

Opposite below left: Mick Jagger on the other hand submits to a savage hairstyle for his role in *Performance*.

Opposite below right: On Keith Richard's 25th birthday on 18 December, he, Anita Pallenberg, Mick Jagger and Marianne Faithfull flew to Brazil to discuss black and white magic with a mystic.

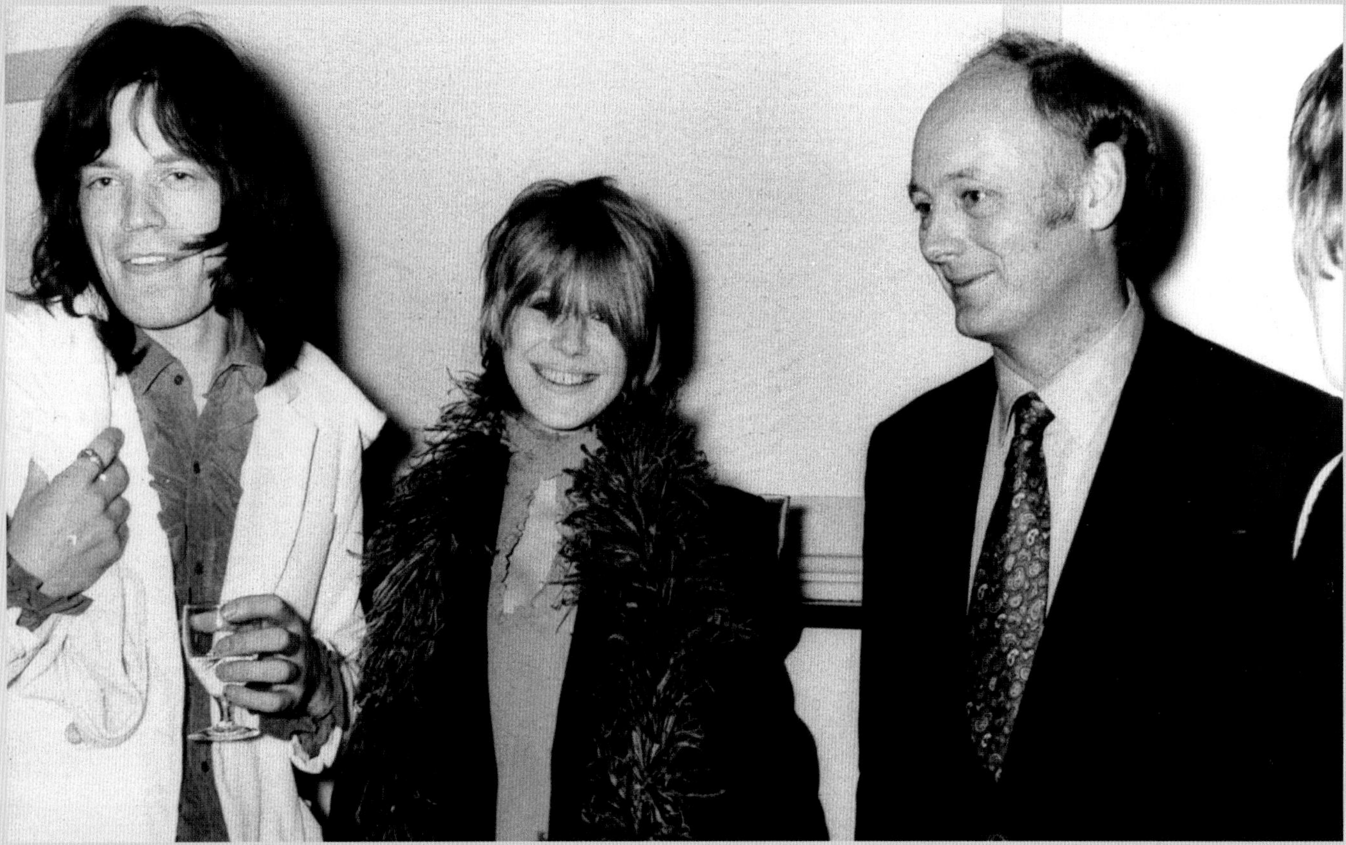

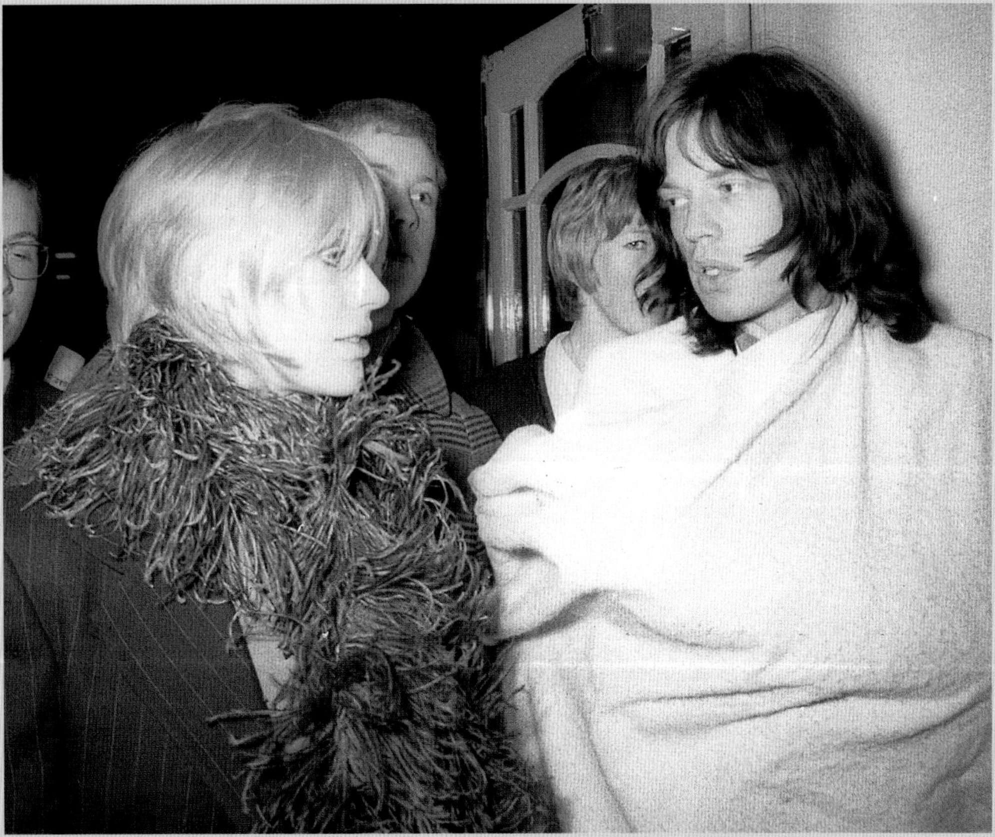

Rock and Roll Circus

Above and left: On 5 December 1968 Mick and Marianne go to see the musical *Hair* in London, their first public outing since Marianne miscarried the previous month, six months into her pregnancy.

Opposite: Five days later Brian is pictured with John Lennon, son Julian and Yoko Ono. Lennon planned to guest in the Stones' TV spectacular, *Rock and Roll Circus*. Much was made of the supposed rivalry between The Beatles and the Stones, but in reality they were great friends and supporters of each other. In fact both Mick and Keith had sung backing vocals on The Beatles' 1967 anthem 'All You Need Is Love'.

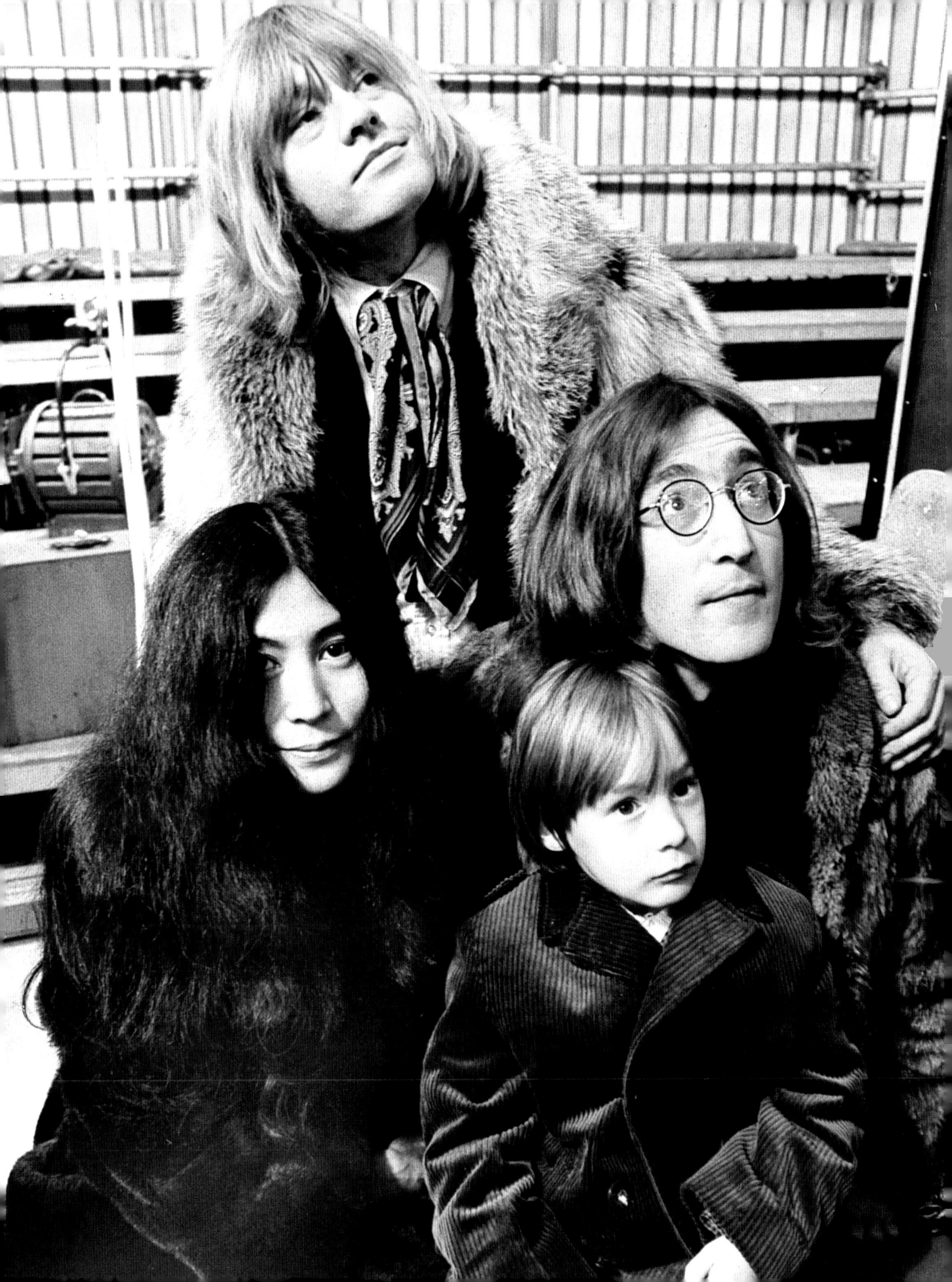

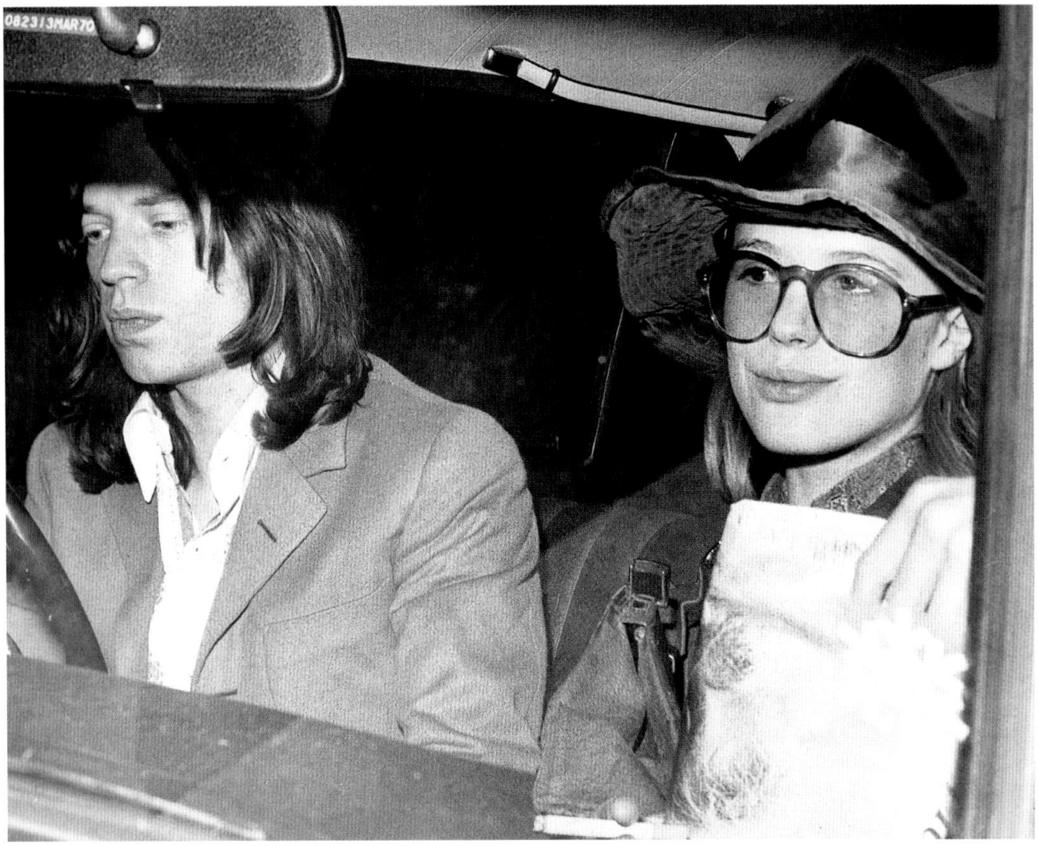

In court again

Left: Mick and Marianne are arrested at their home in Chelsea on 28 May 1969. They are charged with drug-related offences but are released on bail and drive home. Mick maintains that the 'substances' being consumed at the time of the police raid were cherries, toast and honey.

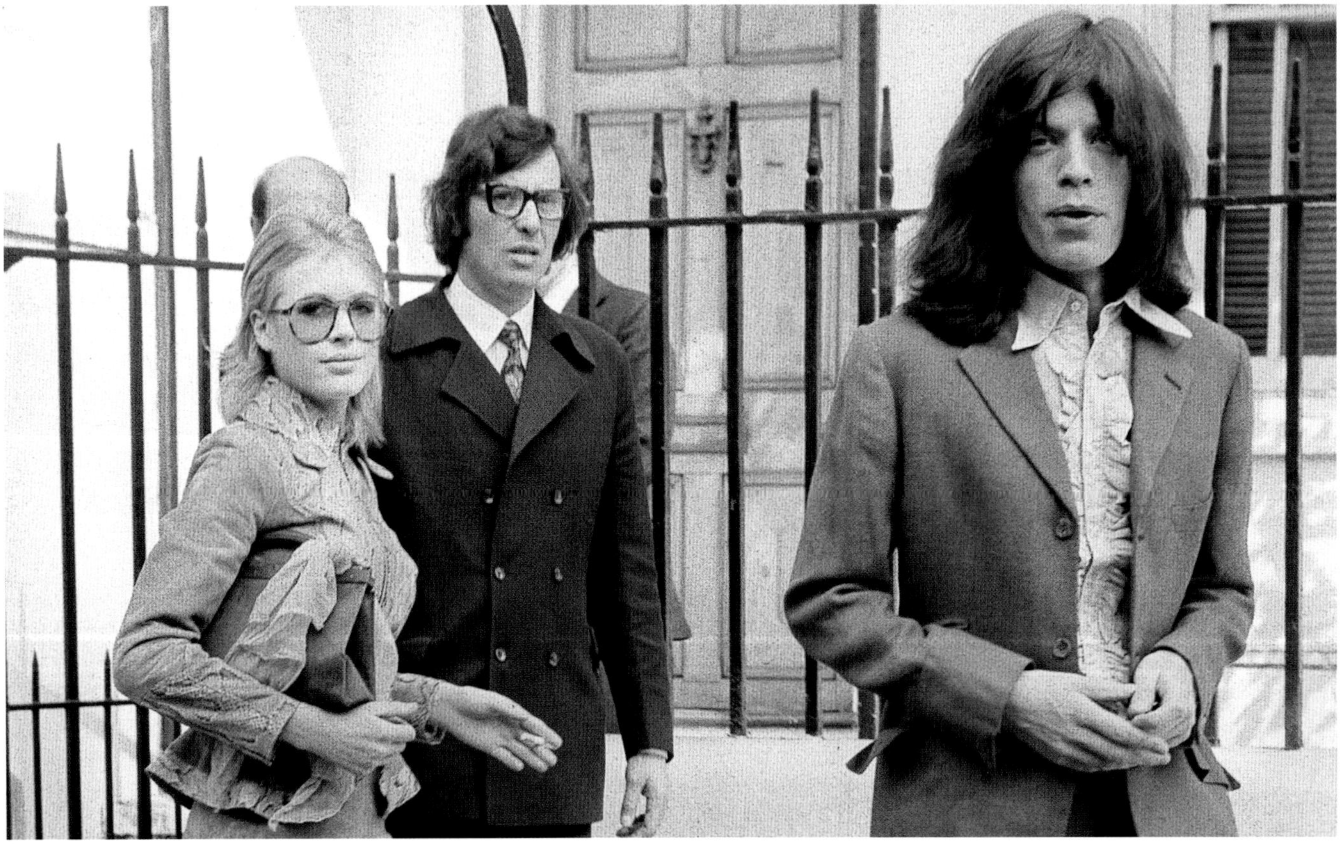

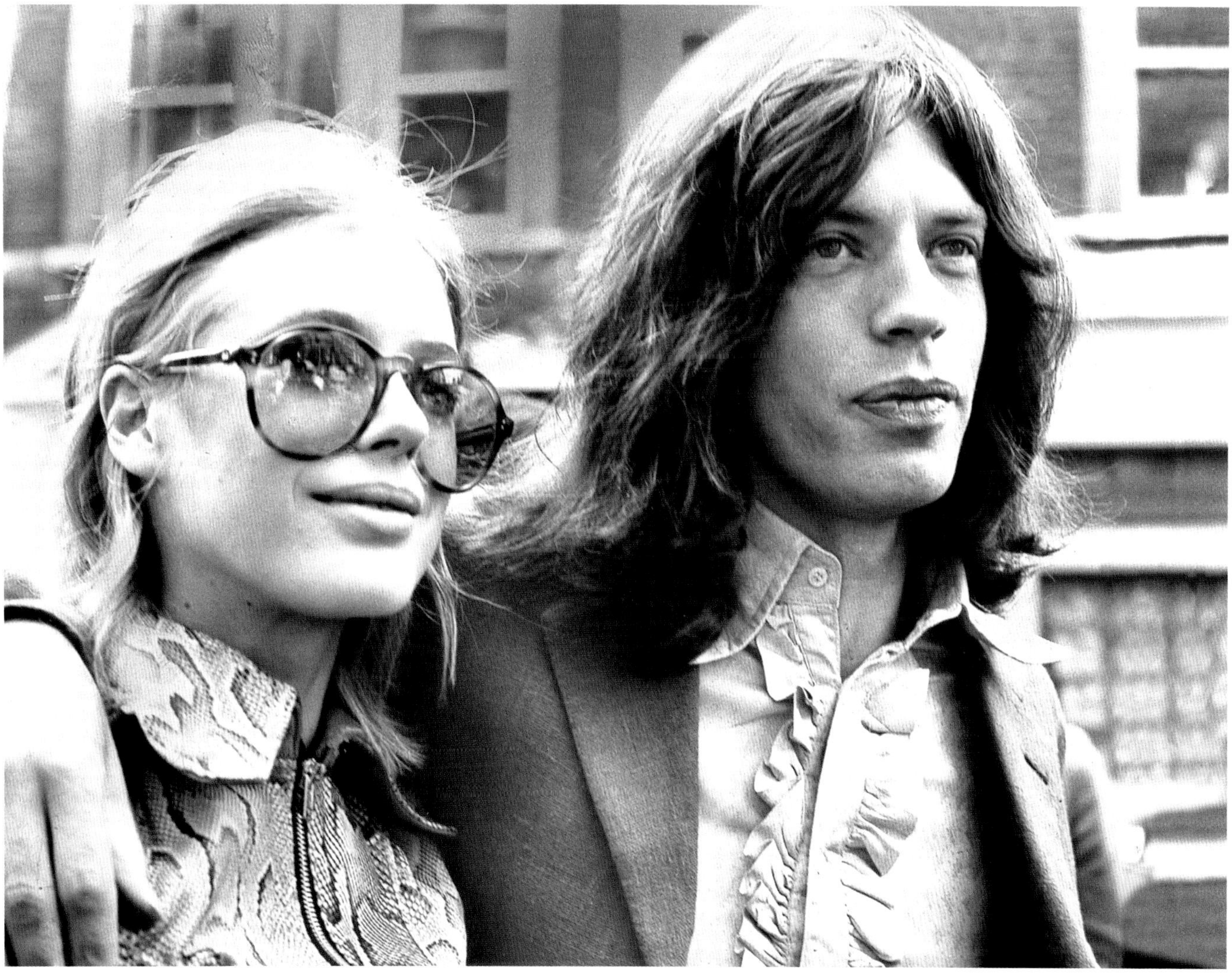

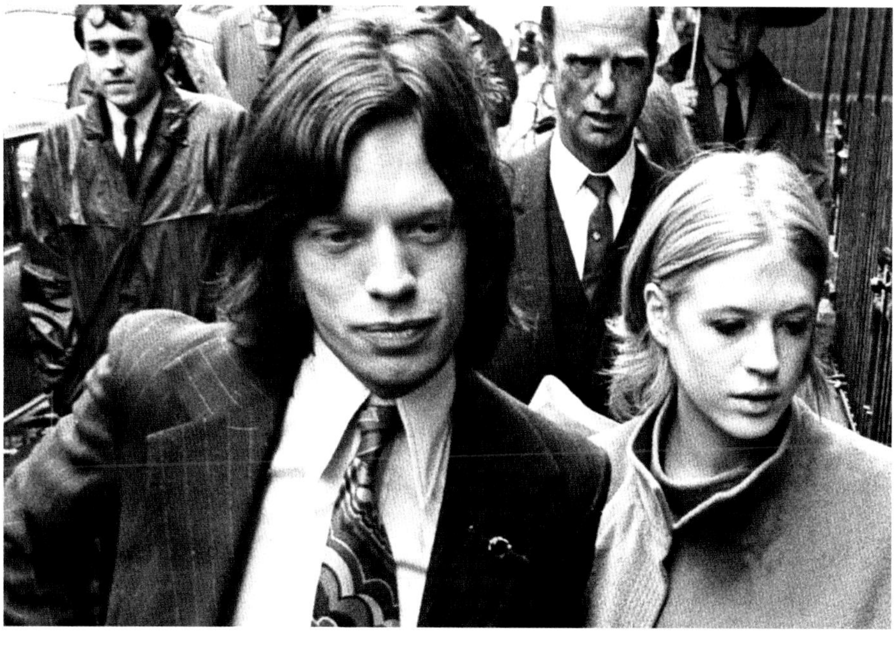

Above and opposite below: Mick and Marianne outside Marlborough Street Magistrates' Court in London on 29 May 1969 after hearing the charges relating to their alleged possession of cannabis. They were remanded on bail until 23 June.

Right: Mick and Marianne dress more formally for their court appearance on 23 June.

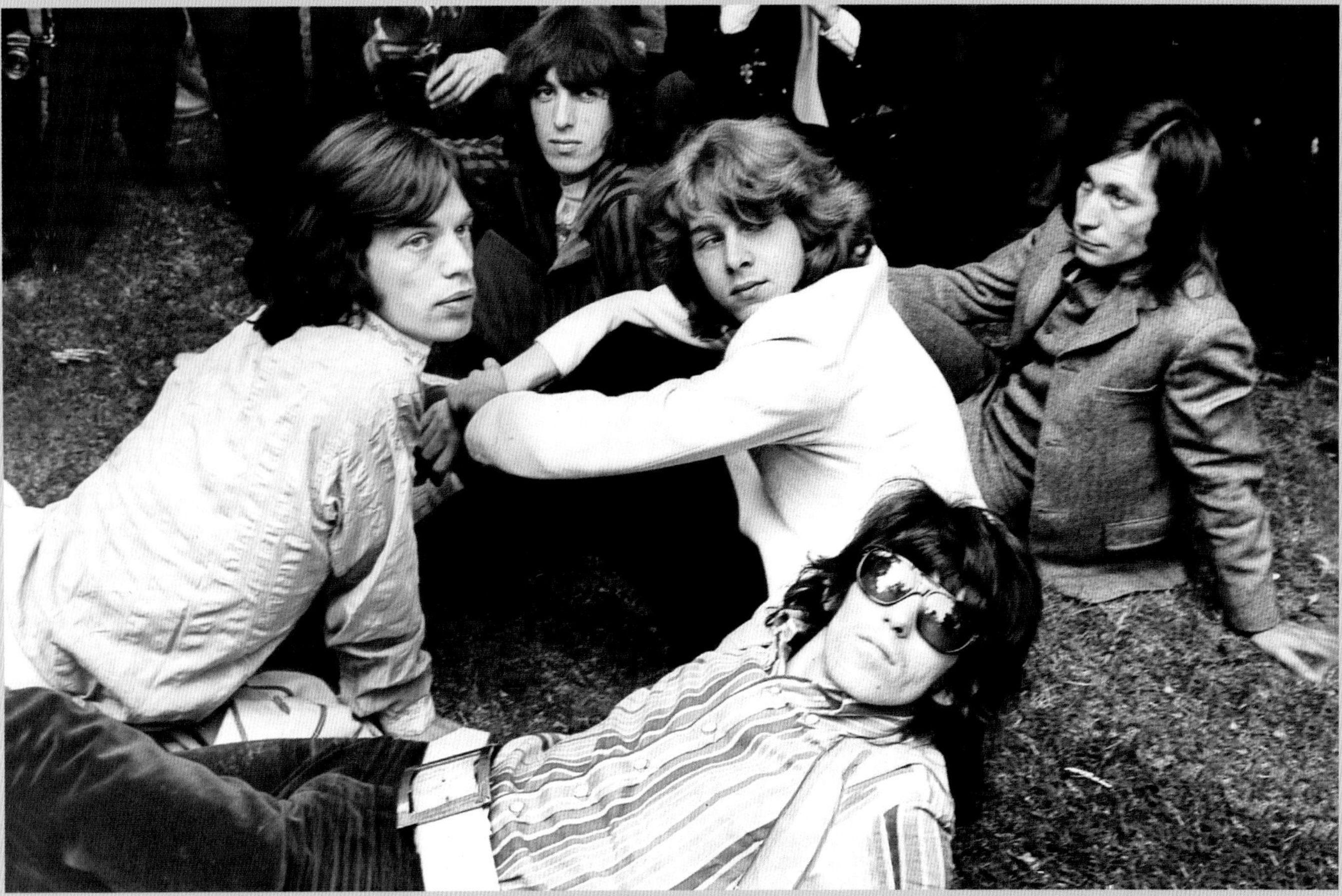

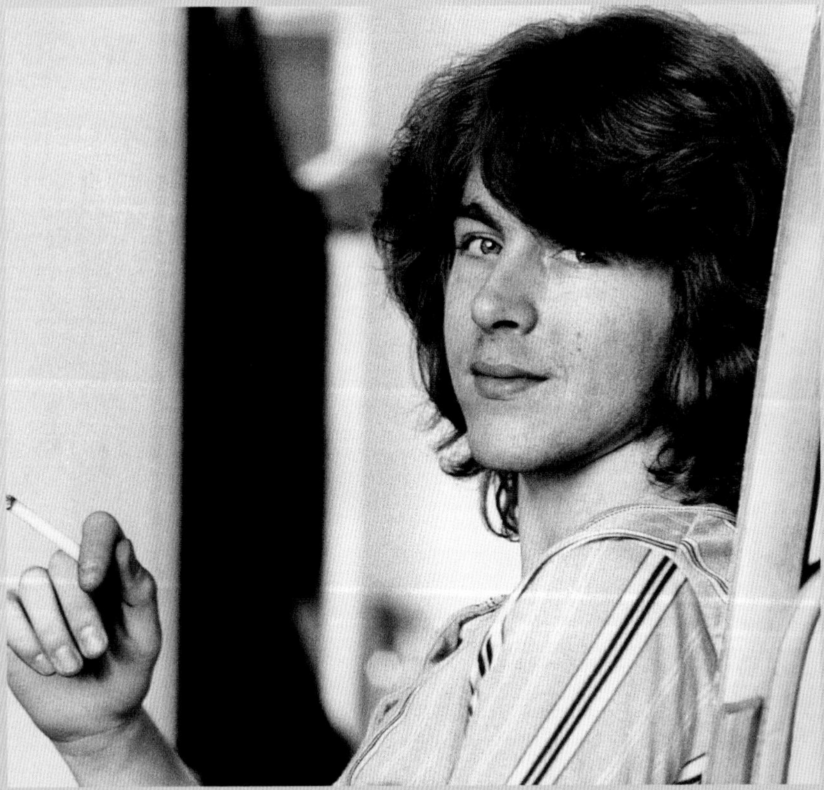

Mick Taylor joins the band

Above: The relationship between Brian Jones and the others was strained and everyone knew that action had to be taken. In May, Mick, Keith and Charlie drove to Cotchford to discuss the future and it was agreed that Brian should leave the band in exchange for a financial settlement. On 8 June Brian Jones leaves The Rolling Stones – musical differences are cited as the reason. Two days later 20-year-old Mick Taylor (*centre*), previously a guitarist in John Mayall's legendary Bluesbreakers, is recruited to replace Jones.

Left and opposite: British audiences were to get their first look at new Stone Mick Taylor at a concert in July 1969 but American fans would see the new line-up first when they recorded a US TV show at the end of June.

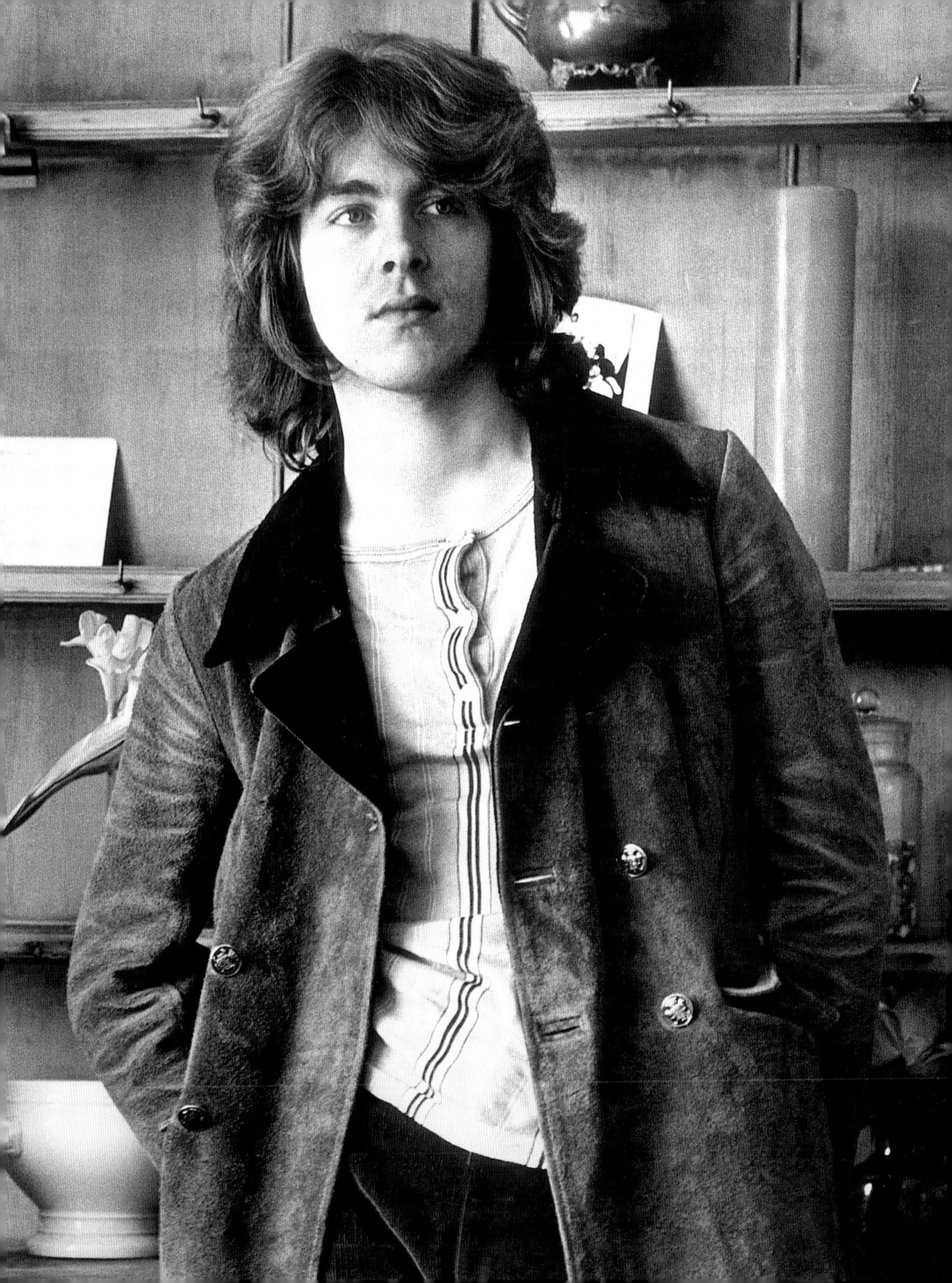

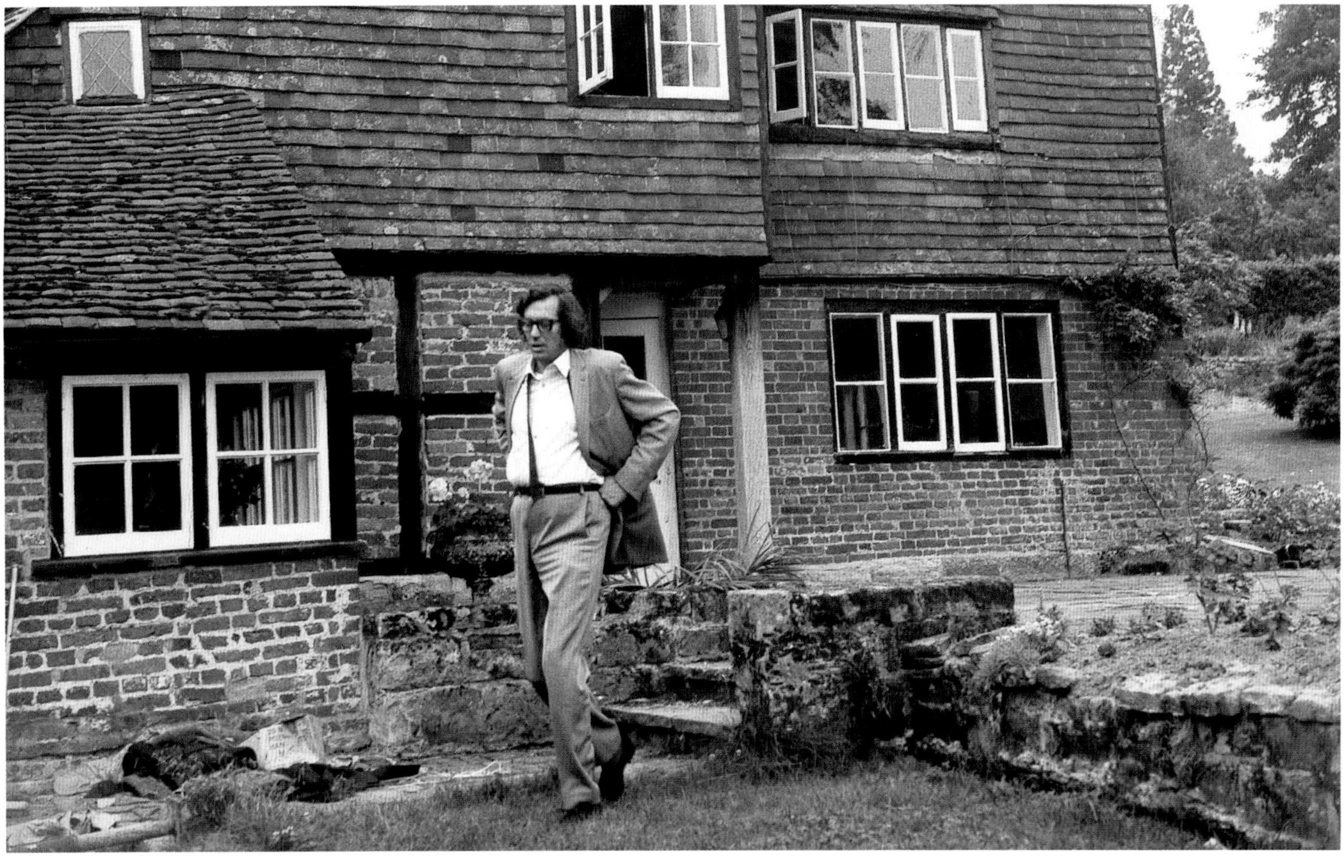

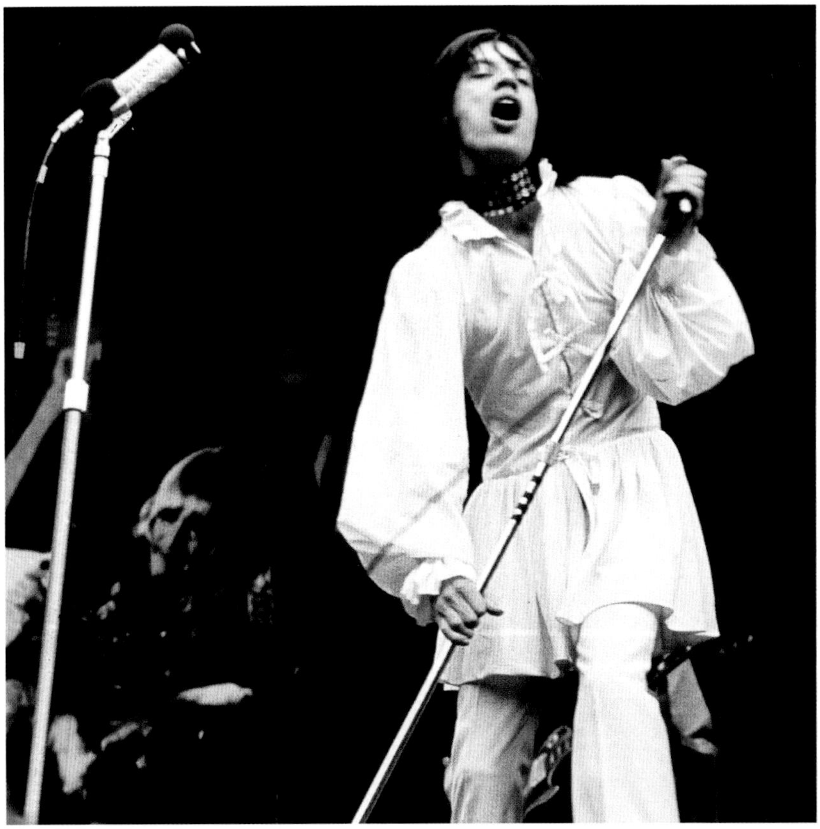

Death of a Rolling Stone

Left: Brian Jones drowned in his Sussex swimming pool on the night of 2 July 1969. The band had already planned a free concert for 5 July to celebrate their re-formation and decided to proceed with it. Inevitably it became an emotional memorial to Brian and remains one of rock 'n' roll's seminal occasions.

Above: Rolling Stones tour manager Tom Keylock stands outside Cotchford Farm, where Brian Jones had lived and died. The house had once been the home of A. A. Milne, who wrote the *Winnie the Pooh* stories there. Brian had been living and working there quietly as he planned his future.

Opposite: A week later, Bill Wyman is granted a divorce from his wife Diane and given custody of their son Stephen. During the proceedings it emerged that Bill was 32 – five years older than had been generally assumed.

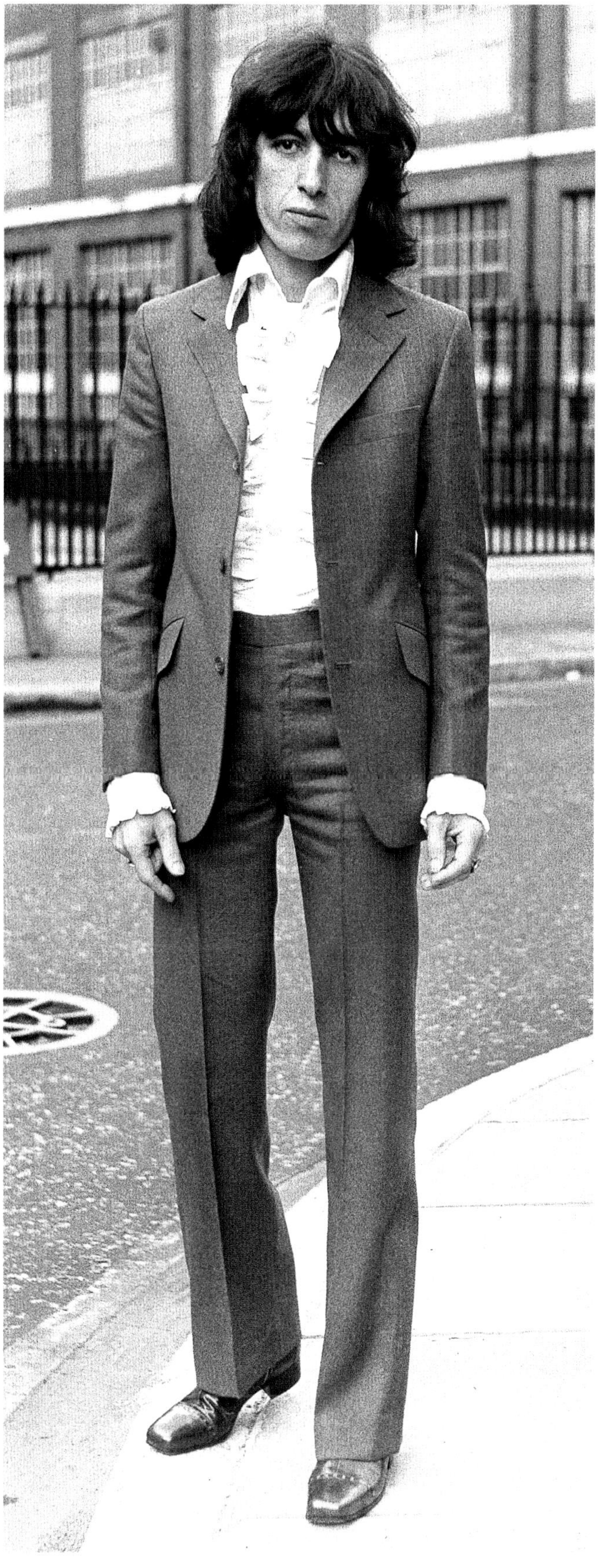

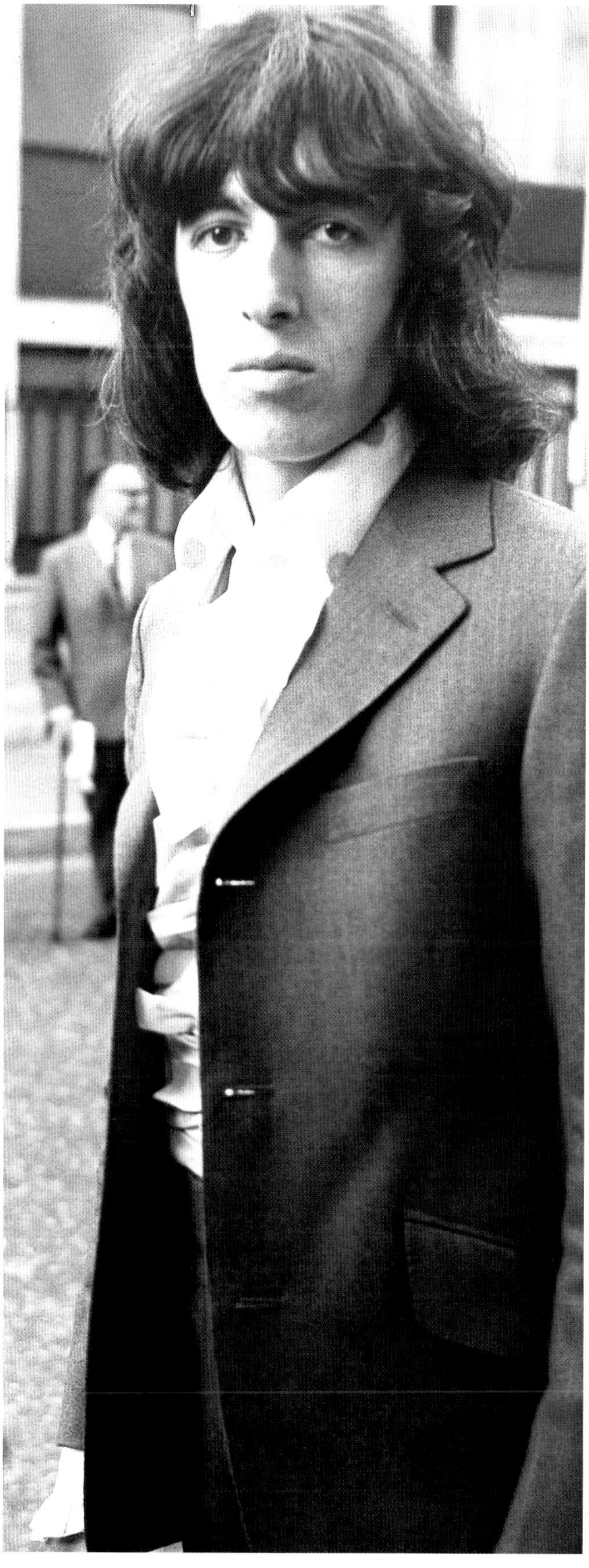

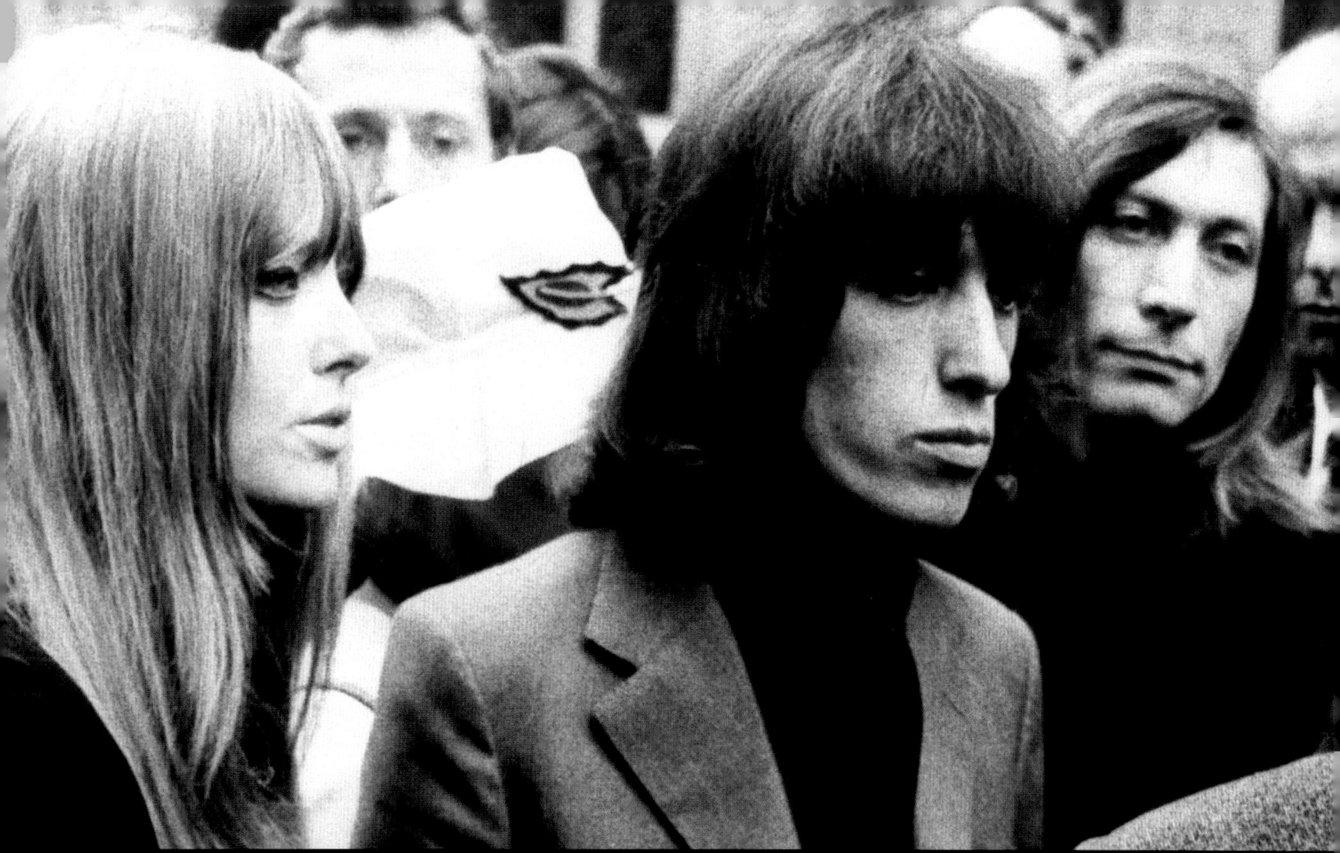

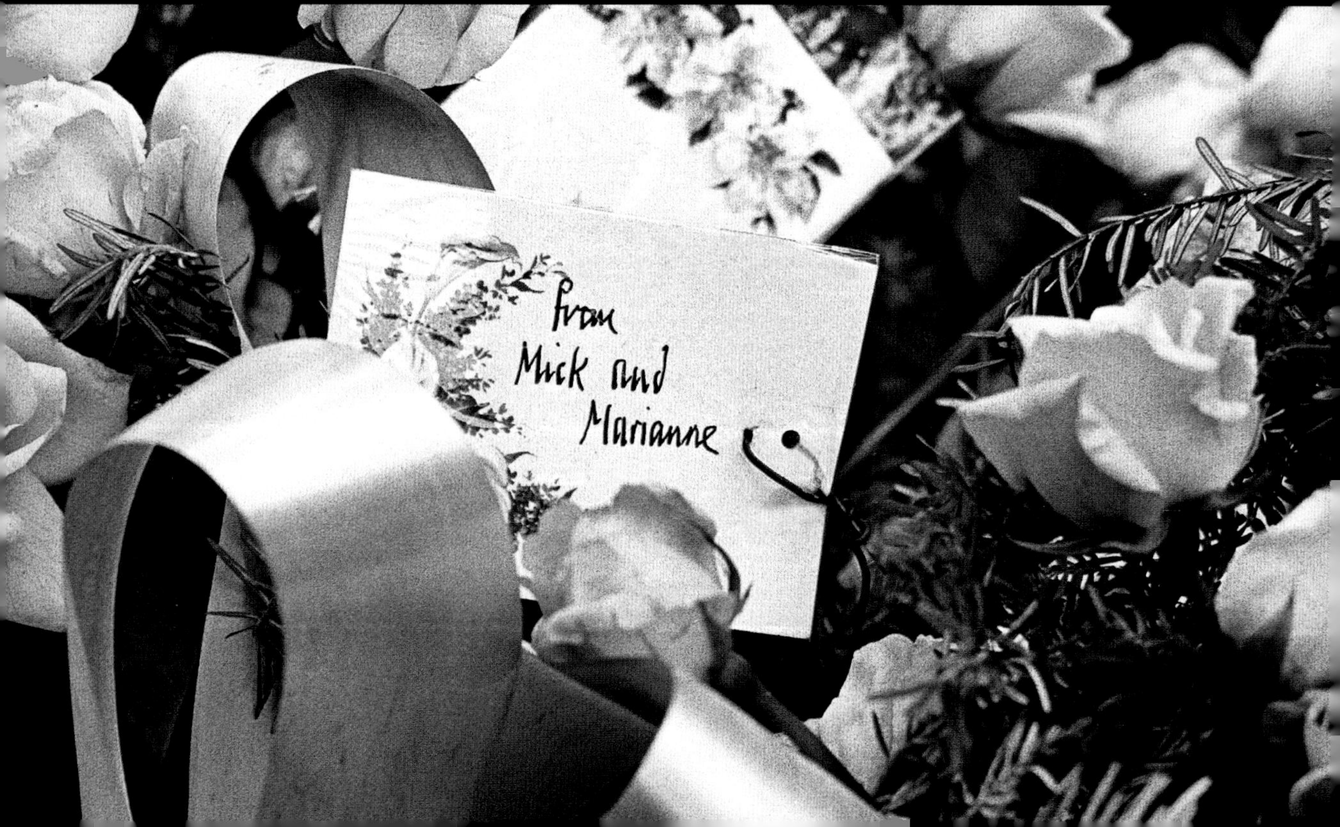
From
Mick and
Marianne

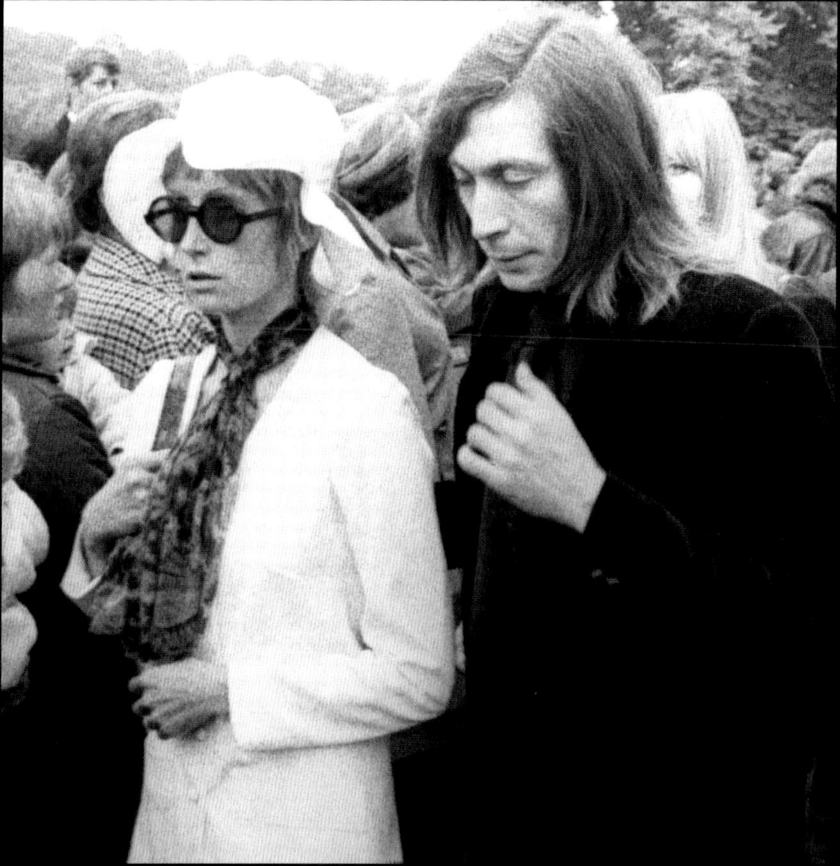

'Please don't judge me too harshly'

Brian Jones was buried in his hometown of Cheltenham on 10 July 1969. All the Stones attended, except Mick Jagger who was filming in Australia, and had to cope with Marianne overdosing and falling into a coma. At the funeral service the priest read from a telegram Brian had sent to his parents after a recent brush with the law saying, 'Please don't judge me too harshly.' In the Cheltenham streets where fans gathered, in the packed church and at the graveside, there were only expressions of affection and sorrow.

Opposite below: Mick and Marianne had sent flowers.

Opposite above: A recently divorced Bill with a female friend.

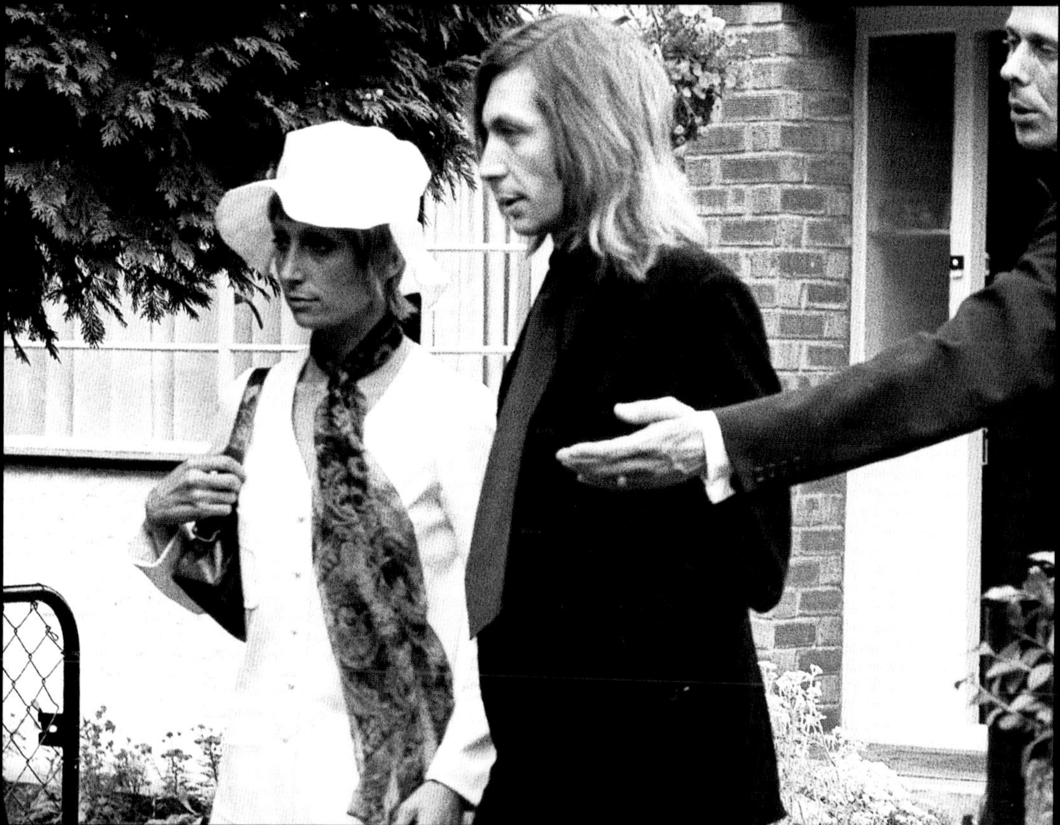

Above and right: Shirley and Charlie Watts, she in the white mourning of Eastern cultures, he in traditional black.

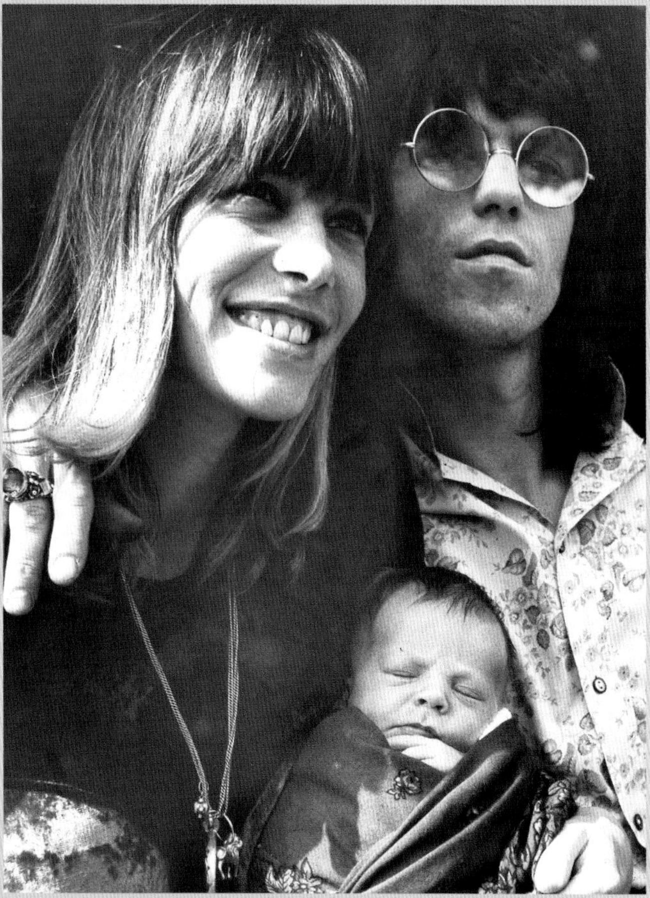

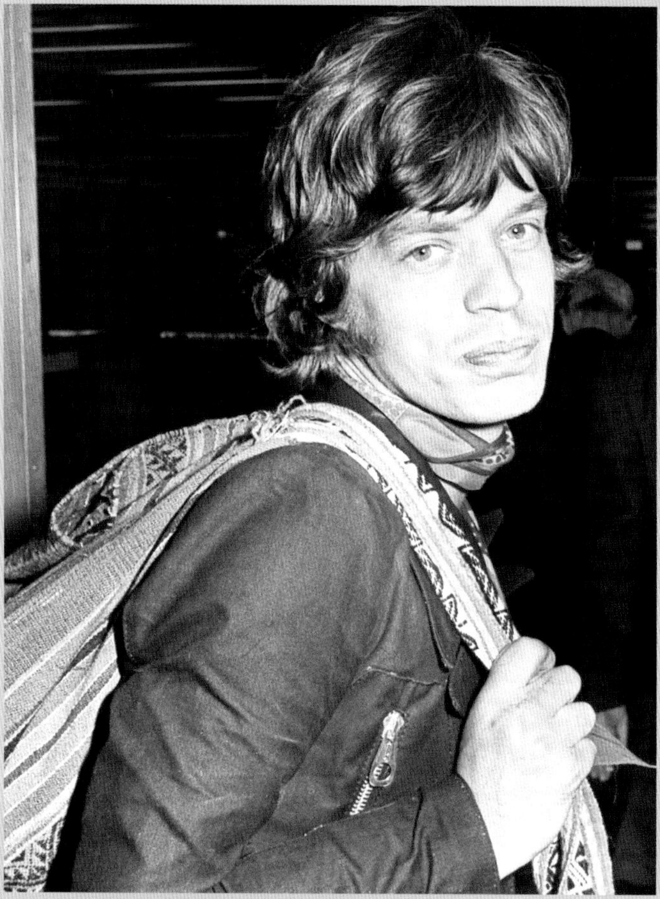

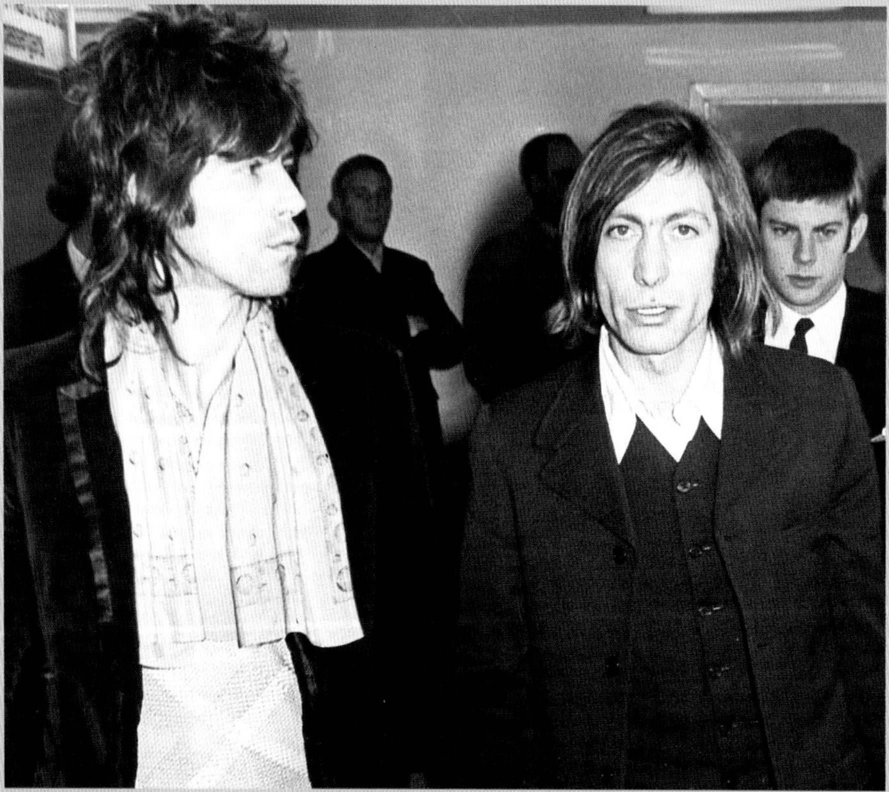

Mick plays Ned Kelly

Above left: Keith Richard, Anita Pallenberg and baby son Marlon, born at King's College Hospital in London on 10 August 1969.

Above right: October 1969. Mick is pictured en route for recording in Los Angeles followed by the band's first American tour for three years. He had all but finished work on *Ned Kelly*. The reasons for going on tour were mainly financial. Most of the tour was organized in the United Kingdom – Ike and Tina Turner and B. B. King were booked as the supporting acts.

Left: December 1969. Keith and Charlie fly back after the dramatic and tragic concert at Altamont, California, during which three fans died and hundreds were injured. The concert had been policed by Hell's Angels, who took the law into their own hands when the crowd became restless.

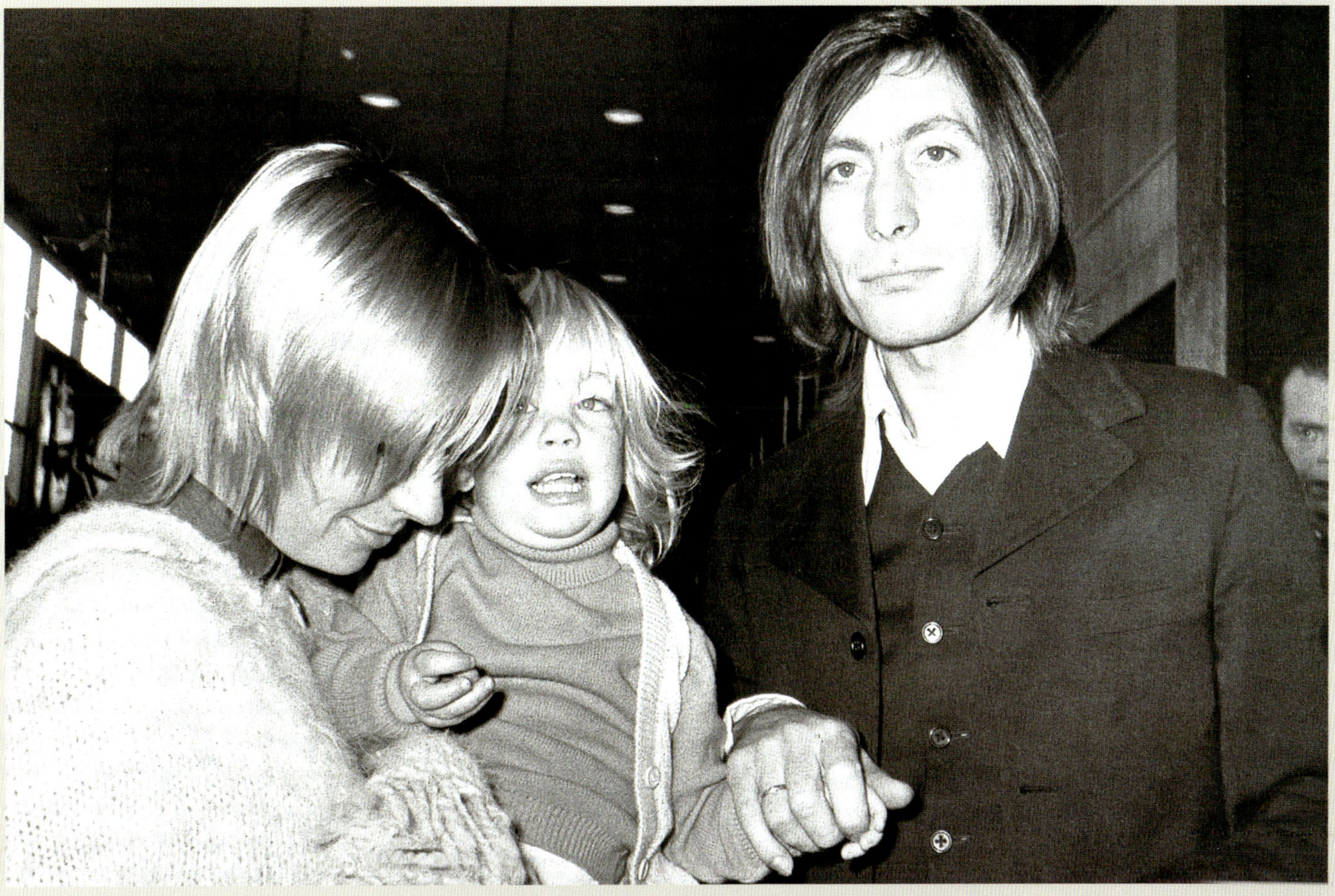

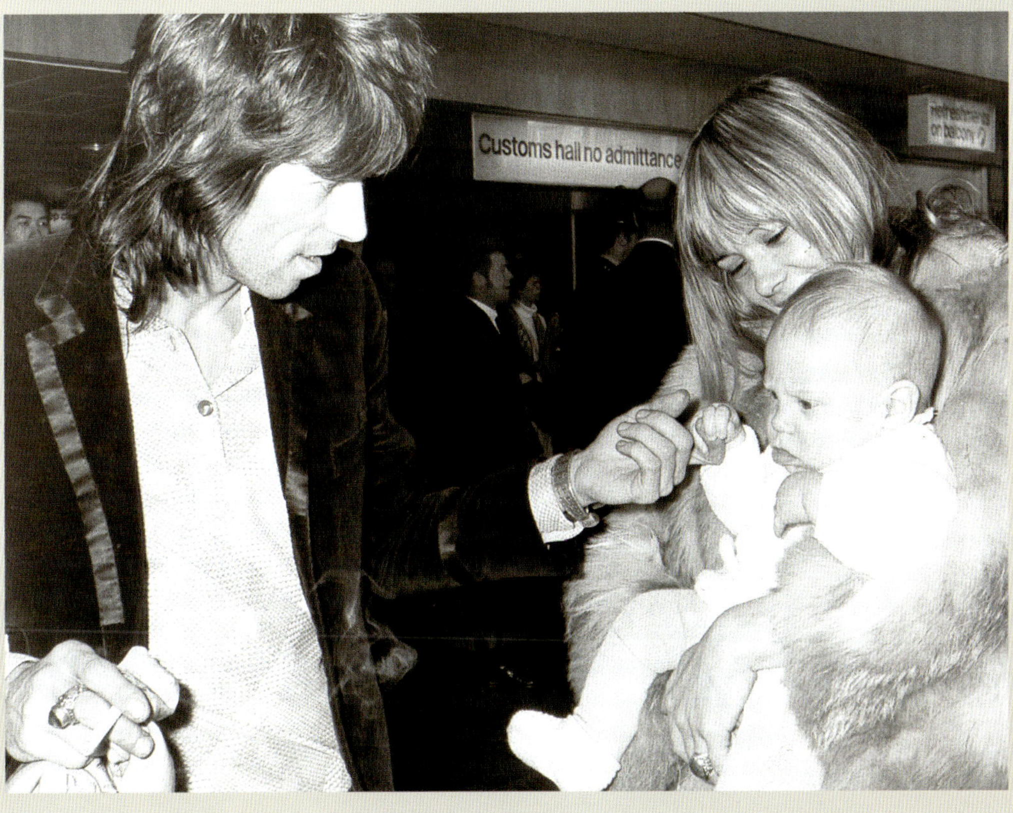

Final tour of the 1960s

Above: Charlie is reunited with Shirley and daughter Serafina.

Left: Keith is greeted by Anita and four-month-old Marlon. People often asked the couple about marriage plans and although there was to be a period when this seemed necessary due to Anita's 'alien' status in Britain, they never married. Long separated now, they remain friends nonetheless.

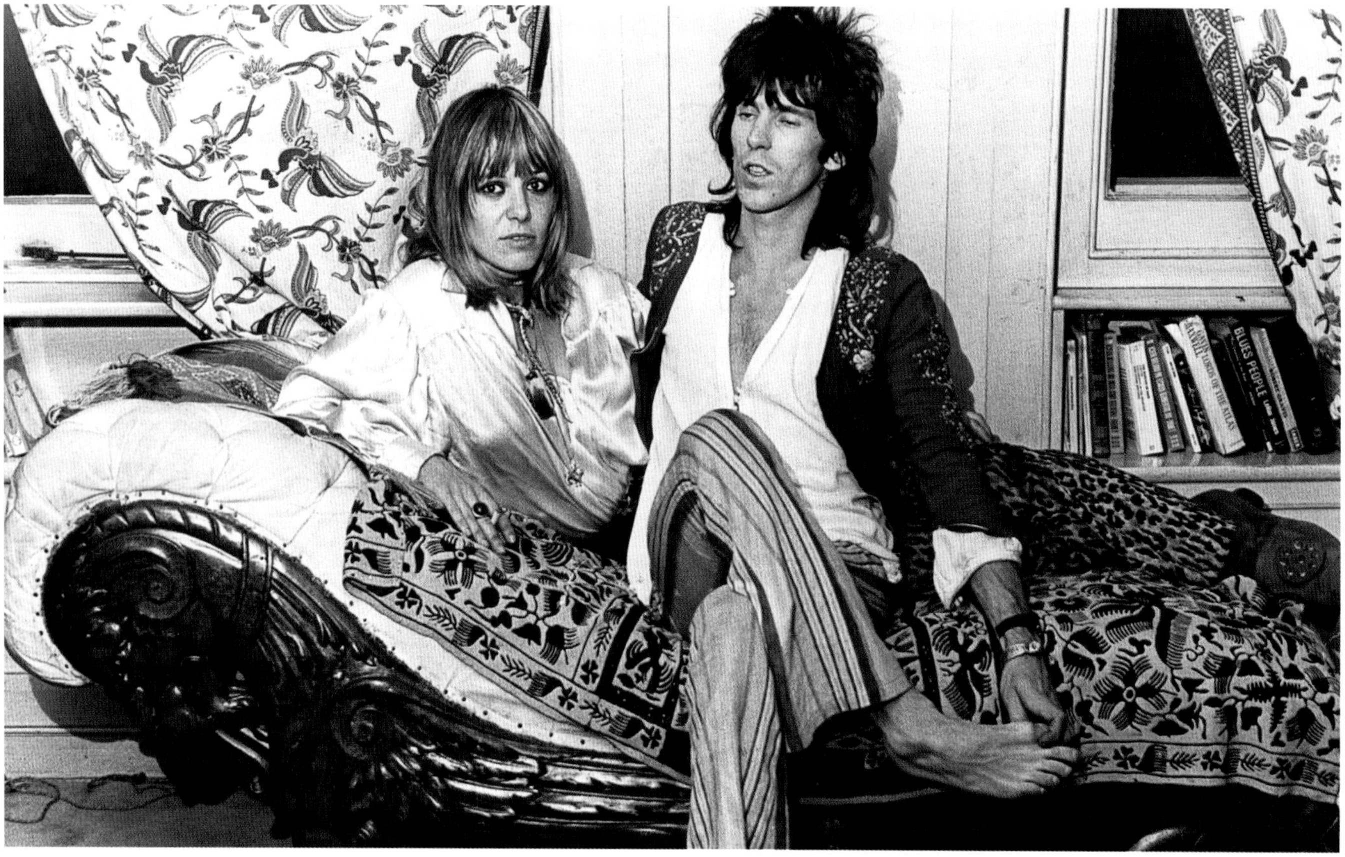

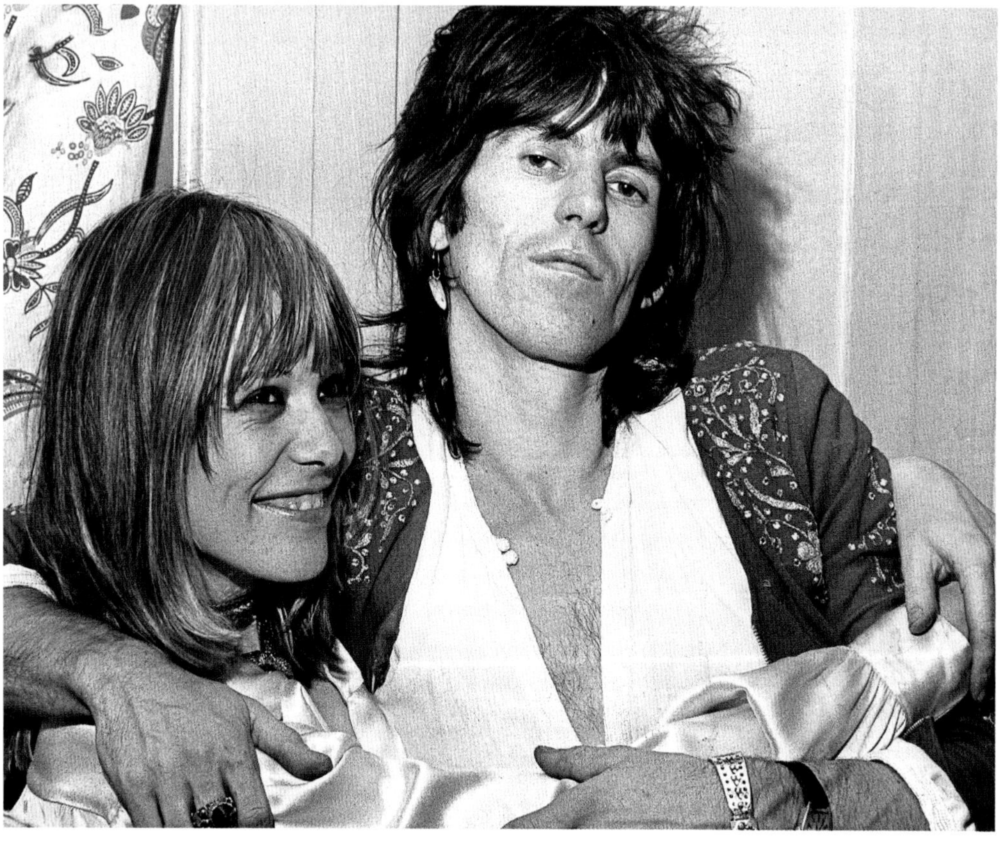

Let It Bleed

Above and left: Keith and Anita relax at home on 8 December 1969. They lived at 3 Cheyne Walk, a few doors down from Mick Jagger at number 48. Although often deemed to have an awesomely unhealthy lifestyle, Keith became a keen and competent skier under Anita's tutelage and the family made a home in Switzerland for some years.

Opposite: 14 December 1969, and just back from California, the Stones (minus Bill Wyman) pose before a concert at the Saville Theatre in London. *Let It Bleed* was released in December 1969 and was the last album to be recorded on the Decca label.

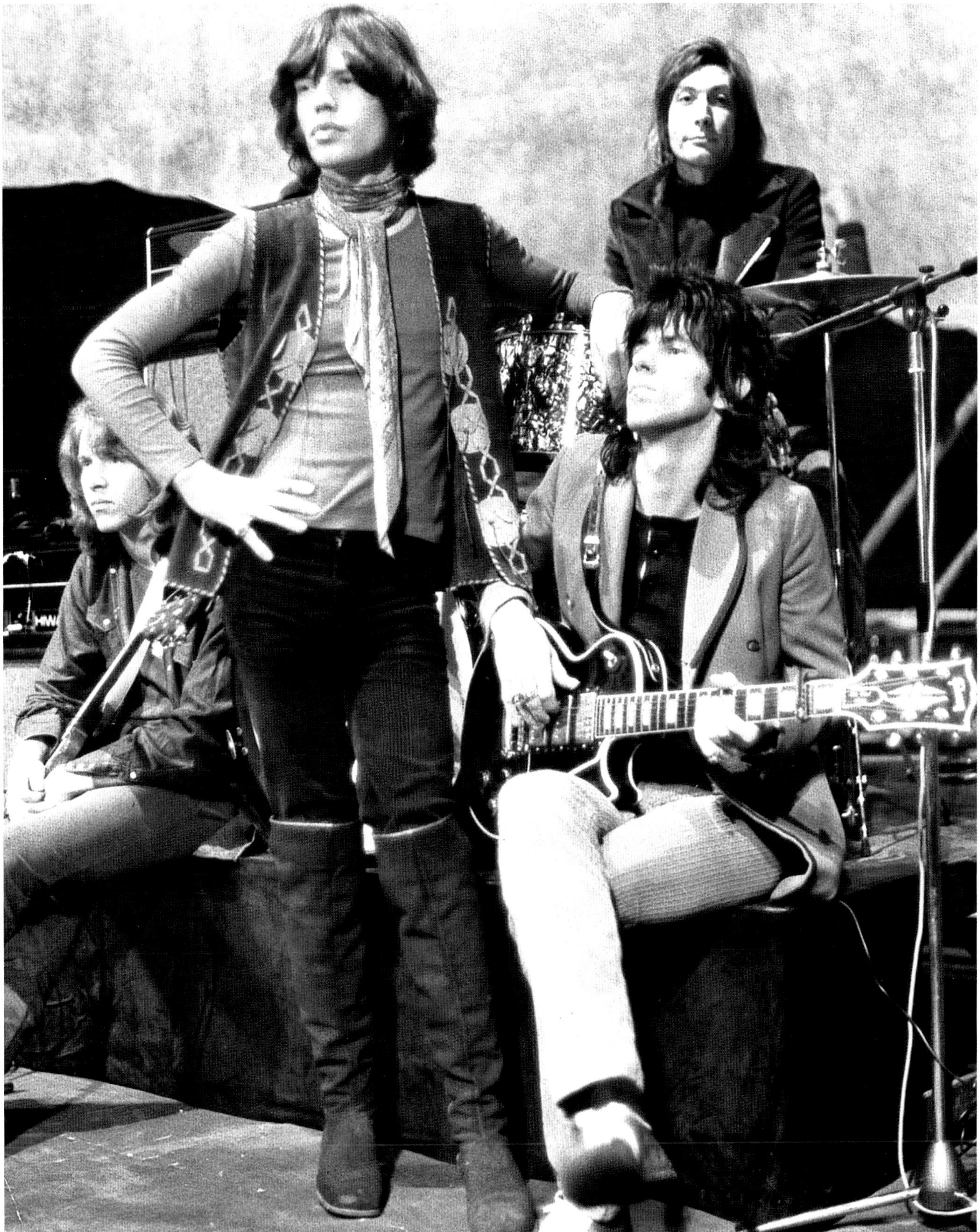

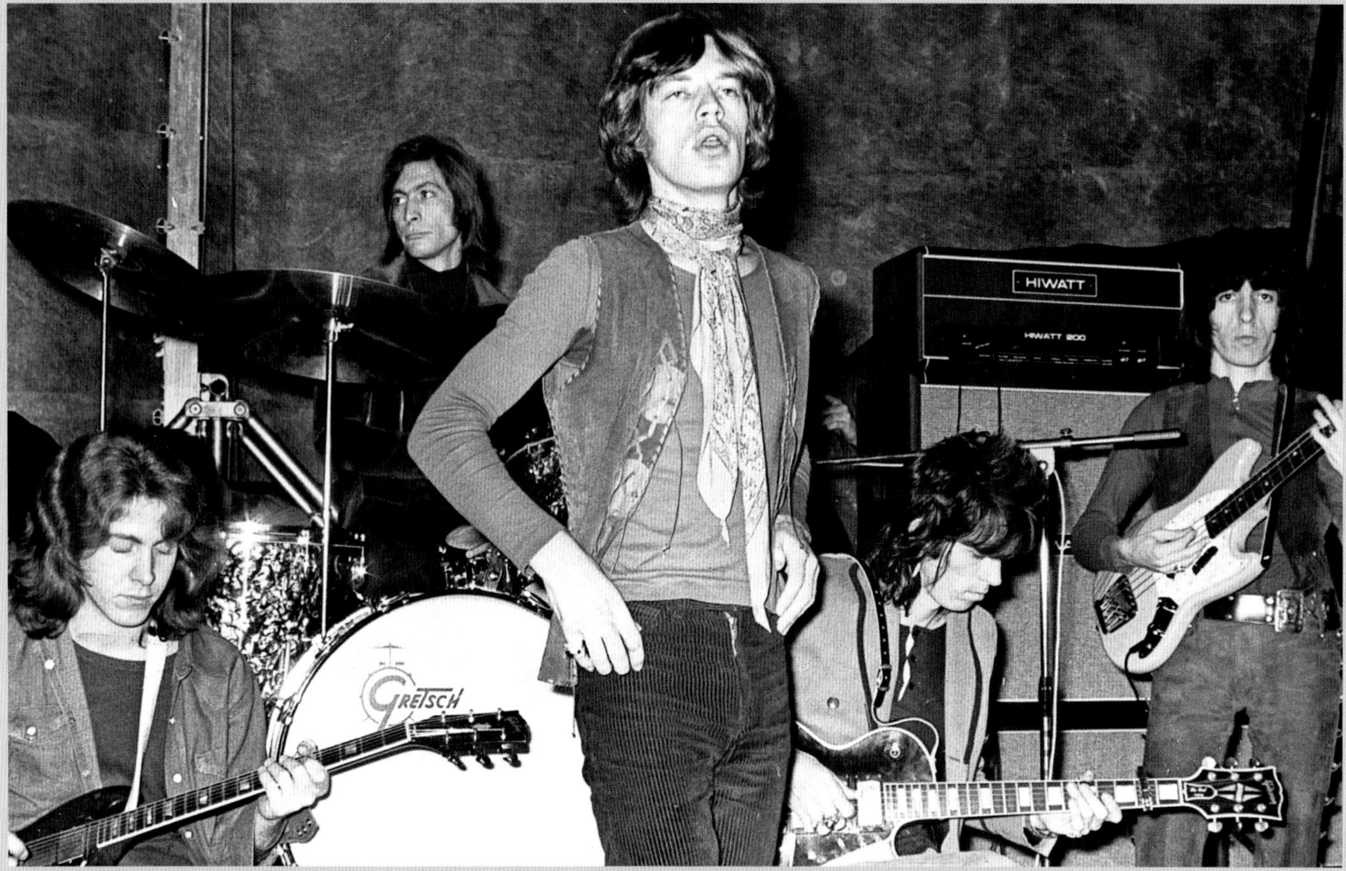

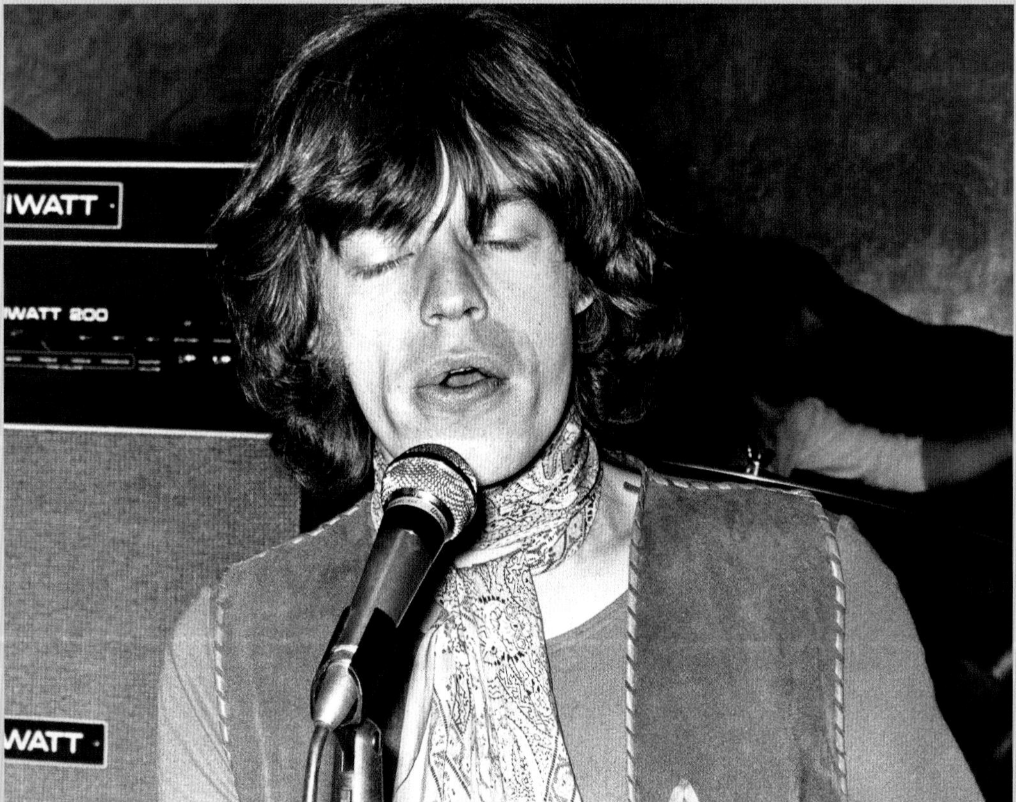

Above and left: The Rolling Stones in rehearsal at the Saville Theatre.

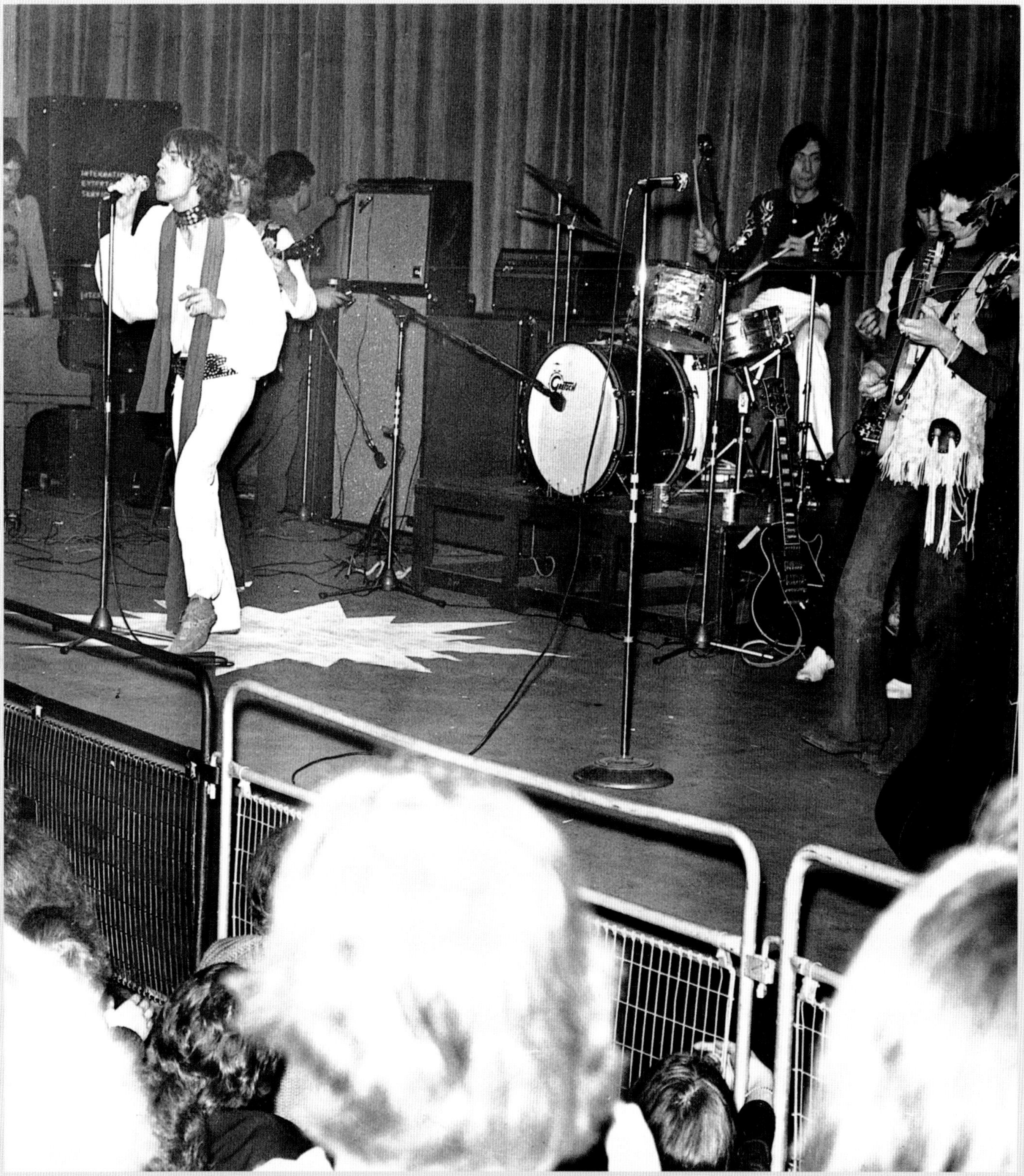

Playing out the decade

Above: On stage at the Lyceum Ballroom in the Strand, London, on 21 December. The Stones played two Christmas shows, at which fans were showered with artificial snow.

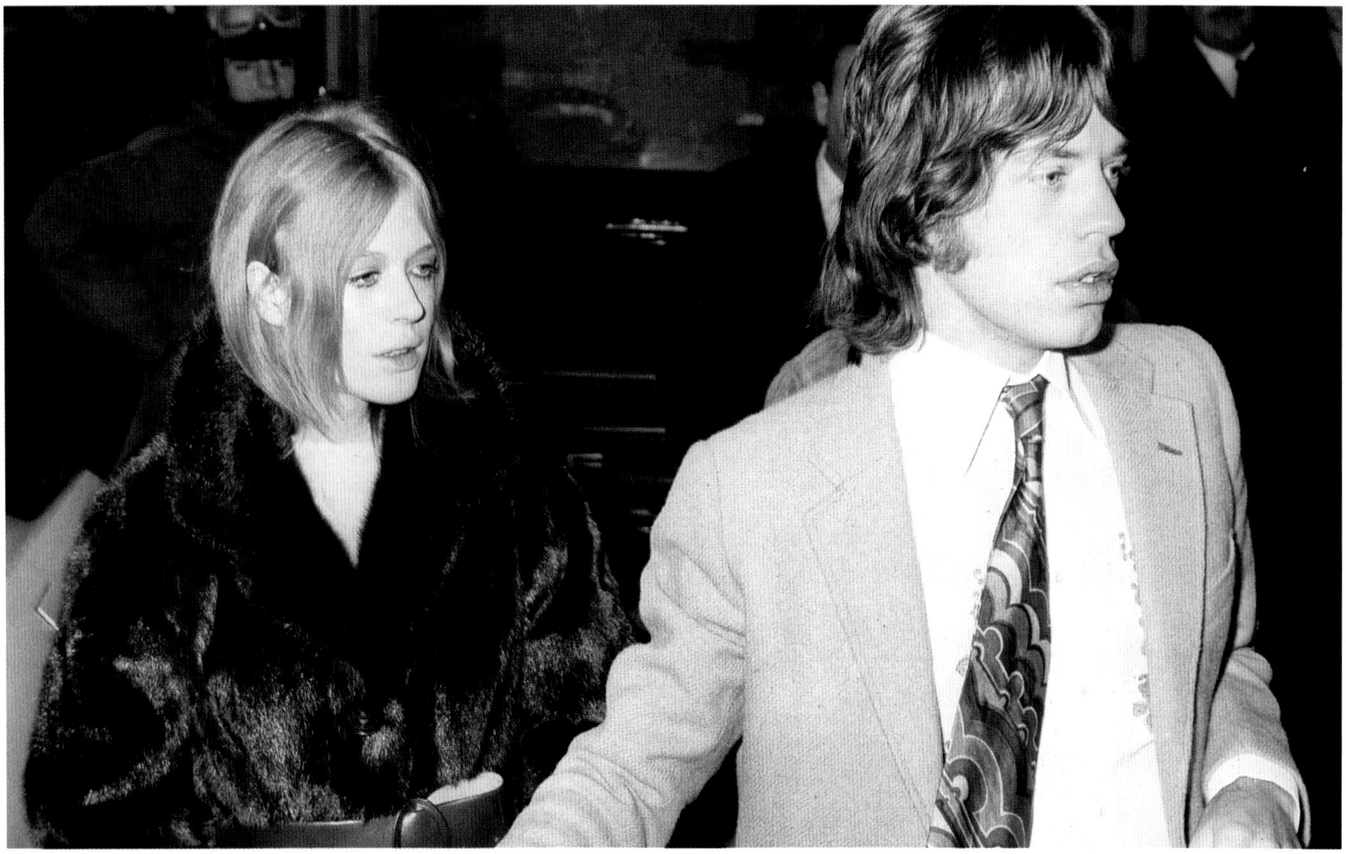

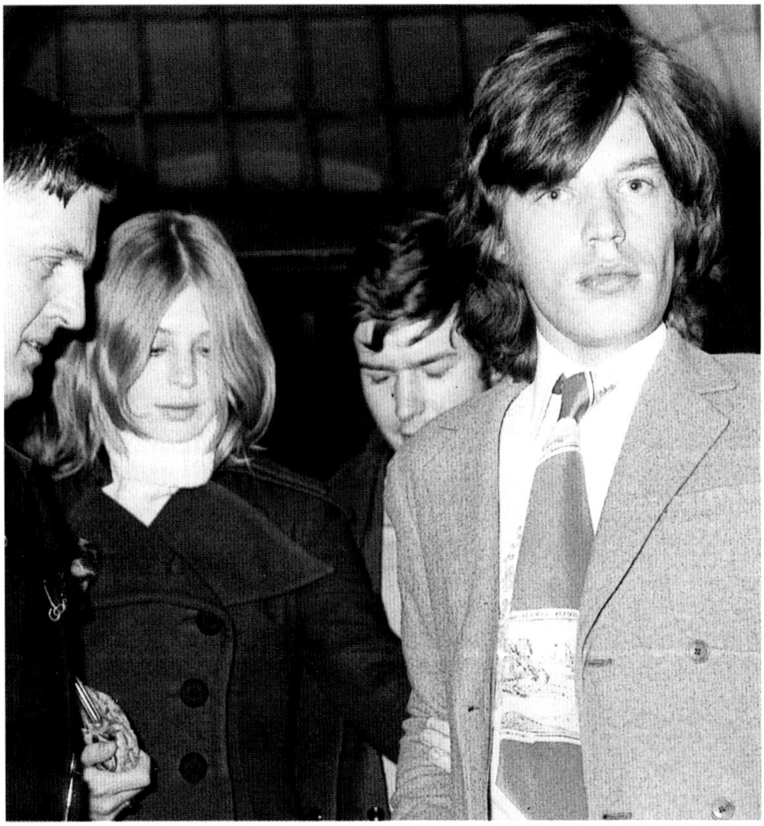

Mick and Marianne plead not guilty

Opposite and above: Mick Jagger pictured on 19 December 1969 with Marianne Faithfull outside a London court where they pleaded not guilty to charges of possessing cannabis resin. This was to be the fourth time their case was heard. Marianne wears a long fur coat, almost as much for protection from more than a hundred photographers outside the London court as for warmth. Mick shields her from the crush. Two days later, Jagger and the band were scheduled to perform their Christmas party show at the Lyceum, London.

Left: The drugs trial at the end of 1969 had taken its toll and the couple had briefly separated, during which time Marianne became involved with an Italian film director. She returned to London but the relationship with Mick was nearly over. Marianne was increasingly using drugs and Mick did not spend much time at home. In the summer of 1970 she left their house in Cheyne Walk and went to stay with her mother. Mick had a number of relationships, but the most significant was with the actress Marsha Hunt, with whom he had a daughter, Karis.

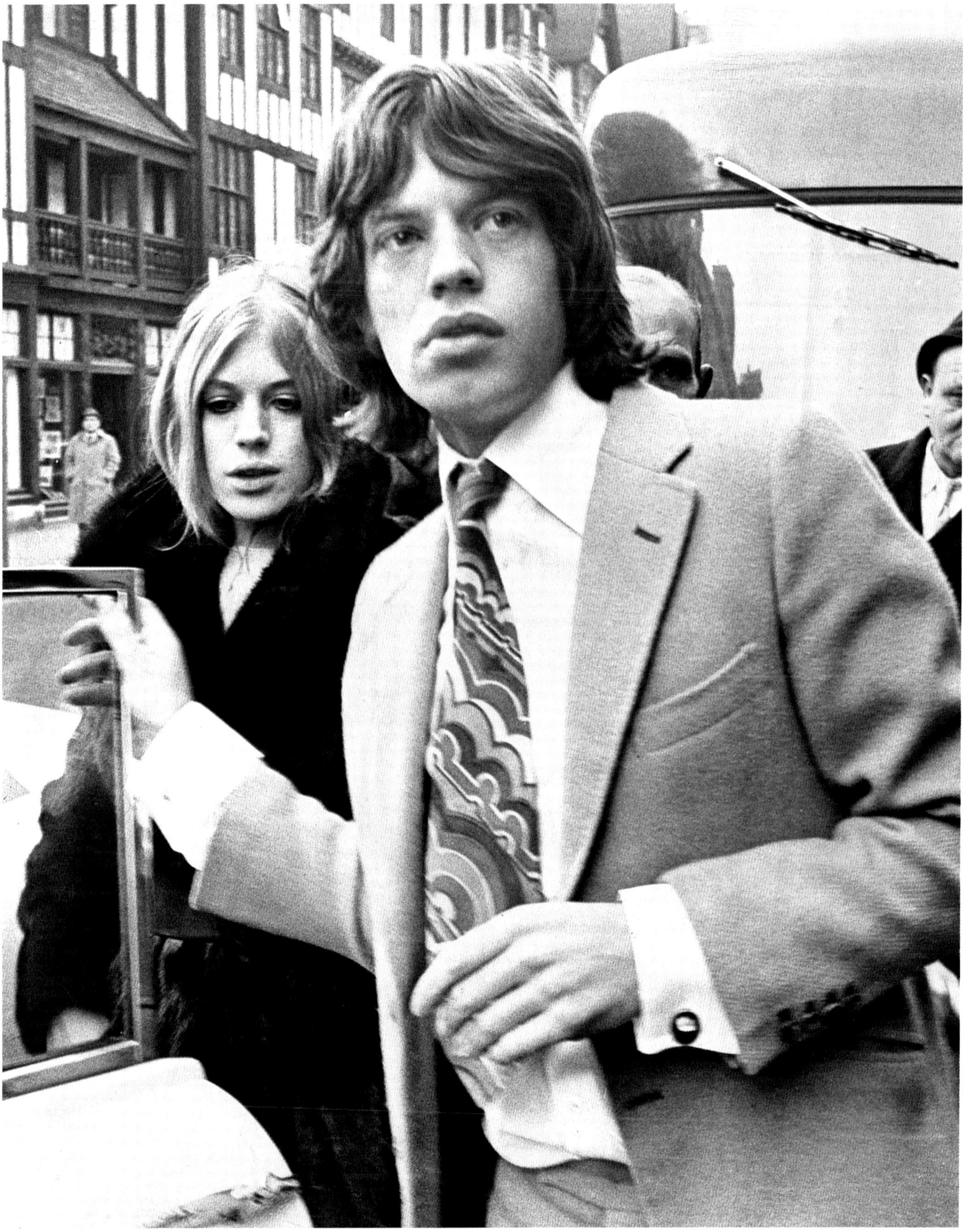

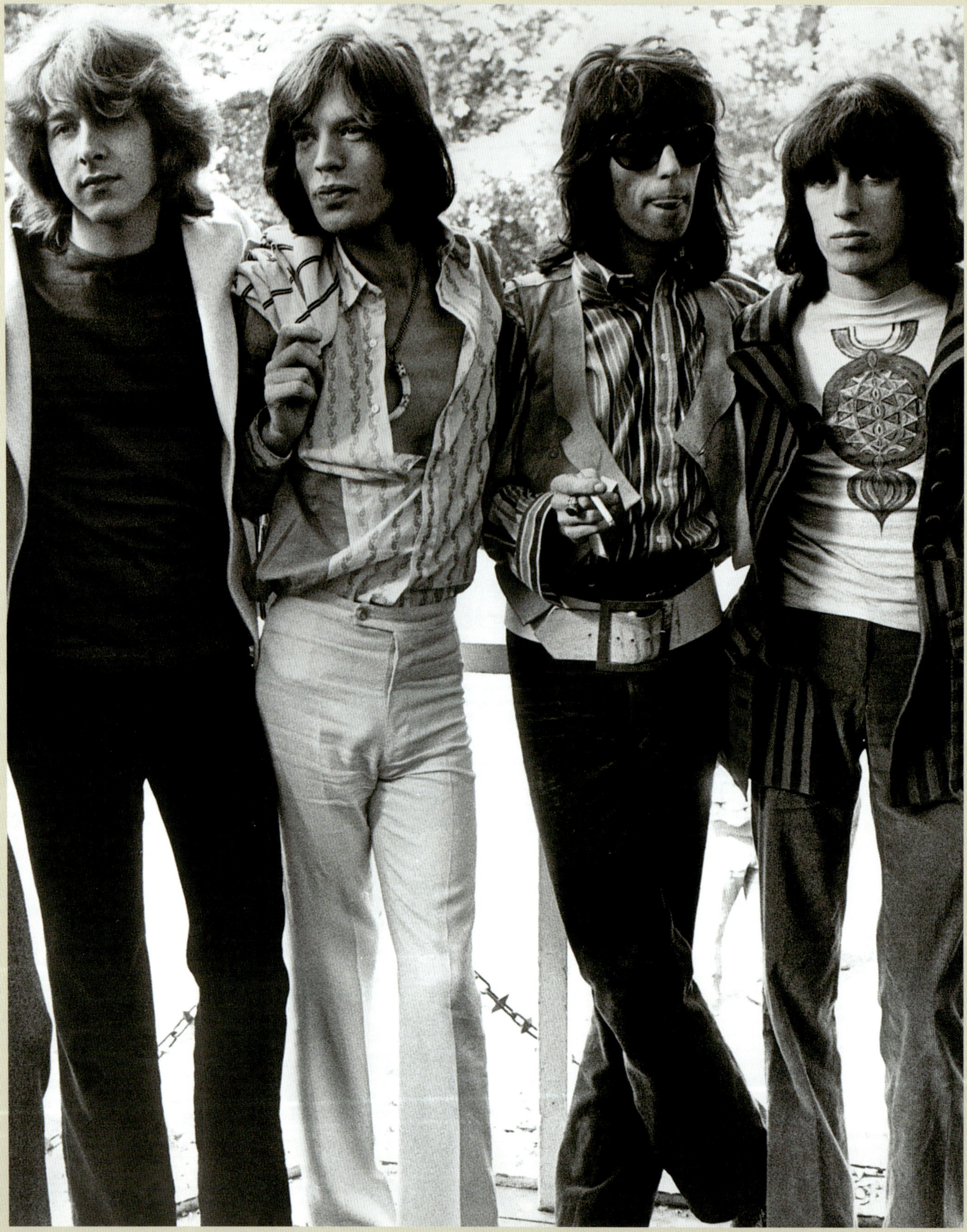

CHAPTER TWO

Exiles on Main Street

And so the decade turned and 1970 was relatively quiet – with a range of emotional rescues and bruises to be nursed. Mick and Marianne's long-term love affair was wilting, and Mick had begun to date other women – including singer and actress Marsha Hunt (who bore him a daughter, Karis) – to take his mind off Marianne and the generally poor reviews given to *Ned Kelly*. By contrast, Keith Richard was increasingly settled with Anita and Marlon. Bill Wyman was recovering from his divorce, and Charlie kept quiet, as ever. Sadly, Mick Taylor began a descent into drugs that eventually worried him enough to find the strength to quit the Stones. There were no serious scandals or busts in 1970. Mick punched a reporter in Rome for 'asking stupid questions', but that was about the extent of it. The contract with Decca expired and the Stones, relishing the freedom that a label of their own could offer, soon began working on a new album.

On 2 September that year, a new European tour began in Helsinki, and on 10 October the final album for Decca, *Get Yer Ya-Ya's Out!*, was released. Marianne was divorced from John Dunbar later that month, around the time that Mick began dating Bianca Perez Morena de Macia. The new album reached No.1 two months later. However, Mick endured another disappointment when Warner Brothers shelved the distribution of *Performance* in the United States, believing American audiences would not be able to understand his English accent. This curious claim must have been irksome to a man whose singing voice had been hitting the spot Stateside for some years. Perhaps the studio was concerned about how middle-class America might react to the film in the wake of the Altamont concert. Certainly when the band played live that year it was mainly in Europe, where demand for tickets was reassuringly high.

Public interest grew in Bianca Perez Morena de Macia. She was variously described as a former Paris hotel chambermaid, and the multi-lingual daughter of a Nicaraguan diplomat. She was neither, although her family had powerful political connections and she had been a political science student in Paris, where she had briefly dated Michael Caine. Bianca was a stunning Latin beauty and could have been Jagger's ravishing twin sister. But rather as Yoko Ono and Linda Eastman would be unfairly blamed for The Beatles' split, the British public did not take well to Bianca's presence on the Stones' periphery. They somehow got the idea that she had ousted Marianne Faithfull (who was, in fact, relieved and happy to have moved on). But Mick was enchanted, and Bianca was with him virtually everywhere he performed. The other Stones' wives and women friends did not seem to warm to her, either. Anita, the most long-standing partner of a Rolling Stone after the reticent Shirley Watts, may well have felt put out by the attention Bianca received. Rose Taylor and Bill Wyman's Swedish girlfriend Astrid Lundstrom were equally put off by Bianca's lofty detachment.

As Mick's commitment to Bianca deepened, work on the new *Sticky Fingers* album was hampered, to the dismay of some others in the band. But it was the 'real thing', and Mick and Bianca were to marry in St Tropez the following year.

The American release just before Christmas 1970 of *Gimme Shelter*, a film about the Altamont tragedy, had restored something of the Stones' bad-boy image – even though Keith Richard associated himself with a charity for drug addicts and offenders at the London premiere of *Performance* in the new year. *Performance* was never granted a general release. It remains a cult classic and invariably fills art-house cinemas.

In the new year, the US's *Billboard* voted The Rolling Stones third best artists of the previous decade. But even this didn't stop them giving a 'farewell tour'. This announcement supported rumours that the band were to leave Britain to become reluctant tax exiles on some main street in France. The result was a stampeding demand for tickets for their concerts. As we know, the band have toured often since, but seldom again claiming it would be for the last time. Any suggestion that The Rolling Stones were moving to escape vast tax debts was scotched, as was the idea that they no longer felt quite admired enough in Britain. The move was, their press agent insisted, simply because they loved France. They would still record in England and did not wish to relinquish British citizenship. The farewell tour finished in London in March 1970 and after a couple of TV shows and a sparkling party in sedate Maidenhead, the band decamped to the South of France. Some 11 years later Bill Wyman was to record his single '(Si Si) Je Suis Un Rock Star', a funny and possibly ironic tribute to this particular part of their lives. Wives, partners, children and staff spent a healing time in France. Photographs of their separate houses show elegant and graceful interiors, terrace tables strewn with the debris of meals for up to 20, overflowing ashtrays, opened bottles, children running about and adults in casual clothes, rather like an extended family party. But there *was* work in progress. However, some Stones missed England and planned to return. Despite their relocation to France, the band remained as popular as ever in Britain, with the release of *Sticky Fingers* in May (the sleeve designed by Andy Warhol and featuring a gentleman's well-packed jeans' crotch) and the hit single 'Brown Sugar' (which jangled a number of sensitive feminist nerves). Both single and album went on to top the UK and US charts.

Previous page: Mick, Keith and Bill are joined by Mick Taylor.

Below: On stage in Paris on 23 September 1970.

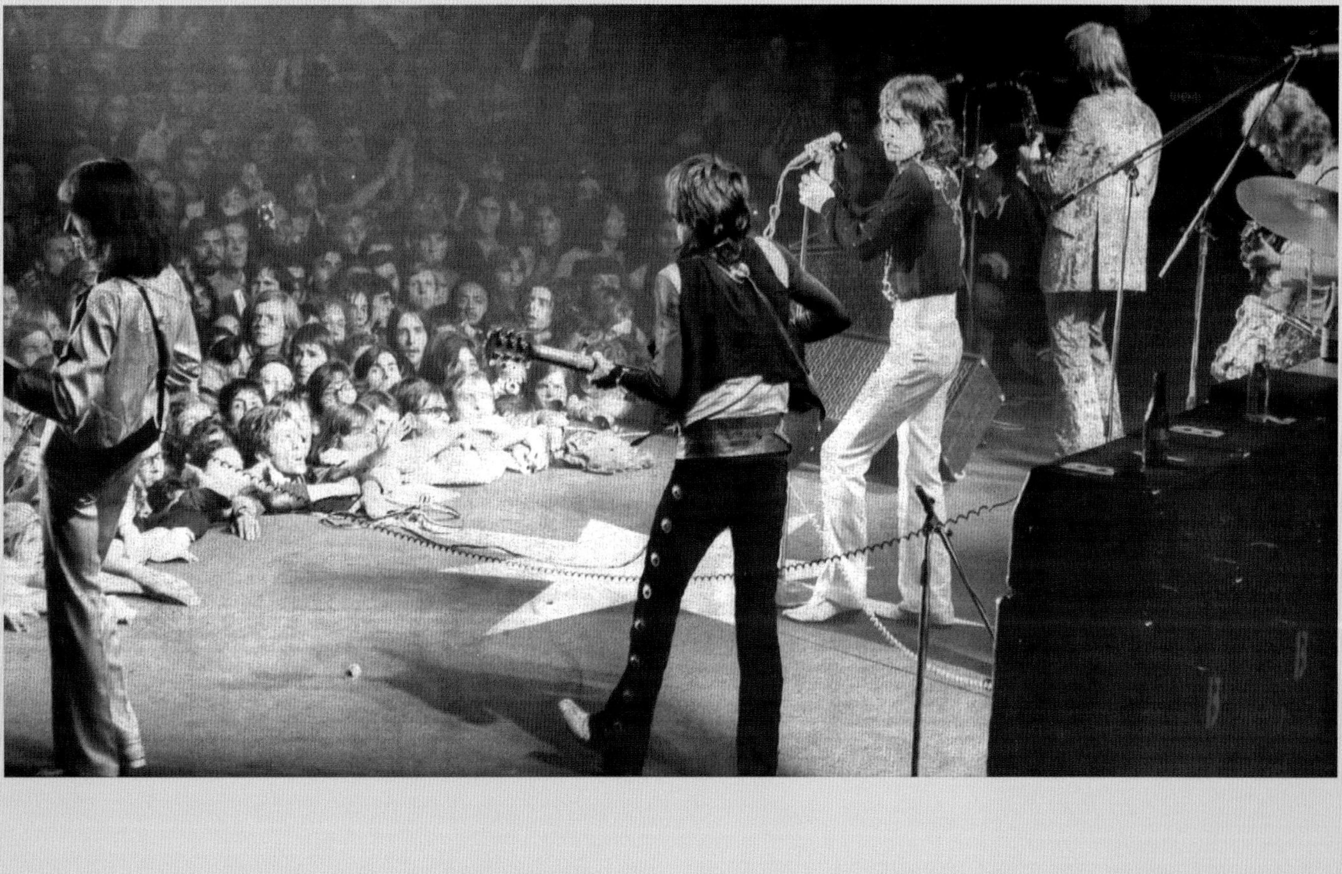

Mick and Bianca's marriage had gained worldwide interest. She was well into her pregnancy with their daughter Jade (who was born in Paris that October), and didn't look radiantly happy in the photographs. That could have been because she resented the paparazzi intrusions. She and Mick both wore white suits, and their guests included Mr and Mrs Paul McCartney and Lord Lichfield, the Queen's cousin. UK media attention intensified whenever the pair visited Britain. Bianca's habitual claim that she spoke no English and her refusal to be a standard rock chick only deepened the public's fascination for the woman who had seemingly made an honest man of Mick.

Meanwhile, plans were laid for a new tour of the United States and there were recordings in Los Angeles. Anita was pregnant again – daughter Dandelion was born in Switzerland in April 1972. And the Jaggers were house-hunting on the West Coast as this most sober of Rolling Stones years drew to a close. The band's relative lack of activity during 1971 left their fans hungrier than ever. By and large the various members had kept out of trouble since Brian's death but had still cleverly managed to retain the public's attention. These hadn't necessarily been vintage times but they had given the Stones a chance to conserve their energy and gather some motivation for their next moves.

Just as the 1960s didn't really begin until well into the decade, the 1970s also took their time to ignite. In the early 1970s Britain was getting used to metrication, worrying about the European Union, enjoying a TV sitcom called *The Good Life* and wondering whether platform soles made you look silly. People were listening to bands like The Faces, Jackson Five and The Osmonds. Bruce Springsteen cut his first album in New York in 1972. These were the times, and The Rolling Stones had to move with them even though they might never again define them. Far from being the dull decade that some dismiss, the 1970s were raunchy and exciting, and the restored Rolling Stones were ready to prove they were up for it all. In the mid-1970s a British Airways advertising campaign featured a stewardess with a fly-hither look in her eye and the legend 'Want to get off with me?' Ten years earlier The Rolling Stones had suggested 'Let's Spend The Night Together'. It had taken the mainstream nearly a decade to catch up with the bold appeal of sexual realities. By then the Stones had moved further along their own path.

In January 1972, Britain's *New Musical Express* voted The Rolling Stones second best British band and second best vocal band in the world. After all these years of being voted 'the best' it must have been hard for them to settle for less. But there were still kicks to be had, and delivered. Over the next few years the Stones proved that they were still the greatest rock 'n' roll band in the world. They weren't deterred when another anthology album, *Milestones*, only charted at No.17. After all, any true fan would already have all the tracks contained on the LP. The band answered back with the single 'Tumbling Dice', released on their own Rolling Stones label. It went into the British charts at once and reached No.5 in May. The *Exile On Main Street* double album, for example, stayed in the album charts for 14 weeks after its release in May 1972, holding the No.1 position for part of that time.

Everything was looking good for the new United States tour, which kicked off in June 1972. However, in July Keith was arrested for assault and Mick was arrested for obstructing a police officer after a scuffle at an airport stopover while on the way to Boston. They were both called to appear before the Rhode Island court in December.

During the tour, Mick's performance outfit of slinky-tight and strategically zipped or laced Lycra jumpsuits, which were studded with rhinestones and worn with tooled belts or floating silks tied around the hips, became a uniform. A wide expanse of hairless chest was usually revealed. Mick explained that he would have preferred to wear denims, but that even the most broken-in jeans did not allow the flexibility needed for his performance athletics. Perhaps he changed from his Spandex for his 29th birthday party after the final concert, at Madison Square Garden, New York, on 26 July. Guests included Truman Capote and Princess Lee Radziwill (Jacqueline Onassis' sister), Bob Dylan, Andy Warhol and Carly Simon. Carly's single 'You're So Vain', released later that year, was widely thought to have been inspired by Mick – who actually provided guest back-up vocals.

A few days later, Mick announced that he would retire from rock music at the age of 33. He would not, he declared, stay in show business at all when he quit rock 'n' roll. In the meantime, though, his schedule included a month of recording in Jamaica (starting in late November 1972) and a tour of the Far East in the new year.

Just before Christmas 1972, an earthquake devastated Managua, Nicaragua – home of Bianca Jagger's relatives. Mick and Bianca chartered a jet from Jamaica to Managua to make a search for her family. She was not to find her parents until 31 December. The couple also took some 2,000 anti-typhoid syringes. This act was to signal Bianca's later work as a dedicated campaigner for international aid. It is also in contrast with the public's image of her as being a hedonist and aloof. When, a few days later, *Billboard* magazine voted the Stones the best band of the year, it looked like being runners-up had been a freak blip.

Despite the first-class travel and luxury hotels, touring was tiring – even punishing at times. It must take real effort to perform with energy and excitement for a new audience night after night, yet The Rolling Stones have never been slackers here. Australasia, Europe, the United States, and painstaking hours in even the best studios can't always have been a party. The Stones worked hard to keep their fans happy. Throughout the early and mid-1970s their schedule was relentless. They even planned to be the first British band to tour the Soviet Union.

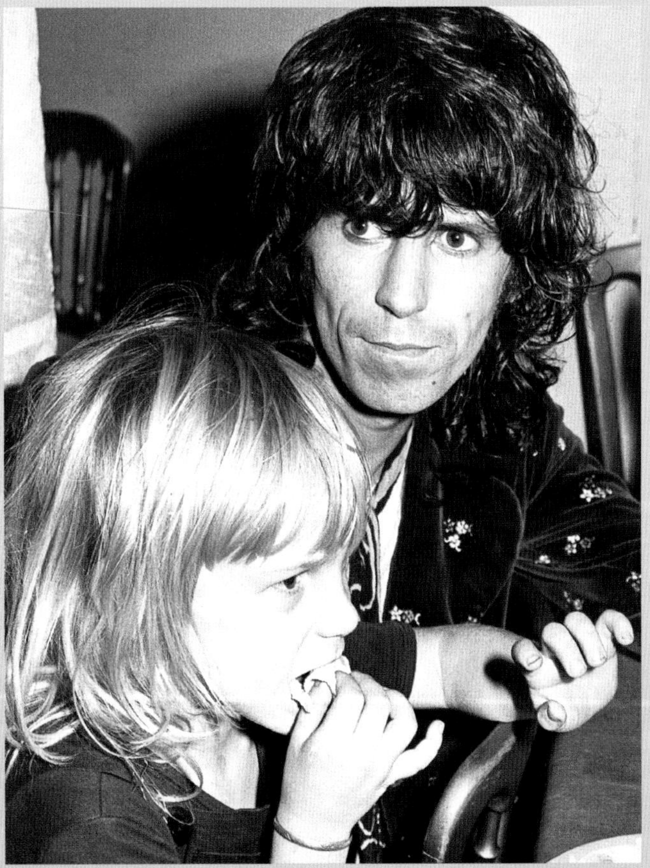

But they still seemed to make the news for the wrong reasons. Mick faced a new legal challenge when Marsha Hunt filed a claim in London about his responsibilities towards her daughter. Mick requested blood tests and eventually accepted paternity of Karis, settling an undisclosed sum with Marsha the following year. He had never shirked interim maintenance payments.

Keith was in different trouble in the summer of 1973, charged not only with possession of cannabis but also with having a revolver and ammunition. He was remanded on bail, but was absent from court as he and Anita dealt with the aftermath of a fire at their Sussex home.

As the decade rolled on, the band's profile stayed high. Still the albums kept coming and still the fans queued for tickets to the regular tours. Not only that, the odd controversy over cover artwork or 'obscene' lyrics kept the band's rebellious image bright. It may only have been rock 'n' roll, but the British fans still liked it. So did the Japanese, who, in 1974, heaped plaudits on The Rolling Stones in general and Mick in particular.

Rumours also kept the fans entertained. There was the one about Mick and Bianca's marriage being shaky. Then there was the one about Mick Taylor's likely departure from the band. There was also the legendary tale of Keith being given a complete blood transfusion in Switzerland in 1974. This, so the rumour went, was to make sure he was 'clean' next time he wished to enter the United States.

As it happens, Taylor did leave the Stones at the end of the year, joining Cream founder Jack Bruce in his new band. Everyone involved was concerned that the split was amicable. But stories persisted that Taylor had been unhappy about the lack of credit (and therefore perhaps royalties?) for his contribution to some songs. After many denials, his place in the band was taken in April 1975 by Ronnie Wood. Despite the arrangement being temporary, with Ronnie 'on loan' from The Faces, he remains with the band to this day.

Weeks later, the Stones embarked on their biggest ever tour, playing to 1.5 million people at 58 concerts across the Americas. Mid-tour, in June, Anita was deported from Keith's home in Jamaica on drugs charges. Weeks later, Keith was arrested in Arkansas for possessing an offensive weapon (he said it was a tin opener with an extra device for removing stones from horses' hooves).

Another exhausting year of tour dates and recording sessions ended with further accolades. In the United States, *Creem* magazine voted the Stones the best group, best R & B group and best live band. The droll and likeable Ronnie Wood won the magazine's award for most valuable musician, and the album compilation *Made In The Shade* was voted best re-issue. *It's Only Rock 'n' Roll* was voted best album and *Ladies And Gentlemen, The Rolling Stones*, best rock movie.

In spring 1976, Anita gave birth to a second son, Tara, named for Tara Browne, the Guinness heir whose death had inspired John Lennon's 'A Day In The Life'. Sadly, the baby died ten weeks later. After these difficult times for Keith and Anita, Dandelion was cared for by Keith's mother, Doris. On 19 May, Keith crashed his Bentley in Buckinghamshire. Police found 'substances', later identified as LSD and cocaine, in the wreckage and he was remanded to appear in court in September. Despite all this, he and the band played on and toured, capitalizing on the success of their most recent album, *Black And Blue*, released in April 1976.

In October 1976, amid strengthening rumours about the fragility of his marriage, Mick Jagger told *Woman's Own* (his interview being something of a coup for a magazine better known for recipes and knitting patterns) that he had married for something to do, that he'd never been madly, deeply in love. Whether it was true or not, this was something that might better have been kept private.

In 1977, Queen Elizabeth II was celebrating 25 years as head of state and of the Commonwealth. Her Silver Jubilee year became one in which punk changed the face of rock music. The Stones would have to guard against looking out of touch with youth culture as bands like The Sex Pistols began to have a massive impact. Indeed, the year began with the almost quaintly traditional sequence of drug-related court appearances for Keith, a wrangle with newspapers about the release of censored photographs, a new record deal (with Britain's ultra-establishment EMI) and Bill weakly complaining to a newspaper about how tiresome it was to find groupies lurking in hotel bathrooms when one checked in on tour.

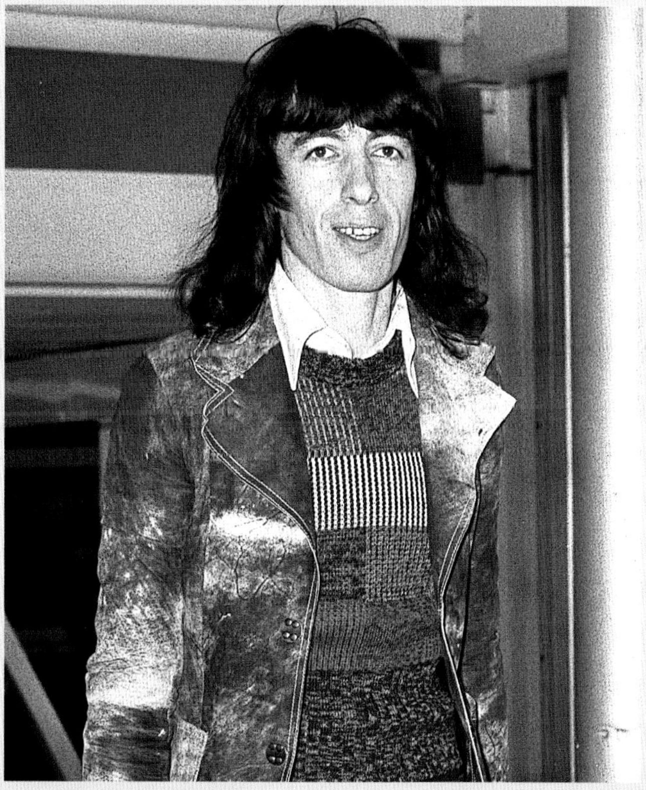

Opposite: Keith poses with his son in 1973.

Above: Bill pictured en route for California in 1973.

Then, in February, the Stones flew to Canada for yet another tour. There was little surprise when Anita and Keith were detained at Toronto customs. Cannabis and traces of heroin were found, and Anita was arrested then released. Three days later the pair were arrested for possession of heroin at their hotel but were released and Keith bailed (albeit facing the threat of a life sentence).

Their first Canadian gig took place on 4 March at a club with an audience of only a few hundred. Afterwards, a party was thrown for the band by Margaret Trudeau, the glamorous young wife of Canada's premier Pierre Trudeau. She had taken a suite at the band's hotel. Mrs Trudeau attended further concerts in Canada and arranged at least one more private party for the band, apparently unconcerned by the weight of Keith's charges or the potential embarrassment for her husband. Inevitably, speculation in the Canadian and world press suggested that Mrs Trudeau was having an affair with a Rolling Stone; a New York writer imagined that she had her eye on Ronnie Wood. There were staunch denials all round.

All the Stones but Keith flew to New York and Mr Trudeau publicly defended his wife, saying she had the right to a private life. However, he added that she had cancelled all forthcoming public engagements. By early April, Keith and Anita had joined the others in New York. The band played some gigs, discussed business, edited some live album tapes and attended more parties. Meanwhile, the brilliant American singer and guitarist Nils Lofgren, on tour in Britain, performed a new song dedicated to Keith Richard. 'Keith Don't Go (To Toronto)' seemed to say it all.

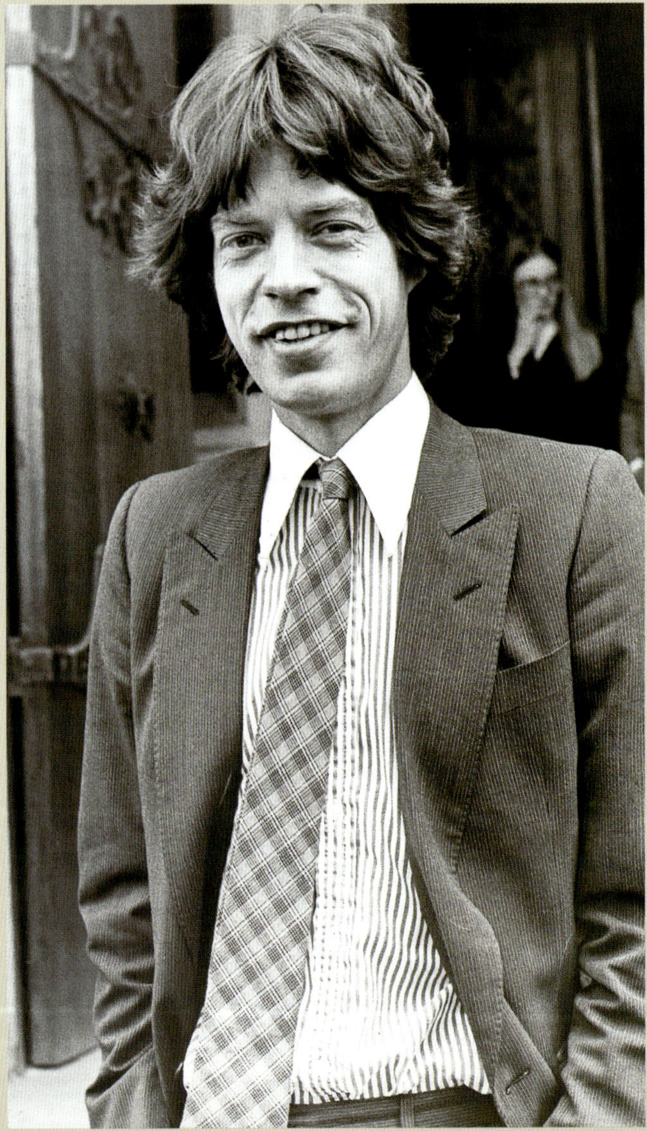

Above: Mick attends preliminary divorce hearings in 1979.

The cloud shadowed them all. Stories about Bianca's friendships with actor Warren Beatty and David Bowie didn't help. Charlie Watts went home to play jazz. Bill Wyman did the same, in Switzerland. Ronnie Wood sold his London home. And, while maintaining that he wasn't a drug addict, Keith was undergoing detox in New York. Kind-hearted German fans launched an appeal to help him finance his tribulations. The band seemed to be in disarray. Their new album, *Love You Live*, was launched with a party in London in September, without Keith.

Recordings in Paris began almost immediately – but where were the songs, the cohesion, the energy? And where was Keith? Actually he made it to some of the sessions. In the context of punk rock, Mick said that Keith was the original: 'You can't really out-punk Keith.'

By this time, Mick had begun dating a tawny Texan model, Jerry Hall. She was clever and humorous, and her rangy beauty had earned her great success, so she was wealthy, too. She used to step out with Brian Ferry of Roxy Music, who did not like her new friendship.

In December 1977, the band stopped recording while Keith faced his trial at last. He was remanded to a higher court the following February. Mick and Jerry used the break to visit Morocco, later spending Christmas in London before flying to Barbados for New Year. Bianca was rumoured to be filing for divorce as the year ended, although she and Mick continued to deny the end of their marriage.

In early March 1978, Keith's trial in Canada was set for October. The suspense must have been almost unbearable; but in the meantime he was free to travel, record and perform. There were no long-distance tours this year. However, the Nanker/Phelge partnership blossomed anew as the Glimmer Twins co-wrote songs for the June-released *Some Girls* LP, the tracks 'Miss You' and 'Beast Of Burden' being among their finest. The album sleeve, which featured less than flatteringly adapted pictures of female film stars with portraits of Stones in wigs and make-up, caused another controversy.

More gigs – mainly in North America – stretched out this strained year. Mick celebrated his 35th birthday in California, after the last concert. No one seemed to ask him about his threat to retire at the age of 33. Maybe everyone was just marking time to see what would happen to Keith. Interestingly, Mick had taken to playing guitar during the course of the tour.

Bill and Charlie attended the London funeral of Keith Moon, The Who's drummer, on 7 September that year. Bill remarked a few days later that he was depressed and thinking of quitting.

On 23 October, almost two years after the original offence, Keith Richards' (he'd recently reinstated the final 's' to his name) trial began in Toronto. His efforts to reform impressed the judge, and he escaped with a year's suspended prison sentence and an order to give a charity concert. He was also commanded to continue with his treatments for addiction. A packed court expressed relief and delight, and demand for the charity concert tickets was massive. Other factions were outraged by the judge's leniency and appealed against the light sentence. But Keith was effectively a free man, although it remained to be seen if the general cloud would lift. Keith was in a dilemma, anyway. If he returned to Canada he could face a subpoena from lawyers who wanted the case reopened, but he'd be in breach of the court if he failed to turn up for the concert. The appeal was heard in June 1979 and, agonizingly again, the decision was reserved.

In October the previous year, Mick had failed to receive Bianca's divorce papers because he was out of London. The documents were served the following April in New York. Her lawyer was the celebrated 'palimony' expert Marvin Mitchelson, who had already represented Marsha Hunt. Meanwhile Mick and Jerry Hall remained together. That Christmas he went to Hong Kong. Keith went to London to be with his family.

In January 1979 *Some Girls* was voted best album of the previous year by the *New Musical Express*. *Rolling Stone* had already given it a similar award and voted the Stones artists of the year. 'Miss You' was named best single. Nonetheless, it is almost miraculous that the beleaguered band (with backing group New Barbarians), managed to play several dates in North America that spring. Jagger had to discuss divorce strategies with his London lawyers. Those concerned may well have been alarmed by reports that Bianca wished to continue helping victims of the Nicaraguan civil war, but claimed she could do nothing without personal funds. Over a year passed before the divorce was finally heard in London in November 1979 – supposedly with neither happy at the eventual settlement. Bianca retained custody of nine-year-old Jade.

Perhaps we shouldn't pry too deeply for reasons for Mick and Bianca's failed marriage. Whatever happened in the past, Bianca would later remark that where Jade is concerned they will always remain united parents for her sake. Both rushed to their daughter's side from different continents when she was involved in a road accident in the Balearics in 2000.

Meanwhile Keith and Anita were in trouble again, this time in New York State. In August, a teenager watching TV in bed with Anita shot himself in the head with a stolen revolver. She was released on bail but her passport was confiscated. She said the boy had a death wish and she had taken pity on him, but that there was no sexual relationship. There were rumours, though, that she was involved with some kind of black magic.

In the face of all this, Keith's relief when the appeal against his life sentence was at last dismissed in recognition that he had kicked his drug addiction must have been enormous. He could get on with his work and life as a free man. Despite a weakening of ties to Anita, he must have been pleased when she was cleared of any involvement in the teenager's death, even though she was indicted on charges of illegal possession of a firearm.

As Christmas 1979 approached and another decade turned, Anita Pallenberg awaited sentence, Bill was again thought to be planning to leave the band and Charlie was playing jazz in small London clubs. Mick and Jerry were relatively untroubled.

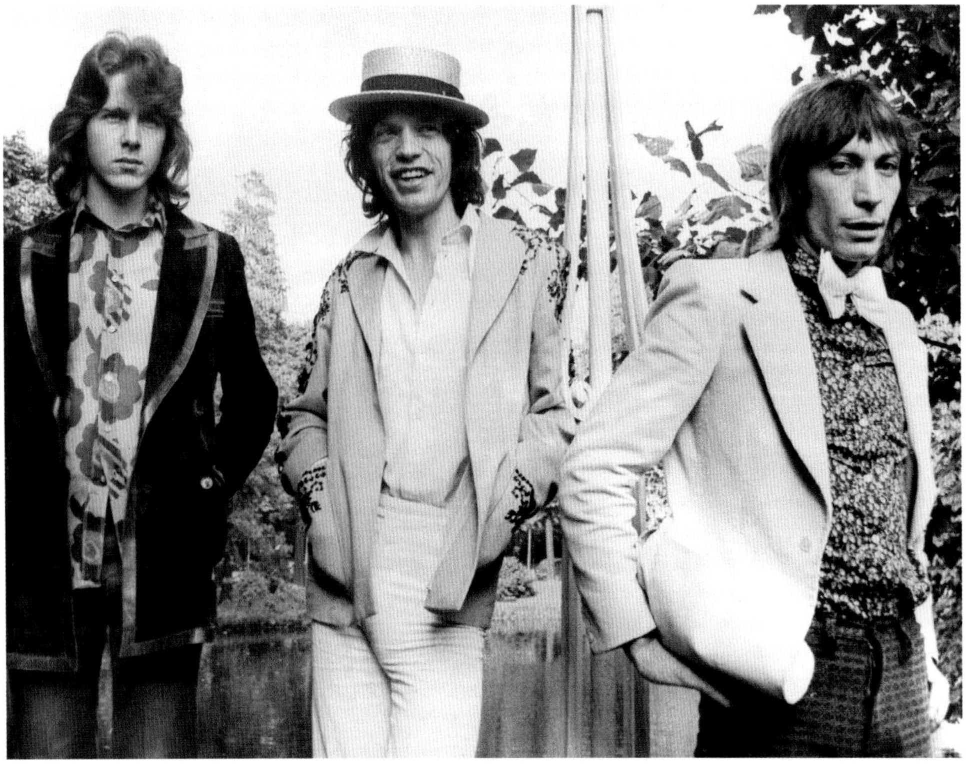

Ned Kelly

Below: On 31 May 1970 Jagger *(far left)* and two other actors pose in Australian policemen's uniforms in a publicity shot for his forthcoming film about the outlaw Ned Kelly. The film was directed by Tony Richardson and premiered in London, but was not well received.

Left: Mick, Mick and Charlie in Paris in September 1970. Early in 1971 it was announced that the Stones were set to leave London and base themselves in France. They began a 'farewell to Britain tour' with a show in Newcastle on 4 March 1971 and ended it with a concert at the Roundhouse in London. The Stones denied that leaving Britain for France had anything to do with tax breaks, but they made use of the 90 days each year they were allowed to spend in Britain.

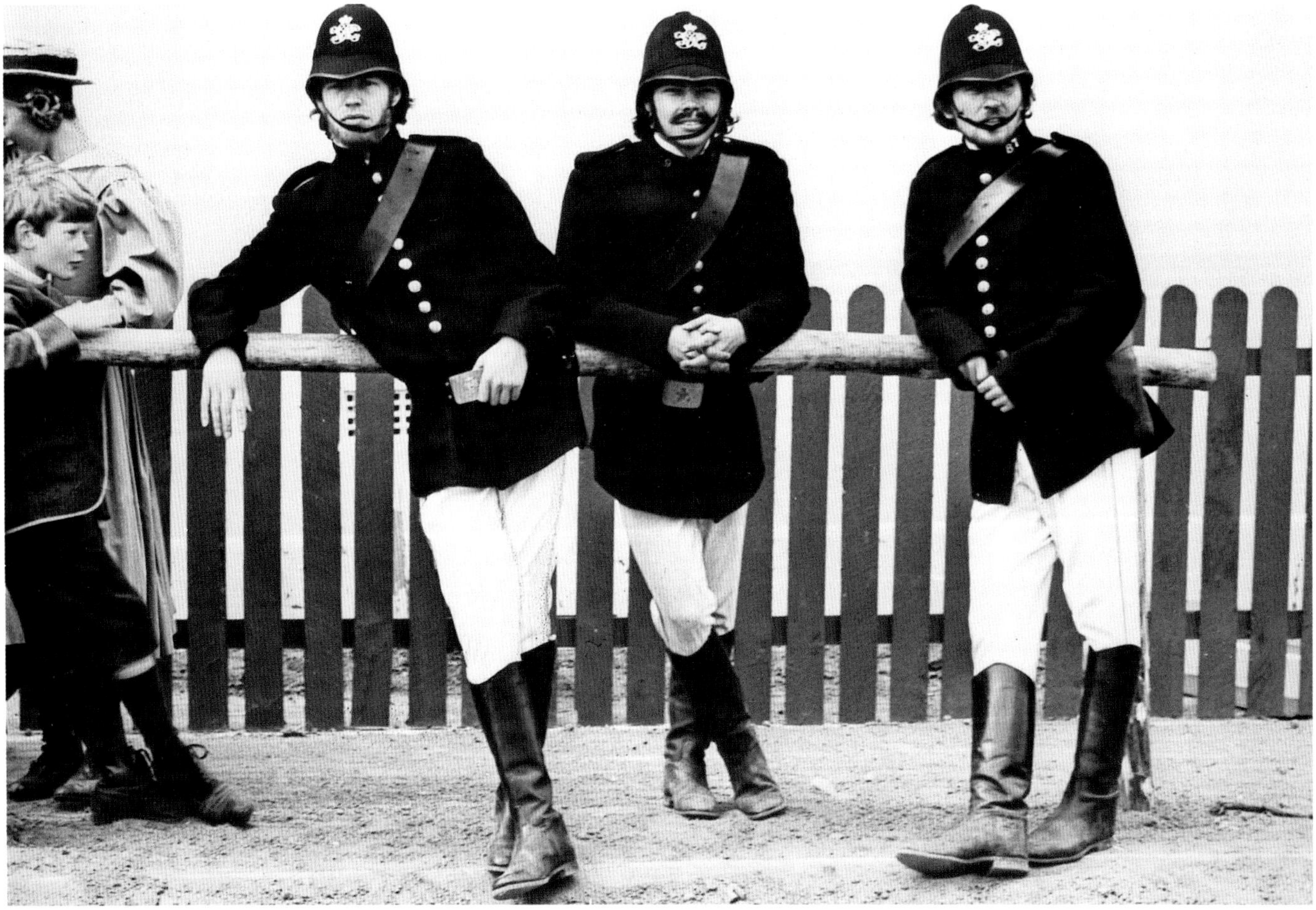

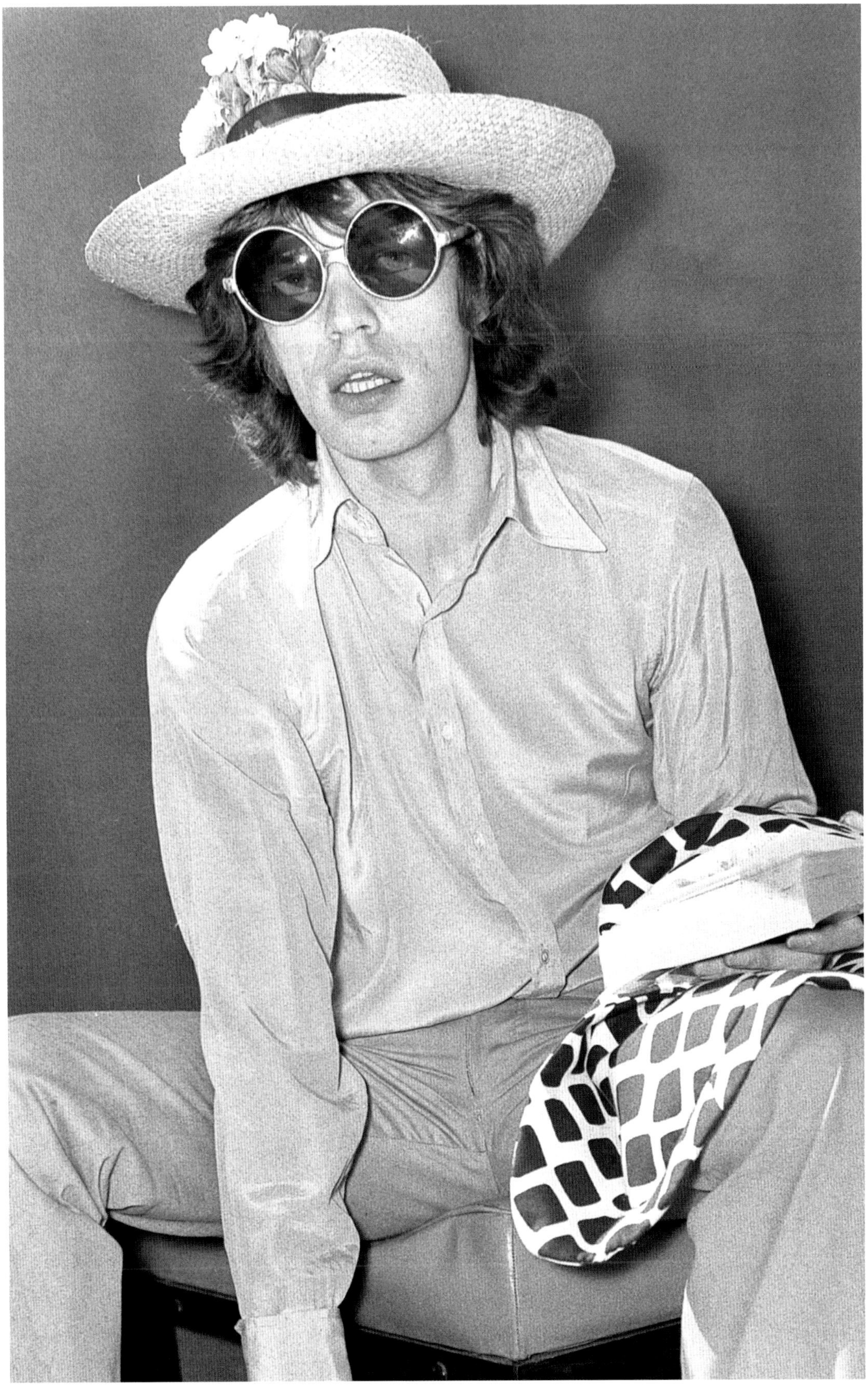

Right: Off to the beach? No, Mick Jagger waits for his flight to Sweden, where the band is touring, on 1 September 1970. On 23 September 1970 5,000 fans enjoyed the show at the Palais des Sports in Paris. Rolling Stones fans had running fights with French police. Some fans had tried to crash the first of three Paris concerts without tickets. The day before the European tour ended, Mick was spotted in London with a new girlfriend, Nicaraguan Bianca Perez Morena de Macia, whom he had met in Paris.

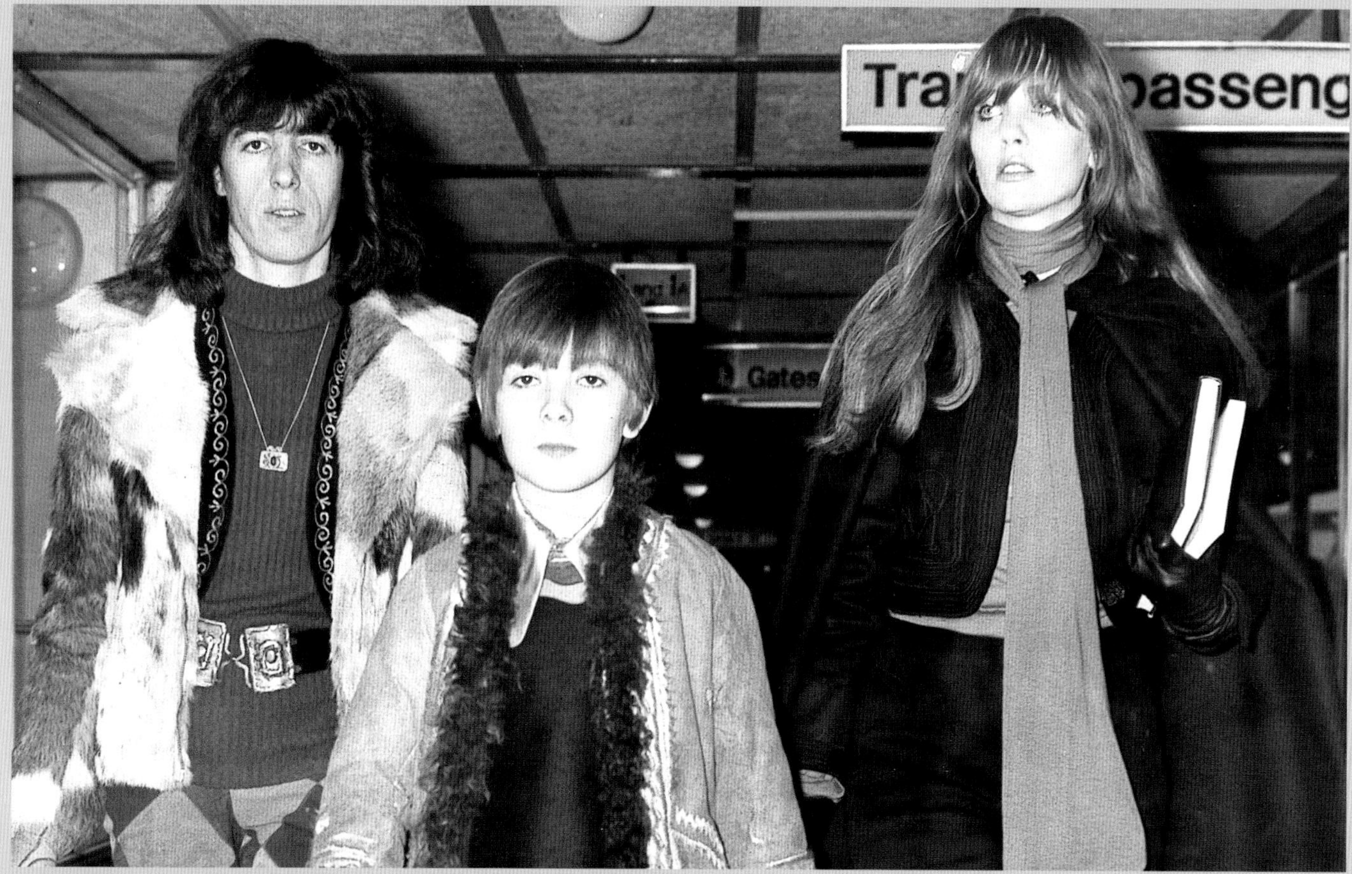

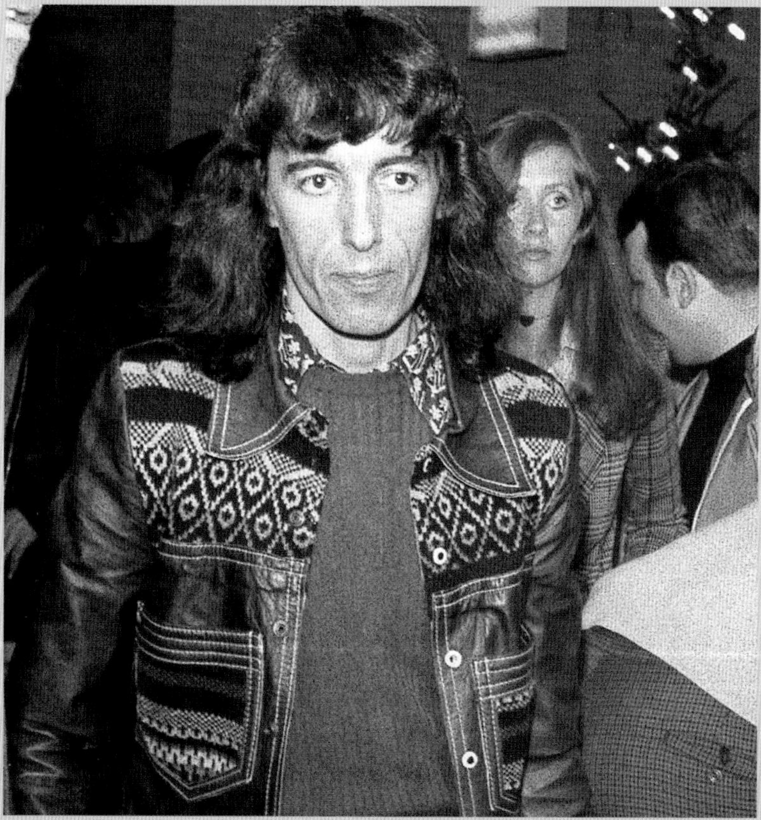

Exiles on Main Street

Above: Bill Wyman, his son Stephen and new girlfriend Astrid Lundstrom head for Astrid's native Sweden for a skiing holiday on 31 December 1970.

At the end of July 1970 the Stones' recording contract with Decca had come to an end. They decided to sign a deal with Atlantic records, allowing them to release albums on their own Rolling Stones label.

Left: Bill Wyman on the move again.

Opposite: Mick Jagger on 17 May 1971. Mick had just married Bianca on 12 May in a civil ceremony in St Tropez. Both wore white suits for the wedding, and the bride was several months pregnant. The marriage was almost cancelled because the press, who were legally entitled to attend the ceremony, refused to leave the building. The witnesses were Roger Vadim and Nathalie Delon. At the religious ceremony, held later in the day, Lord Lichfield gave away the bride. A daughter, Jade, was born in Paris on 21 October and Mick commuted back and forth from the South of France where the band was recording the *Exile On Main Street* album.

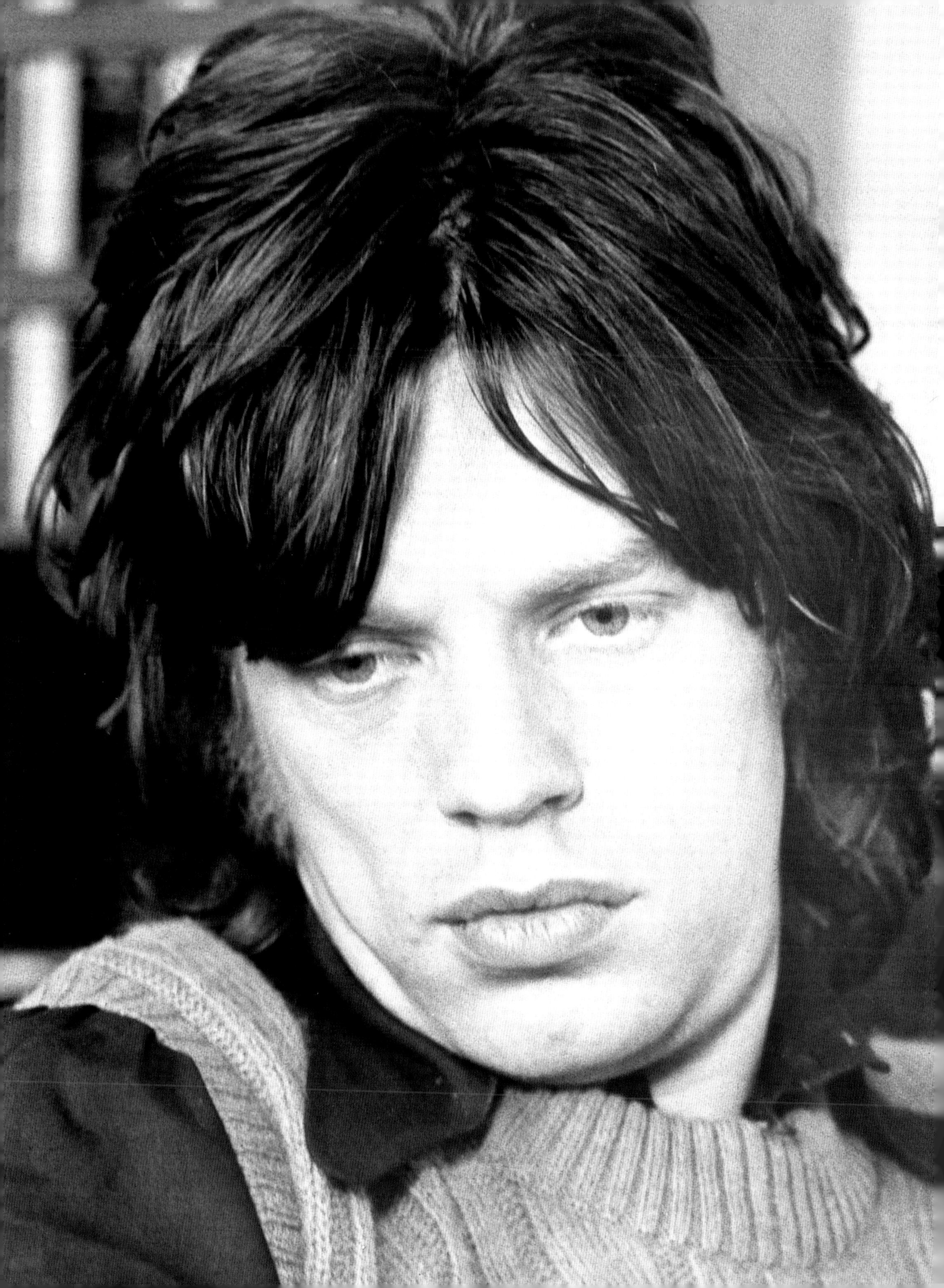

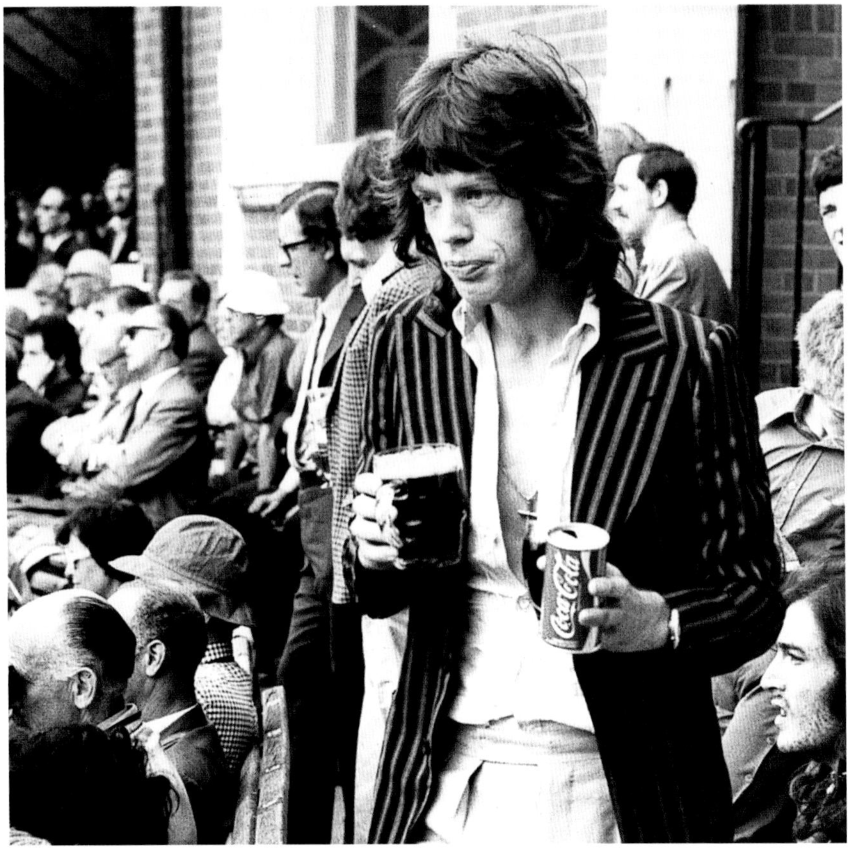

Warm beer and cricket

It wasn't long before Mick was back in the country. During an interview on 11 May 1971 he spoke of the likelihood of pursuing solo musical projects as well as film work. However, an enduring love affair with France and many things French deepened during his time there and he now owns a chateau in the Loire valley. Just a small one, he assures us.

Left: Mick enjoys the warm beer (and indeed the dress code) of an English cricket match on 11 August 1972. His passion for cricket was sometimes dismissed as a pose but no one could deny it is real now. He is often seen at Lords, at the Oval, and at Test matches in the West Indies.

Below: Mick Jagger and friend at the Oval Test on 12 August 1972.

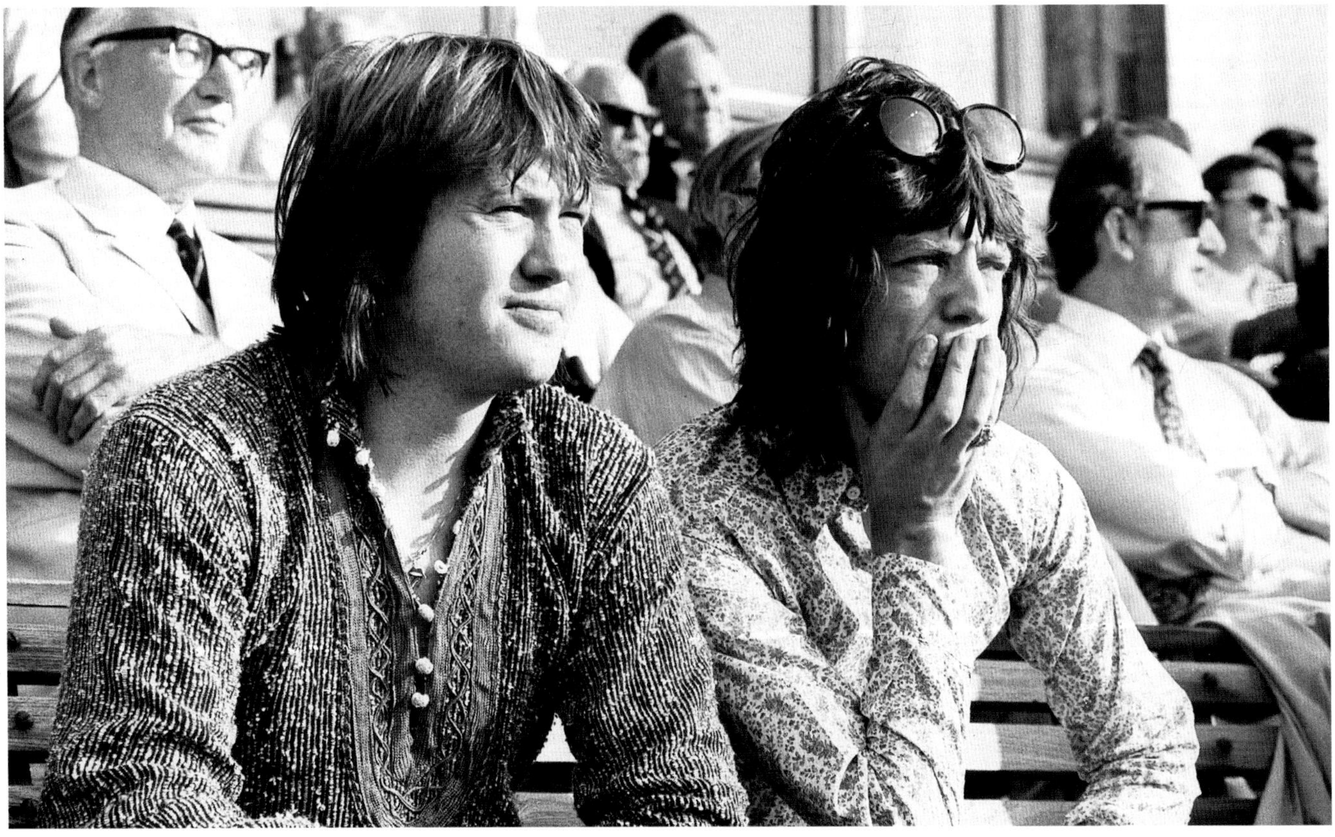

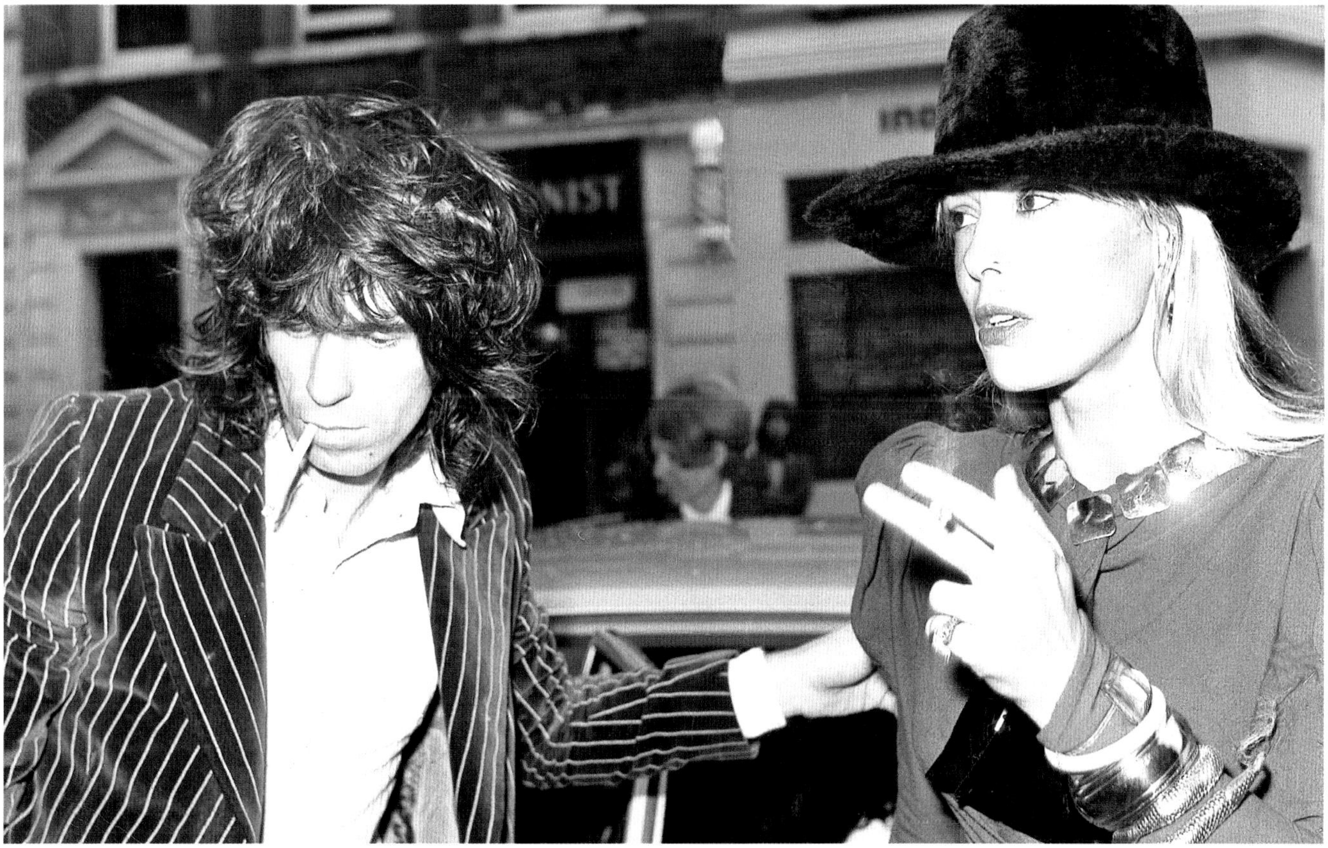

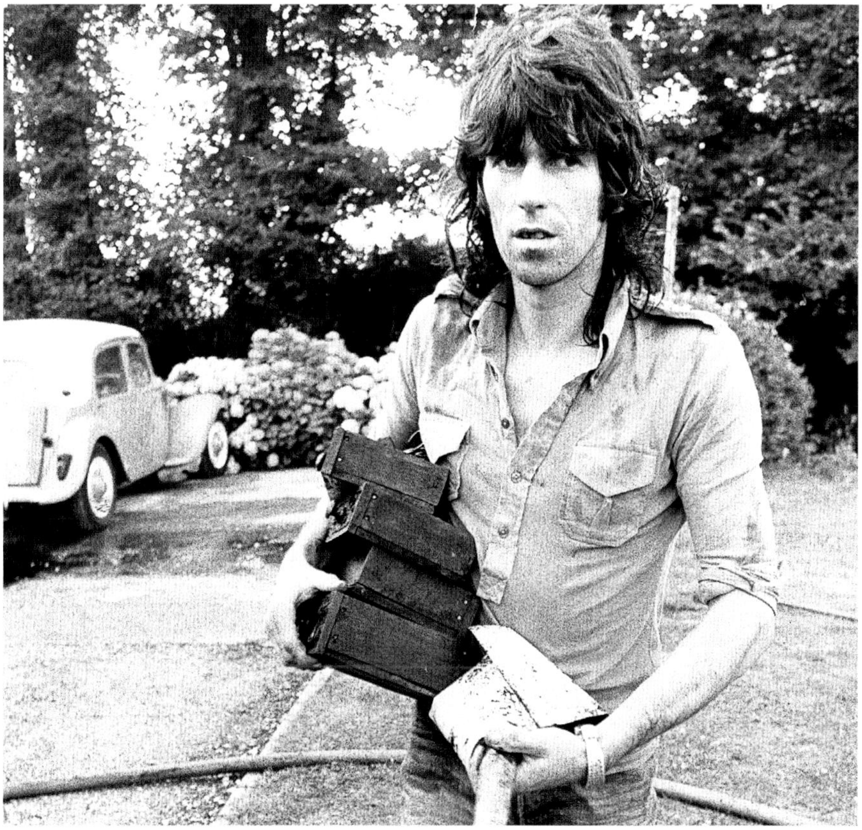

Keith arrested

Above: On 27 June 1973 Keith, Anita and a friend were in a London court on drugs charges, having been arrested the previous day. Keith was also charged with possession of a firearm and ammunition without a licence. They were released on £1,000 bail apiece.

Right: Keith Richard on 1 August 1973. After their court appearance Keith and Anita, accompanied by their children Marlon and Dandelion, had returned to Redlands, their Sussex home. During the night a fire caused serious damage to the house.

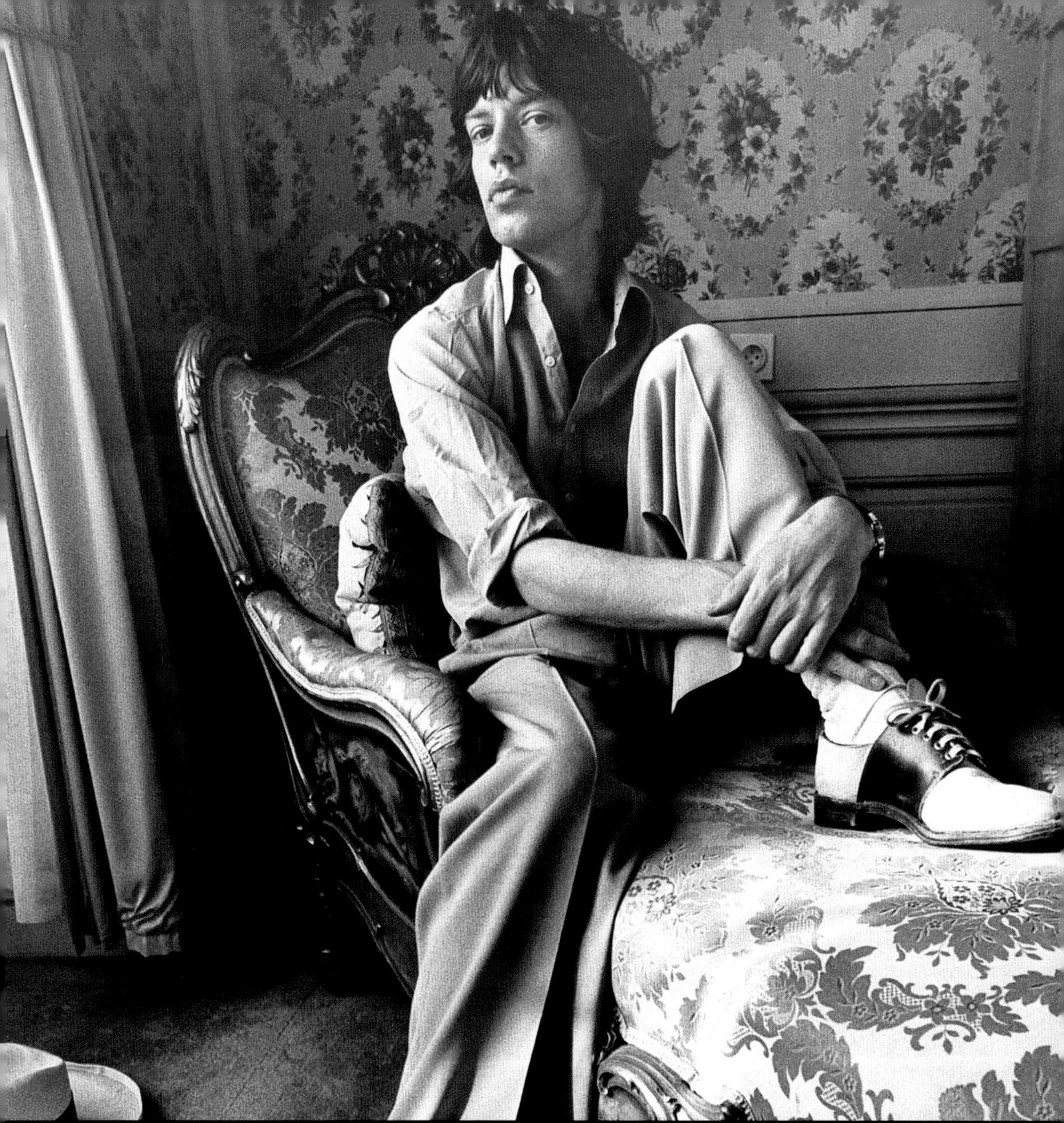

Angie' charts

bove: Mick Jagger tilts his best side for the camera in Vienna on 3 September 1973. The band had just begun a wo-month European tour, starting in Mannheim and finishing in Berlin. 'Angie', a return to the type of ballad that he Stones had not recorded since the early days, entered the UK singles chart at No.2 in August, and both the ingle and *Goats Head Soup,* the album it came from, would be No.1 in the United States in October 1973.

pposite: Mick and Bianca could not have looked happier or better matched at the party they threw at Blenheim alace on 7 September 1973. It confounded scandalmongers who had been linking Bianca with actors Ryan O'Neill

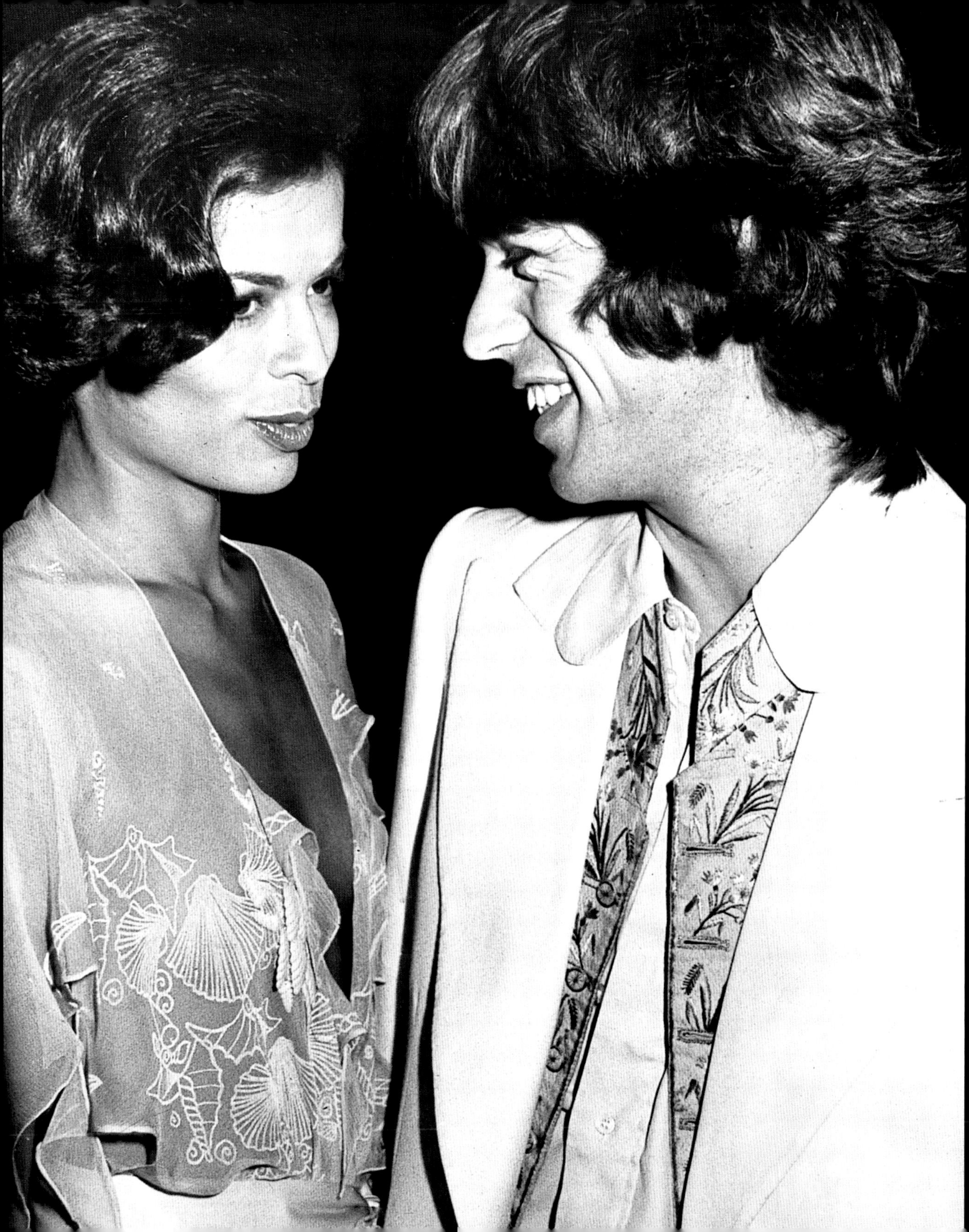

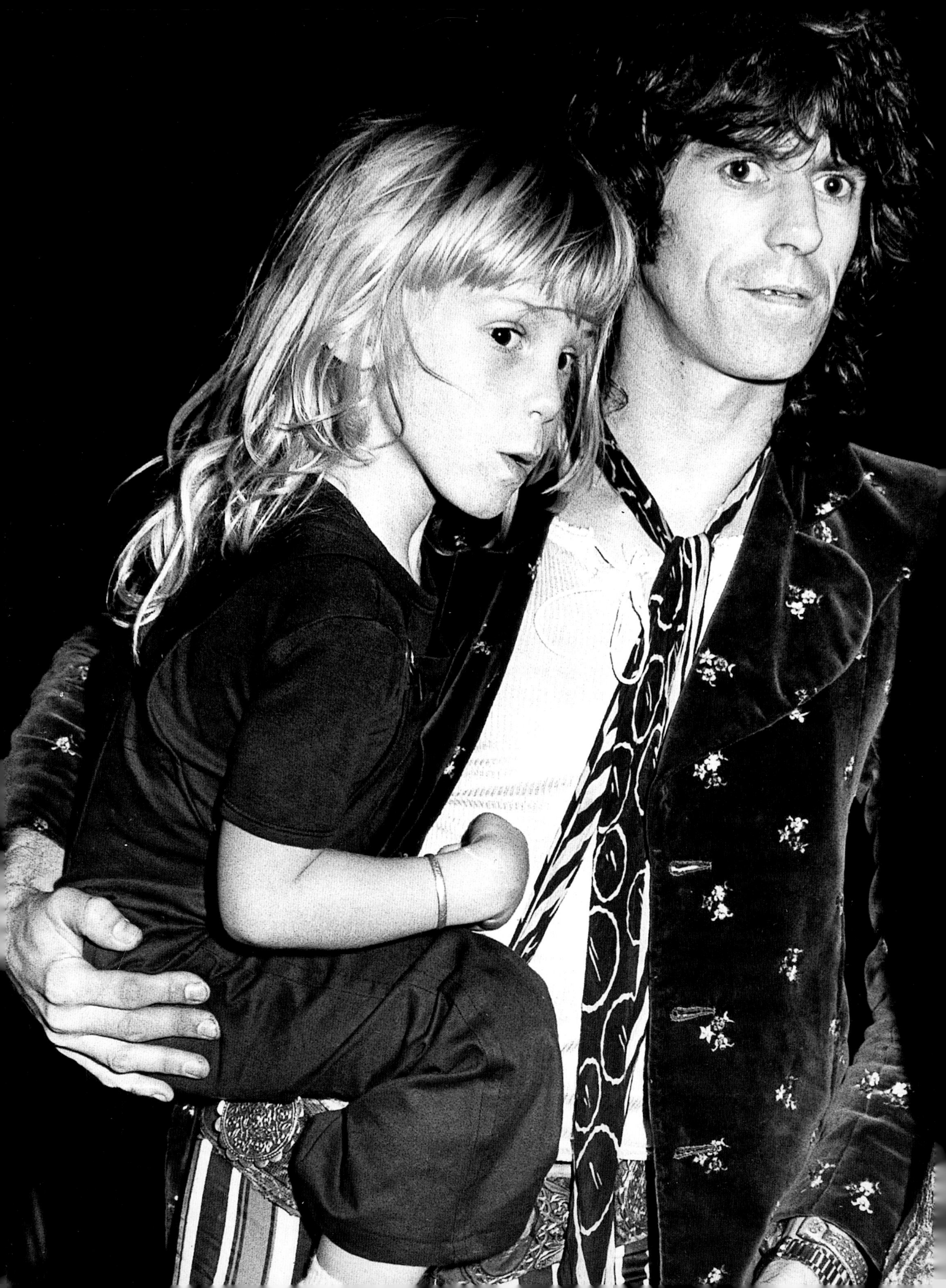

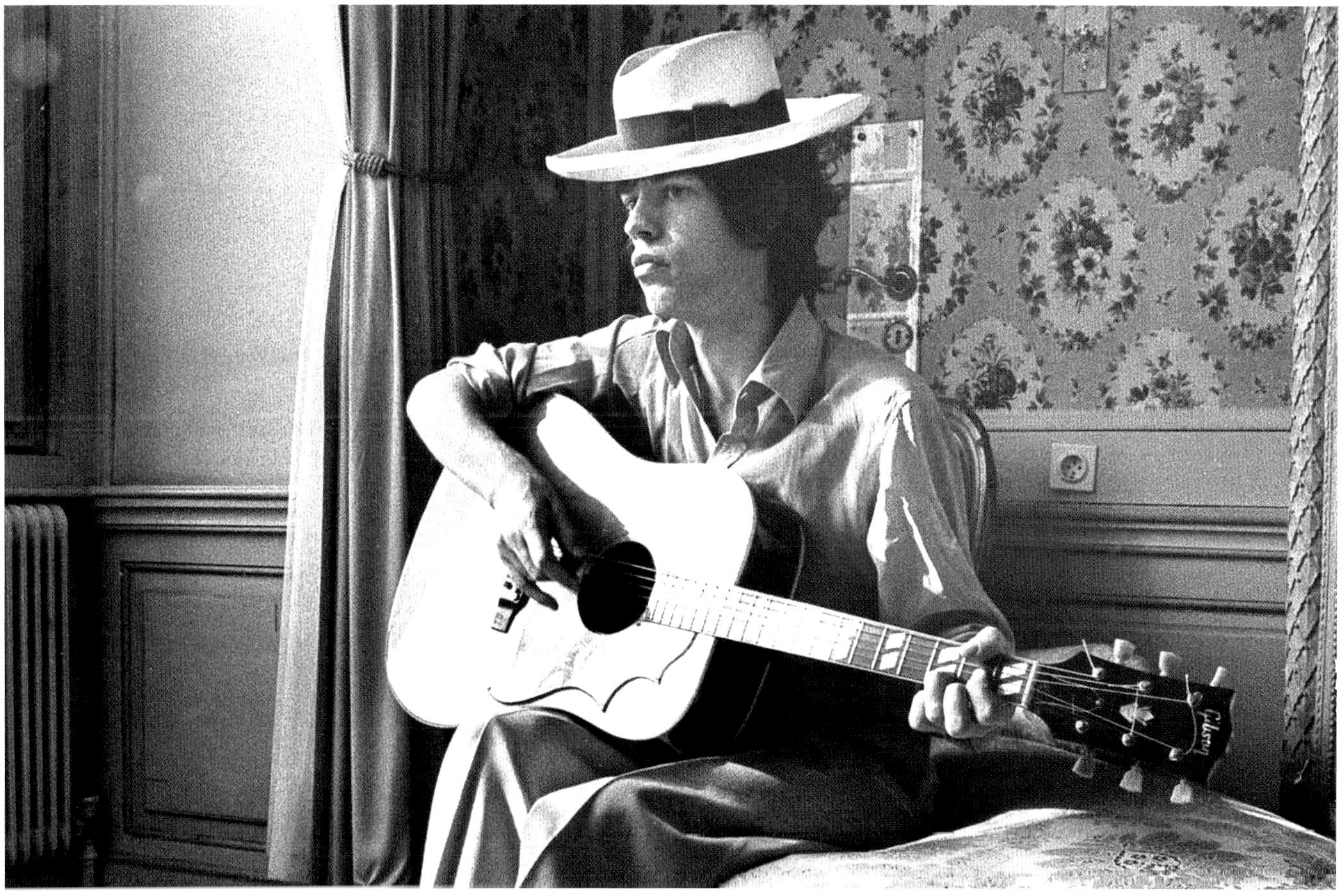

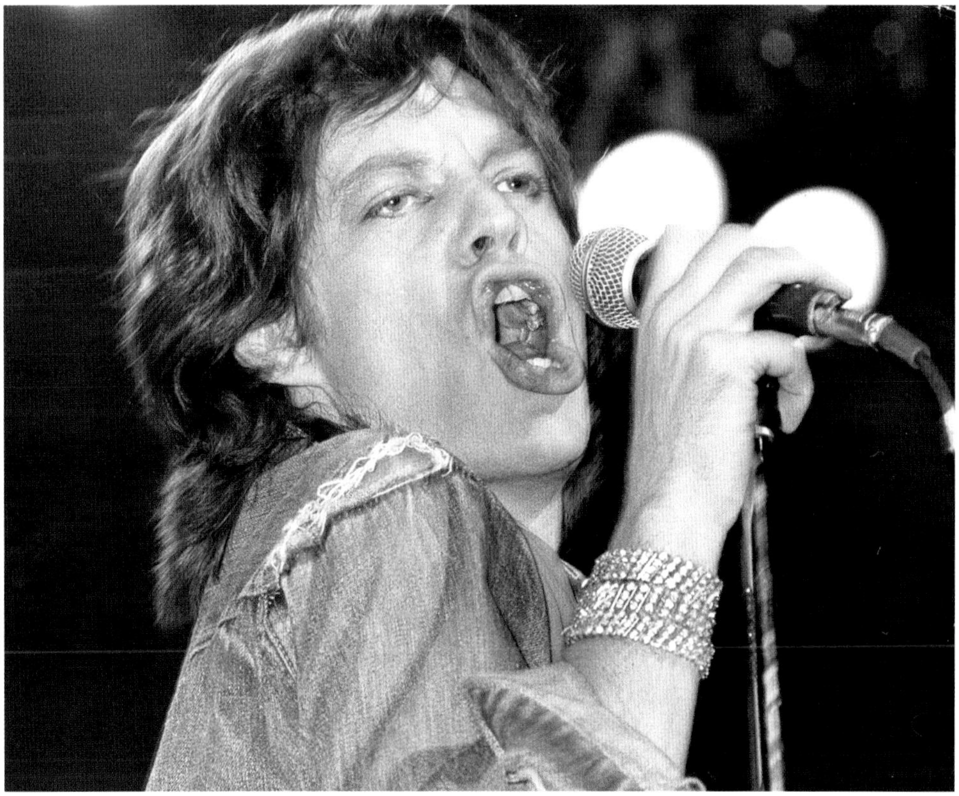

Proud dad

Opposite: Keith Richard spends some quality time with his children in September 1973. A month later, after the end of the European tour, he was charged with possession of various drugs, firearms and ammunition. Mick Jagger went to court to lend moral support to Keith, who was fined £205 for possession of heroin and cannabis. Anita Pallenberg, who had been found in possession of Mandrax, was conditionally discharged.

In 1973 the Stones had returned to Britain and tickets for the UK tour were an almost instant sell-out. More dates were hurriedly arranged.

Above: Mick in Vienna.

Left: Mick Jagger on stage in Vienna in September 1973. The tour reached Wembley on 7 September – one of four dates there.

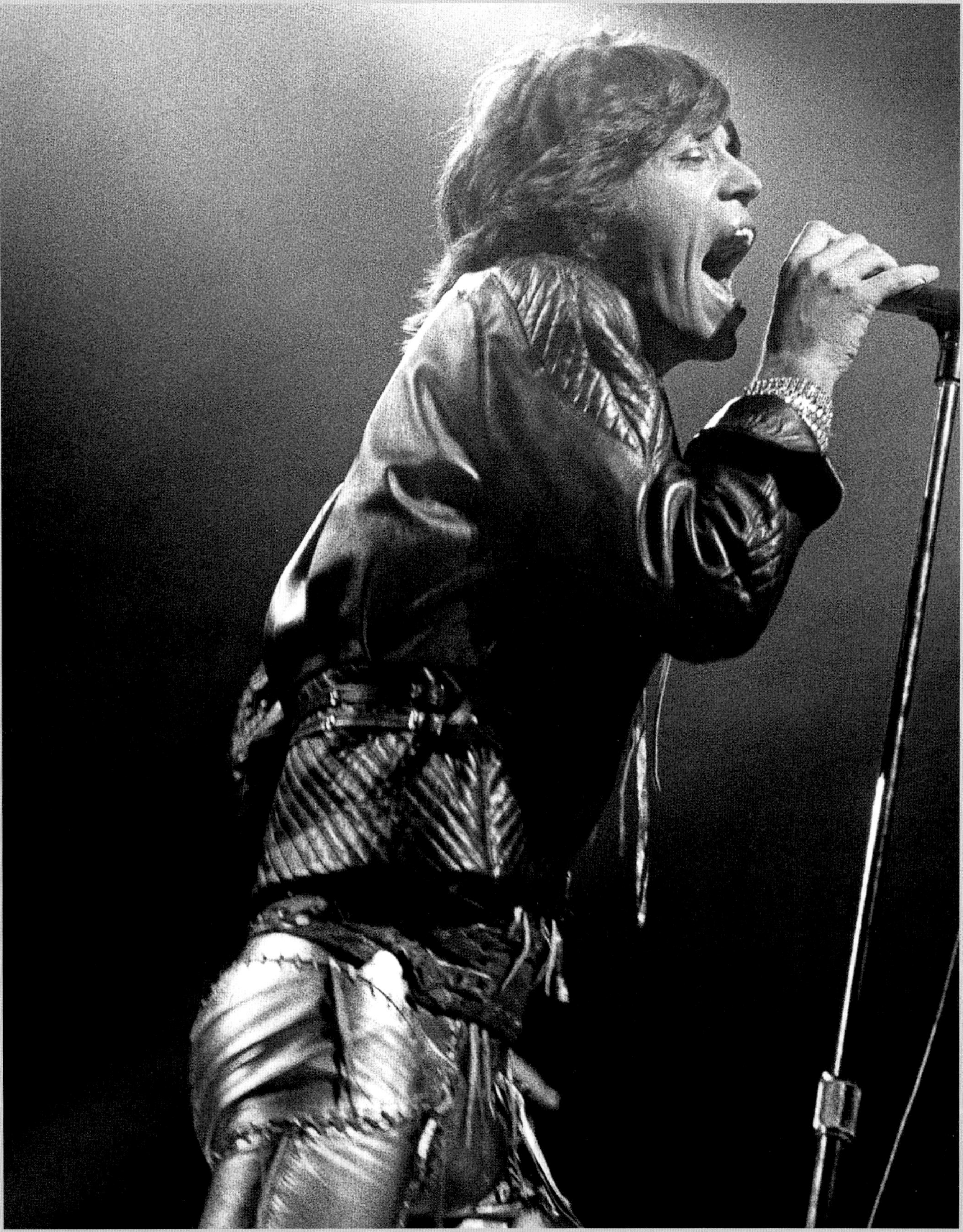

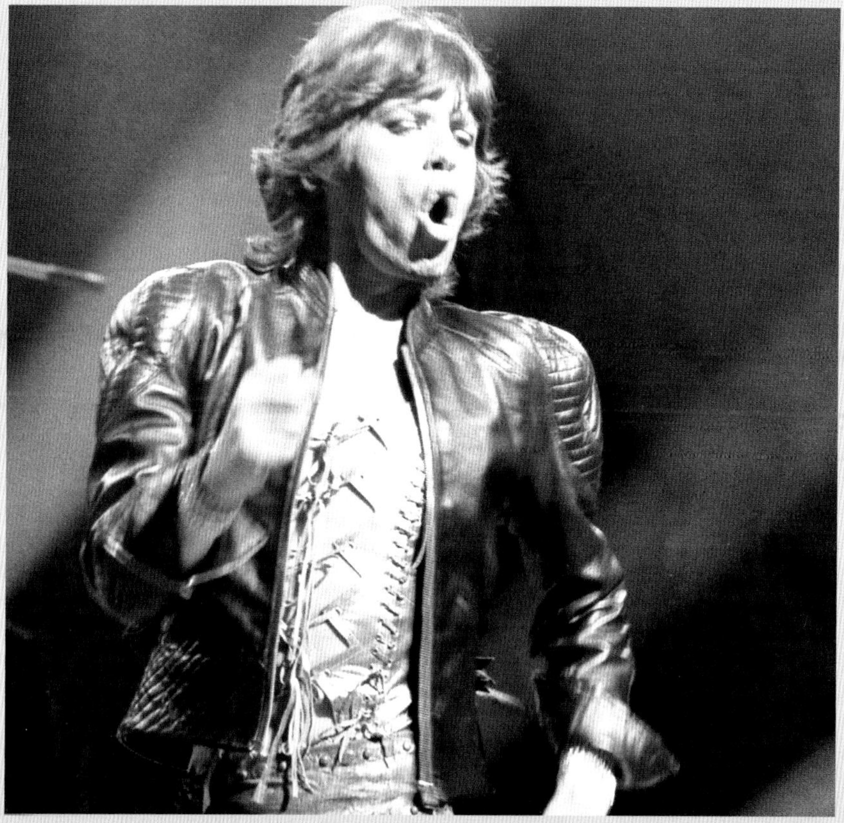

Rocking Wembley

Among the audience at the first Stones show at Wembley on 7 September 1973 were M*A*S*H stars Donald Sutherland and Elliot Gould (the latter rumoured to be sweet on Bianca Jagger). Ryan O'Neill was also there, as were hundreds of would-be gatecrashers who attempted to gain entrance to the sell-out gig by mingling with the 10,000 ticket-holding fans. A leather-clad Mick Jagger worked the crowd into a frenzy, to the consternation of some pundits who, even then, were beginning to suggest that the Stones were too old to be rock 'n' roll stars.

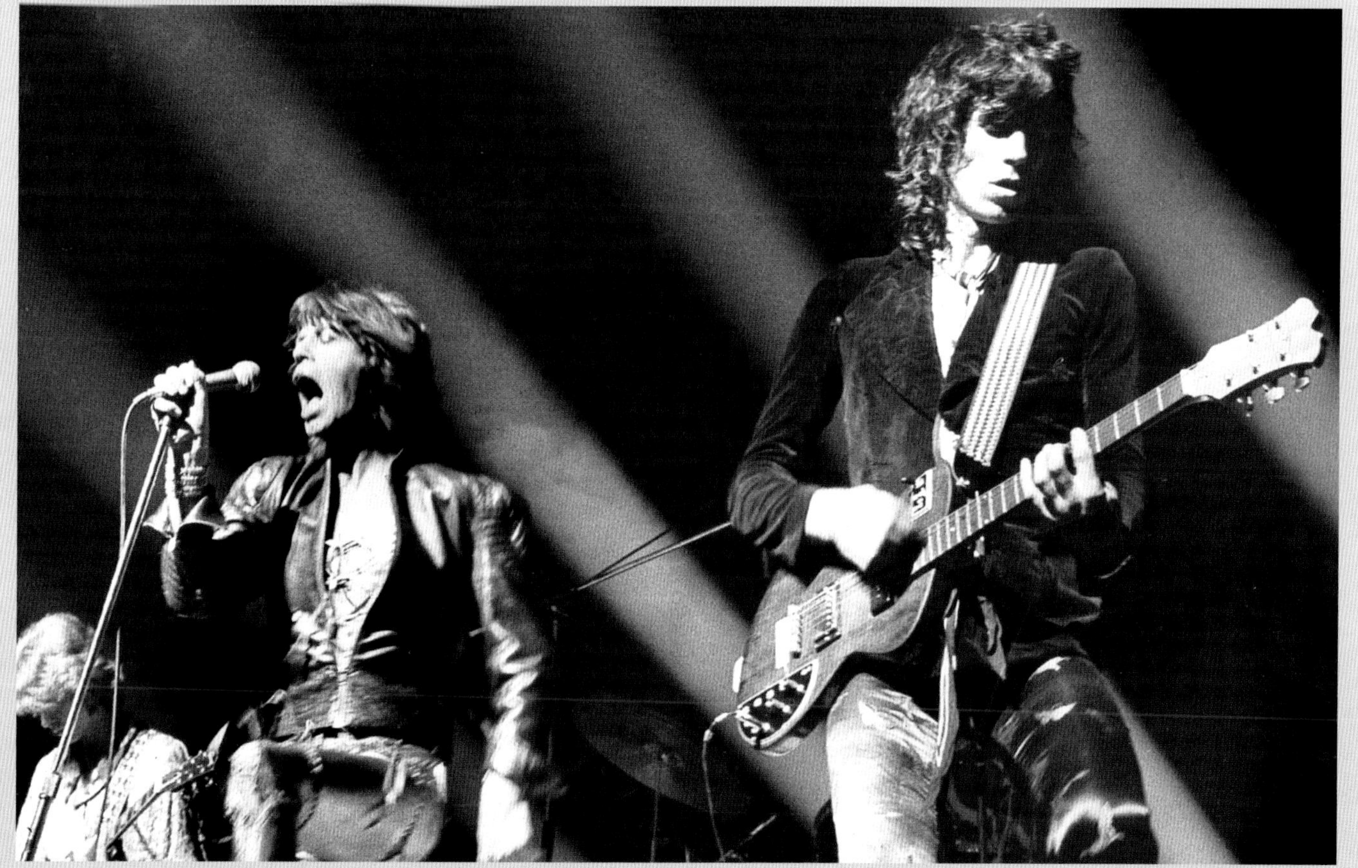

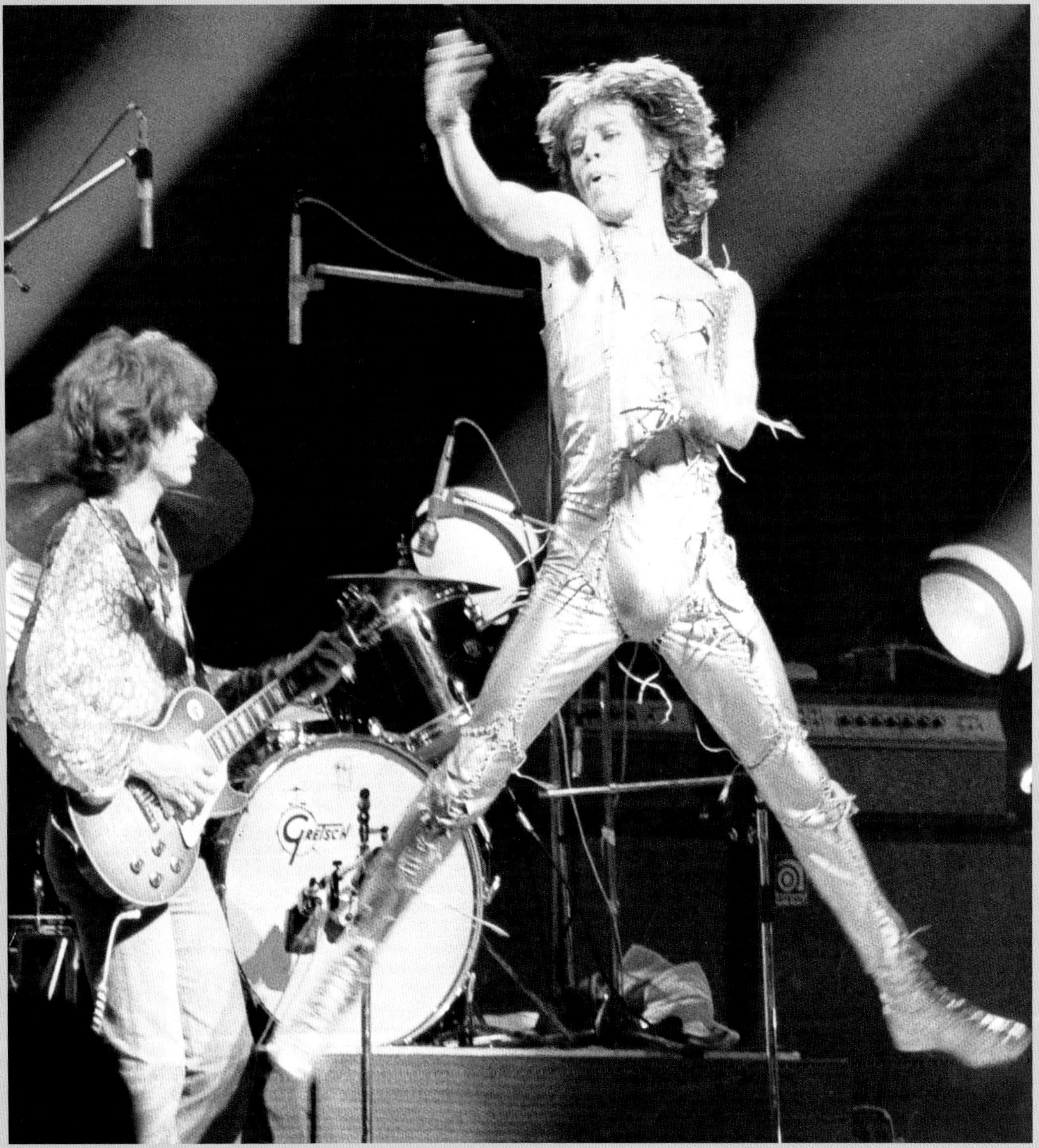

Hitting the heights

Above: The band on stage during the Wembley shows in September 1973. At the time The Rolling Stones were No.1 in the album charts.

Opposite: Bill Wyman's impassive stage demeanour and subtly brilliant base licks helped to keep the band focused on stage. Wyman was beginning to think about working on his solo album *Monkey Grip* which was recorded in Los Angeles in January 1974.

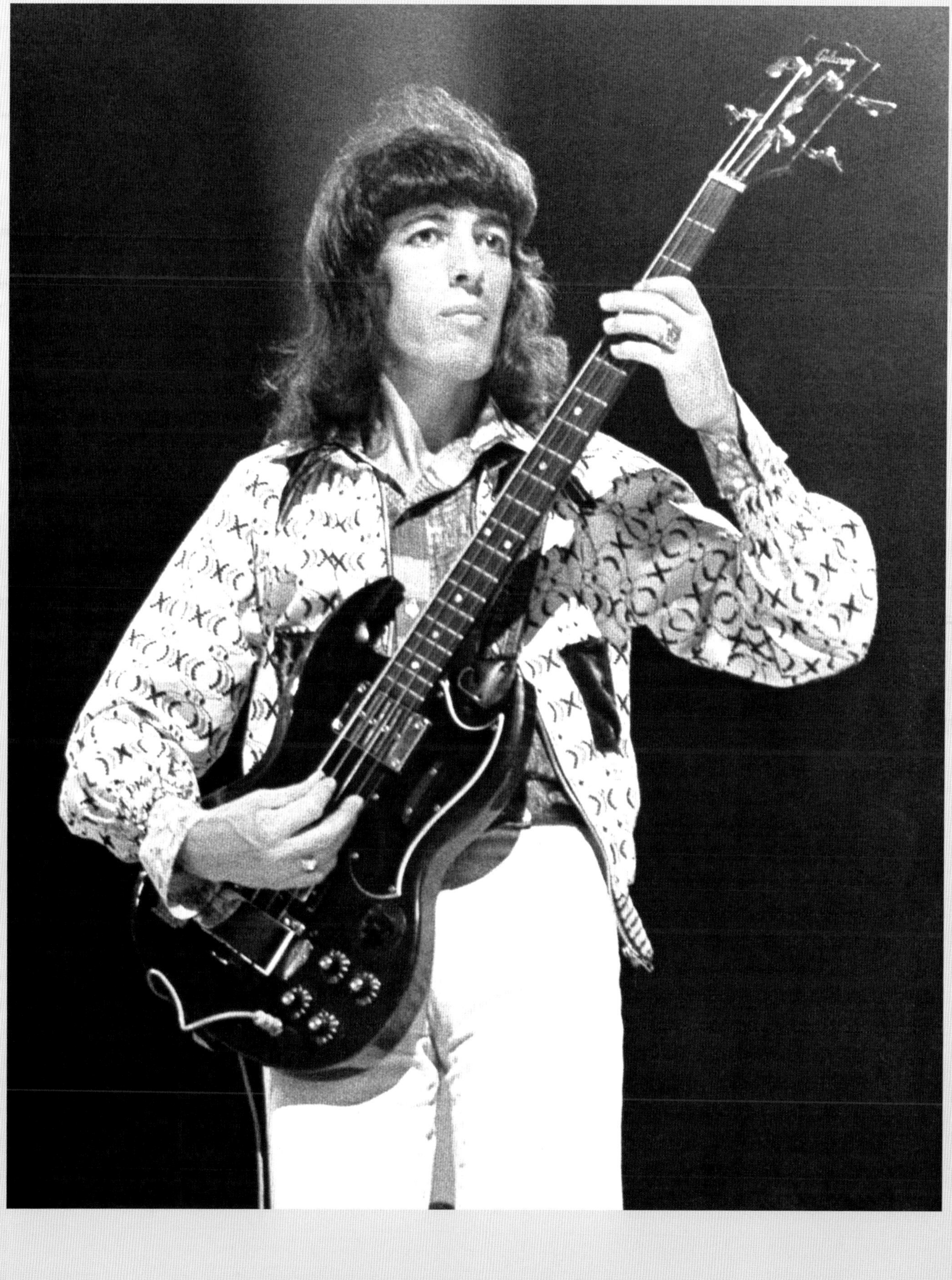
Gibson

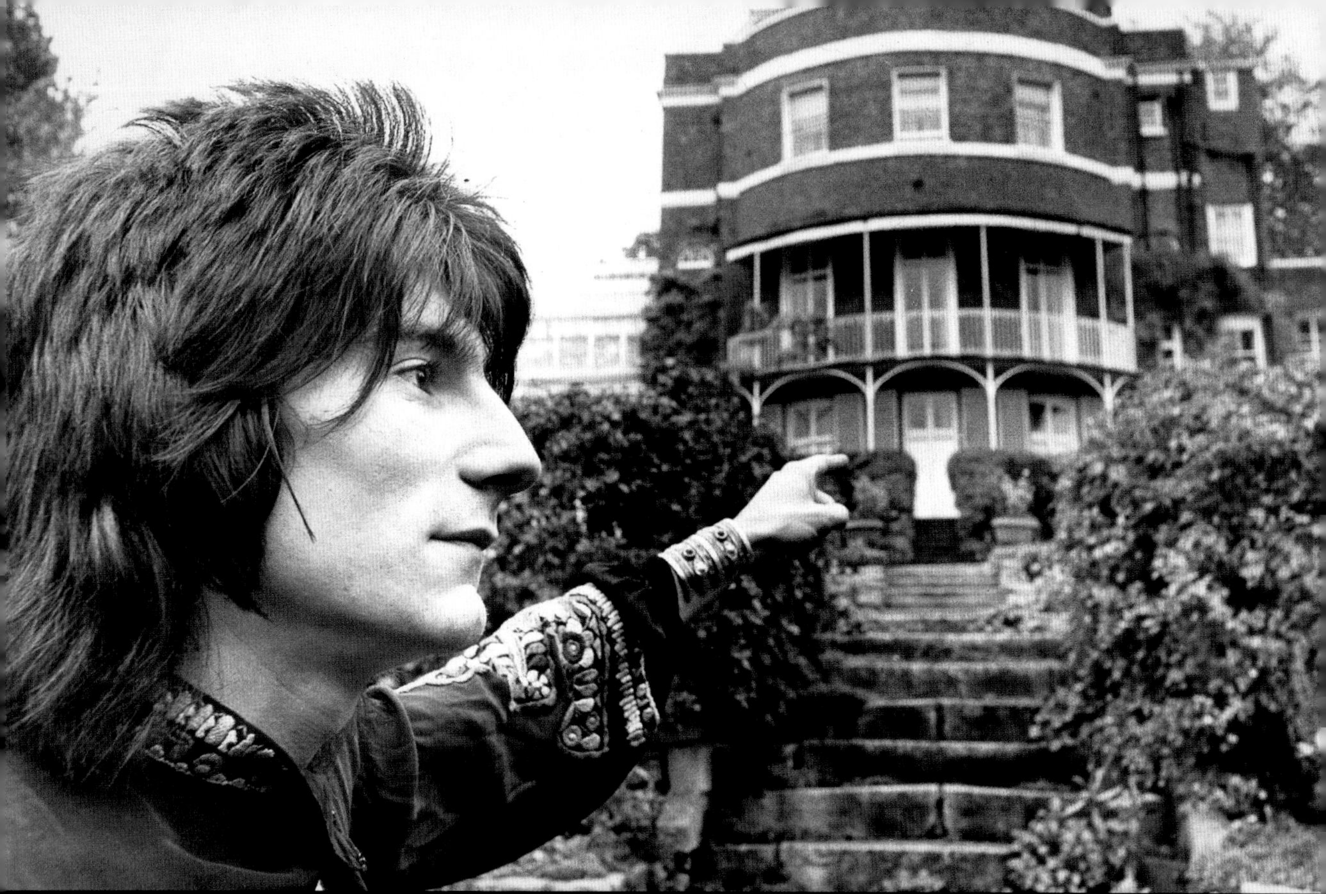

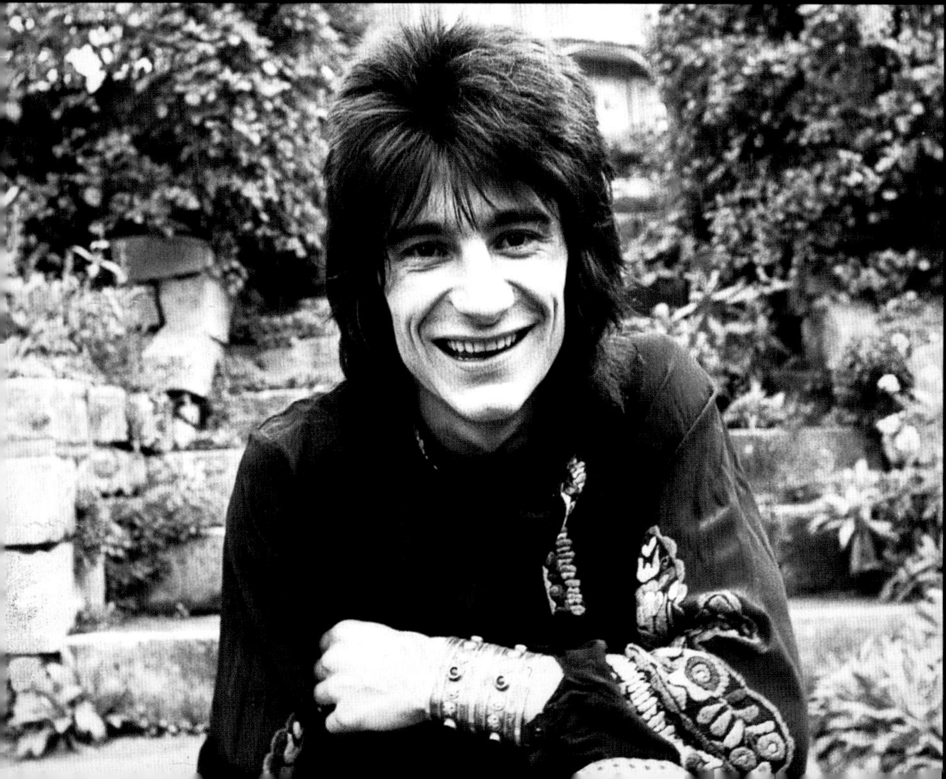

Left and above: Ronnie Wood at his south London home. Ronnie was a member of The Faces, and a friend of Keith Richard. Ronnie often hung out with Keith and the boys.

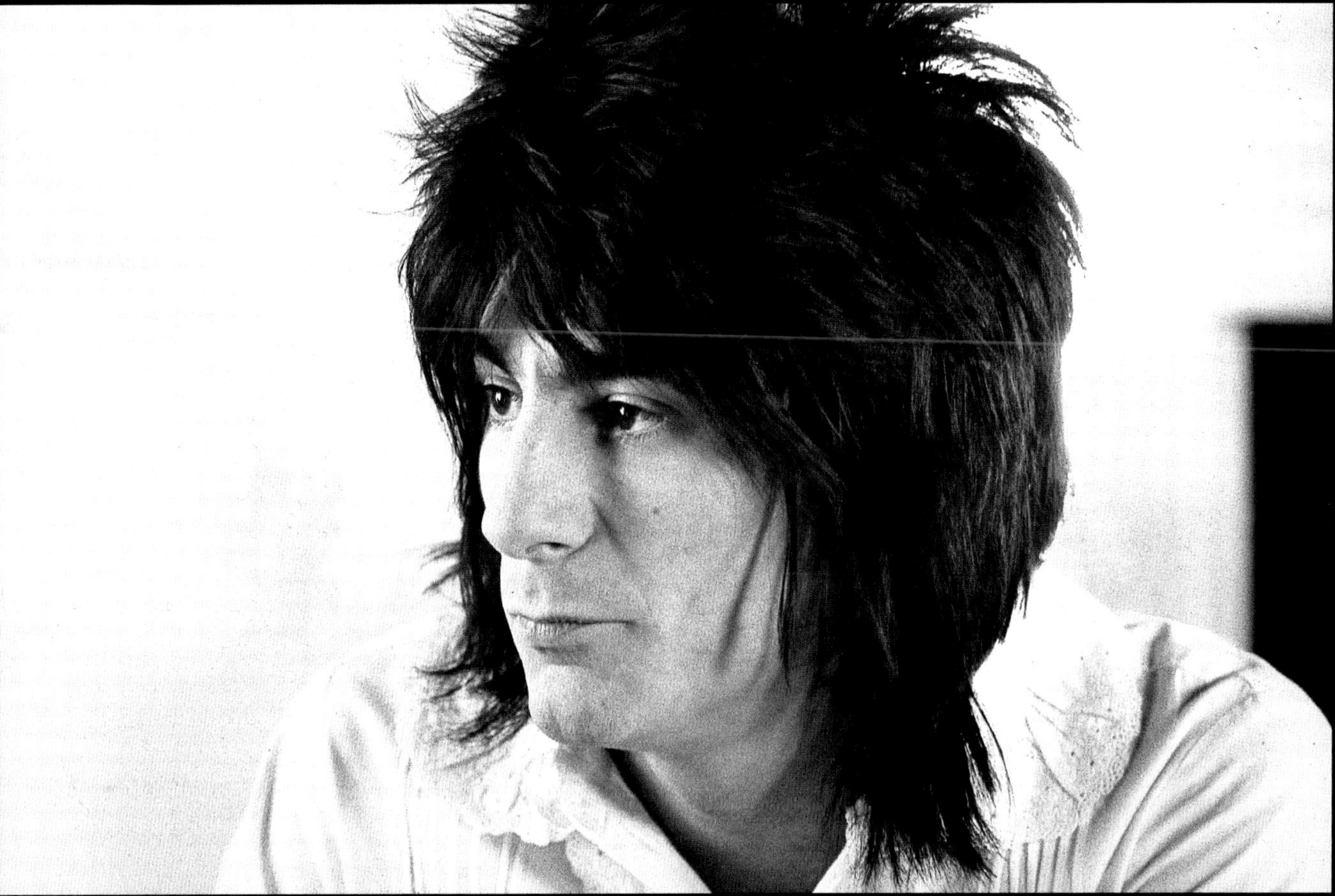

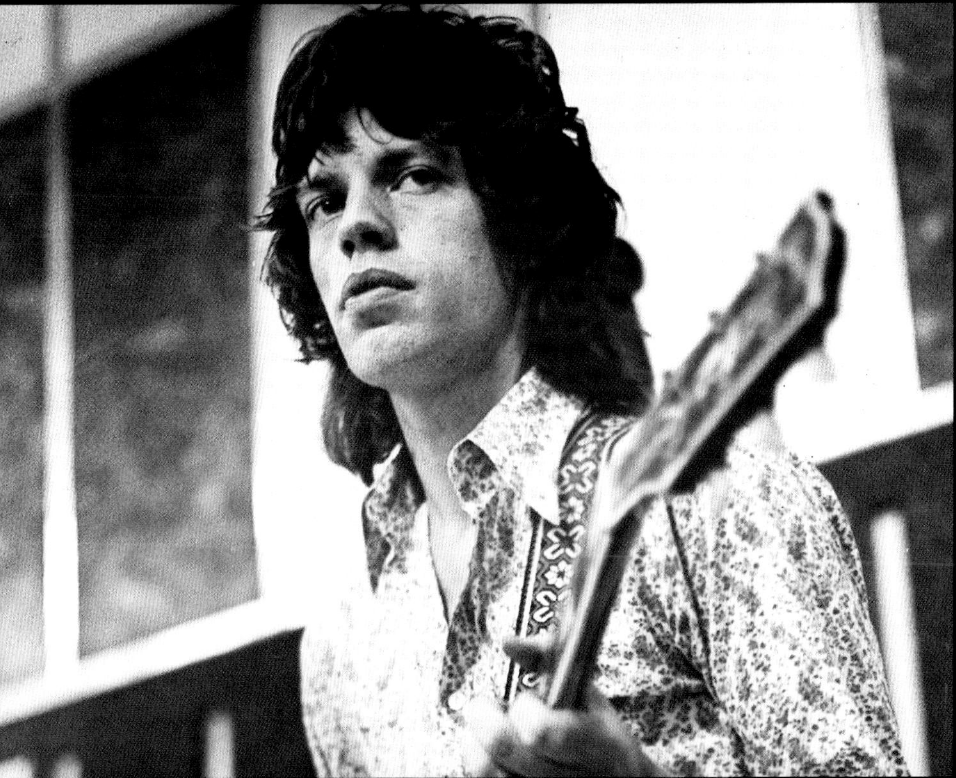

Wood set to replace Taylor

Above: At the end of 1974 Mick Taylor decided that it was time to leave the band. Ronnie Wood, who had occasionally jammed with Keith during the previous year, was considered as a candidate to replace Taylor. However, Wood said that he was committed to The Faces.

Left: A rare picture of Mick Jagger holding a guitar, 6 May 1974.

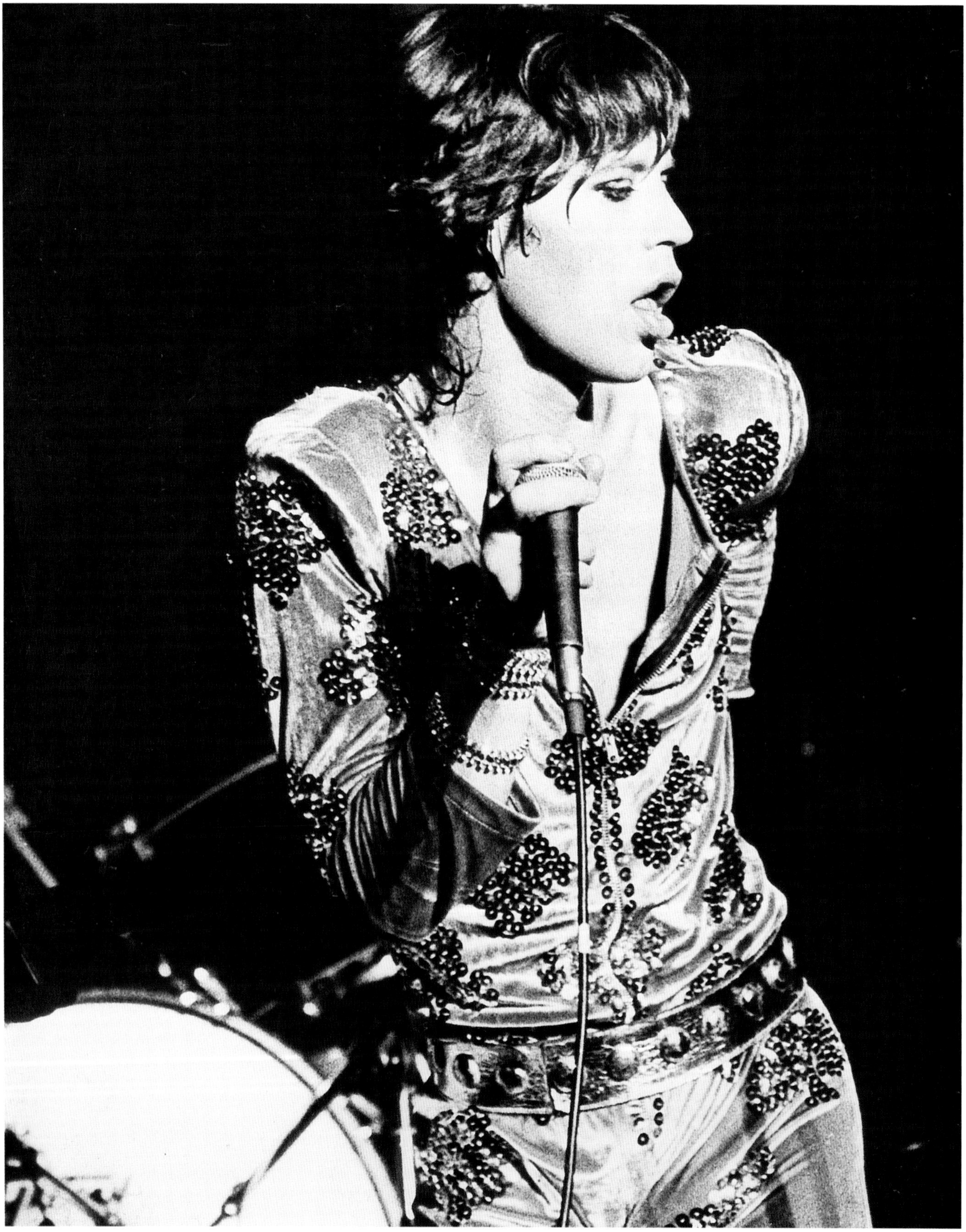

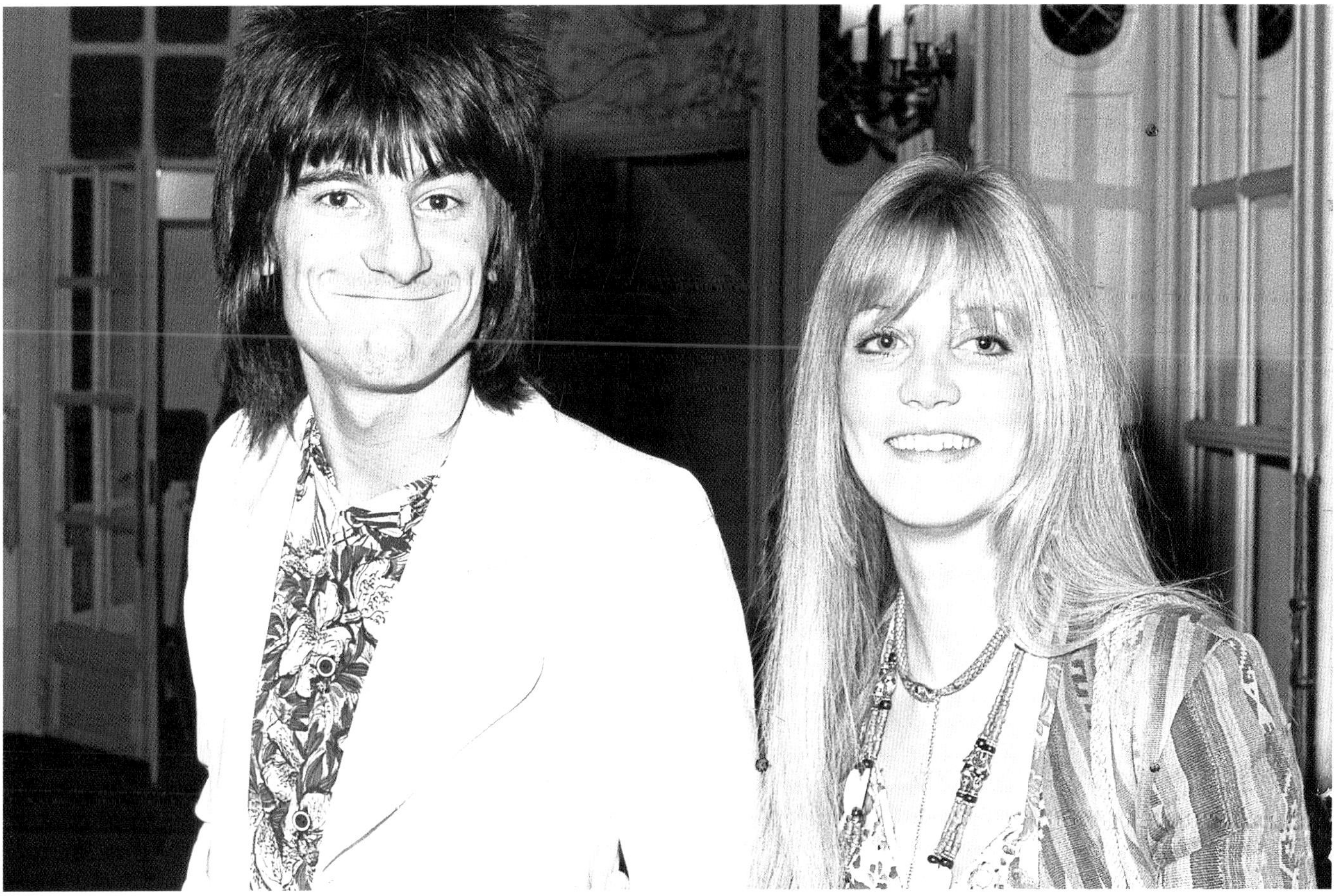

On loan from The Faces

Above: Ronnie Wood with wife Krissie. When Mick Taylor announced he was leaving the Stones in December 1974, just as the band were about to leave for Munich to start work on a new album, Wood was touted as his successor. Various guitarists worked on the album, to be entitled *Black And Blue*, including Wayne Perkins and Harvey Mandel, as well as Ronnie Wood.

Right: Ronnie joined Jagger and other musicians in LA in March 1975 to jam, then went back to Munich to finish *Black And Blue*. In April he joined the Stones' American tour 'on loan' from The Faces, but had to leave part way through in order to rejoin The Faces, whose tour overlapped with that of the Stones. Rod Stewart was to quit The Faces in 1975, apparently unhappy with the Stones' frequent 'borrowing' of Ronnie.

Opposite: Jagger in full Spandex and rhinestone regalia, May 1974.

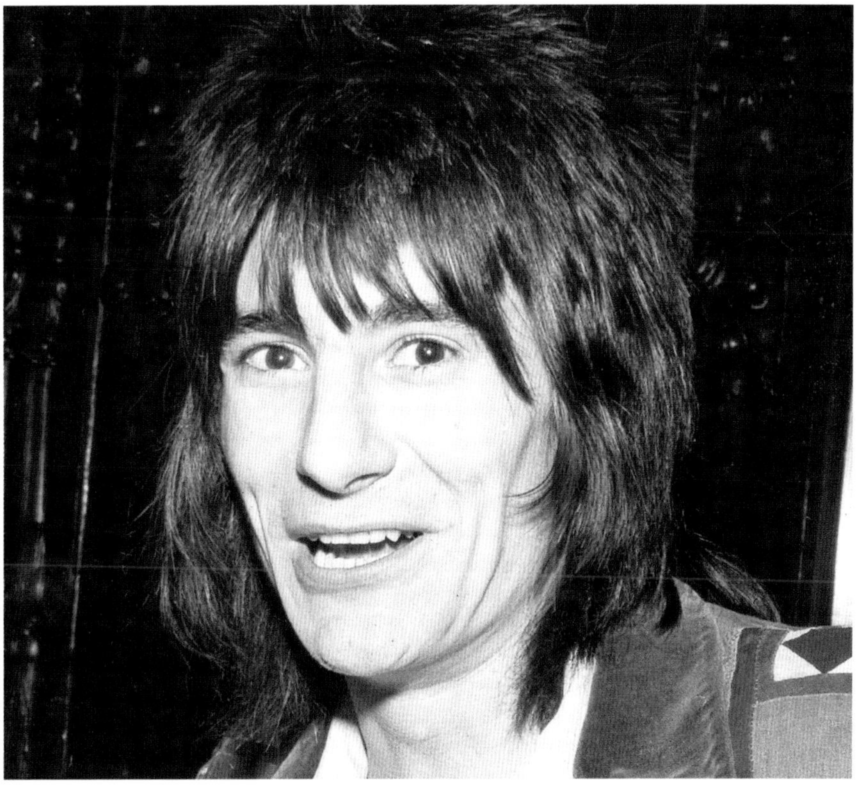

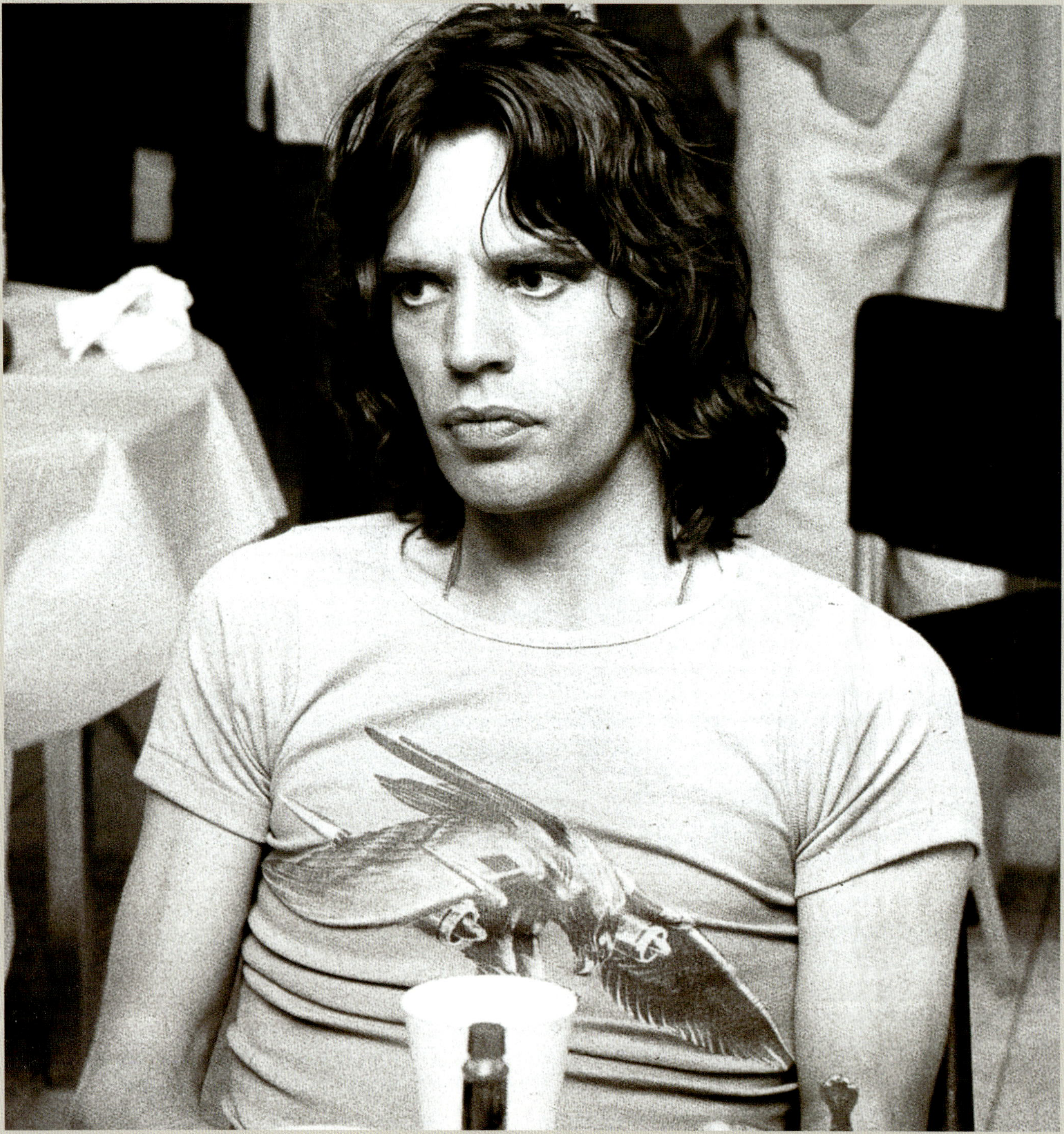

'How come you taste so good?'

Above: The American tour began in New York when the band sang 'Brown Sugar' on the back of a truck travelling along Fifth Avenue on 1 May. By June Mick said his larynx was becoming strained and observers noted him resorting occasionally to nips from a medicinal Jack Daniel's bottle resting on a stage amp.

Right: Mick Jagger in Baton Rouge, Louisiana, in June 1975. Time is still on his side during this longest-ever Rolling Stones tour of the Americas, but the lines are drawn – especially around the eyes. The tour finally finished in Buffalo in August, but they had planned it to be even longer – a number of shows in South America were cancelled in the end.

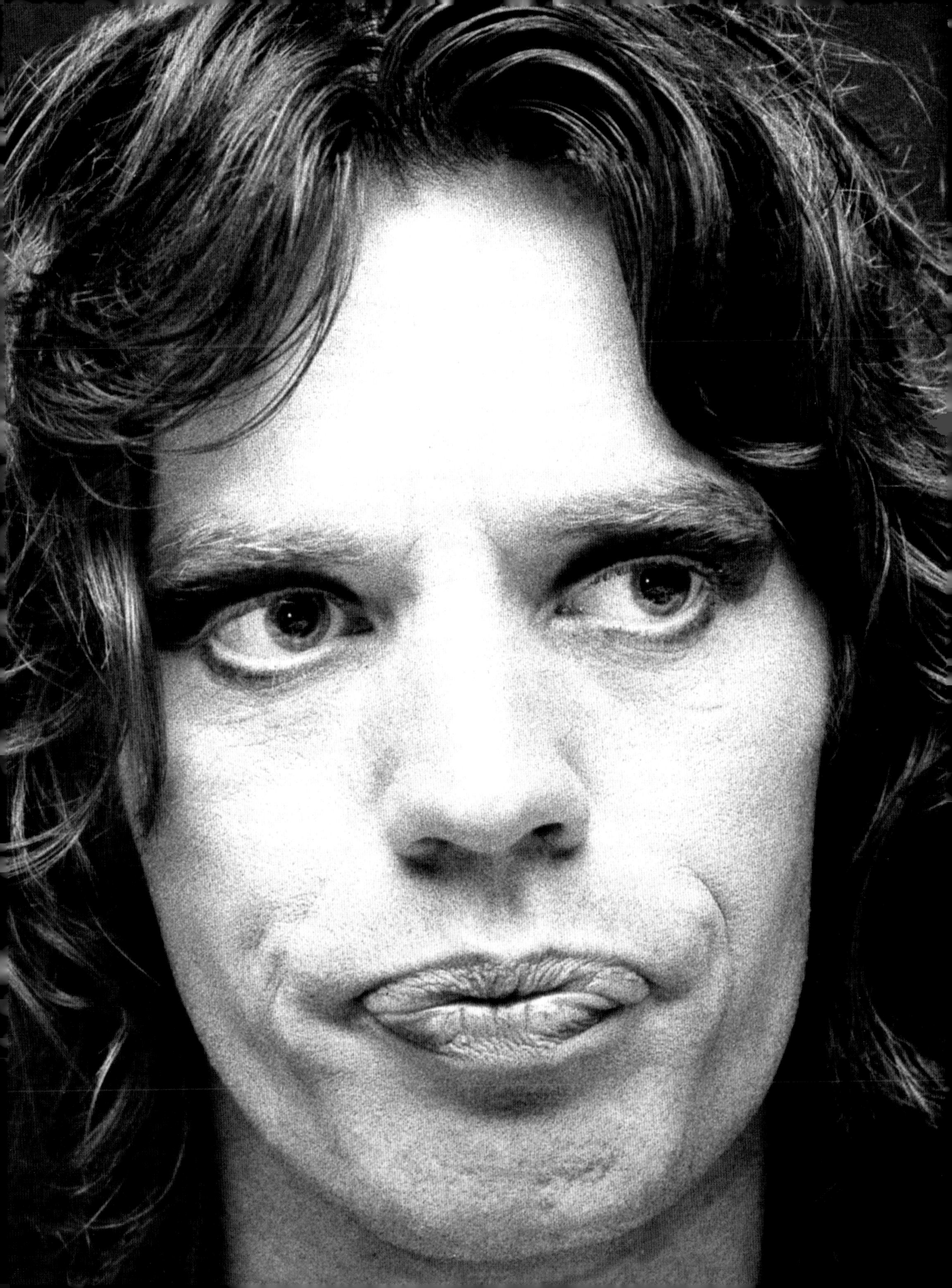

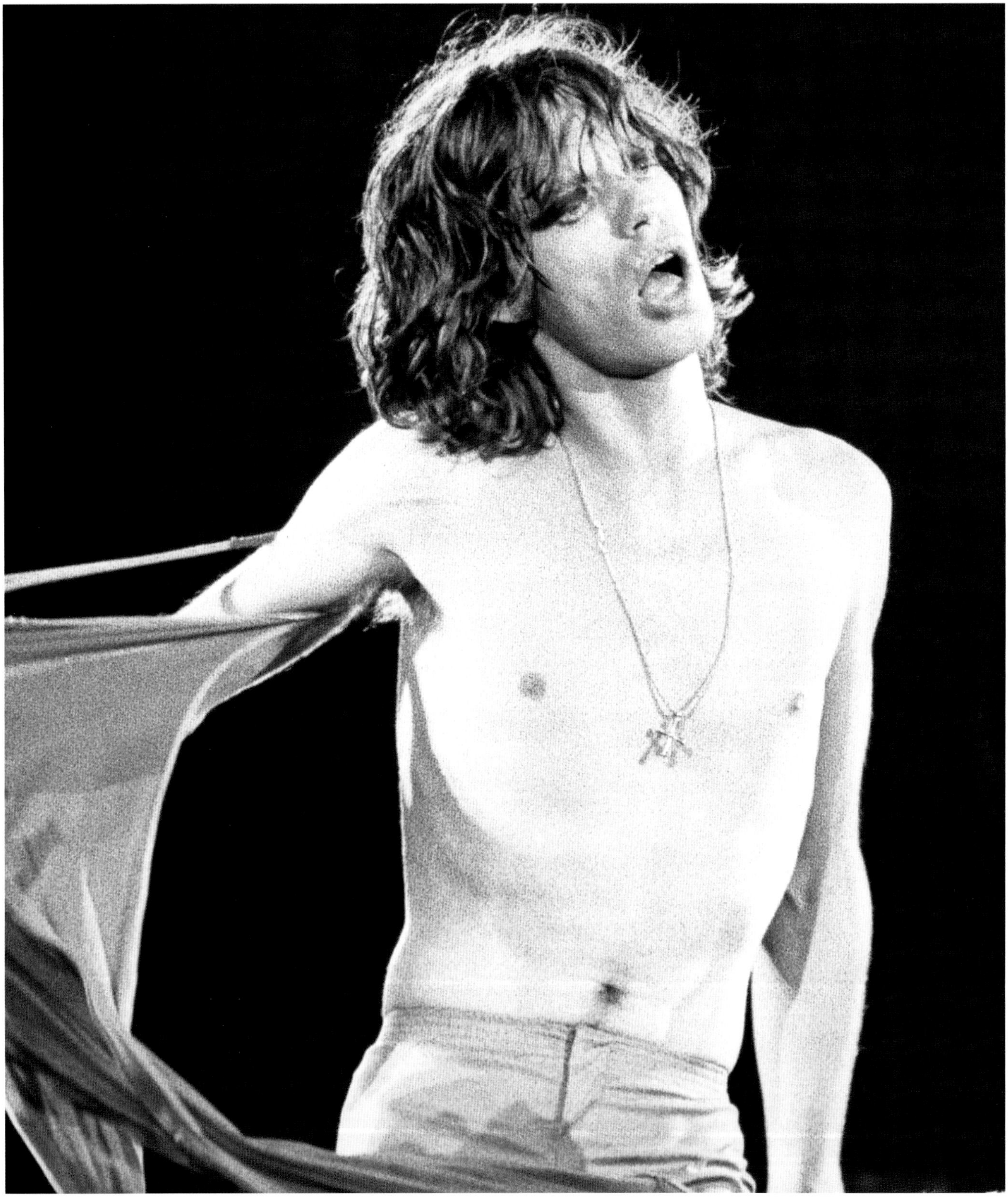

Above: A crucifix may dangle across his naked chest, but Mick was dubbed 'Disciple of Dirt' by scandalized newspapers and parents across America during their 1975 tour.

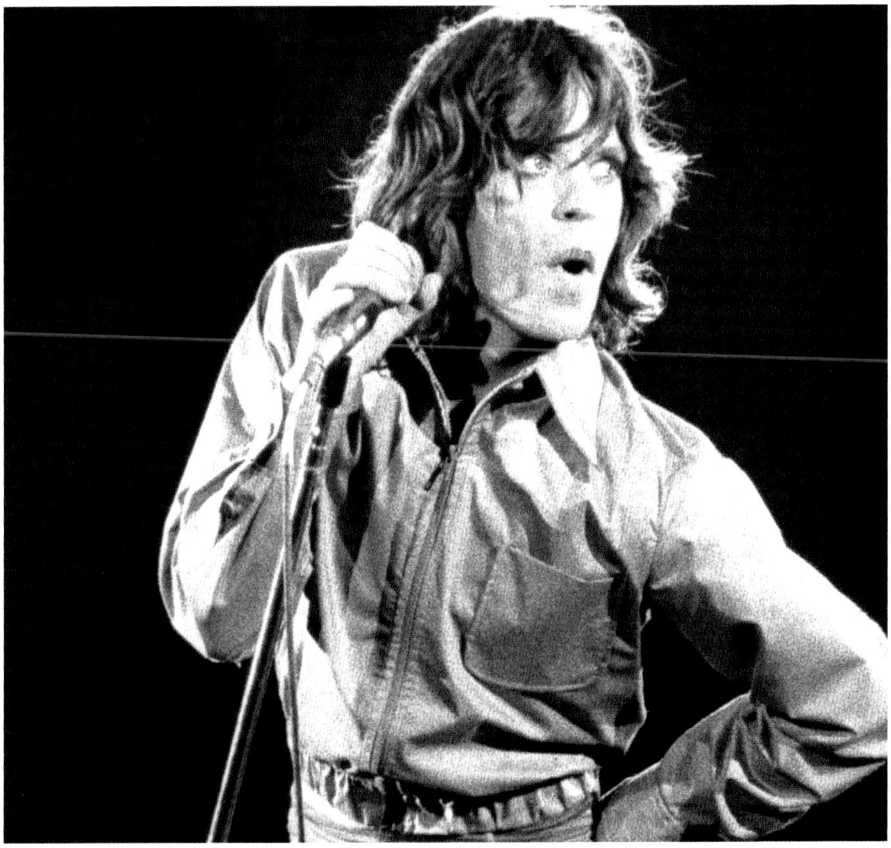

Provoking outrage

Left:. Mick on stage during the US tour. One paper deplored the Stones' 'demonic influence'. During the Baton Rouge shows in June outrage was particularly strong when a massive inflated phallus took centre stage as Mick sang 'Starf*cker'.

Below: Keith and Mick share the microphone. In July Keith and Ronnie were arrested in Arkansas and charged with carrying an offensive weapon. They were released on bail and later explained that the weapon was a can opener with an attached blade.

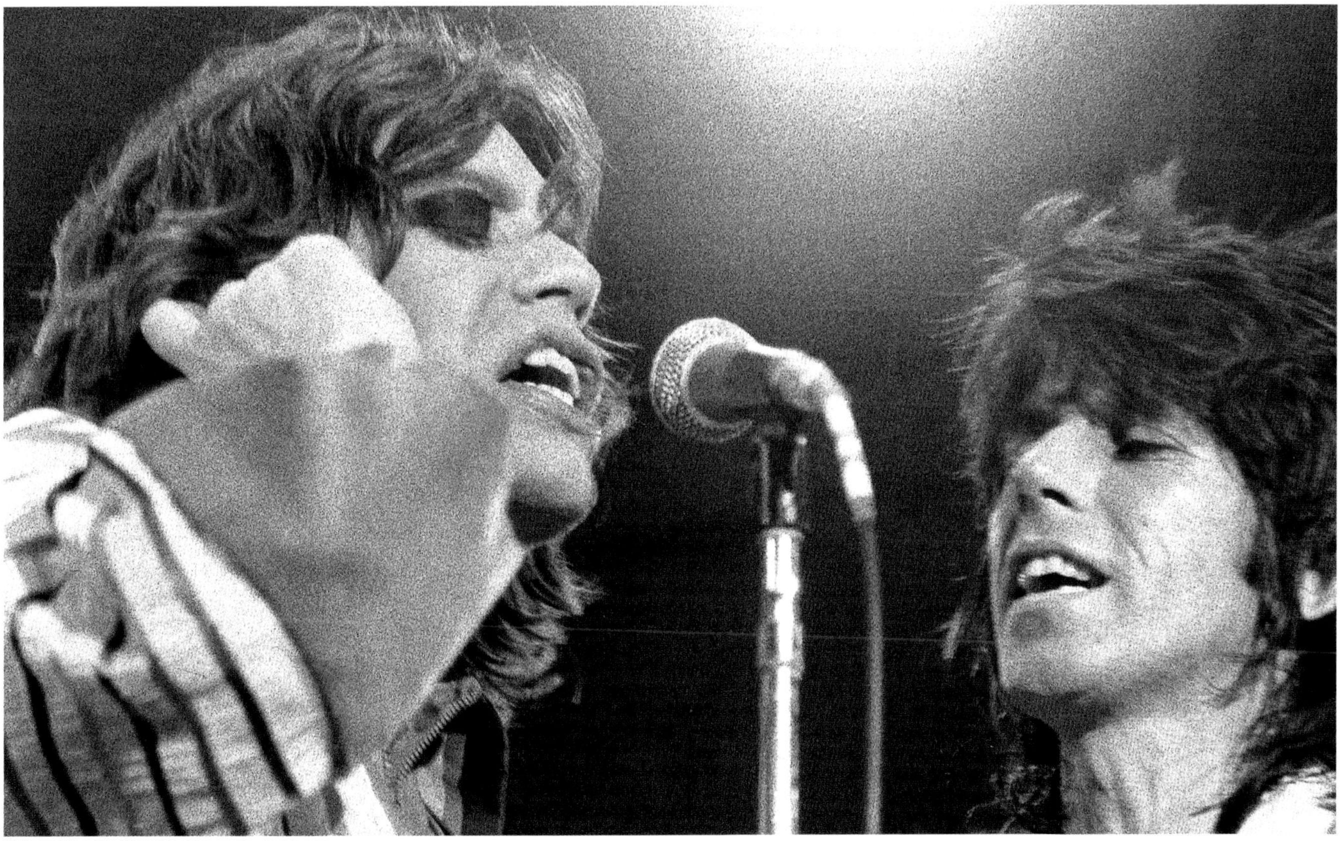

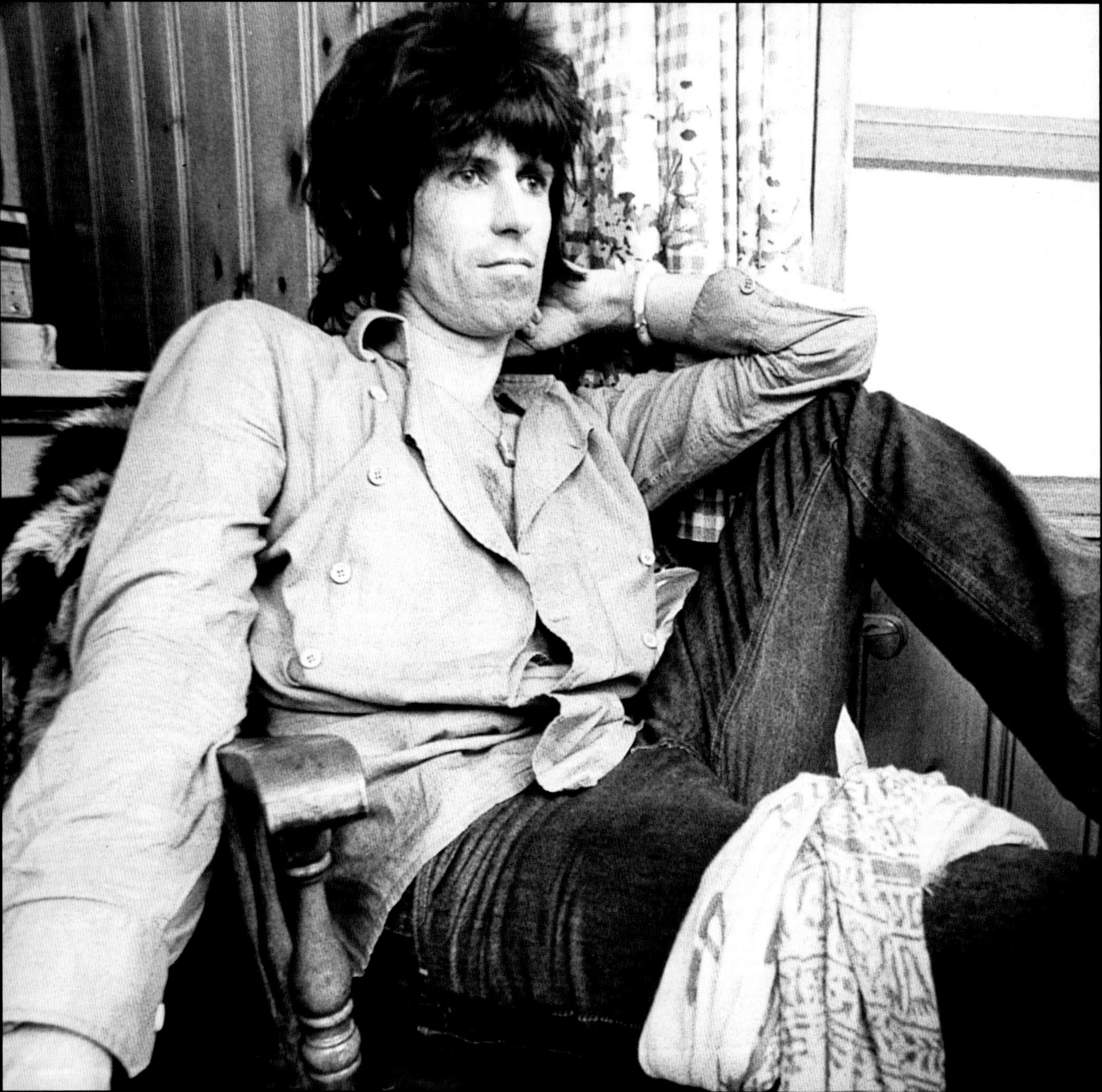

Longest tour

Above: Keith wears an appropriate and unbuttoned Confederate-style shirt in Baton Rouge and looks more relaxed than Mick has at times on tour.

Opposite below right: Bill Wyman, Fellow of the Royal Horticultural Society, among the hothouse blooms at Kew Gardens in 1976. His interest in botany started when the Stones first toured in exotic places and he'd photograph the local plant life when he had time off.

Opposite above: Bill is interviewed at Kew Gardens by music journalist John Blake, now a successful book publisher. Despite the long face, he said in a newspaper interview in March that year, 'I'm content with my career, my family, my hobbies. I wish everyone was as happy as me.'

Opposite below left: Bill photographed in 1976.

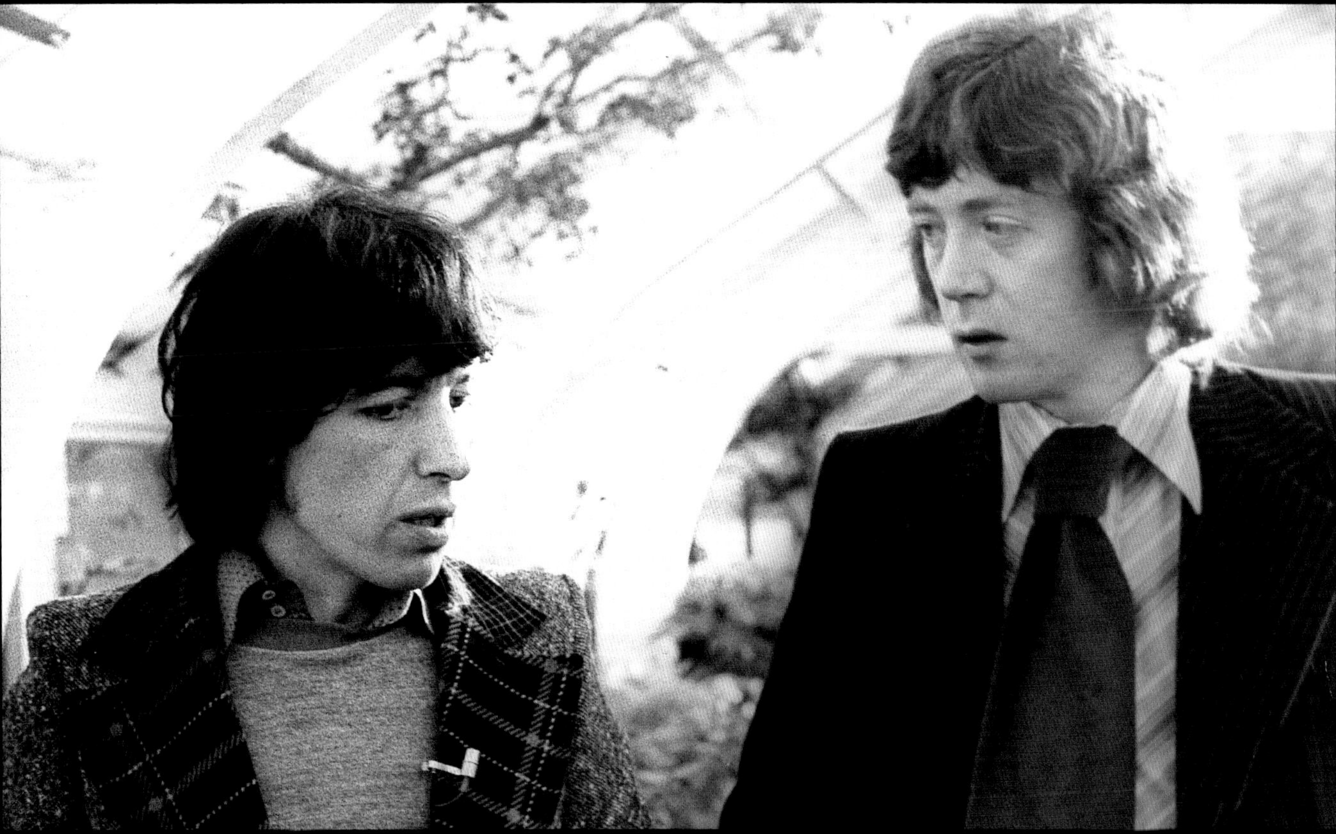

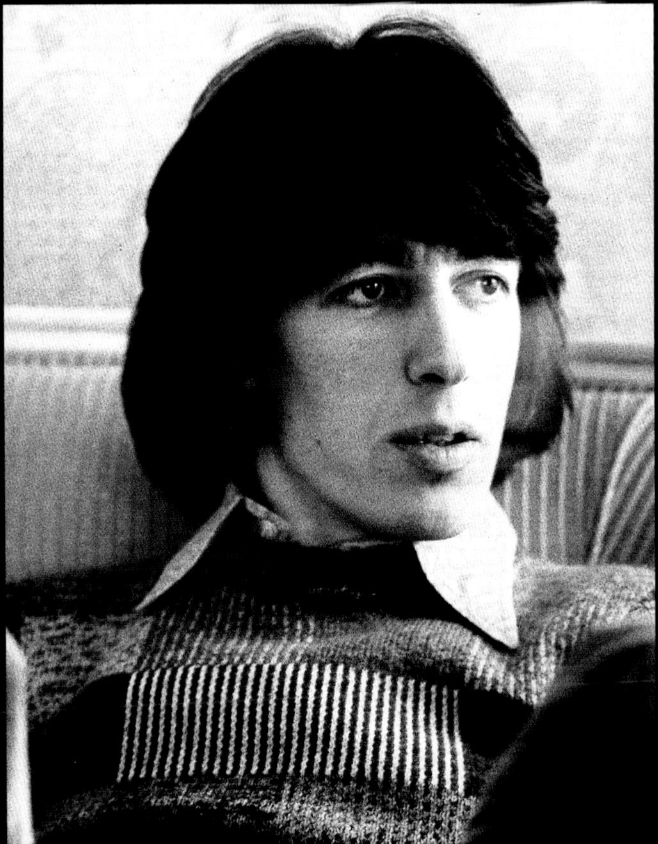

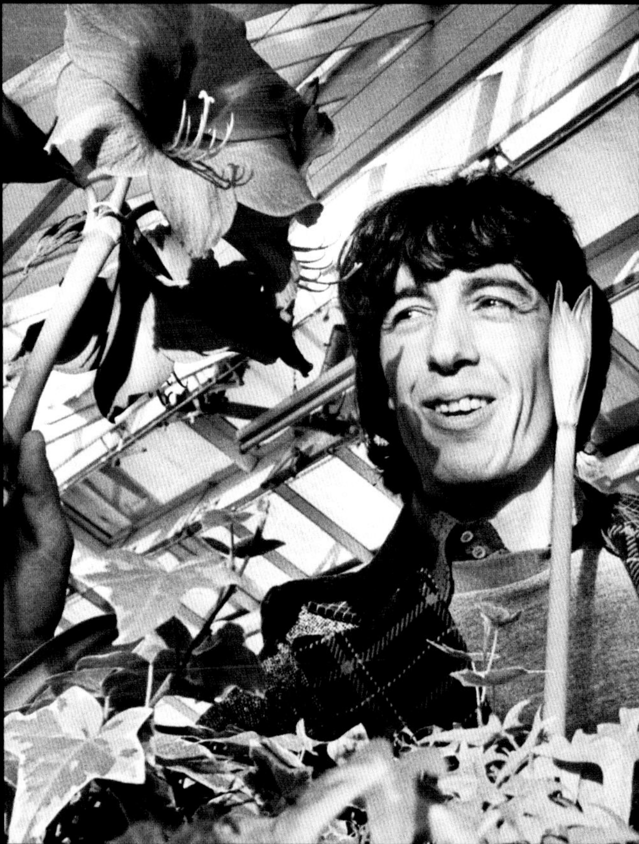

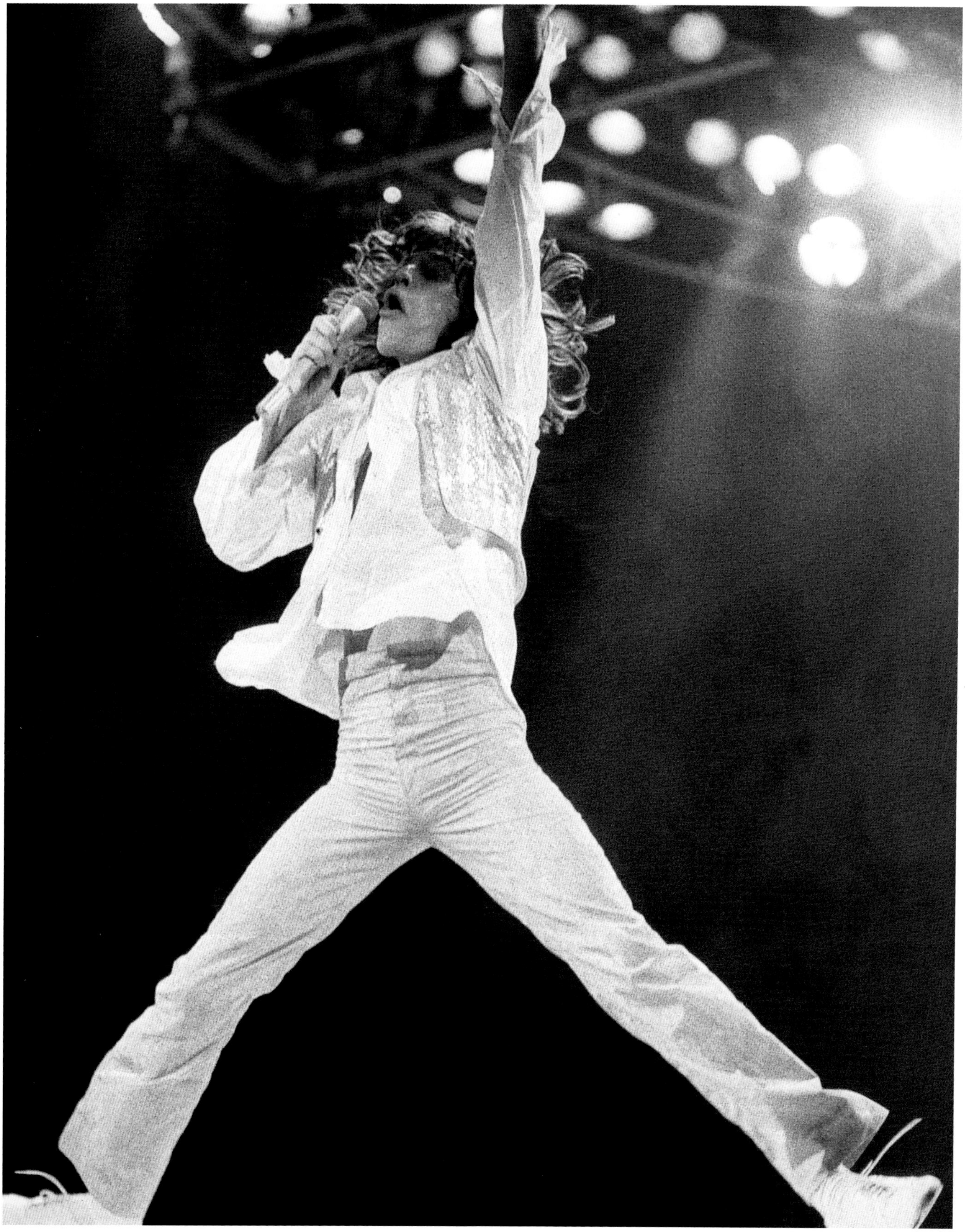

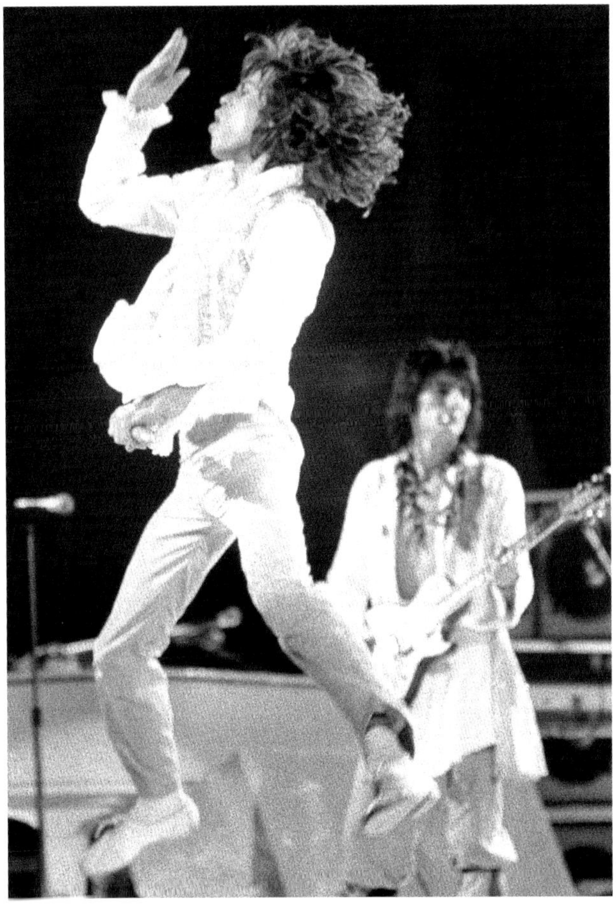

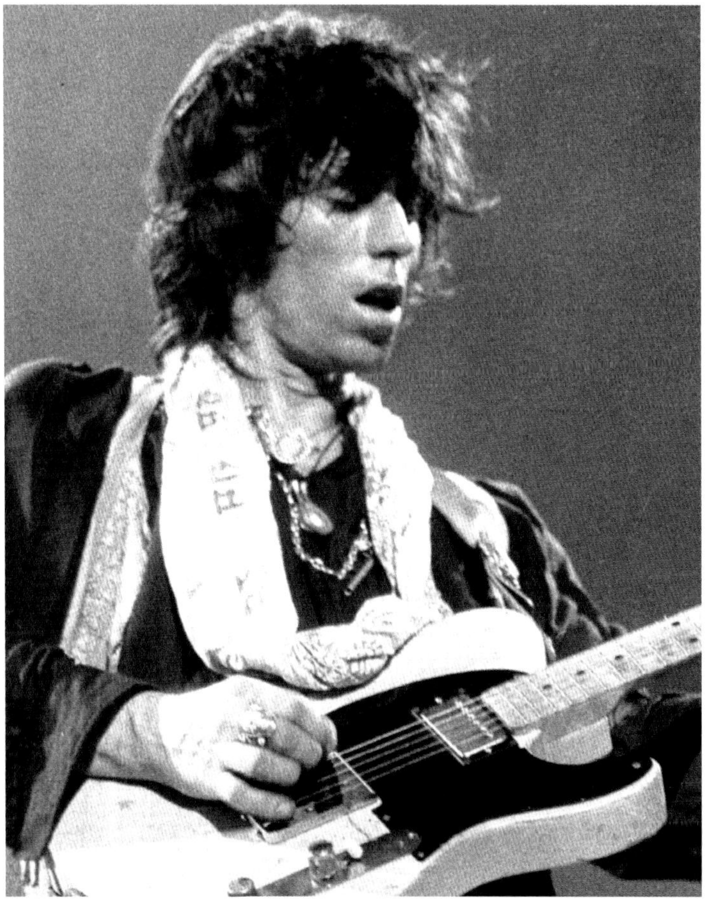

One million apply for tickets

Above right and right: The kings of rock 'n' roll at Earls Court in May 1976. A million people applied for tickets to the six London shows, the first in the capital for three years, but only 100,000 fans were lucky enough to get in. The British tour cost over £1 million to produce, thanks in part to stage props such as an 25-metre silk dragon that was suspended over the audience.

Opposite and above: The Nijinski of rock 'n' roll? Mick Jagger seems to have springs on his heels as he gives his all at Earls Court in May 1976. Towards the end of the shows, the band pumped confetti over the audience and threw buckets of water over those fans nearest the stage. Then, naked to the waist, Jagger tipped water over himself too.

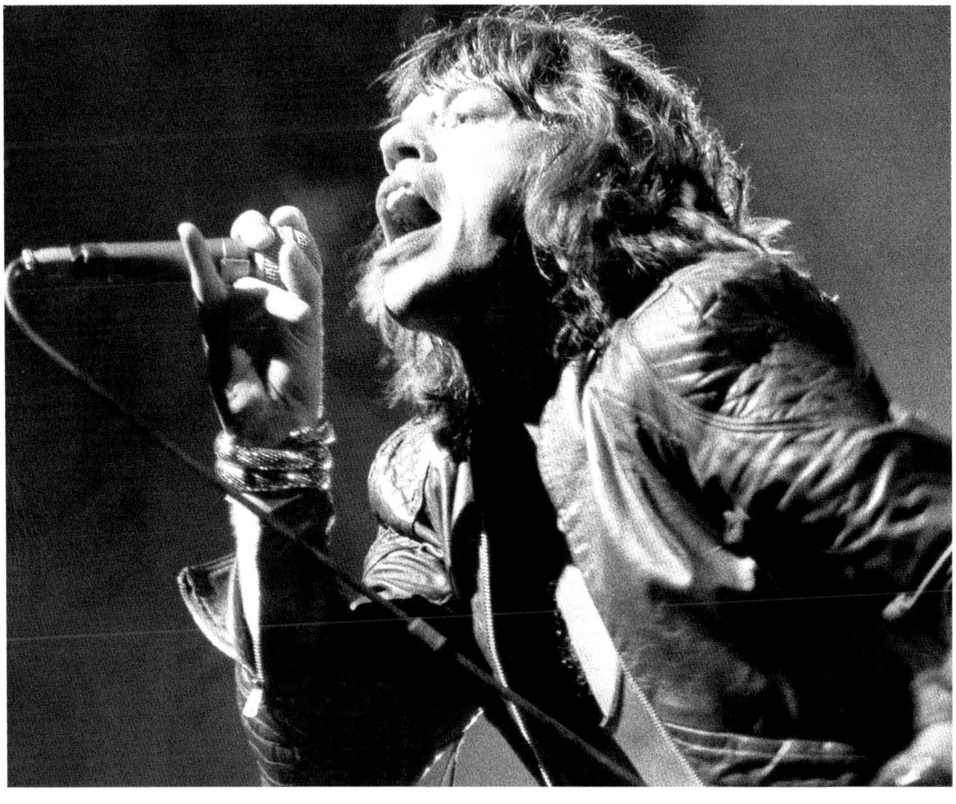

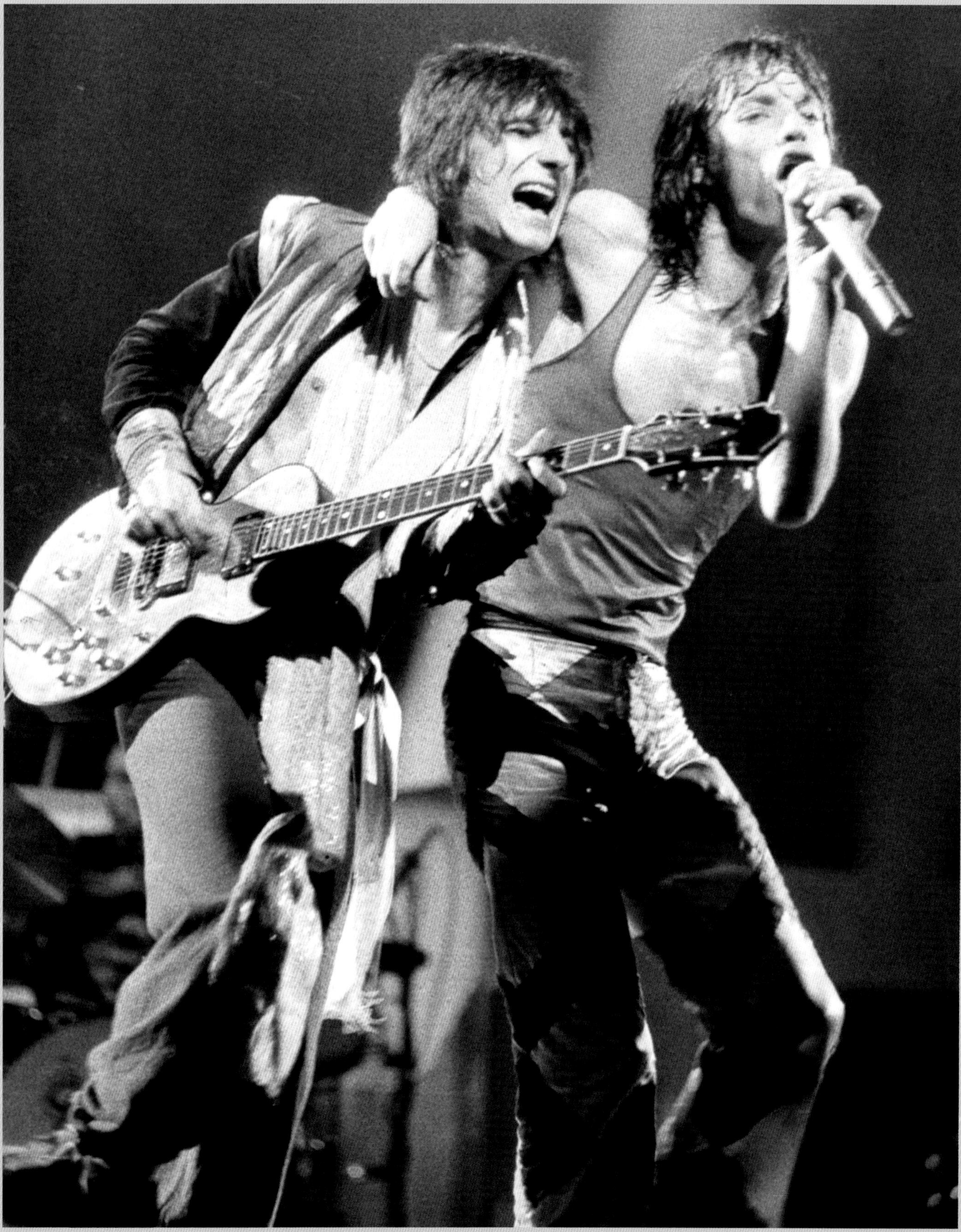

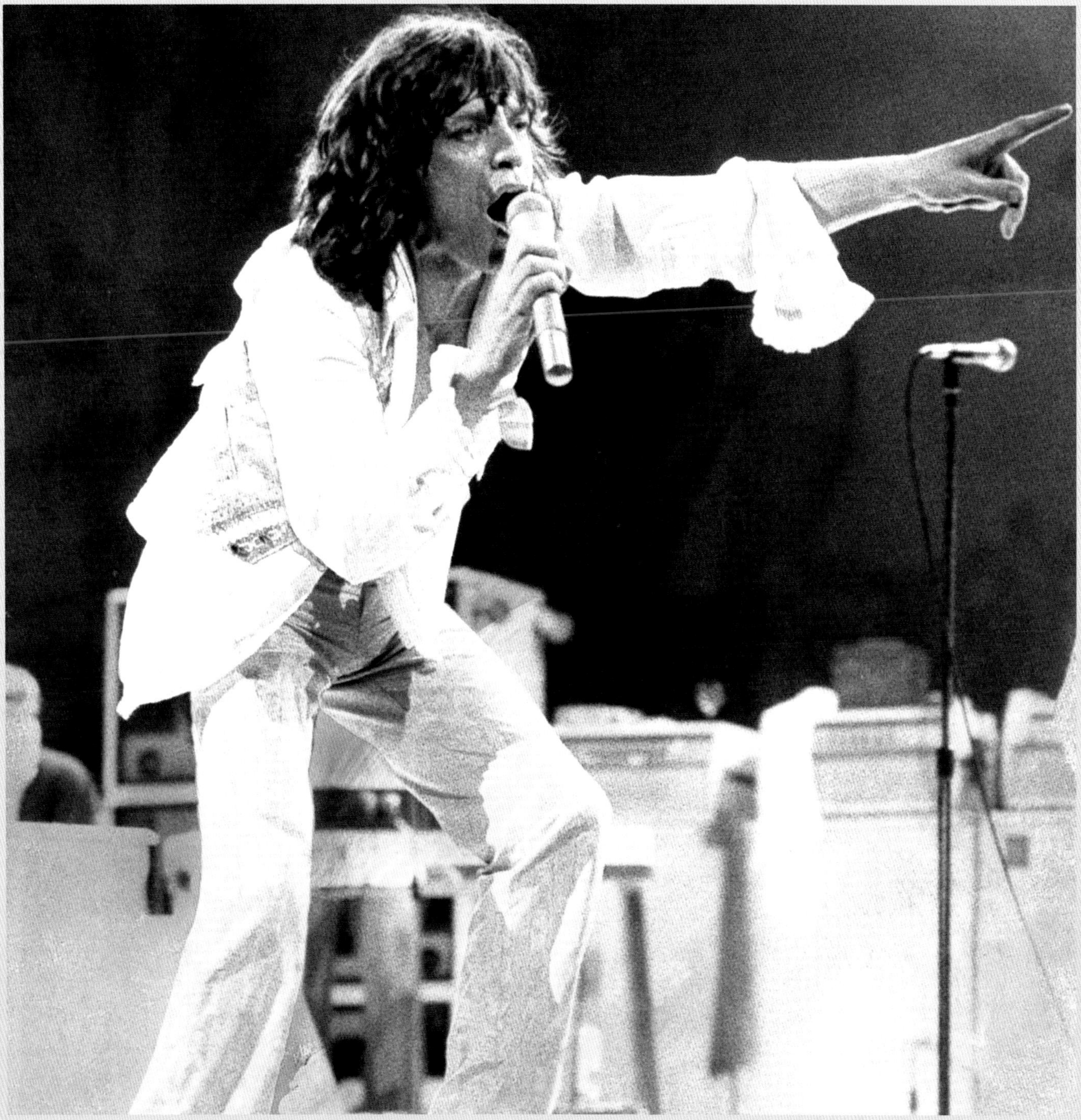

'Fool To Cry'

Opposite: Ronnie Wood had to learn the riffs and words of over 100 songs when he joined The Rolling Stones – not only the old hits but new ones such as 'Fool To Cry', which reached No.4 in the British charts. 'Fool To Cry' was considered sentimental by many fans and Keith is said to have fallen asleep while peforming it at a concert in Germany in 1976.

Above: The Earls Court shows, with all the elaborate embellishments of clowns, dragons, cannon fire and wartime-type searchlights, established a pattern in which each concert gave fans far more for their money than a simple set of songs, however electrifying the performance was. Every show was to be a spectacle, often themed, as well as rock music at its most powerful, and Mick Jagger was always in control.

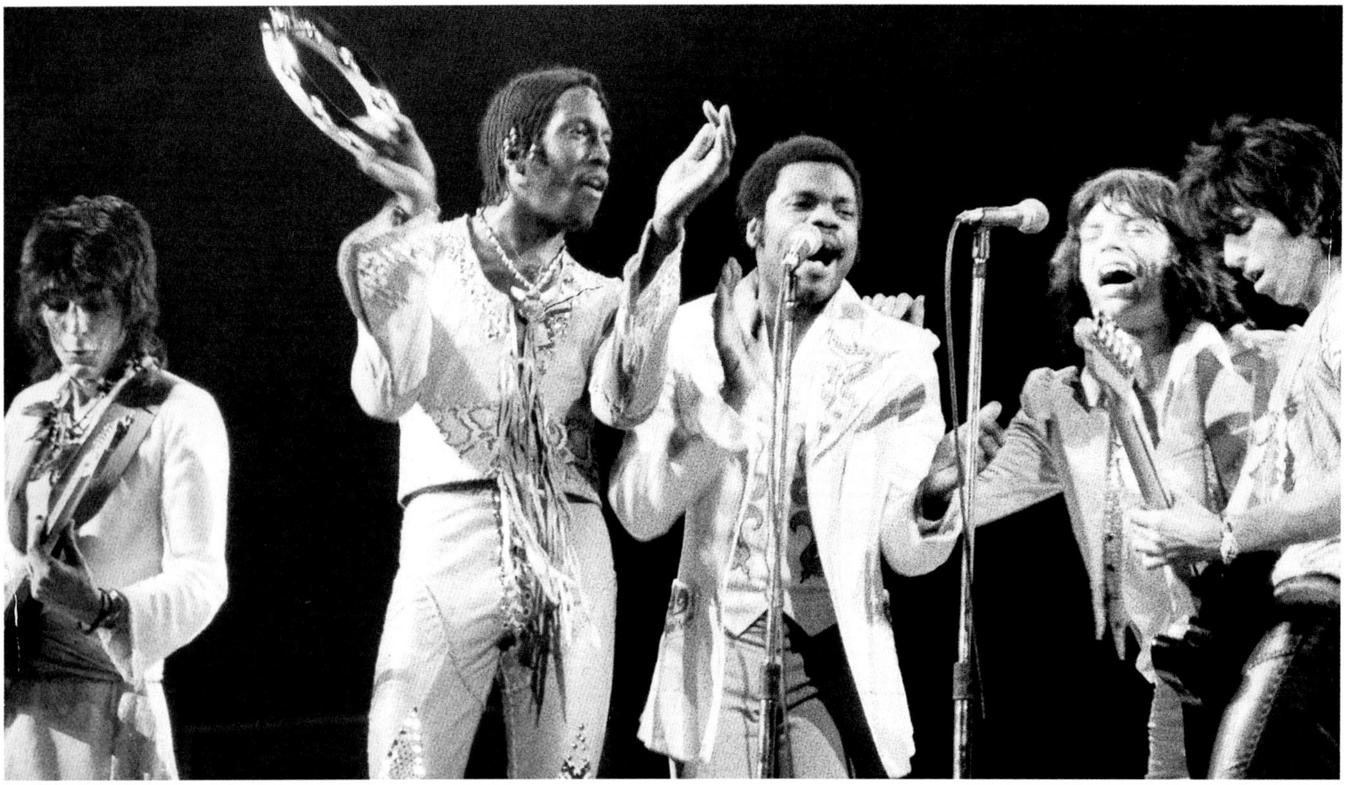

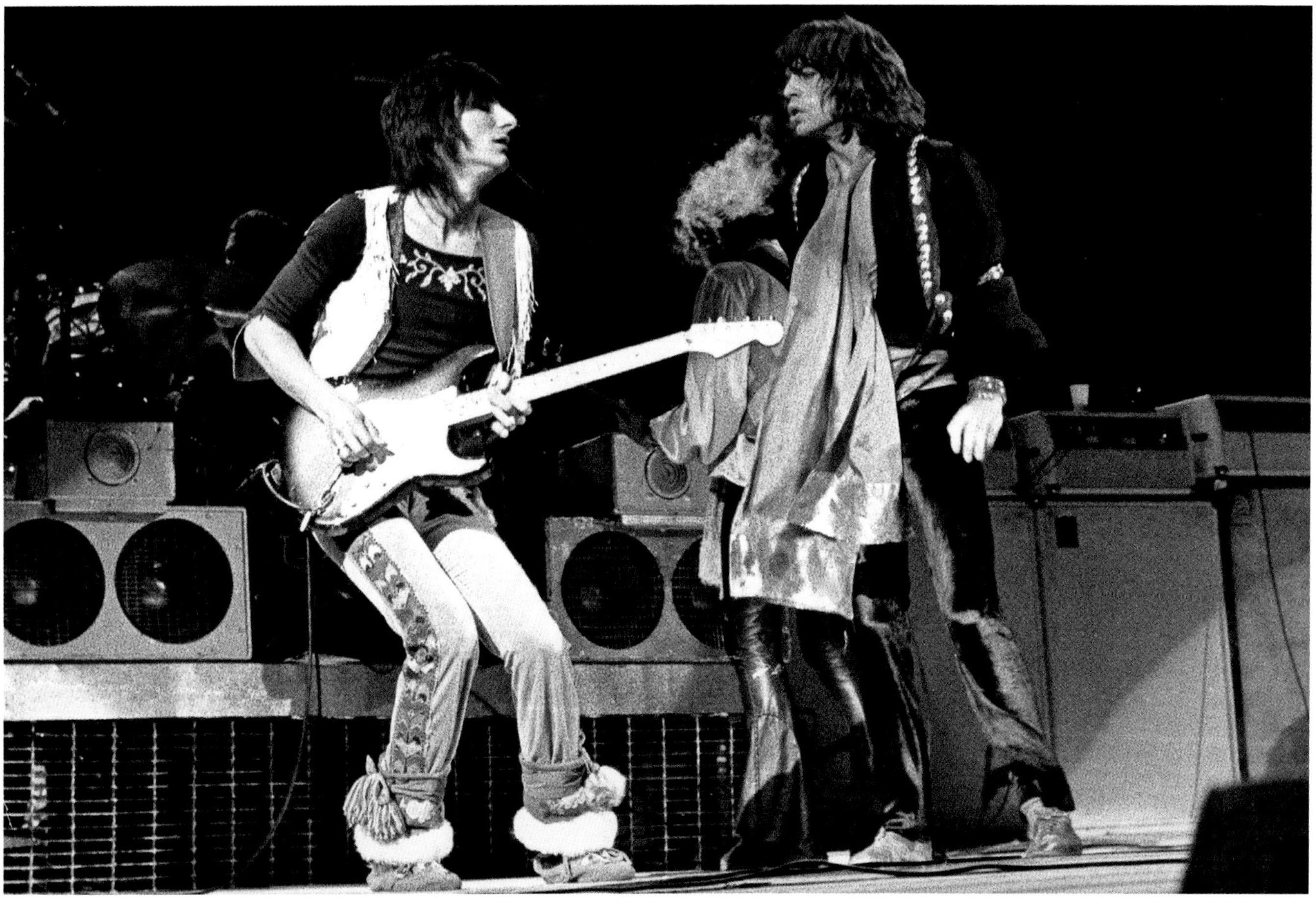

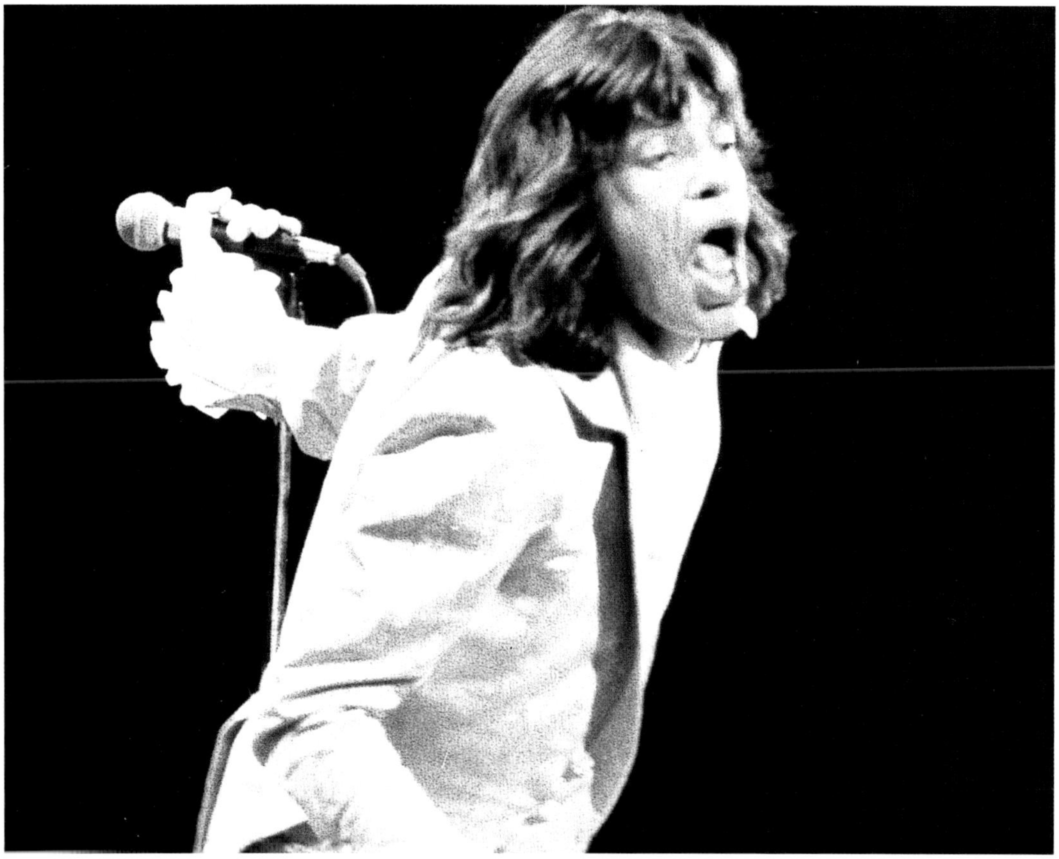

Hot in Earls Court

Mick Jagger always gave his all in every show, training like an athlete and gradually removing items of clothing as the show hotted up. Starting out at Earls Court in a turquoise suit, he was stripped to the waist by the time the show closed.

Opposite top: The band is joined on stage by Ollie Brown and Billy Preston at Earls Court on 21 May 1976.

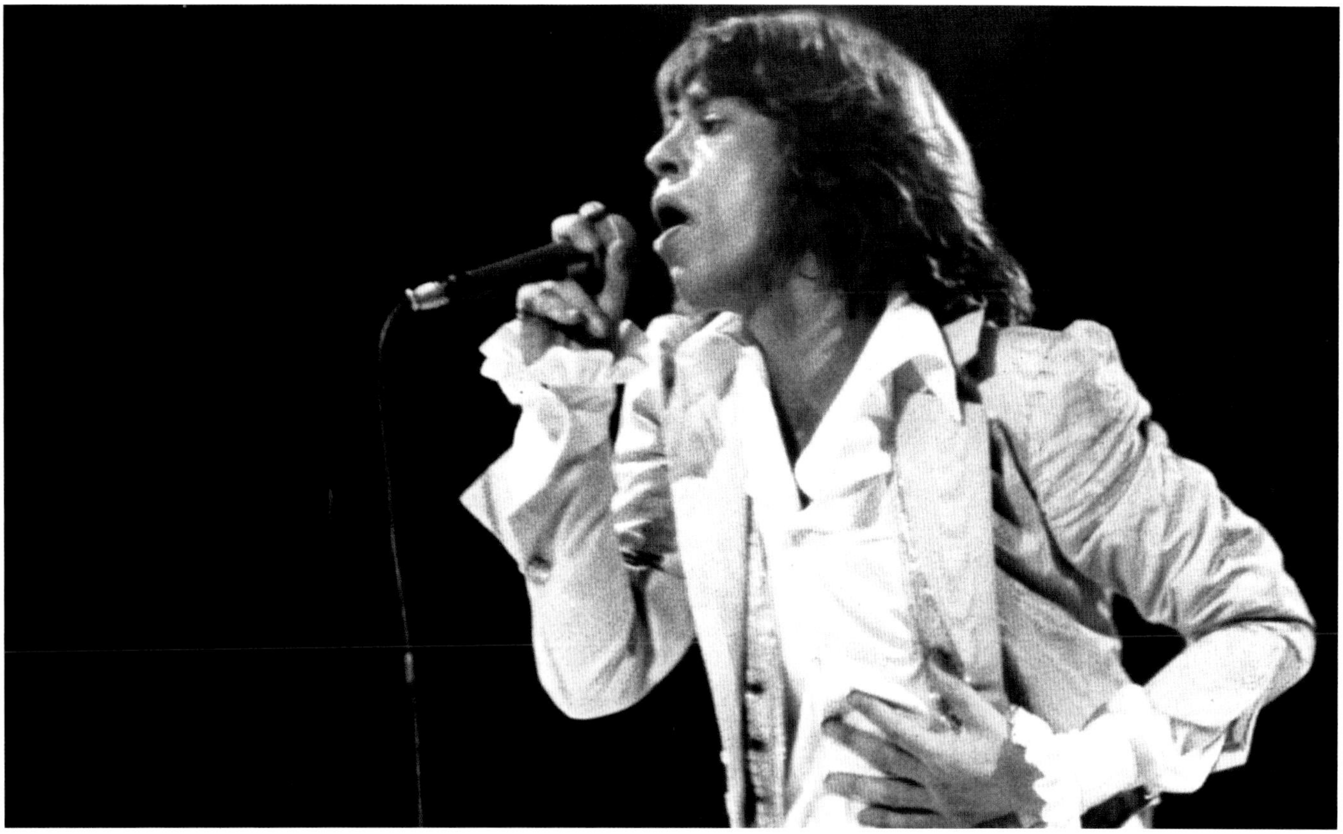

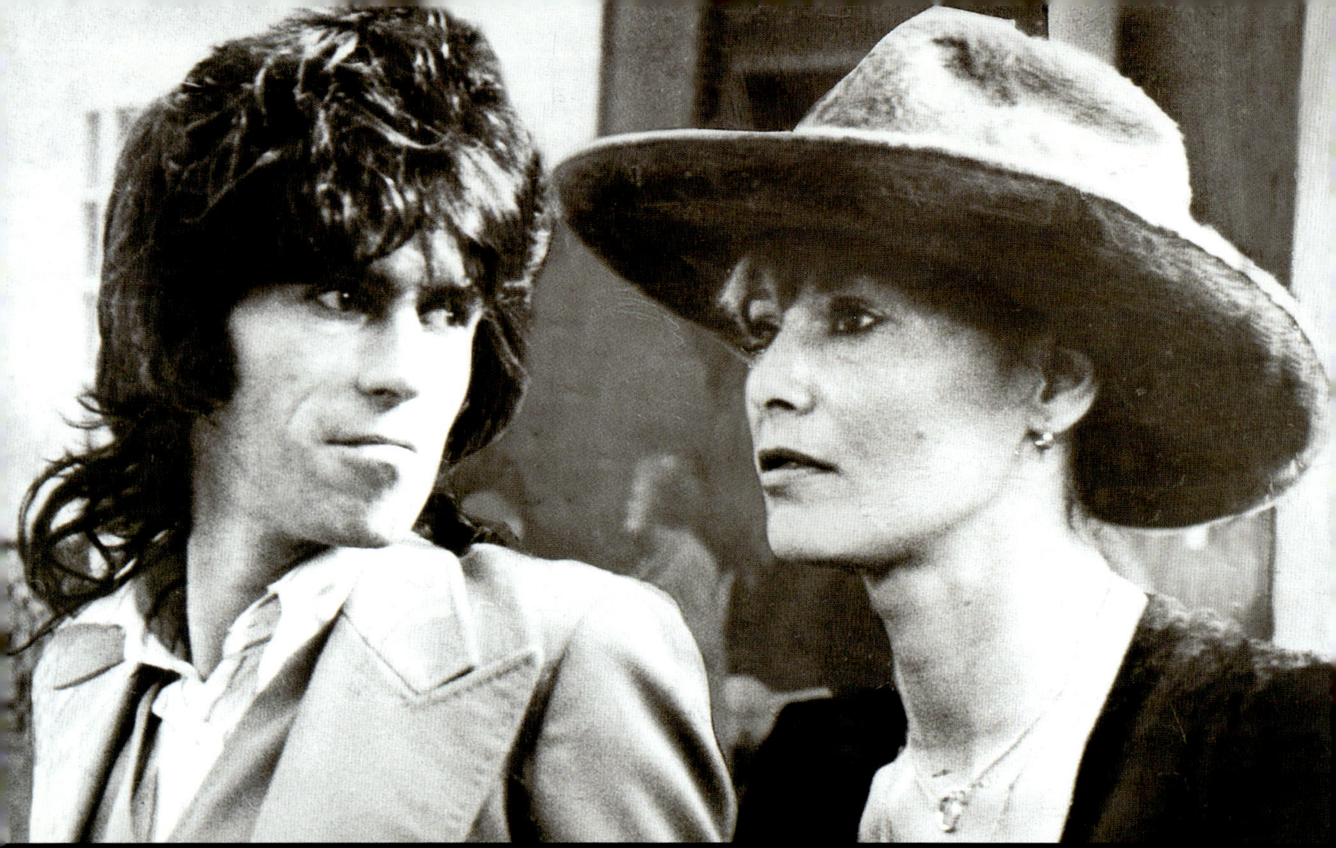
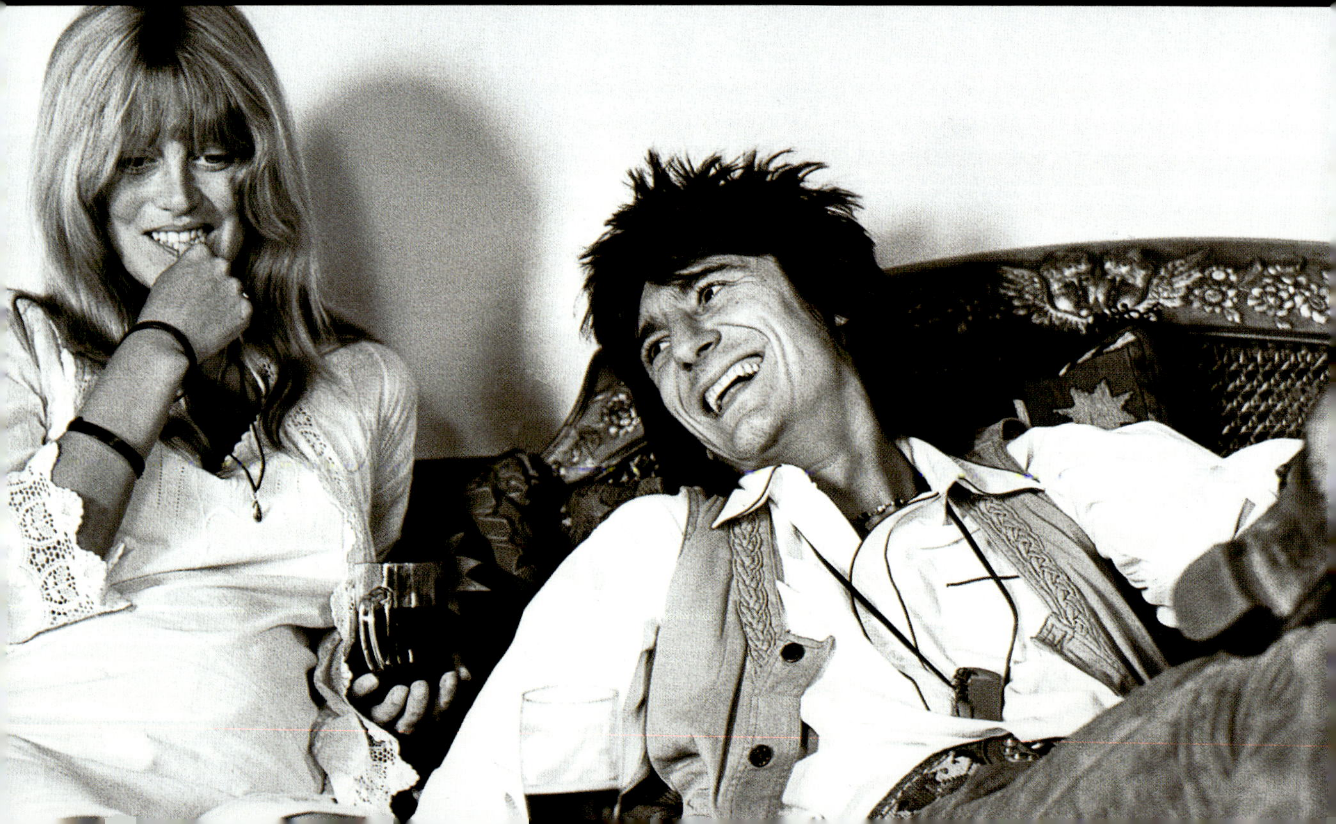

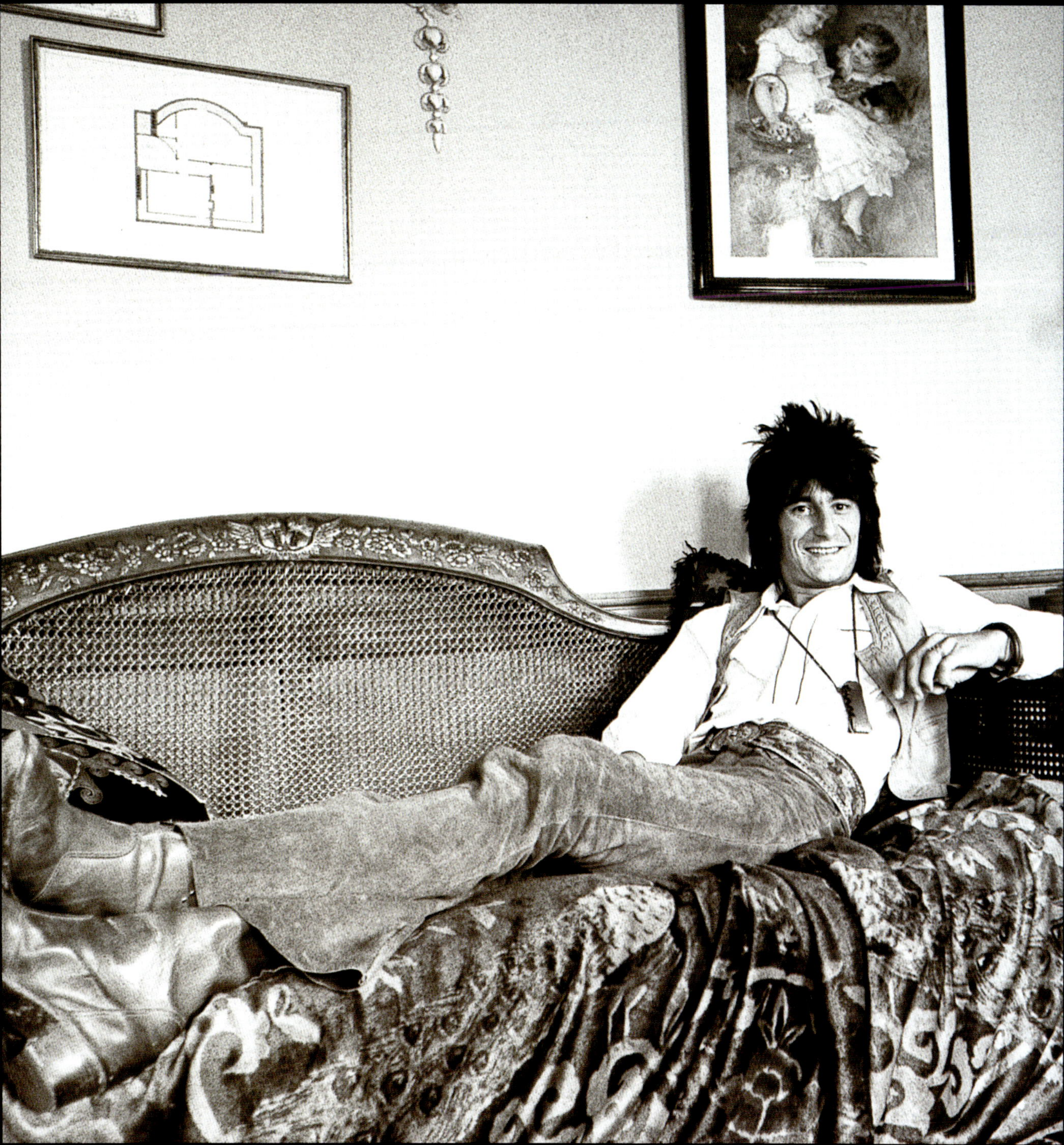

Keith's grief

Opposite above: In June 1976 Tara, the ten-week-old son of Keith Richard and Anita Pallenberg, died of a mystery virus. Keith was grief-stricken but insisted that the tragedy should remain a secret for now, and that the current tour should continue.

Above and opposite below: Ronnie and Krissie Wood relax at home in Richmond amid a comfortable clutter of pictures, antique pieces and rugs. Krissie is six months pregnant – a son, Jesse James, was born on 30 October 1976. Ronnie was soon to be involved with model Jo Howard.

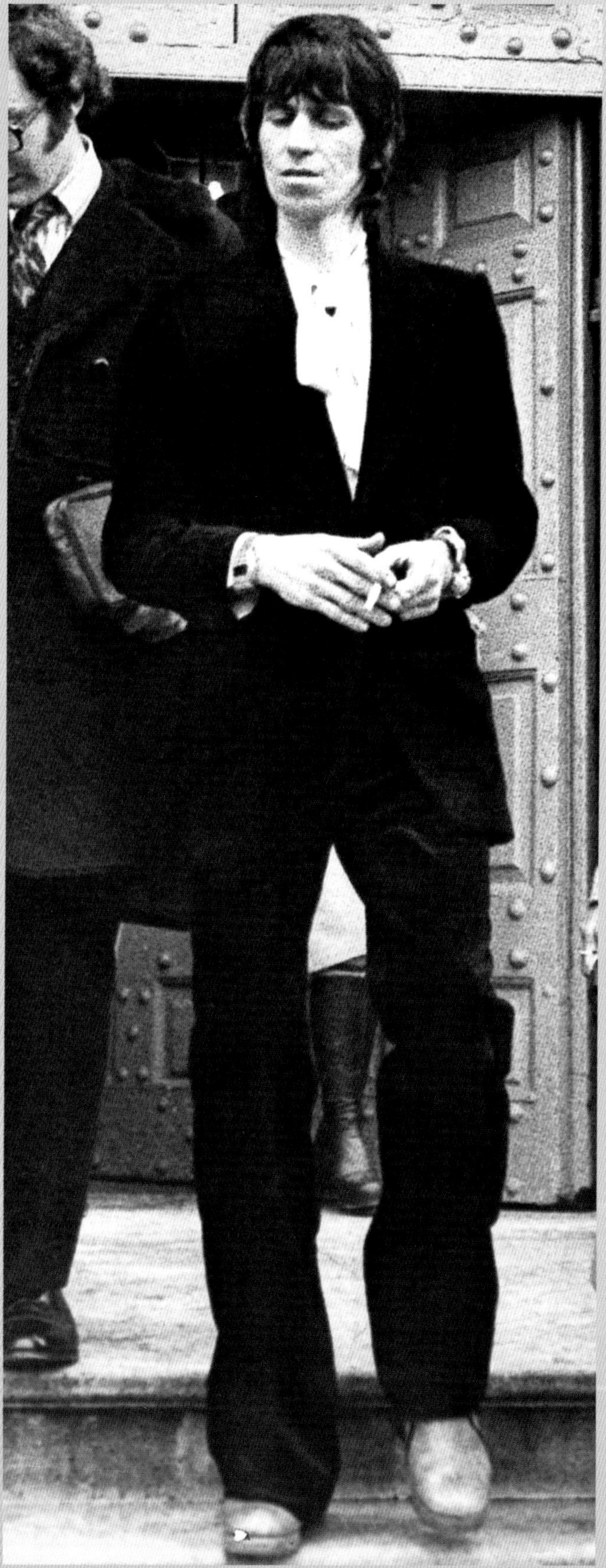

Crashing the Bentley

Left and below: It was a bad start to 1977 for Keith Richard. While he and Anita were still grieving after the sudden death of their third child, Keith appeared in court in Aylesbury, Buckinghamshire, accused of possession of LSD and cocaine discovered by the police in his Bentley after he'd crashed it in the area the previous May. Anita and son Marlon had been in the car with him at the time, and although the car was written off, no one was hurt.

Opposite: Mick attends Aylesbury Crown Court to lend support to Keith during his current drugs trial. On a sartorial note, Mick's striped purple jacket was worn over green suede trousers tucked into high red boots.

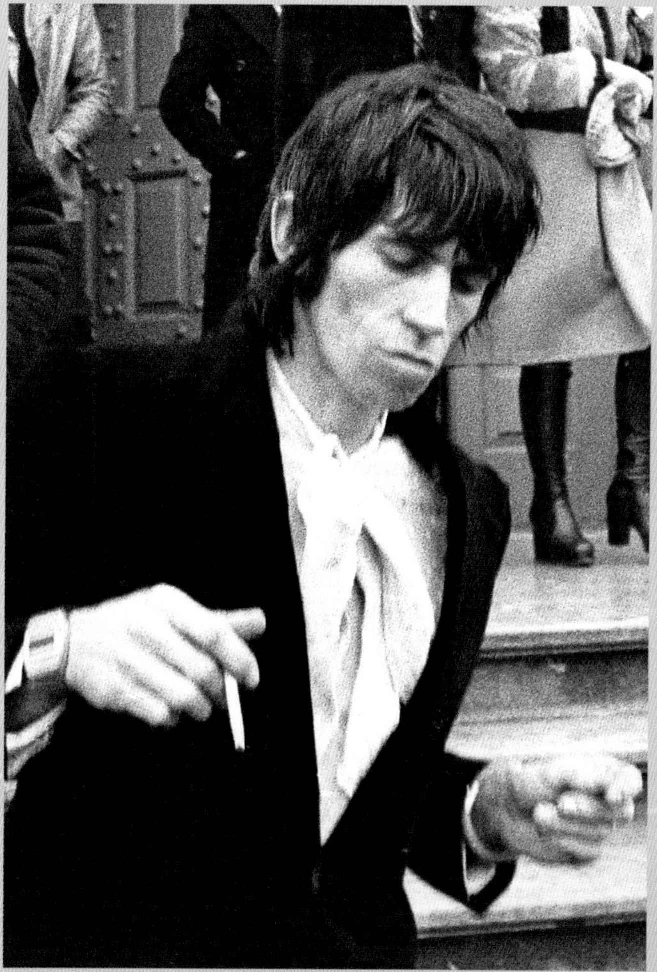

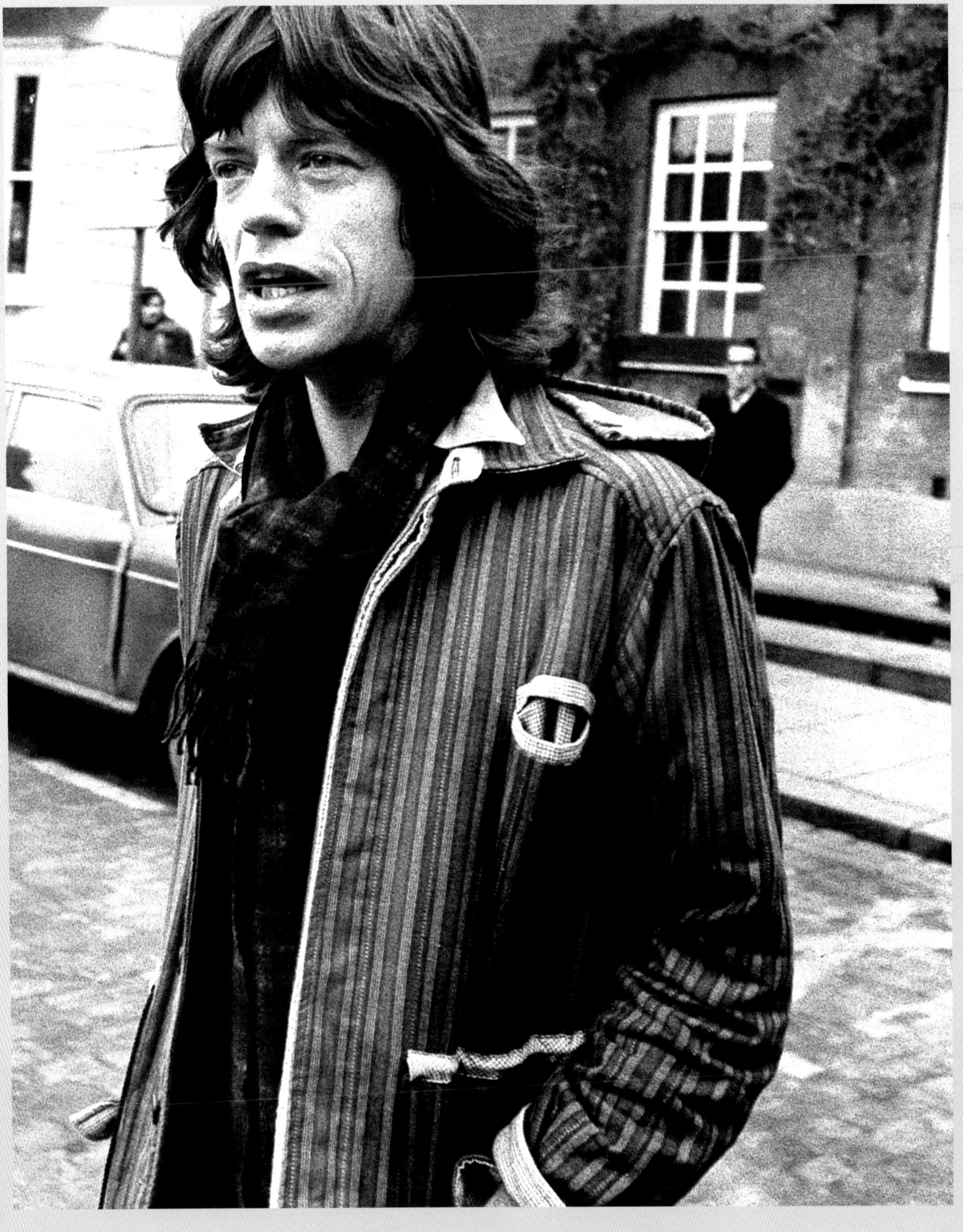

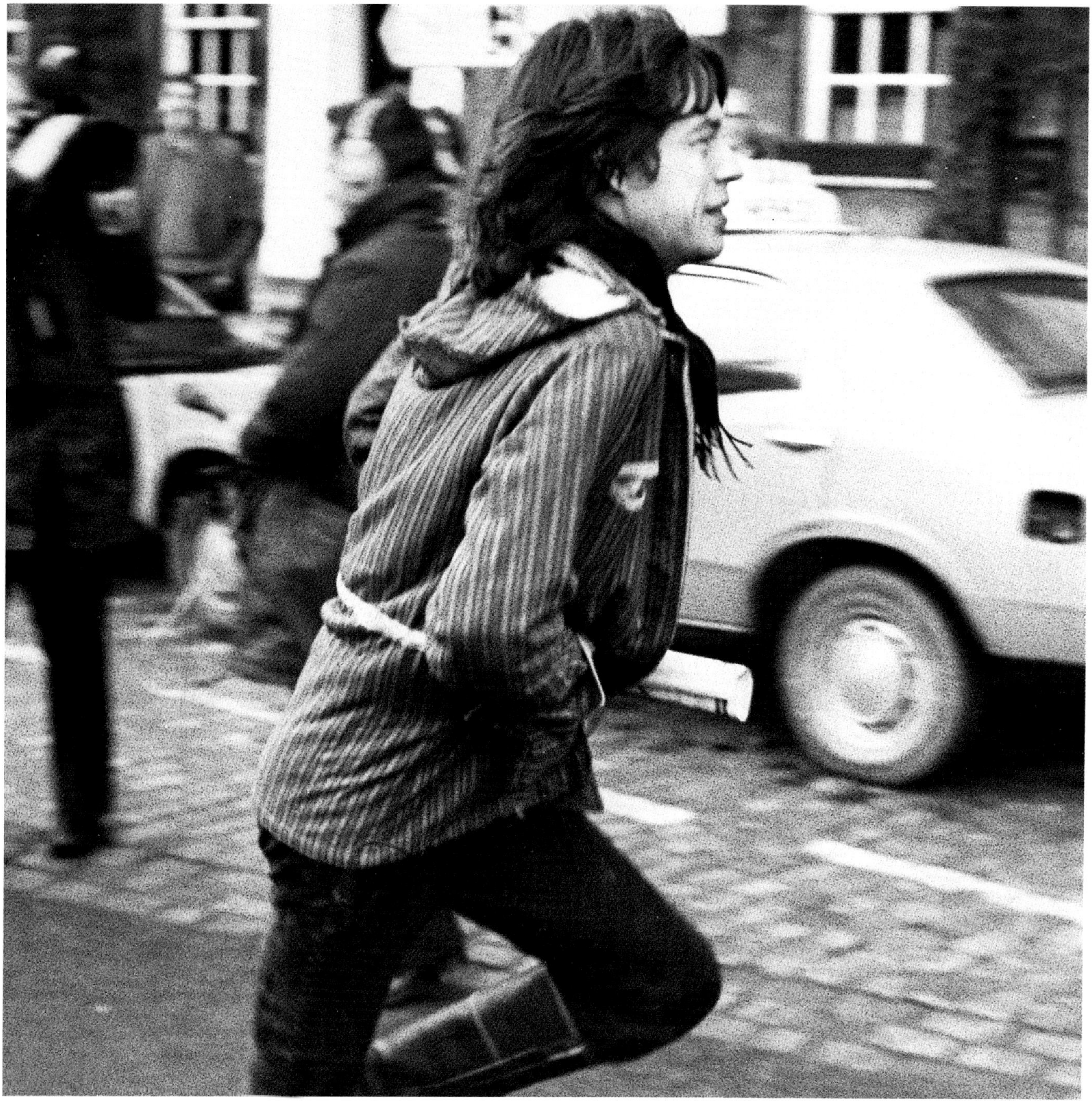

A friend in need

Above: Mick sprints back to his gold-coloured Rolls-Royce, attempting to avoid fans and photographers outside the Aylesbury courtroom. No one denies that Keith and Mick have had their differences over the years, but the friendship and loyalties have always prevailed in a crisis. Mick flew in from Los Angeles to help Keith.

Opposite above: Keith arrives at the court looking gaunt and understandably apprehensive, and dashes away after proceedings end for the day. He pleaded not guilty. His defence counsel suggested that the various drugs found on the night of the Bentley crash had been given to him by misguided fans, and that his client had no idea what the packages contained.

Opposite below: Mick at the court – it was speculated that he may be called as a witness.

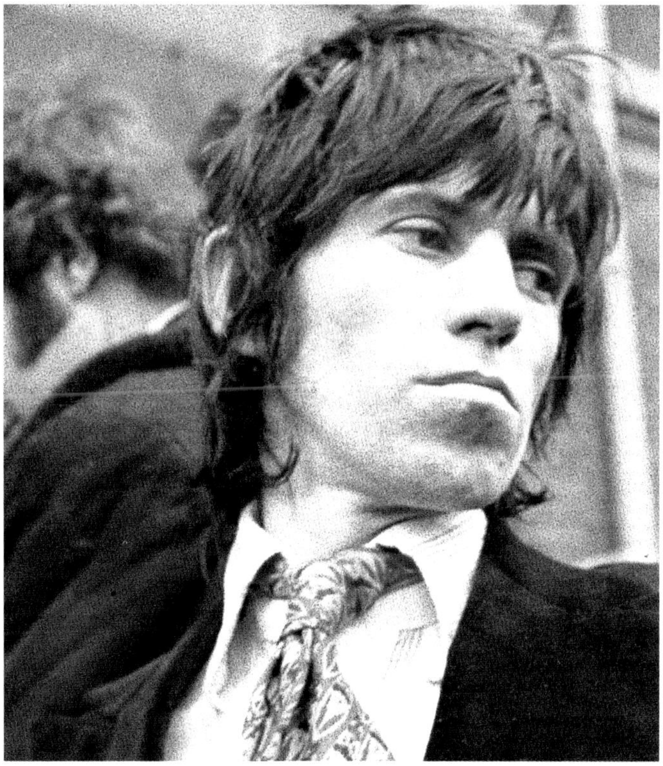

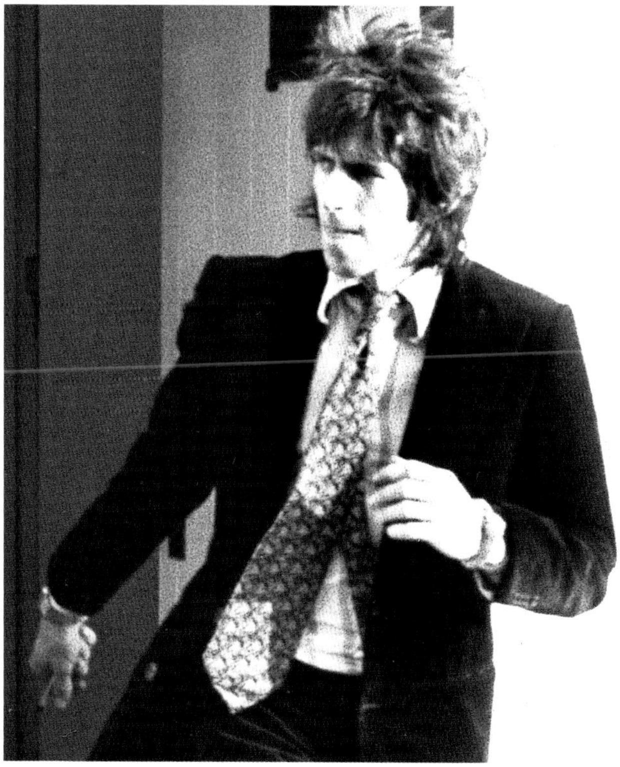

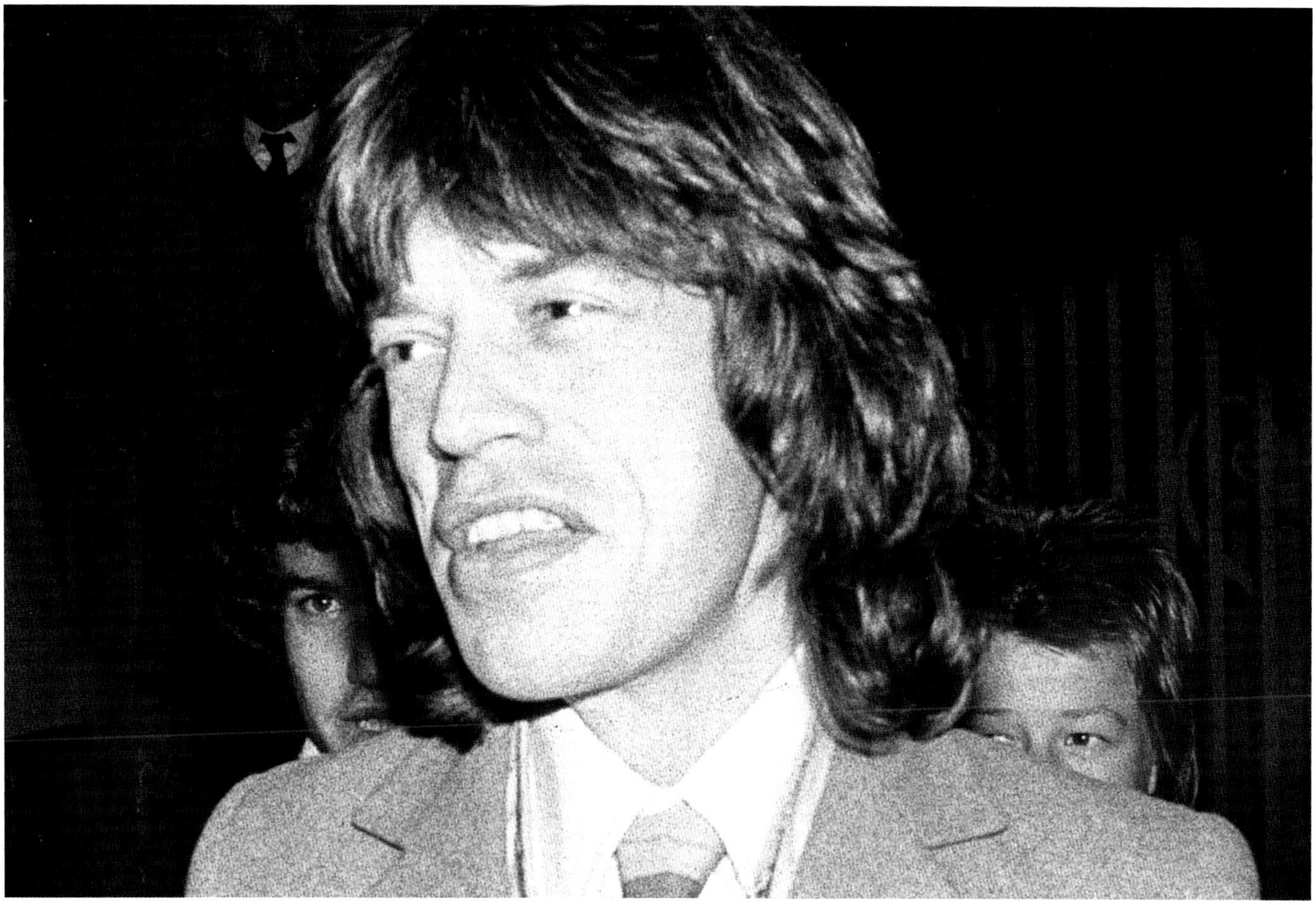

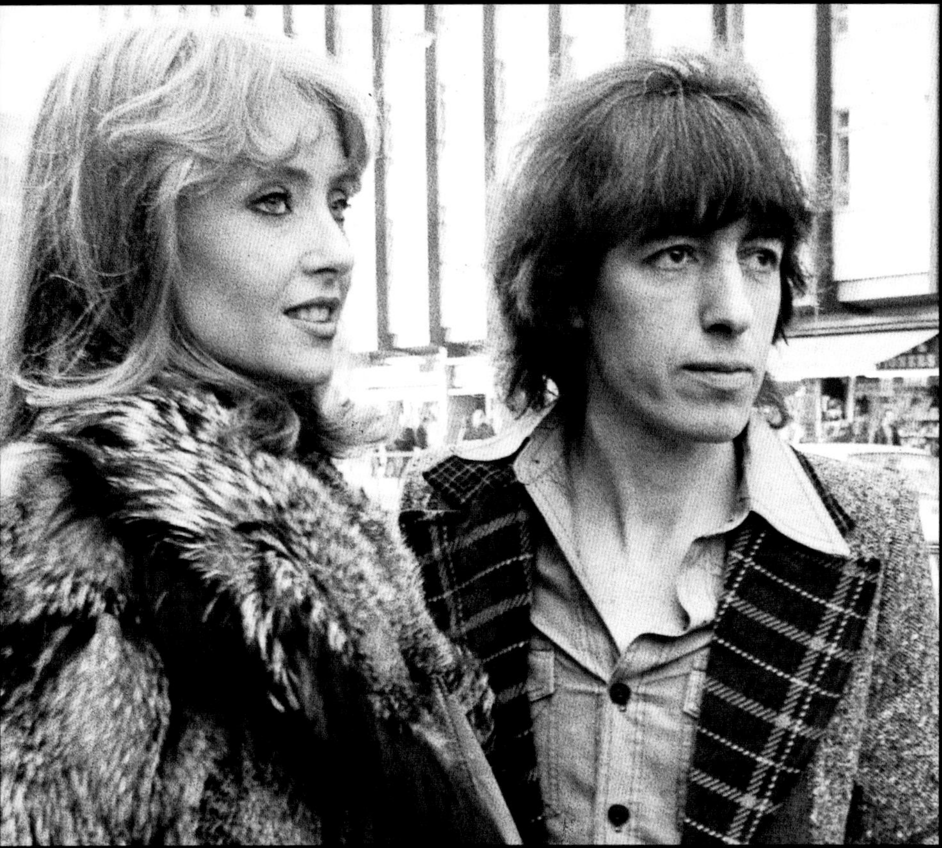

Celebrating a compromise

Opposite: On 12 January 1977 what Keith described as a true British compromise was reached: he was found guilty of possessing cocaine, and fined £750 plus costs, but not guilty of the LSD charge. Broad smiles as he and Mick celebrate at the plush hotel near Aylesbury where they've been staying. However, celebrations were short-lived. When Keith and Anita flew to Toronto in February to join the rest of the band, they were in trouble again.

Left and below: On 14 February 1977 Bill and Astrid attend the London wedding of Judy Garland's daughter Lorna Luft and musician Jake Rogers.

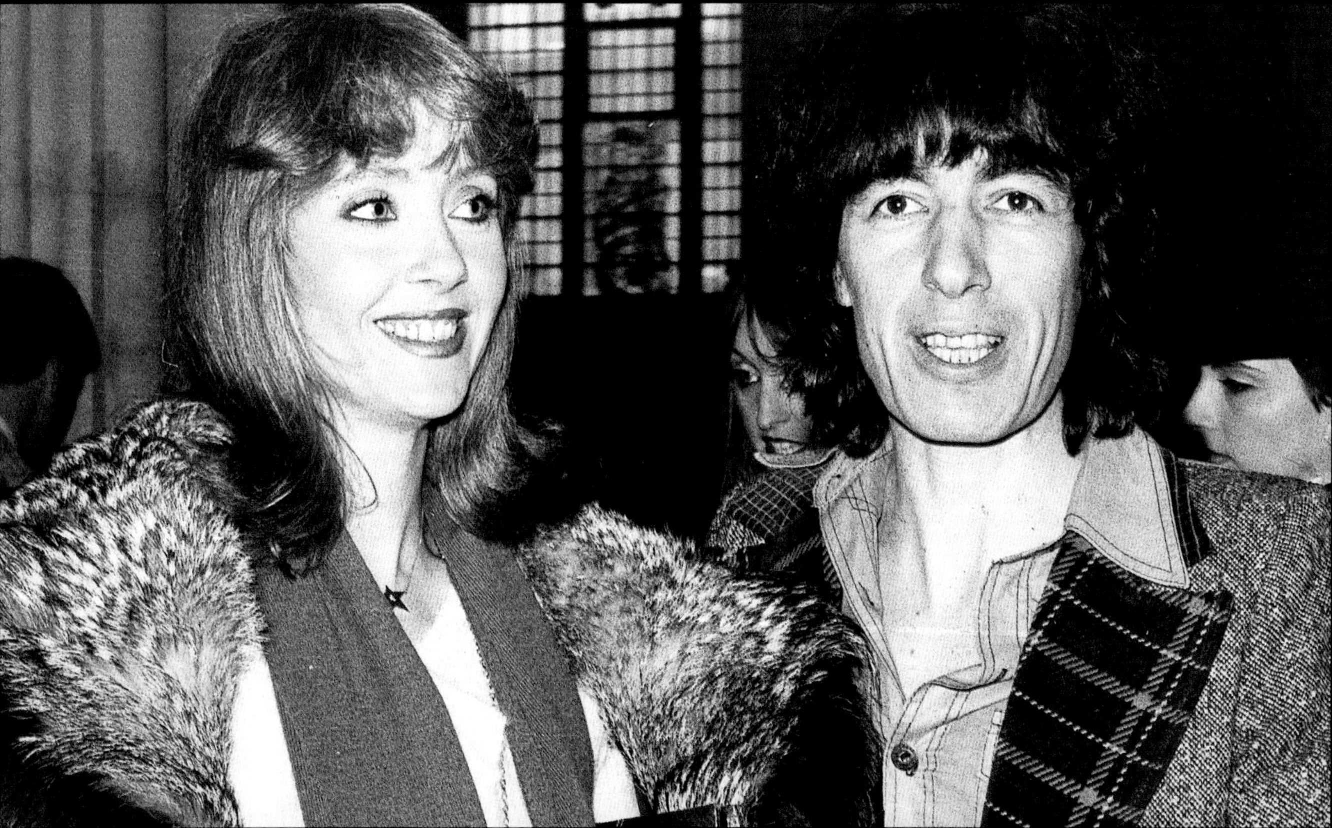

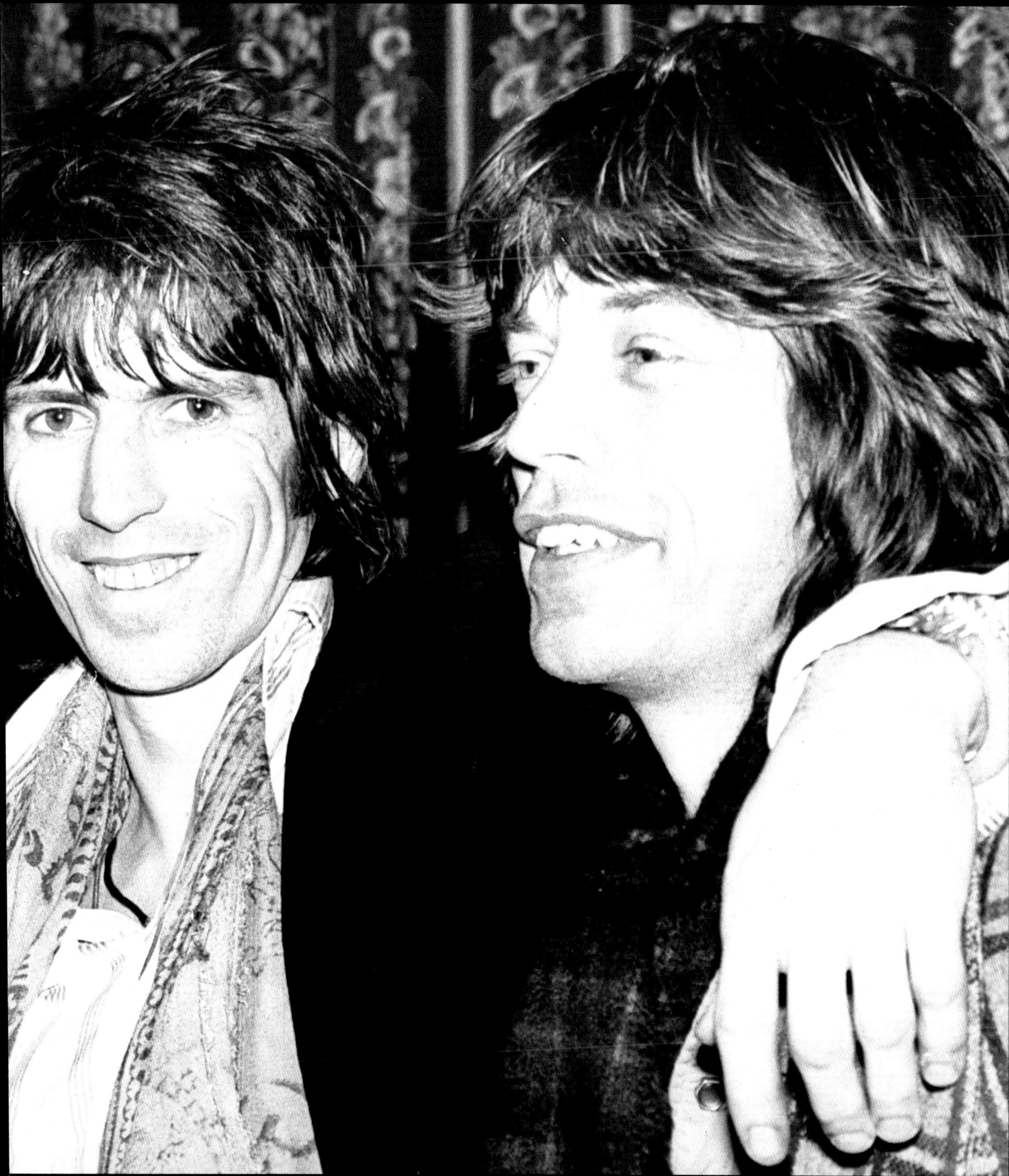

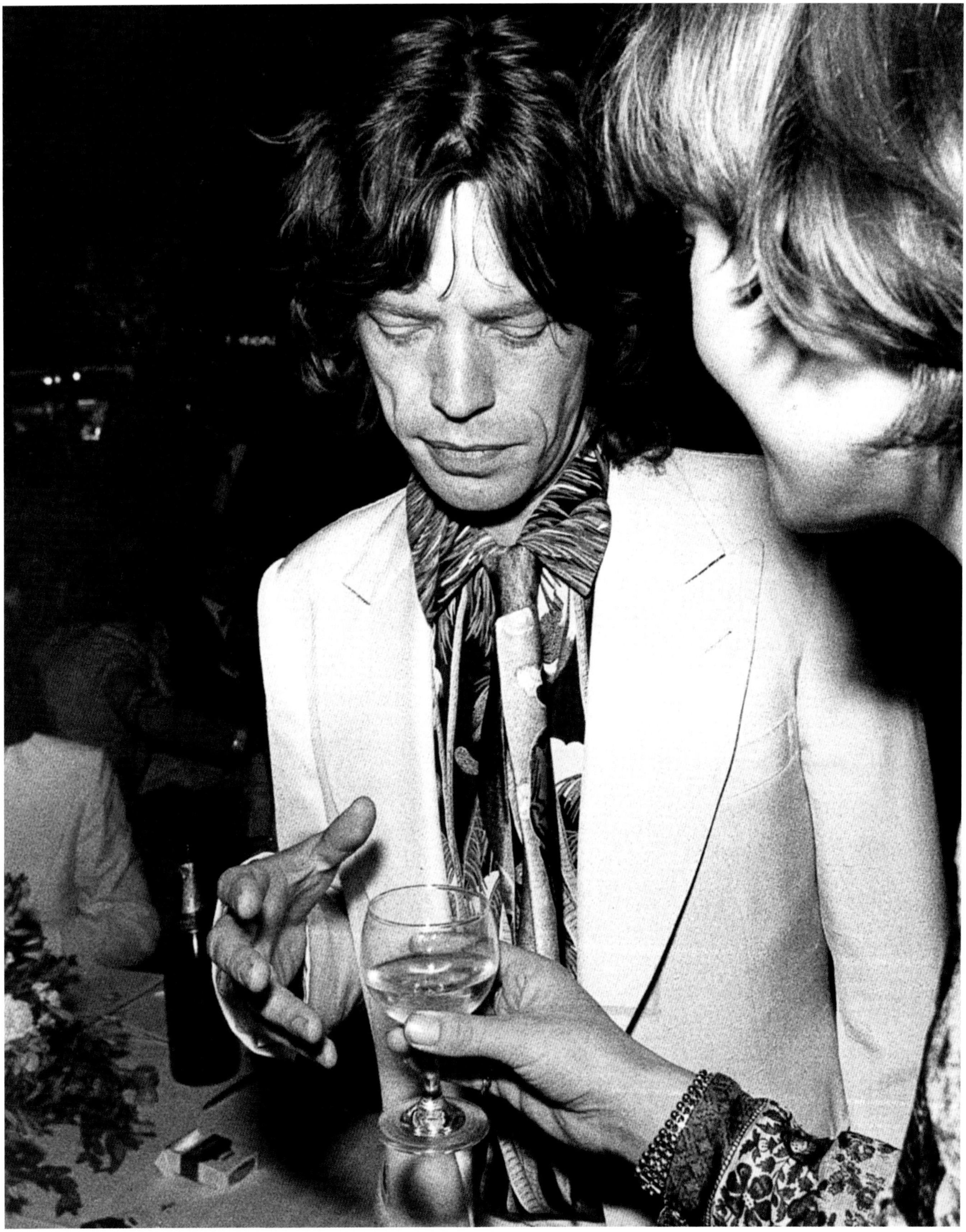

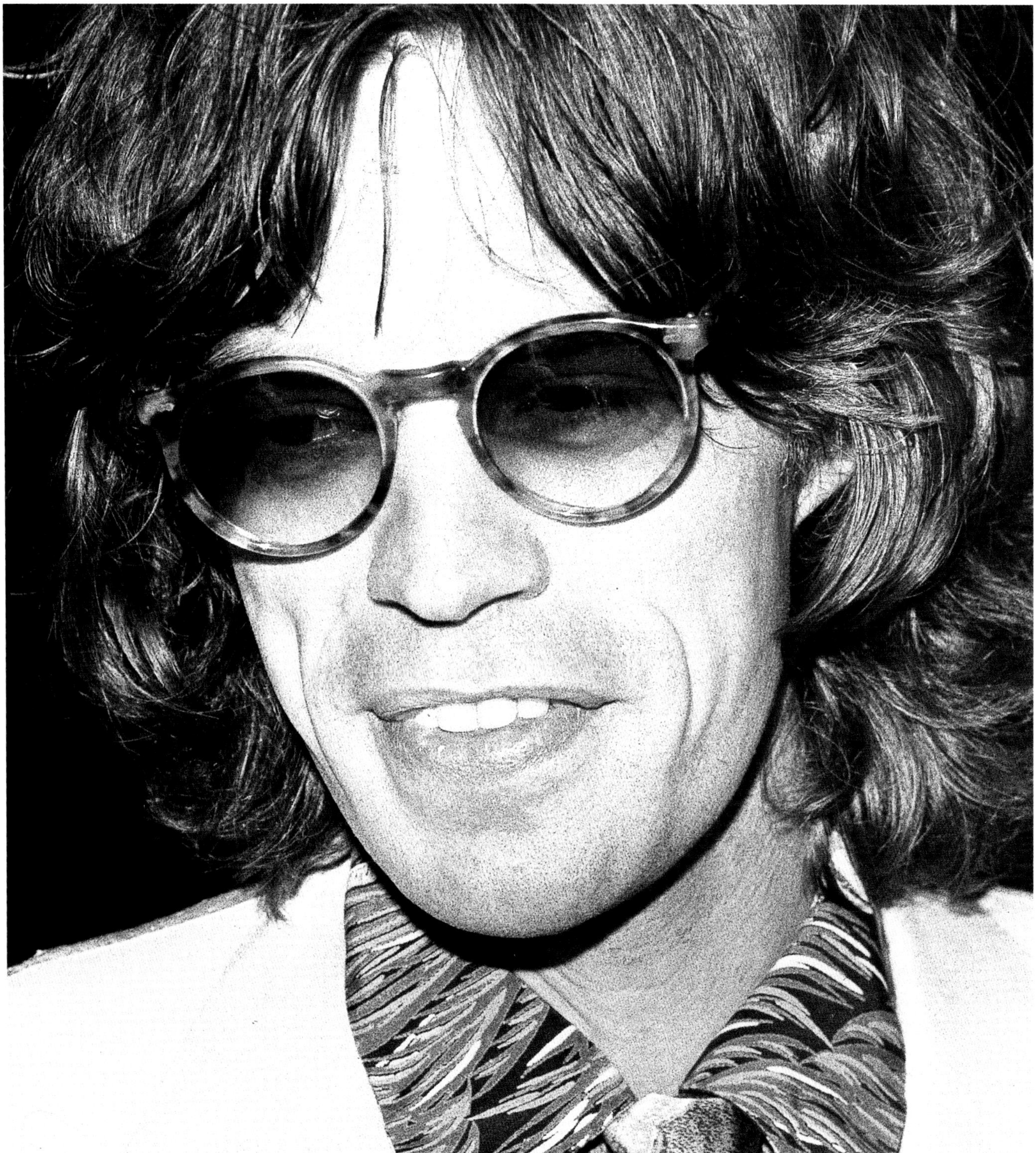

Mick joins the Establishment?

Above and opposite: While Keith continued to live the life of the rebellious rock star, Mick joined the cream of London society at the Bond Street Jubilee Ball in Berkeley Square, marking the Queen's Silver Jubilee, on 7 July 1977. Bianca is not with him, although they are still together, despite persistent rumours about Bianca's friendships with Warren Beatty and David Bowie.

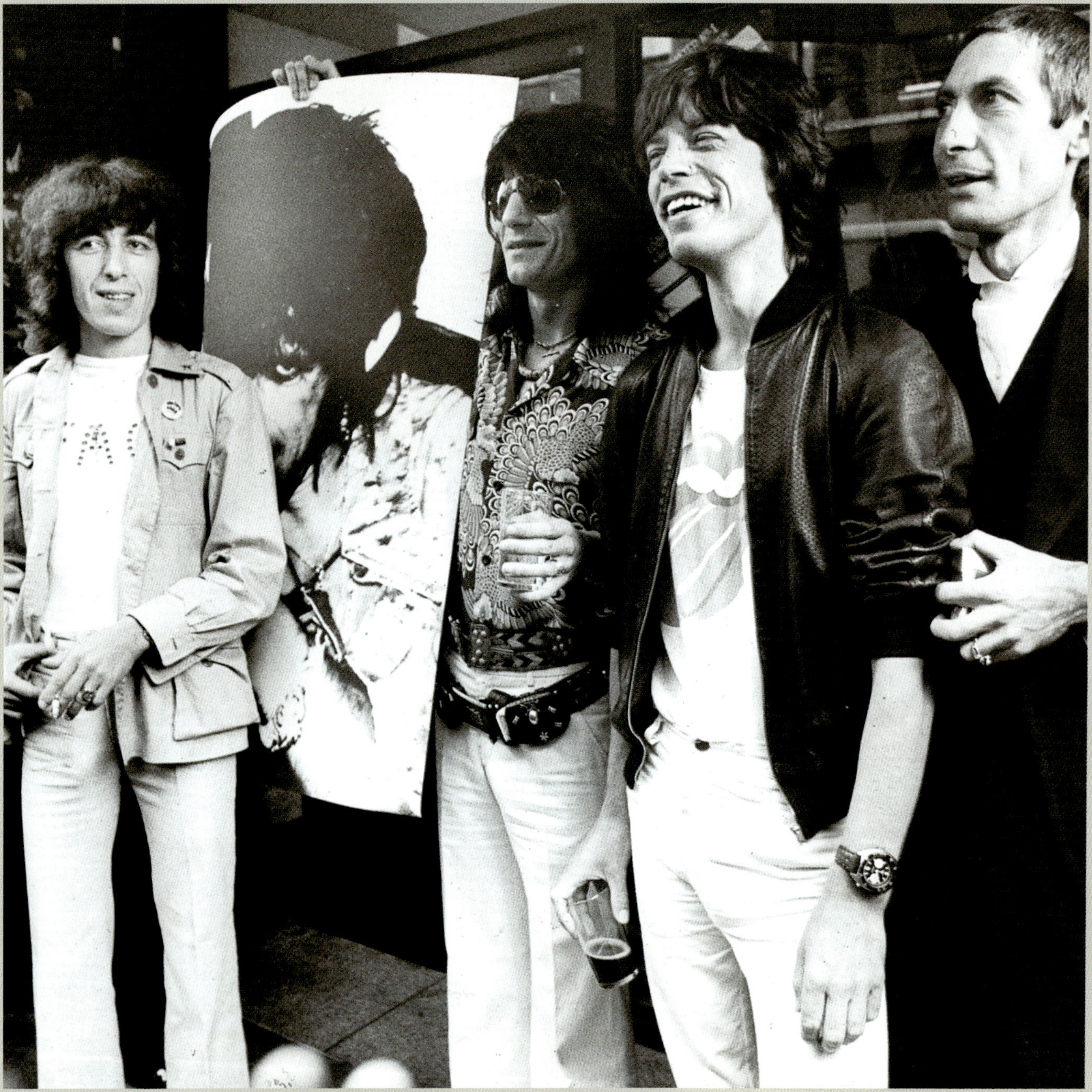

Keith faces serious charges

Above: Ronnie Wood holds aloft an enlarged photograph of Keith Richard, who was unable to attend the launch of the band's album, *Love You Live*, at London's Marquee club in the summer of 1977. Keith was in the United States undergoing rehabilitation therapy for drug dependency. A few months earlier Keith and Anita were arrested at Toronto Airport and charged with possession of drugs found in one of Anita's 28 pieces of luggage. Some days later quantities of drugs were found in their hotel room and Keith was charged with trafficking, with a potential penalty of life imprisonment. The whole future of the band was in jeopardy.

Opposite: At the Marquee Mick denied that he and Bianca were having problems, and said they had no intention of splitting. However, two months later, he headed off to Morocco with Texan model Jerry Hall, until recently the girlfriend of Bryan Ferry, the lead singer in Roxy Music.

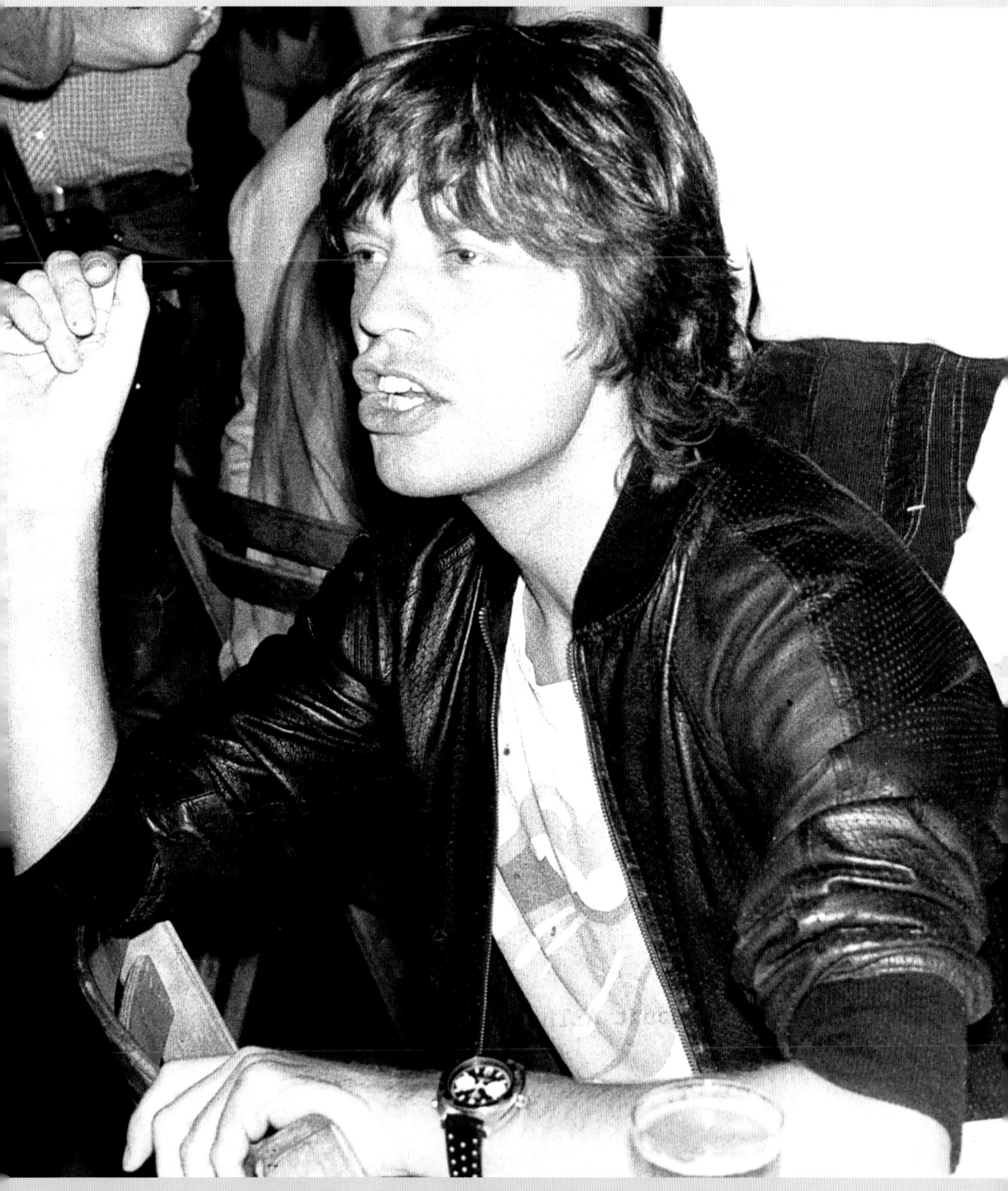

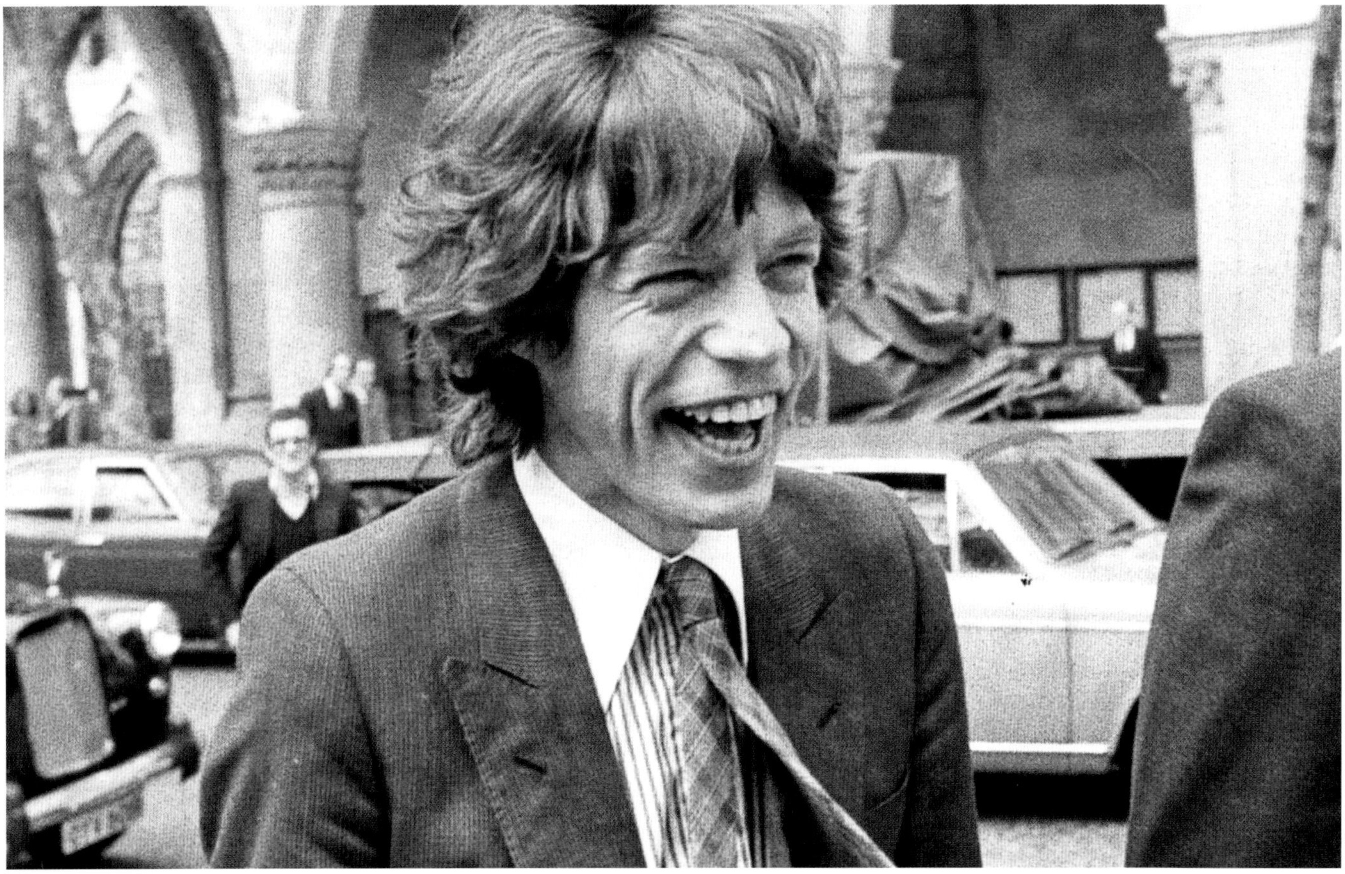

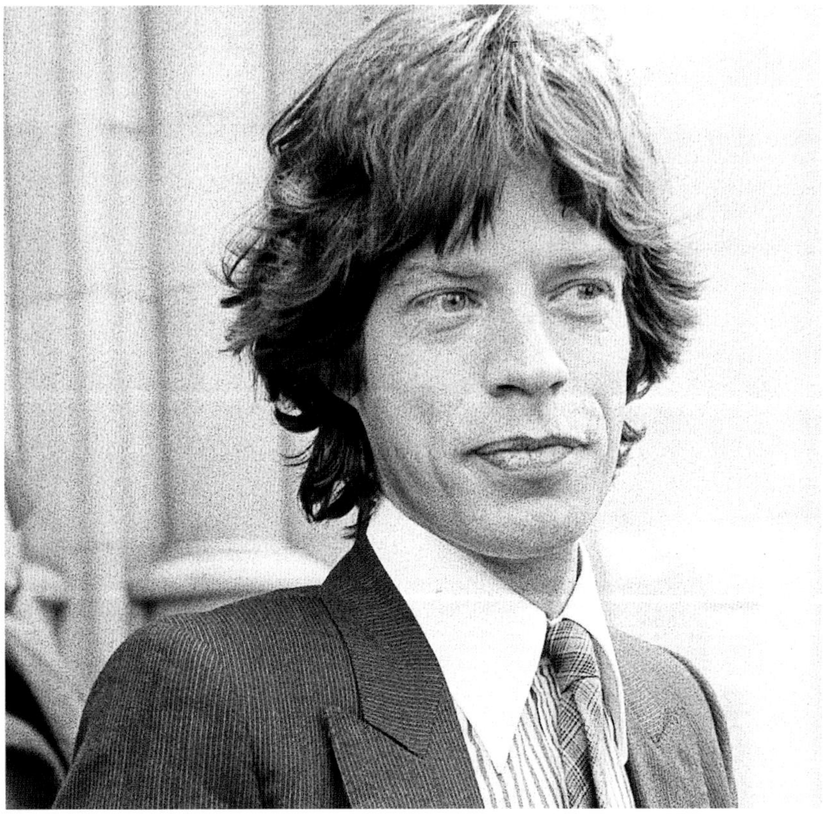

Bianca's divorce proceedings

Above and left: Mick Jagger, photographed on 3 May 1979, outside the High Court in London where his preliminary divorce proceedings are under way. Bianca would have preferred to have the case heard in America, where the financial settlement might have been more generous towards her.

While Mick was in court dealing with his divorce, Keith was still involved in legal processes in Toronto. Having been given a one-year suspended prison sentence, he was now fighting an appeal against the leniency of the sentence. Keen to prove there was more to him than bad publicity, he allowed Barbara Charone to write his biography – the first Stone to do so. The ties between Keith and Anita were weakening. Further strain was put on their relationship when Anita was arrested after a teenage boy shot himself in her bed.

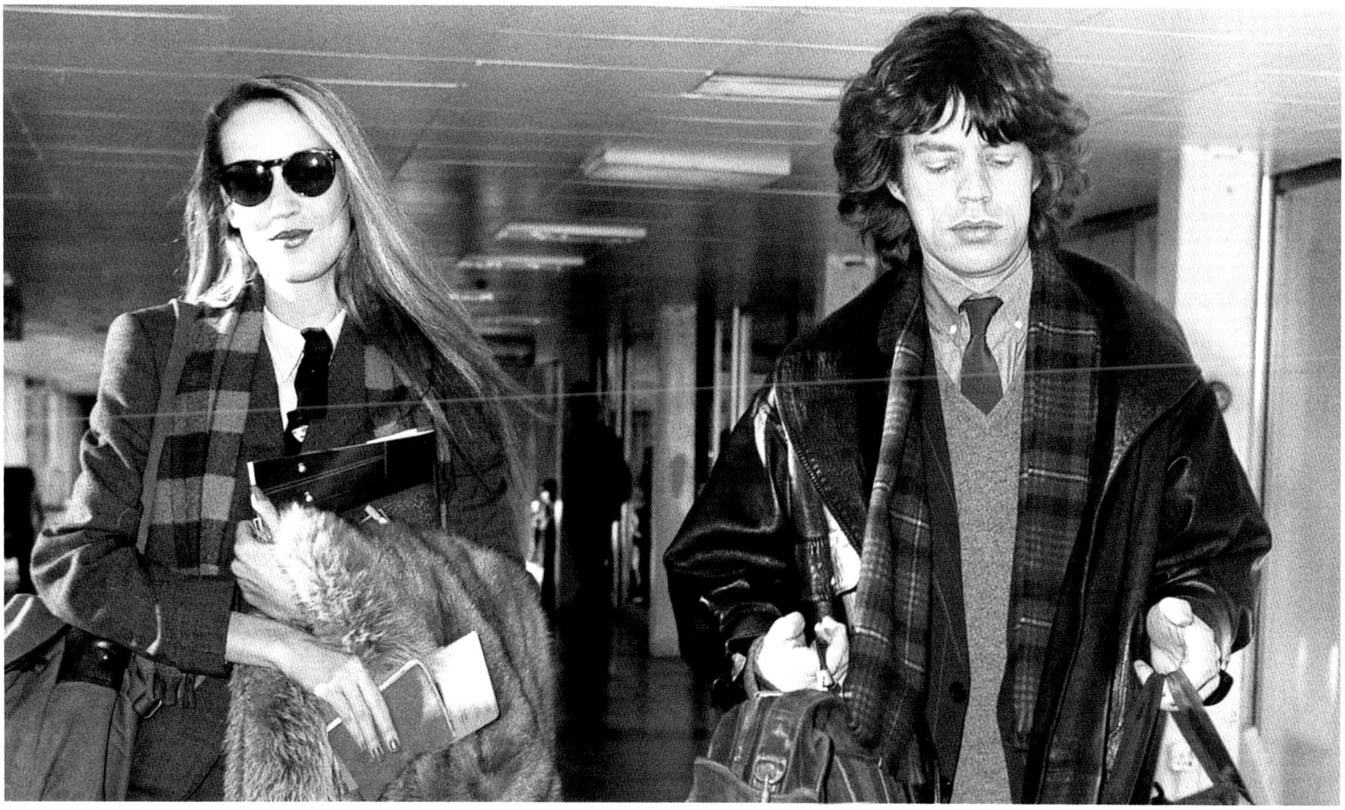

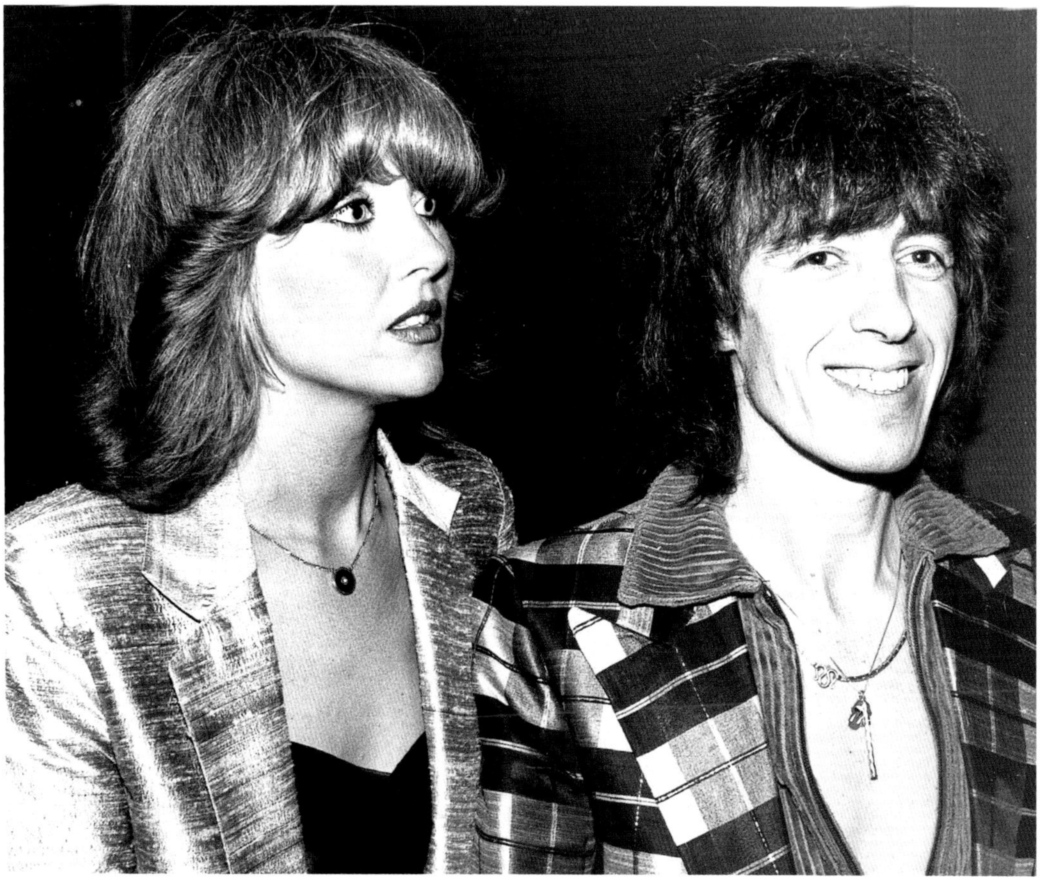

Mick's new love

Above: Mick Jagger and new love Jerry Hall at Heathrow Airport in March 1978 en route for New York. Bianca had filed for divorce on 14 May. Jagger was not the only one with marriage problems – on 19 March Krissie Wood filed for divorce from Ronnie, citing Jo Howard in her petition.

Left: Bill and Astrid still look to be a solid partnership at the opening of a 'tri-sexual' nightclub in London.

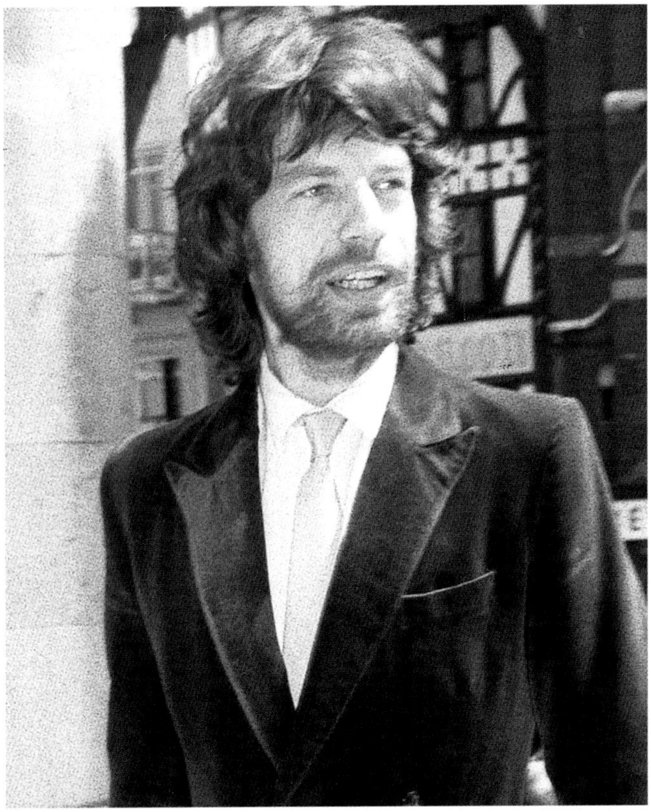

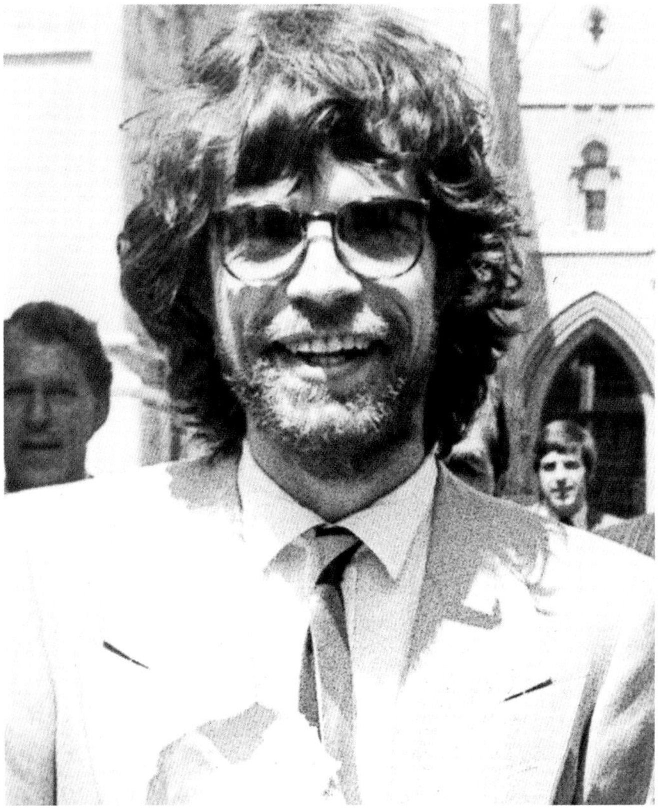

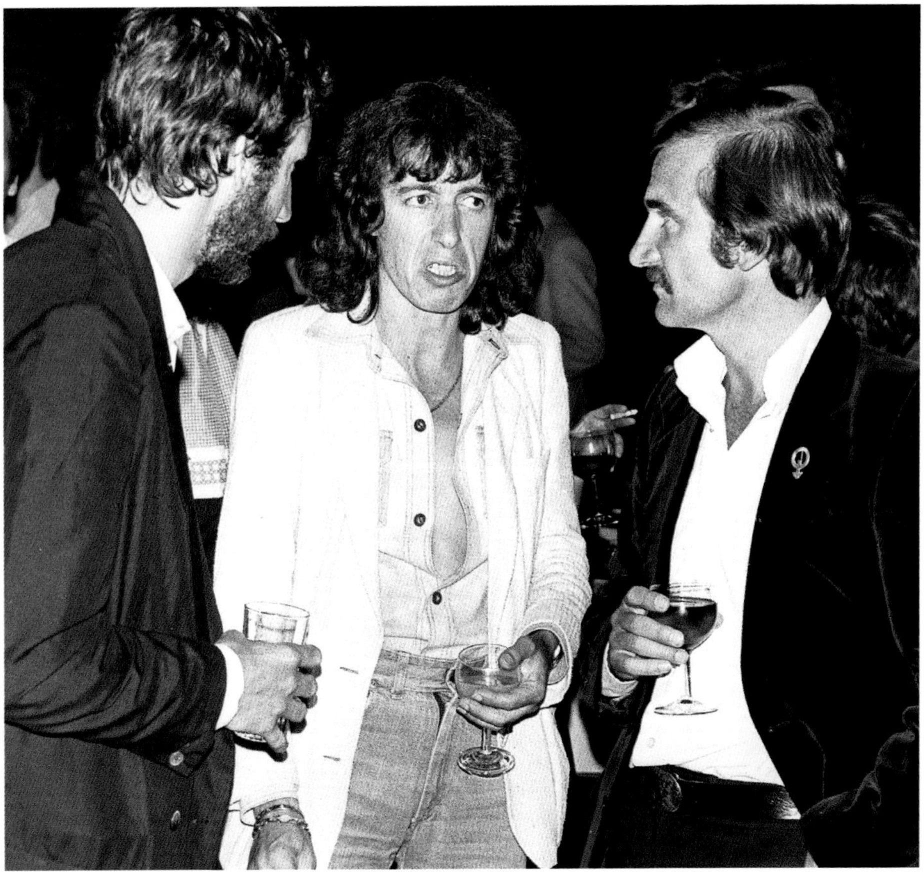

Some Girls sells 7 million

Above left: Despite looking relaxed, Mick Jagger was unable to comment about how things were going in the complicated matter of his divorce and the custody of seven-year-old daughter Jade.

Above right: Mick looks cheerful as he takes a lunchtime stroll outside the court on 3 July 1979.

Left: Bill Wyman in May 1979. The Stones had just given their only live performance of the year in Toronto, arranged by Keith Richards to meet his recent sentencing stipulation. But they did release *Some Girls*, recorded in 1978 despite all the legal difficulties. It was both a commercial and critical success, selling / milllon copies in 1979.

Opposite: The publicity-shy Charlie Watts sitting comfortably, doing what he likes and knows best. In the gaps between recording and touring with the Stones, Charlie pursued other musical interests. Rocket 88, the band led by Charlie and Ian Stewart, released a live record of a concert in Germany.

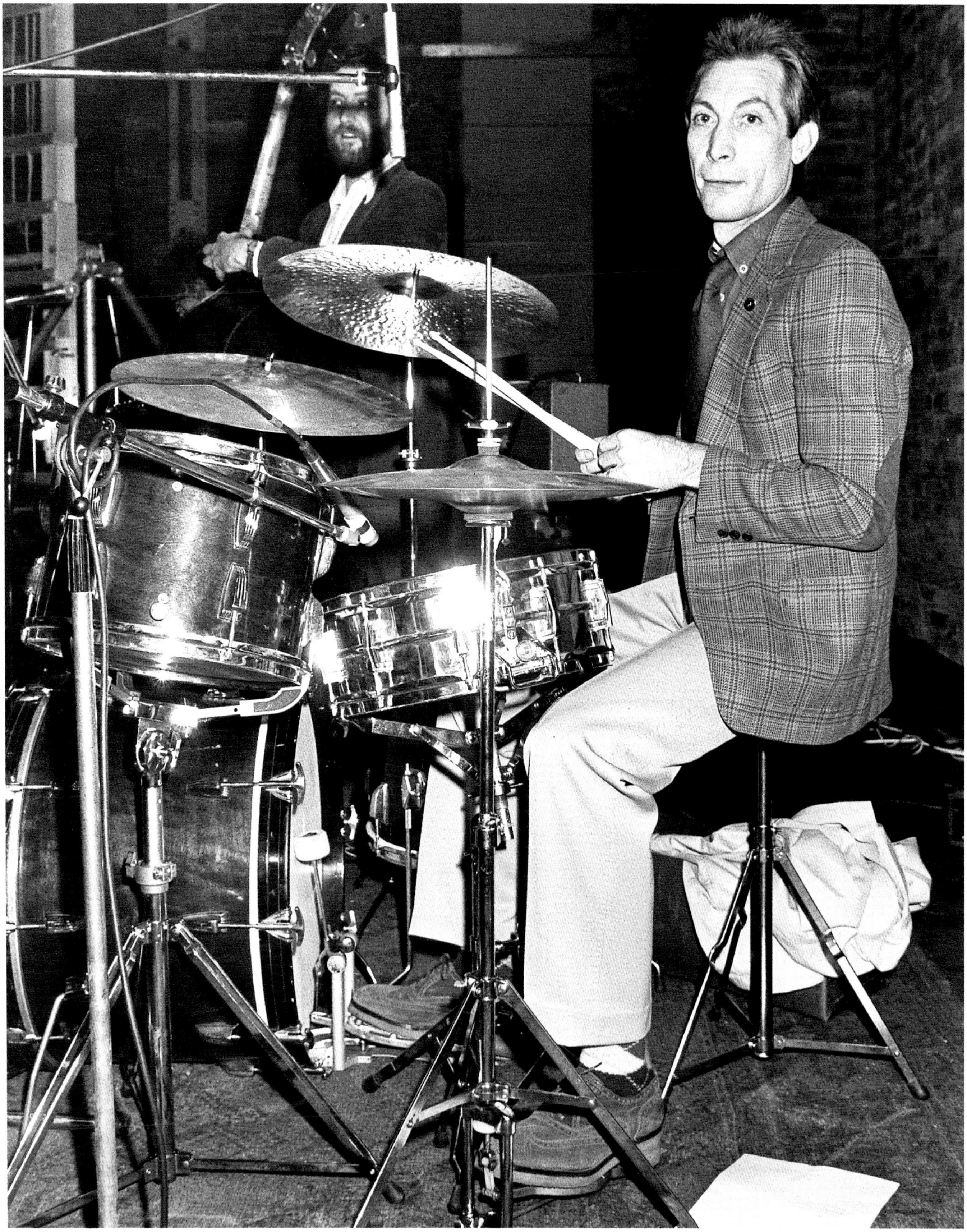

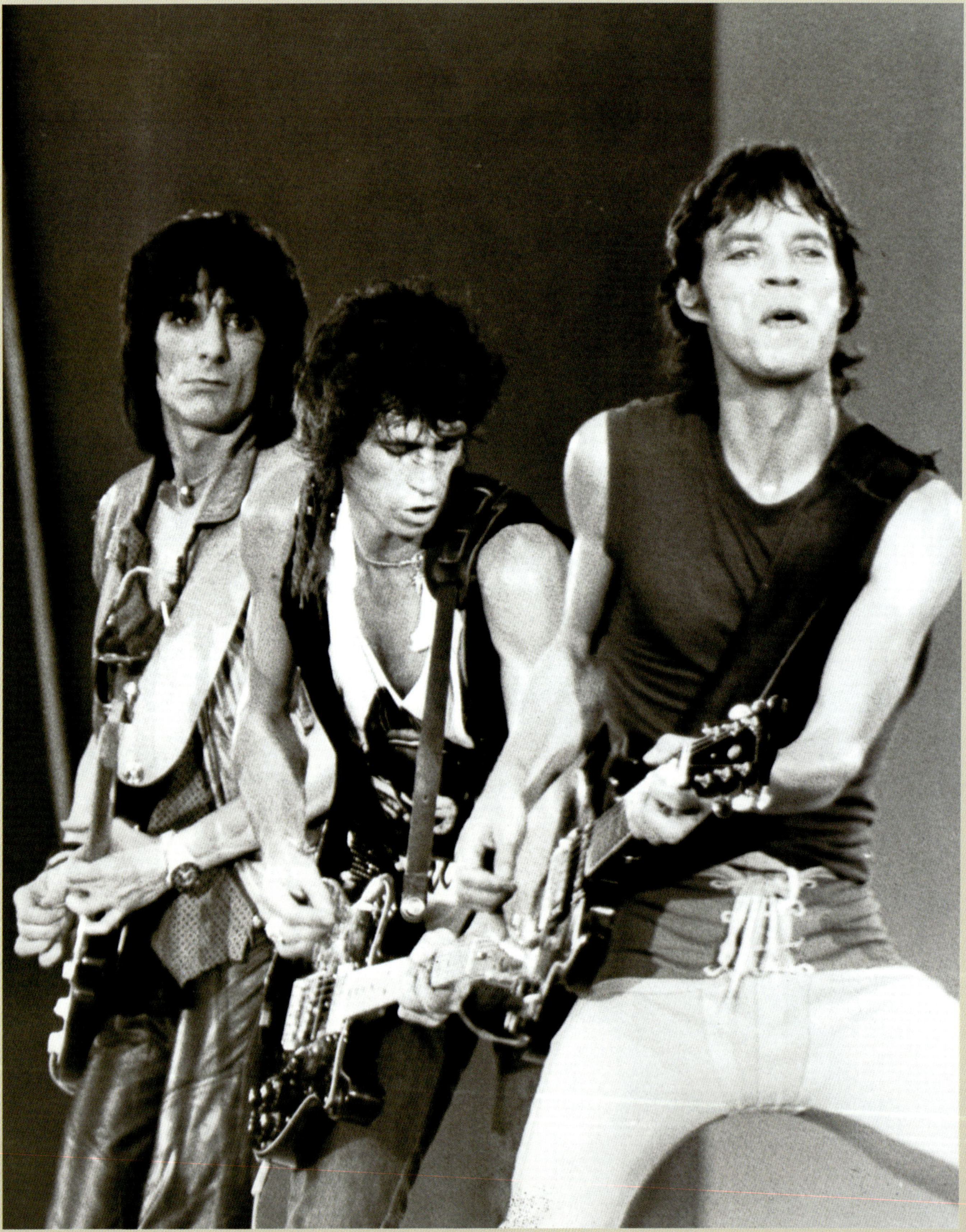

CHAPTER THREE

Emotional Rescues

The Rolling Stones were more or less intact as the 1980s beckoned. But the axis of pop music had shifted again, with New Romantics and bands like ABC, Spandau Ballet and Soft Cell poised to carry the torch through this decade. Even though The Rolling Stones had confounded critics, overcome personal troubles and survived to flaunt their 'trademark' of wide, slack lips on every piece of promotional material, they may have struggled to remain both men of wealth and taste *and* ageing rebels. Words like 'veterans' and 'survivors' seemed unflattering. But more than one generation had grown up to a Rolling Stones soundtrack. The band were still rocking, and so were the fans.

Bill told the *Daily Express* in February 1980 that he would leave the Stones in September 1982, the band's 20th anniversary, the year that Charlie would profess to hate rock 'n' roll and to dislike being a full-time Stone. Also in February 1980, Ronnie and new partner Jo Howard were arrested for possession of cocaine. The charges were dropped when it was established that the drug had been planted. Could some of the Stones be considering a calmer way of life?

Increasingly, Bill and Charlie 'guested' on recordings and made appearances with jazz and blues musicians. They also scored music for mainstream films. But Mick remarked later in 1980 that he might remain a rock 'n' roller forever. The band's logo of those swollen lips with the sensuously lolling tongue had already become a design icon. The Stones, to some extent, had become a simple branded business – albeit a massive one.

Mick's interest in film was waning; he abandoned plans to star in Werner Herzog's (later celebrated) film *Fitzcarraldo*, and to produce and act in another film. He also declined a reportedly huge sum of money to appear in the American TV drama *Dallas*. His relationship with Jerry survived separations and stories about his affairs with actresses and models, and was one of rock 'n' roll's most enduring (and productive) unions: Elizabeth Scarlett, the first of their four children, was born in March 1984.

Keith seemed to remain the sole unreconstructed rocker. His relationship with Anita Pallenberg was over, and he married Patti Hansen, an American actress and model, on 18 December 1983 – his 40th birthday. He remained a devoted father, which called for some stability and responsibility. However, he had remarked in 1981 that he'd be playing rock 'n' roll in a wheelchair – it was what he did for a living.

The band's 1981 single 'Start Me Up', cut from *Tattoo You*, went to the UK No.1 slot, and their 1982 tour was their most successful ever. But Mick and Keith were approaching 40 in 1983, and incredulous and faintly patronizing things were said and written about superannuated rock stars. Needless to say, the Stones were untroubled – the facts spoke for themselves. During an American tour that year, the band filled venues with up to 90,000 capacity. Polls, such as those among *Rolling Stone* readers, kept voting them best band, Mick best vocalist and their albums best of the year. It has been suggested that the energy Mick spent during any one performance was comparable to running 20 miles.

Mindful perhaps of a landmark birthday, or simply being in reflective mode, he began a programme that included running, rowing and training in the martial arts. He also accepted a large amount of money to write his memoirs – which have never been completed or published, since he famously claimed that he couldn't remember enough about the early years to tell the story. It was also said that Bill declined to assist because he was saving up the best bits for his own story. In May 1984, it was reported that Mick was considering returning his advance. Soon after, Wyman was reputed to have trumped Jagger by signing an even bigger financial deal for his own diaries.

Around this time members of the Stones became involved in fundraising. Bill and Charlie supported ARMS, the multiple sclerosis charity, and the band performed before the Prince and Princess of Wales at a Prince's Trust gala in September 1983. Then it was announced that Mick was sponsoring Britain's gymnasts for the 1984 Los Angeles Olympics, partly to acknowledge the value of his father's work as a PE teacher. Charlie played in Edinburgh to raise money for famine-blighted Ethiopia. Yet the band's power to outrage was undiminished. In November the BBC banned a video for 'Undercover Of The Night' for its depiction of a terrorist murder. Mick maintained that the film was a protest against totalitarian regimes. The song went to No.11 in Britain before Christmas 1983 in spite of – possibly because of – these constraints.

In spring 1984, Bill was reported in the *Sun* newspaper as having made critical comments about two fellow band members. A week later he denied it. In the summer, as Mick prepared for the release of his solo album *She's The Boss*, he dismissed rumours that the band was disintegrating. He said individual projects did not threaten the Stones' future and that there was enthusiastic planning rather than dissent.

Simultaneous London and Philadelphia Live Aid concerts took place in July 1985. Mick sang in the United States with Daryl Hall and John Oates, and with Tina Turner. Ronnie and Keith joined Bob Dylan later, and Mick also joined David Bowie in a rendition of 'Dancing In The Street', which became a major hit single and video classic. It was a nice welcome to the world for James Leroy Augustine, Mick and Jerry's first son, born on 28 August. But 1985 closed sadly, with the death in December of Ian Stewart, who had been the heart and spine of the Stones as driver, sometime pianist and wise friend since the start. The band played a memorial gig for him in London in the new year.

Amid new rumours of a split, particularly of disagreements between Mick and Keith, the latest album, *Dirty Work*, made a respectable No.3 in the UK charts in April 1986. But the Glimmer Twins did sometimes seem to be in separate cities, and other members of the band were increasingly interested in solo projects – especially Charlie with his jazz orchestra. Attention was diverted from this by 16-year-old Mandy Smith's revelations about her affair with 49-year-old Bill. Altogether, 1987 was not a vintage year for the Stones.

In January 1988 Ronnie Wood opened a nightclub, Woody's, on Miami's South Beach, designed by Barbara Hulanicki, the genius behind Biba. Sadly the club didn't stay open long because of complaints about noise. The band may not have collected quite so many awards for being best something-or-other at the new year's music business polls, but this didn't break any hearts: tickets for Mick's forthcoming Japanese shows had been an instant sell-out. By May 1988 there was something of an armistice when all five Rolling Stones convened for the first time in two years at a London hotel. They agreed that they would work together again, in the studio and on tour. *Rolling Stone* magazine would shortly announced that '(I Can't Get No) Satisfaction' was the best single of the past 25 years, which may well have provided some motivation for the band to continue.

Mick had the separate satisfaction of seeing Jerry reprise the Marilyn Monroe role in a New Jersey stage production of the play *Bus Stop*. They celebrated his 45th birthday on her first night. While still planning solo gigs, Mick and Keith met in New York to further discuss and strengthen the Stones' future. Mick also announced the following month (in Australia where he was touring) that he would retire when he was 50.

In the autumn Keith, whose live solo gigs had been cheerful (if unremarkable) affairs, spoke to *Rolling Stone* about his relationship with Mick. He may well have alluded to Mick having a Peter Pan complex and controlling tendencies, but he also stressed that Mick had always stood by him as a faithful friend throughout the years. Finally, he confirmed that the Stones would soon be rocking together again. So the band seemed to be in harmony once more. They talked of their joint future together in New York in 1989 and in meetings between two or three of them. Talk of reconciliation wasn't idle chit-chat. In March, the Stones signed rock's biggest ever tour deal. They also gathered in Montserrat in May to record.

Fifty-two-year-old Bill managed to find time during the sessions to phone a marriage proposal to 19-year-old Mandy. She displayed her Asprey's engagement ring at the launch of Bill's new Kensington restaurant, Sticky Fingers, on 9 May. The restaurant still flourishes. Wedding arrangements were so secret that even Bill's 76-year-old mother didn't know about them. Afterwards she said she was disappointed but not surprised, commenting that he had always been a rebel. A few days later the marriage was blessed in London before a party for 400 guests.

Meanwhile, the new album was mixed. But there were reports that Mick and Charlie were less than happy with each other after a group meeting in Amsterdam. Mick had apparently referred to Charlie as 'my drummer'. Charlie, quite reasonably, responded by referring to Mick as 'my singer'. The squabble seems to have resulted in someone landing face first in a plate of smoked salmon. Nonetheless, plans for the next American tour proceeded.

The tour began in the late summer, including concerts in Toronto to promote a new album, *Steel Wheels*, and single, 'Mixed Emotions'. Almost 20 years after Altamont, some of the Hell's Angel fraternity still bore a grudge about comments Mick was reported to have made about them. He was therefore given round-the-clock security protection. Despite that, the Steel Wheels tour was a sell-out and it became clear that the restless spirit behind the Stones' boast to be the greatest rock 'n' roll band in the world was still as strong as ever.

Previous page: Ronnie, Keith and Mick line up at Wembley.
Below: Mick on stage in New York in 1989.

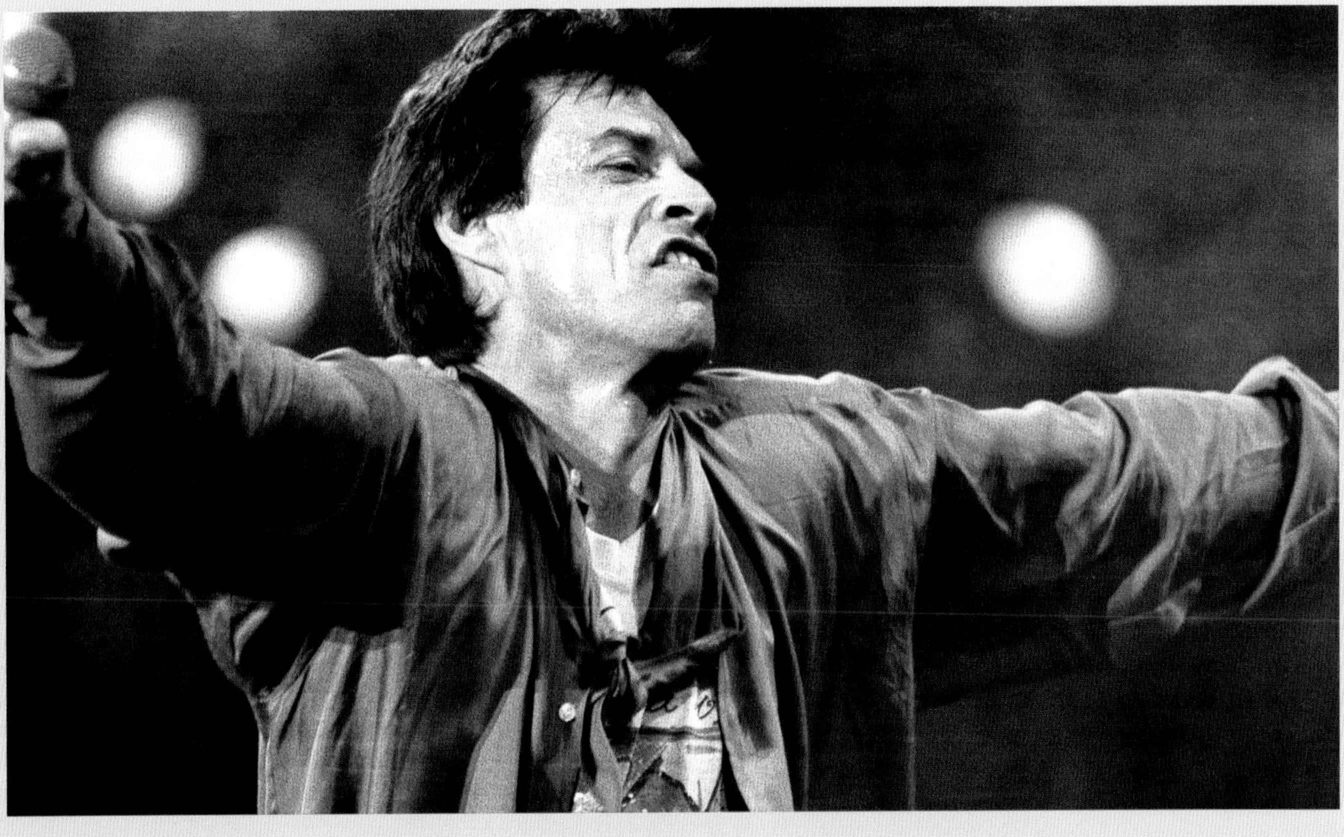

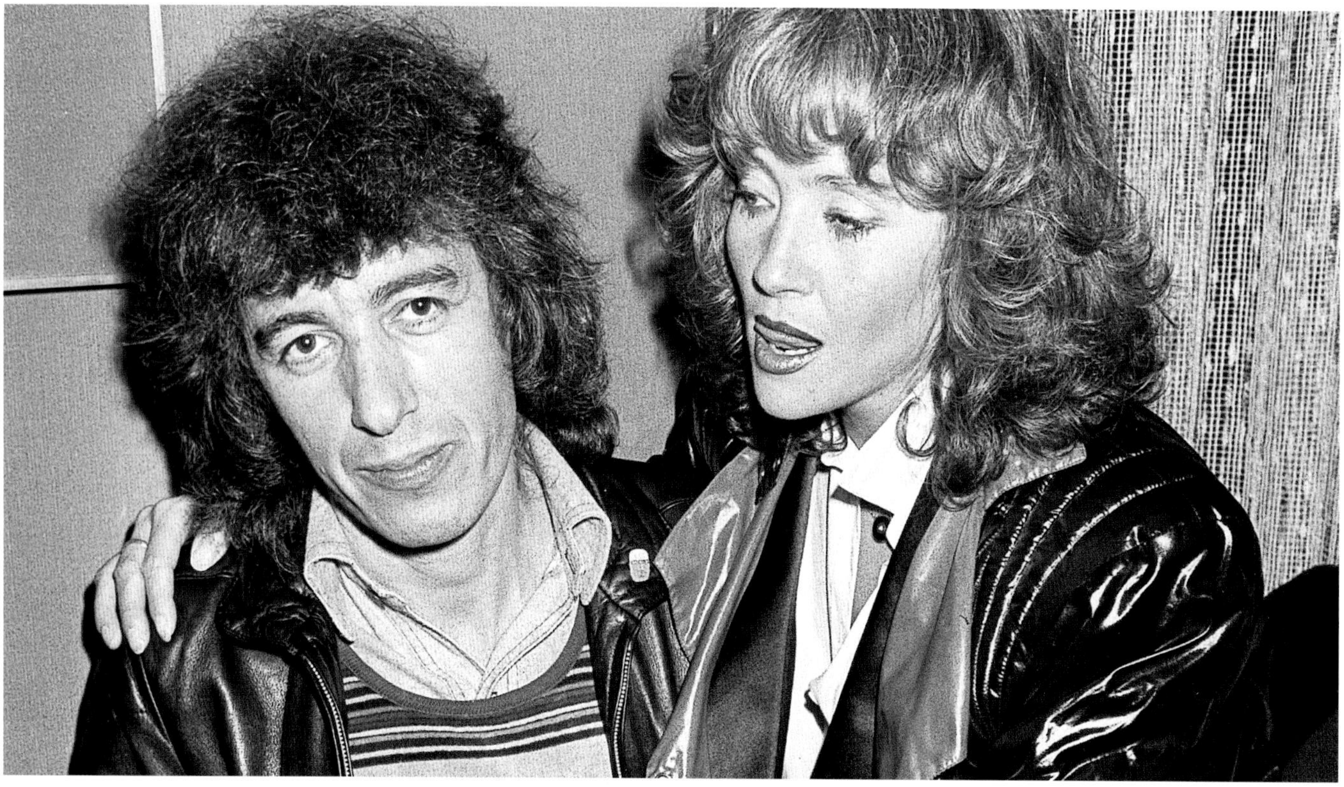

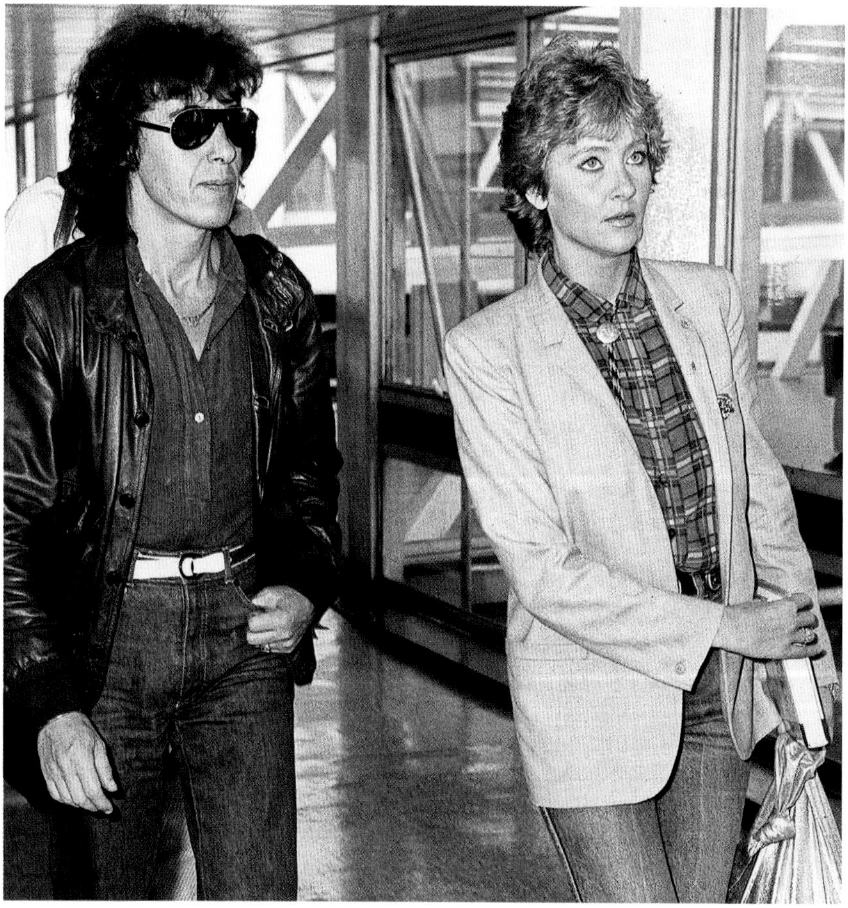

'Je Suis Un Rock Star'

Above: Bill and Astrid on 2 May 1980. Astrid announced with some sorrow that she was considering a split. The couple had weathered many years and she had miscarried several times. They were still together on 6 July 1981 (*left*), despite the reported fragility of their relationship. Bill was busy during the summer of 1981 before the band began the North American tour. There were rumours that he was set to leave the Stones. These were in part fuelled by an interview in which he said he planned to quit in 1982 to coincide with the band's 20th anniversary. In June his solo single 'Je Suis Un Rock Star' was a hit in the UK charts, and he composed music for the film *Green Ice*.

Tattoo You was released in August 1981 and was greeted more enthusiastically than the previous album, *Emotional Rescue*. In fact, *Tattoo You* was more a compilation of tracks originally recorded for *Goats Head Soup*, *Black And Blue*, *Some Girls* and *Emotional Rescue*. Mick Taylor, who left the band in 1974, played guitar on two of the tracks taken from the *Goats Head Soup* sessions.

Opposite: Mick Jagger on stage at Shea Stadium, New York, during a tour of North America.

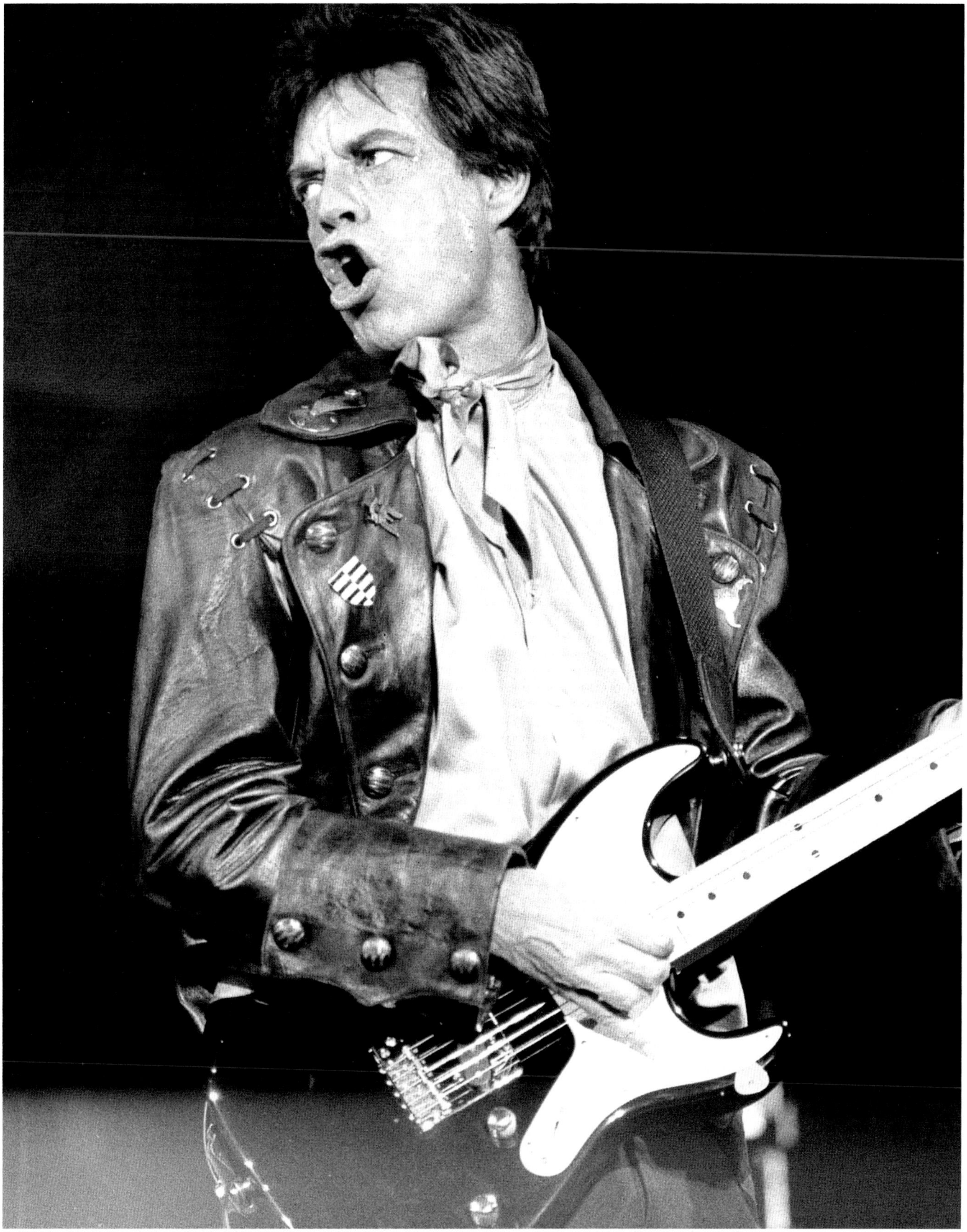

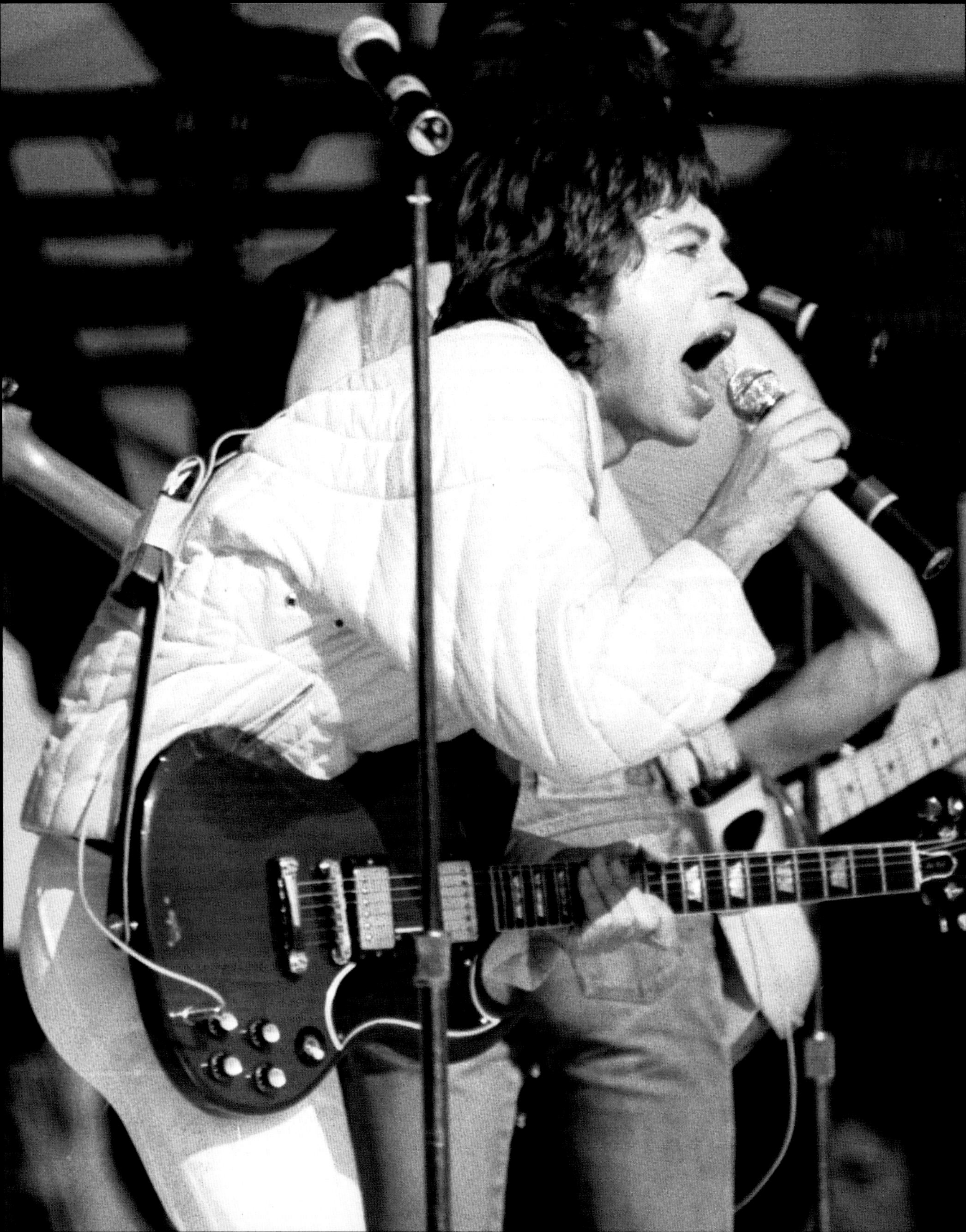

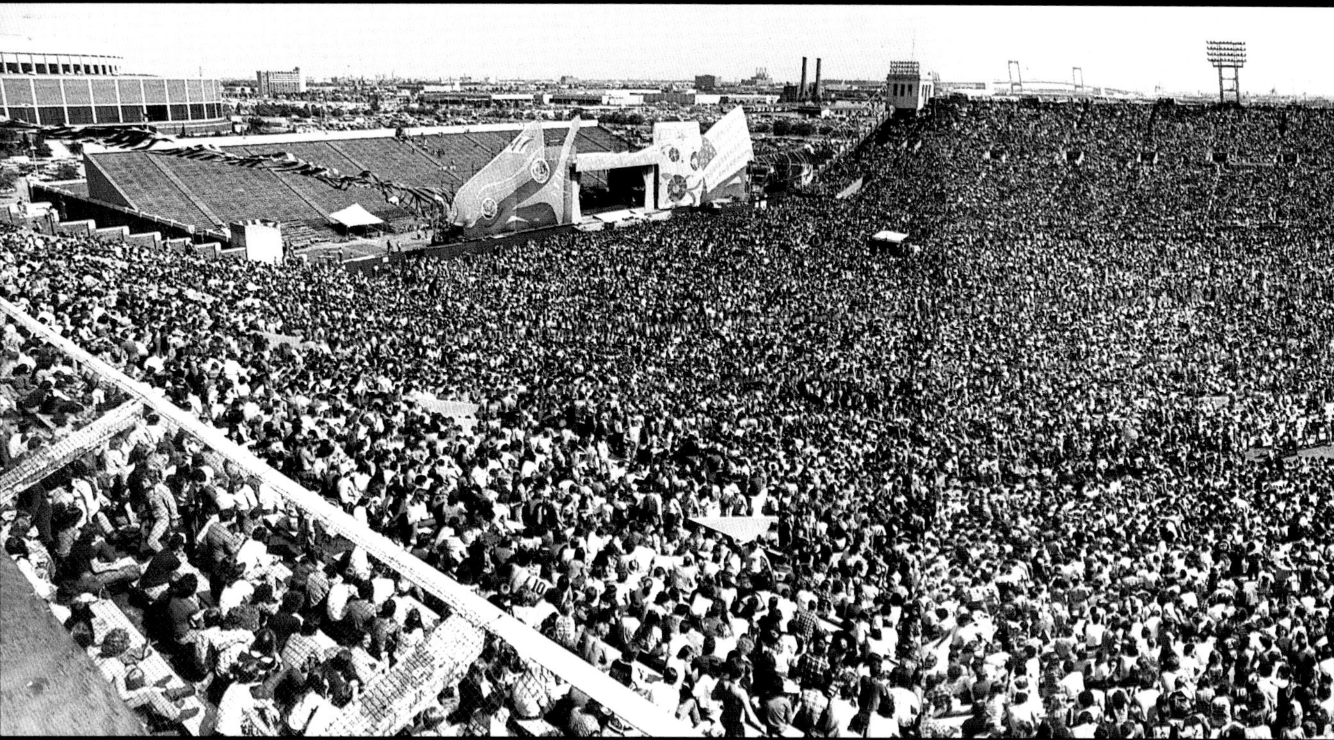

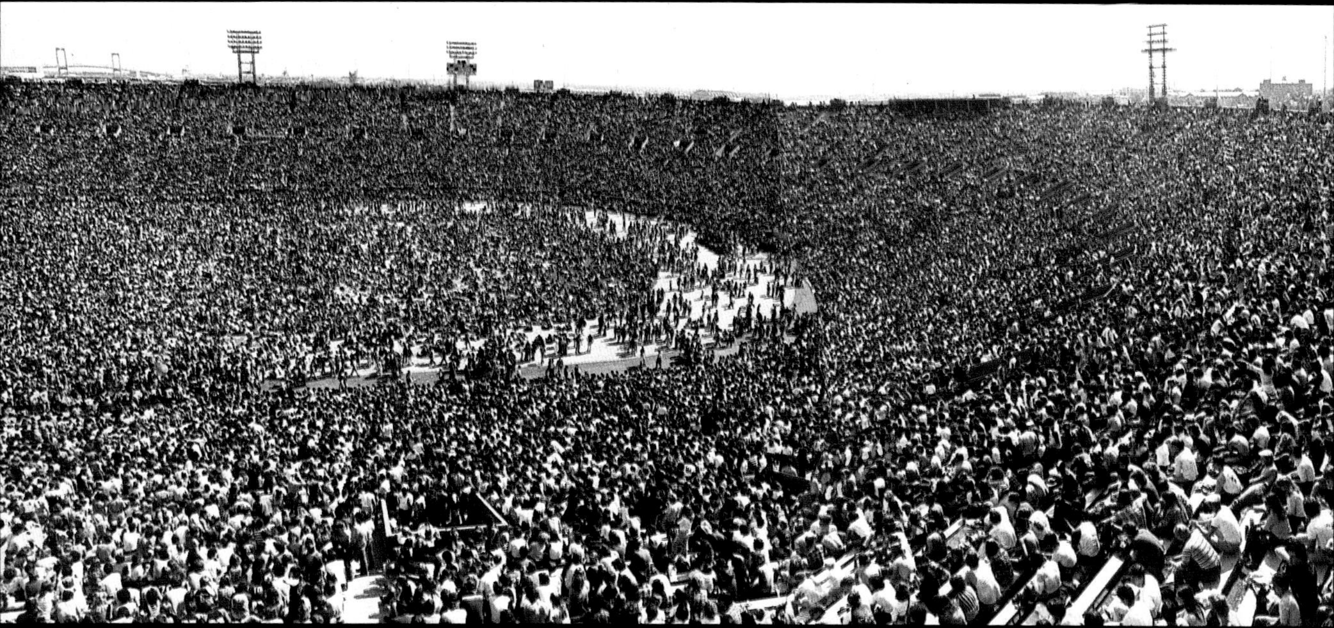

'Start Me Up'

Above: The Rolling Stones opened a North American tour on 25 September 1981 at the JFK Stadium in Philadelphia. Some estimated the crowd to be 90,000 on this blazing day. The band had just released a new single, 'Start Me Up', taken from the *Tattoo You* album. The single sold a million copies in the first week. 'Start Me Up' had been recorded using a reggae beat during the making of *Black And Blue* and was briefly considered for inclusion on *Some Girls*. The version on *Tattoo You* became a classic Stones track in the style of 'Brown Sugar' and provoked an instant response from the fans.

Opposite: Mick leans forward, still wearing a yellow quilted blouson jacket early in the show.

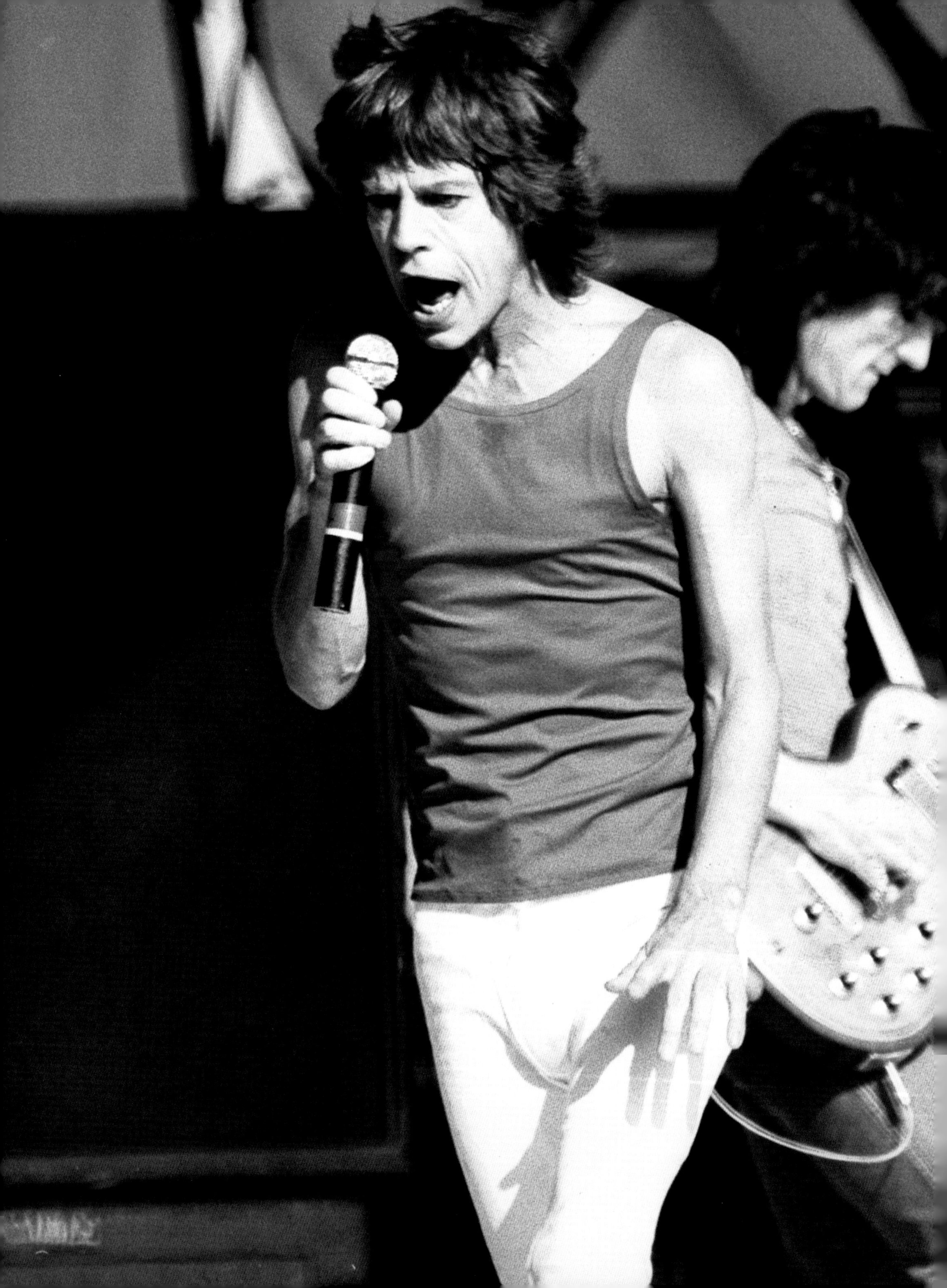

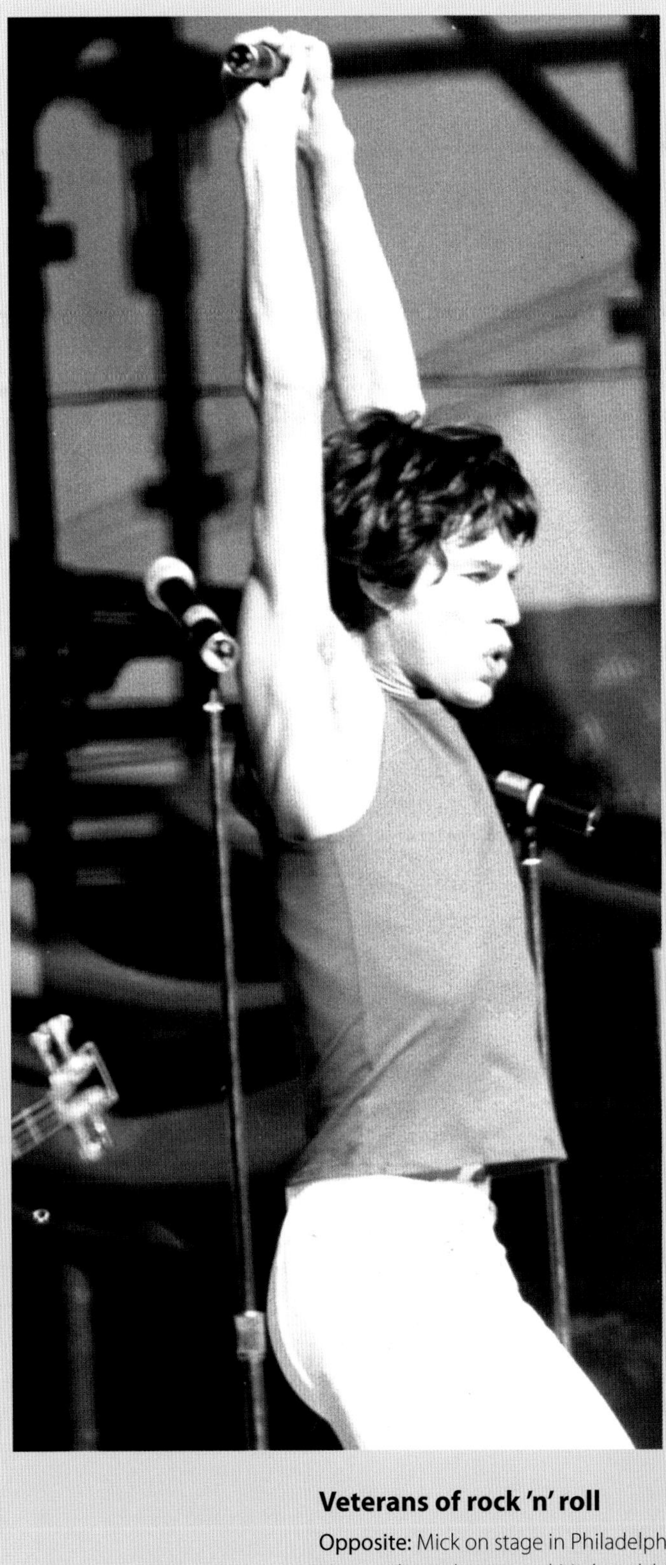

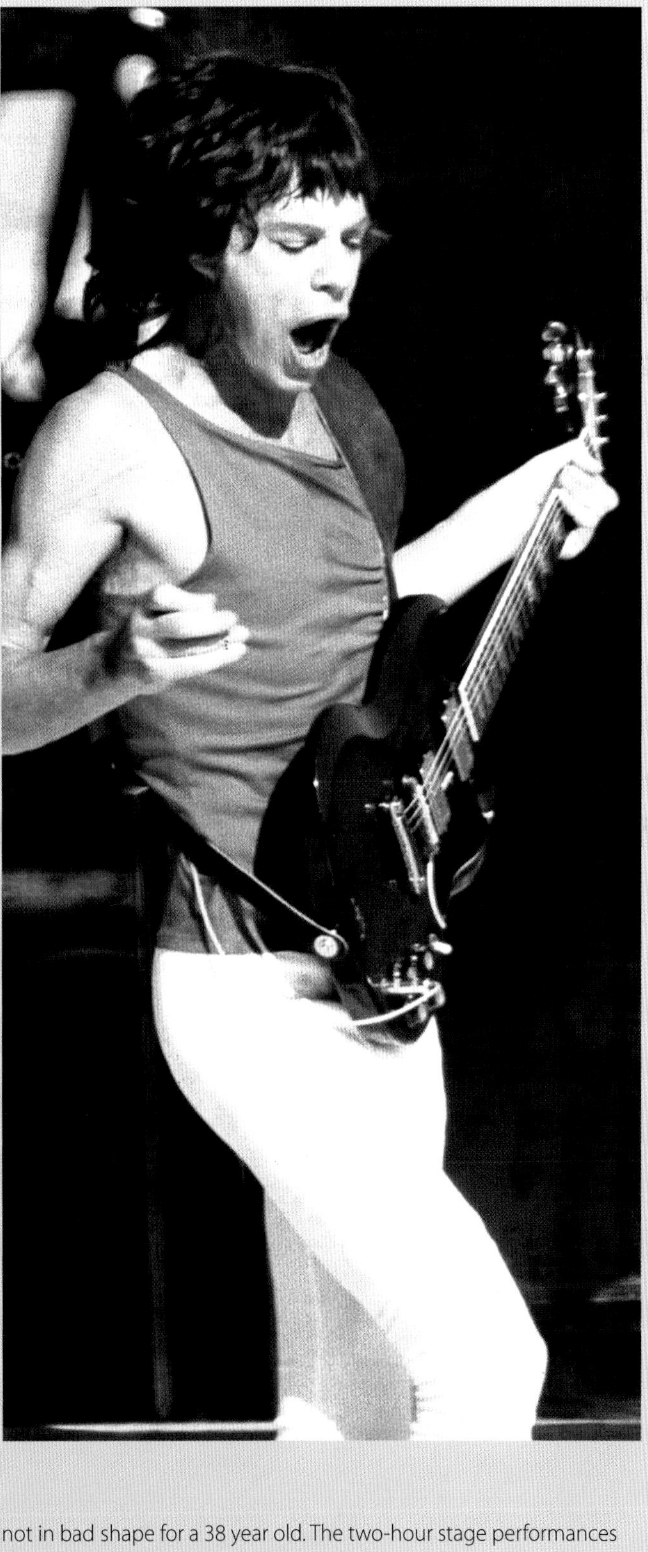

Veterans of rock 'n' roll

Opposite: Mick on stage in Philadelphia – not in bad shape for a 38 year old. The two-hour stage performances were a physical strain and Mick took his preparation seriously, limbering up before he went on stage and running and excercising regularly. Bill Wyman may well be the oldest man in the stadium – he is several years older than the other band members.

Above: Mick whips up all his customary crowd-pulling energy. The tour was another mammoth one, finishing three months later in Virginia.

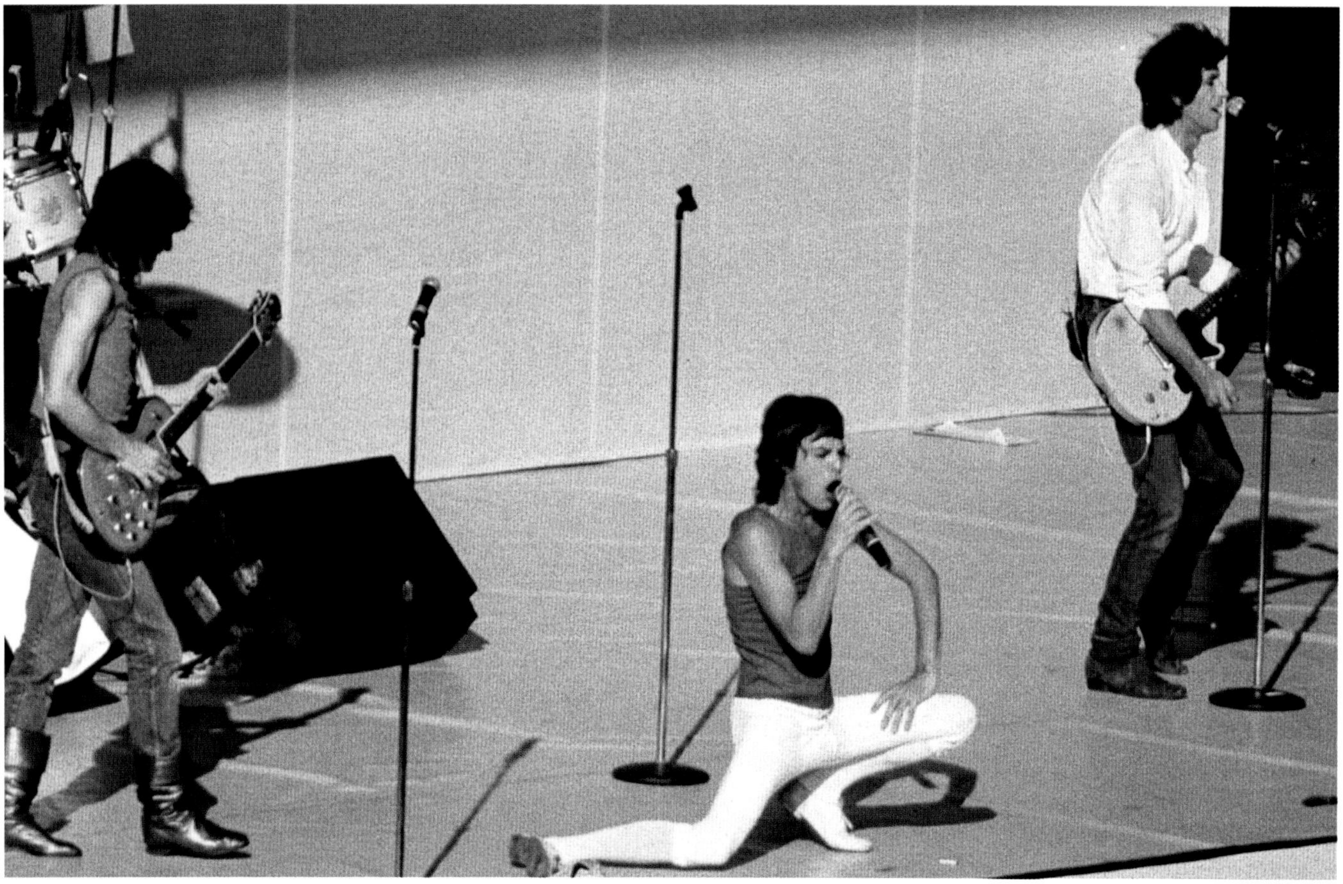

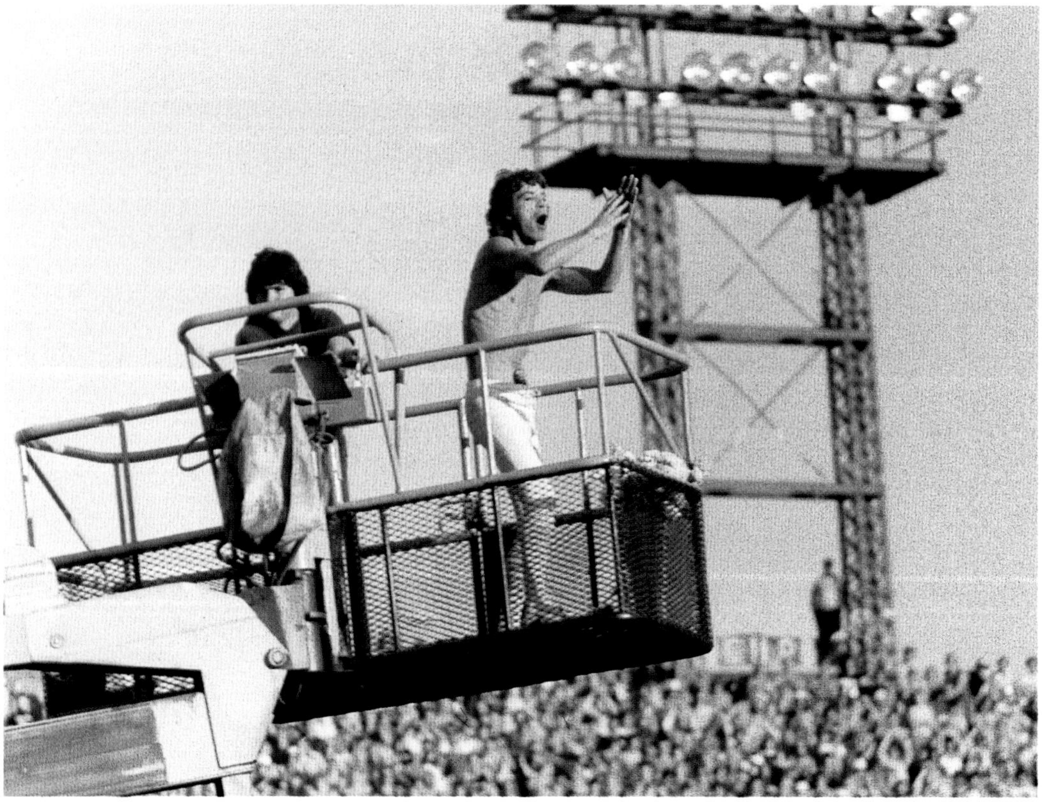

'It's A Gas'

It was estimated that the tour grossed $50 million, including ticket sales, merchandise and TV and film rights. There was also money raised by sponsorship from the Jovan perfume company, which paid to have its name associated with the concerts.

A film was made of the 50-date tour by Hal Ashby. Mick and Keith assisted with the editing.

Left: A long version of 'Jumpin' Jack Flash' is the finale to the show and Mick sings part of it suspended above the crowd.

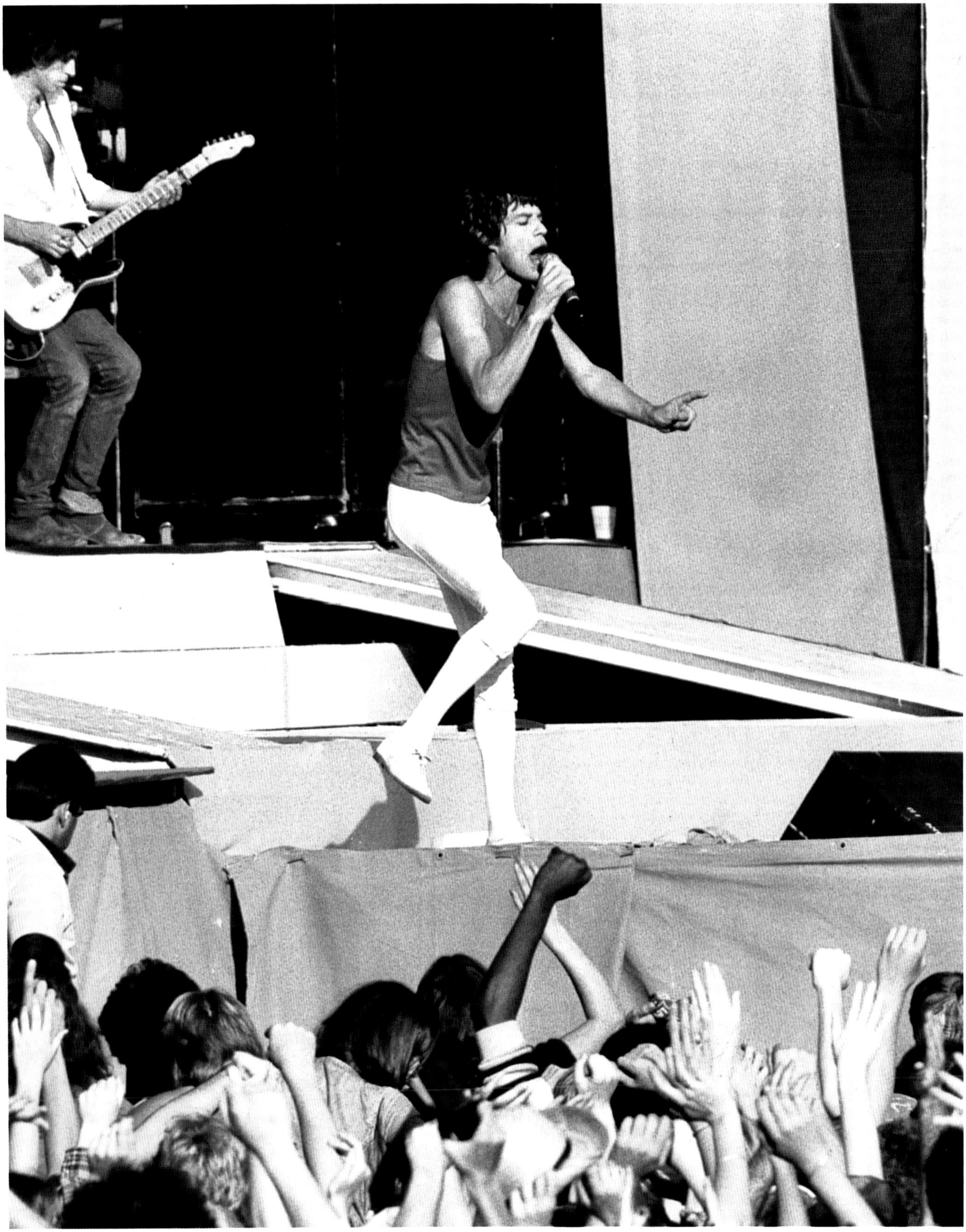

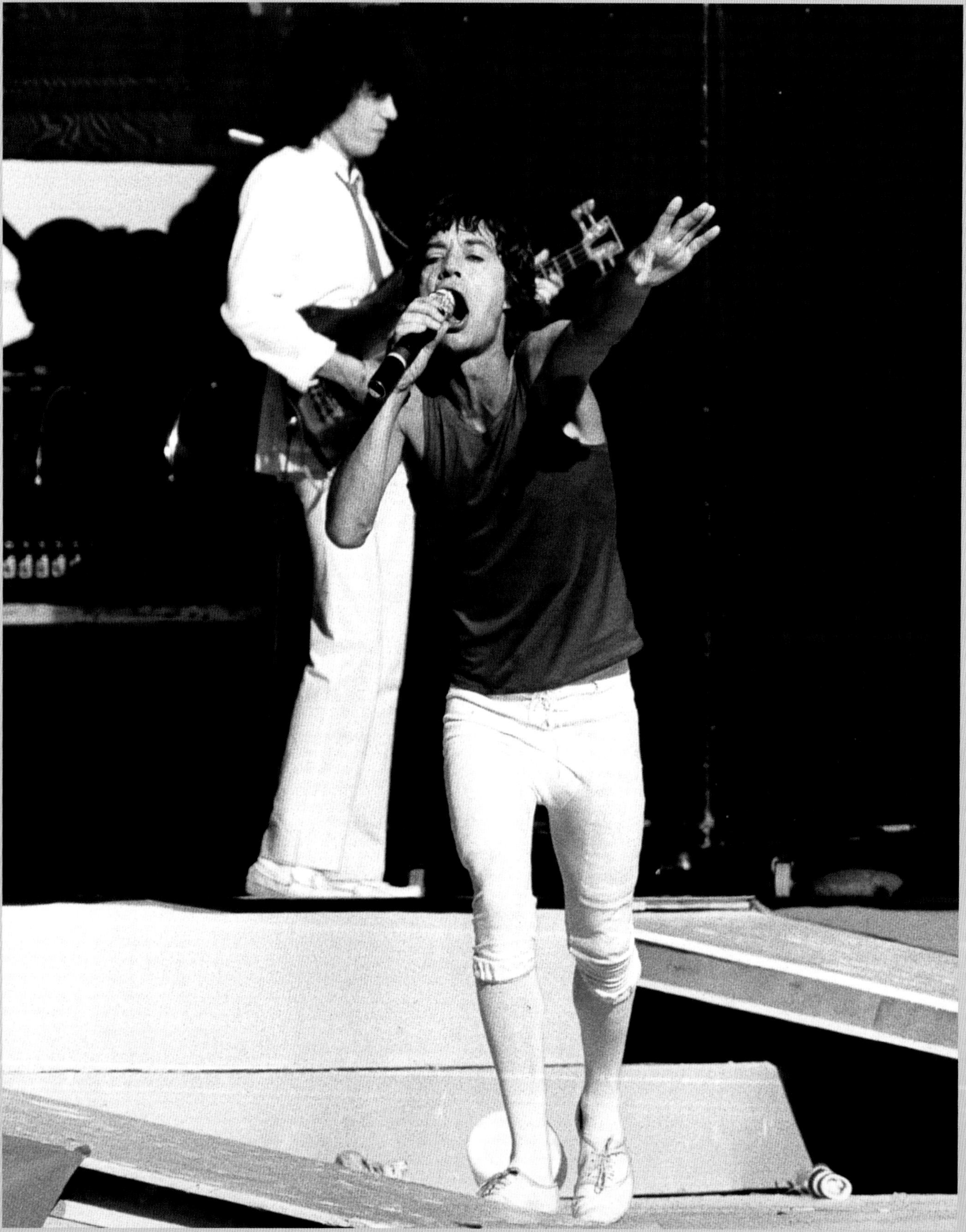

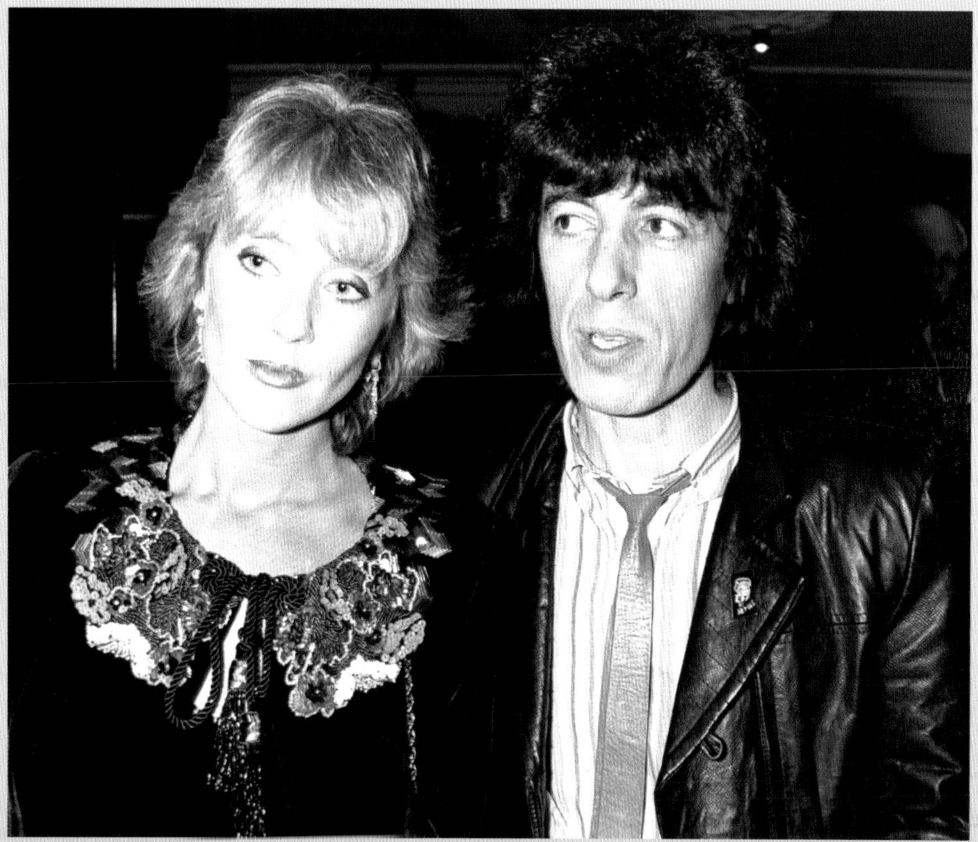

Birthday Bill

Opposite: The man in the white suit is Bill Wyman. The band and their entourage celebrated his 45th birthday in October with a party at Walt Disney World, Florida.

Right: Bill Wyman and Astrid, seemingly having got through the tough times in their relationship. Bill told reporters that there were still no marriage plans.

Below: On 9 October 1982 Bill and Astrid leave London for an eight-week break in Hawaii, which will coincide with their anniversary. It is also a reward for completing a two-month tour of Europe, which included the band's first British concert for six years.

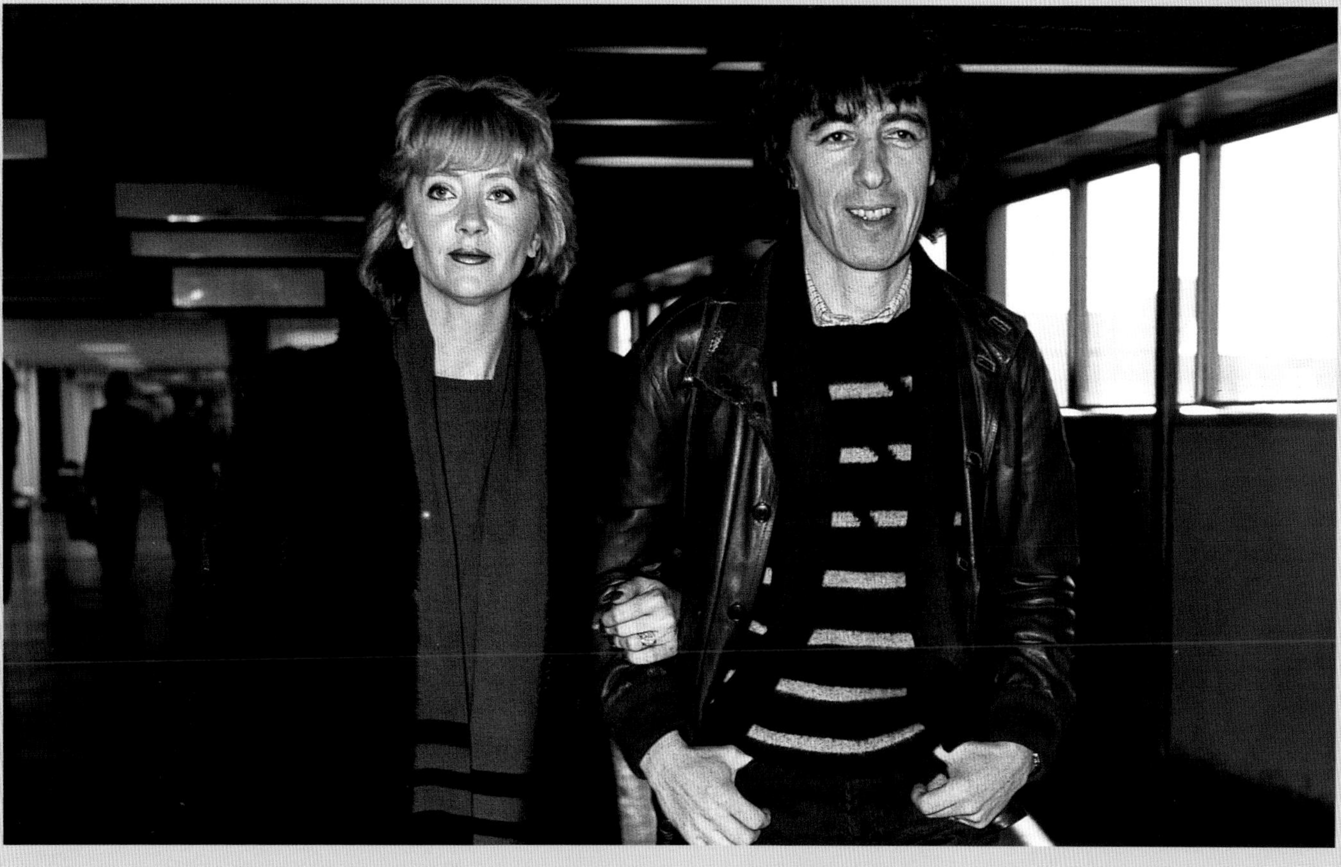

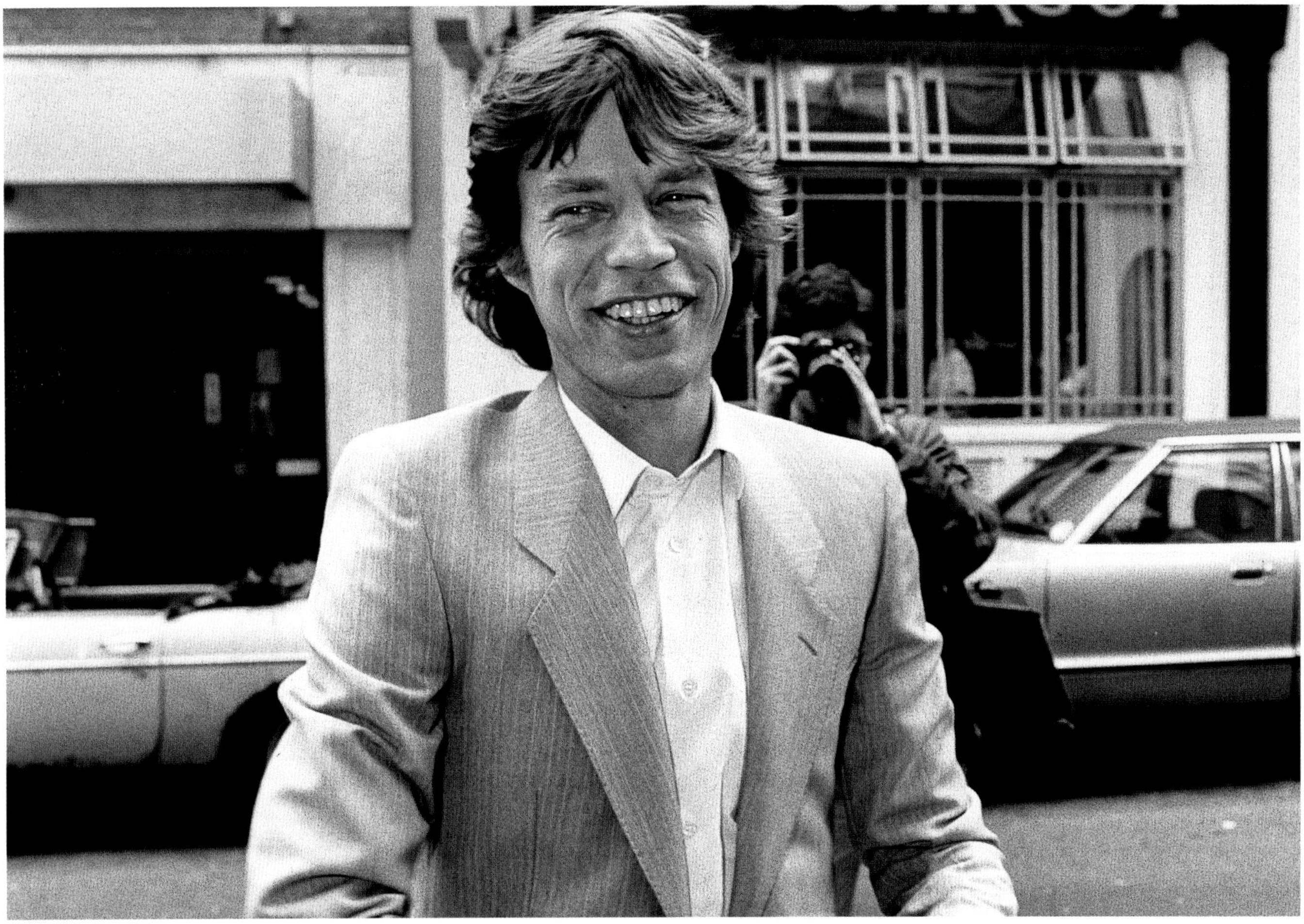

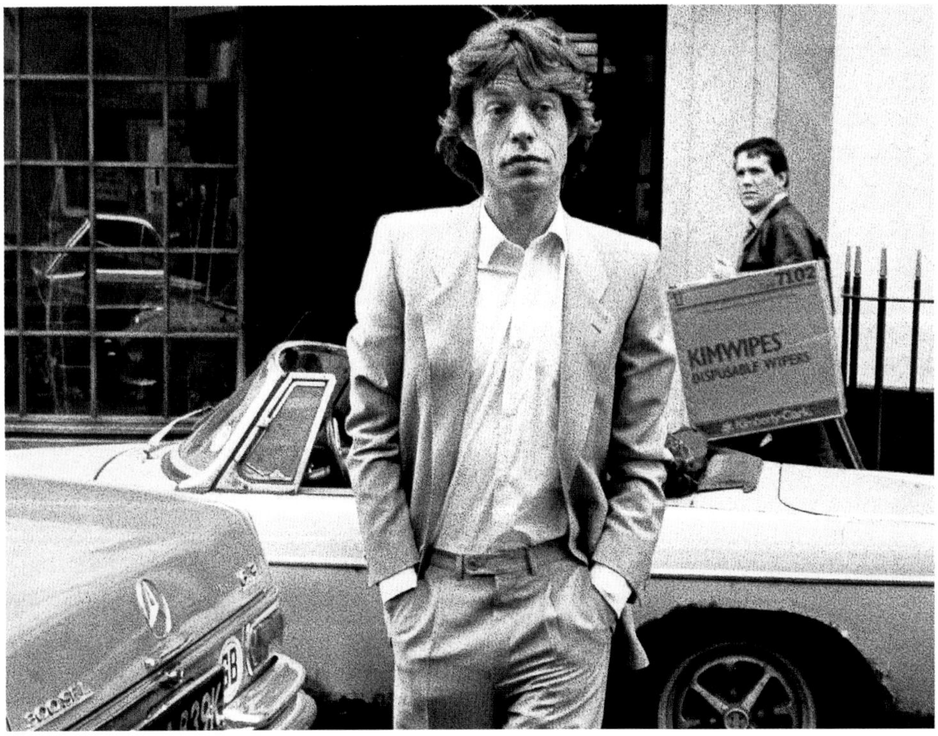

Mick in training for European tour

Above, left and opposite: Mick Jagger at L'Escargot, the fashionable Soho restaurant, before a press conference on 28 April 1982. Mick tells an assembly of journalists that The Rolling Stones are planning their first European tour for six years, due to open on 4 June in Rotterdam. He was, he said, already in training for it. Even when pressed he was non-committal about current music trends and about the financial advantages of touring.

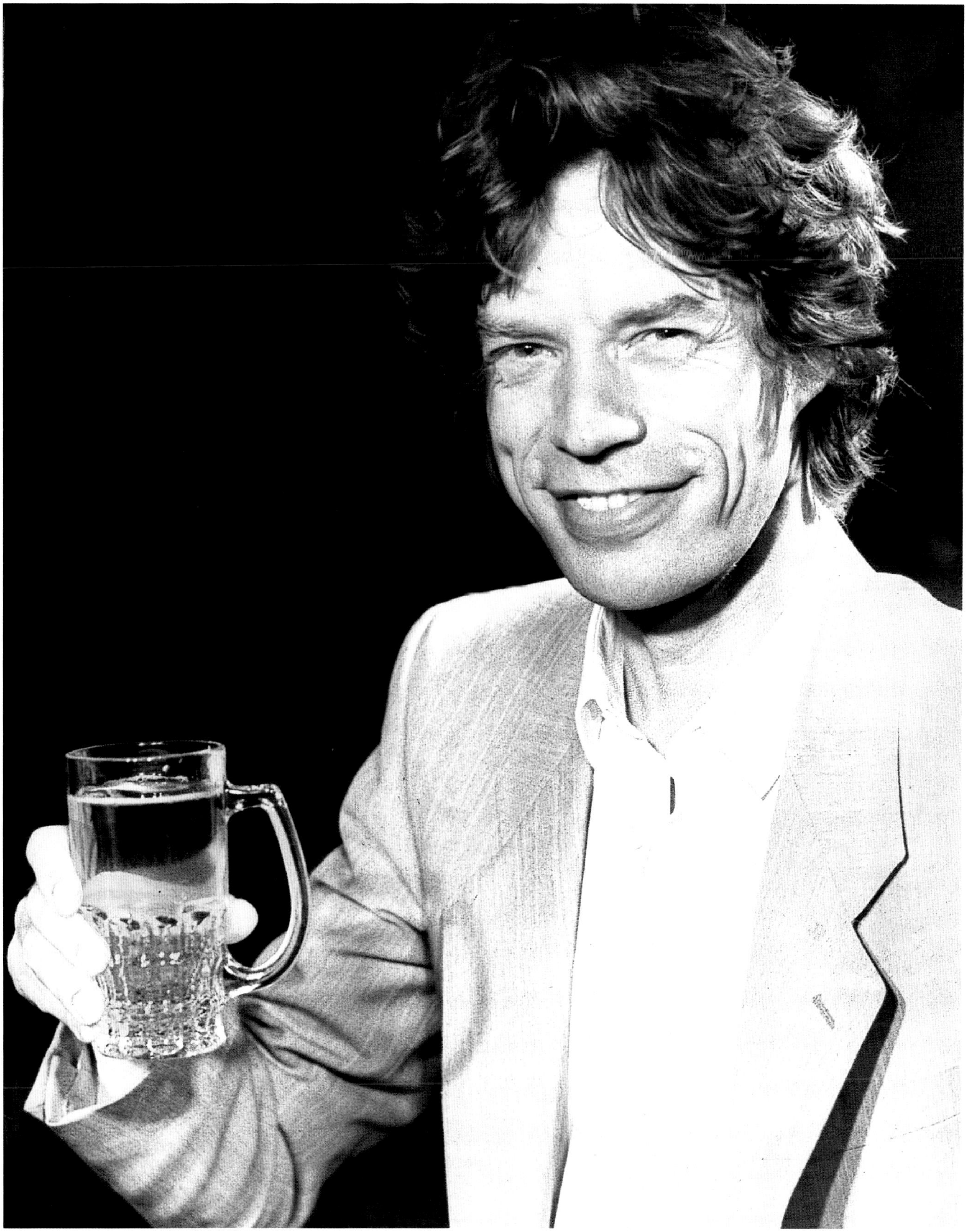

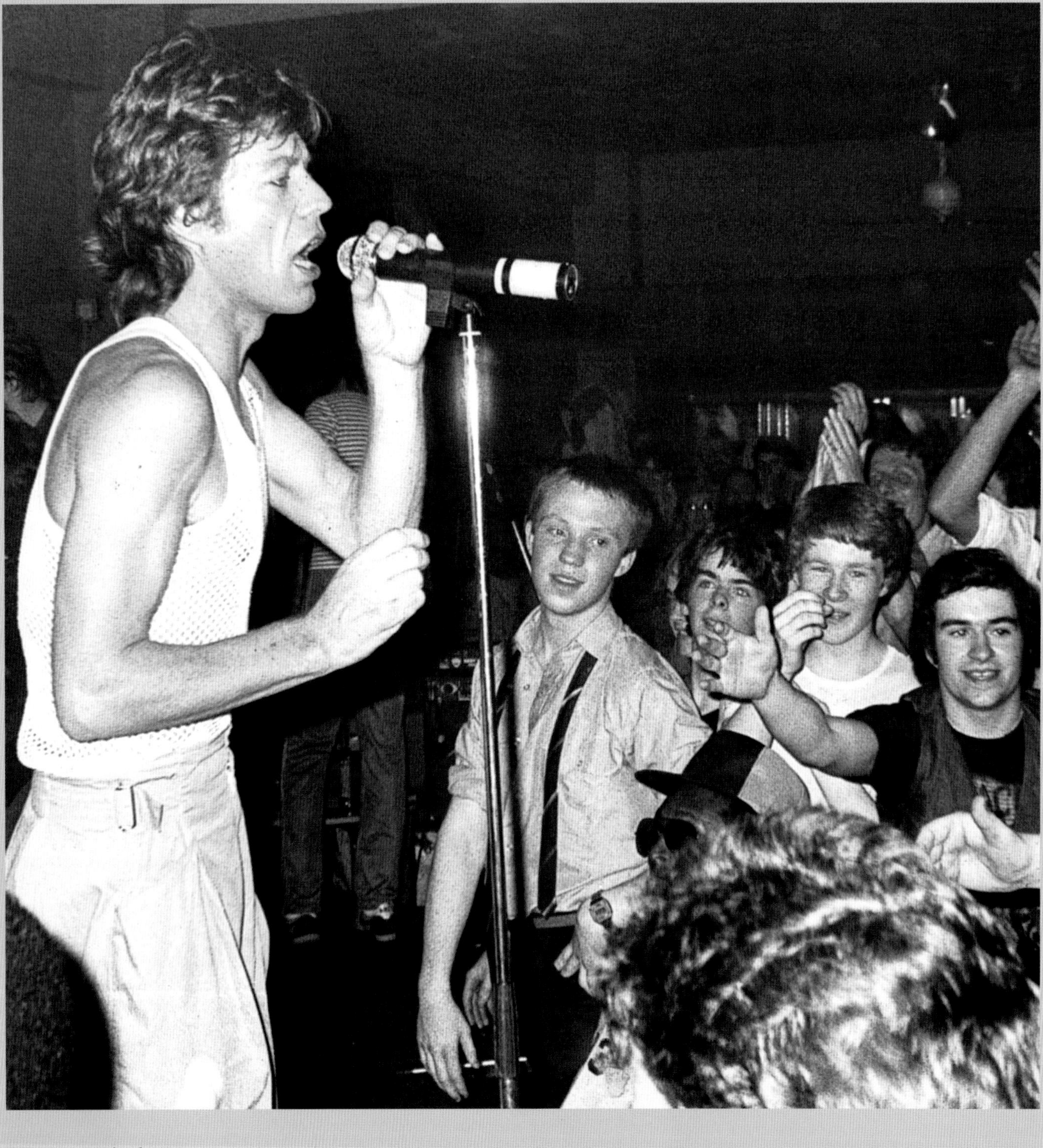

Stones get intimate

Above: Mick warms up for the new tour with an intimate gig at the 100 Club in London on 31 May. The band had attempted to play surprise concerts at small venues in America in the run-up to the 1981 tour. However, the first show was mobbed by thousands of fans and the performance had to take place outside.

Opposite: During the Wembley shows on 25 and 26 June, Mick chose a variety of flamboyant trousers. Keith mostly preferred his trusty beaten-up jeans.

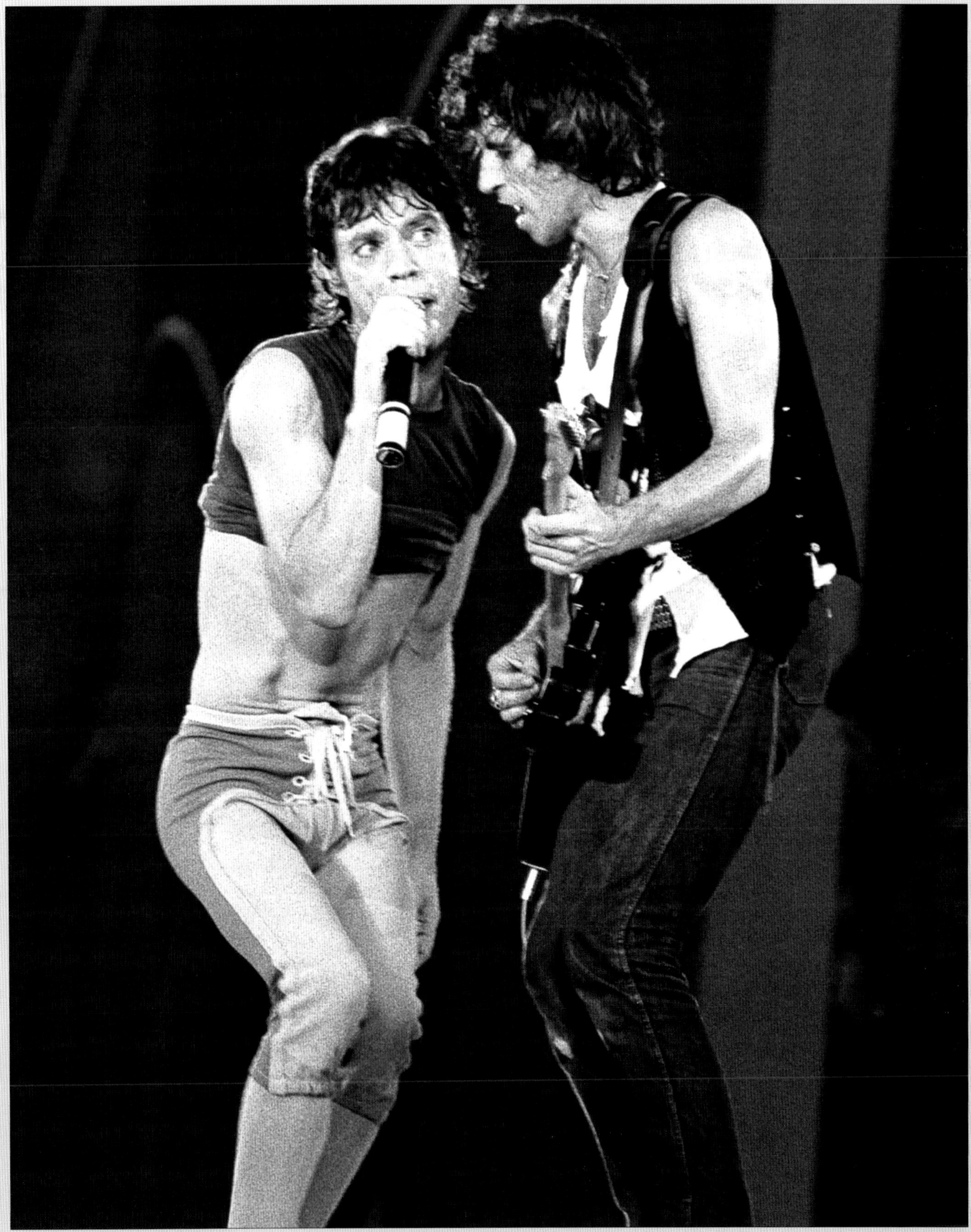

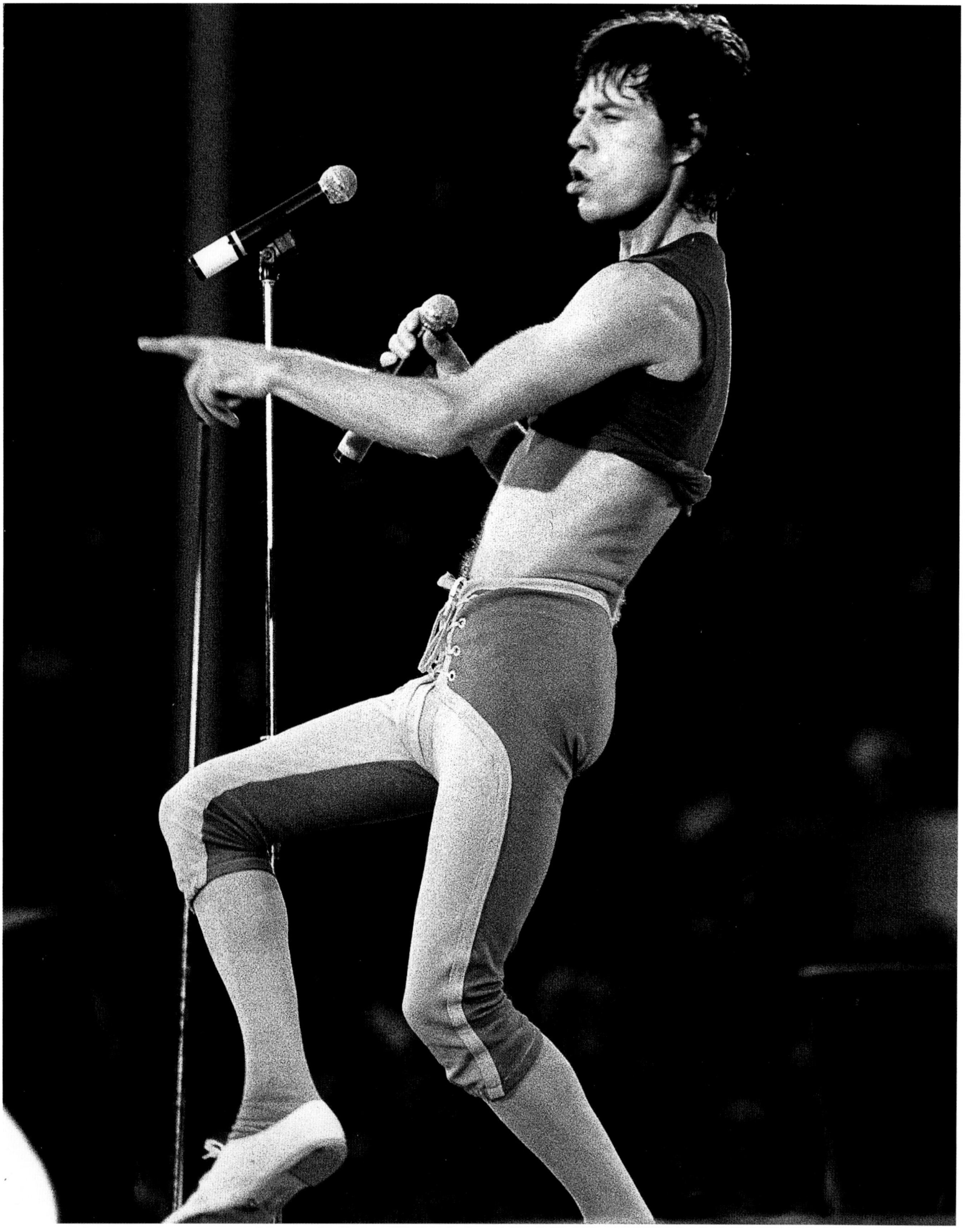

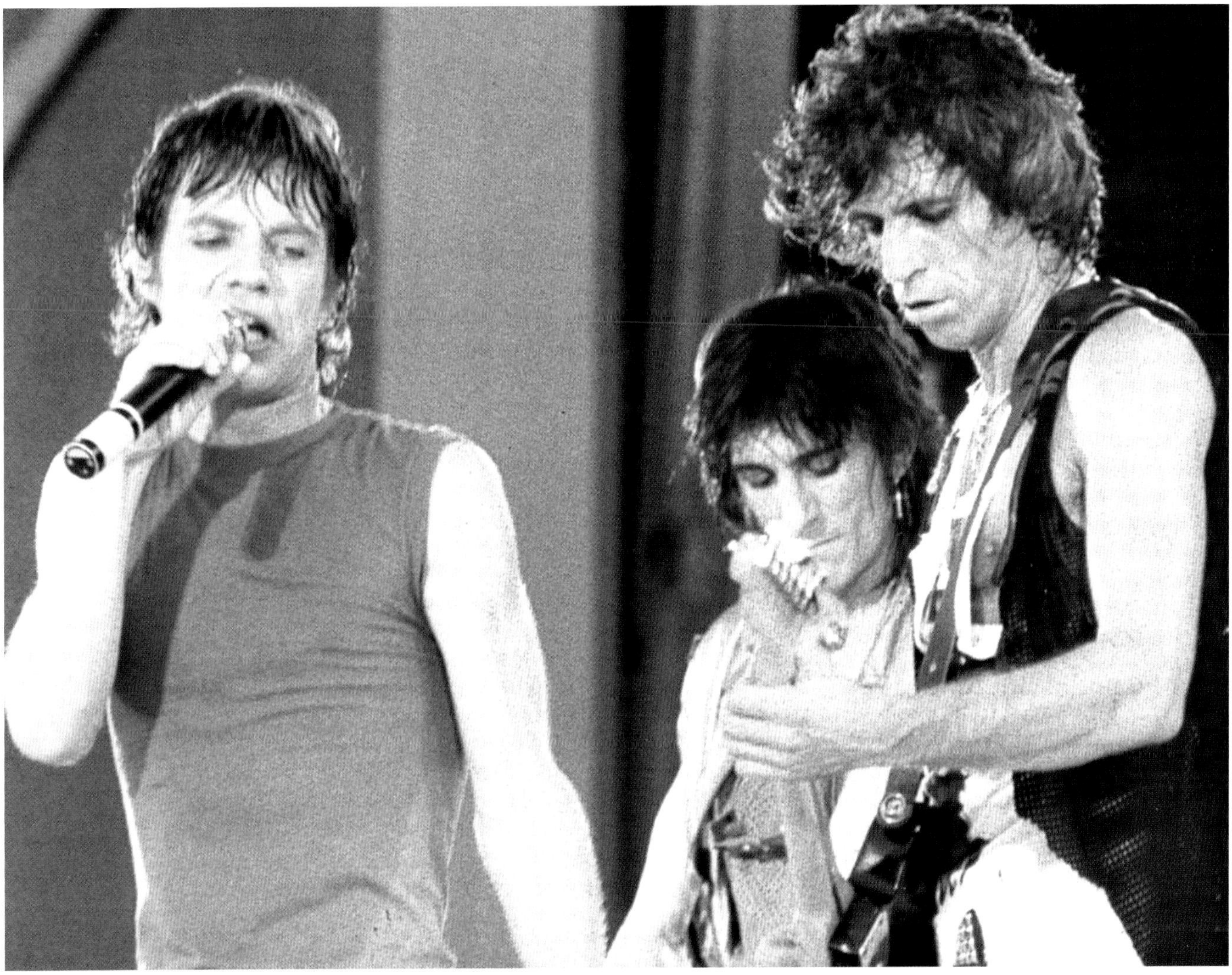

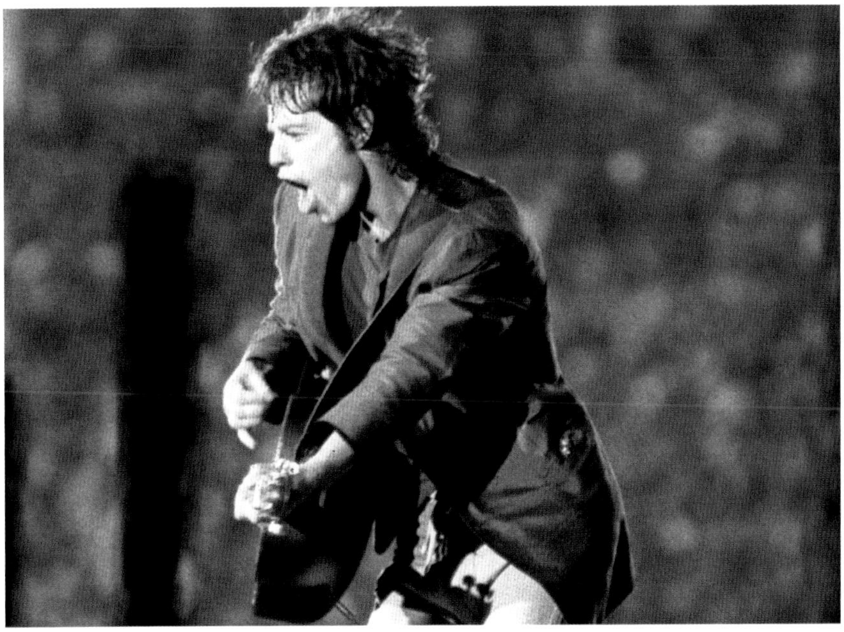

'Outstanding' Stones

Above, left and opposite: The band on stage at Wembley. The day before the London dates, Bill collected a British Music Industry award on behalf of the band, given for outstanding achievement. Keith was also interviewed on BBC2's *Newsnight* programme.

Ronnie, Keith and Mick formed a line-up of almost menacing power at Wembley. The tour closed in Leeds on the night before Mick Jagger's 39th birthday. About 80,000 fans were at the city's Roundhay Park for the gig. Hundreds of thousands attended the British dates of the tour alone – it was a triumph. Some observers muttered that the long tour had taken its toll and that the band looked tired that night – but the Stones' road still stretched far ahead in 1982.

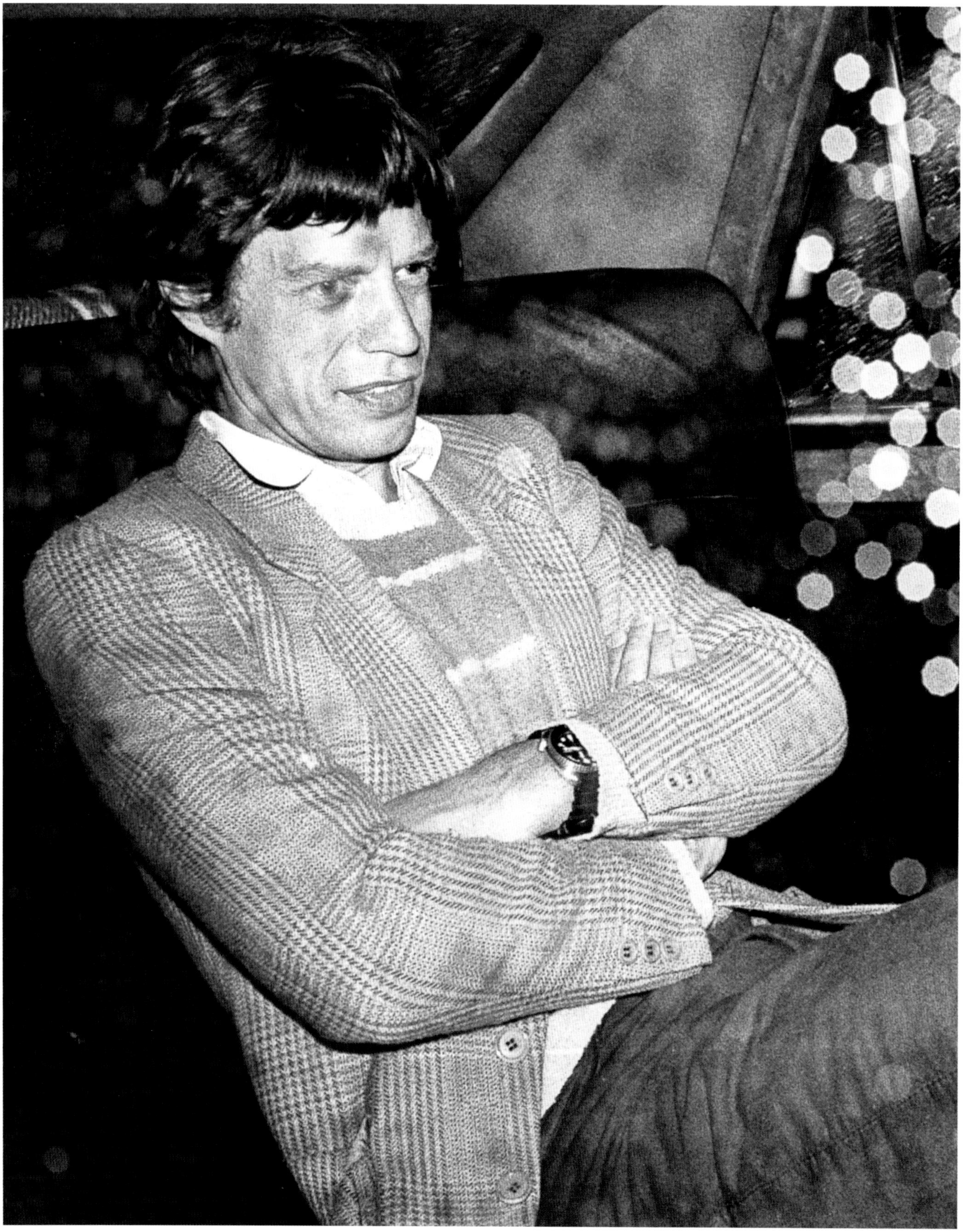

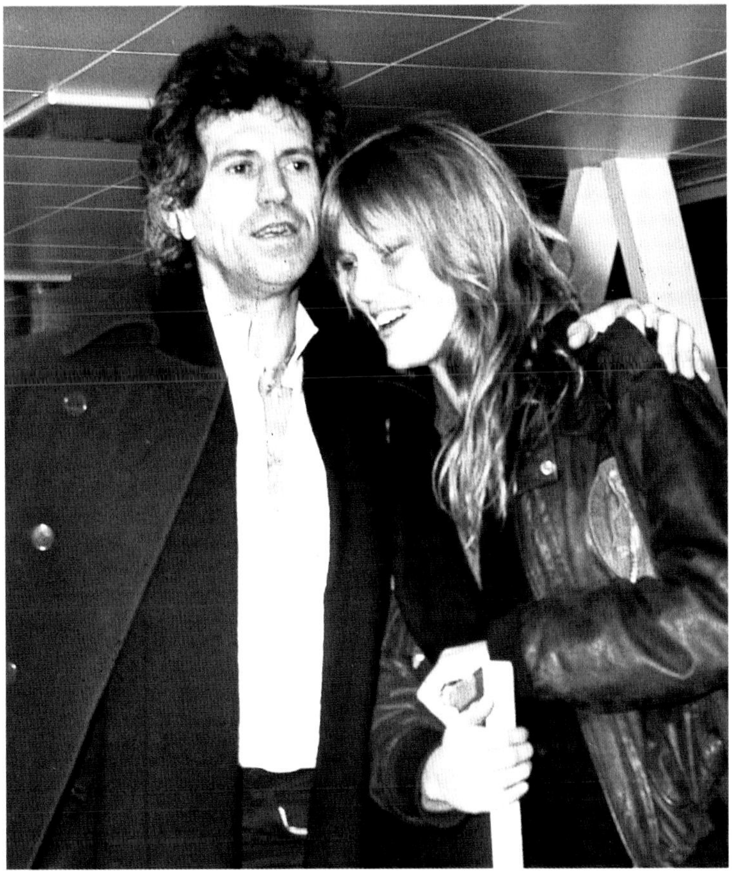

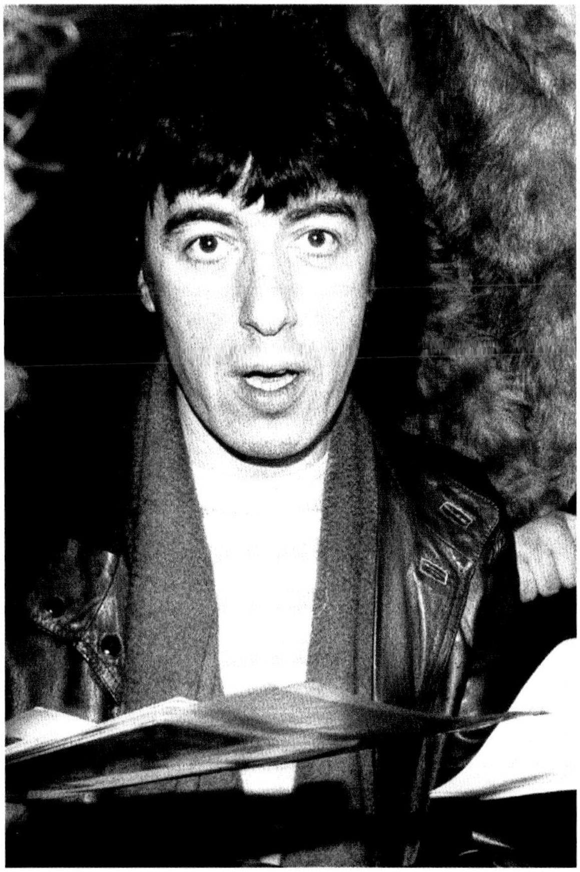

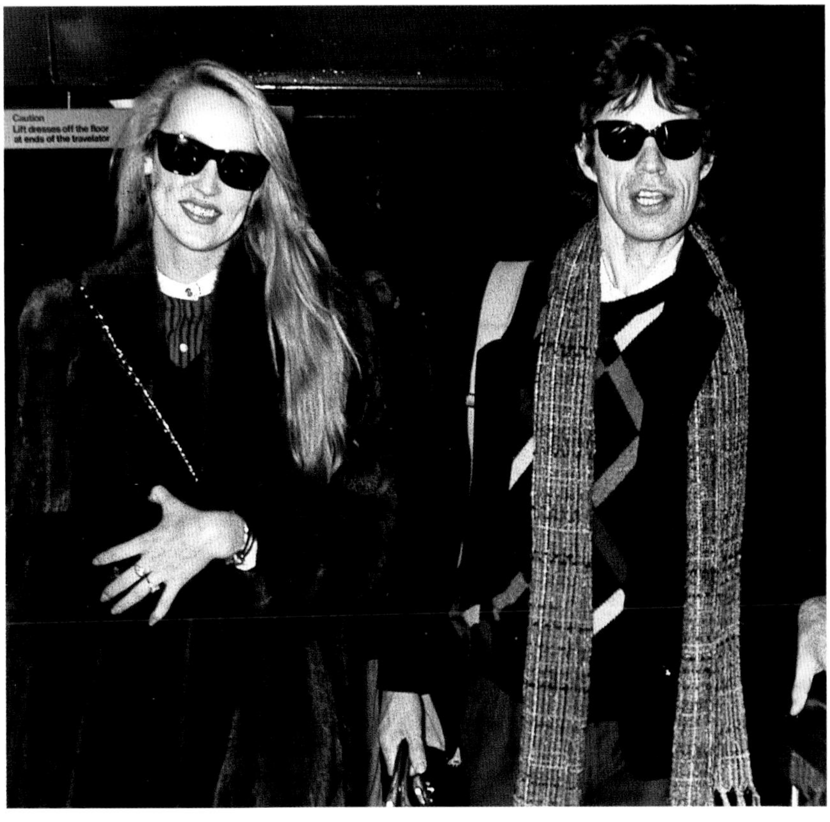

'Undercover Of The Night'

Opposite: Mick enjoys a moment of repose. 'Undercover Of The Night' was released in October 1983 and was, unusually for the Stones, a political song, dealing with the situation in Latin America. It was not the lyrics but the video, directed by Julian Temple, that attracted most publicity. The BBC refused to show the film, in which Richards plays an assassin wielding a gun. The album *Undercover* reached the Top Ten in both the United Kingdom and the United States.

Above left: Keith Richards and Patti Hansen. They married on 18 December 1983, Keith's 40th birthday.

Left: Just before Christmas 1982 Mick Jagger and Jerry Hall left London for Barbados. Their relationship had ridden a little strain when Jerry had briefly flirted with millionaire racehorse owner Robert Sangster earlier in the year. But Mick was not irreproachable either. When Jerry left New York for Paris, Mick was joined by Venezuelan model Victoria Vicuna.

Above right: Bill Wyman leafs through some Beatles memorabilia at Sotheby's, London, on 22 December. Wyman was always known to be the archivist of The Rolling Stones.

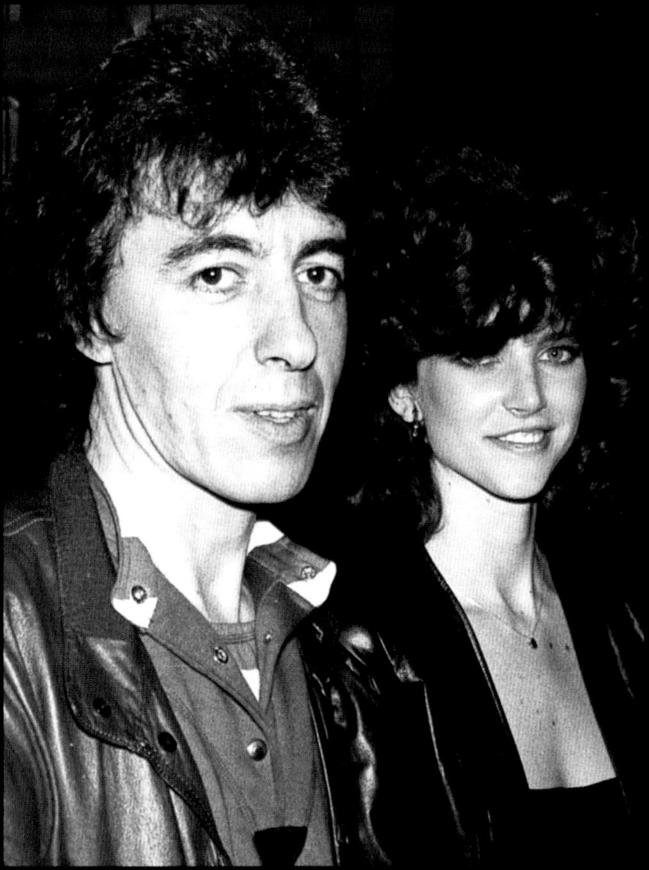

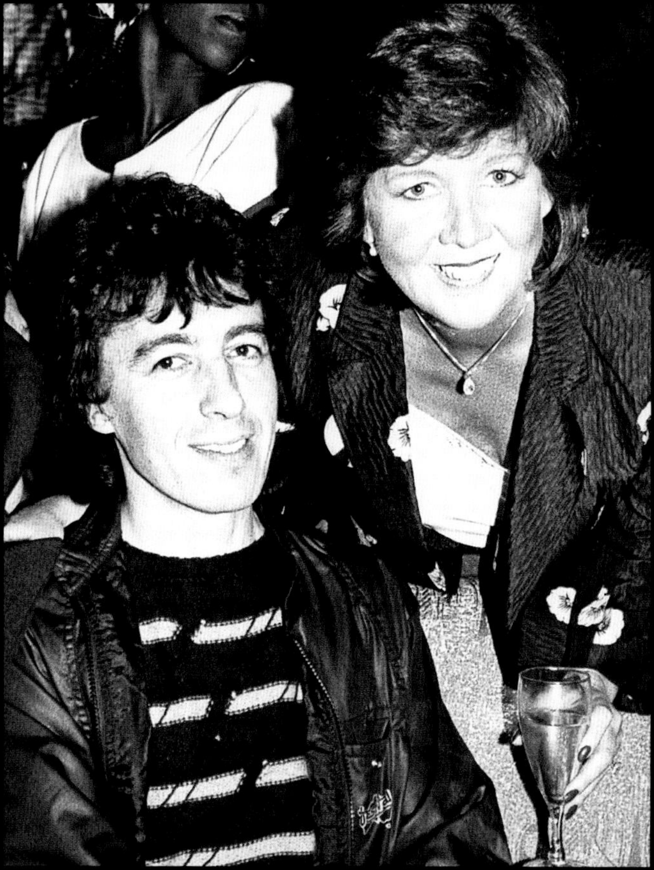

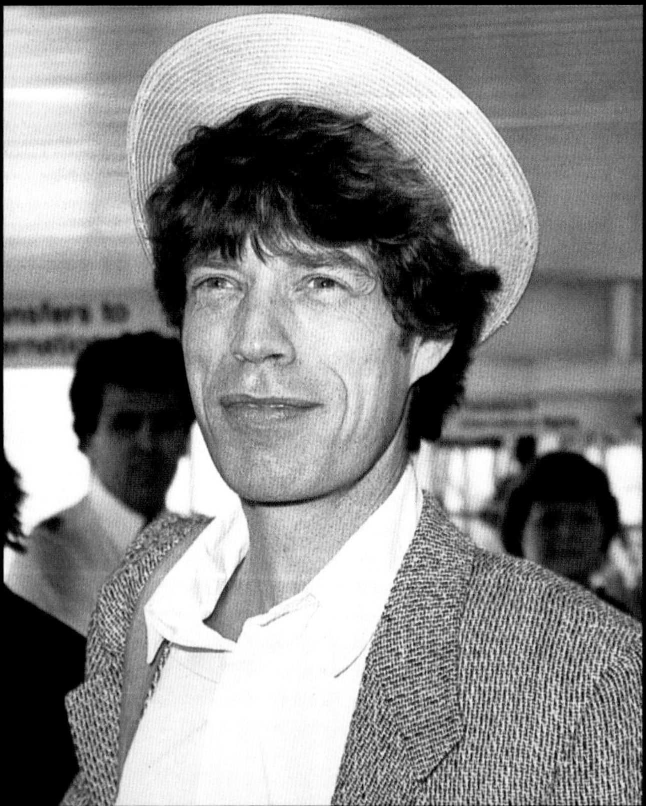

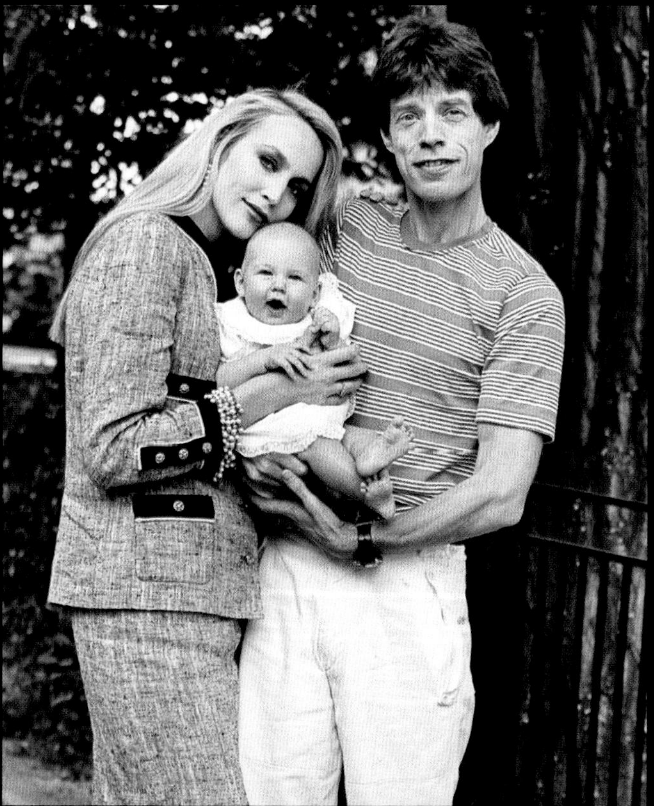

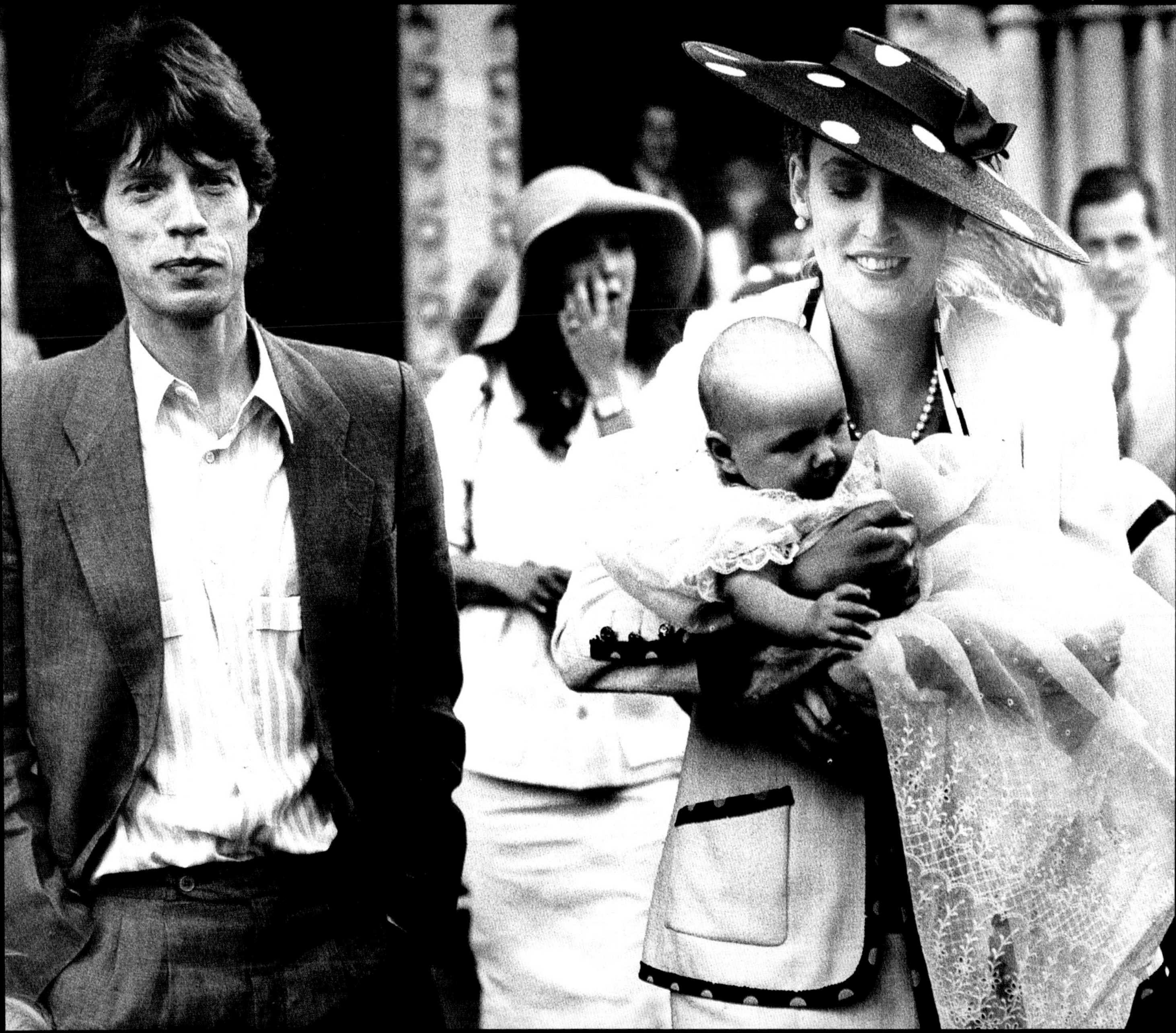

Proud father

Opposite below right and left: June 1984 and Mick Jagger is enchanted by being a father again. Elizabeth Scarlett was born on 2 March in New York, the first of four children Mick and Jerry eventually had.

Above: The christening of Elizabeth Scarlett at the parish church near Mick and Jerry's rented Kensington home on 24 June 1984. Jagger already has two daughters: 13-year-old Karis by singer Marsha Hunt, and 12-year-old Jade from his marriage to Bianca. He would later have another girl, Georgia May, with Jerry Hall.

However, rumours had been circulating for a while about discord within the band. Bill Wyman had been quoted in the *Sun* newspaper as making critical remarks about fellow band members, and had also reportedly refused to help Jagger with his autobiography. News of Jagger's forthcoming solo album caused further speculation.

Opposite above left: Bill Wyman with new girlfriend Kelly Winn and (*opposite above right*) with Cilla Black at the 1,000th show party for *Top of the Pops*.

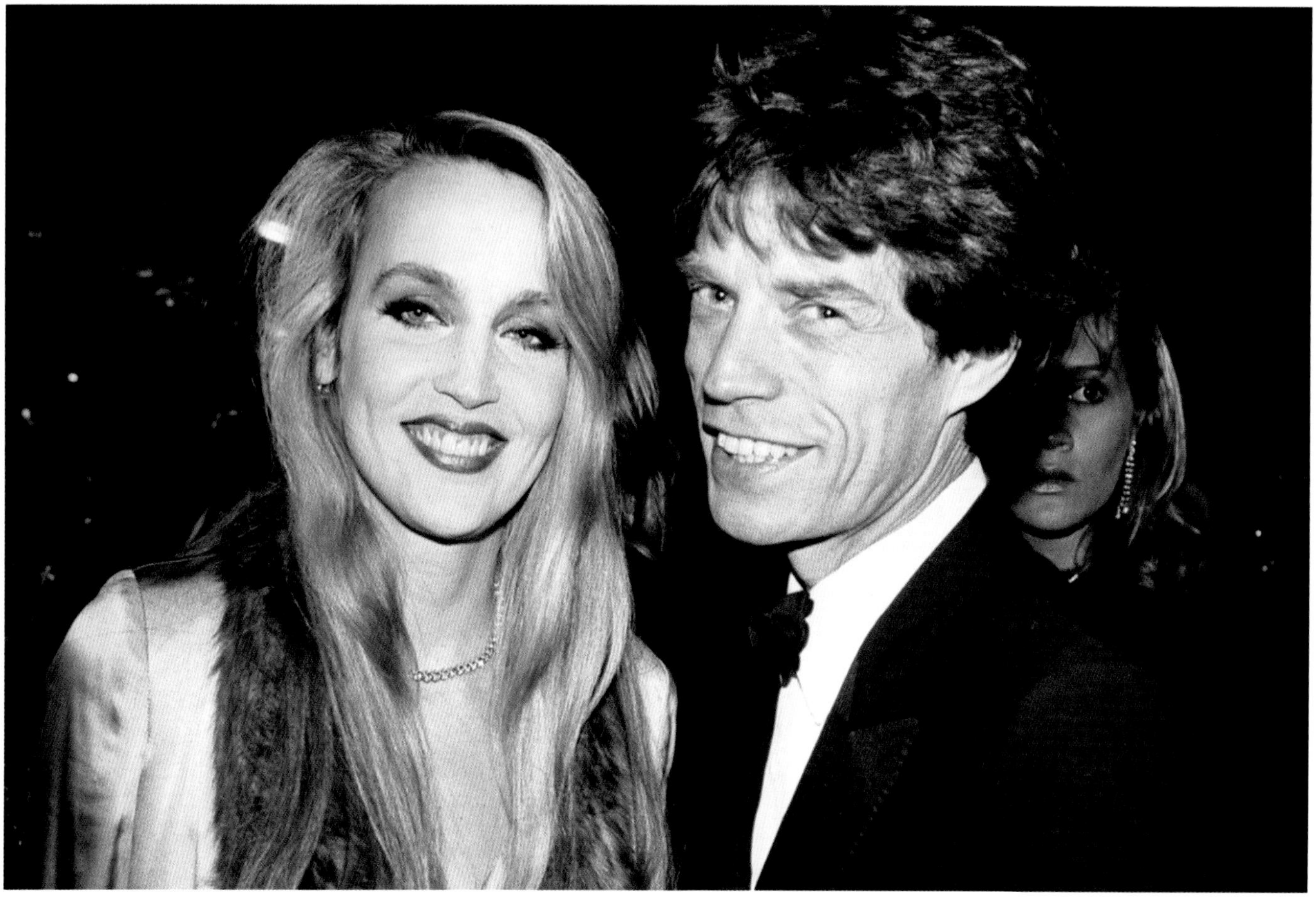

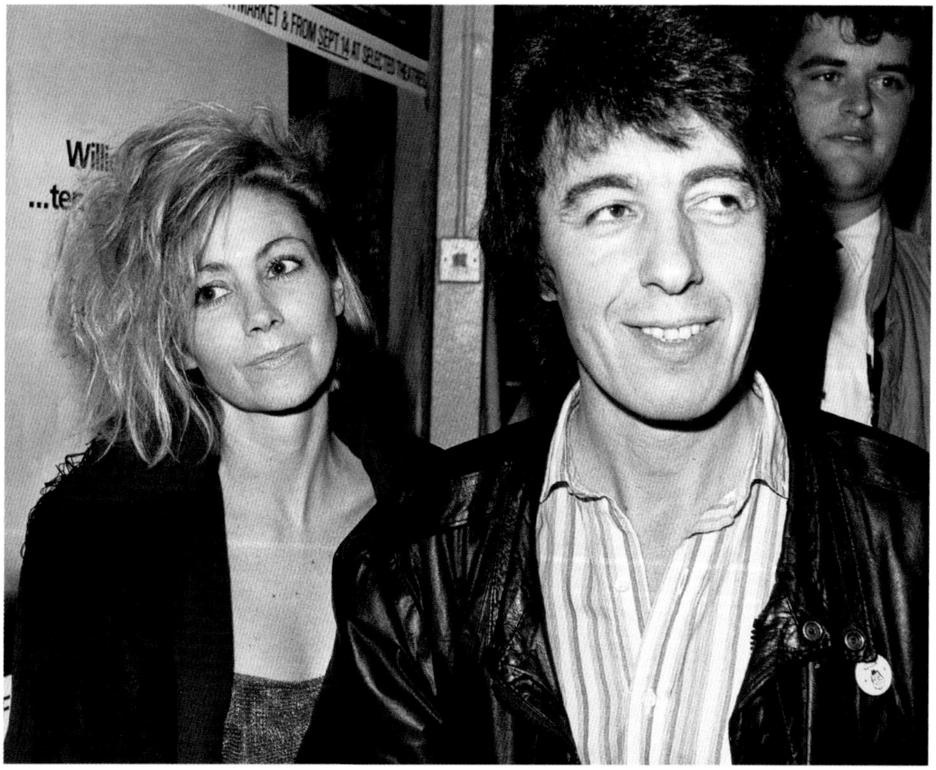

Mick can't go to the ball

Above: A radiant Jerry Hall after the birth of Elizabeth Scarlett, with Mick Jagger at the Berkeley Square Ball in London in July 1984. Mick's first choice of a blue and green suit was deemed unsuitable and he had to go home and change into more conventional attire for the event.

Left: Another party and another girlfriend for Bill Wyman, pictured with Wendy Jewel at a nightclub in September 1984.

Opposite: October 1984: a sharply dressed Charlie Watts. Charlie and Ronnie, along with with Chris Rea, Andy Fairweather Low and The Who's Kenney Jones, have just recorded an album produced by Bill Wyman, calling themselves 'Willie and the Poor Boys'.

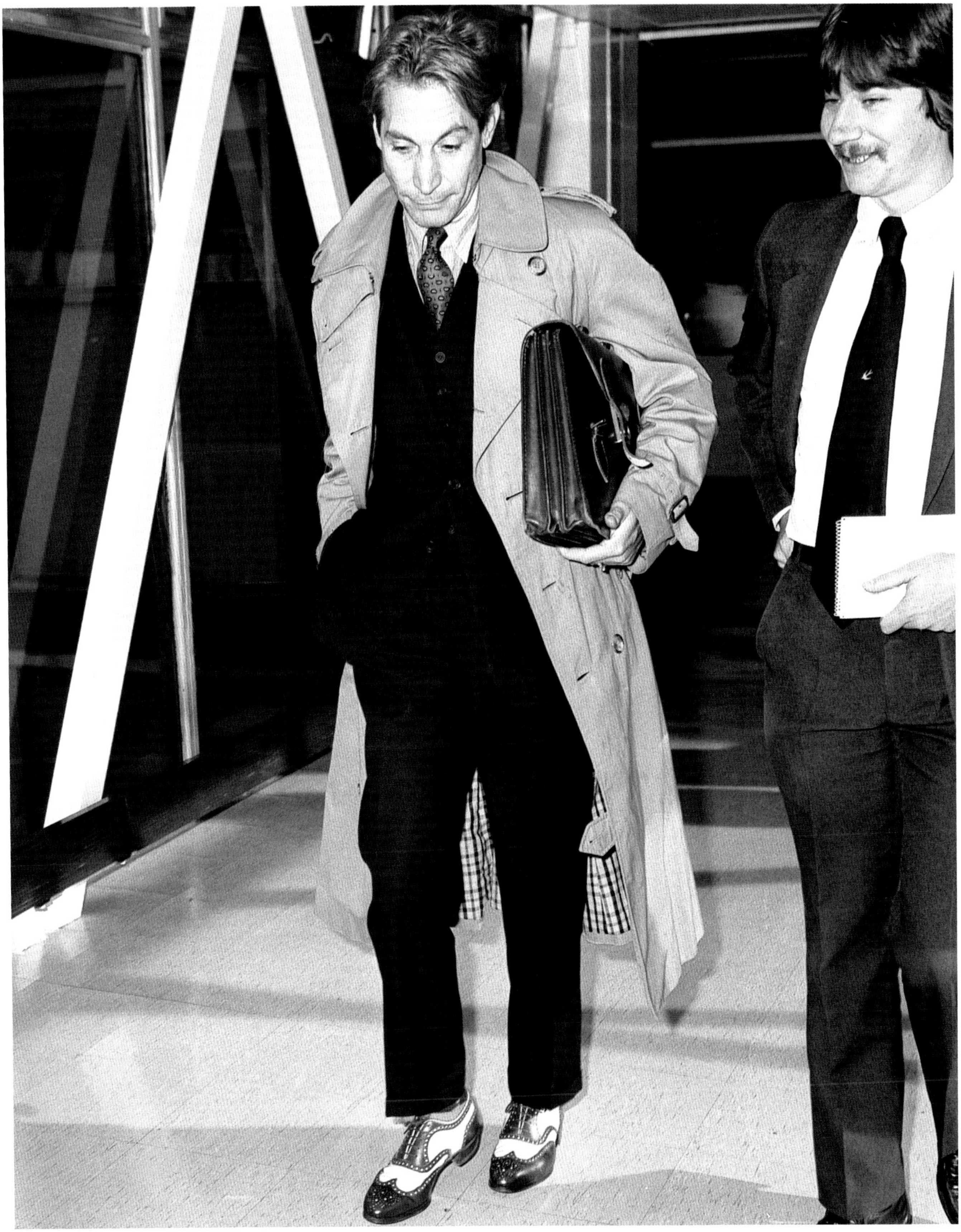

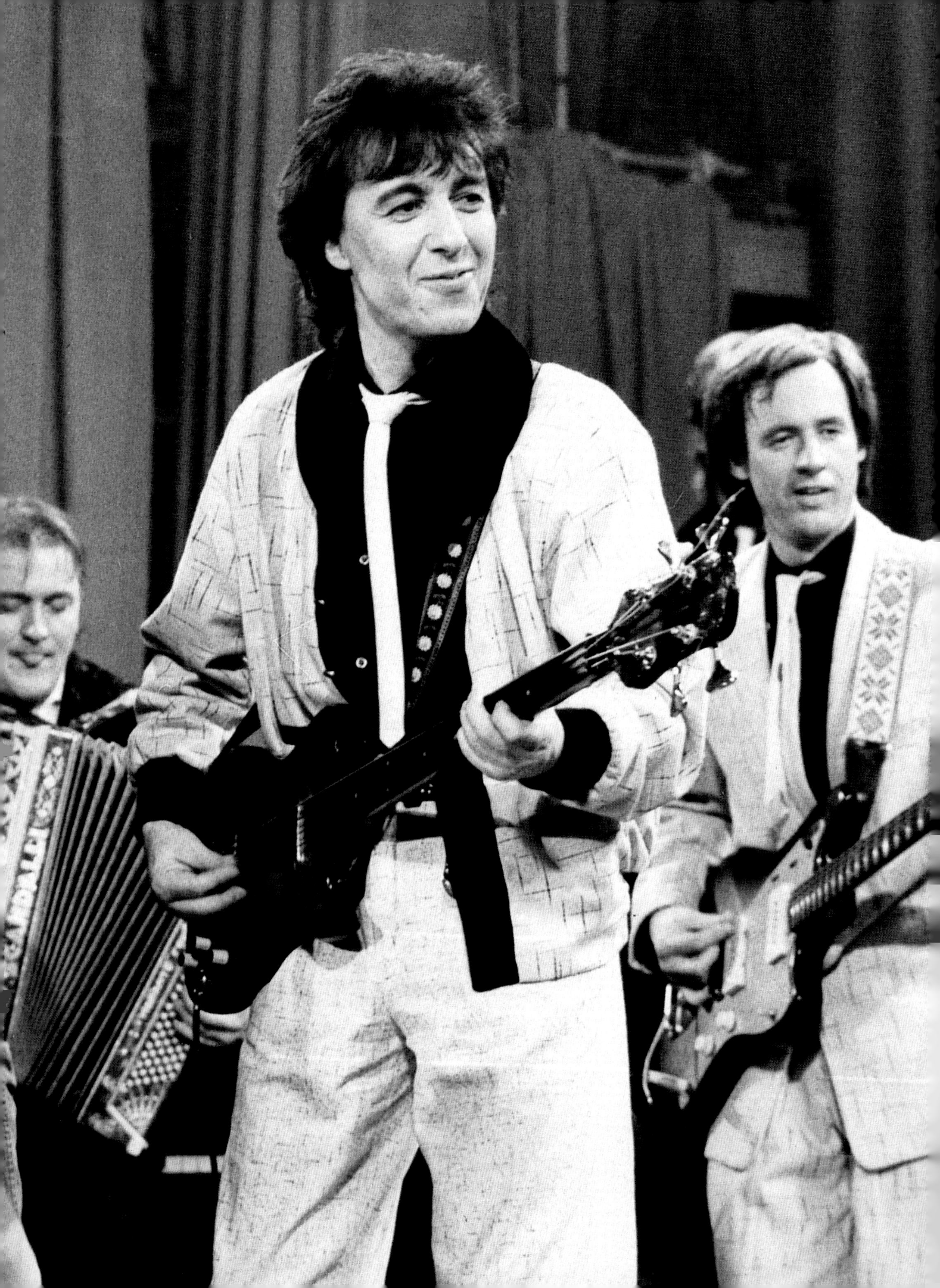

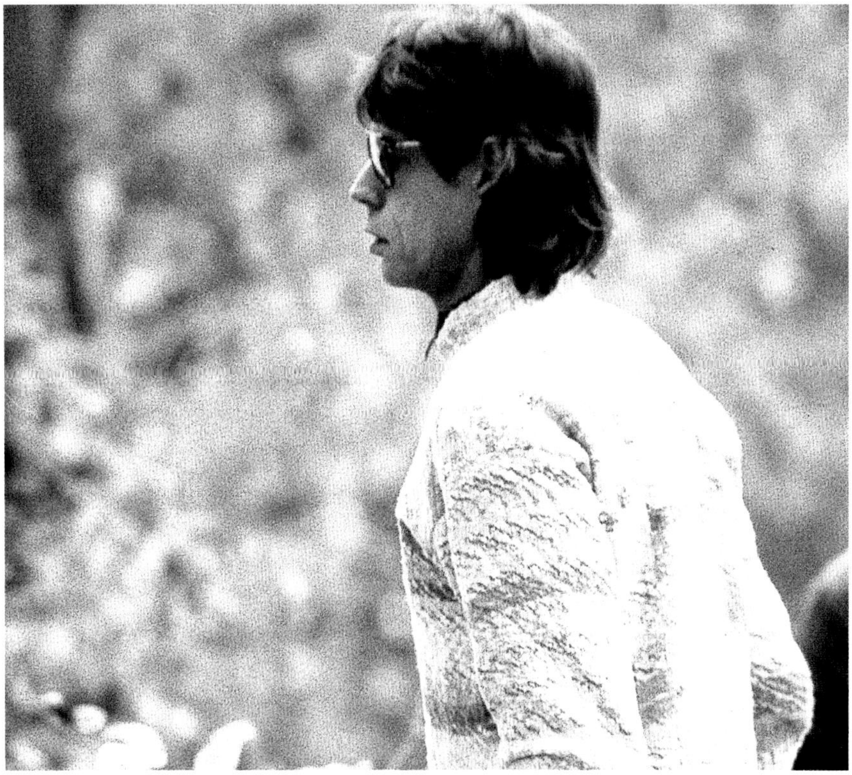

Hearing Aid

Opposite: July 1985, and Bill Wyman proves his commitment to multiple sclerosis research by organizing a fundraising show with fellow musicians Andy Fairweather Low (*right*), Chris Rea, Kenney Jones and Charlie Watts. Following the Live Aid concerts, they call themselves 'Hearing Aid'.

Some of the Stones had played in the Live Aid concert in Philadelphia but not together, perhaps because of the tensions between them. Mick performed solo, backed by Hall and Oates, and also with Tina Turner, while Keith and Ronnie appeared with Bob Dylan.

Right: Just back from India in October 1985, Mick Jagger at his garden gate in Kensington, and a few days later (*below*) with his agent. In August Mick had a No.1 single with David Bowie. 'Dancing In The Street' topped the UK charts immediately after its release.

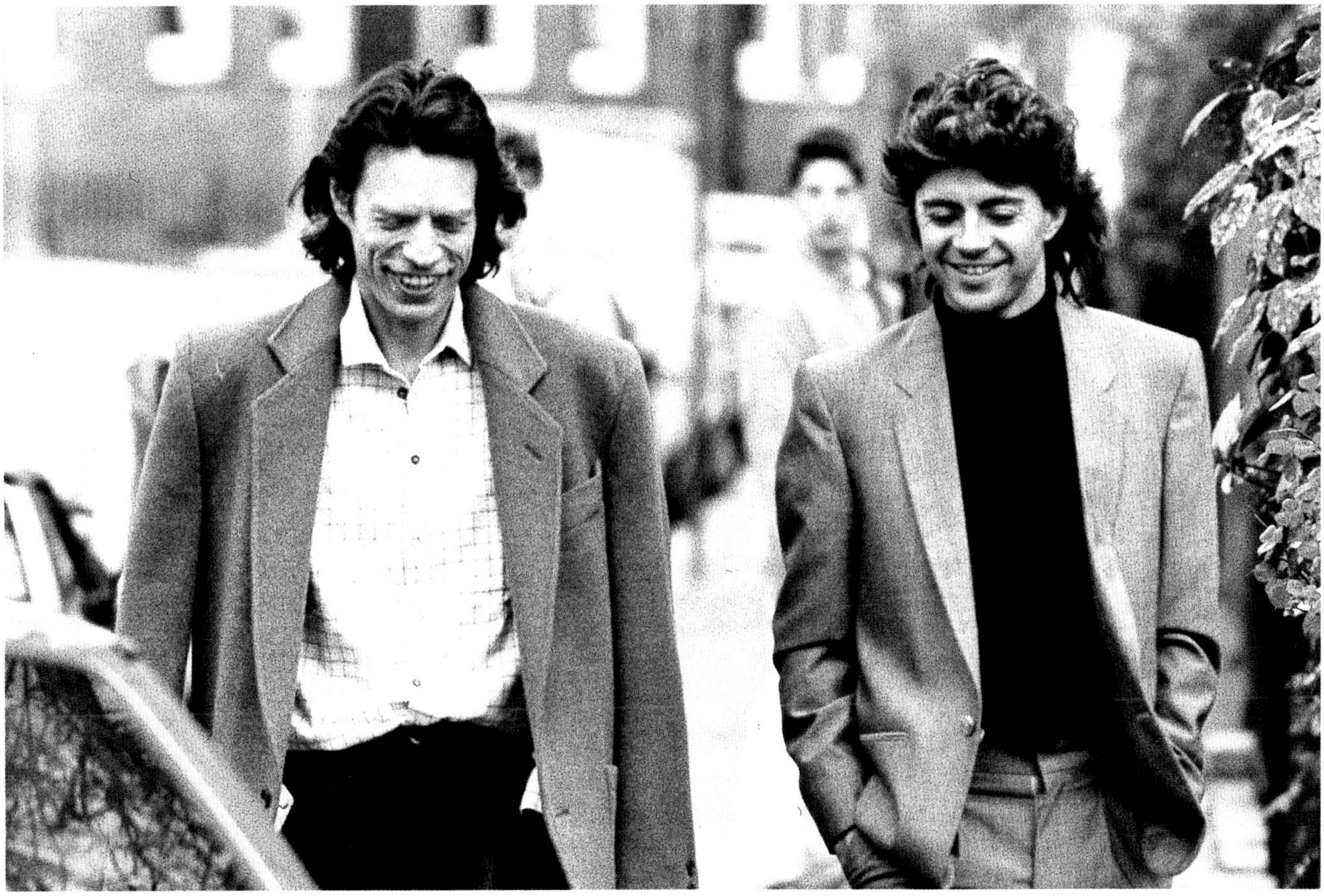

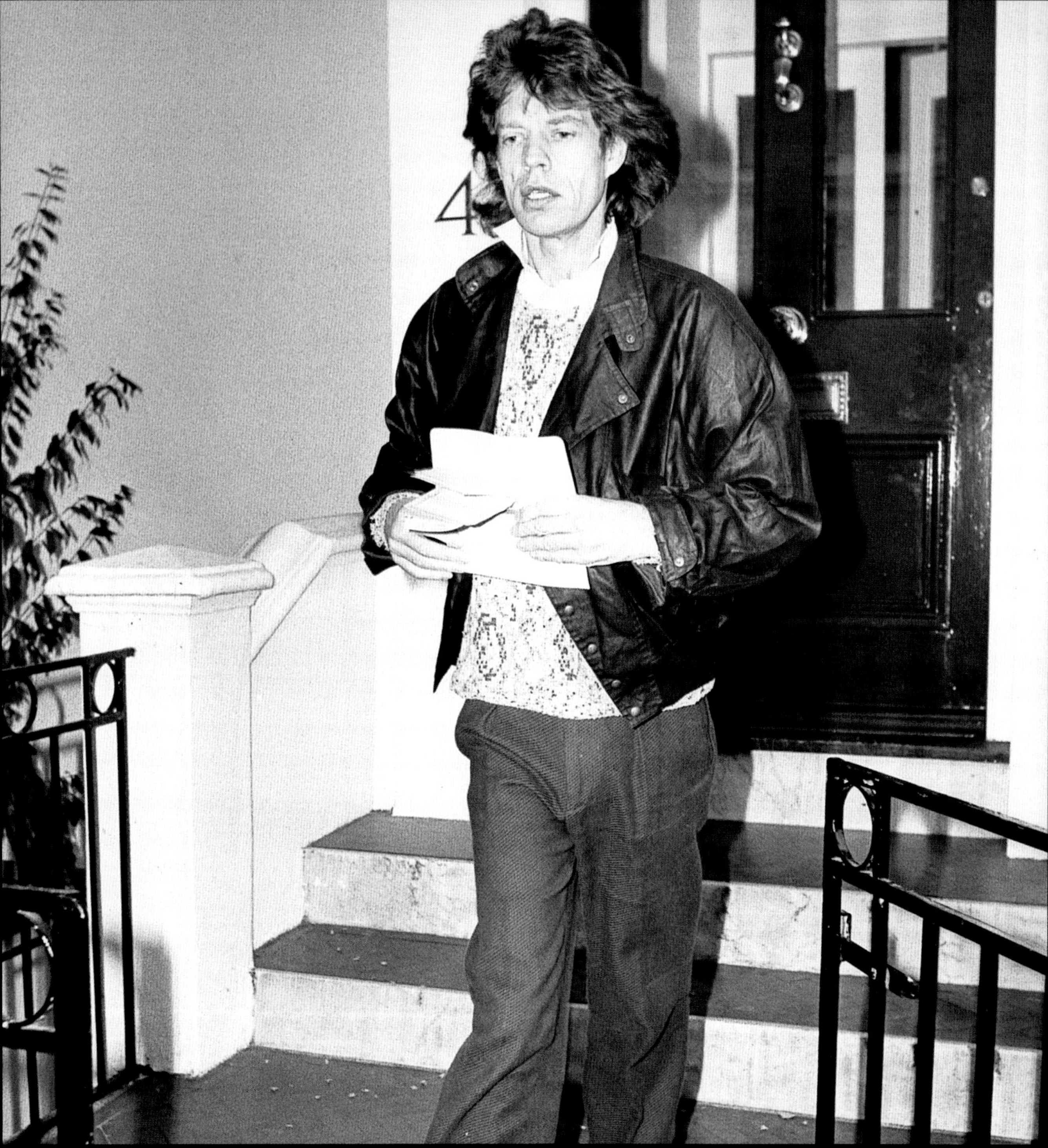

James Leroy Augustine arrives

Above: Mick Jagger outside his Kensington home on 31 October 1985 and (*opposite above*) with Jerry Hall and the new baby, James Leroy Augustine, before the christening at St Mary Abbot's Church, Kensington, on 8 November.

It had been two years since the last Stones album, *Undercover*, and an unusually long time without recording, but during 1985 the band were back in the studio together.

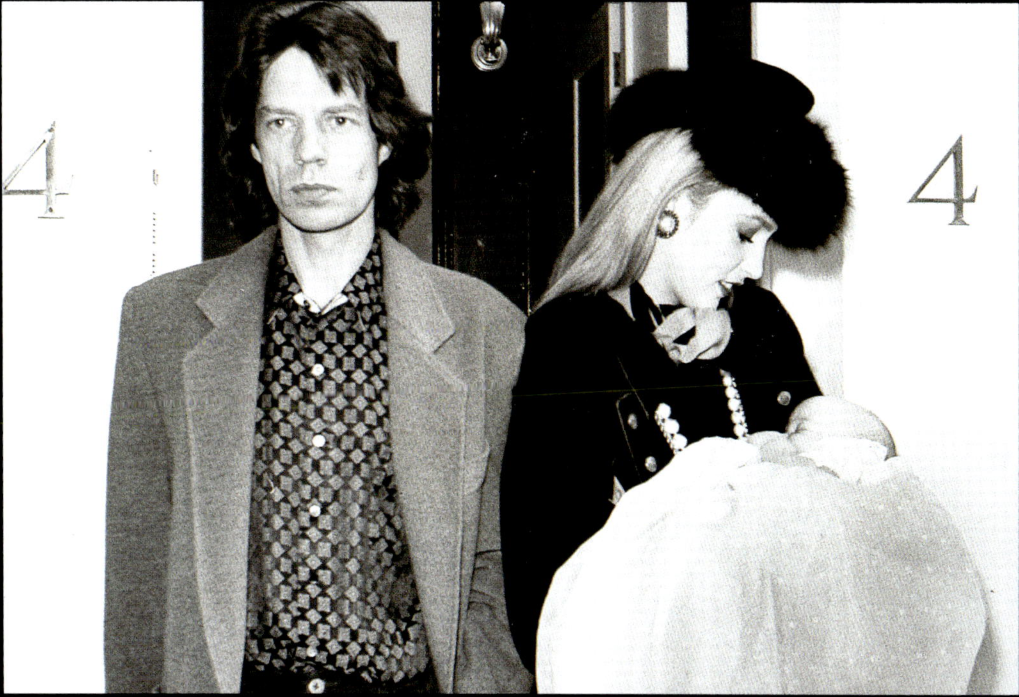

Below: Despite reported tensions between the members of the band, Mick, Keith, Charlie and Ronnie appear to be enjoying an evening out on the town.

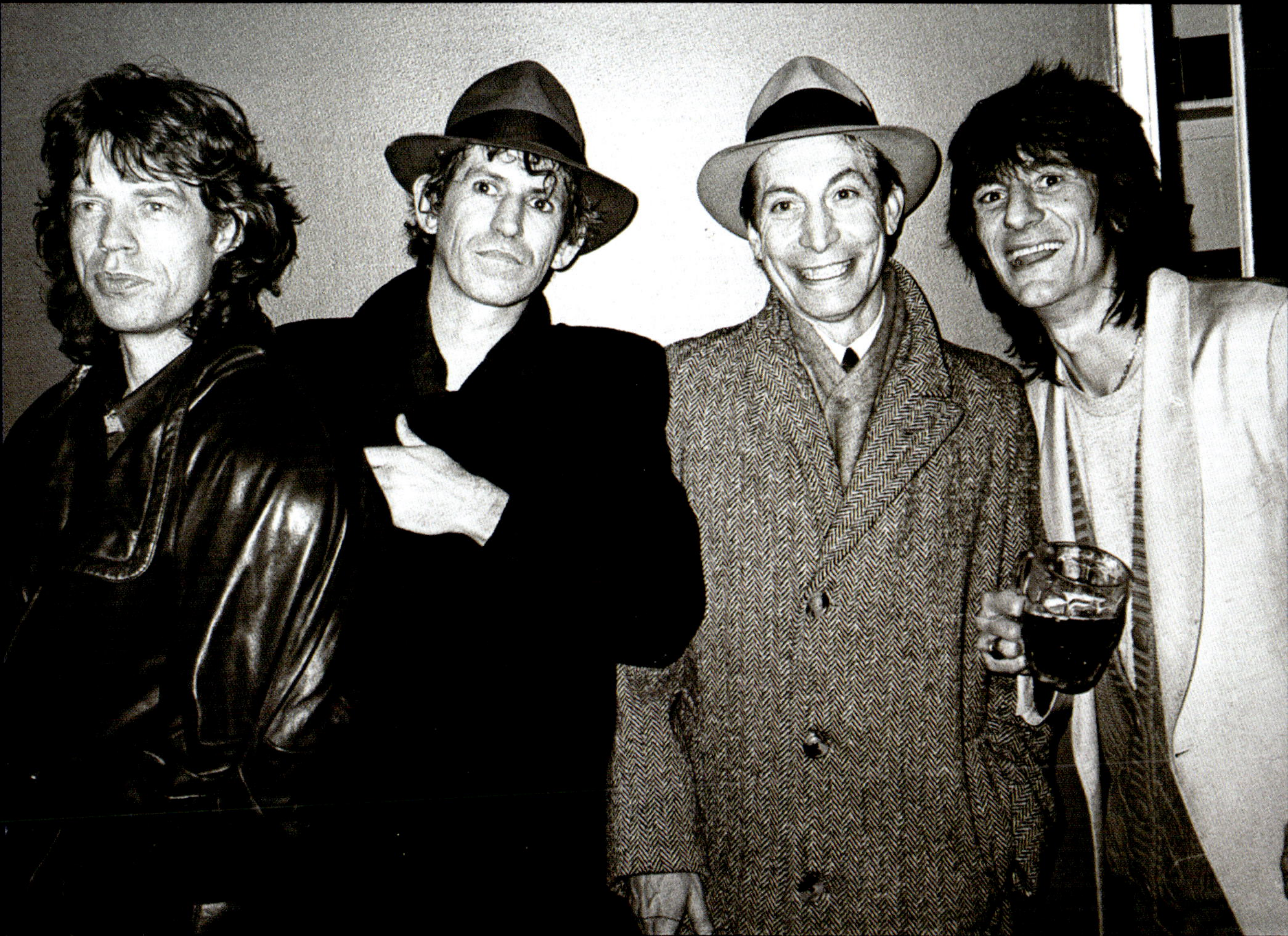

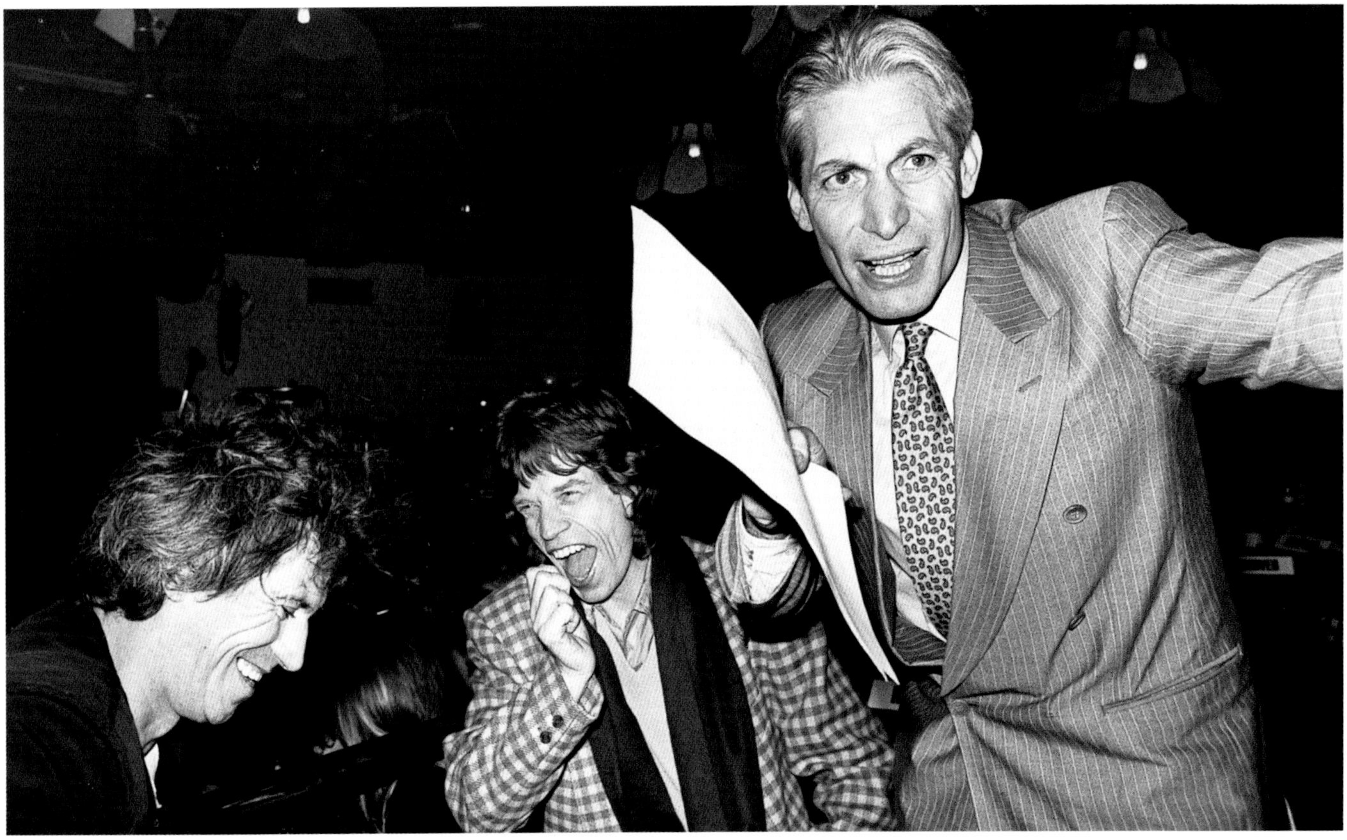

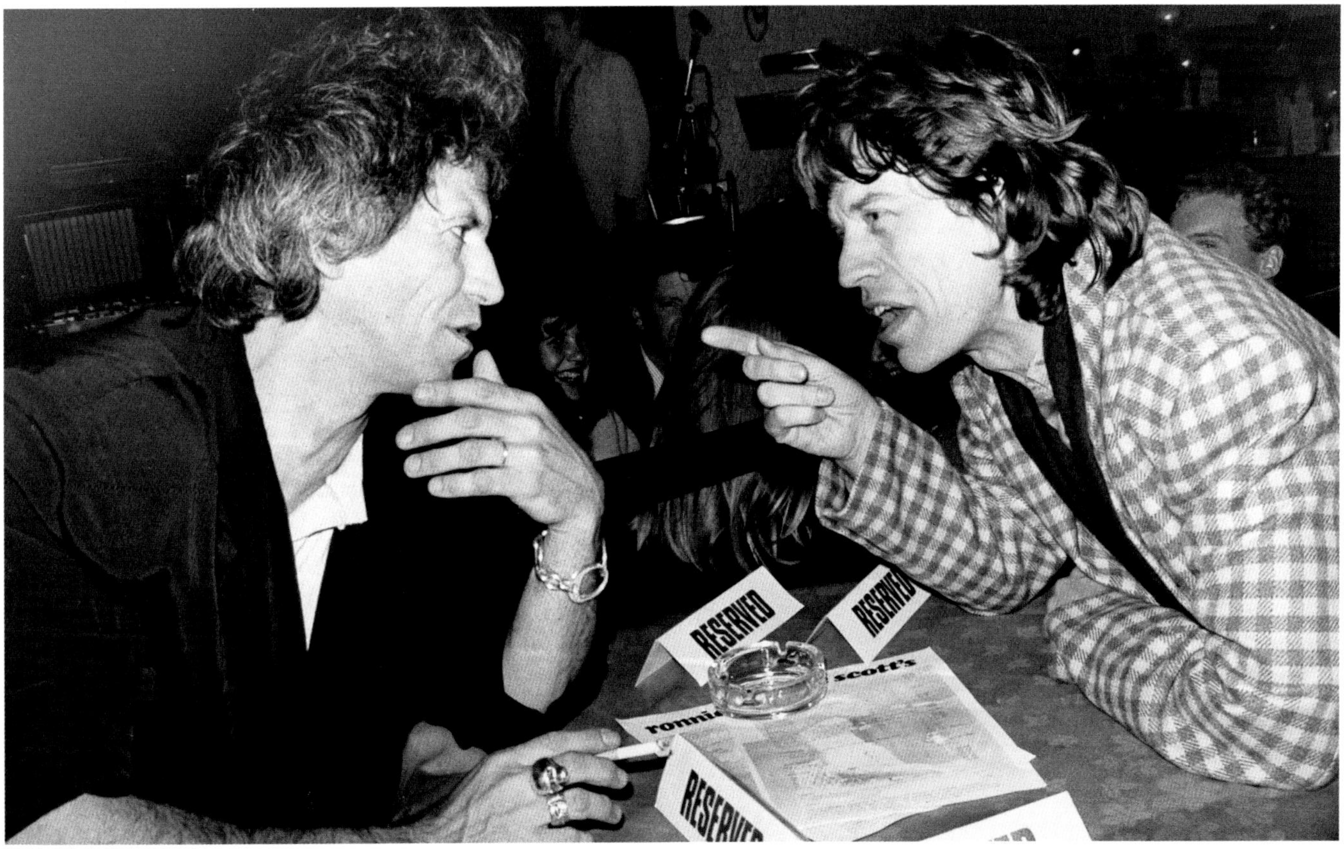
RESERVED
RESERVED
scott's
RESERVED

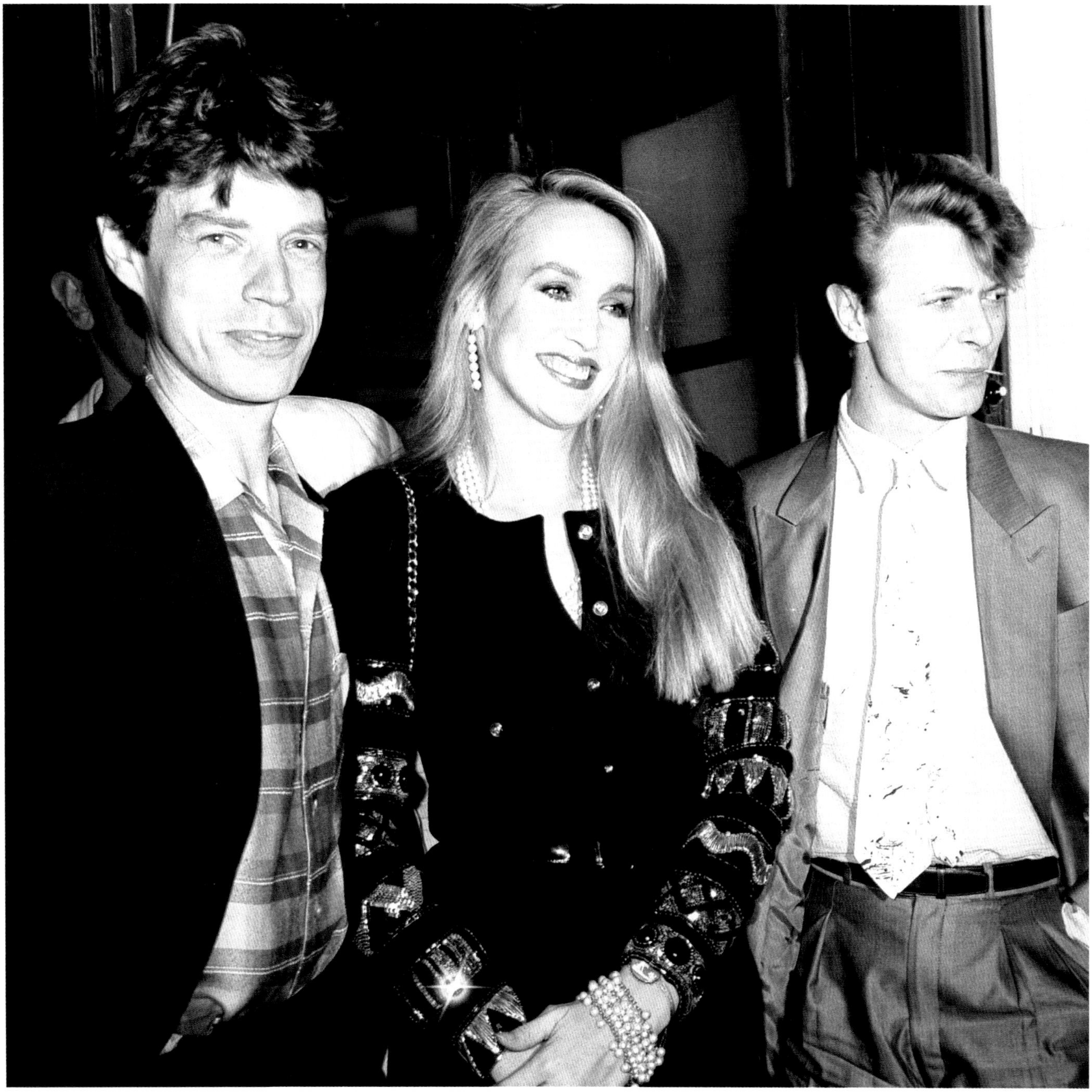

Playing Ronnie Scott's

Opposite above: Charlie Watts may not look like a musician, but he's playing at Ronnie Scott's jazz club in London on 18 November 1985. Mick and Keith (*opposite below*) came along on the first night of Charlie Watts and his Big Band's engagement – a fulfilment of Charlie's long-held dream of playing with top jazz musicians in Britain's leading jazz club.

Above: Jerry Hall, flanked by Mick Jagger and David Bowie, celebrates her 27th birthday at a party at London's Langan's Brasserie. Jagger and Bowie are to collaborate on the single 'Dancing In The Street' and the accompanying video, which is to be shown at the Live Aid concert in July 1985.

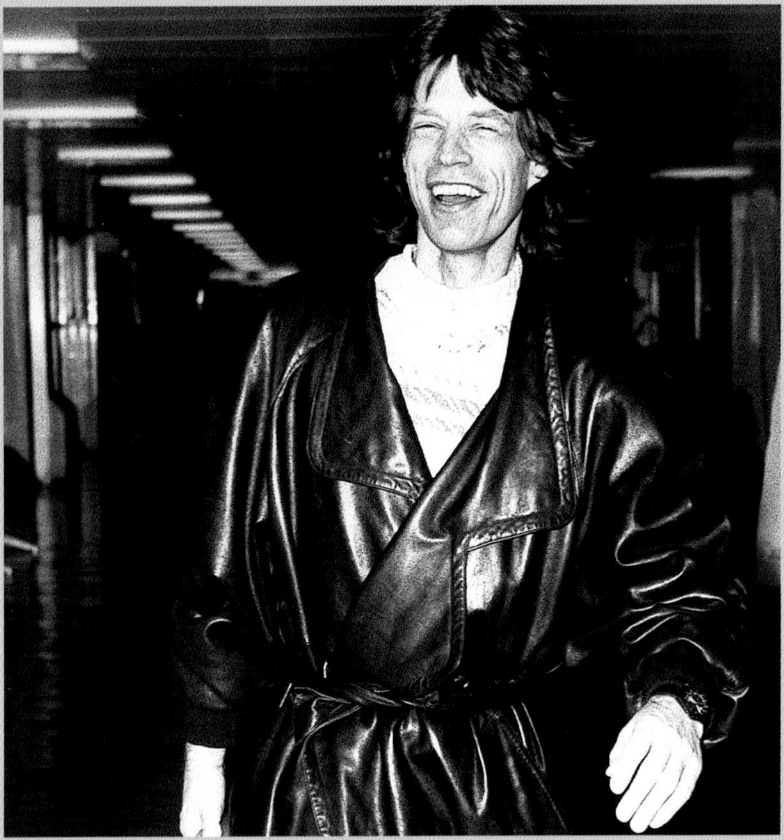

Farewell to a friend

Left: Mick Jagger heads to New York to resume work on the Stones' new album, *Dirty Work*. But Mick, who was concentrating more on his solo career and promoting his own album *She's The Boss*, was often unable to attend recording sessions.

Mick's absence antagonized Keith, who felt that the Stones should come first. *Dirty Work* took nearly a year to make and the relationship between Keith and Mick was severely strained. The likeable Ronnie Wood often took the role of peacemaker between them.

Below: Along with all other band members and musicians, including Eric Clapton and Jeff Beck, Mick Jagger attended the funeral of Ian Stewart on 20 December 1985. Stewart, who had been a friend, colleague and back-up musician for the band since it began, died from heart failure aged 47. The Rolling Stones sang the 23rd Psalm at the service, and later organized a memorial concert at the 100 Club in London. At the end of *Dirty Work* a short piece of boogie woogie piano was added in his honour.

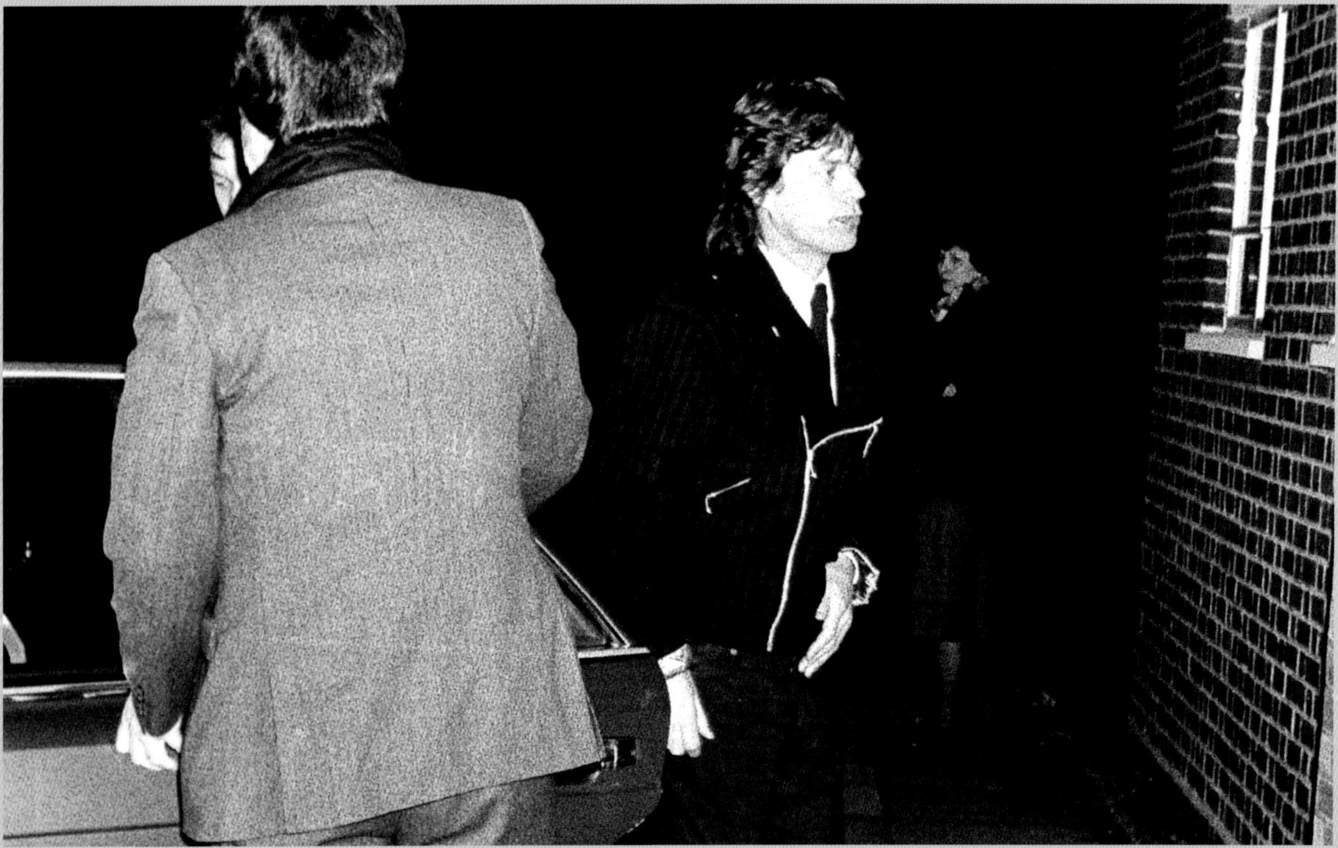

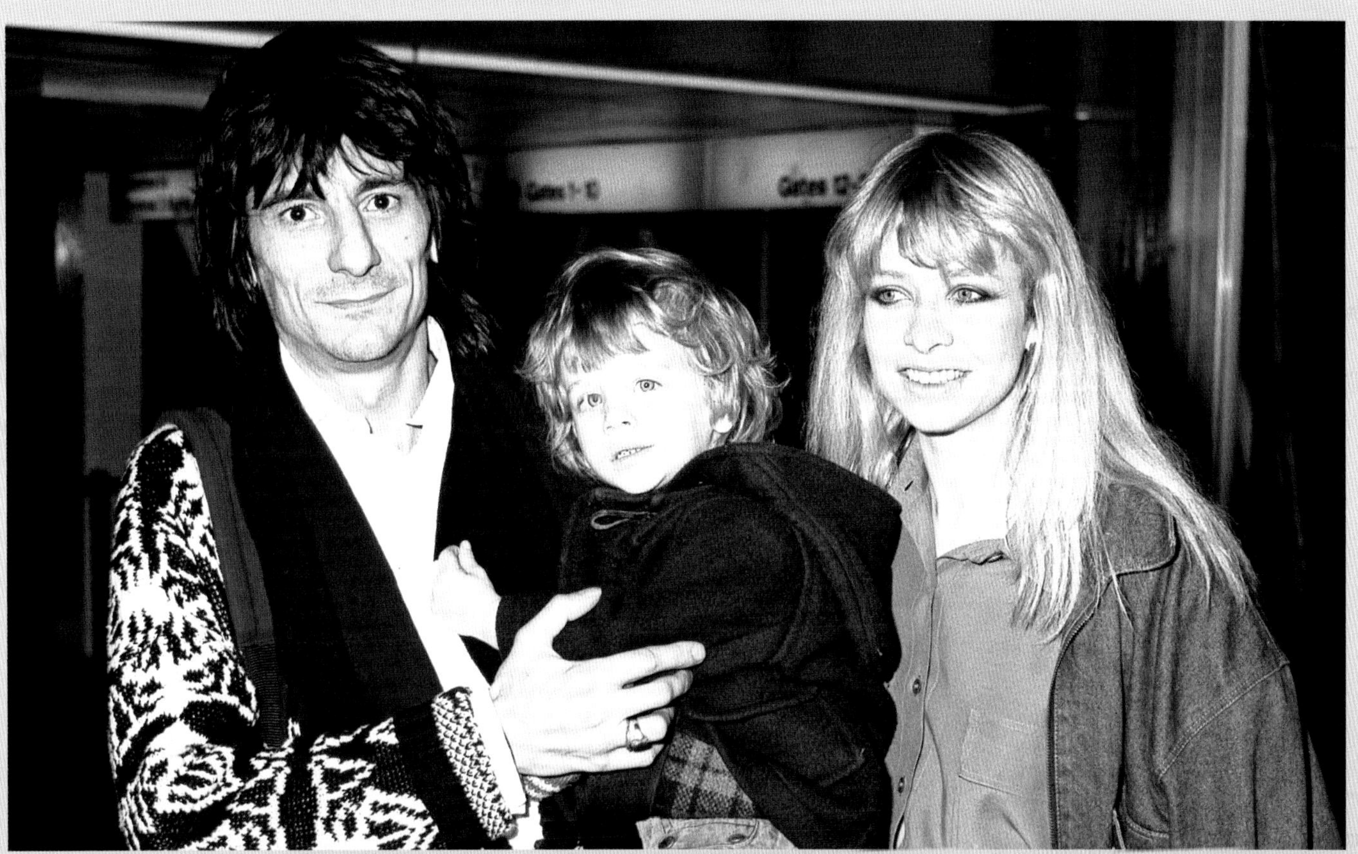

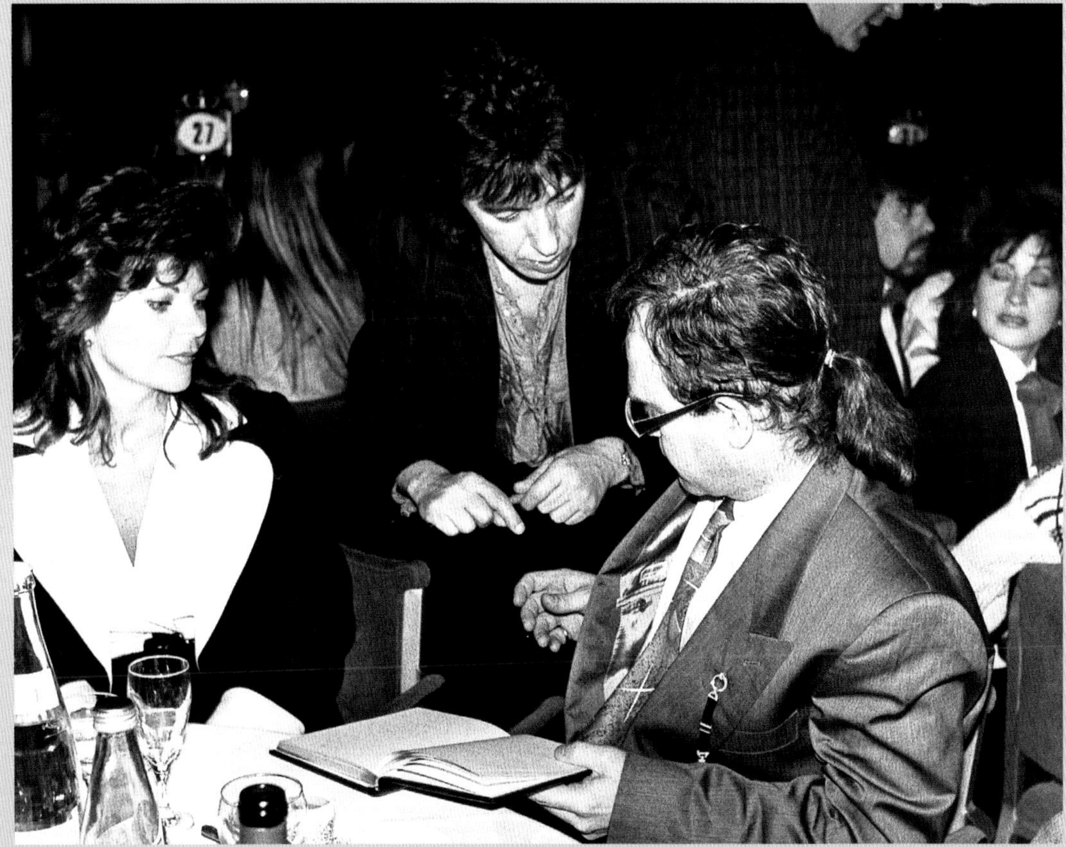

Dirty Work

Above: Ronnie and Jo Wood leave for New York, where *Dirty Work* is being recorded, with their two-year-old son Tyrone in March 1986.

There were many visitors to the New York recording sessions, especially around the time of the Live Aid concert. Bob Dylan came along, and Jimmy Page played a solo on 'One Hit (To The Body)'.

Right: In April 1986 Bill gets an autograph from Elton John.

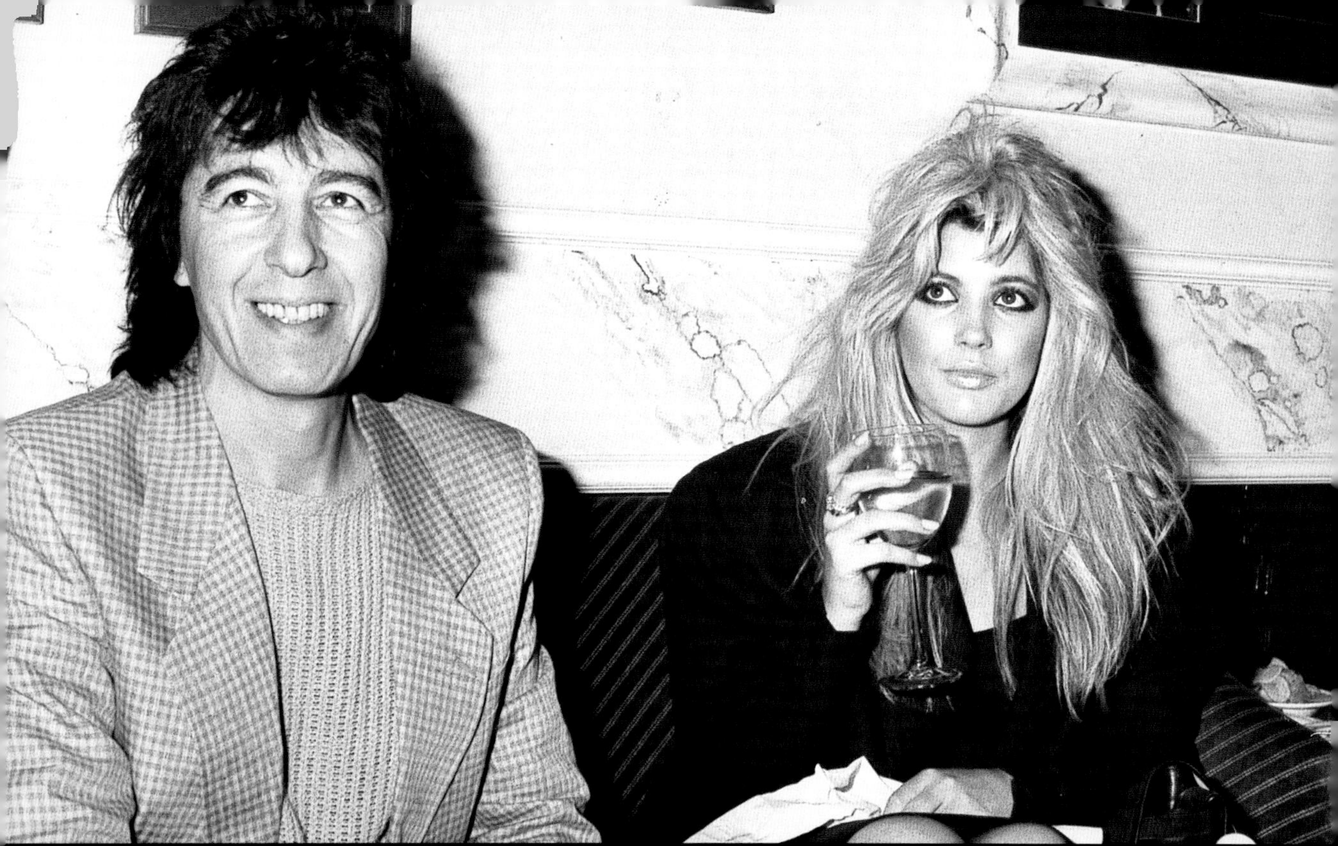

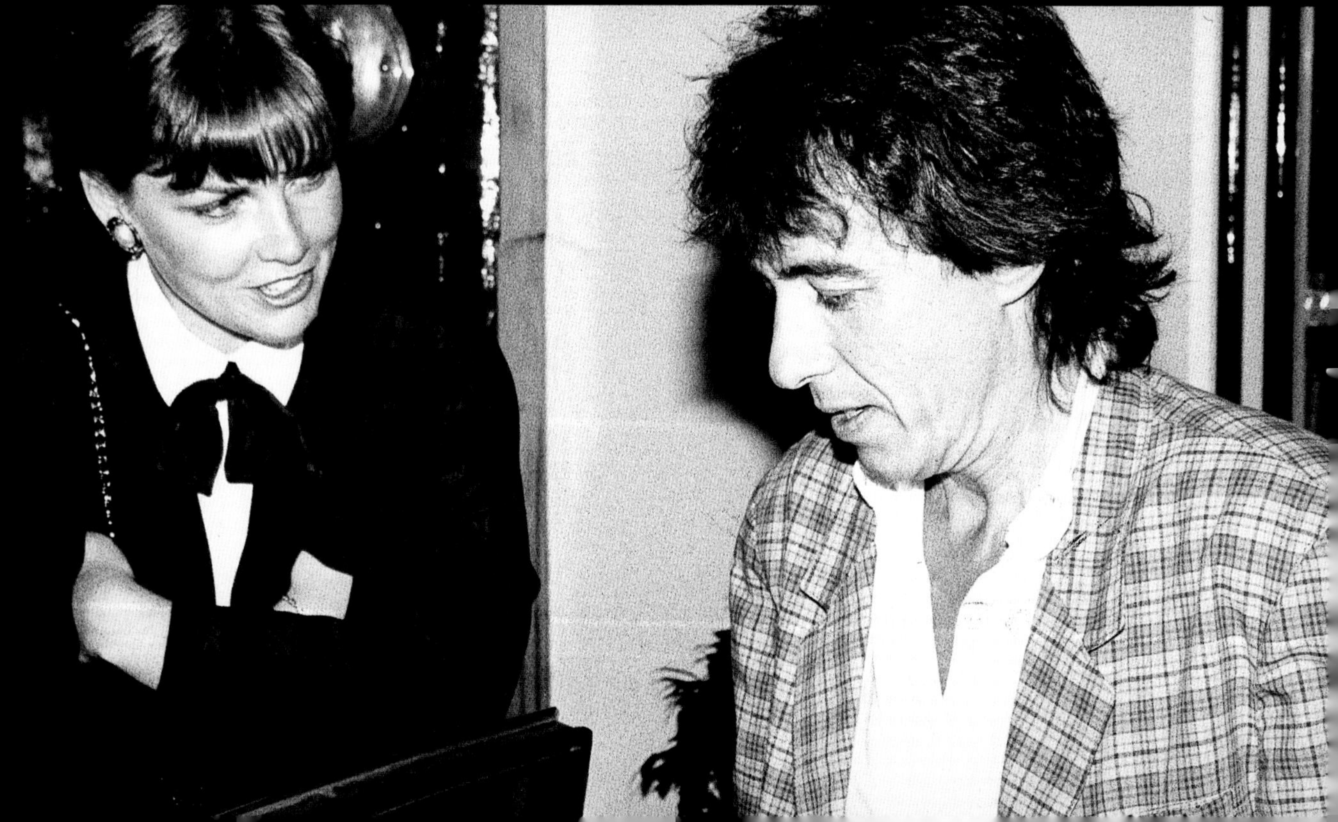

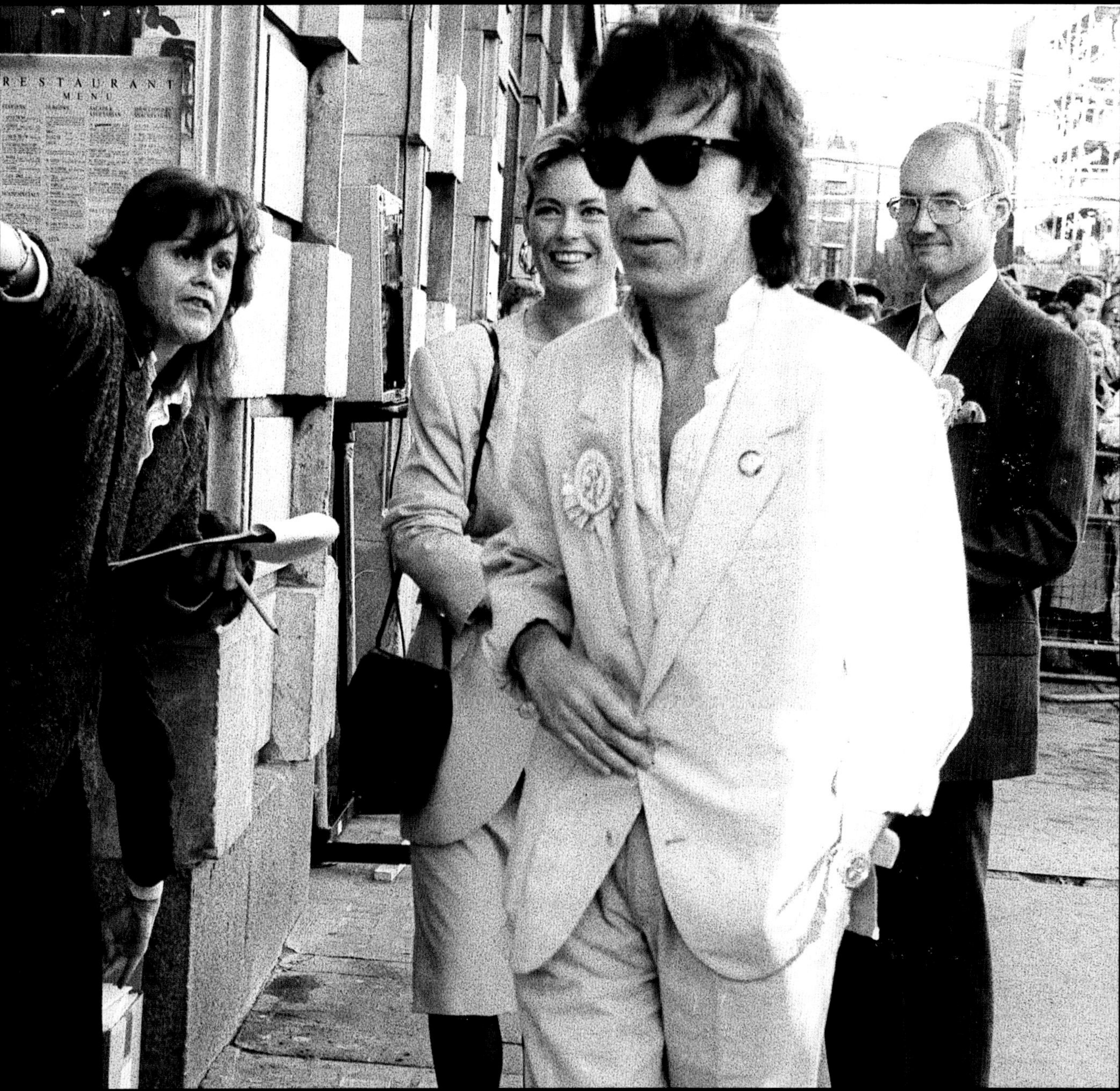

Wyman signs

Above: In November 1986 Bill Wyman signed his name beneath Princess Diana's on a petition displayed at a fashionable Covent Garden bar and restaurant. It urged young people to avoid drugs. Other signatories included Cliff Richard and John Entwistle of The Who.

Opposite above: Bill pictured in September with teenager Mandy Smith, whom he'd first met two years previously at the Lyceum Ballroom. Their relationship caused a scandal when made public because of her young age, but they would eventually marry in June 1989.

Opposite below: Another admirer detains Bill as he leaves Tramp nightclub.

Bill was less active musically than the other members of the band during this period. Charlie and Mick pursued their own interests and Keith eventually formed a band and recorded 'Talk is Cheap'. But when Ronnie Wood reunited with Rod Stewart and The Faces at Wembley in 1986, Bill took the place of Ronnie Lane

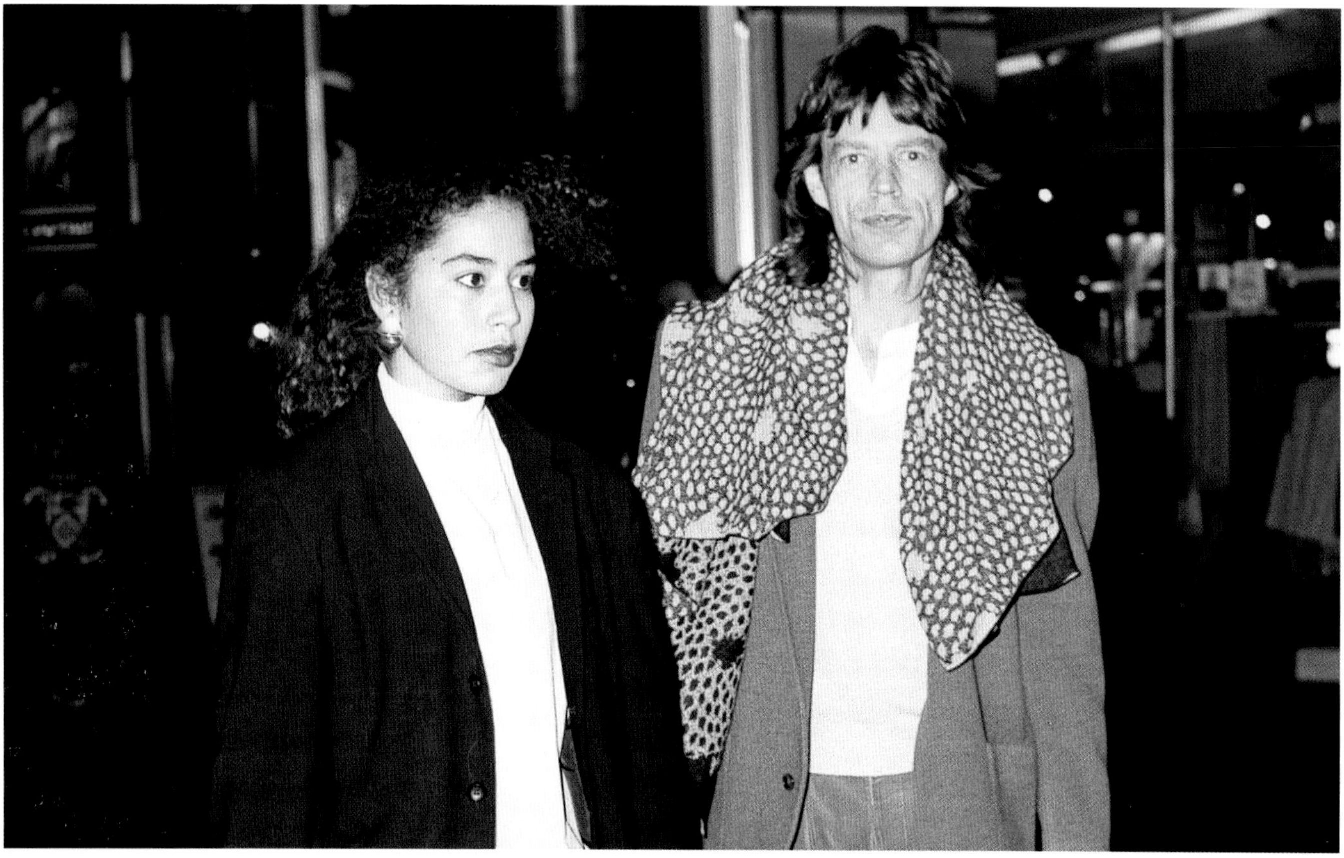

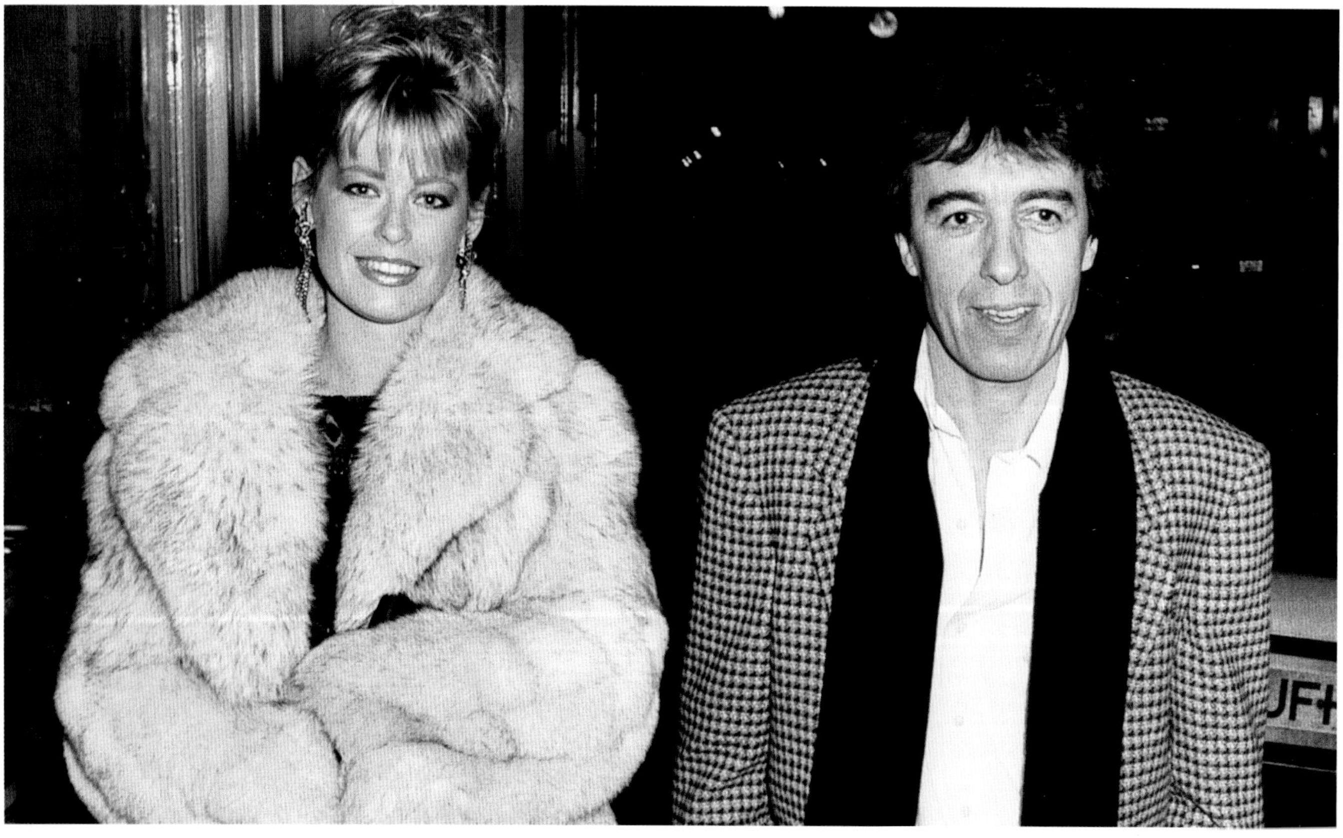

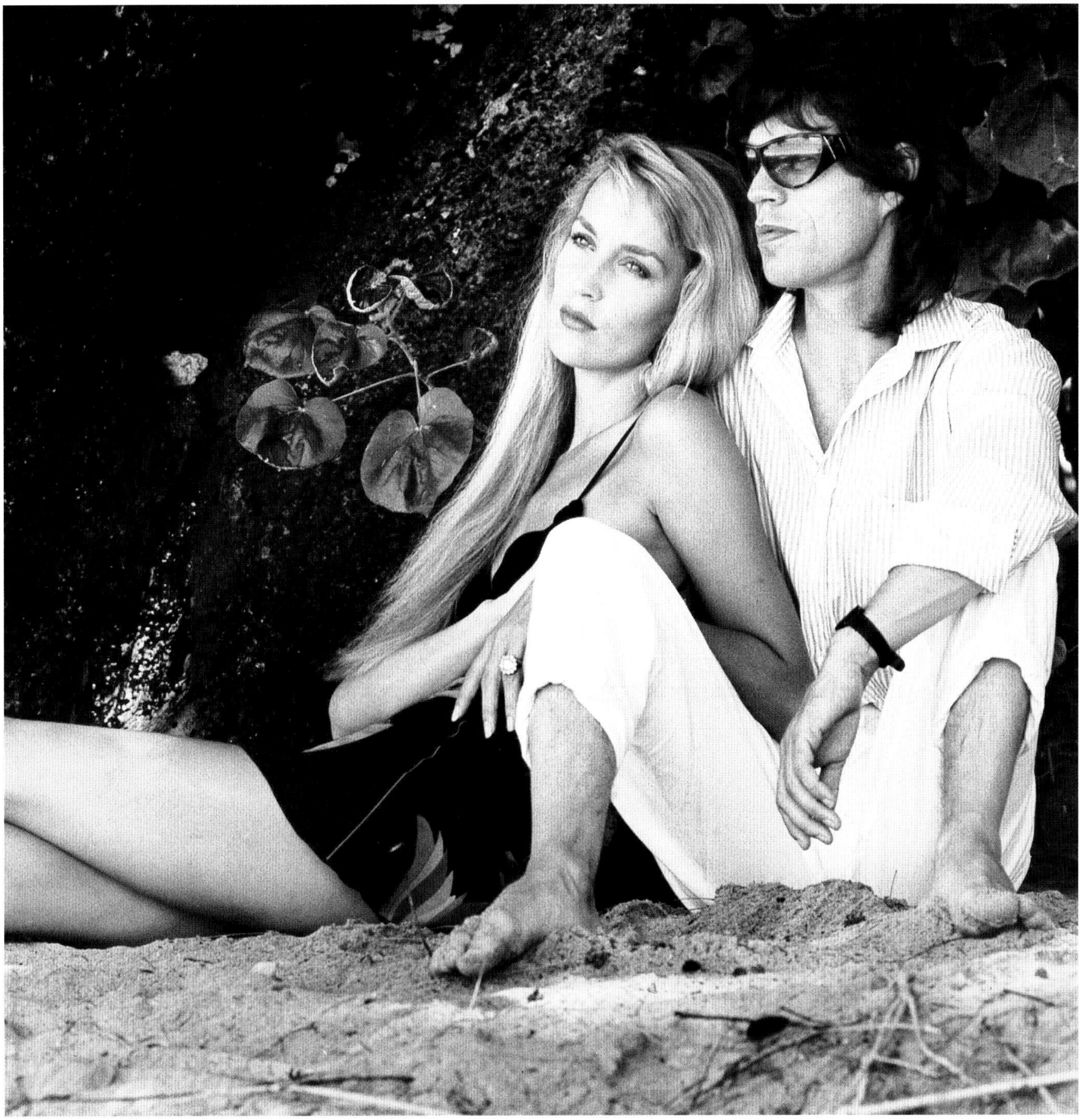

Christmas in the sun

Opposite above: Mick Jagger flew to Barbados with 16-year-old daughter Karis for a Christmas break in the sun on 19 December 1986.

Opposite below: Early in 1987 Bill Wyman saw a lot of American model Nike Clark. This particular evening they dined at Langan's Brasserie and went on to Tramp.

Above: A serenely beautiful Jerry Hall leans against Mick Jagger in Barbados in January 1987. Her thoughts are likely to be on her forthcoming court appearance. Customs officials found a large quantity of marijuana in her luggage when Jerry flew in to the island.

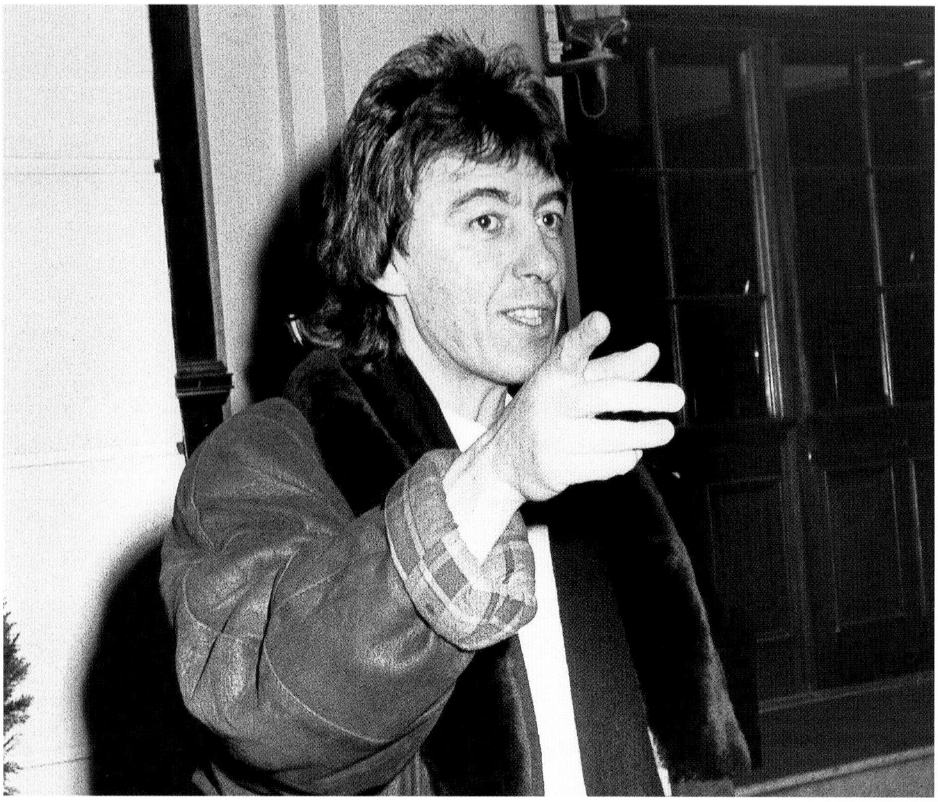

Playboy Jazz

Opposite above: Charlie Watts views the cricket memorabilia at an MCC auction at Christie's in April 1987. Charlie was continuing his jazz career, playing with his orchestra at the Playboy Jazz Festival in Hollywood the following June.

Opposite below: Charlie buys a distinguished portrait for a little under £1,000.

Left: Being a Rolling Stone doesn't open every door. Bill Wyman was refused entrance to Regine's nightclub in London. His crime? Not wearing a tie.

Below: Mick en route for New York in April 1987, where he was recording a solo album, *Primitive Cool*. Jeff Beck was again to be involved, and this time Dave Stewart of Eurythmics helped with production.

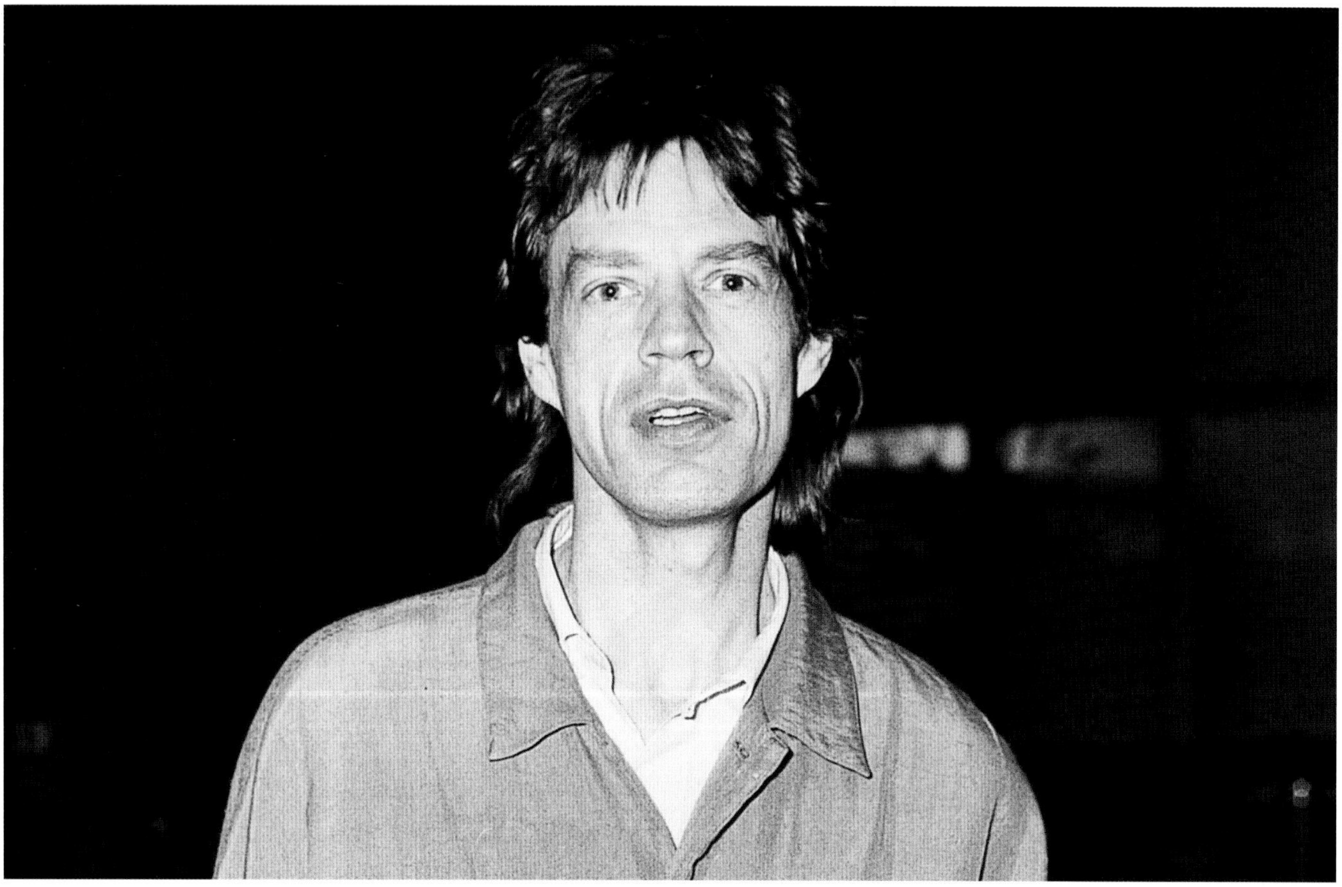

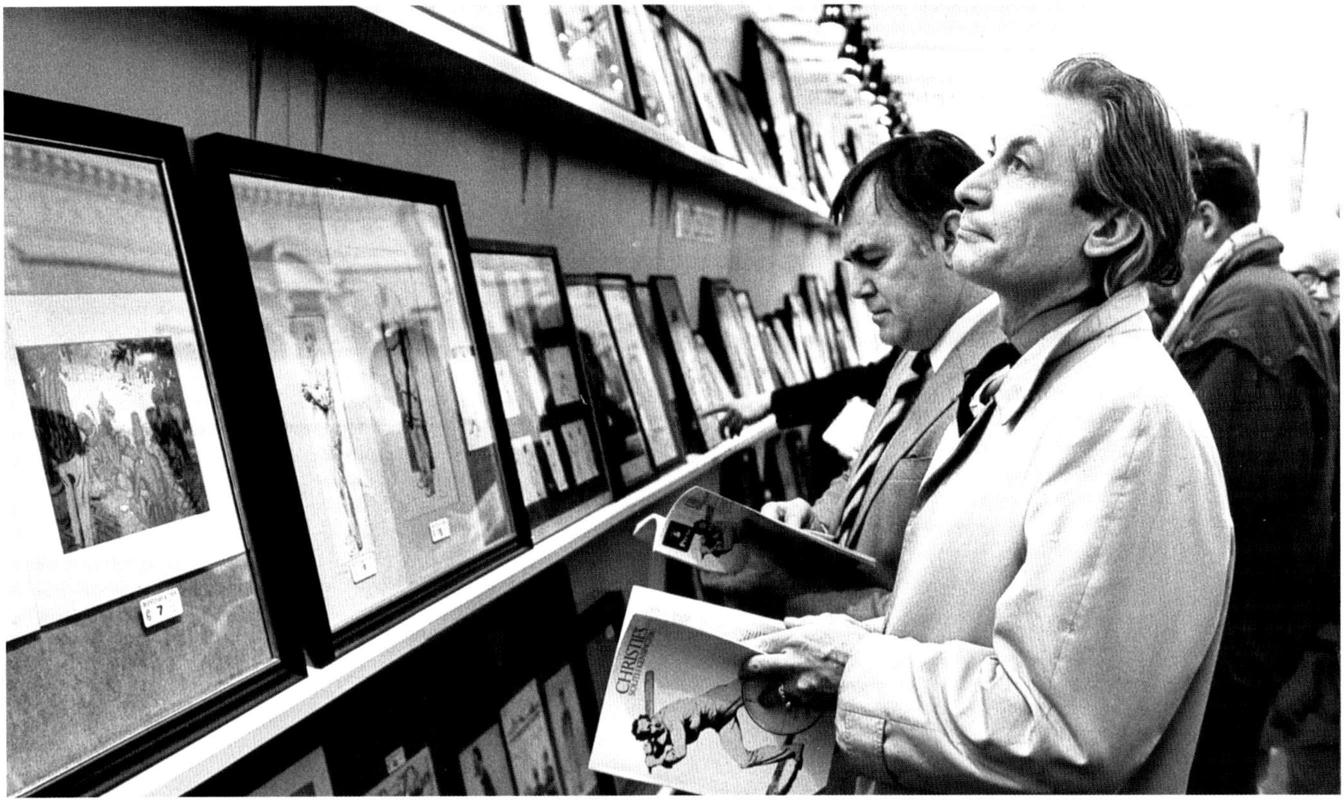
CHRISTIE'S

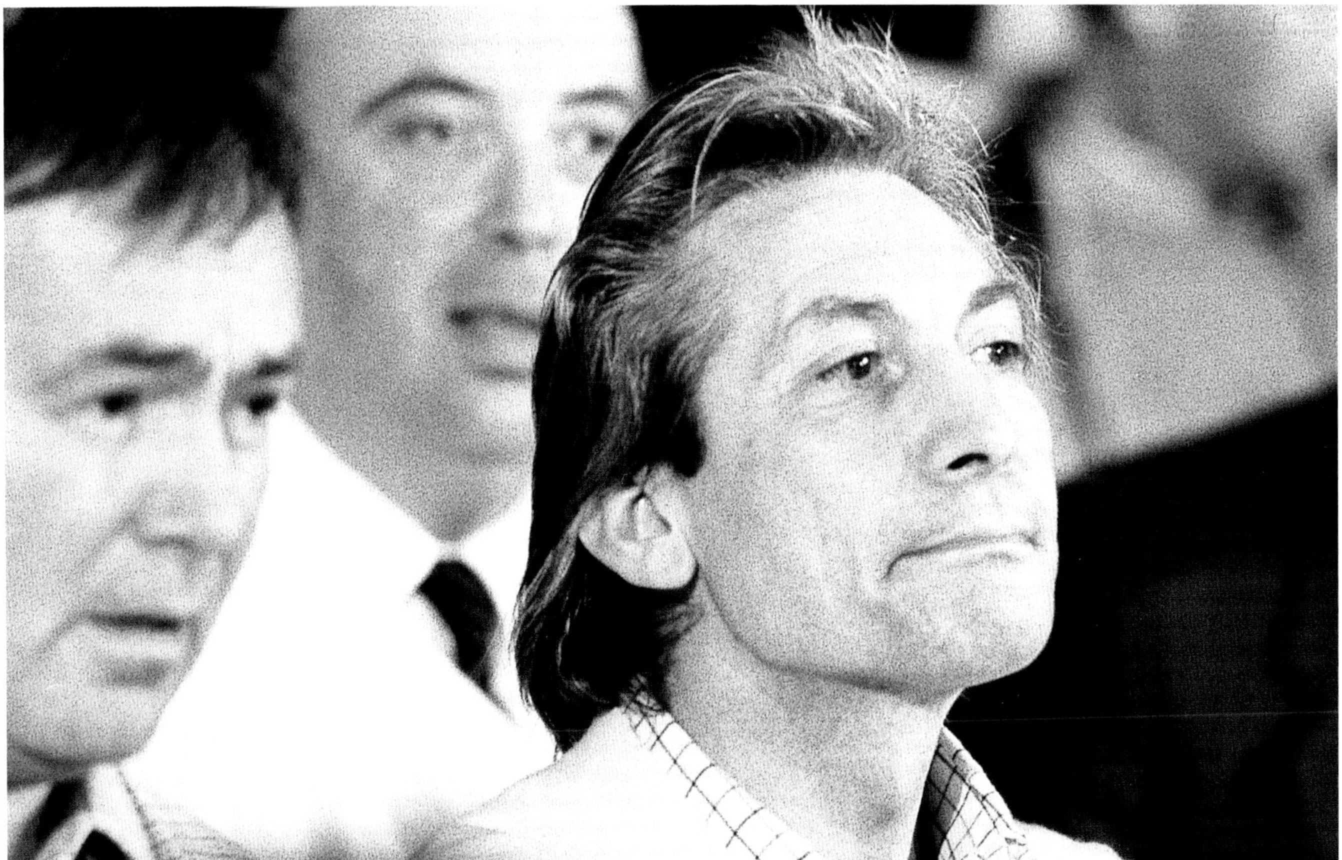

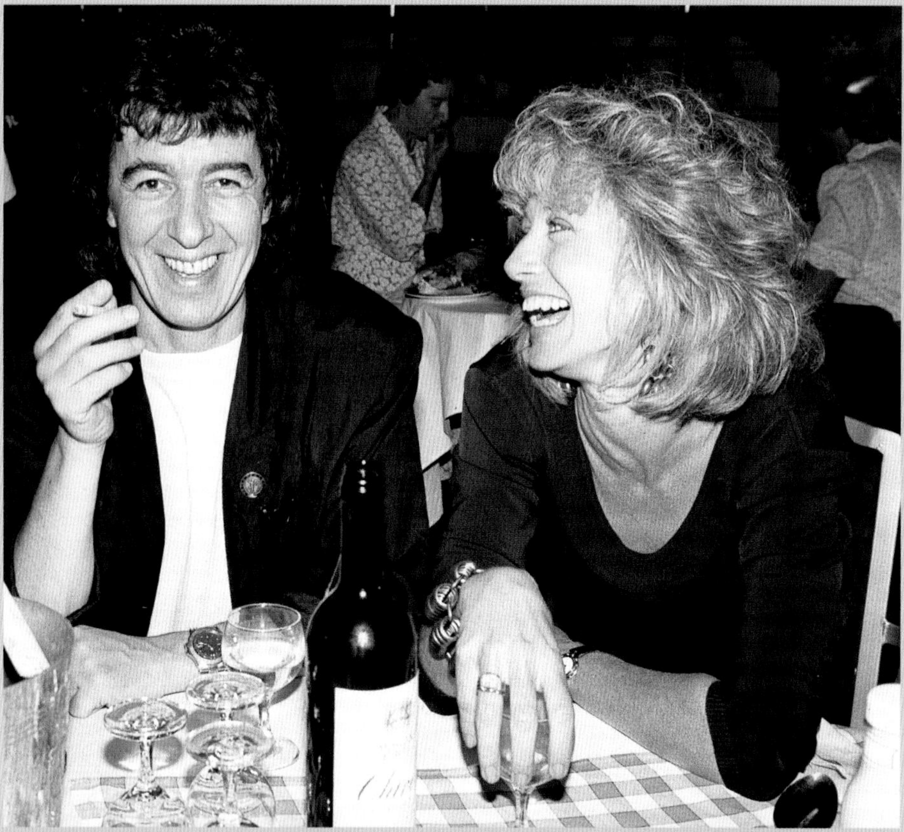

Back live

Opposite: In September 1987 Mick recorded his forthcoming single 'Let's Work' for the BBC's *Top of the Pops* – the first 'live' Stones appearance on the programme since 1970. It charted briefly later in the month.

Left: Bill Wyman with his current date at Stringfellows nightclub in London.

Mandy Smith had announced in August 1986 that her relationship with Wyman was flagging, but it wasn't the end of the road – they announced their engagement in March 1989.

Below: Ronnie Wood with wife Jo. Even though the Stones hadn't been doing much collectively, Ronnie had been busy – there was to be an exhibition of his paintings and he was also involved with his own nightclub and restaurant in Miami.

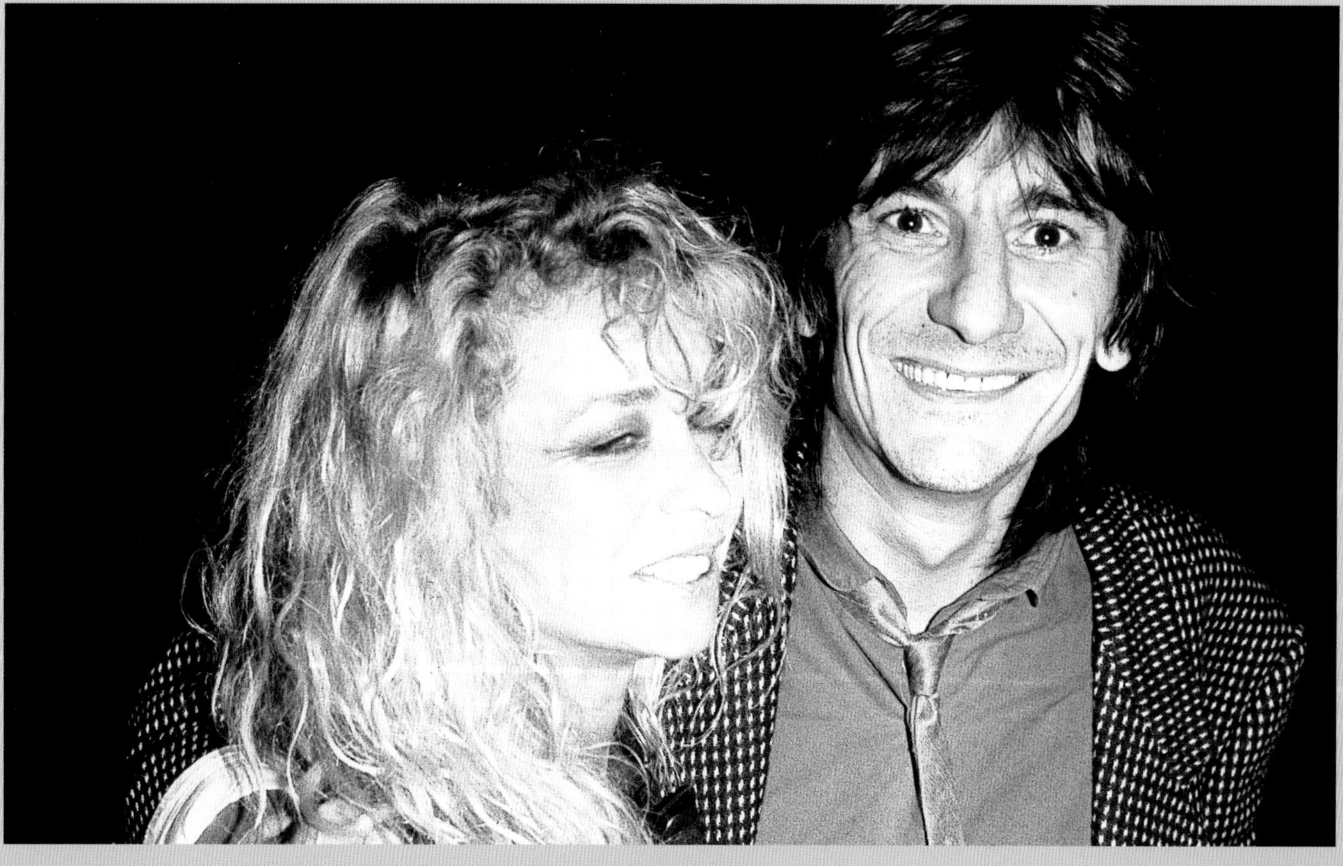

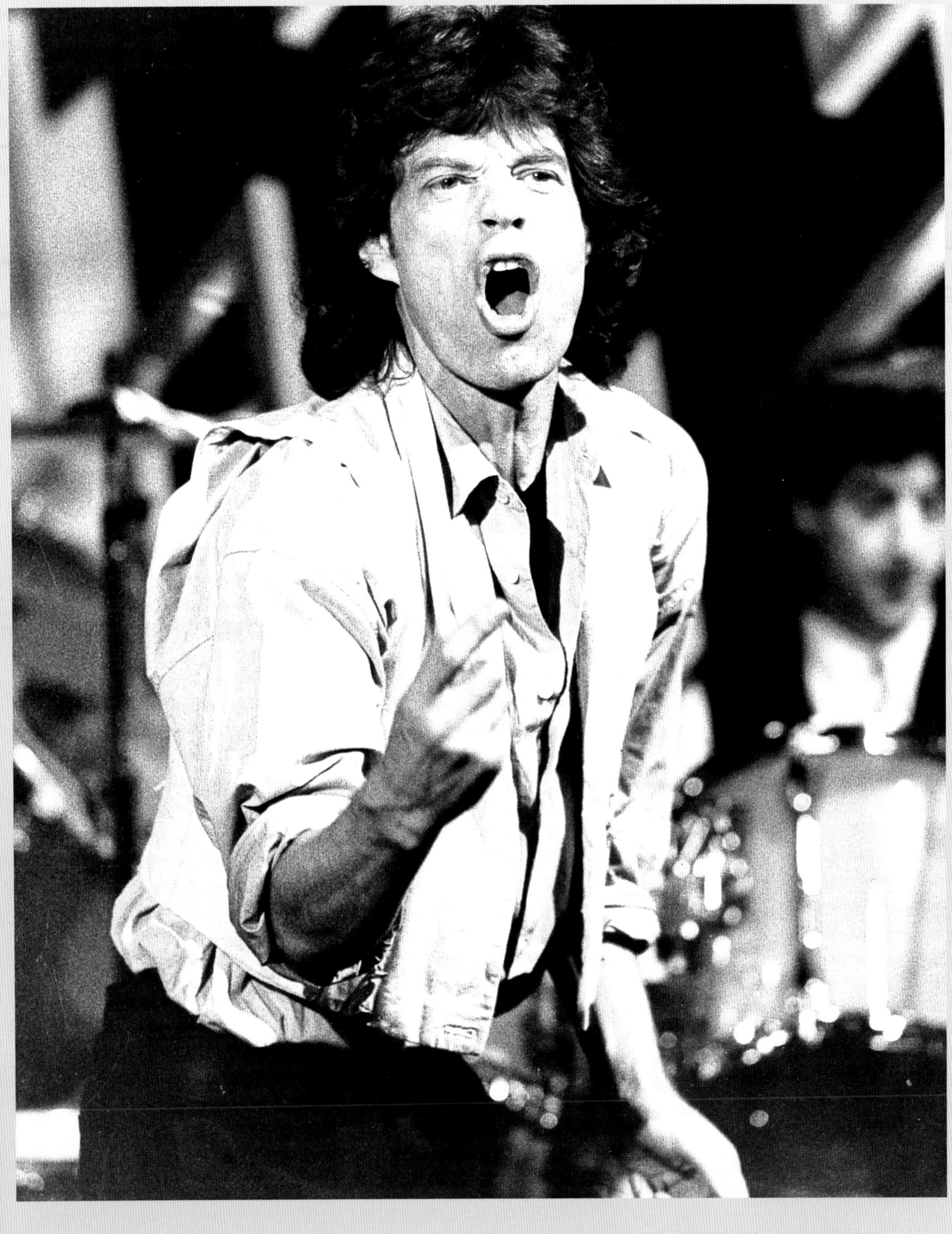

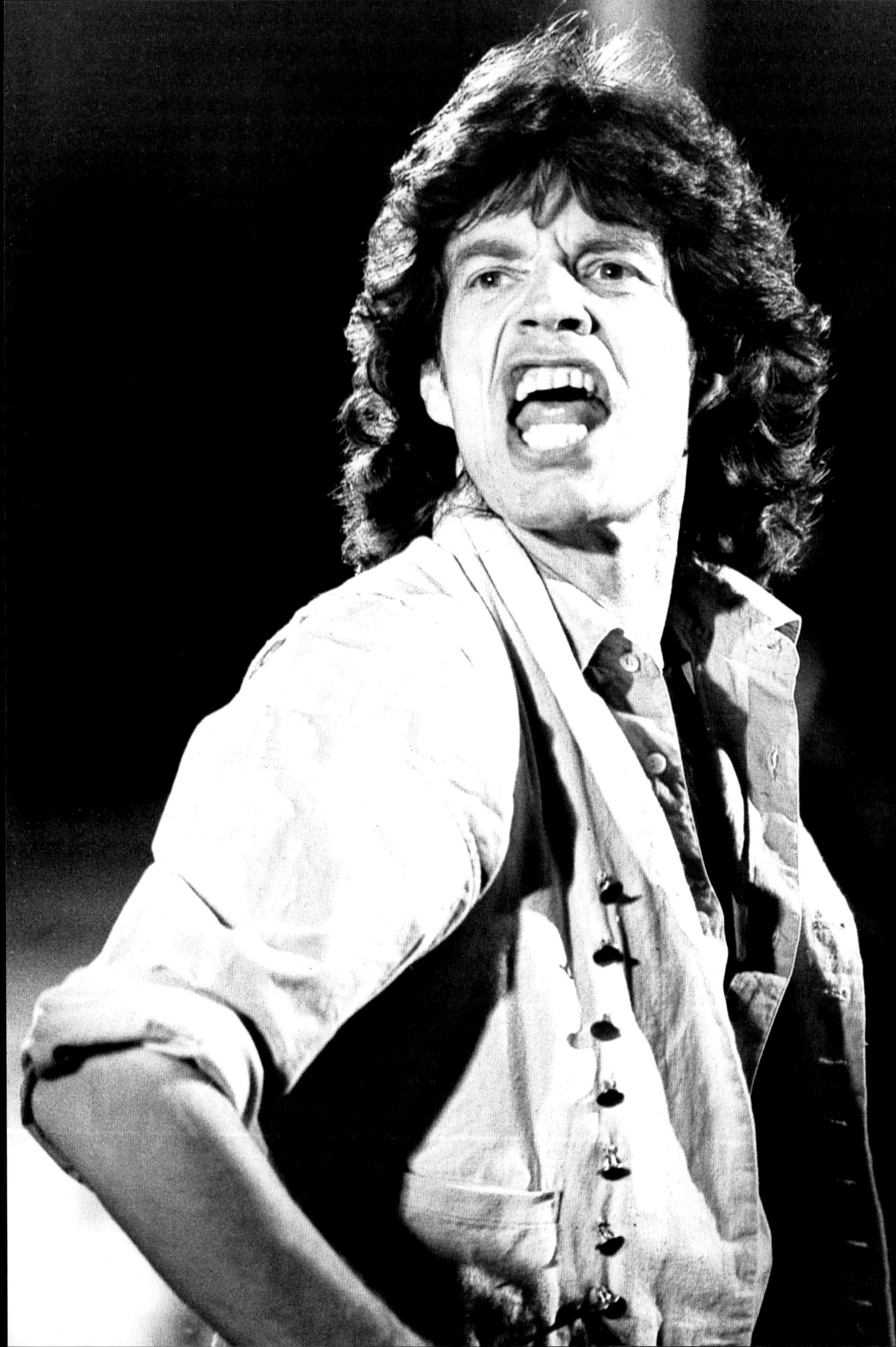

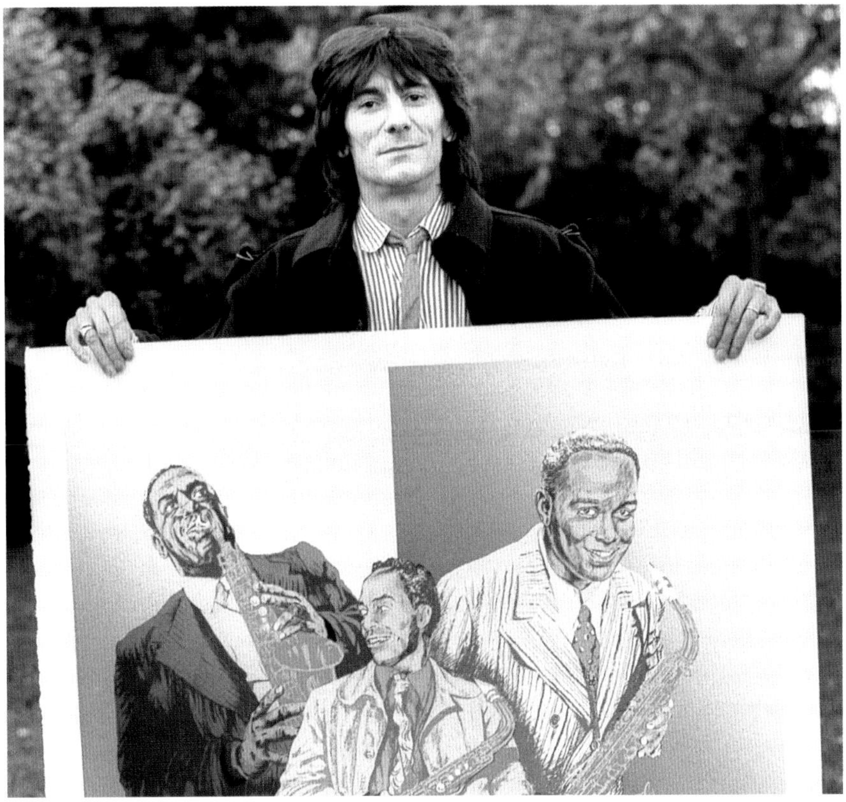

Mick's Primitive Cool

Opposite: Mick roars. His second solo album, *Primitive Cool*, was released in September 1987 and reached No.18 in the charts. In 1988, instead of performing with the band, Mick has just completed a solo tour of Japan, reportedly receiving £1 million per show. By the time the tour closed, over a quarter of a million tickets had been sold. Ronnie was also on tour in Japan and the two met up in Osaka.

Left: In October 1987 an exhibition of Ronnie Wood's pictures of legendary musicians opened in London. The exhibition, 'Decades', would later open in the United States.

Below: Bill Wyman out on the town with Lorna Luft, who is passing through London.

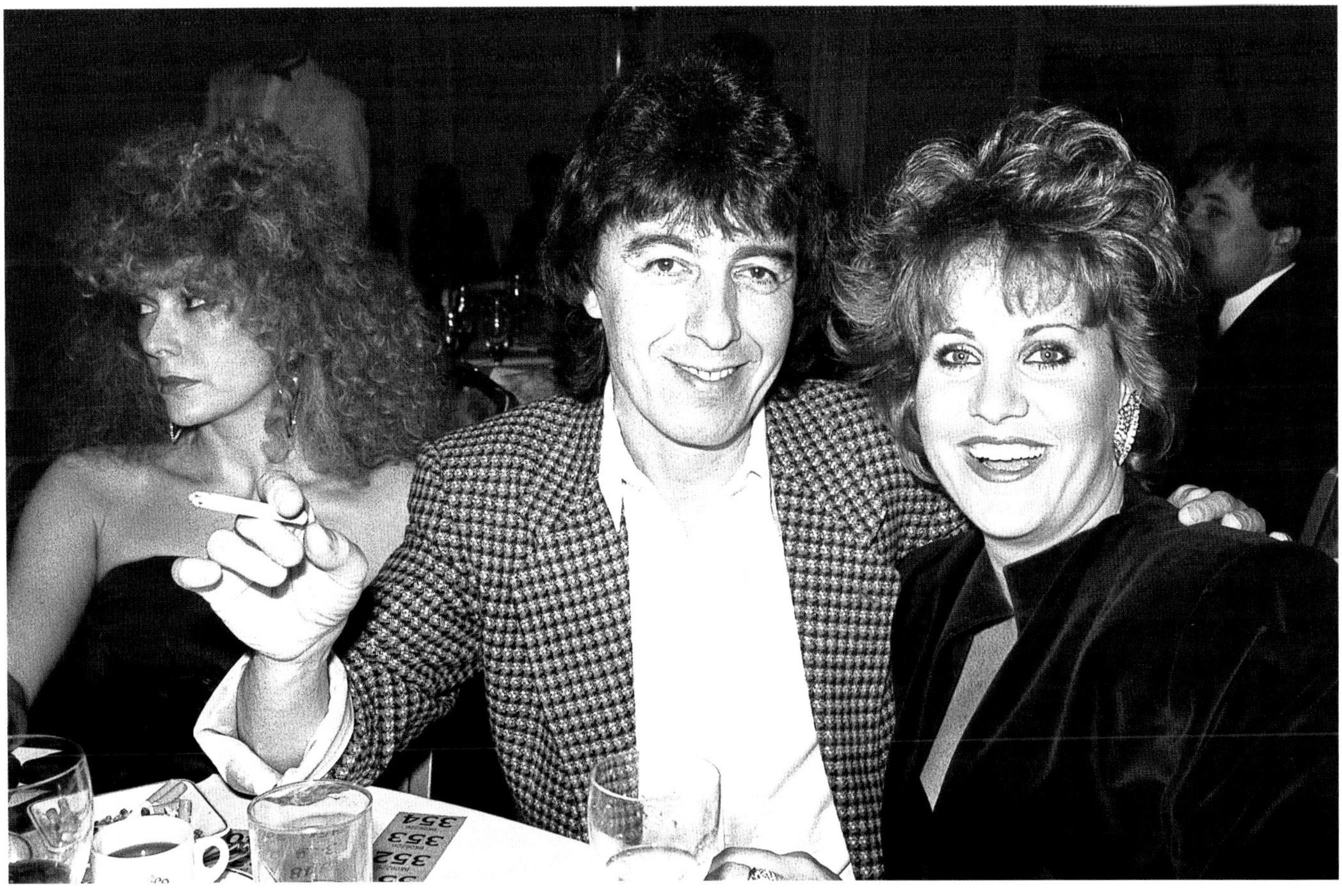

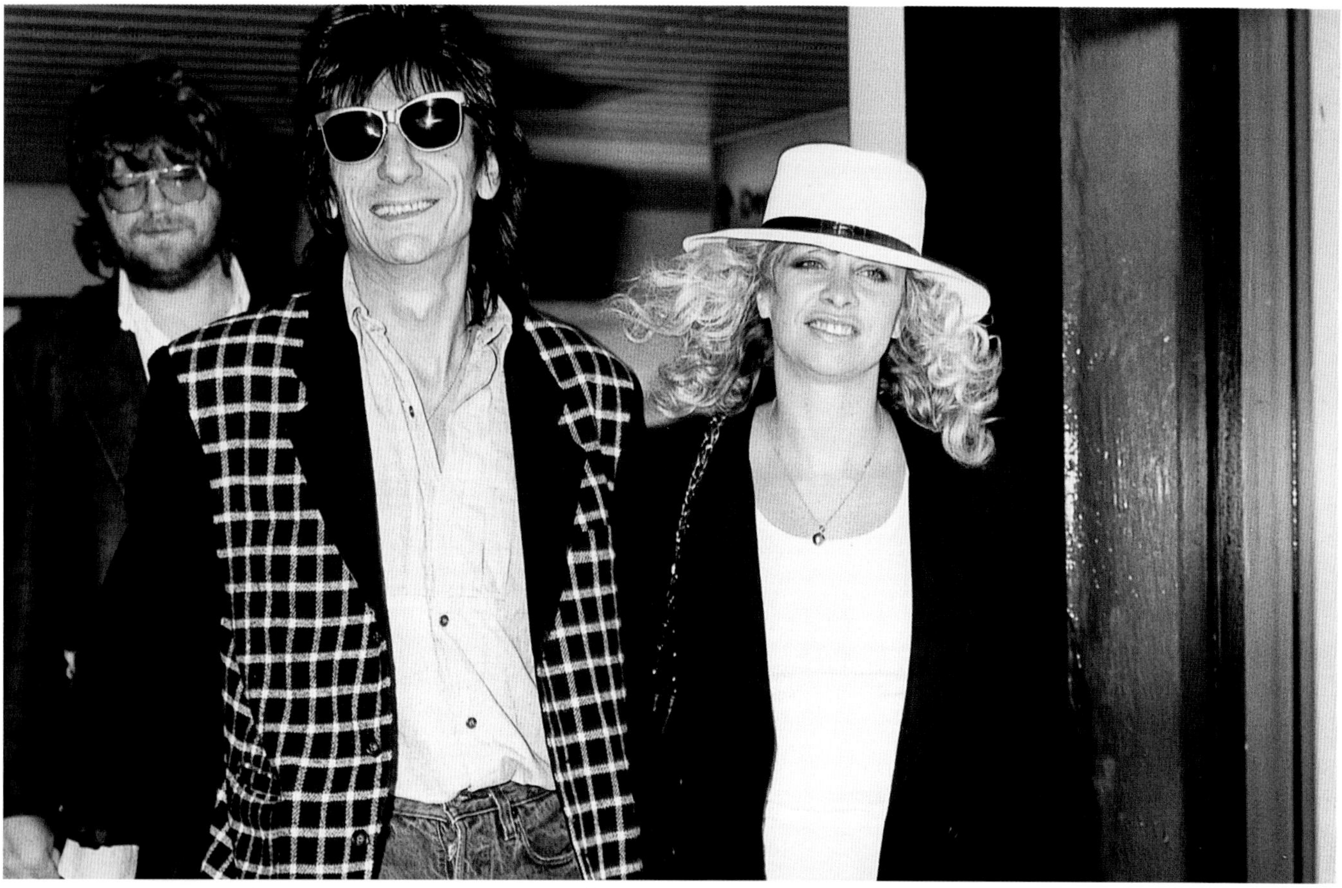

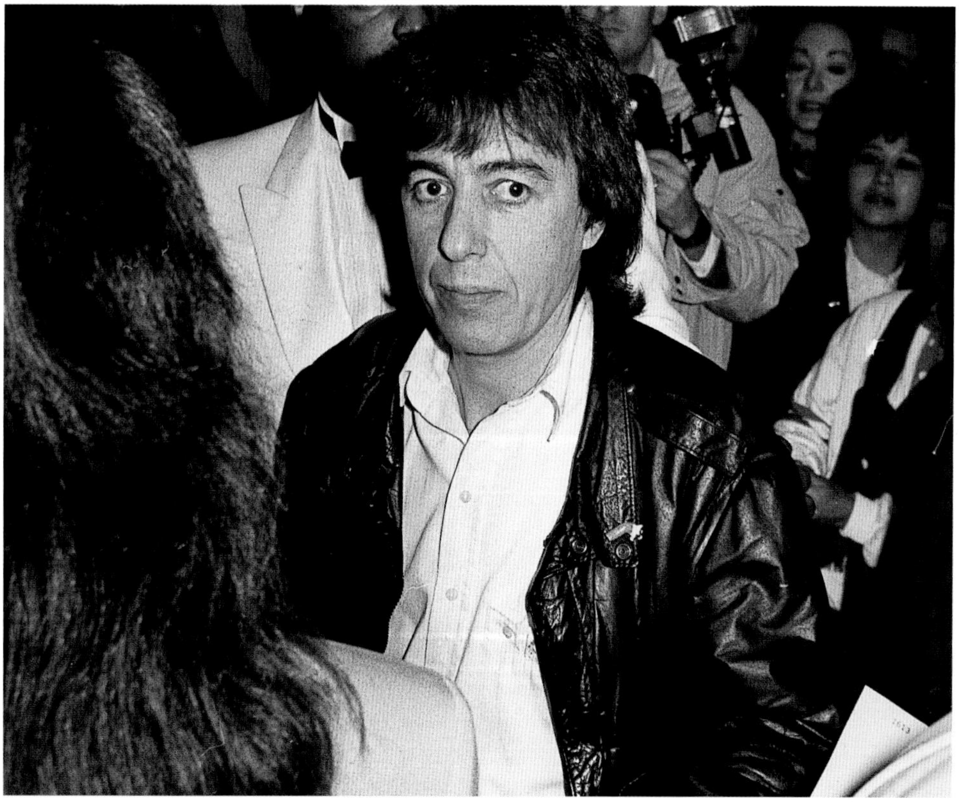

Working together again

Above: Ronnie and Jo in July 1988.

Just when it seemed that the Stones might split, all five members of the band met for the first time in two years and it was announced in August that The Rolling Stones would record and tour together the following year.

Left: Bill Wyman had signed a book deal with Viking/Penguin. He was credited with being the most organized member of the band and having the best memory.

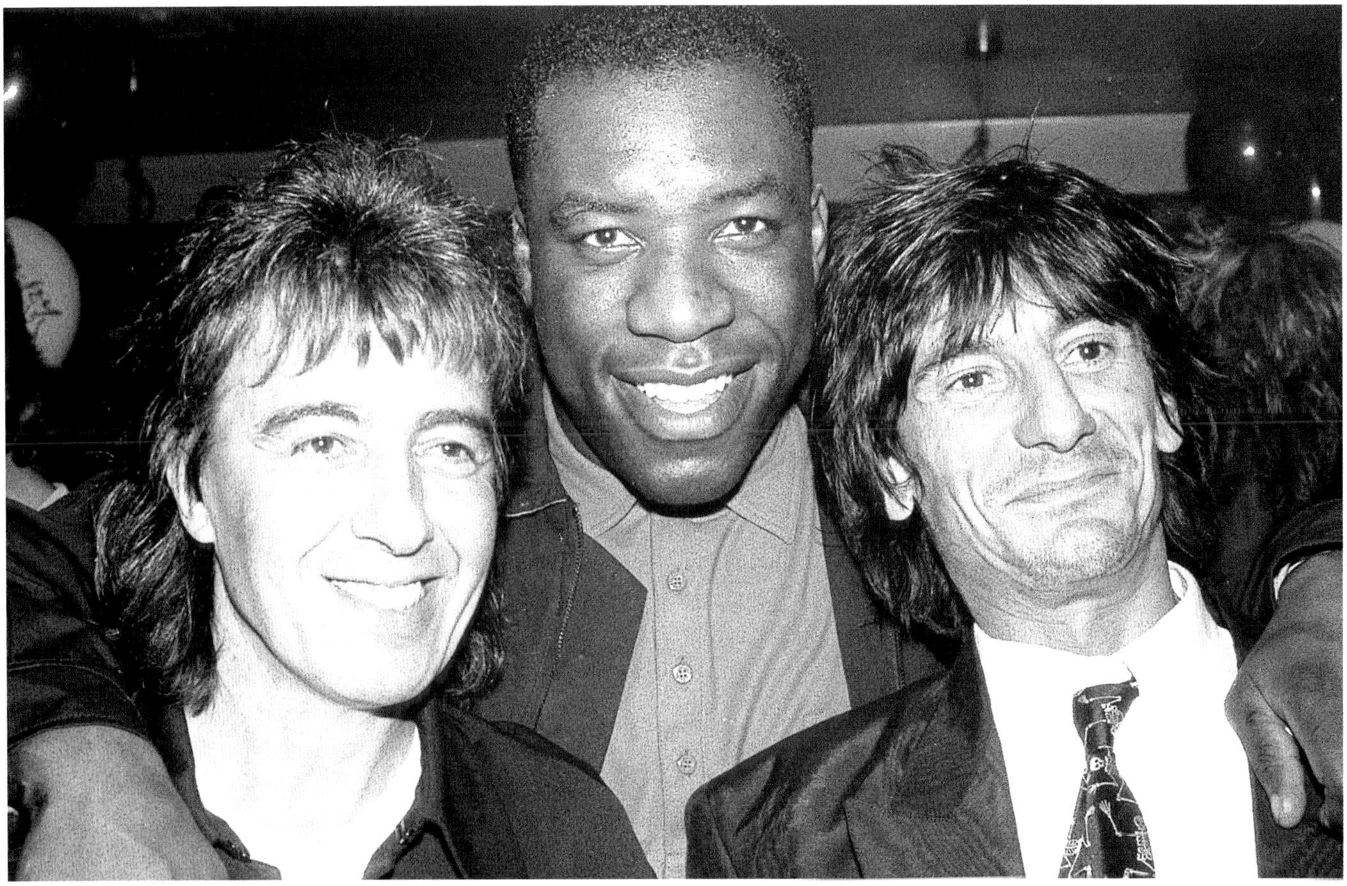

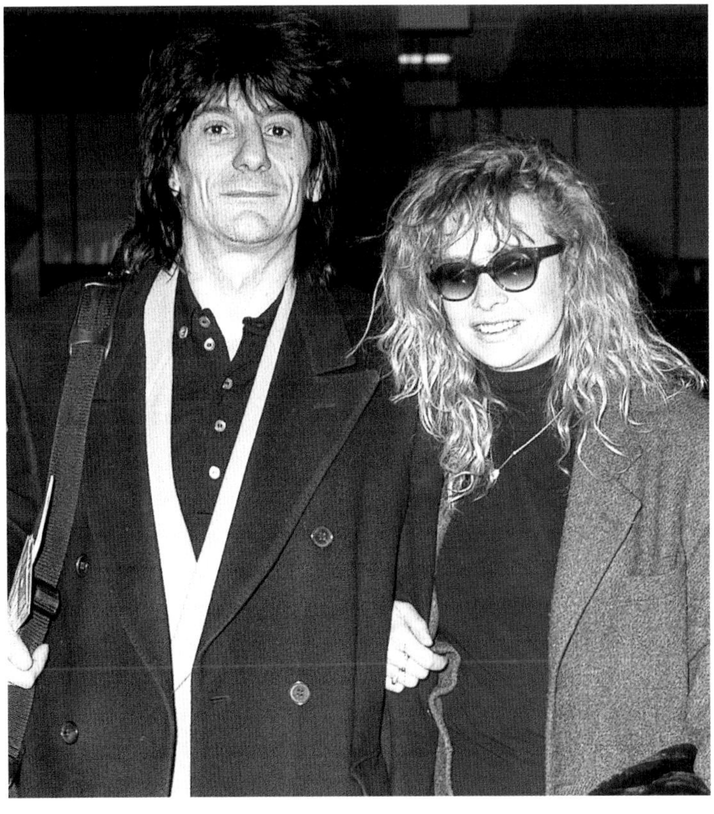

Hall of Fame

Left: Ronnie and Jo Wood, en route for New York in January 1989, where the band is being inducted into the Rock and Roll Hall of Fame. Bill Wyman and Charlie Watts were absent due to other commitments, but Mick Taylor was reunited with the other band members.

In February 1989 the Stones headed for Barbados to discuss a new album and future plans with their financial, legal and business advisers. In March they signed a multimillion-dollar contract – the biggest in rock 'n' roll history – relating to the promotion and merchandising of their next tour.

Mick and Keith settled down to write immediately, and most of the recording was done over a period of five weeks in Monserrat. Bill Wyman had to leave before the album was completed to deal with the press once the news of his forthcoming wedding to Mandy Smith was made public. Although Keith and Mick had patched up their differences, the future of the band was still in doubt because of Charlie's ill health and Wyman's announced intention to leave the band.

Above: A photo opportunity at the launch party for boxer Gary Mason, posing with Bill and Ronnie.

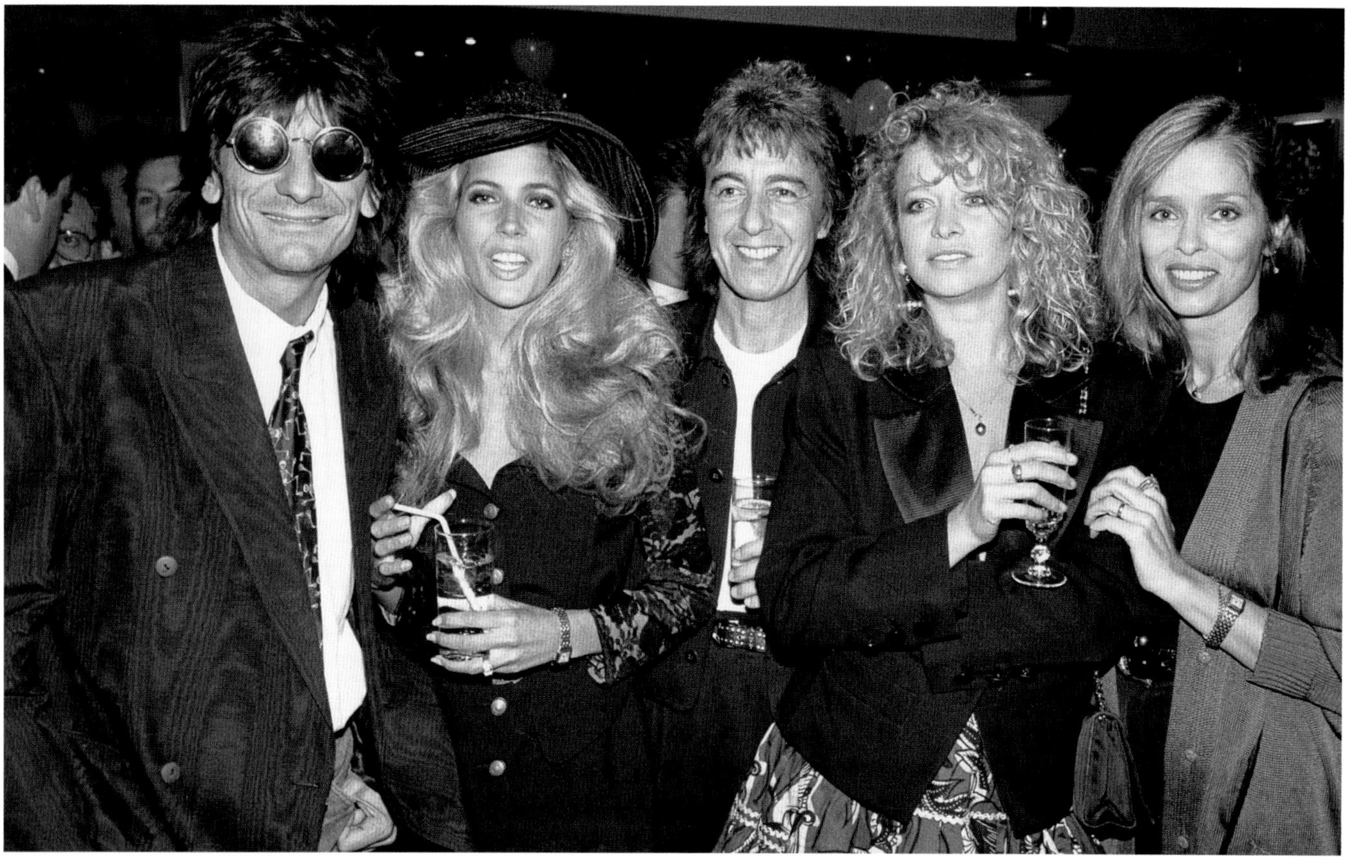

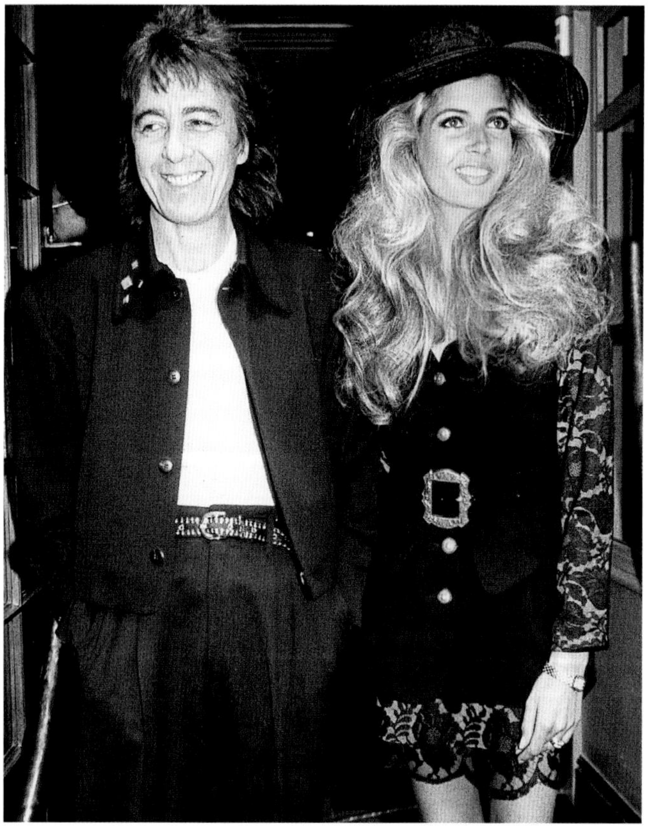

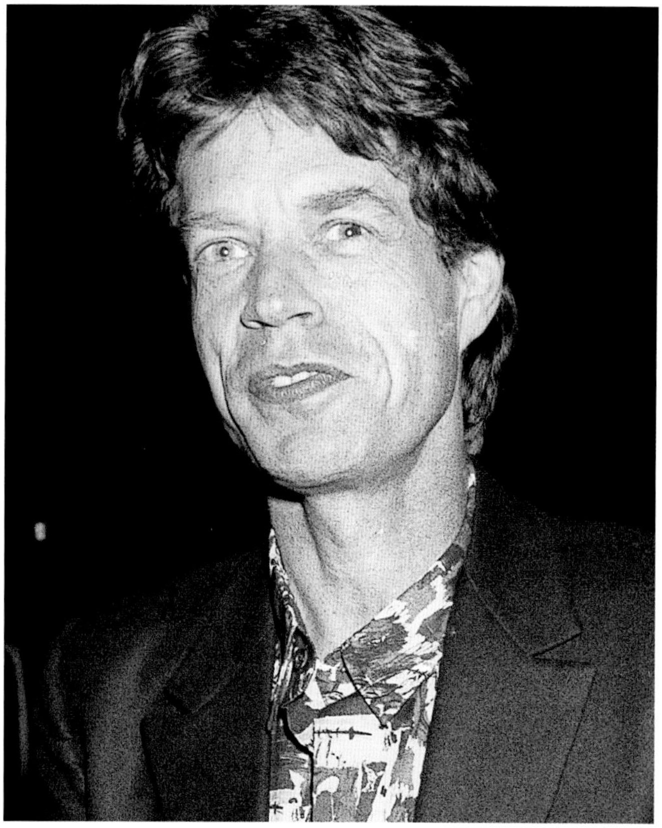

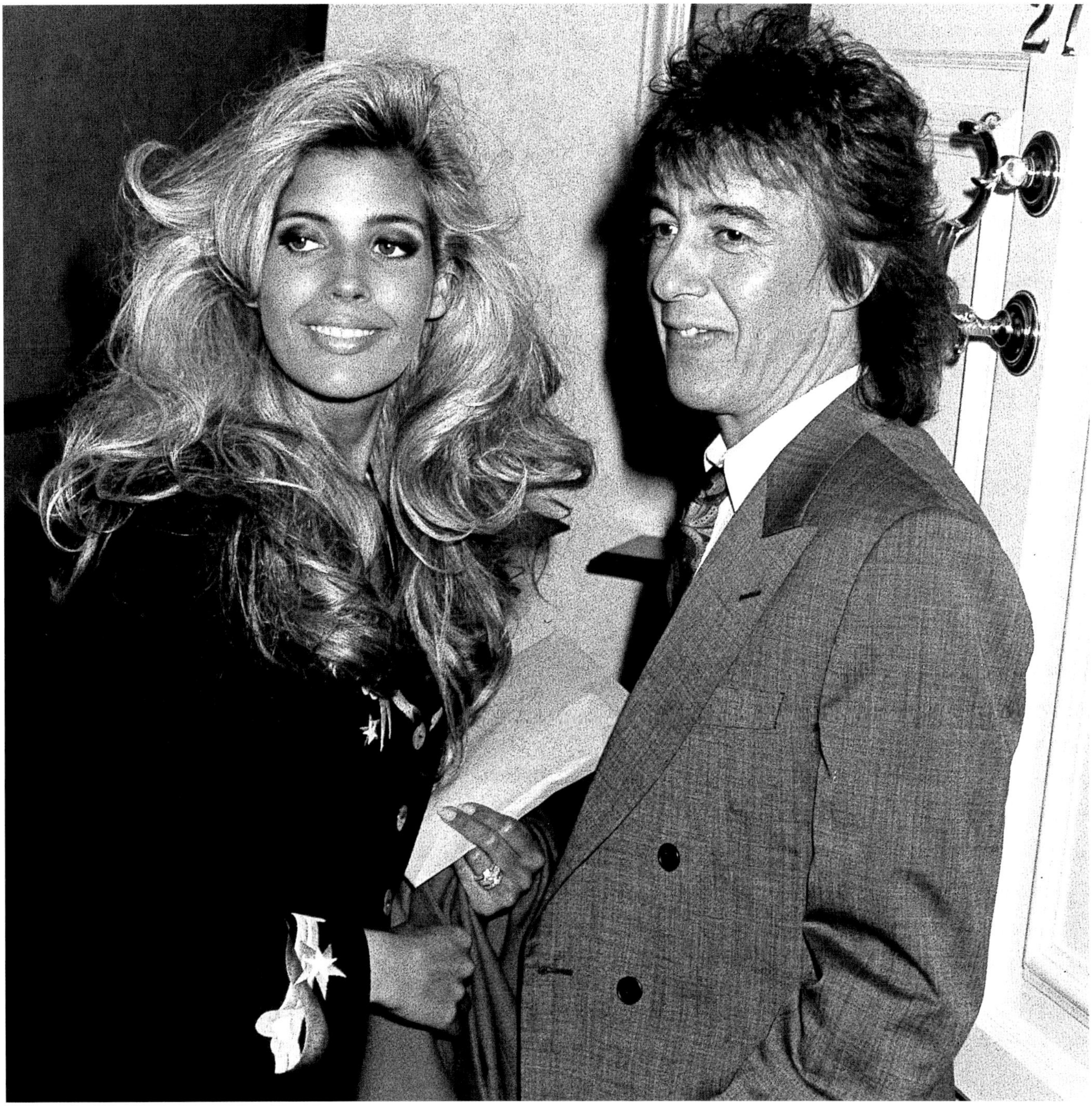

Bill's Sticky Fingers

Opposite above: Mandy Smith, Jo Wood and Barbara Bach, aka Mrs Ringo Starr, party with Ronnie and Bill in May 1989. They were attending the opening of Bill's new Tex/Mex restaurant, Sticky Fingers – named after the band's 1971 album.

Opposite below left: Bill and Mandy at the launch party.

Above: Mandy Smith wears a sober black outfit for her civil marriage ceremony to Bill Wyman on 2 June 1989. The ceremony was a quiet one in Bury St Edmunds, and was followed three days later by a church blessing in London.

Opposite below right: Also on 2 June, Mick Jagger arrives late at a party to celebrate the 21st birthday of the top model agency Models One.

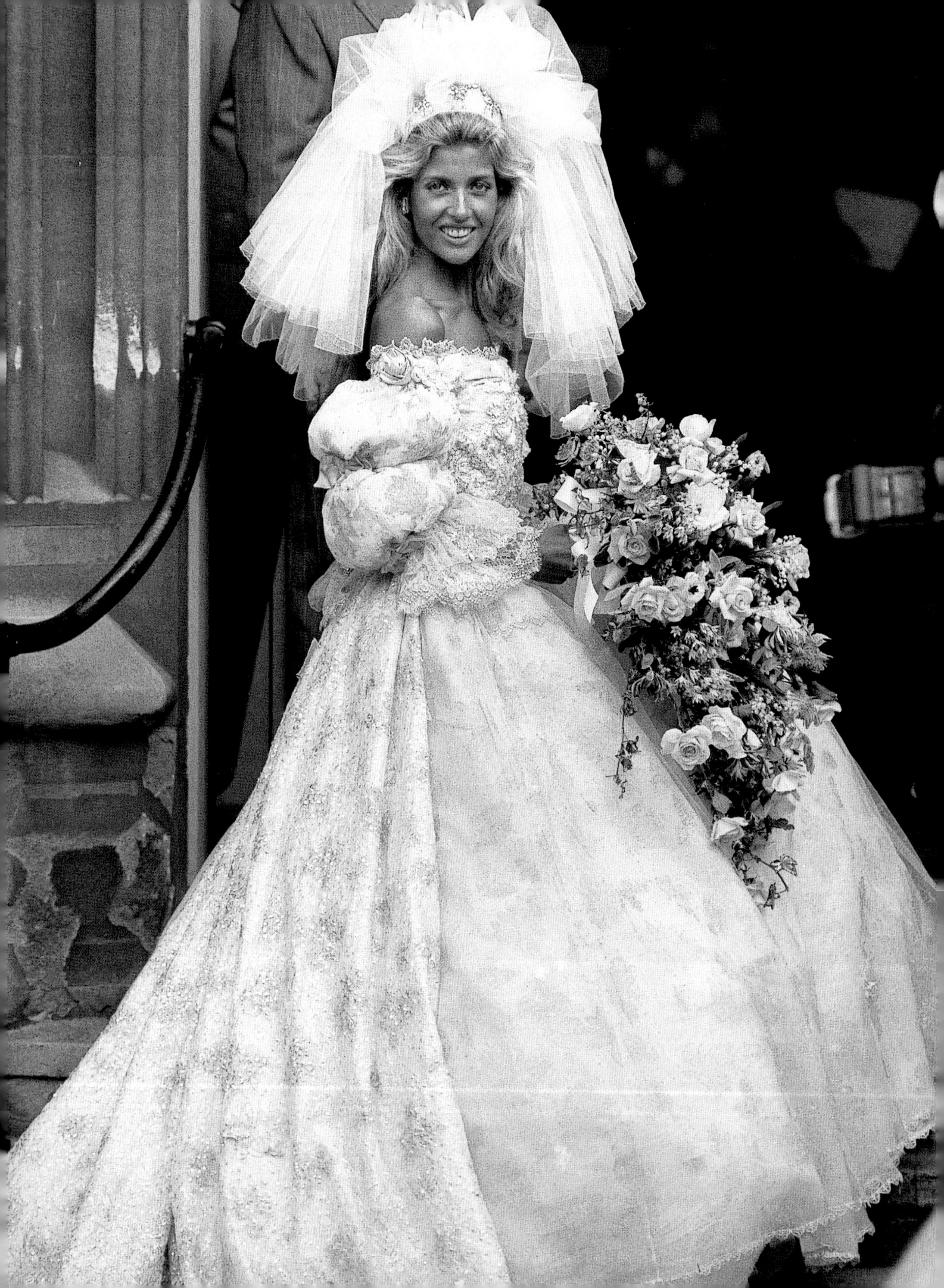

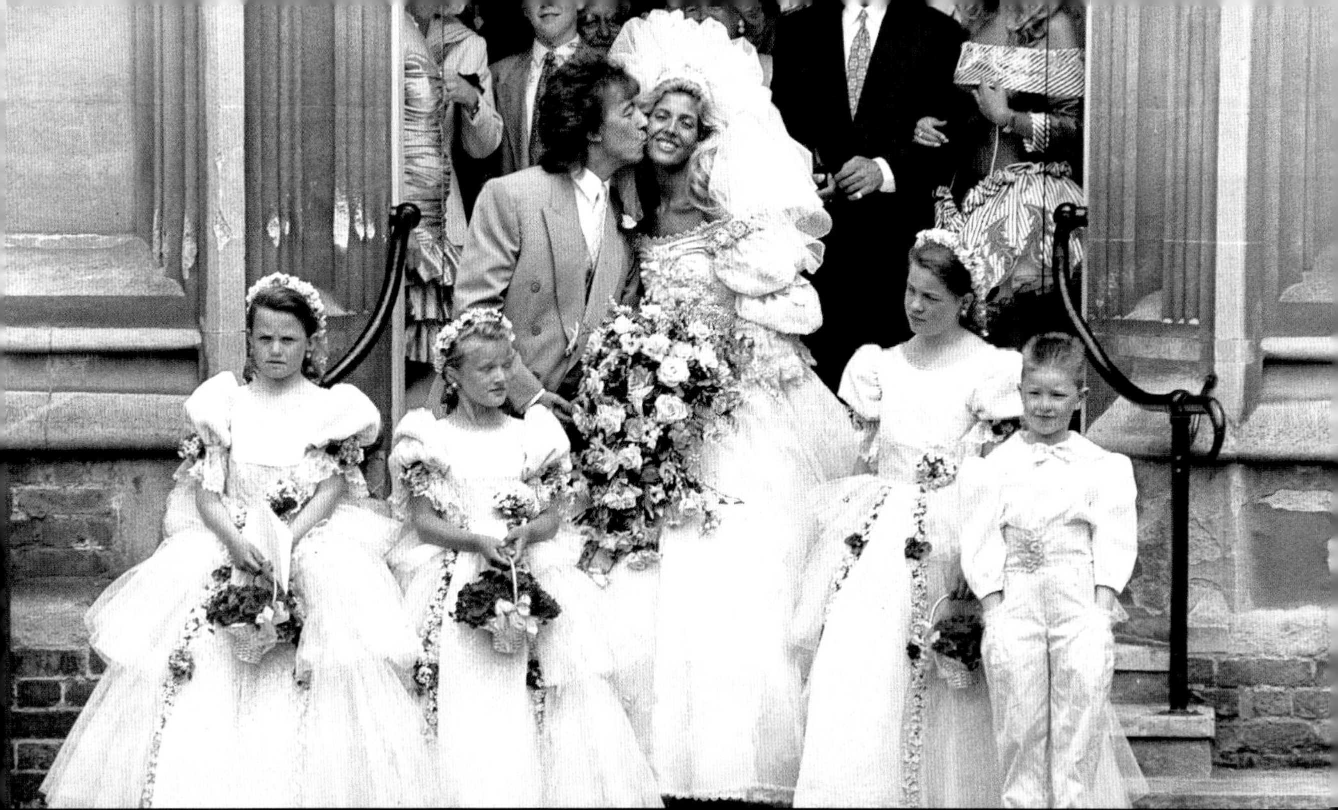

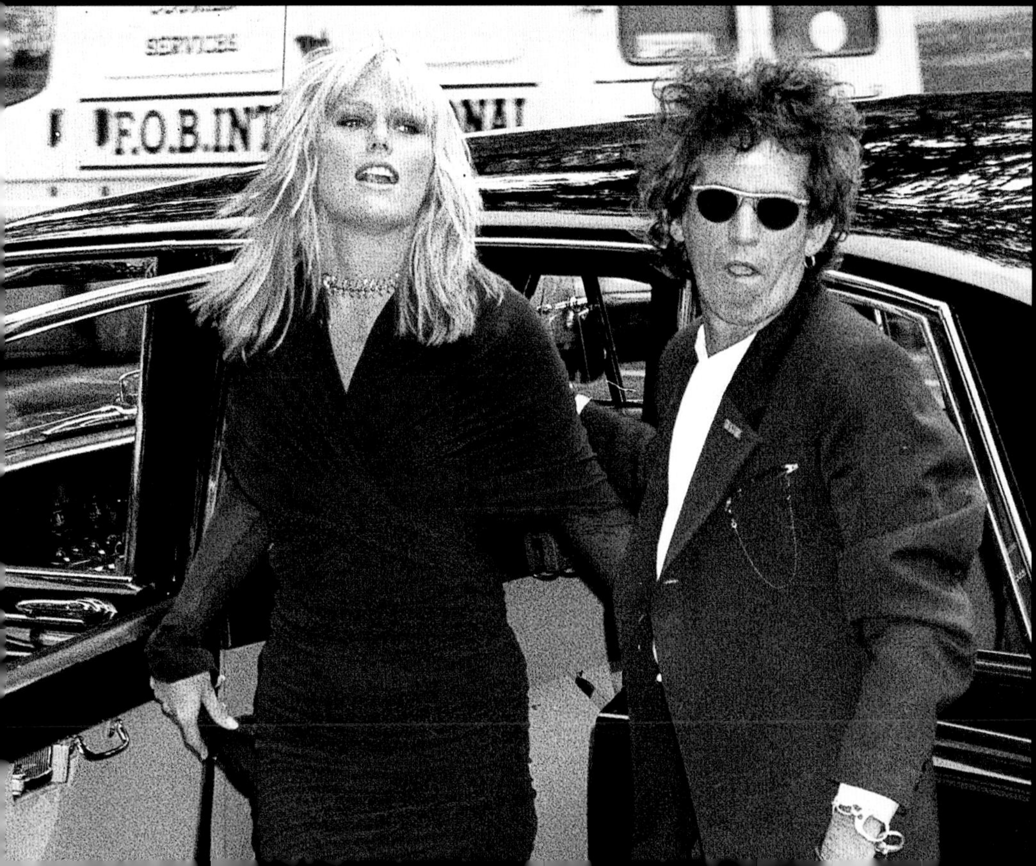

Princess bride

Opposite: Mandy arrives at the blessing at the Church of St John the Evangelist in London. The bride's dress is a £10,000 sequinned lace gown with silk panels of pastel green, pink and lilac.

Above: Mr Wyman kisses the cheek of the new Mrs Wyman, surrounded by three perfect bridesmaids and a page – all Mandy's cousins.

Left: Keith and Patti Richards were among a huge crowd of celebrity guests at a party at the Grosvenor House Hotel that followed the blessing.

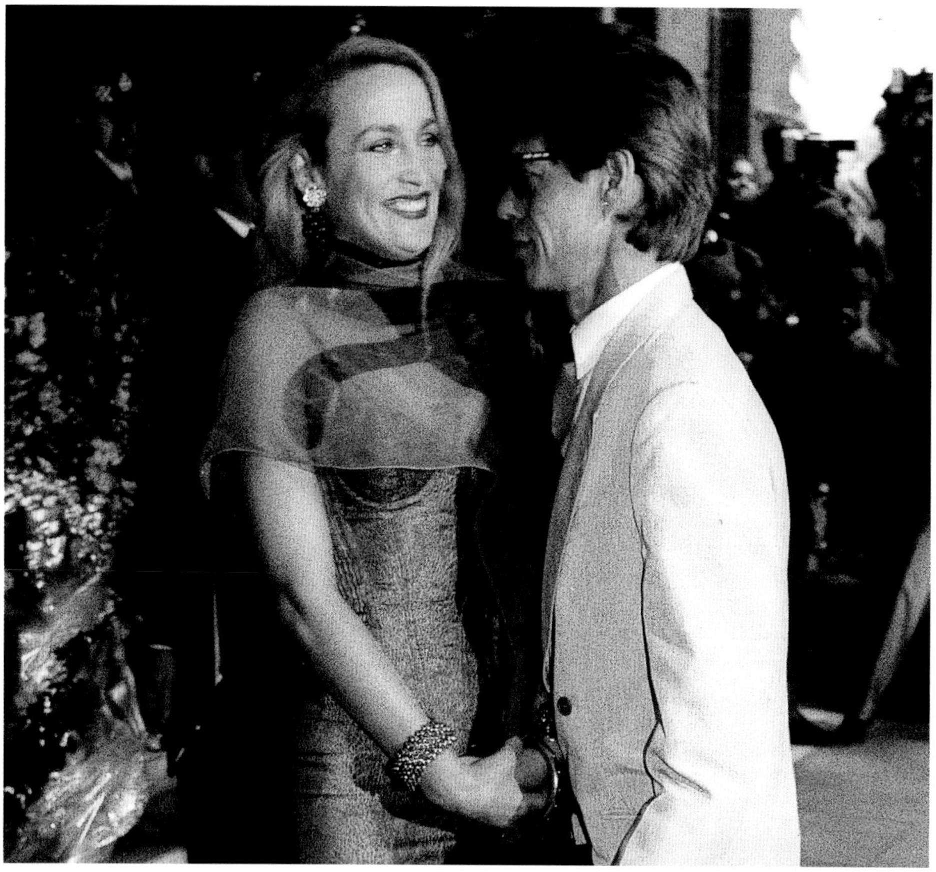

Happy families

Opposite: Keith Richards attends a bash at London's Hard Rock Café with his 19-year-old son Marlon in June 1989.

Left: Jerry Hall and Mick Jagger arrive at Bill and Mandy's party. There were more than 500 guests at the celebration, including singers Paul Young and Cyndi Lauper, and comedian Spike Milligan. One of the more unusual wedding presents came from Spike – a walking frame for Bill, 'to help him through the honeymoon'.

Below: Bill Wyman and new wife Mandy outside Sticky Fingers in June 1989, just days after their marriage.

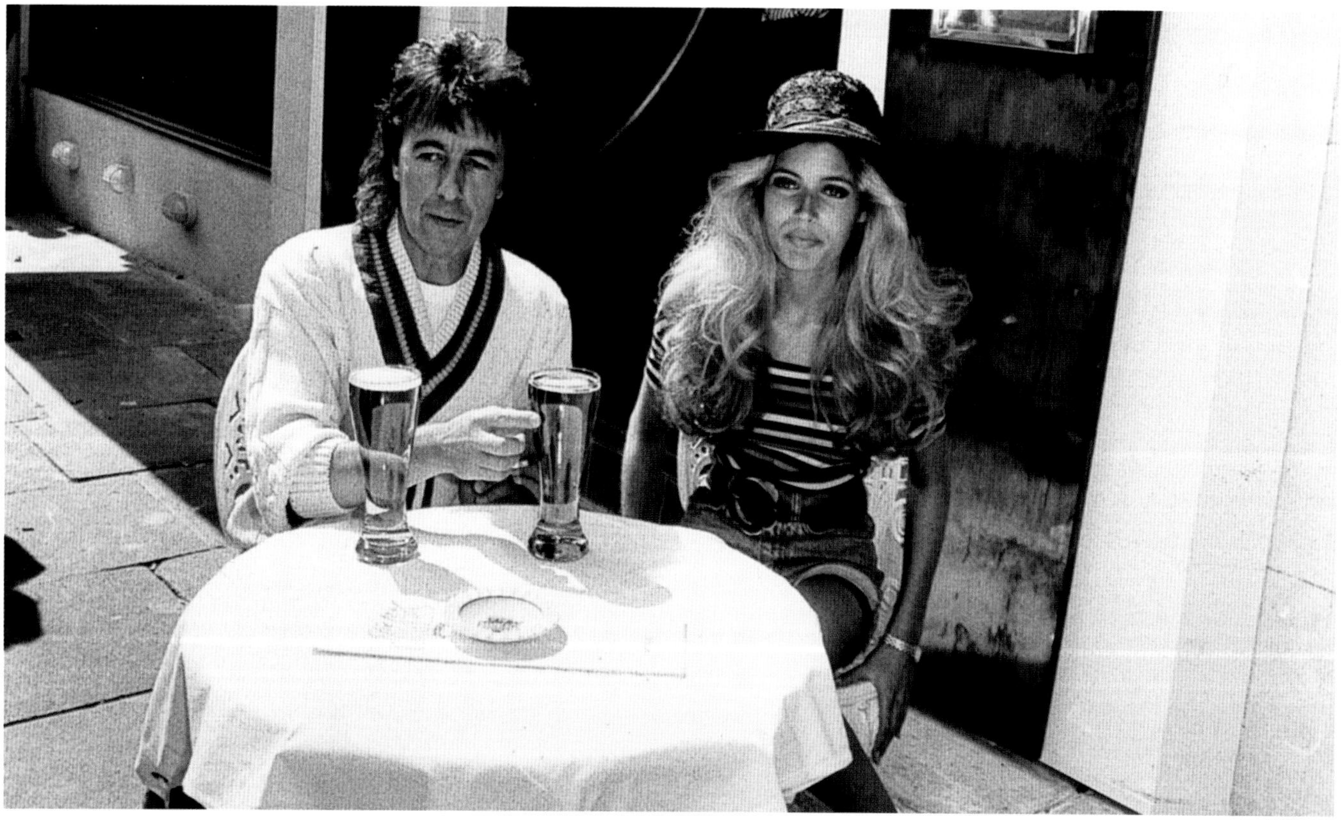

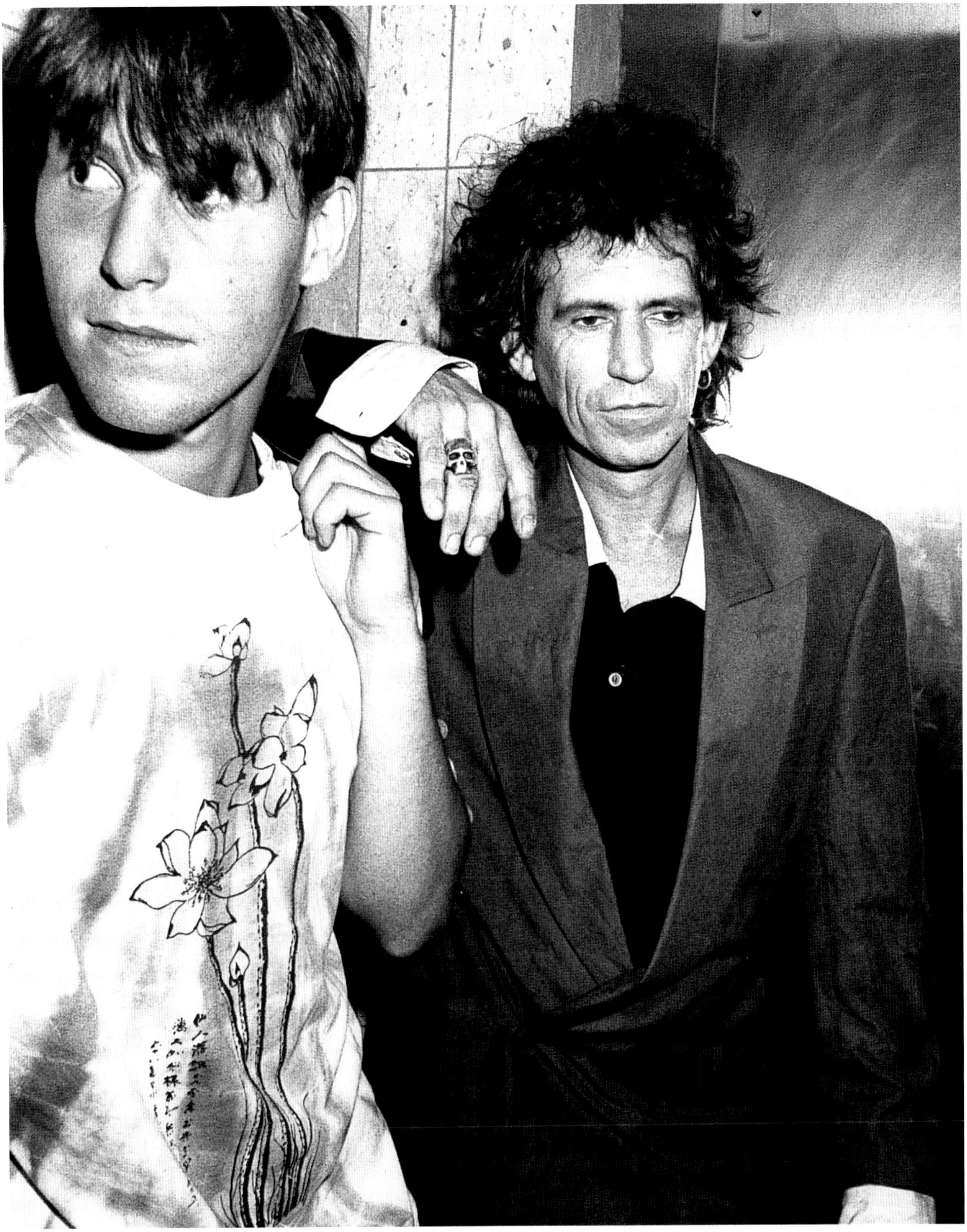

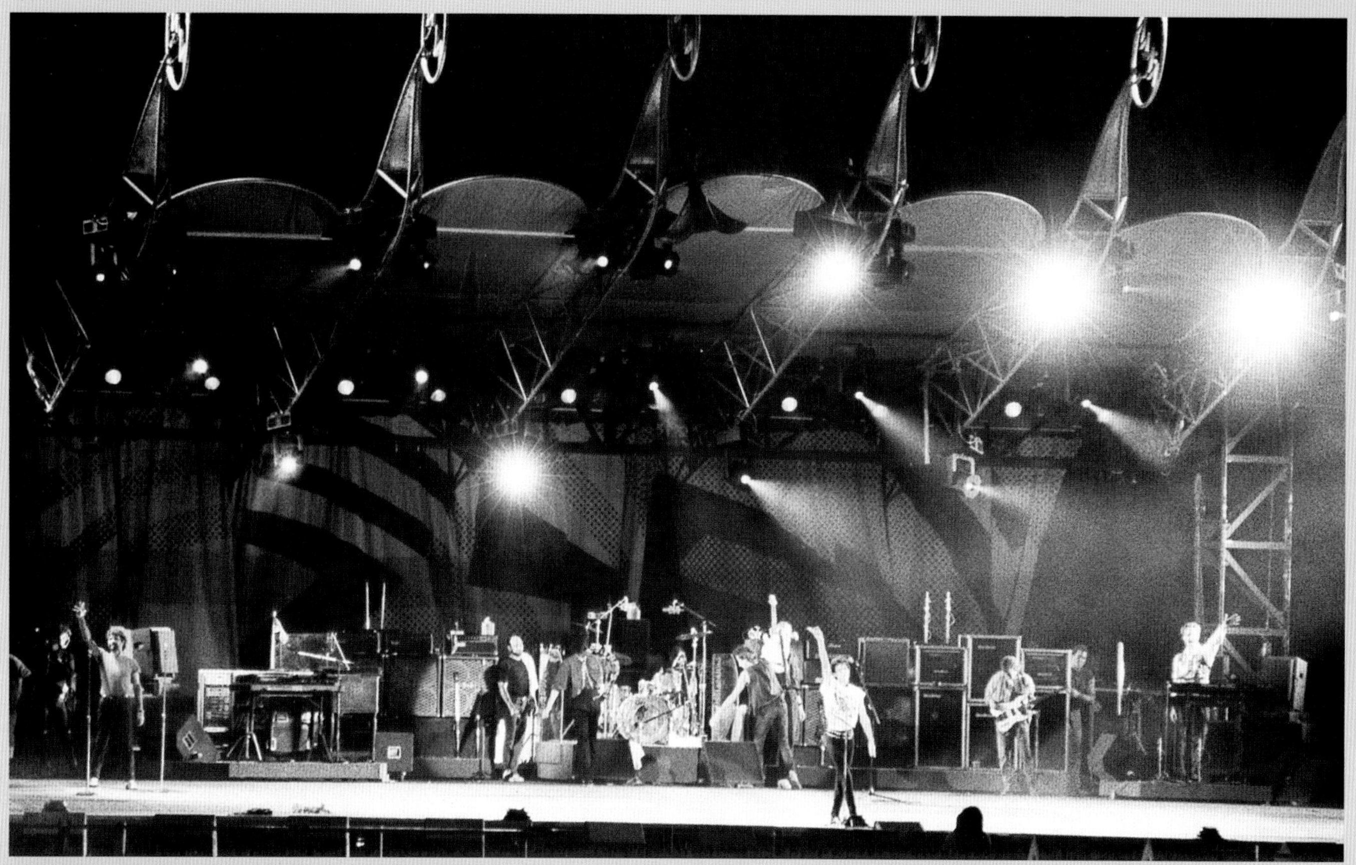

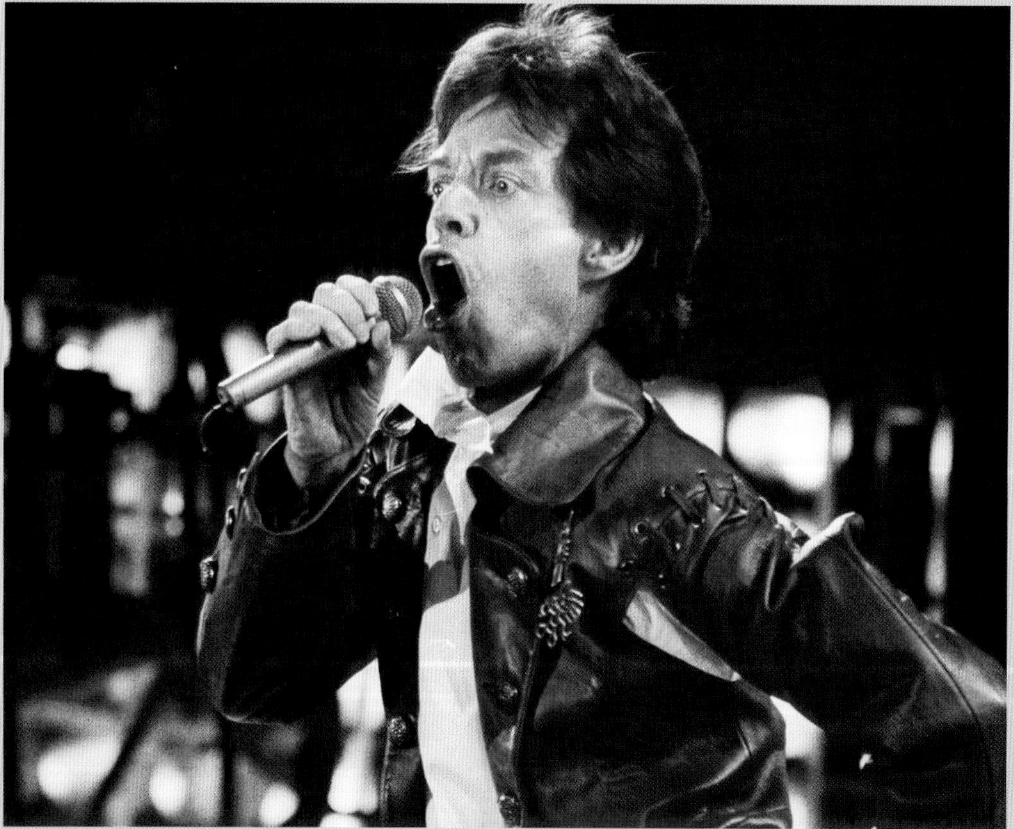

Steel Wheels

The Rolling Stones on the opening night of the Steel Wheels world tour in Philadelphia on 31 August 1989. Advance ticket sales for the shows had broken all records. The American leg consisted of 55 dates, finishing in Atlantic City. The album of the same name reached No.1 in the US charts and No.2 in the United Kingdom. The single 'Mixed Emotions' reached No.5 in the US charts.

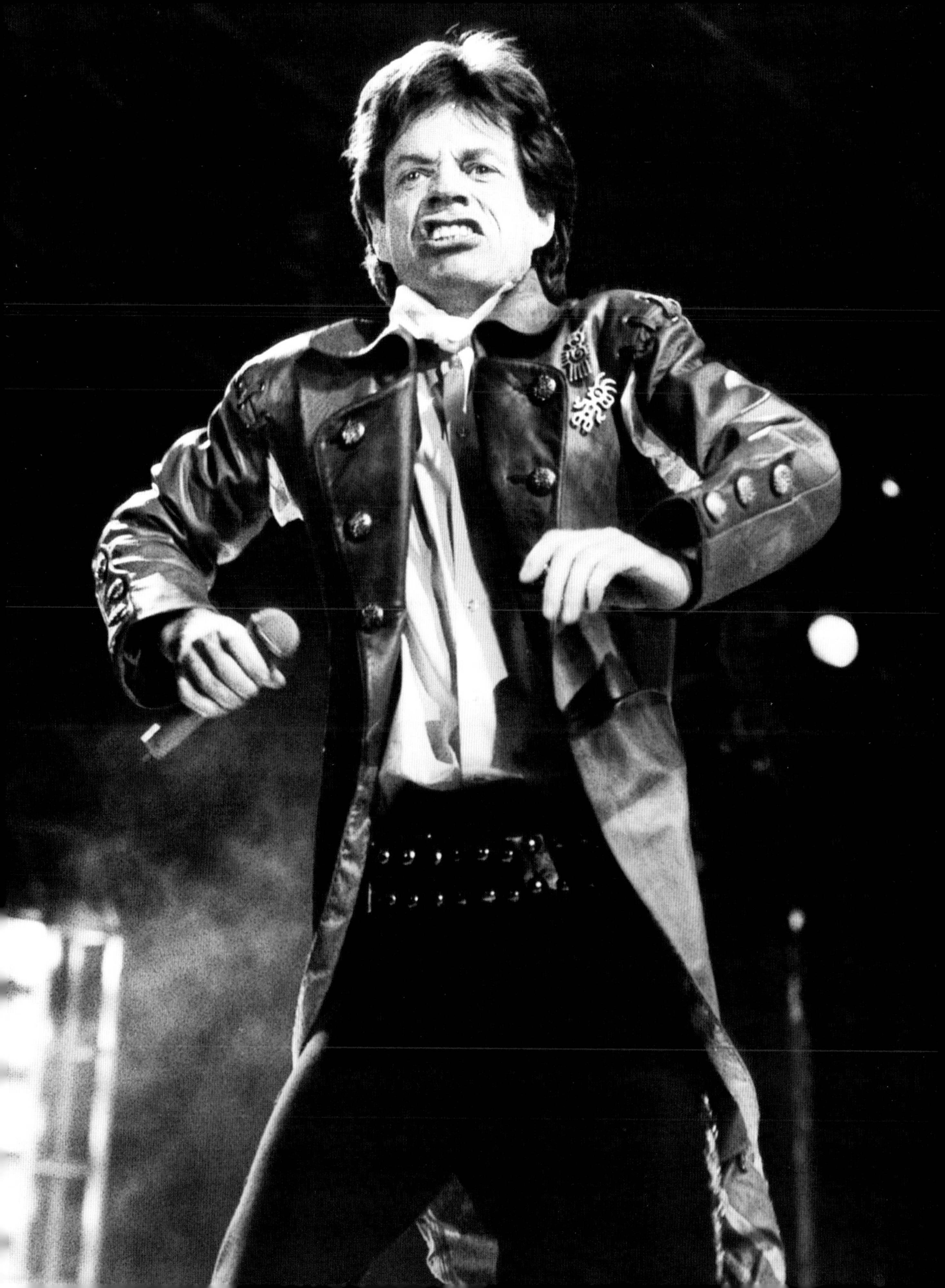

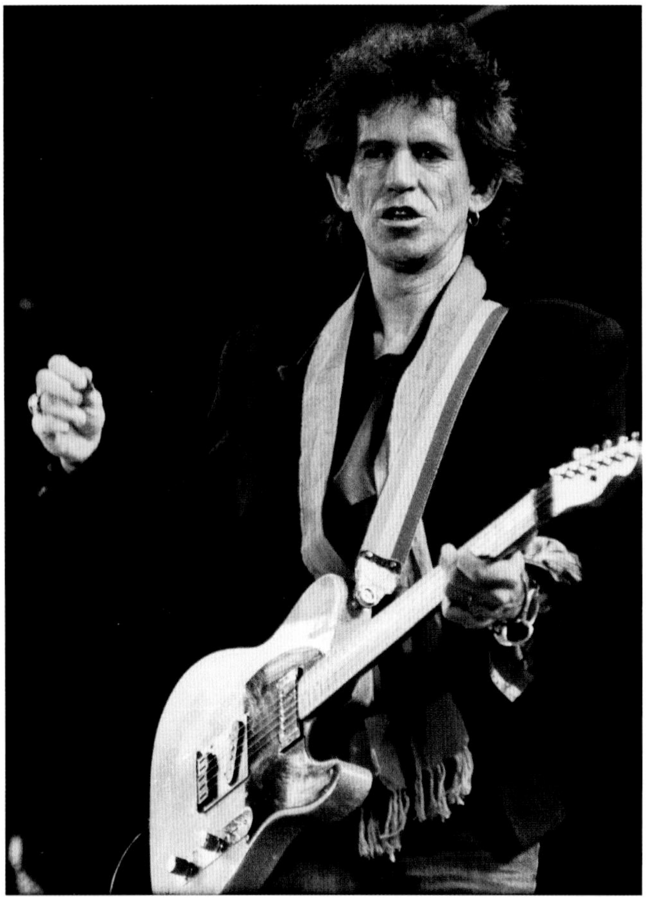

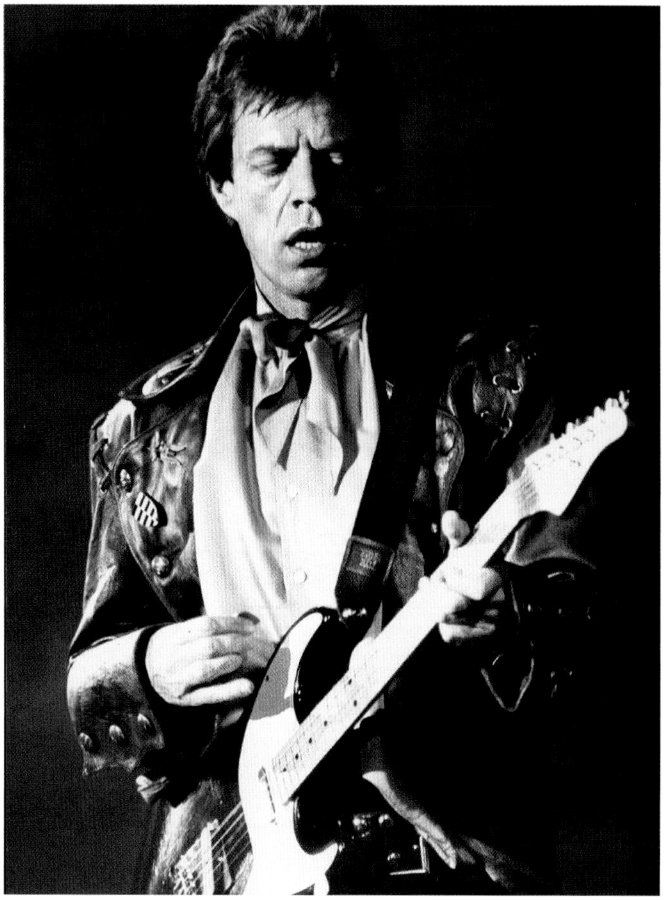

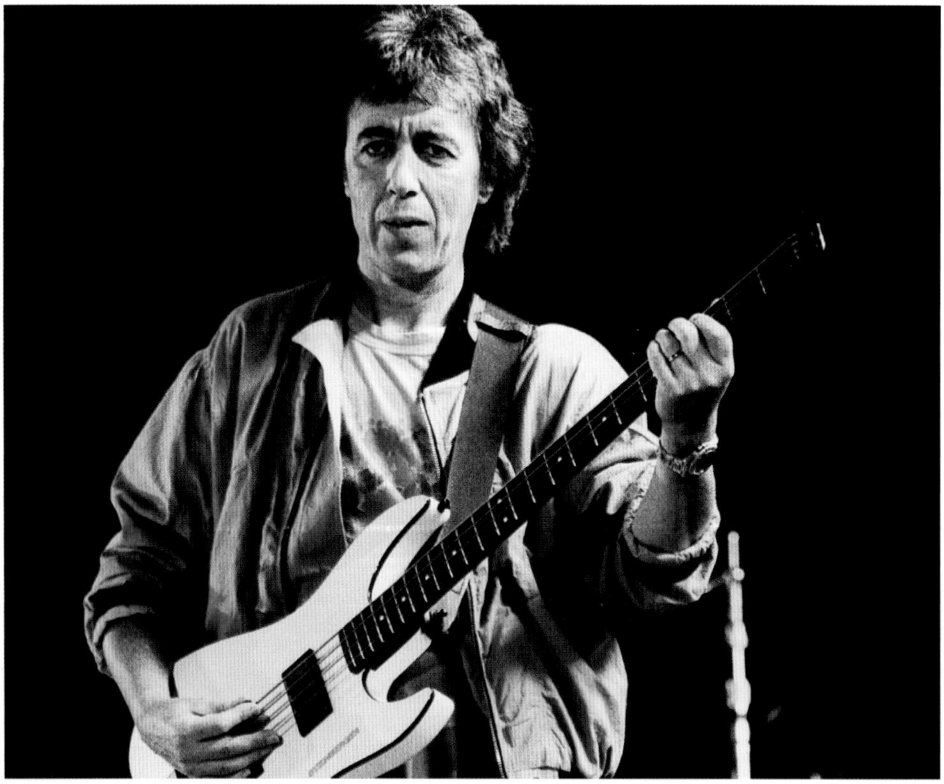

Concert in Philadelphia

Keith Richards (*above left*), Mick Jagger (*above right*) and Bill Wyman (*left*) on stage in Philadelphia. Tickets for the gig had sold for up to 40 times the original price on the black market. Ten days later 'Mixed Emotions' entered the British singles charts, reaching a disappointing No.33.

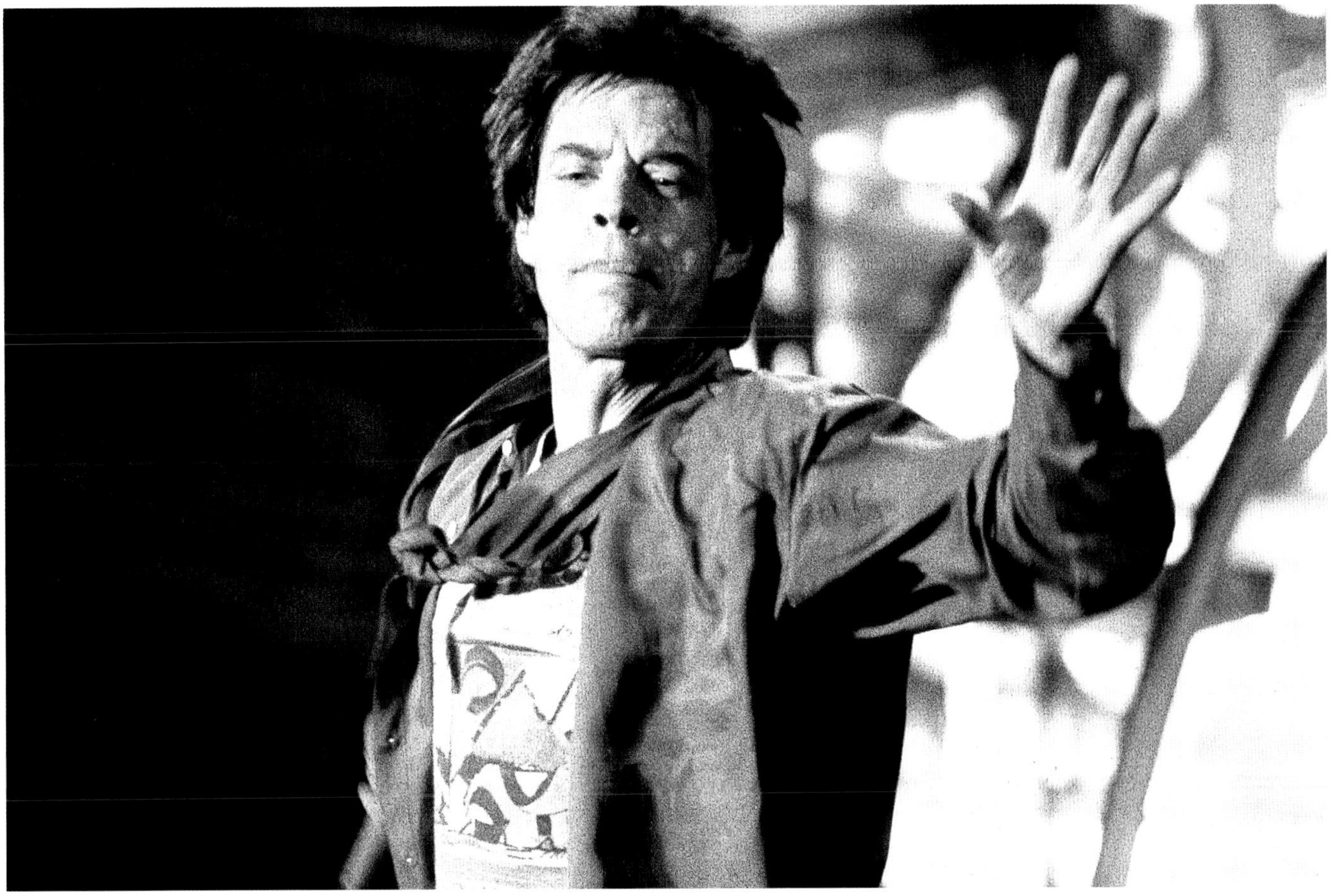

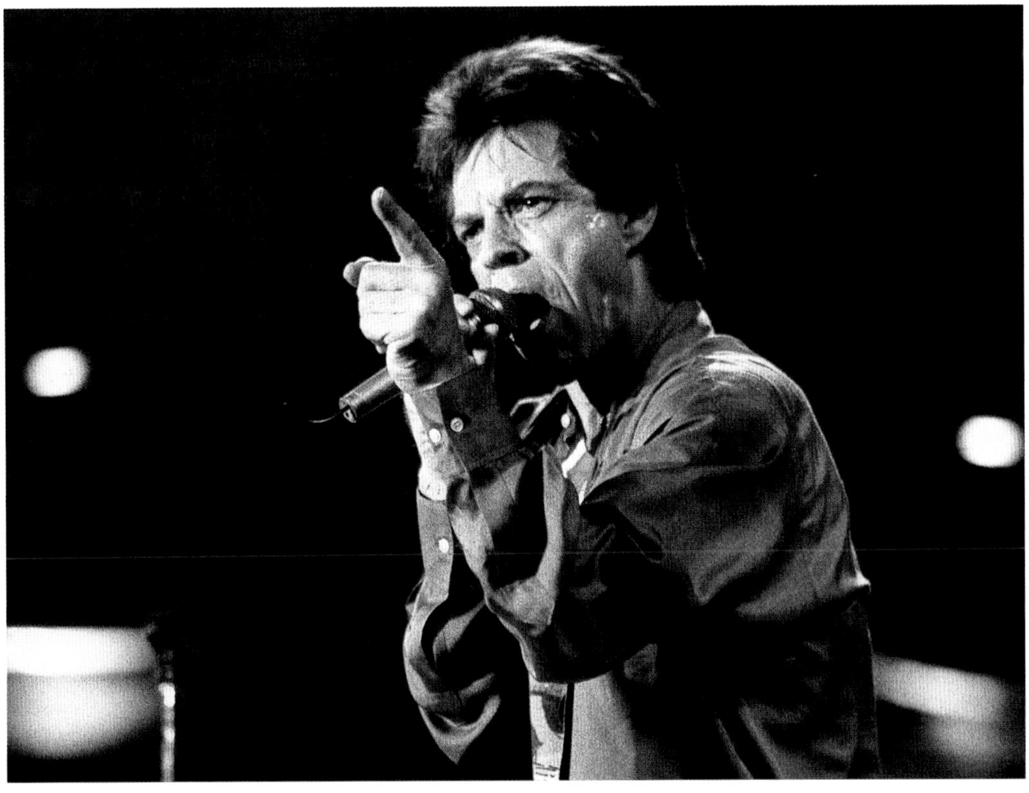

Show stopper

Above and left: Holding an audience, as ever, in the palm of his hand, Mick Jagger gives a sensational performance in New York in October 1989, fronting the Steel Wheels tour, which astonished crowds in every North American city where the band played that autumn. The sets, effects and stagecraft almost eclipsed the sheer energy and magnetism of the rock 'n' roll. The New York concert was held at Shea Stadium, home of the Mets baseball team. Seventy thousand fans attended, some over a third of a mile from the stage and depending on binoculars.

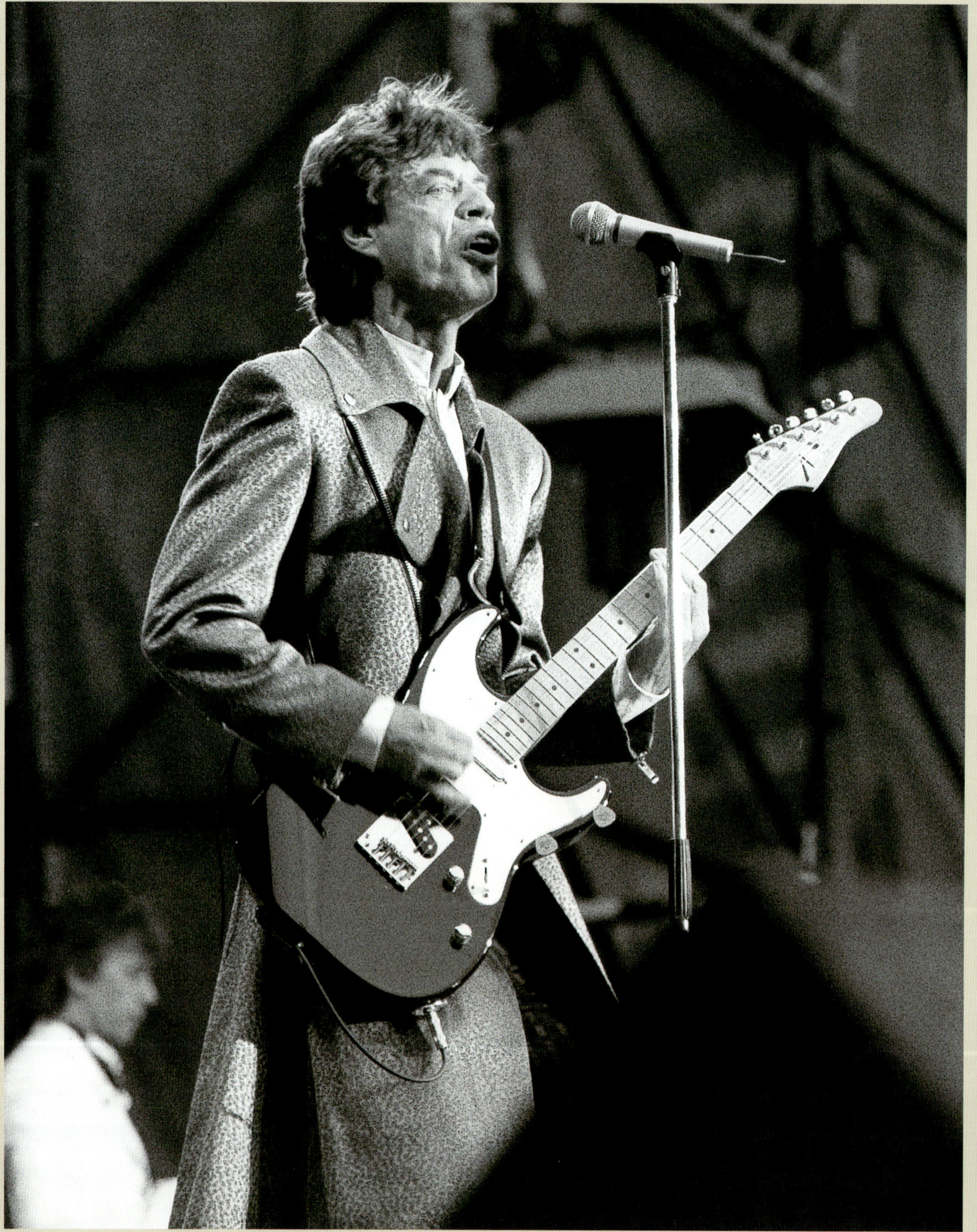

CHAPTER FOUR

Bridges To Babylon

After covering North America and Canada, the Steel Wheels tour travelled to Japan during February 1990. The European leg of the tour, with a different logo and renamed the Urban Jungle, began the following May and continued throughout that summer, culminating in a concert at Wembley towards the end of August. Ronnie Wood had finally been made an official band member, but this proved to be the last Rolling Stones tour for Bill Wyman, who after 30 years of being a Stone was keen to explore other musical areas – although his decision to leave wasn't made public until the end of 1992. After all his hints over the years few were surprised – Bill had always been a little detached, on stage and off, and he hated flying. While he considered his future options, Bill used the meticulous diaries that he had kept regularly since he was a child to write his autobiography, *Stone Alone*, which was published in 1990. Among other things, it offered startling revelations about his adventures with young female fans while playing away from home.

After the tour the other band members also took a break to pursue their other interests. Charlie Watts released two jazz albums, *From One Charlie* and *Tribute To Charlie Parker With Strings*. Ronnie Wood made his fifth solo album, *Slide on This* – his first in 11 years – and went on tour to promote it across North America and Japan. In 1993 he appeared with former bandmate Rod Stewart on *MTV Unplugged*, which led to another album, *Unplugged . . . and Seated*. Keith released his second solo album, *Main Offender*; and did a solo tour that included major concerts in Spain and Argentina. Mick released a third solo album, *Wandering Spirit*, which received good reviews and went on to sell 2 million copies worldwide.

Meanwhile the Stones' new record company, Virgin, decided to remaster and repackage all the band's back catalogue of studio albums. They also issued a sixth hits compilation, *Jump Back: The Best Of The Rolling Stones*, which covered material from 1971 to 1989.

By 1993, the Stones were ready to begin work on a new album: *Voodoo Lounge*. Darryl Jones was selected to replace Bill Wyman on bass guitar, but as a salaried employee rather than a full member of the band. The new album proved to be a great success, debuting at No.1 in the United Kingdom and No.2 in the United States and quickly going platinum. The Voodoo Lounge tour began in August 1994 in North America and ran for more than a year, covering most of the world. Keith reportedly said of the tour – which included the Stones' first Australian and New Zealand gigs for over 20 years – that their performance had improved every night, so the best show of the whole tour was probably the last gig at Wembley.

Although the music was still going well, in their personal lives some of the Stones had a mixed time during the 1990s. Bill wasn't alone and broken-hearted for long after his marriage to Mandy ended in 1991; he married Suzanne Accosta, a Californian fashion designer in her 30s, five months after his divorce was finalized in 1993. The first of their three daughters, Katherine Noelle, was born in September 1994, followed by Jessica Rose in November 1995 and Matilda Mae in May 1998. The ex-Stone seemed far happier with a settled family life, running his restaurant and pursuing his many other private interests.

Mick and Jerry also weathered some personal storms during this time. At first Mick's constant womanizing had not seemed to perturb Jerry much, and after the birth of Elizabeth in 1984 and James in 1985, two further children arrived in 1992 and 1997 to loudly make the point that all was well. Mick and Jerry had always had a tolerant and understanding relationship, and the couple even went through a marriage ceremony in 1990 in Indonesia. But towards the end of the decade Mick plucked one dusky beauty too many. In May 1998, when the 29-year-old Brazilian model Luciana Morad gave birth to a son, Jerry's patience finally expired. At first, Mick denied paternity. But DNA tests decided that he was the father and he committed to modest maintenance payments. Mick also disputed that Jerry and he were ever legally married and in 1999 their marriage was anulled.

However, after a slightly rocky patch in the 1980s, Charlie and Shirley Watts remained as stable as ever, while Jo and Ronnie Wood seemed to have forged a rock-solid marriage. And Keith … well, Keith and Patti were still together and now had two daughters. Keith's heroin addiction appeared to be a thing of the past – although, as he said himself in 1994, his image was 'like a long shadow. Even though that was nearly 20 years ago, you cannot convince some people that I'm not a mad drug addict.'

The Bridges To Babylon tour, which opened in Chicago in 1997 and lasted until the end of the millennium, featured (appropriately enough) a bridge flung across the world's auditoriums. It seemed to symbolize the band's ability to reach across generations, across time and into the hearts and hips of every single person throughout the world who'd bought a piece of The Rolling Stones experience for the price of a ticket. However, perhaps Mick and Keith had begun to feel that the complicated staging and crowds of up to 100,000 that featured on the enormous Bridges To Babylon tour were moving too far away from their performance of the music. At the beginning of 1999 the Stones took a break from Bridges To Babylon to do a short US tour of smaller venues with crowds of less than 20,000, featuring fewer special effects and concentrating on the music and band. The No Security tour ran from January to April 1999 and supported their new album of the same name, which was a live recording of concerts in the Bridges To Babylon tour. After it finished, the full Babylon tour resumed for a final month in Europe.

By 1997 Bill Wyman was also touring again; he had founded a new blues-rock band, Rhythm Kings, which quickly became renowned for live performances during frequent tours of the United Kingdom and Europe. The band members frequently change as established musicians move from project to project, but the touring line-up has included Martin Taylor, Georgie Fame and Andy Fairweather Low, with studio guests such as Mick Taylor, George Harrison, Eric Clapton, and Mark Knopfler. Much of Rhythm Kings' material is written by Bill with his long-standing musical partner Terry Taylor.

During the 1990s, Mick also resumed his deep interest in movie projects, appearing in *Freejack* in 1992 and *Bent* in 1997. In 1995 he started his own production company, Jagged Films, which in 1999 produced the wartime drama *Enigma* from the Robert Harris novel. However, all this was of little consequence for the band. Even without Bill as corner Stone, even without Mick Taylor, and now with the memory of Brian distant indeed, even with Charlie Watts quietly diversifying and the extensive responsibilities of his jazz orchestra, the Stones could still do the business like no other. And as Keith said in an interview towards the end of the decade, 'Moneywise, we haven't had to work for years. But it's for the pleasure of the music, pride, the quest of the Holy Grail.'

Previous page: Mick on stage at Wembley in 1990. One hundred and twenty thousand tickets for the Wembley concerts were sold within a day of the dates being announced.

Opposite: Keith Richards on stage in New Jersey, 1997.

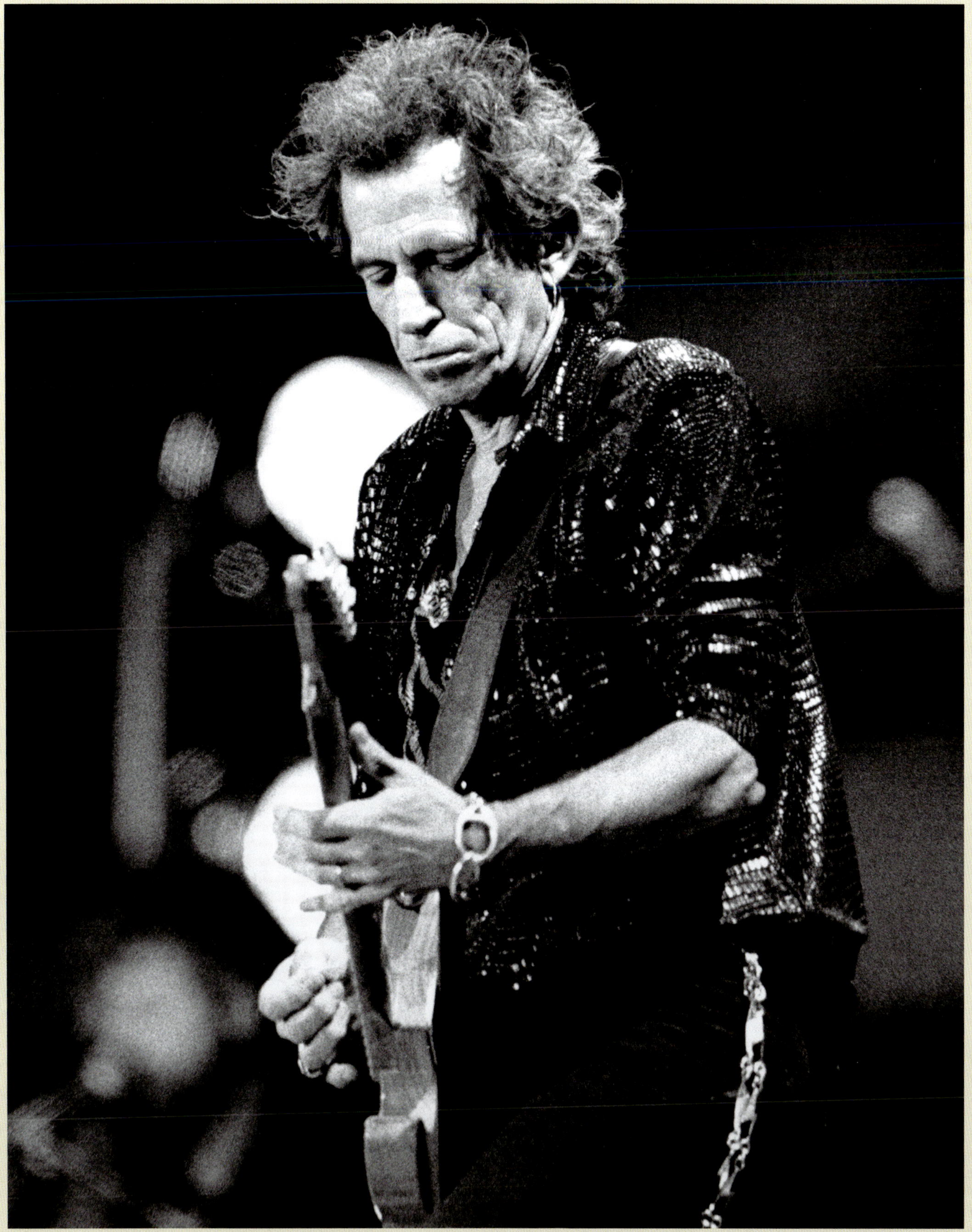

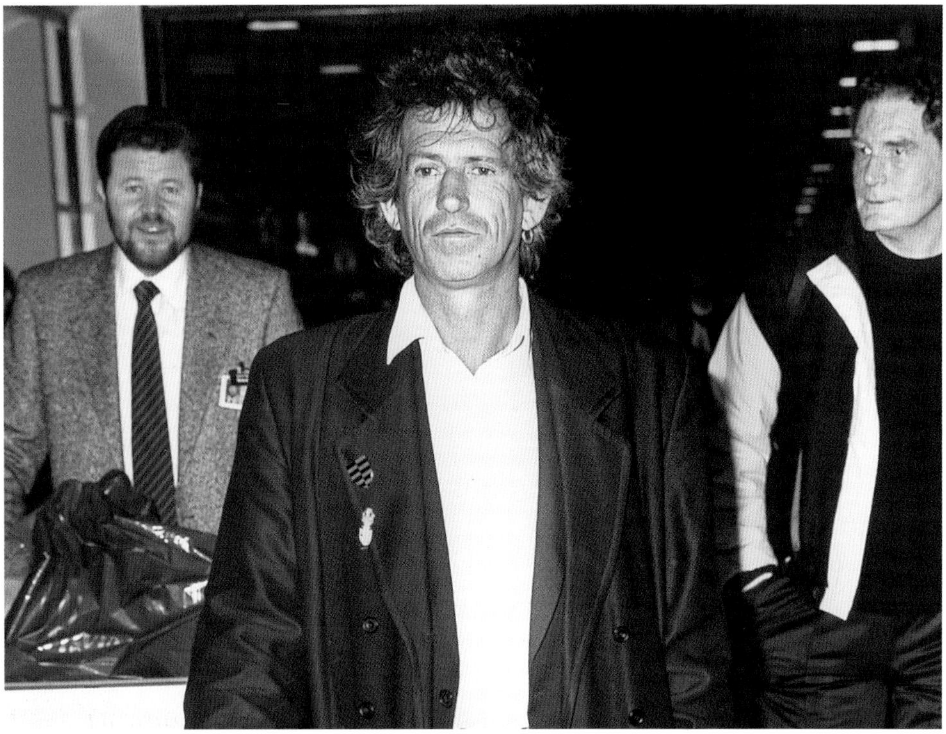

Big in Japan

Left and below: On 4 February 1990 Keith and Ronnie leave for the next leg of the Steel Wheels tour in Japan. Ronnie is with his wife Jo and children Tyrone and Leah.

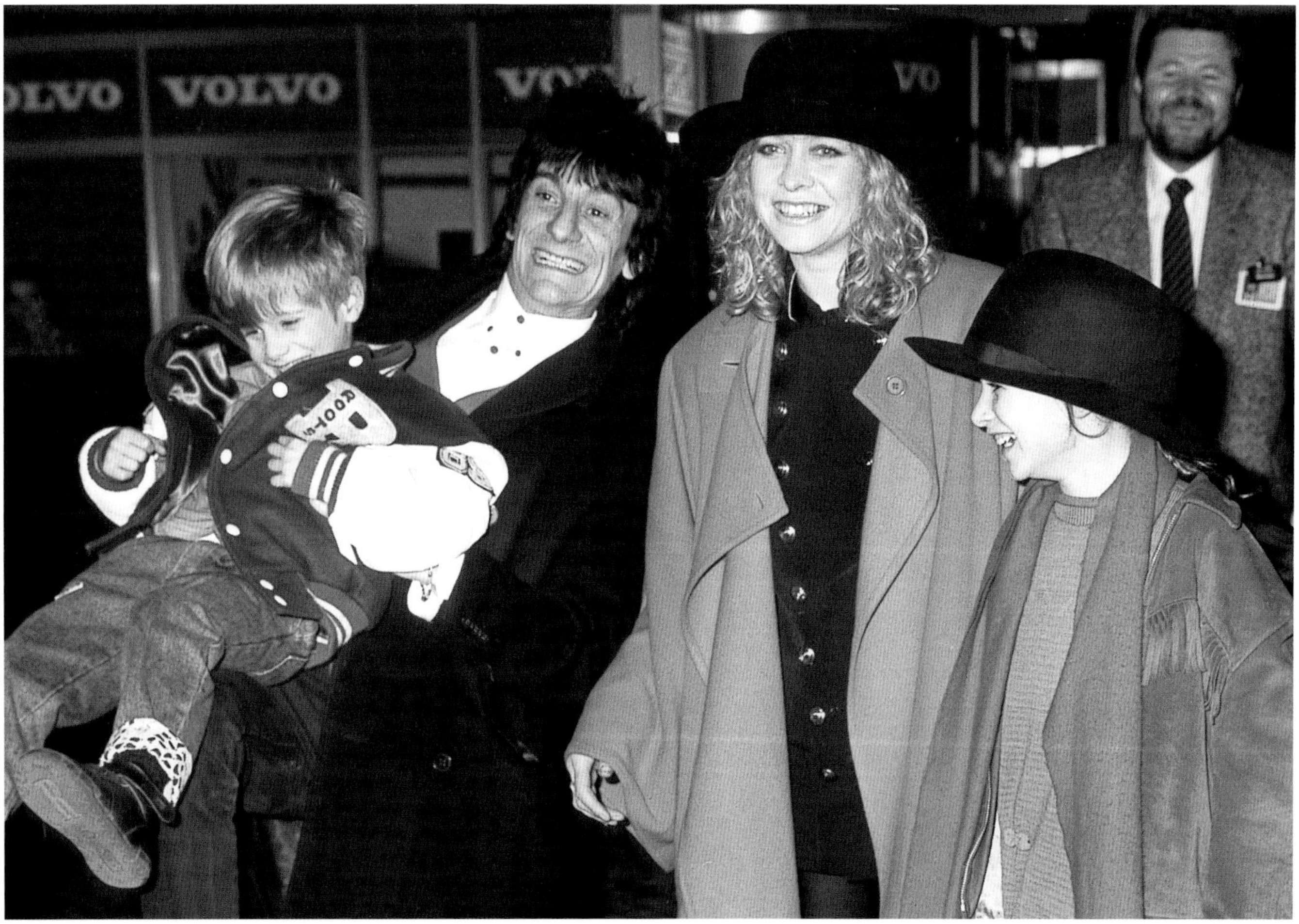

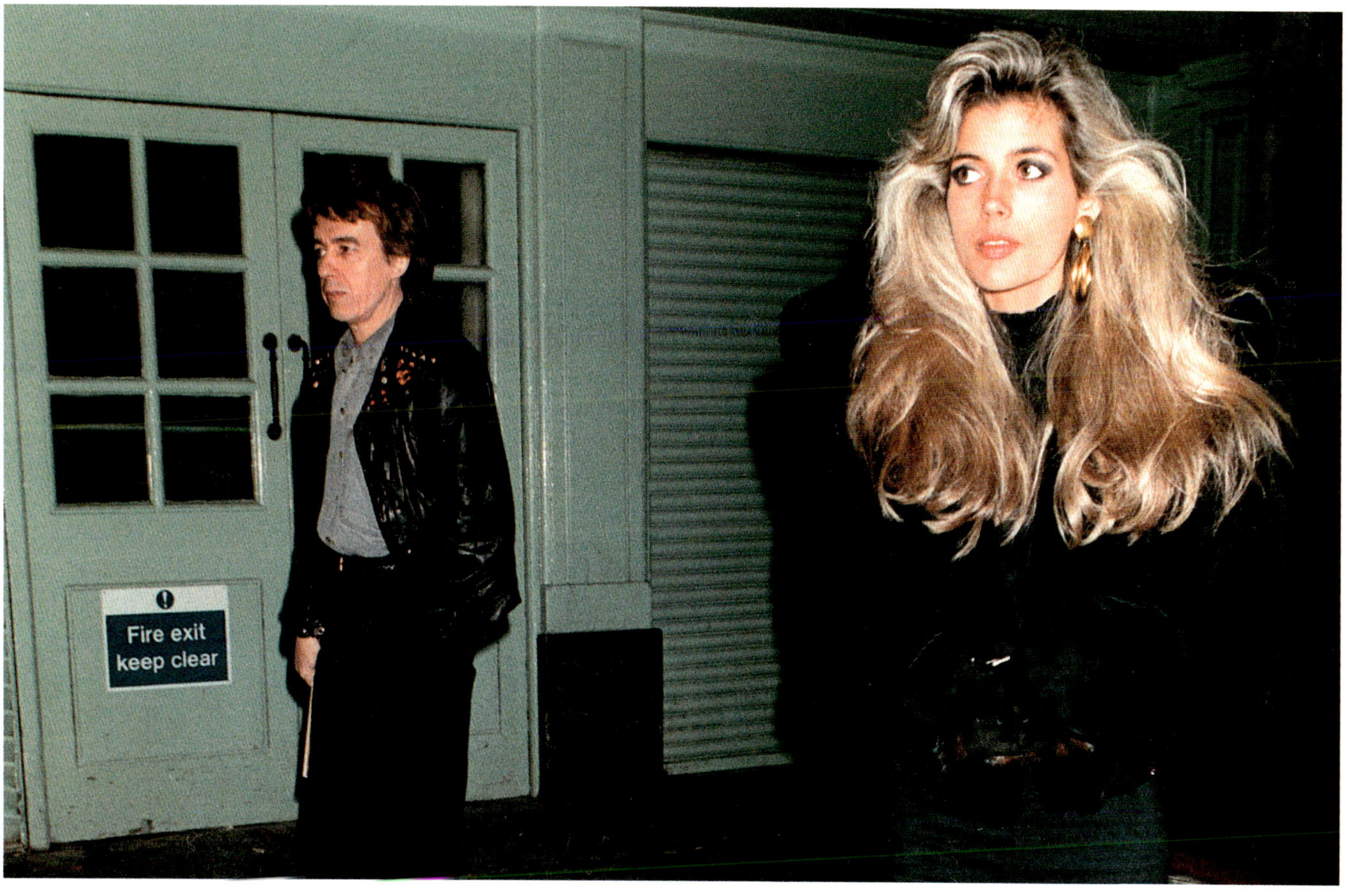

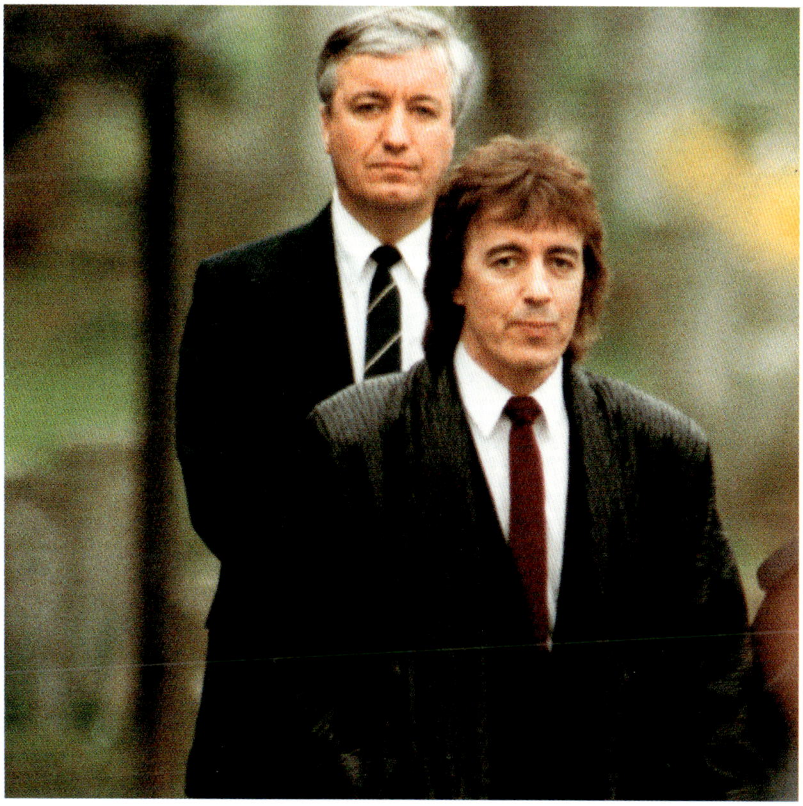

Rumours of a rift

Above: When Bill and Mandy Wyman celebrated New Year 1990 at Tramp they took along her mother and Bill's son Stephen. The older woman and younger man were shortly to embark upon a romance of their own. Since their wedding the previous June, Bill and Mandy had only spent five weeks together – both denied rumours of a rift.

Left: On 5 March Bill attends his father's funeral at Beckenham Crematorium. Floral tributes were sent by Mick Jagger and Jerry Hall, among others.

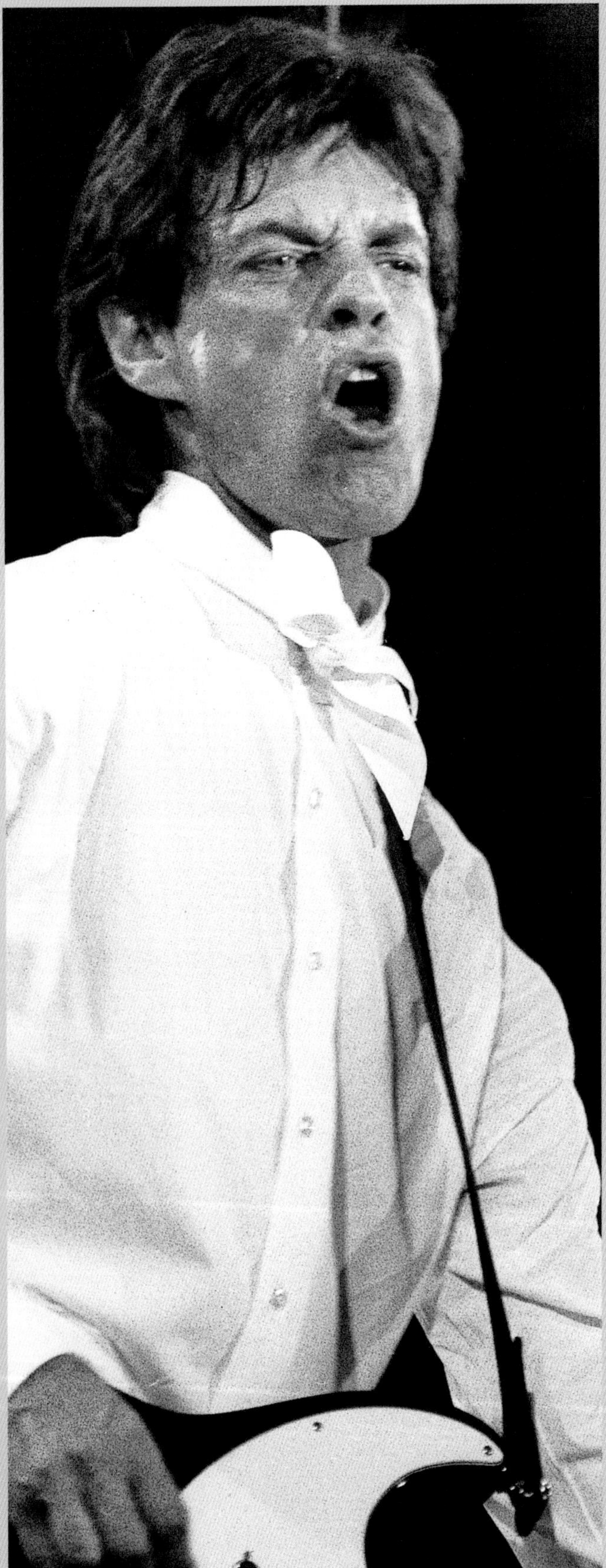

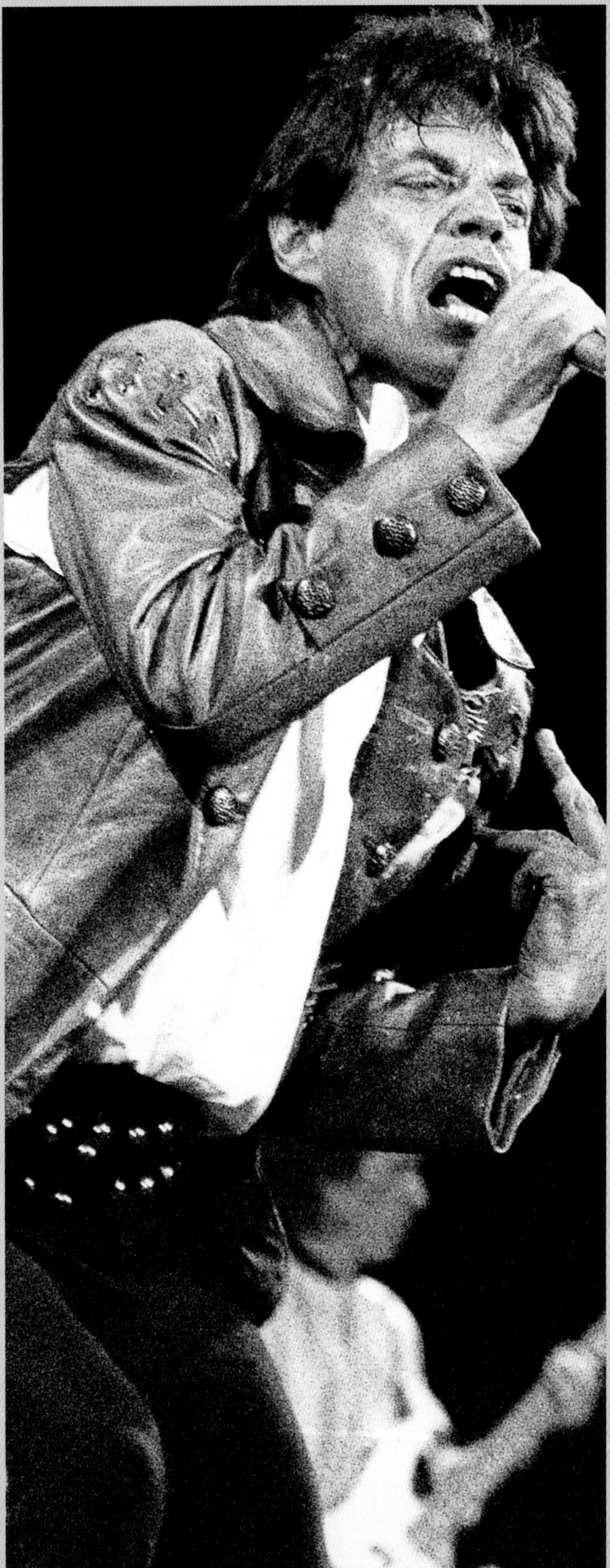

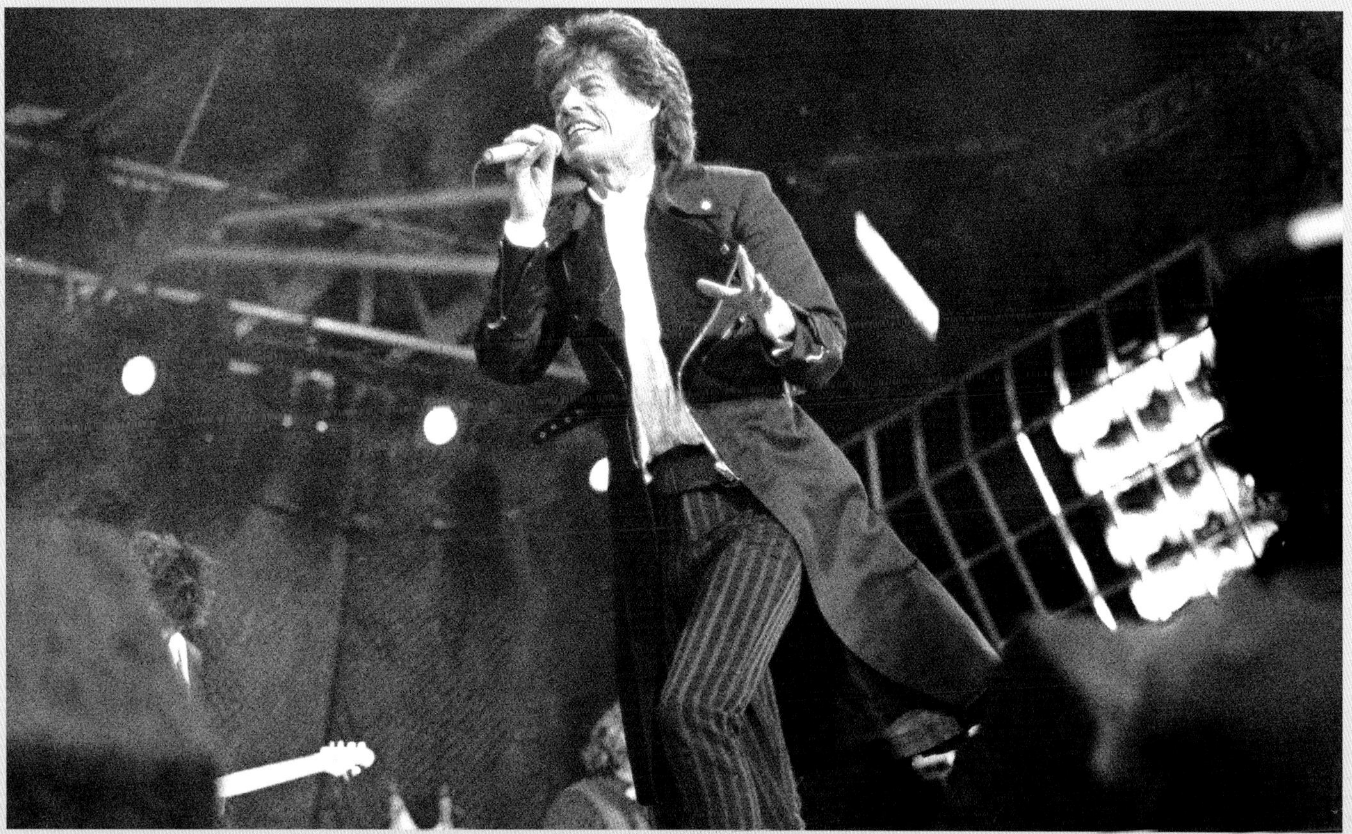

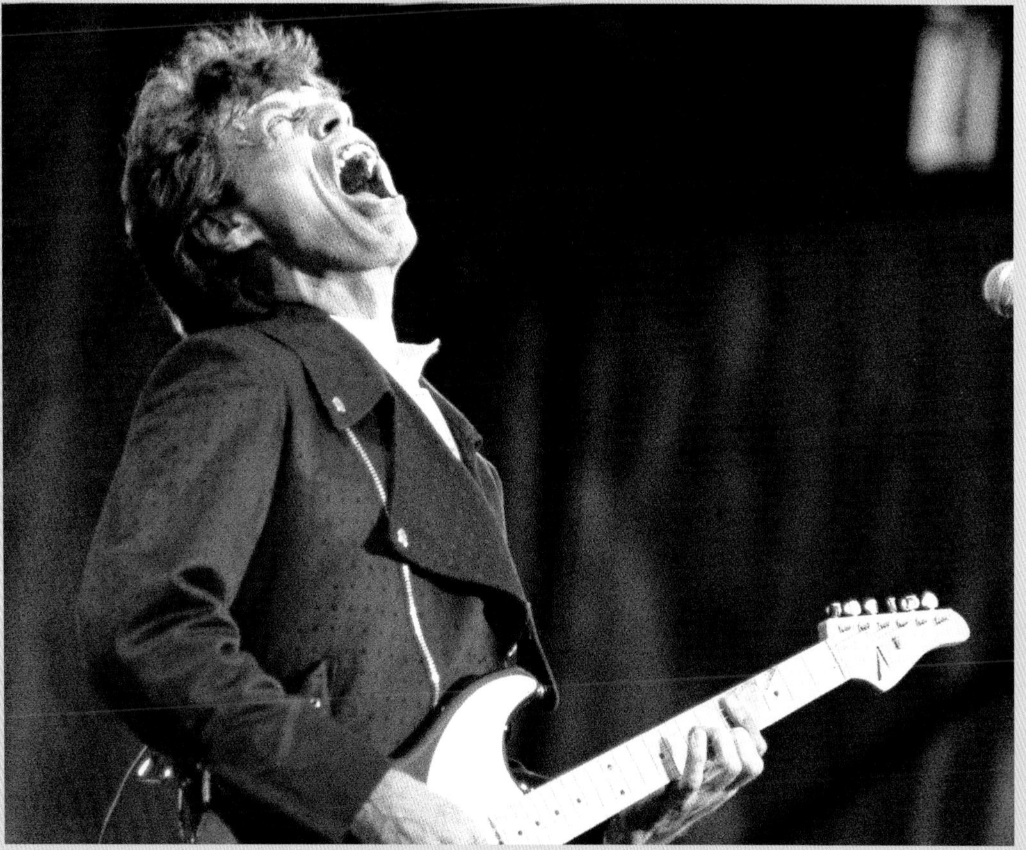

Best single, best tour, best comeback

Opposite: On 8 March 1990 *Rolling Stone* magazine nominated the Stones for a host of awards for 1989, including best album *Steel Wheels*, best single 'Mixed Emotions', best tour and best comeback. Later that month Jagger announced a new tour, the Urban Jungle European tour. It would feature a new stage set and lighting, and a different playing order from the Steel Wheels shows.

Above and left: The tour opens in Rotterdam on 18 May 1990 and will move to Australia later in the year.

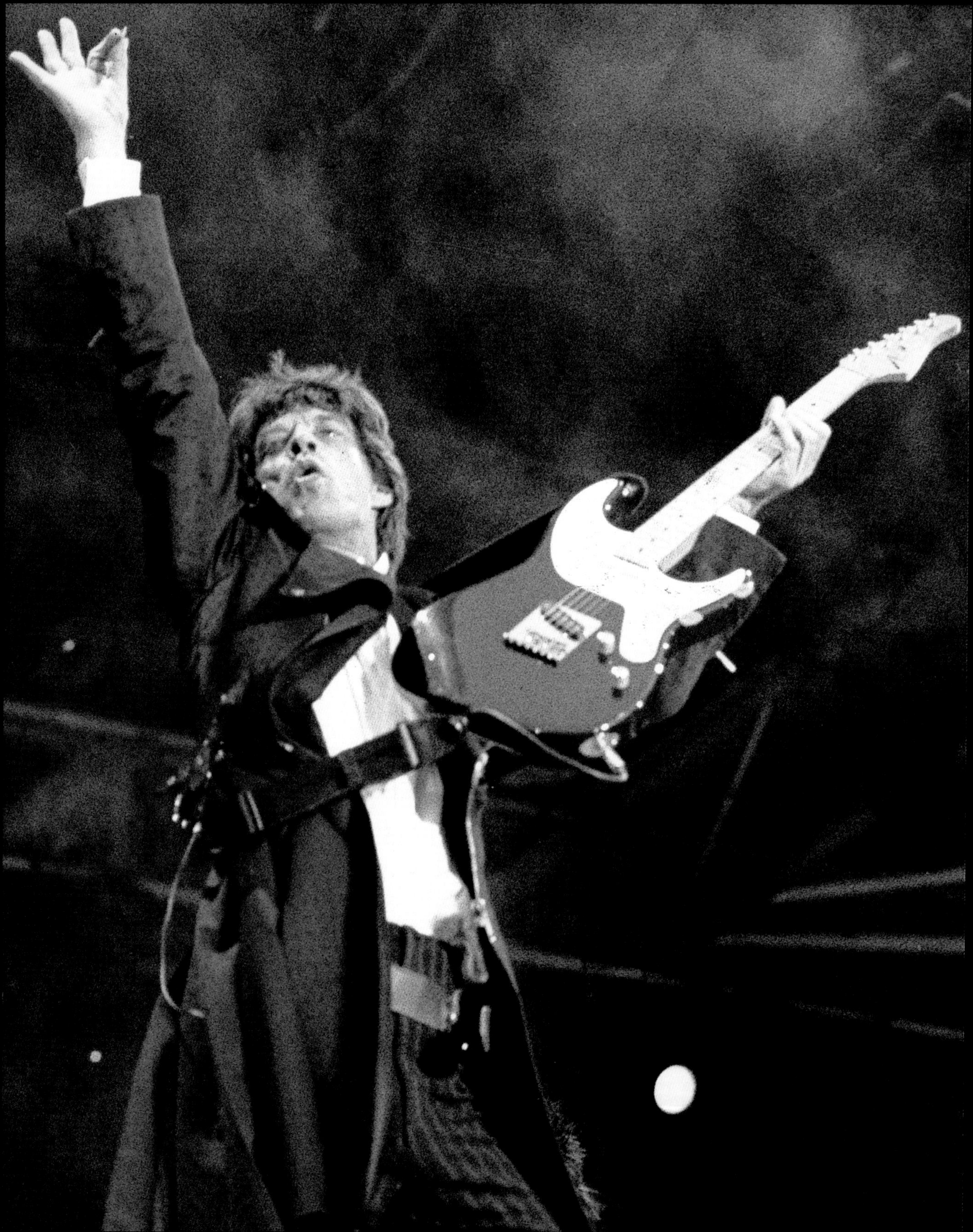

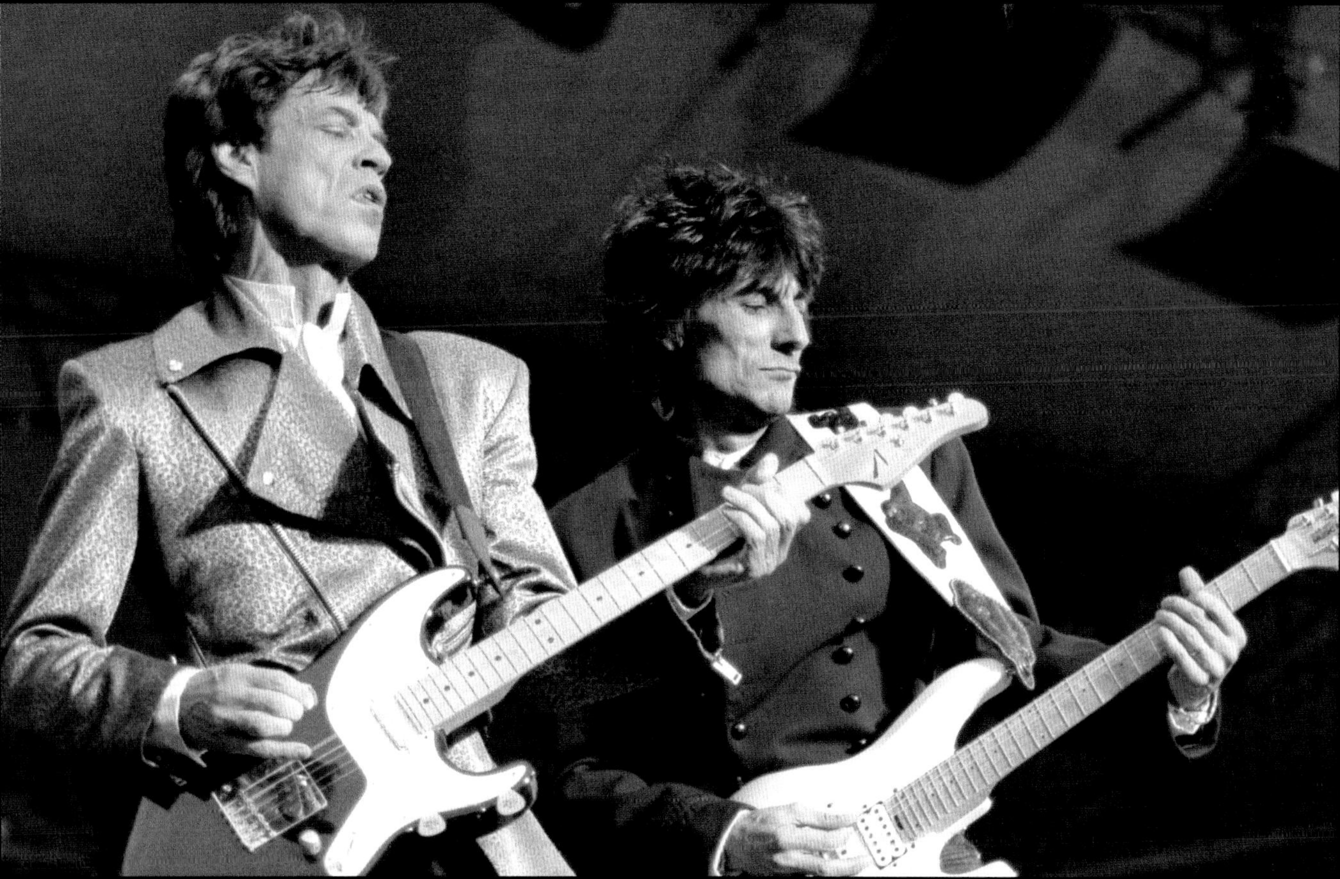

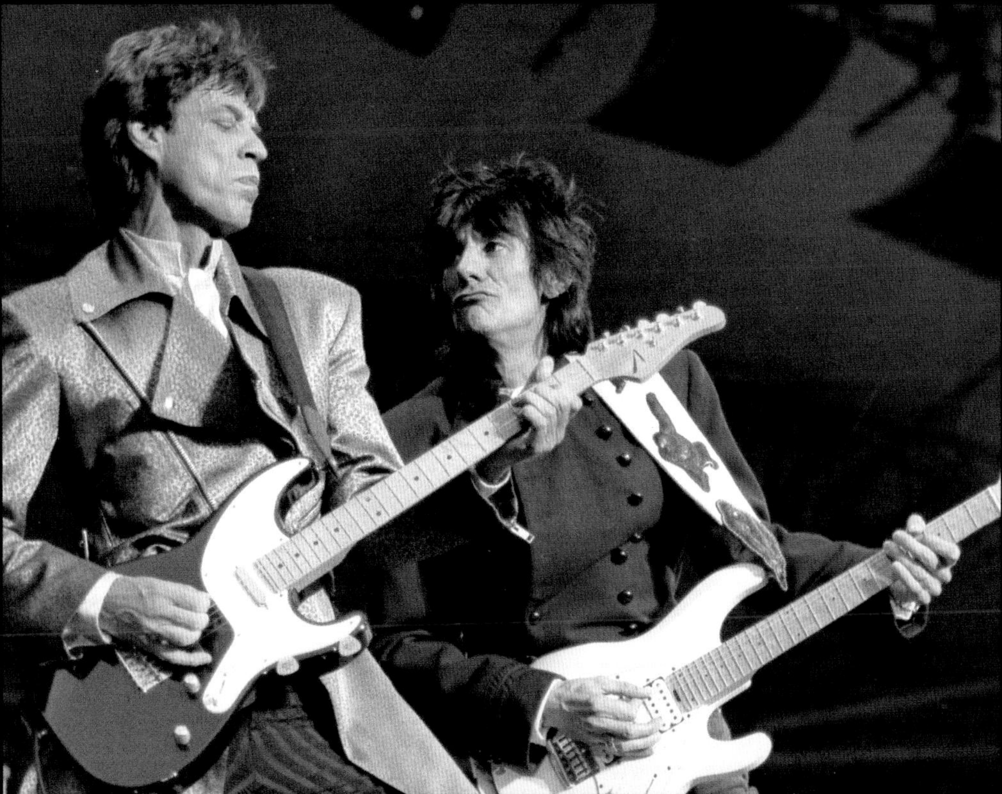

Playing Wembley

Above and left: Mick and Ronnie in the groove. When the Stones played Wembley Stadium on 4 July 1990, there were 'mixed emotions' as some fans had ears cocked to radios to tune into an England World Cup football match. There were several dates at Wembley, and all 120,000 tickets were sold in one day.

During the Wembley concerts the fans' attention was rapturous as the music was accompanied by astonishing visuals including gigantic blow-up dolls during 'Honky Tonk Women' and an inflatable dog during 'Street Fighting Man'. Mick's many costume changes enhanced the sense of theatre.

Opposite: Mick on stage in Rotterdam.

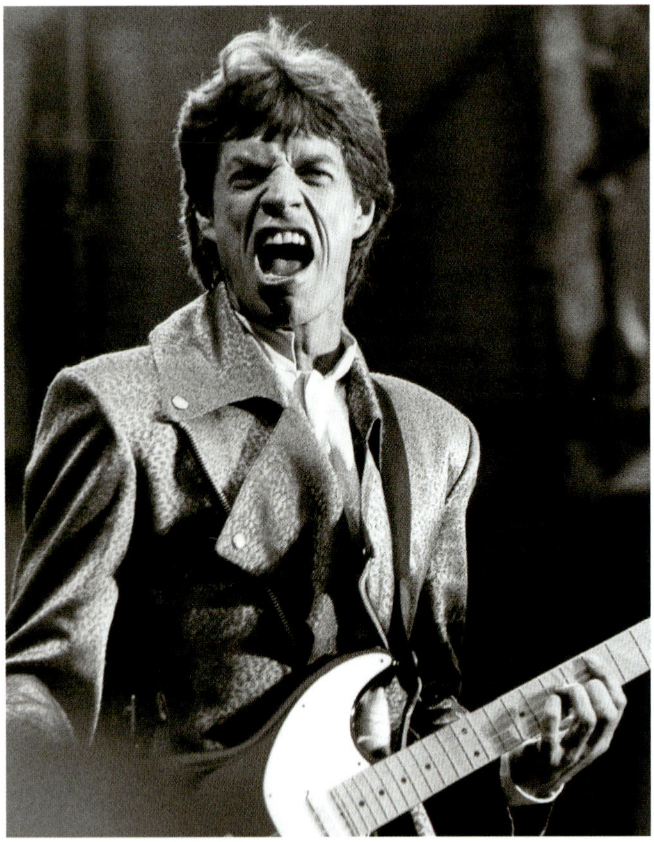

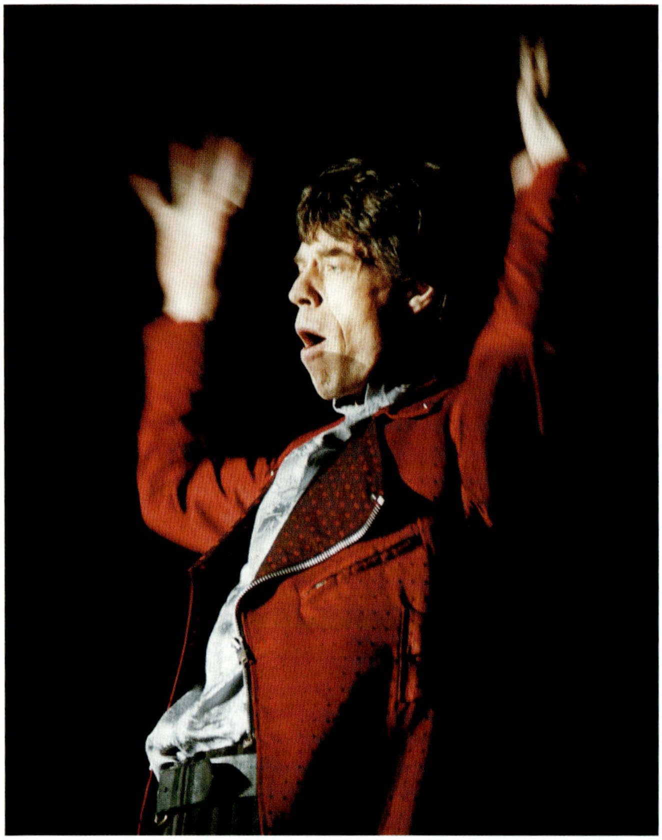

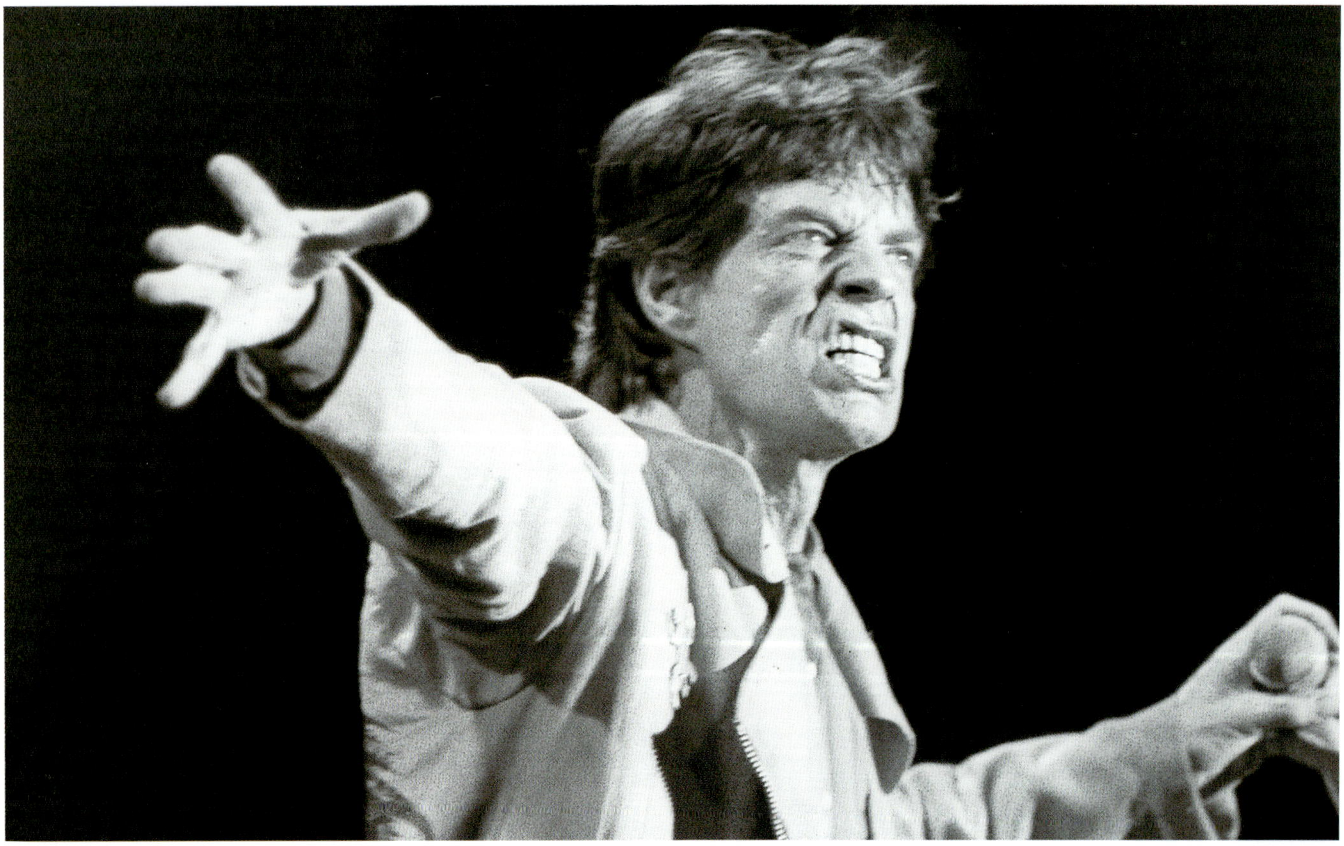

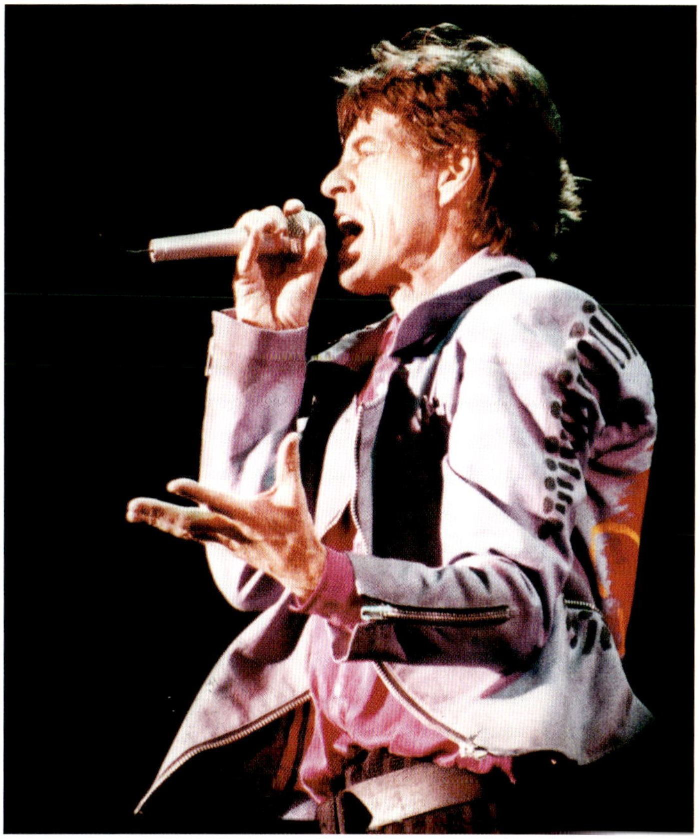

Steel Wheels

Opposite and right: The Stones were at full throttle during their sequence of gigs at Wembley. The British concerts finished with a date in Glasgow before the band headed back to Europe, beginning with a show in Dublin.

'Mixed Emotions' was the first track from the *Steel Wheels* album to be released as a single. Mick sang the line 'Lets bury the hatchet, wipe out the past.' Even Keith speculated that it might be about their relationship but Mick maintained this was not so. *Steel Wheels* was warmly received by the fans, who had waited some time for a new studio album. It was to be the last one on which Bill Wyman played. On the track 'Continental Drift' Mick and Keith returned to Tangier to record rhythms that Brian Jones had introduced them to in the 1960s.

Below: Wembley, August 1990, and the band salute the loyal fans. Among the crowd of 72,000 were old flames Marianne Faithfull and Anita Pallenberg.

The European tour even took in parts of Eastern Europe – Mick is seen in Prague, Czech Republic (*opposite top right*). While in Prague the band were invited to dinner by President Vaclav Havel. Each member of the group was reputed to have earned £10 million from the Urban Jungle tour.

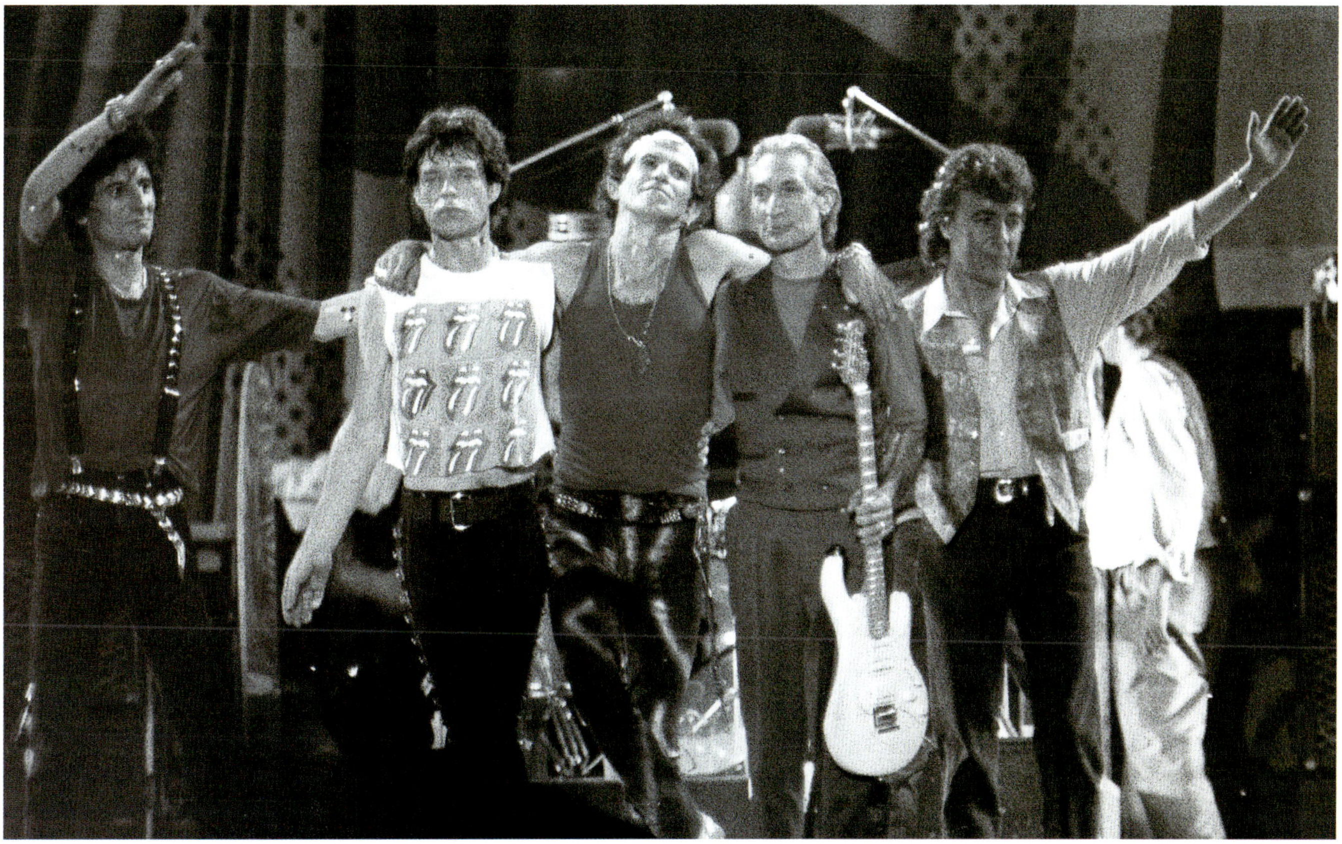

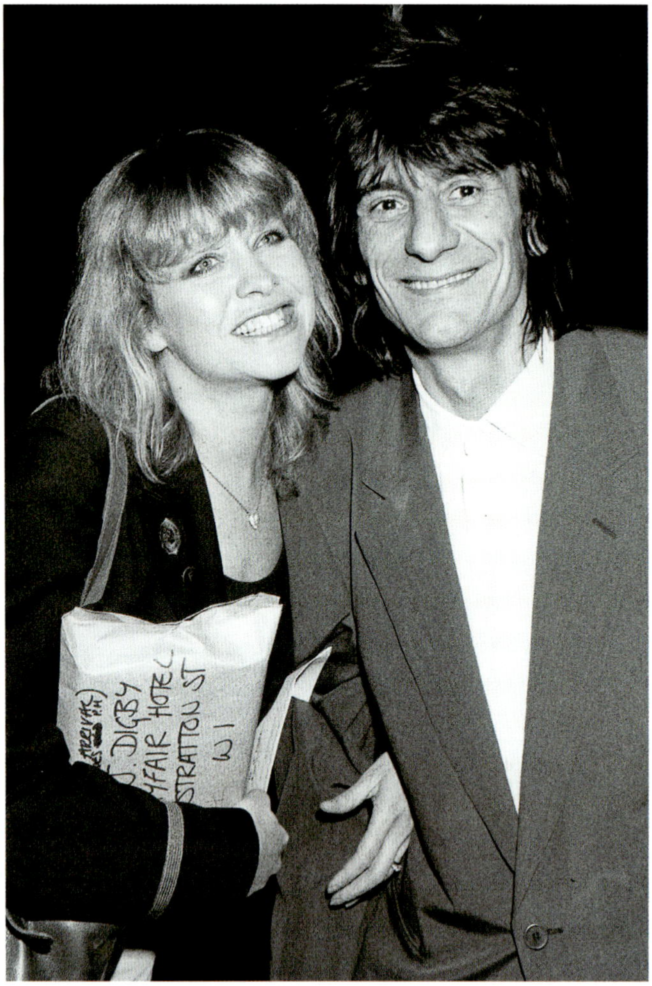

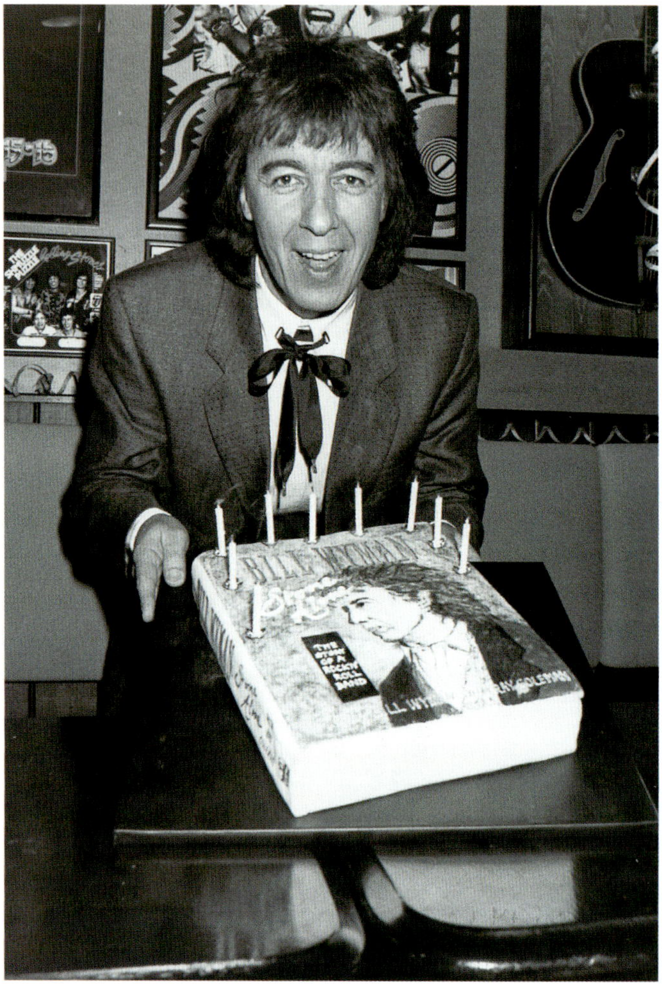

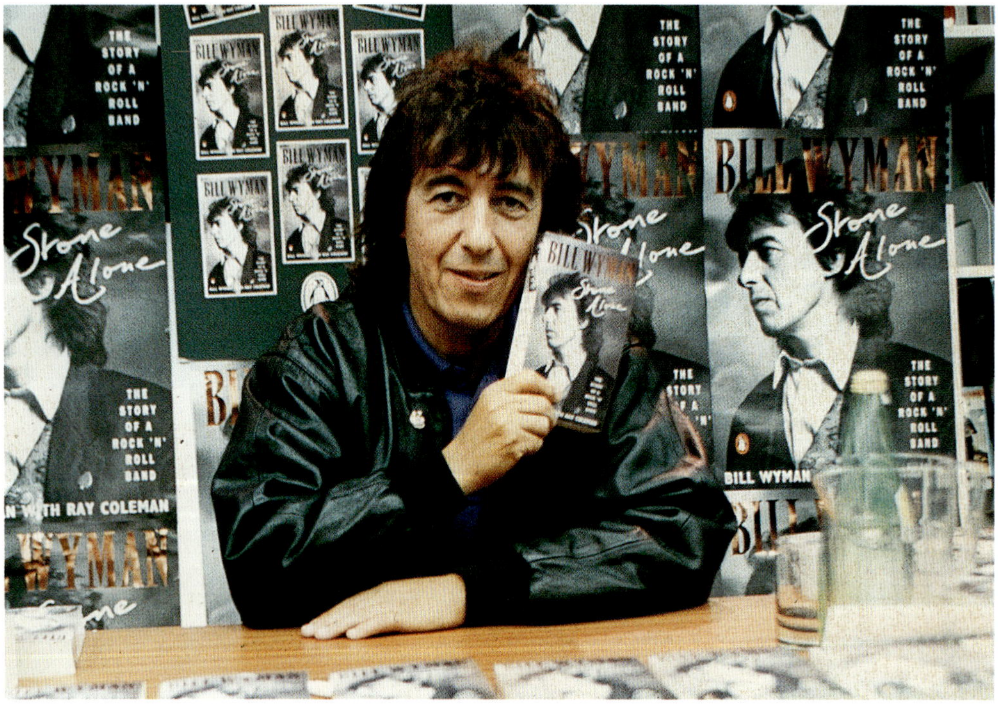

Stone Alone

Above right: Bill Wyman prepares to blow out the candles on his book-shaped birthday cake at Sticky Fingers on 24 October 1990, his 54th birthday. The restaurant is decorated with priceless rock 'n' roll memorabilia, including a guitar given to him by Brian Jones and his collection of gold discs.

Above left: Ronnie and Jo Wood in July 1990.

Left: Bill Wyman autographs more copies of his bestselling memoir.

Opposite: More book promotion – Bill Wyman with a copy of his book propped on the neck of a double bass.

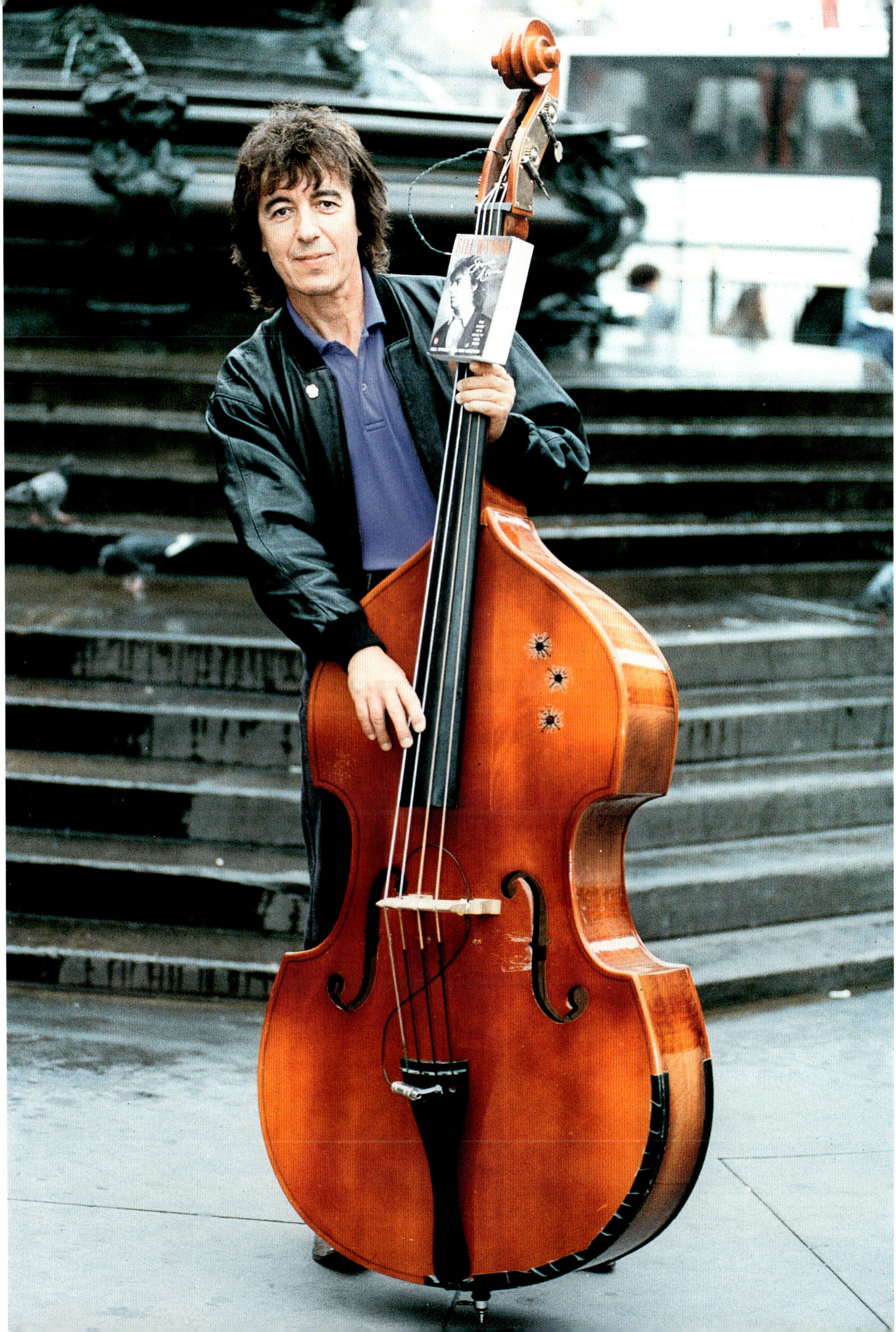

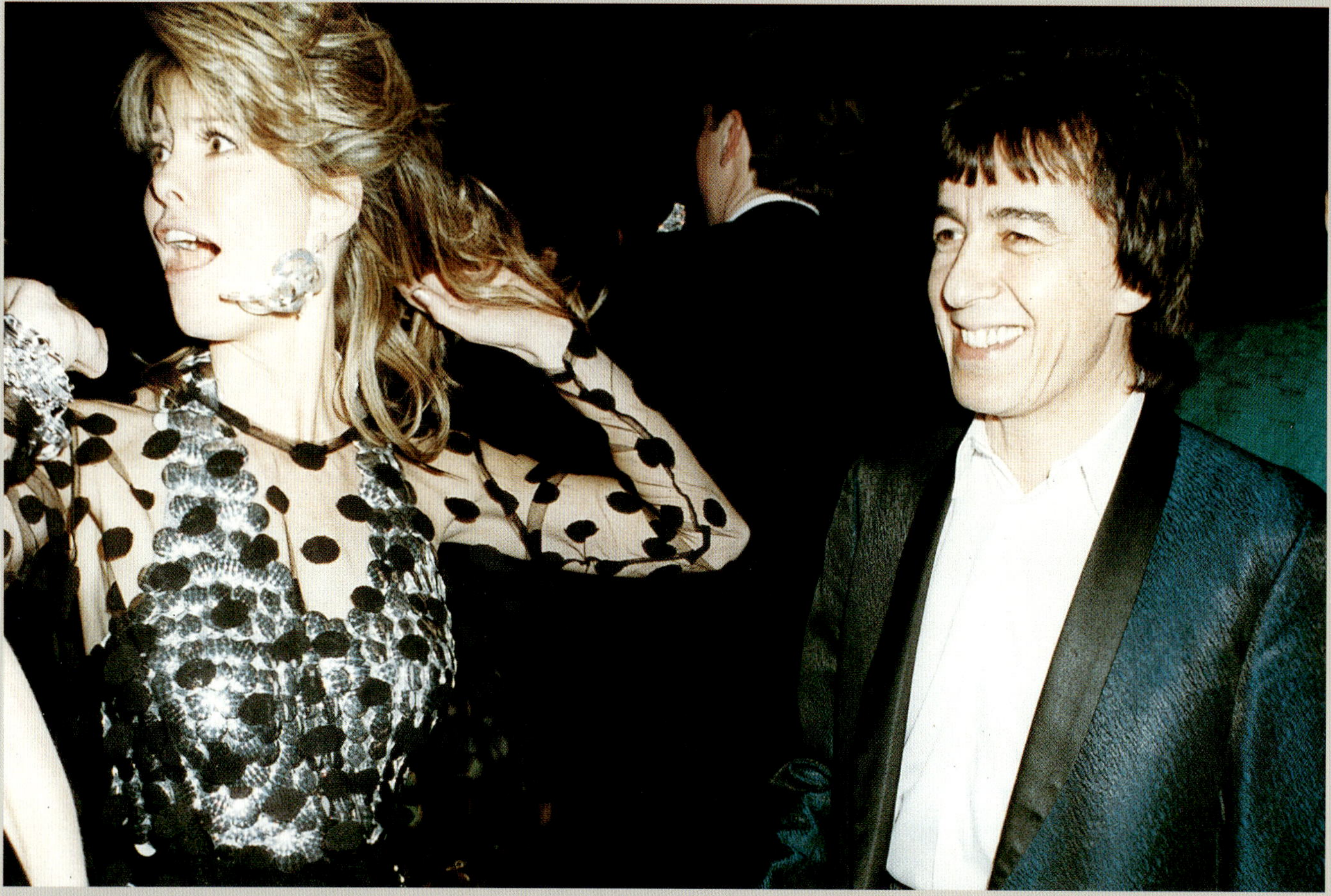

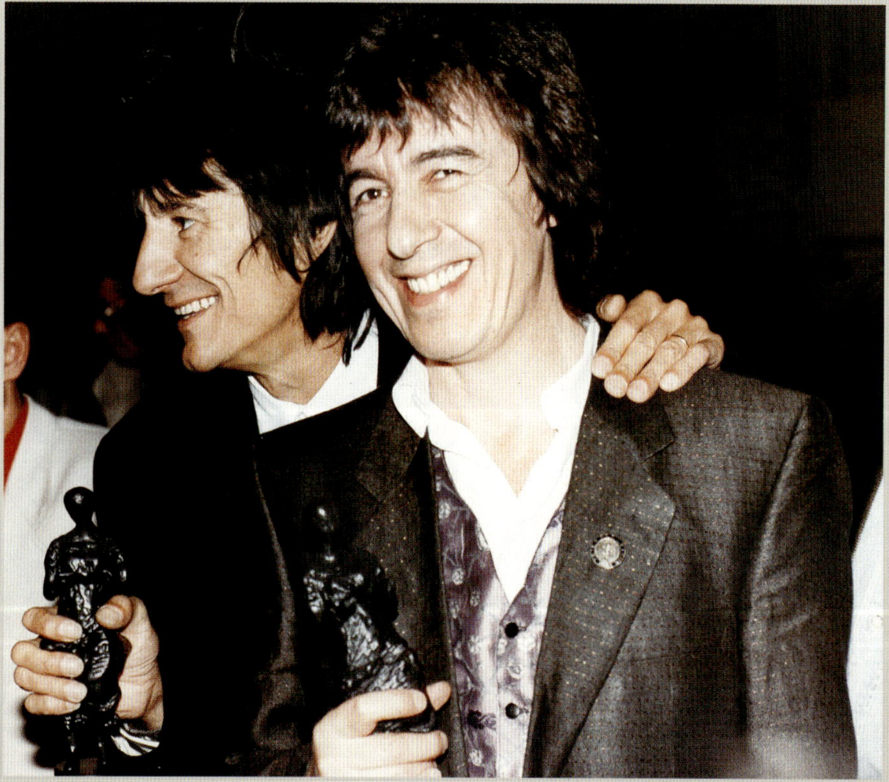

Having a ball

Above: A 1960s-themed charity ball was staged at the Royal Albert Hall in London on 12 March 1991. Bill Wyman was among the 2,000 revellers. His marriage to Mandy was slowly disintegrating and the divorce courts loomed.

Left: Bill and Ronnie clutch trophies received at the Ivor Novello awards ceremony on 2 May. They won the Novello award for outstanding contribution to British music.

Opposite above: Bill chats to 1960s icons Petula Clark (*left*) and Patti Boyd, the former model who was married to George Harrison and then Eric Clapton.

Opposite below: Charlie Watts smiles at the relaunch of his book about Charlie Parker, *Ode to a High Flying Bird,* on 3 April at Ronnie Scott's. The book had only sold a handful of copies when first published in the mid-1960s.

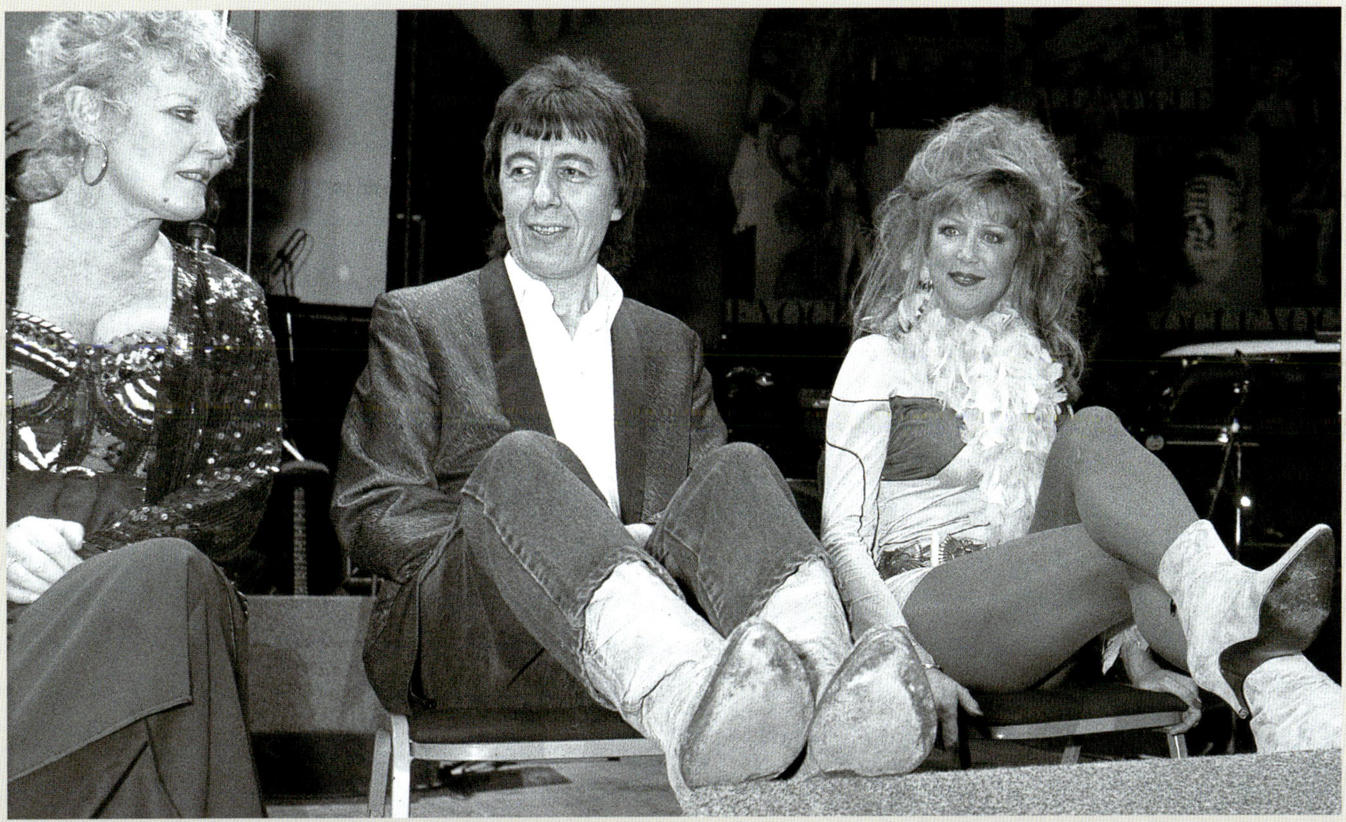

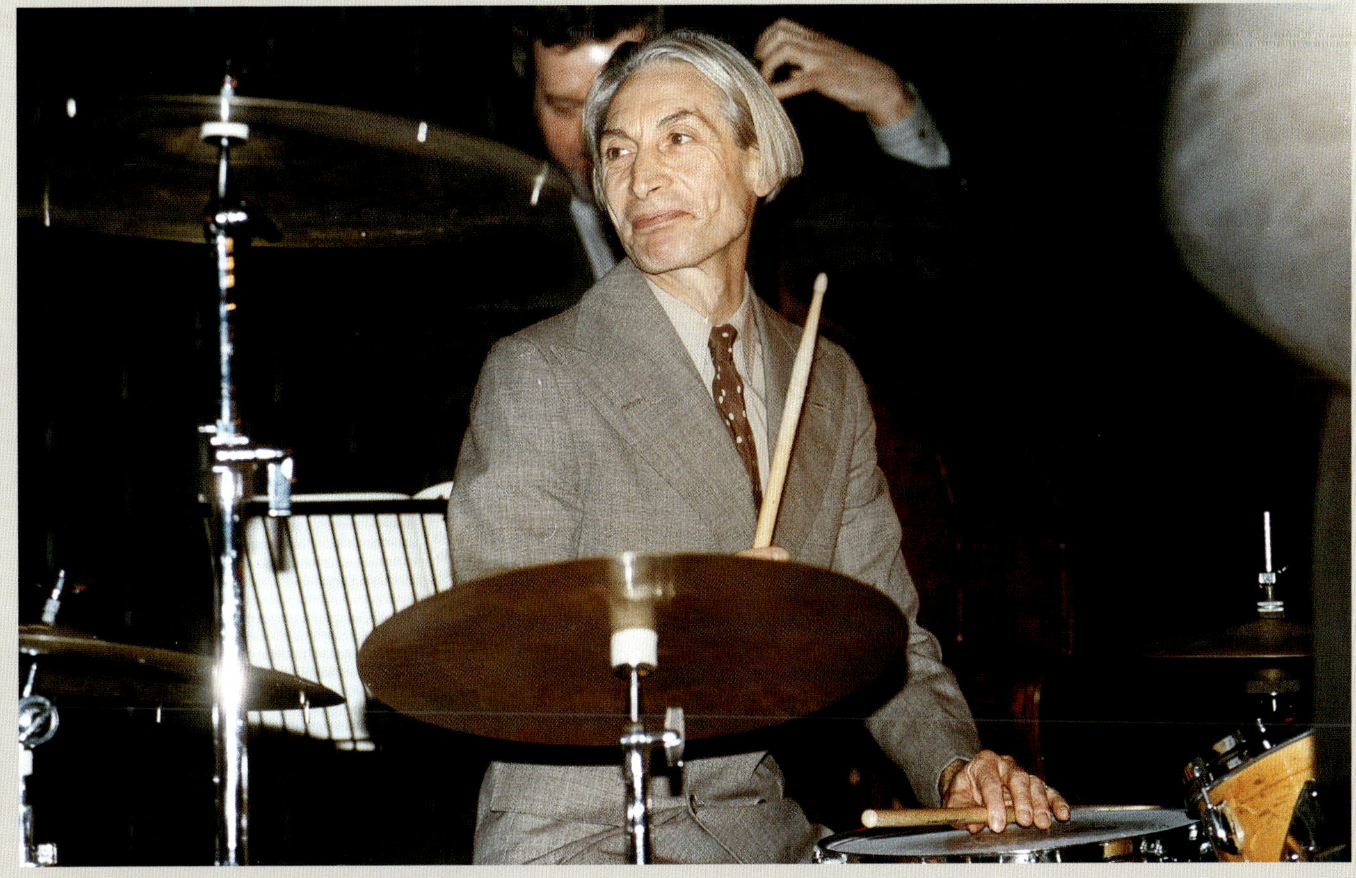

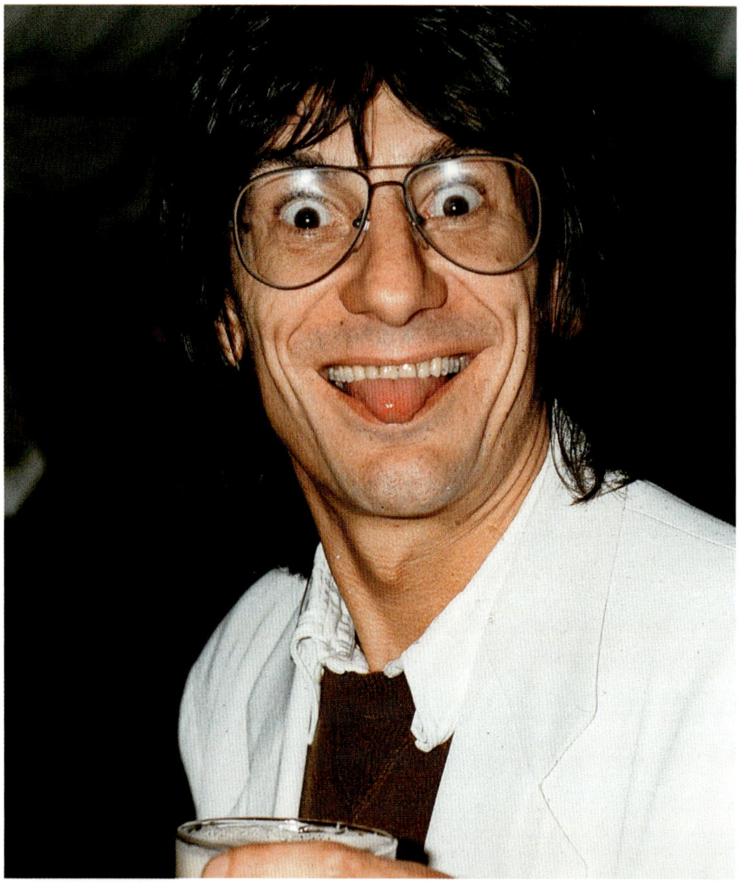

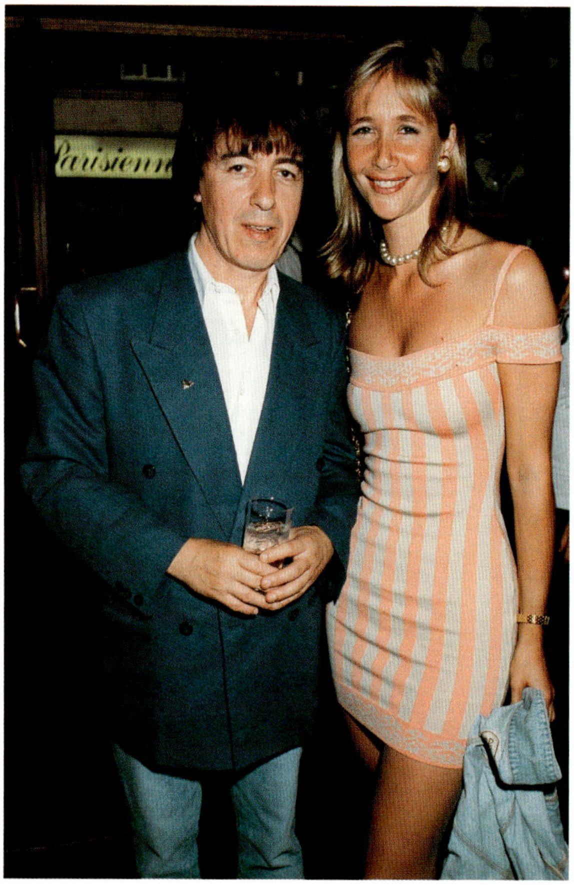

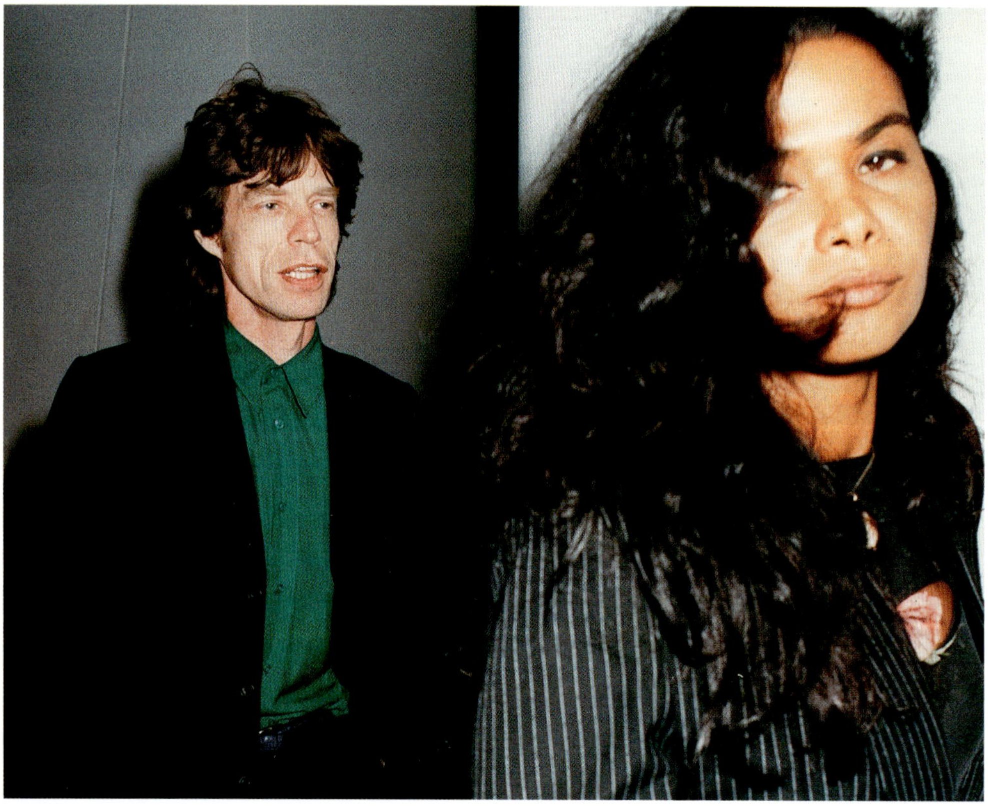

£25 million deal

Above left: Ronnie Wood's grin is as wide as some of the deliveries at a charity cricket match on 14 June 1991.

Above right: Bill Wyman seemed to be enjoying some time to rest after 20 years of being a Rolling Stone. TV presenter Tania Bryer was his guest at Sticky Fingers on 20 May 1992.

Left: Mick follows 19-year-old daughter Karis into a party hosted by former Eurythmics star Dave Stewart.

The Stones were soon to agree a deal worth £25 million with Virgin Records but Wyman did not want to sign. It seemed like he really was getting ready to leave the band.

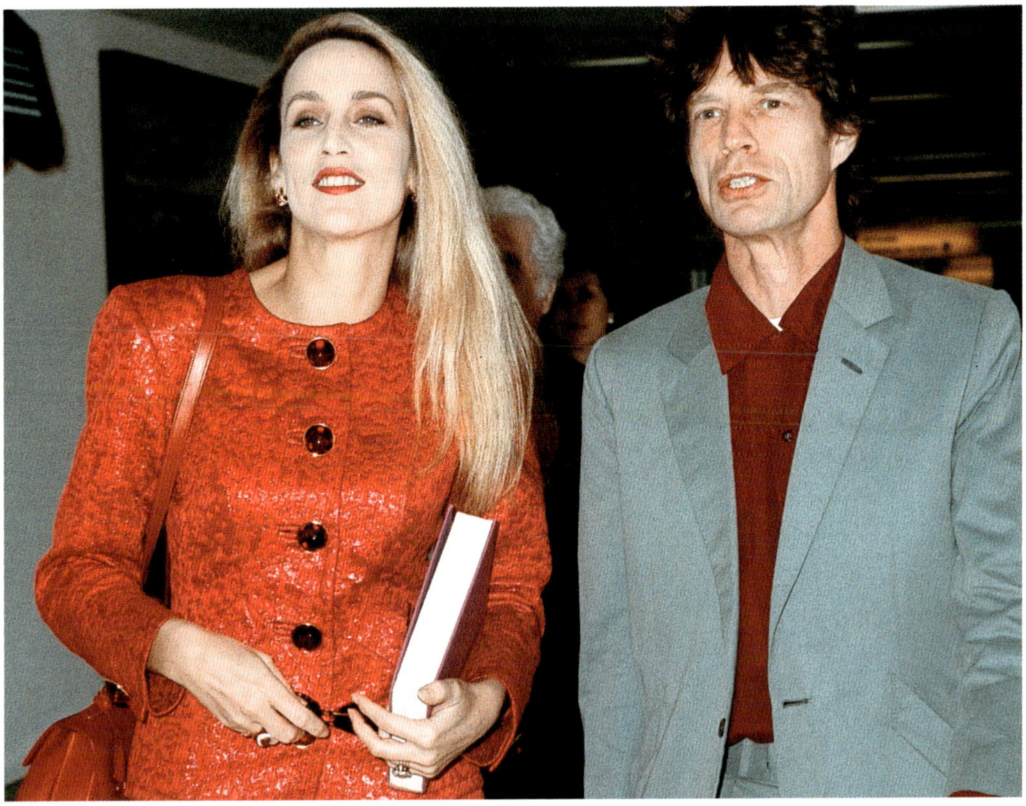

Left: Mick and Jerry on their way to Nice in 1991, the year after they finally decided to marry in Bali, Indonesia. Although there were no plans for the Stones to get back into the studio together, most members of the band were working. In 1992 Mick began his third album, to be called *Wandering Spirit*. Ronnie released *Slide On This* and Keith produced his second solo album later in the year.

Below: Keith Richards takes part in the Guitar Legends festival in Seville, Spain, in October 1991. He received better press coverage than some of the other legends present, including Bob Dylan.

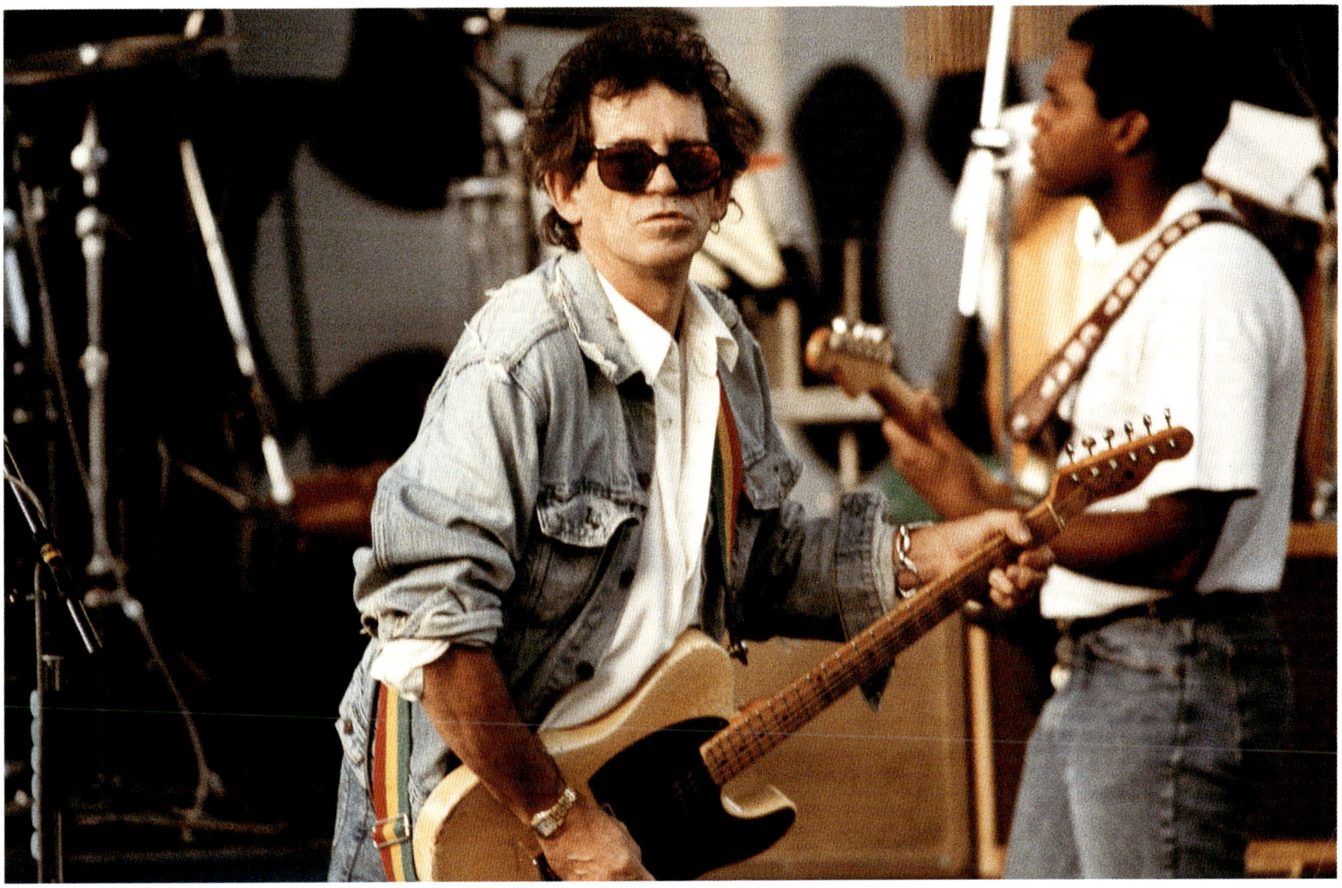

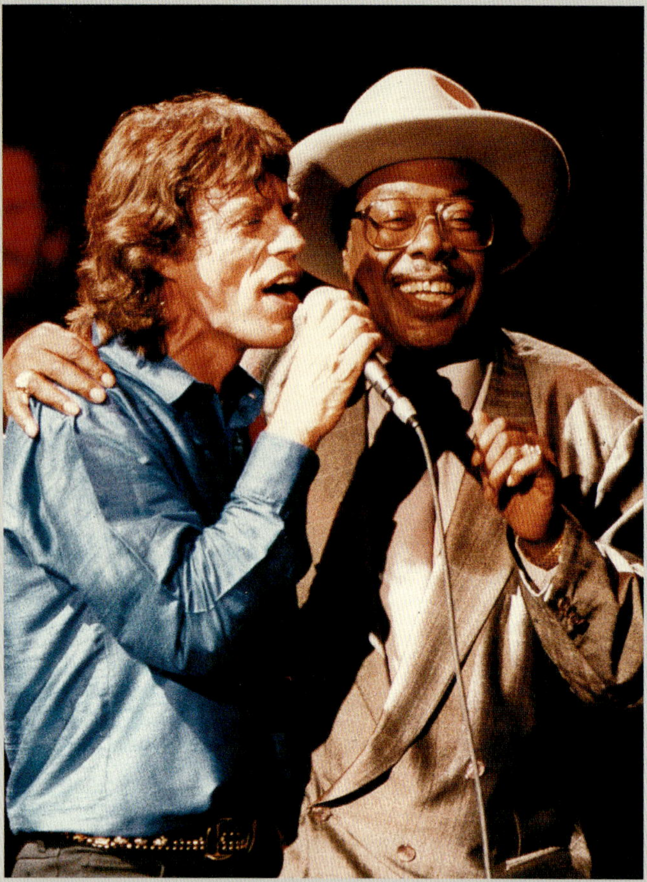

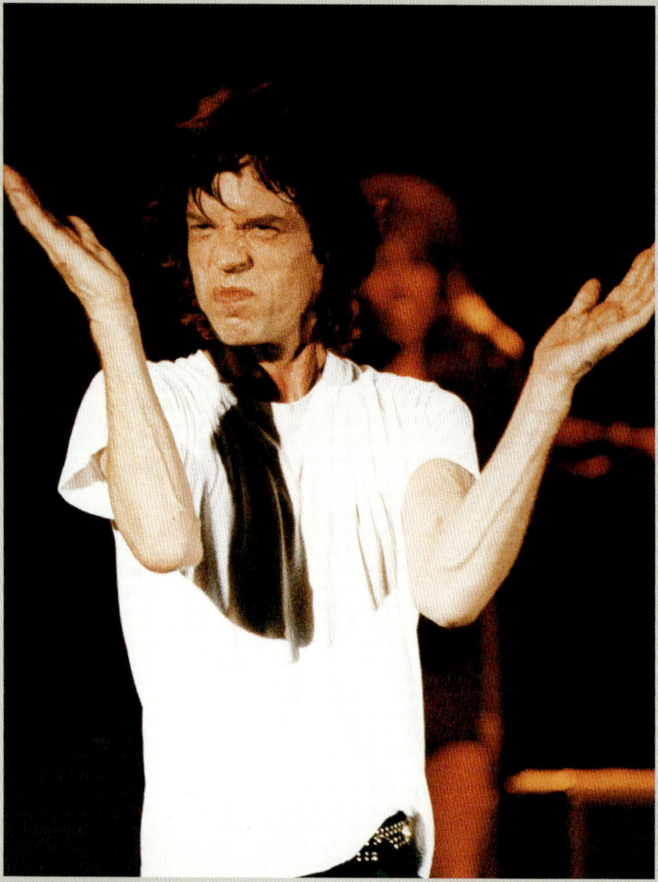

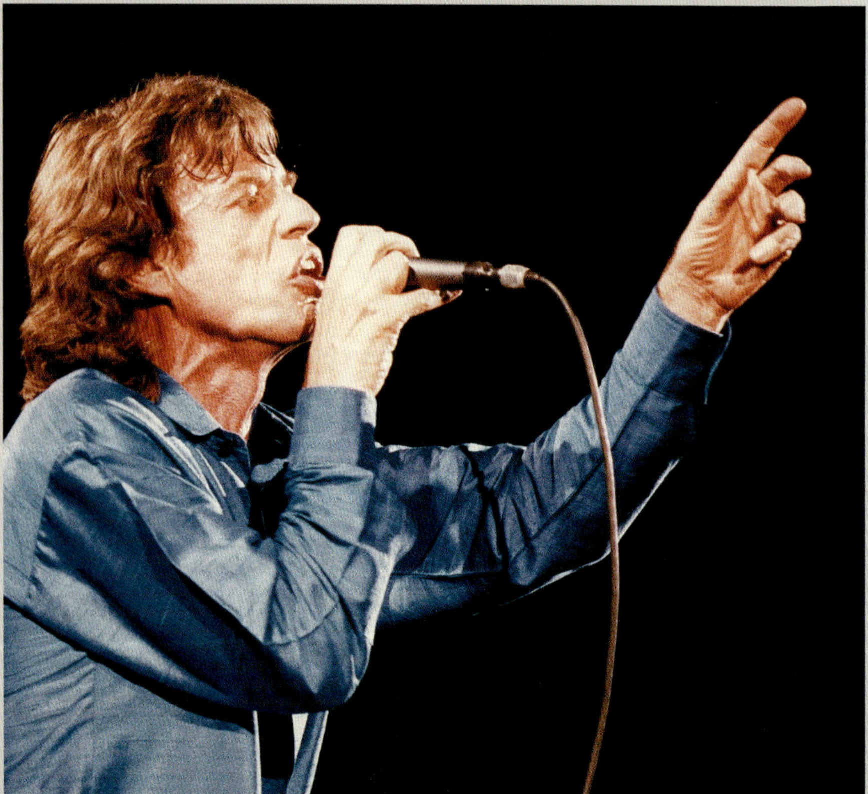

National Music Day

Above left: Mick Jagger put the hammer back into 'Hammersmith' when he played there the night before National Music Day in June 1992 – it was his first solo concert for two years. The show was a special blues tribute – here he duets with blues hero Jimmie Rogers.

Left: Mick on stage in Hammersmith. Thousands of people supported 1,500 music events around the country, and singers such as Cliff Richard and José Carreras participated as well as rock 'n' rollers such as Eric Clapton, Elton John and Jagger. Sadly it did not become an annual fixture.

Above right: Mick encourages the crowd in Hammersmith.

Opposite: Fellow Stones Ronnie Wood (*pictured*) and Charlie Watts also took part in Jagger's 'Celebration Of The Blues'.

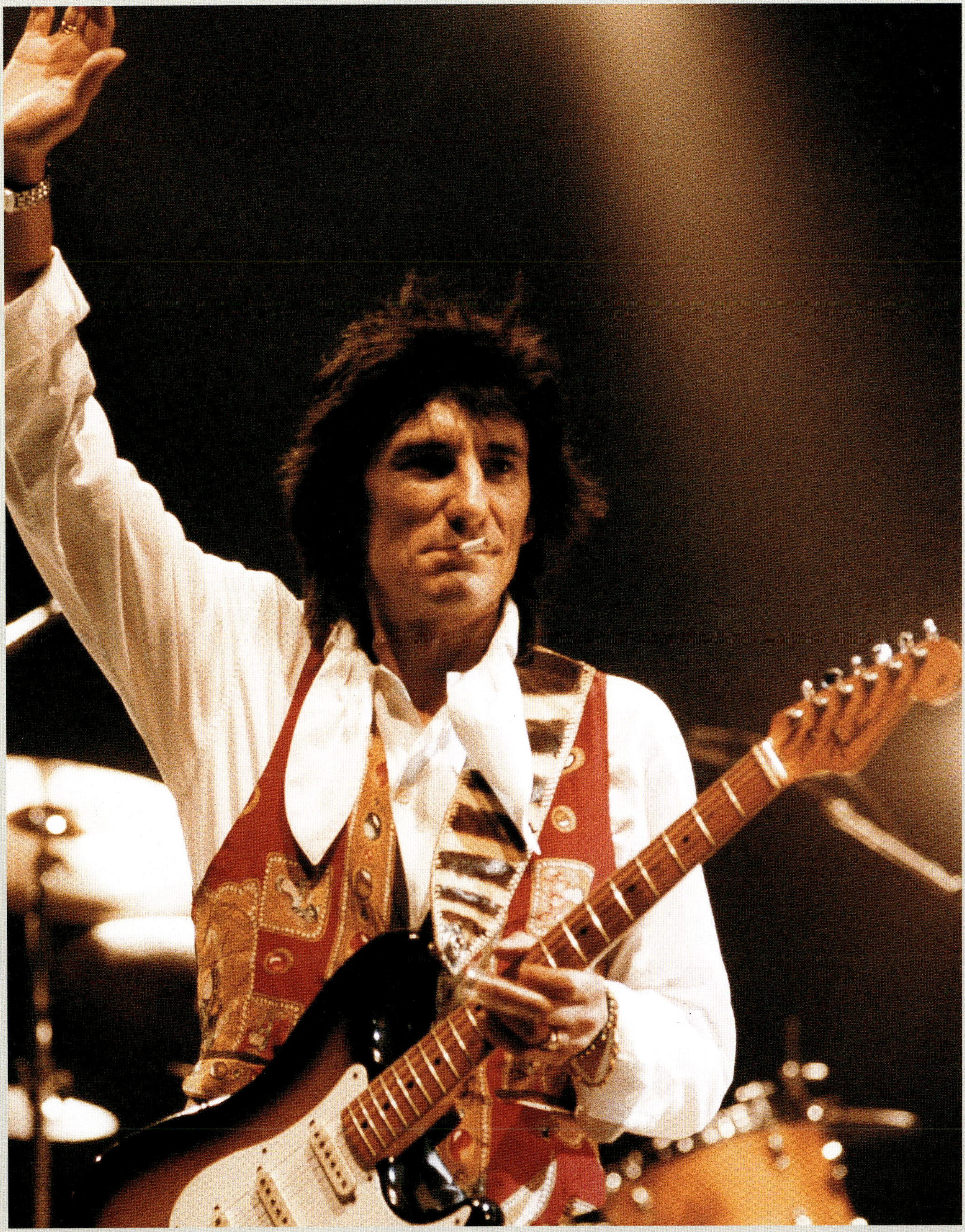

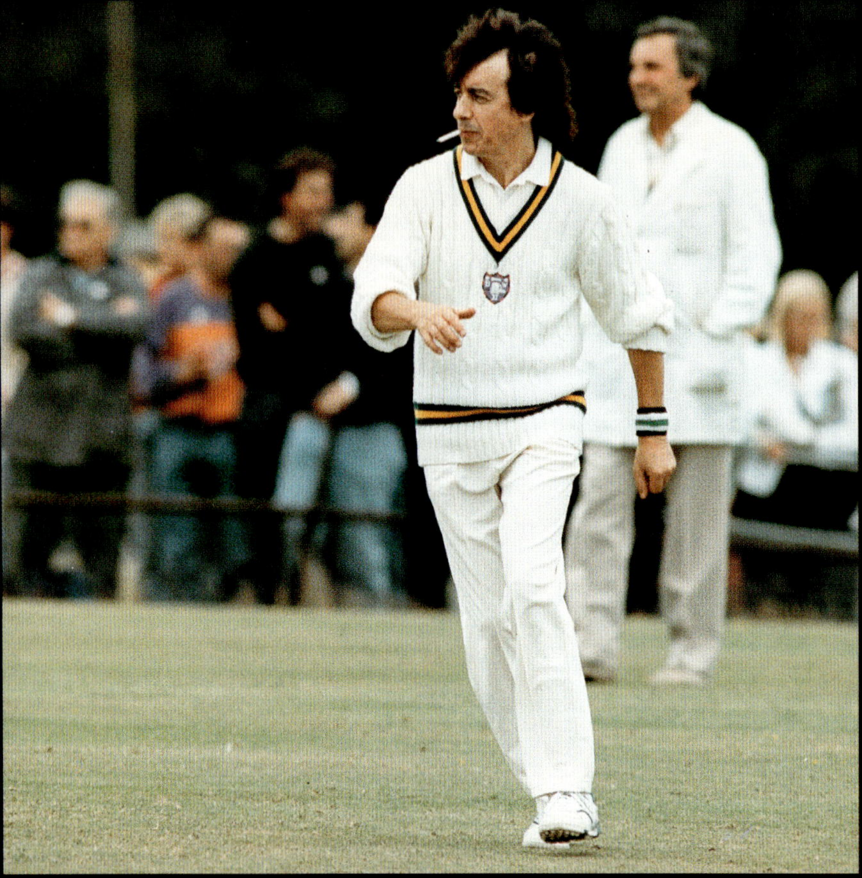

Good sports

Left: Bill Wyman on the outfield at a charity cricket match in Kent on 15 August 1992.

Below: The Wood family – Ronnie, wife Jo and children Leah, aged 13, and Tyrone, aged 9.

Ronnie left early in January 1993 to give a series of solo concerts in Japan.

Opposite above: Bill is driven to the High Court for his divorce proceedings. His marriage to Mandy Smith had been brief and troubled – they spent little time together owing to work commitments and illness.

Opposite below right: Bill Wyman looks purposeful yet sad as he strides out of court after the final settlement has been agreed in his divorce in November 1992. Mandy had hoped for £5 million but settled for £580,000. Both were sufficiently recovered to find new love before long. Mandy was seeing a professional footballer, and Bill remarried just five months after the divorce. His new wife, Suzanne Accosta, was a Californian fashion designer in her 30s.

Opposite below left: Bill turns out to support a cancer charity.

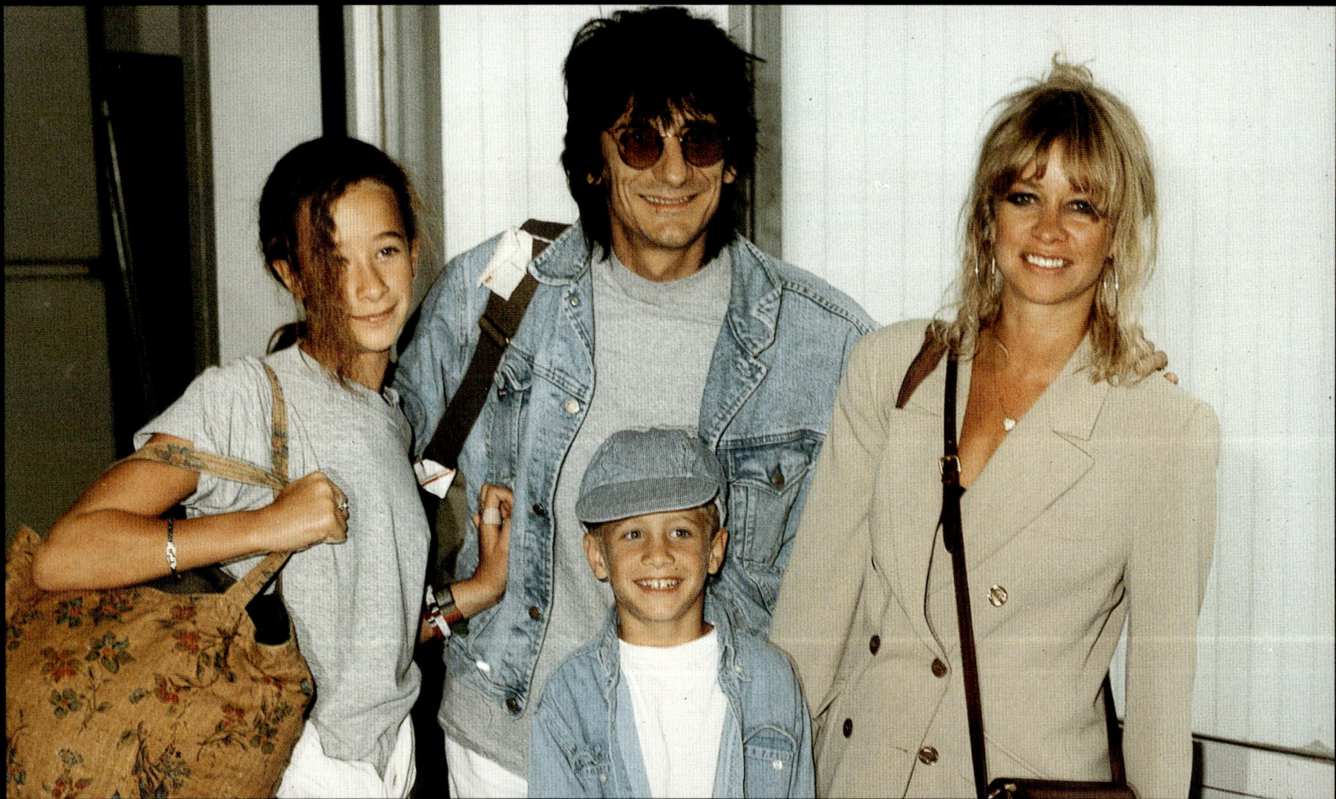

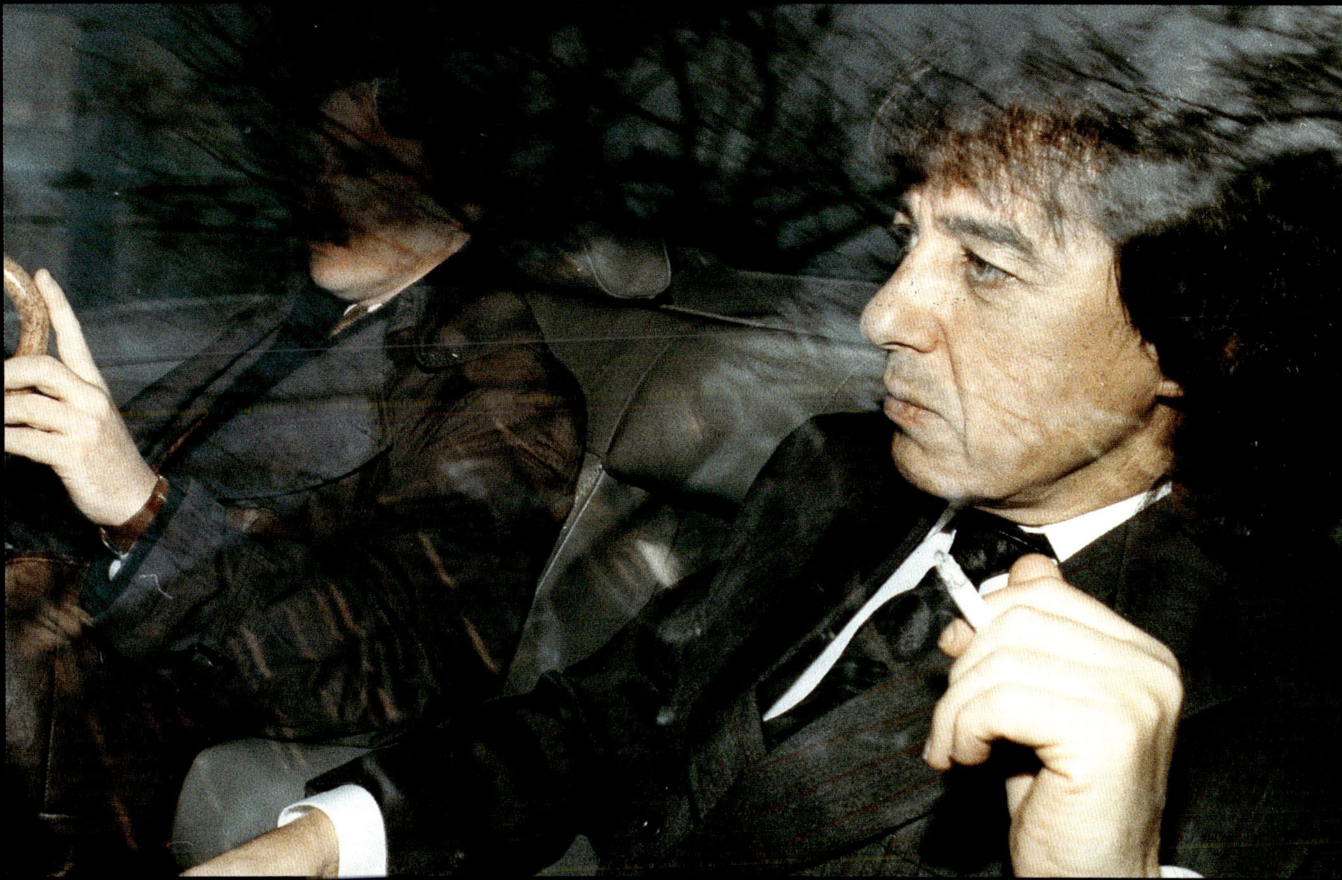

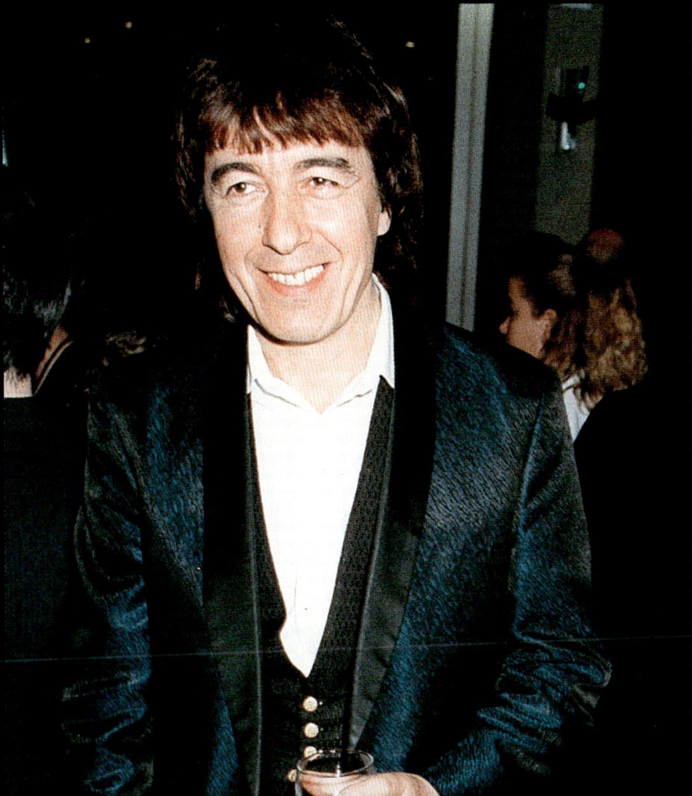

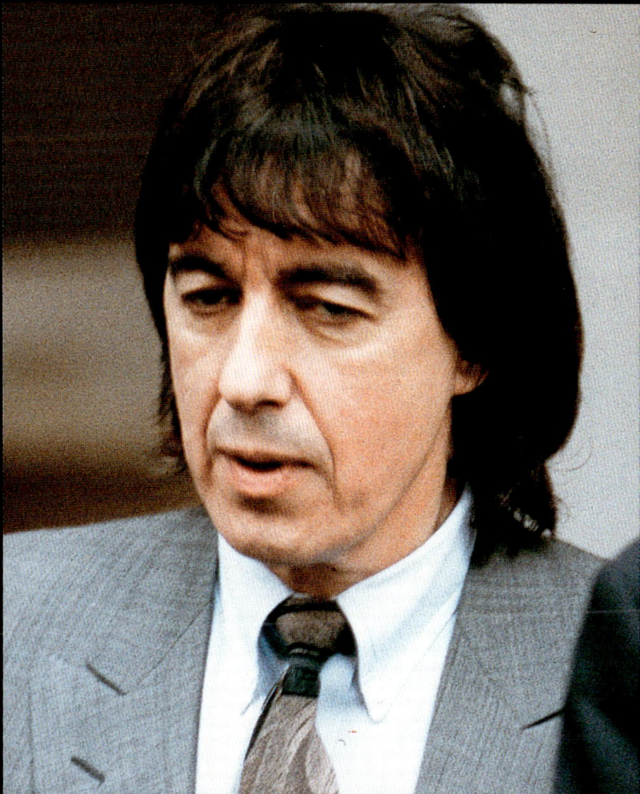

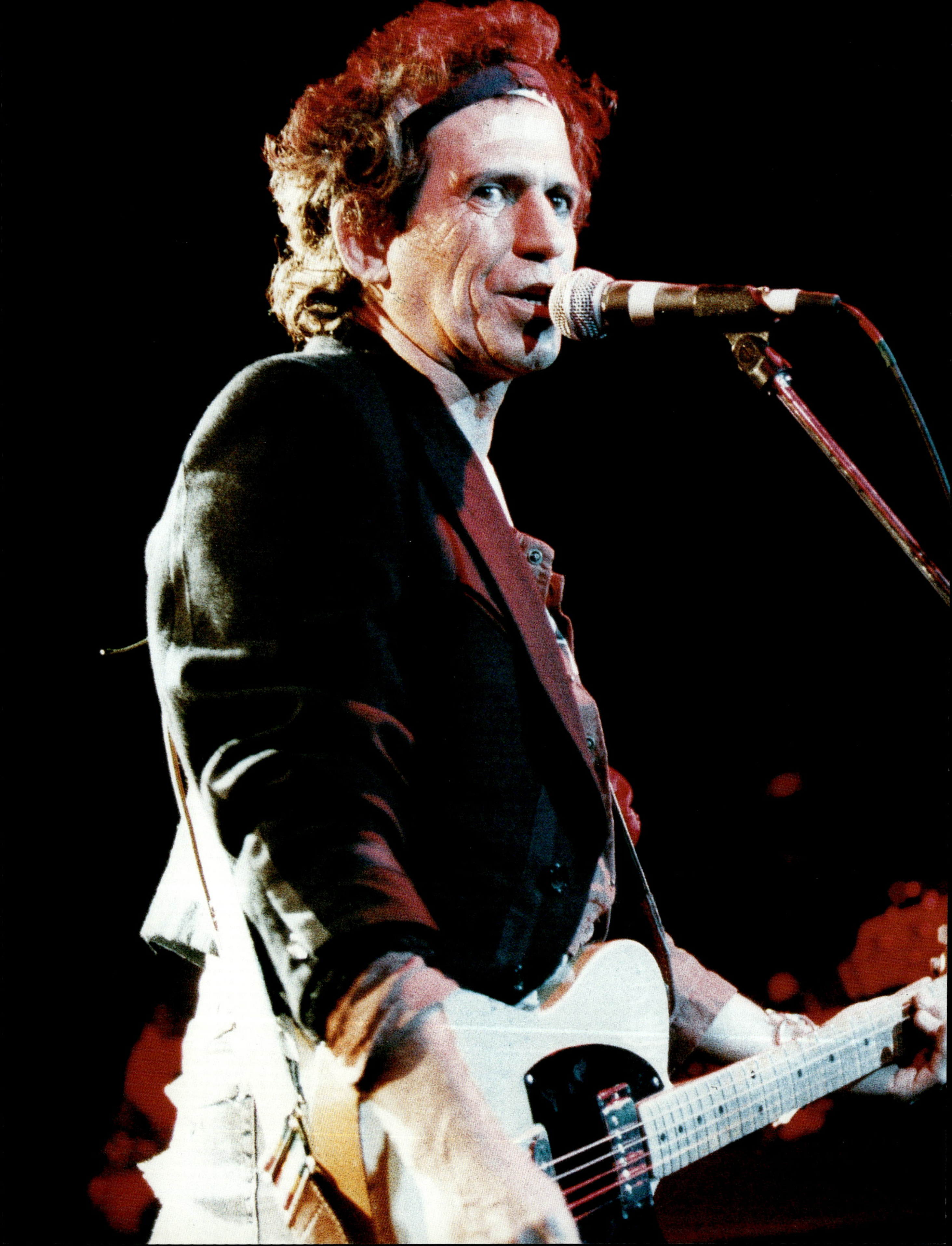

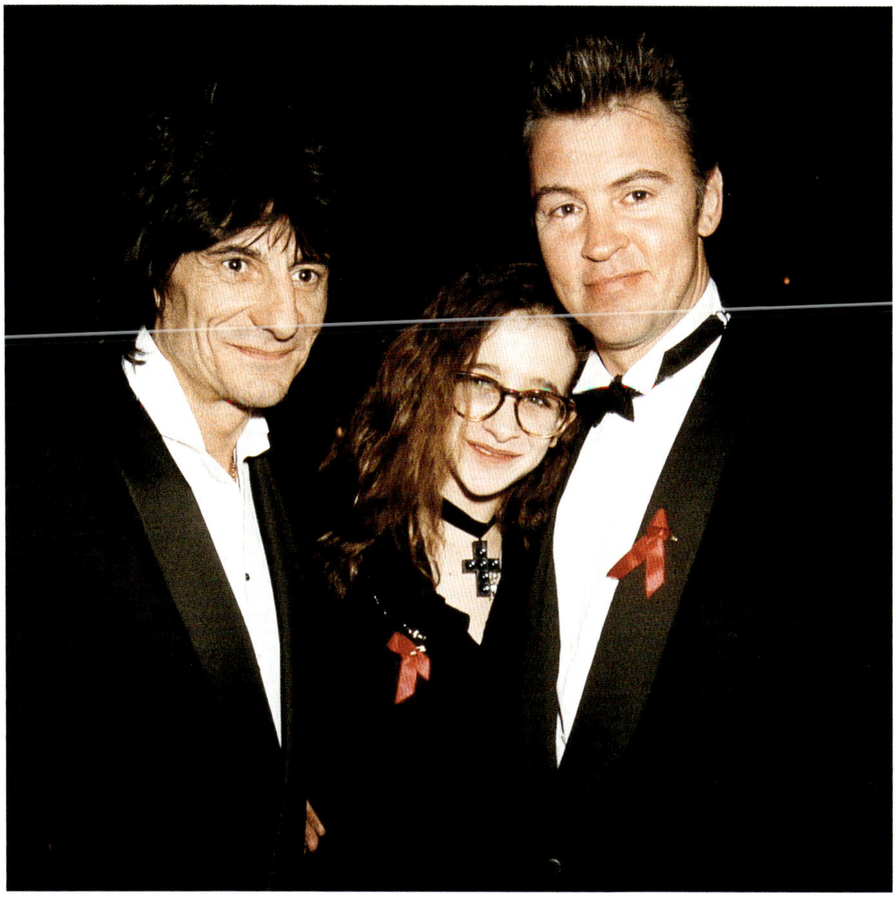

Going solo

Opposite: Keith goes solo – and suited – at a Marquee Club gig in London in December 1992. Mick attended but declined fans' entreaties to join his Glimmer Twin onstage.

Right: Ronnie at the Brit awards in February 1993. Paul Young (*right*) was a big star. Ronnie's daughter Leah (*centre*) was set to become one. A few years later she was to appear on stage with the band on the Bridges To Babylon tour.

Below: February 1993: Mick and Jerry are all smiles, clearly confounding rumours of any estrangement. It was reported that their relationship was in difficulties the previous year.

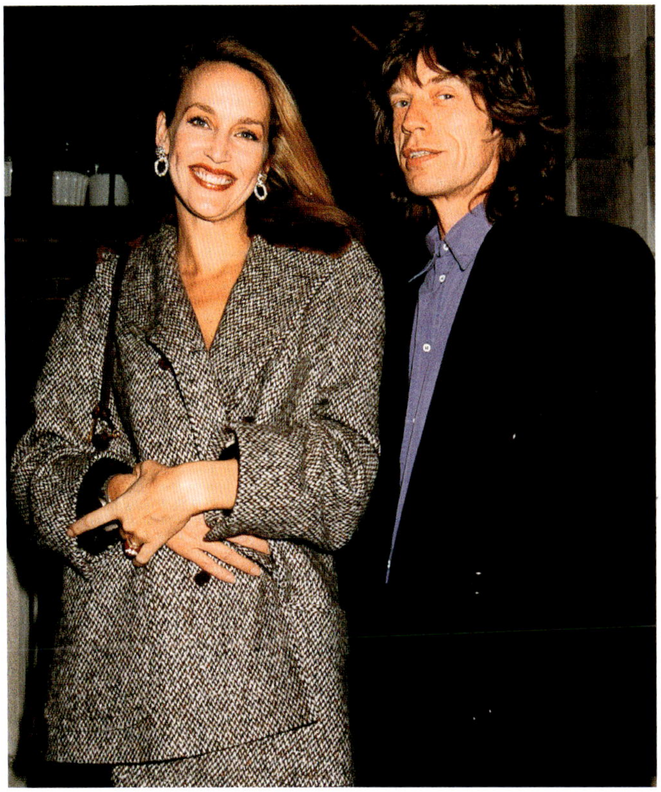

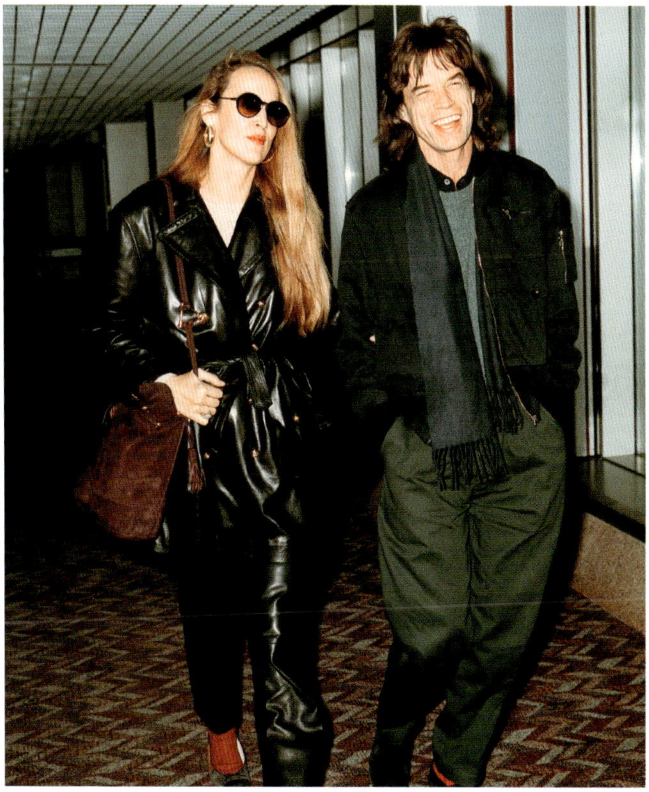

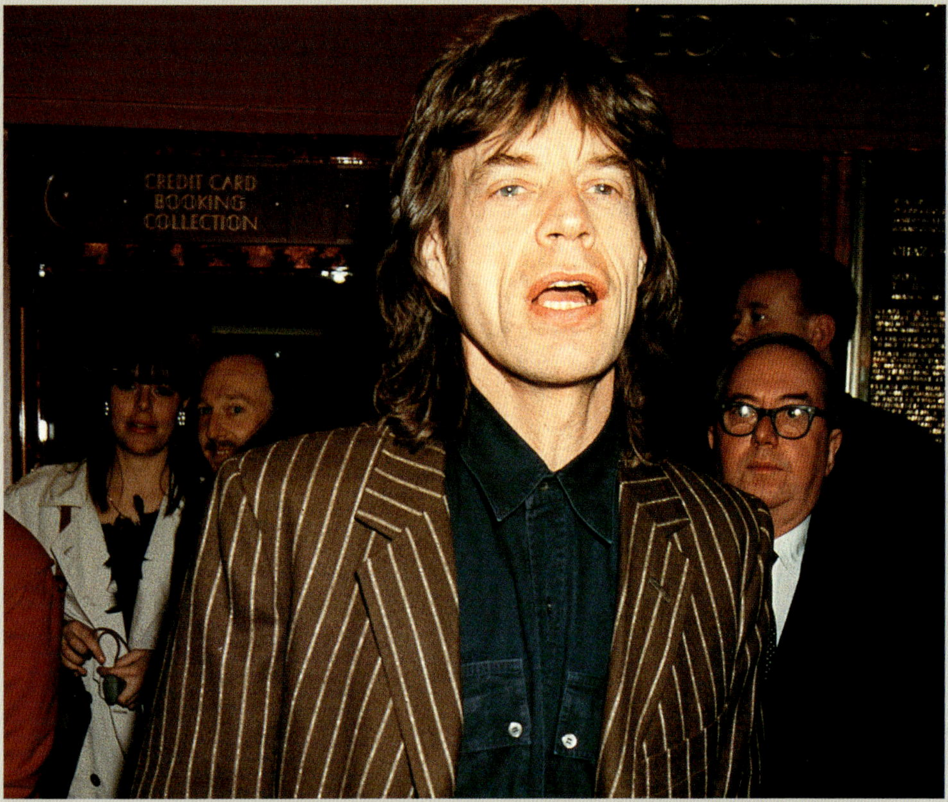

True Brits

Opposite: In February 1993 Bill Wyman guested at the Brit awards. Ronnie Wood was there to congratulate Rod Stewart, his ex-Faces colleague, on receiving a special award for services to the music industry.

Left: In March Mick attended a first night party for *Crazy for You*, before joining Keith in the West Indies to start writing for the forthcoming Stones album to be produced by Don Was. Although relationships between members of the band were good, it was five years since they had worked in the studio together.

Below: Charlie and Shirley Watts fly into London from New York in March 1993. Charlie went on to Barbados to meet Mick and Keith.

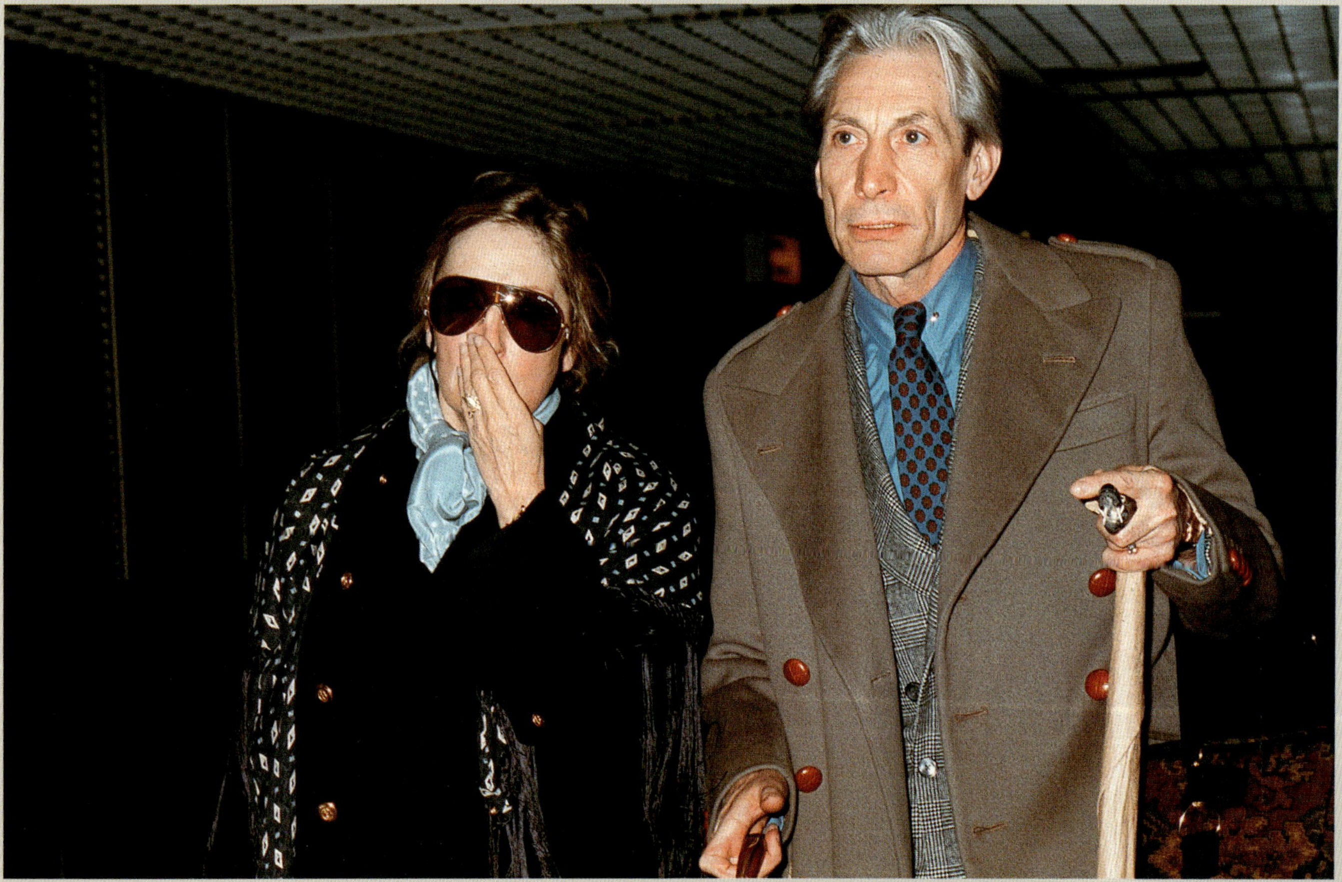

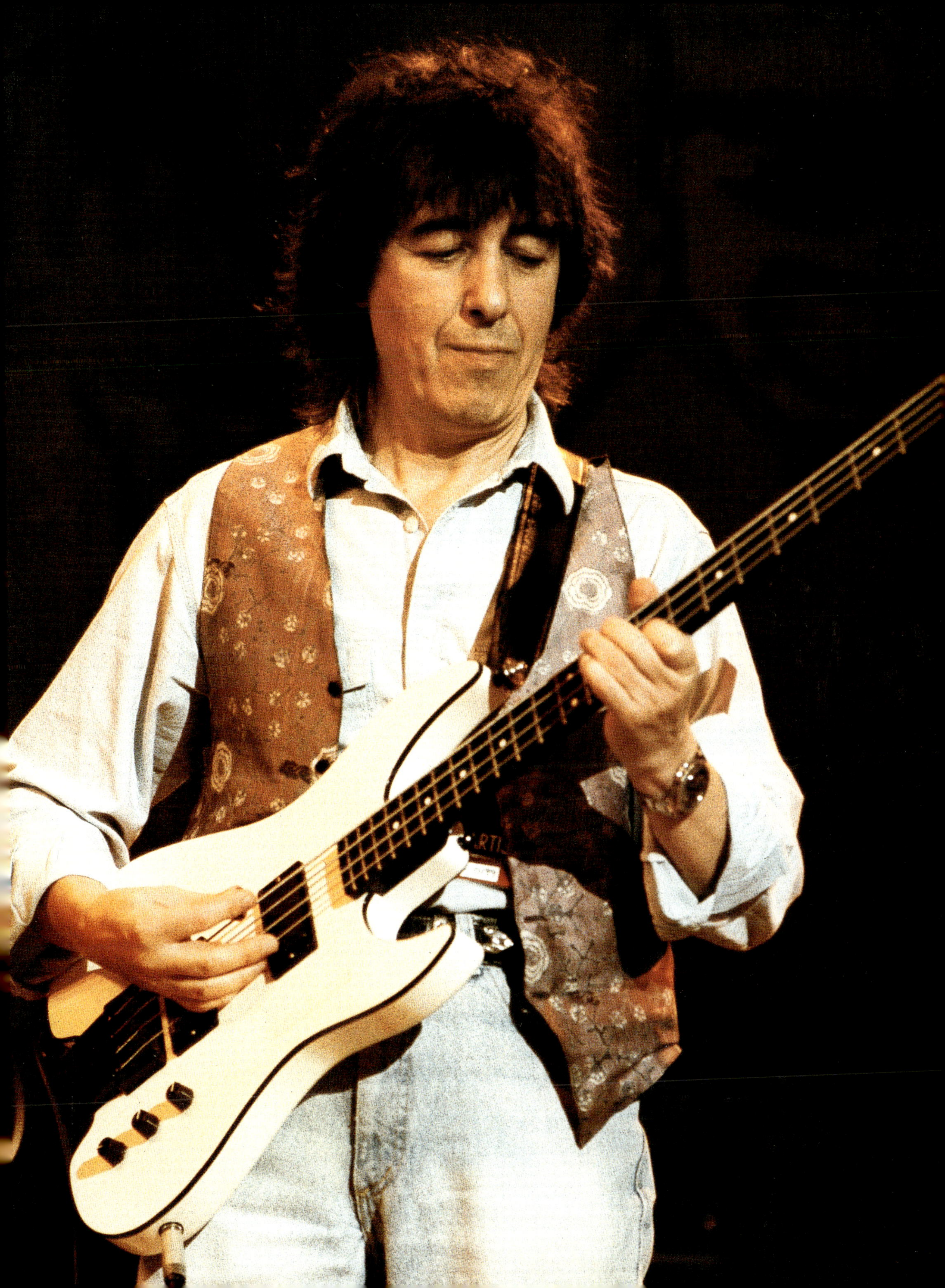

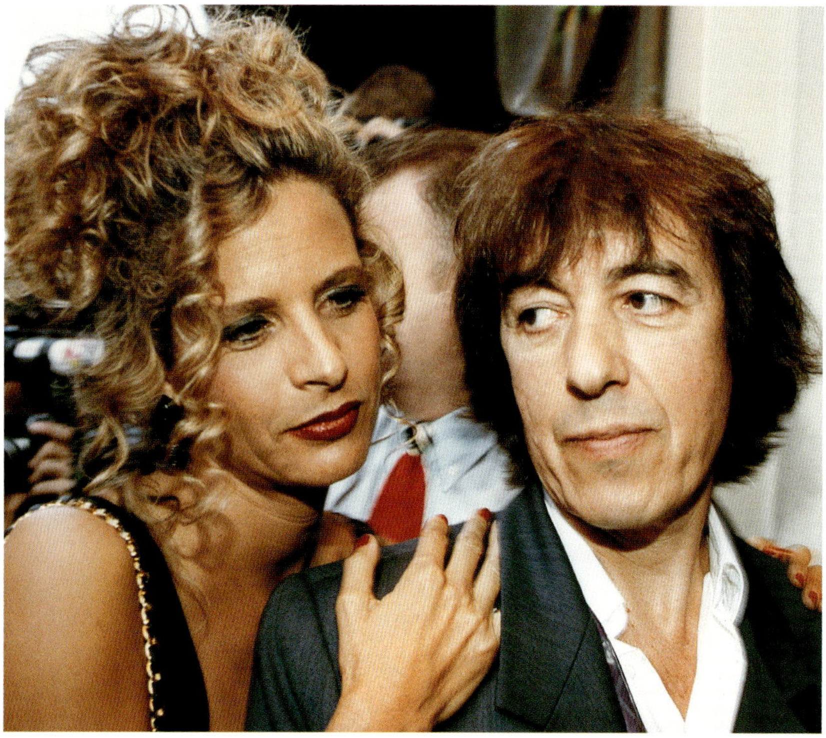

Party time

Left: Bill struck lucky when he married third wife Suzanne. Here they celebrate the fourth anniversary of his Sticky Fingers restaurant.

Below: The Wood family visit Planet Hollywood, the celebrity restaurant in central London, in May 1993.

Opposite above left: Bill is joined on stage by former Amen Corner singer and guitarist Andy Fairweather Low at a concert in March 1993. He played classic blues and rock 'n' roll rather than reprise any Rolling Stones songs.

Opposite above right: Mick looking relaxed in April 1993. While in Barbados he and Keith had written 15 new songs for the new album, *Voodoo Lounge*.

Opposite below: At a gathering of the clans to mark Mick's 50th birthday. Mick declined to be snapped but various other band members, including Ronnie in Napoleonic costume, were in the firing line at Walpole House. The theme of the party was the French Revolution. Charlie Watts came dressed as Robespierre, while Jerry Hall was Marie Antoinette.

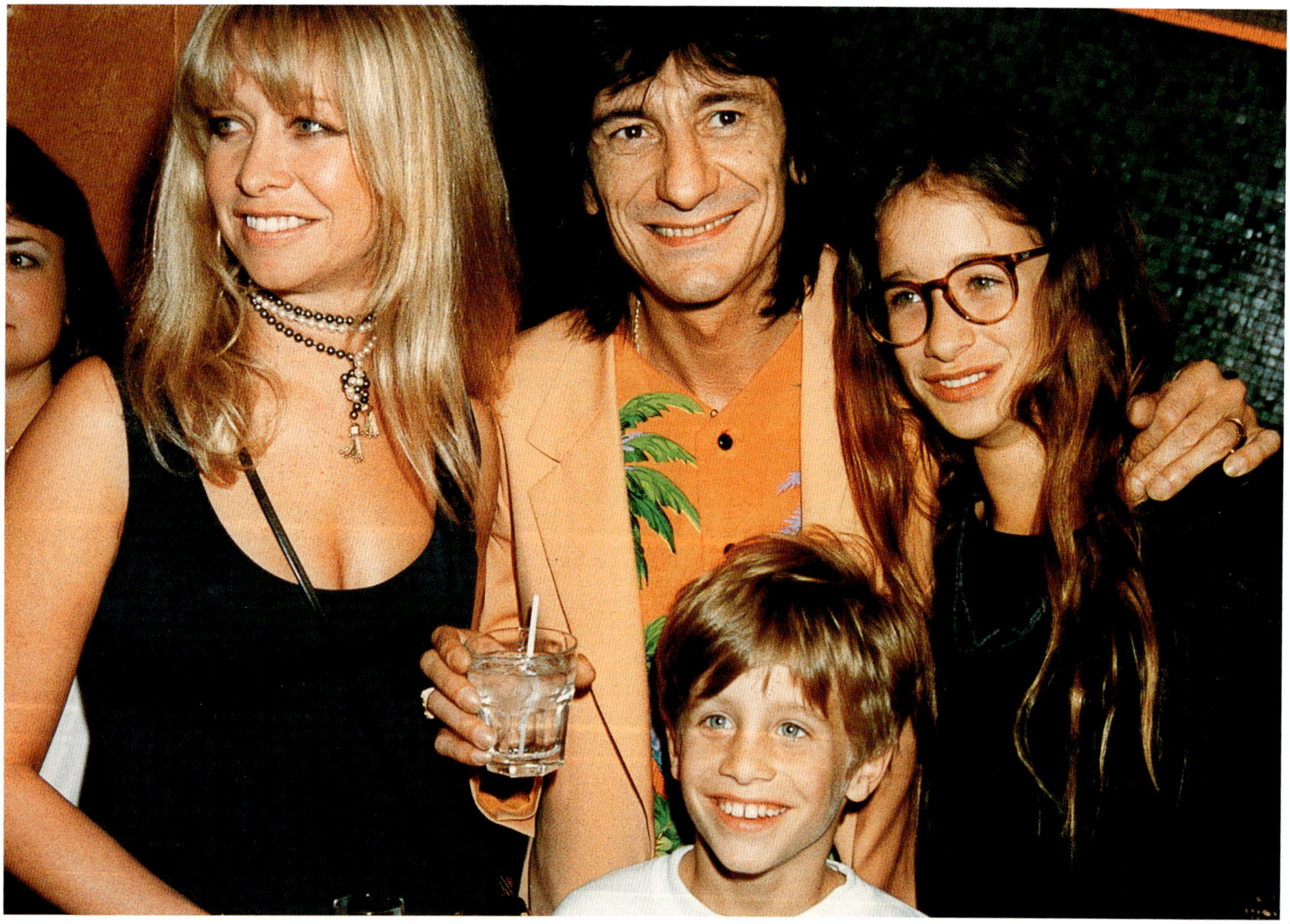

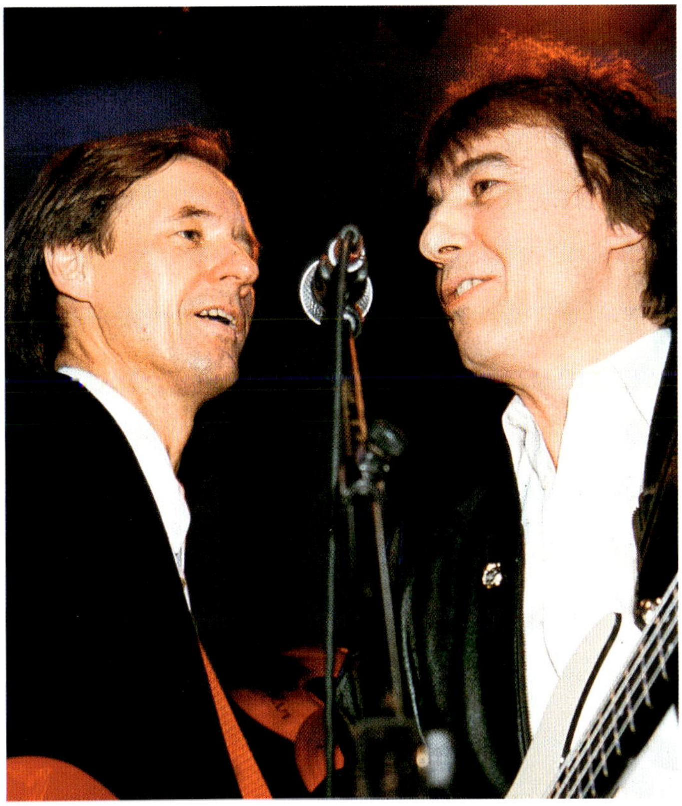

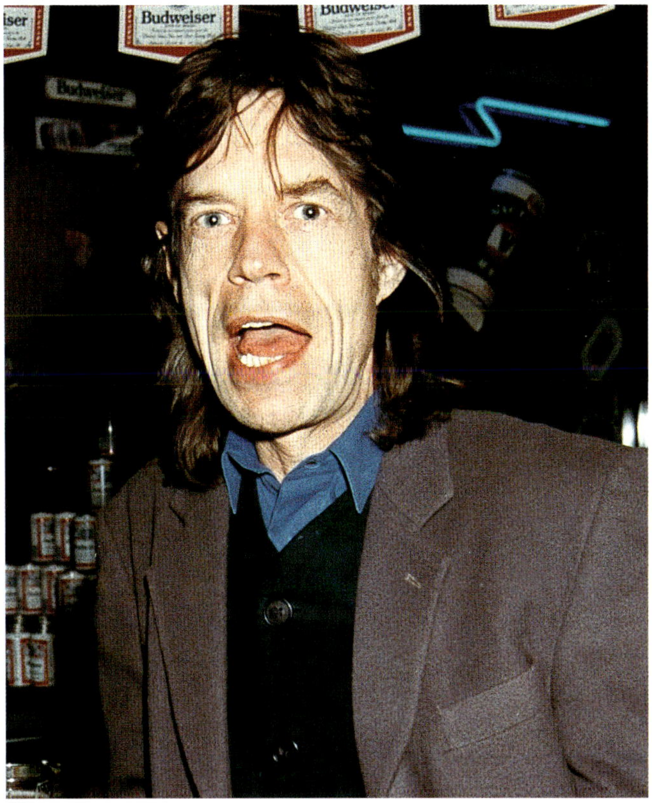
Budweiser

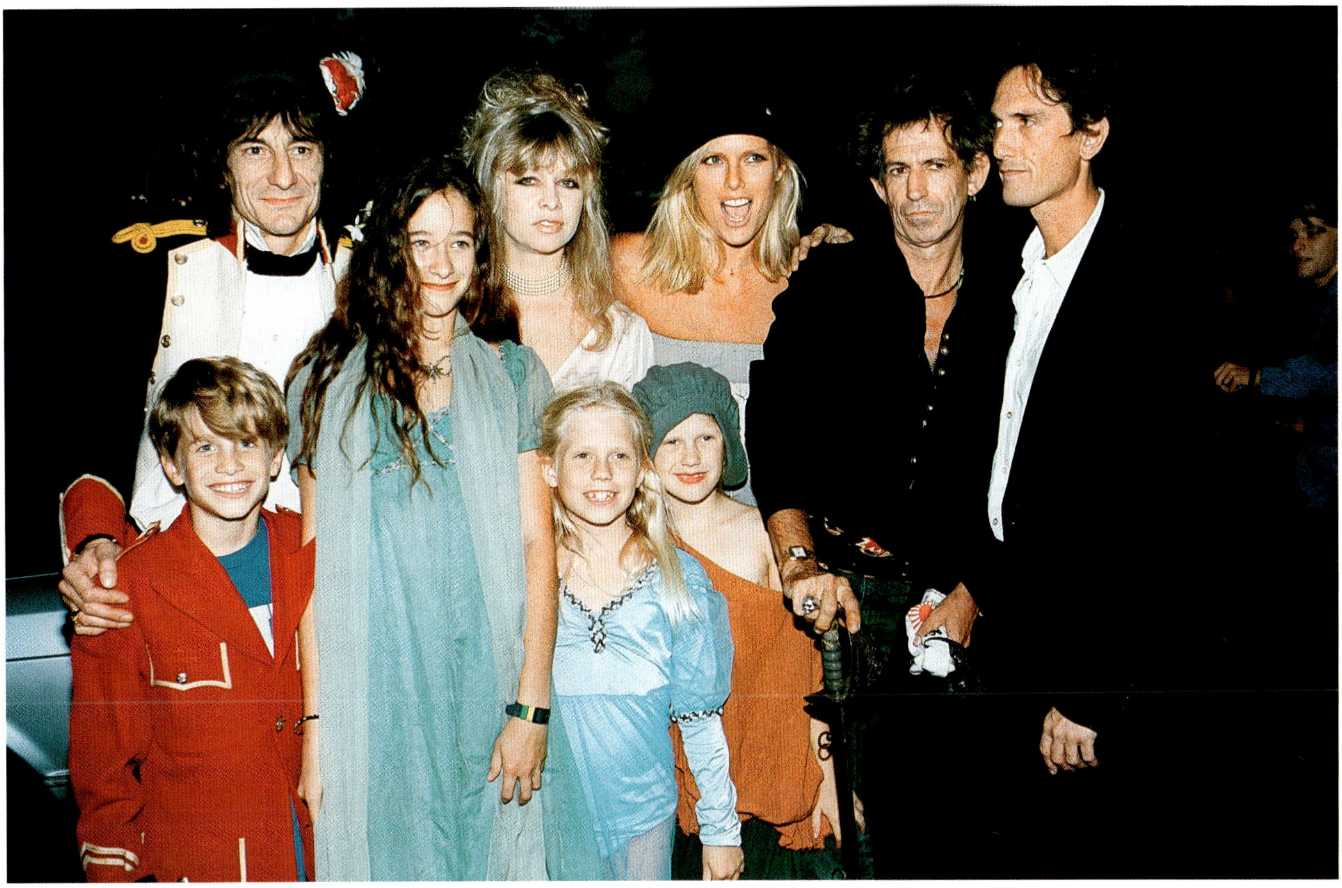

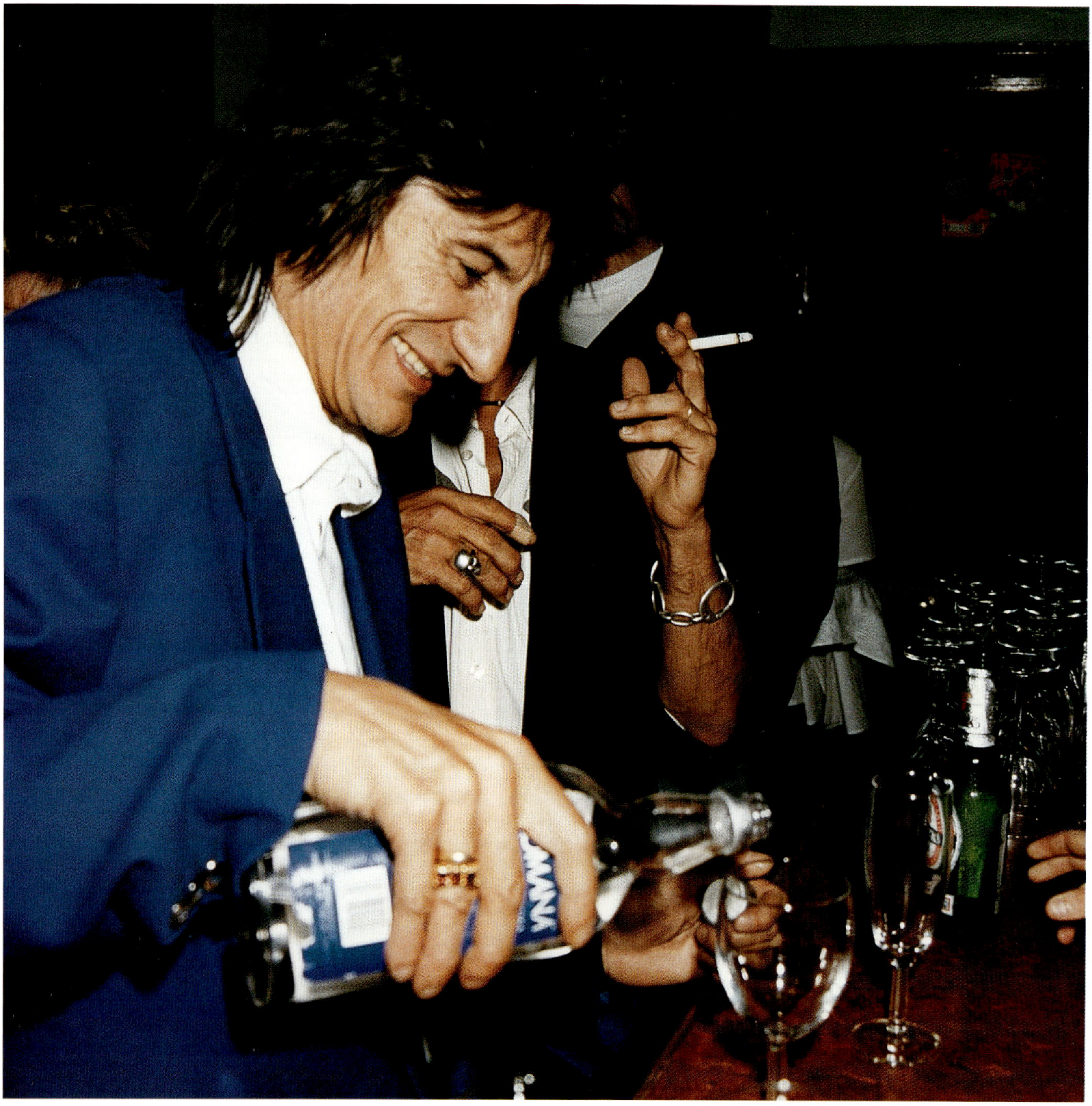

Having a laugh

Above: Ronnie at a party hosted by comedians Peter Cook and Dudley Moore to celebrate the release of a new video. Various Monty Pythons were present, as were golfer Sam Torrance, actor Alan Bates and musicians Dave Stewart and Ian Dury.

Opposite above left: Mick Jagger leaving Quaglino's restaurant in London. He had recently returned from a trip to New York to launch publicity for the Stones' forthcoming worldwide tour.

Opposite above right: Ronnie Wood celebrates his birthday on 1 June 1994 at the 606 Club with Guns and Roses' guitarist Slash.

Opposite below: The party continues with wife Jo and Eric Clapton.

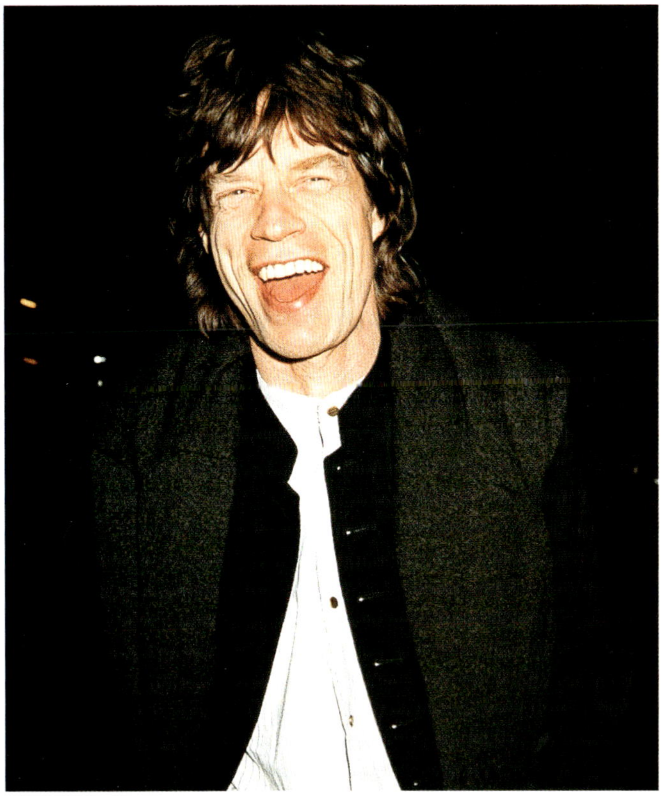

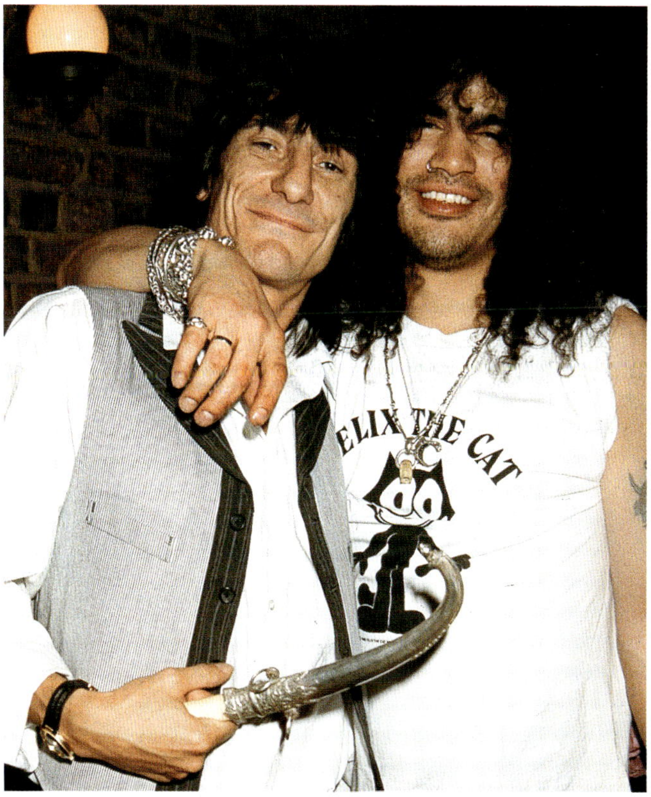
ELIX THE CAT

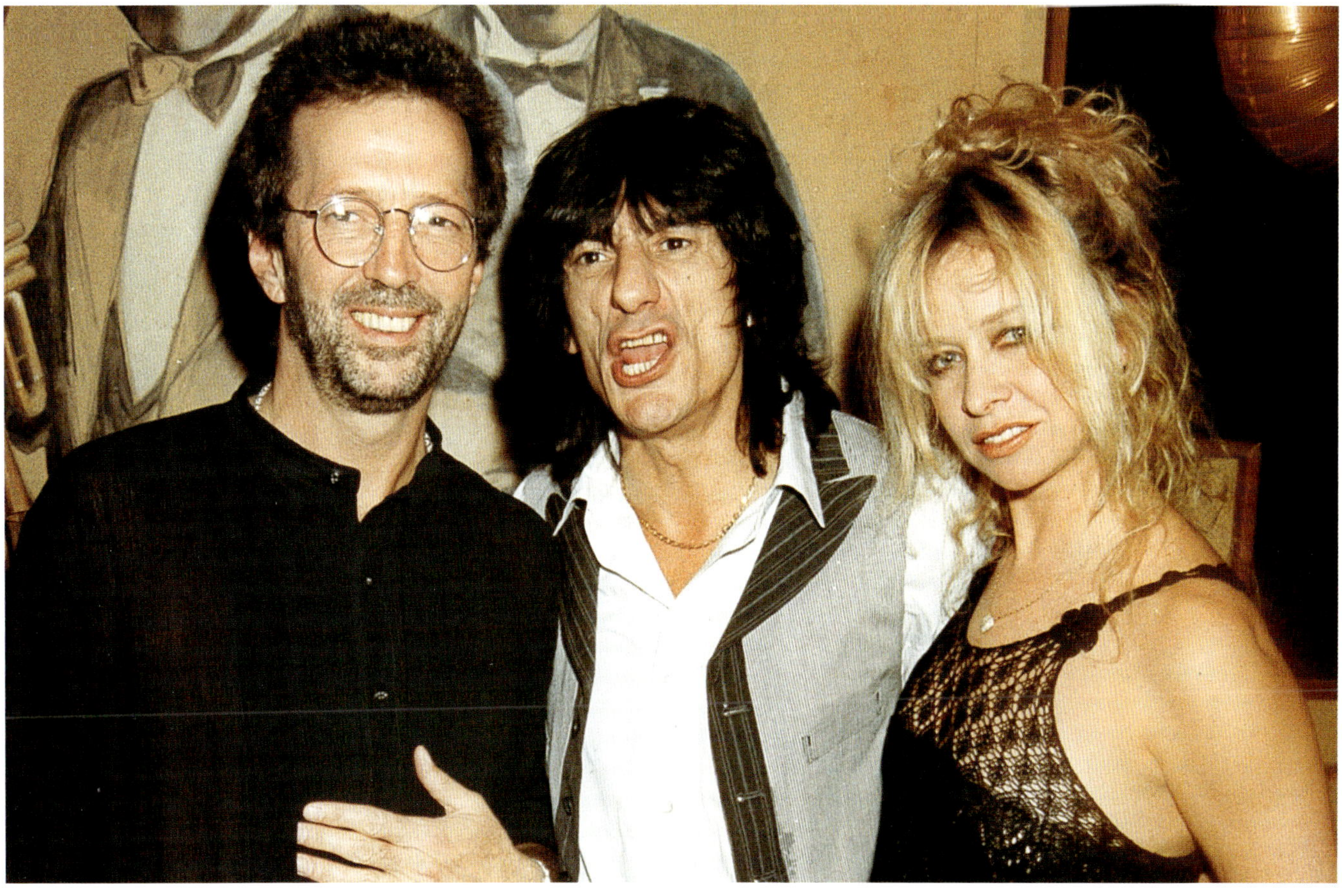

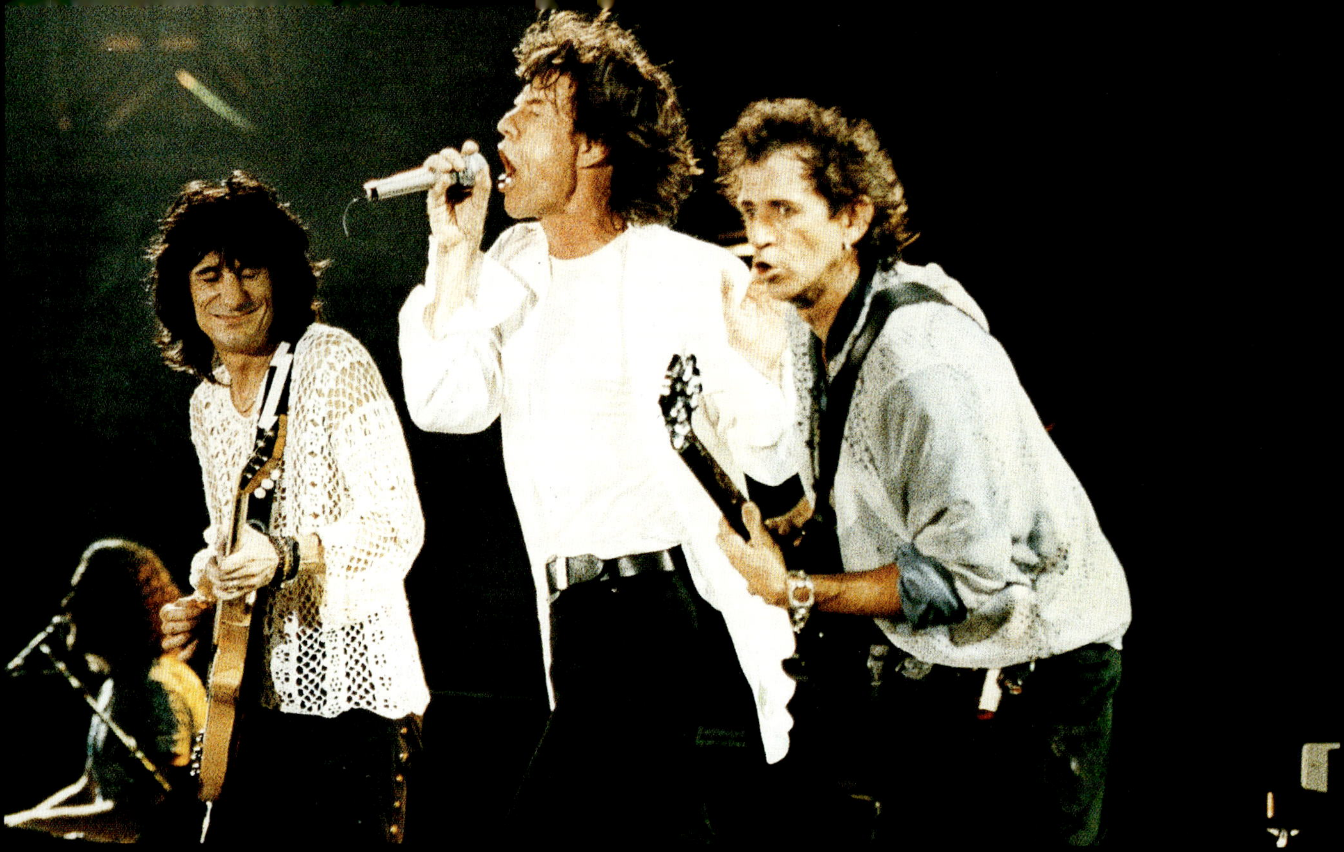

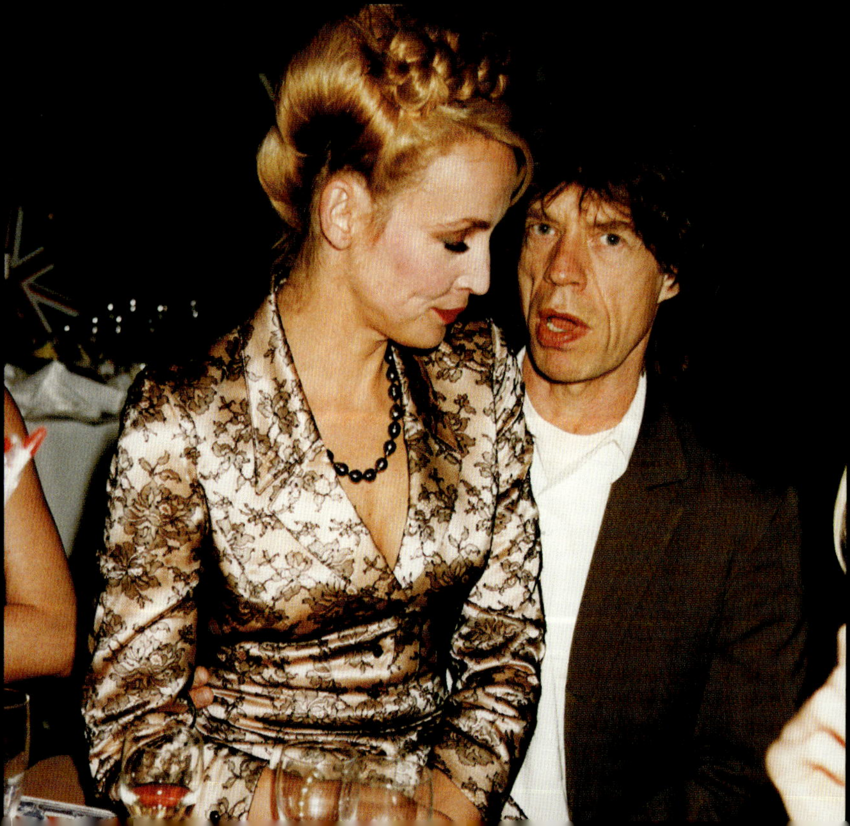

Voodoo Lounge

Above: By 8 August it was back to work: the opening night of the Stones' Voodoo Lounge tour in Washington, DC.

Opposite: Mick and Ronnie on stage in Washington, DC. The Voodoo Lounge tour included dates in North and South America, Europe, South Africa and Australasia, with Darryl Jones replacing Bill Wyman. *Stripped*, a live album taken from the tour, sold 3.5 million copies and *Voodoo Lounge* was even more successful, chalking up sales of around 5.5 million.

Left: Jerry Hall and Mick Jagger attend a hospital fundraiser in May 1995. The long relationship between Mick and Jerry endured many ups and downs.

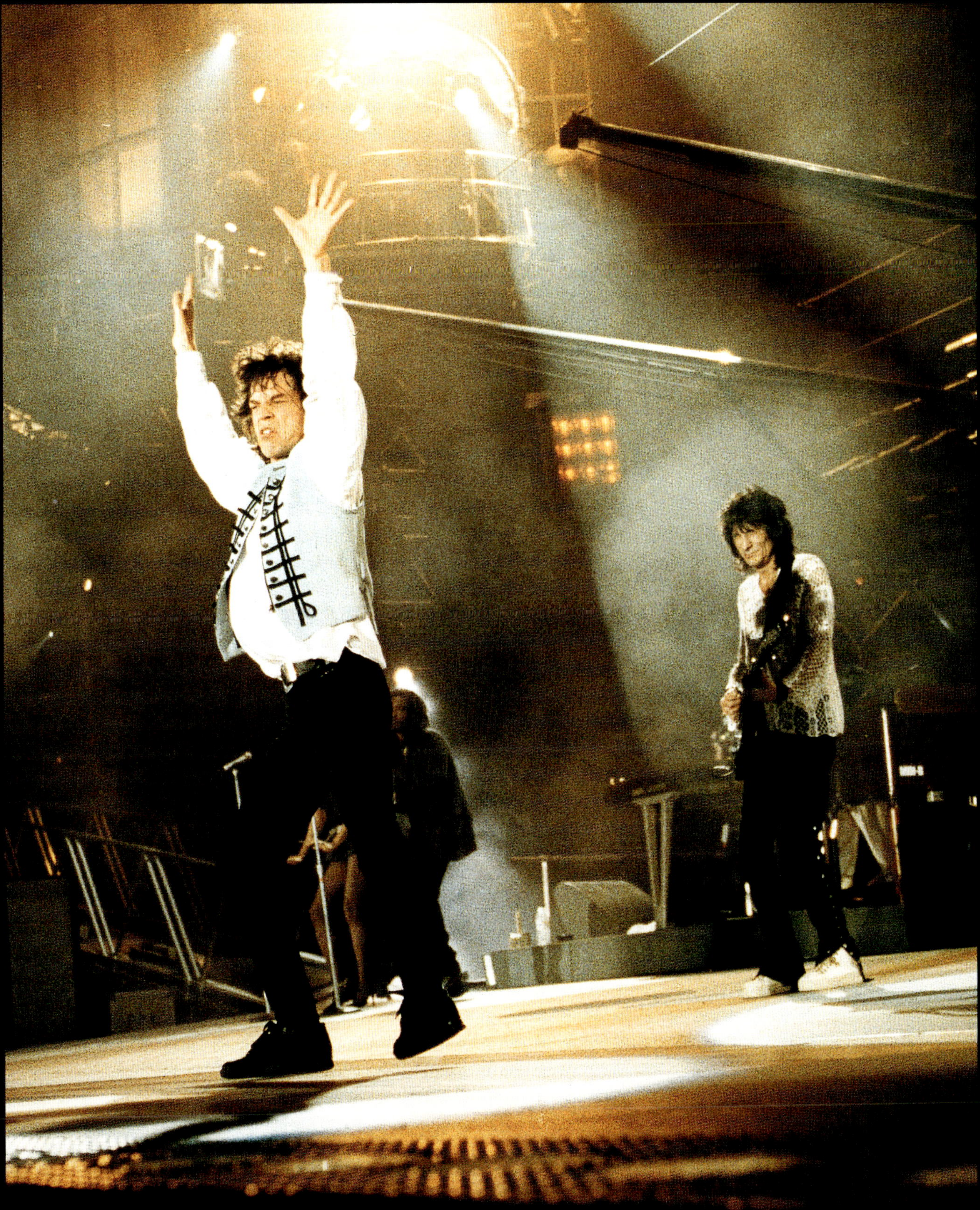

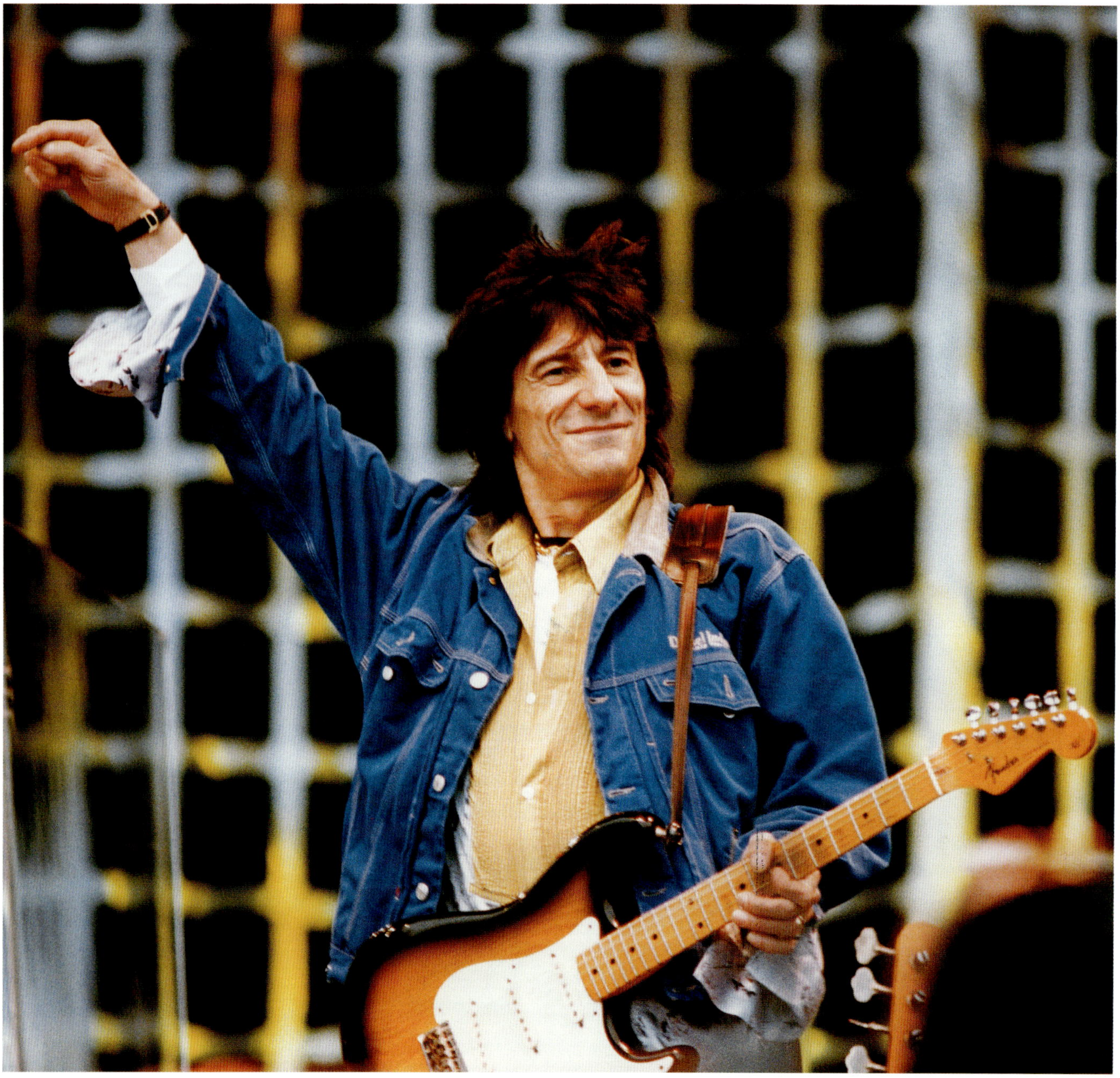

Prince's Trust concert

Above: Ronnie raises a triumphant arm at the Hyde Park concert in June 1996 to raise money for the Prince's Trust. Prince Charles attended and the concert was broadcast to an estimated 120 million people as the Stones and others, including The Who and Bob Dylan, jammed in the open air.

Opposite above left: Ronnie and Jo Wood at home.

Opposite above right: Mick and Jerry at a function in February 1997. Just before Christmas Jerry gave birth to their fourth child, Gabriel Luke Beauregard Jagger, in New York.

Opposite below: Jerry looks radiantly happy at a theatre awards ceremony in London. Her marriage to Mick was annulled in 1999, but since then they have remained good friends, he moving back into the former 'marital' home for a time after the court case was resolved. Mick attended the West End first night of *The Graduate* in which Jerry took the role of Mrs Robinson.

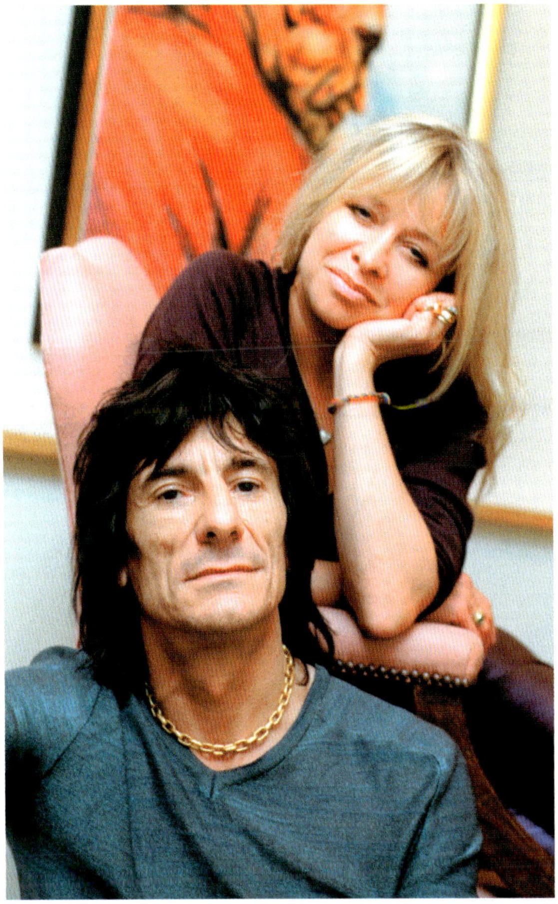

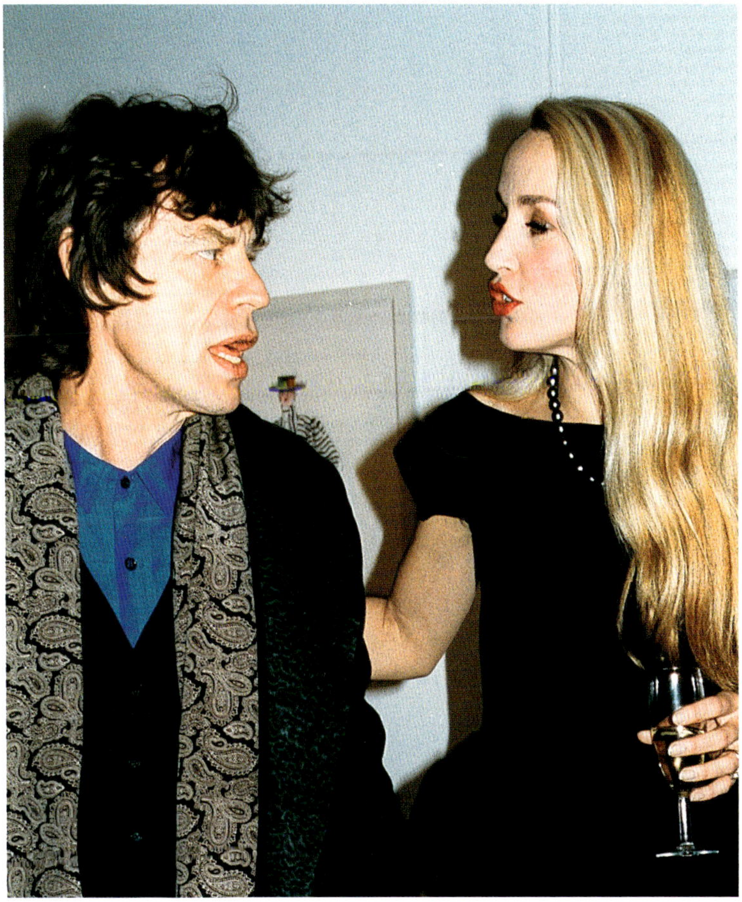

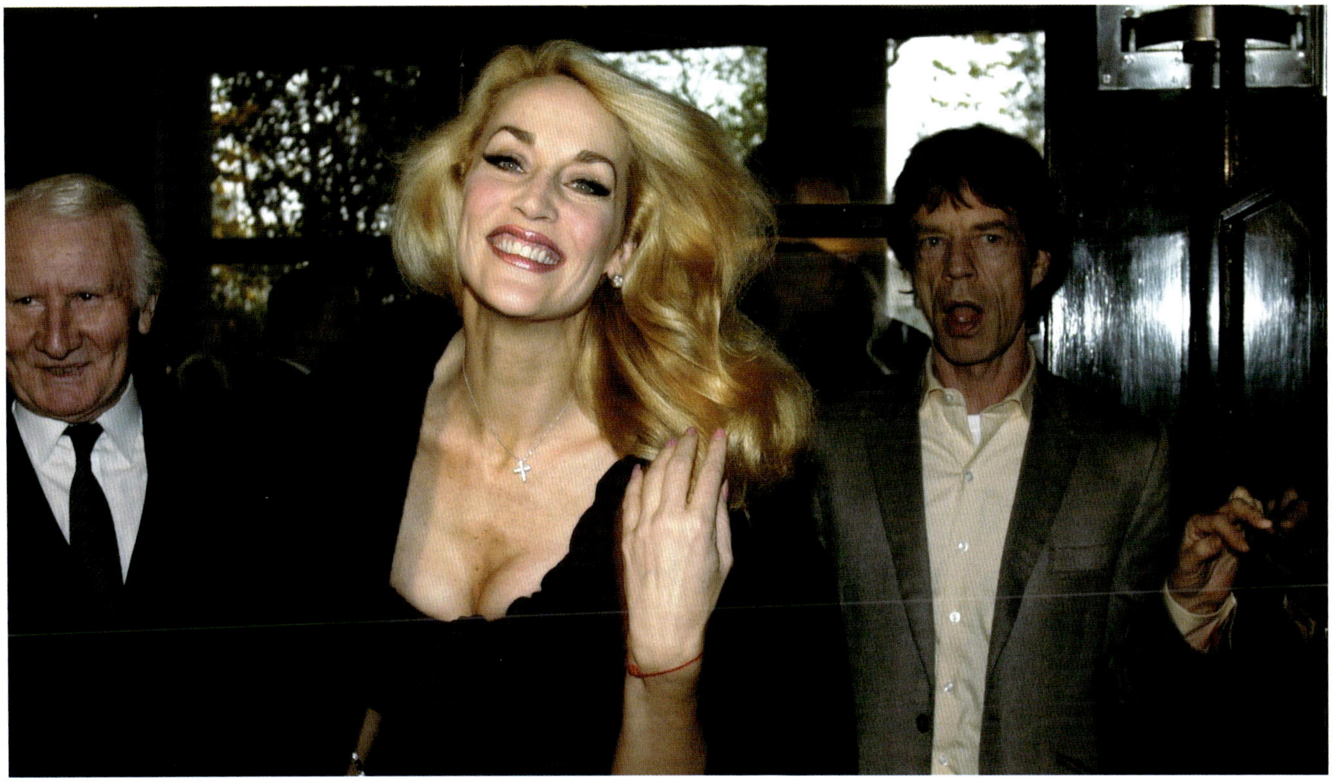

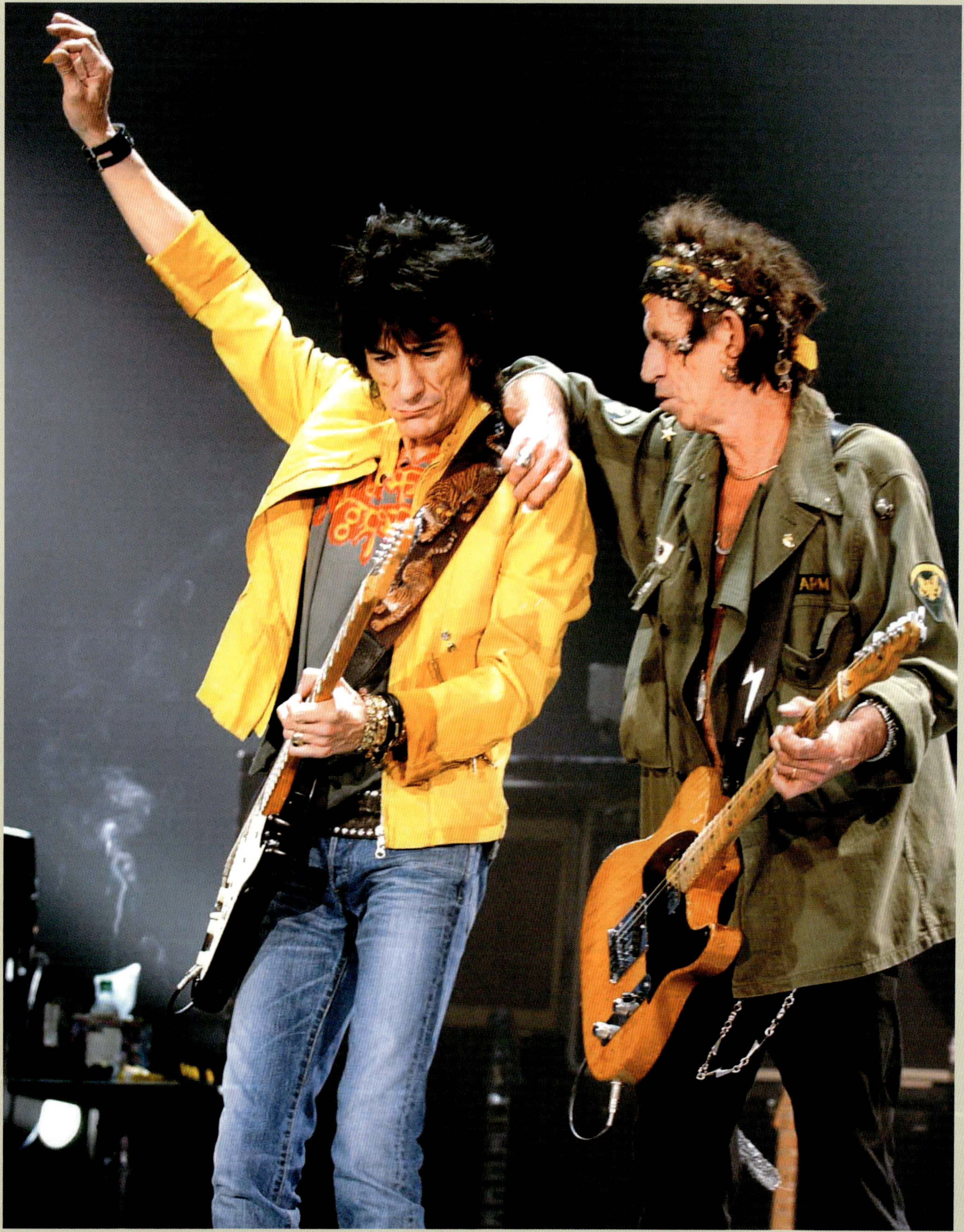

CHAPTER FIVE

Don't Stop

It seems that The Rolling Stones are much more than the sum of their various parts. This is not to dismiss individual talents and separate enterprises. Far from it. Such solo expressions of great talent have served to strengthen the Stones as a band whenever they gather on stage or in the studio. So however marvellous private passions indulged may be, it is when the band collide and convene that the brilliance and magic return.

Touring may well bring with it an element of rather boring repetition. But truthfully life on the road can't have been quite as tough as waiting in the rain morning after morning for a bus or enduring mindlessly repetitious office tasks. One can only conclude that the Stones still enjoy the circus after all these decades – and feuds. One can also hope that Mick Taylor, who managed to escape, is happier now.

Despite their 1999 divorce, Mick Jagger and Jerry Hall seem warmly amicable today, even comfortable together, and determined that their four children should not be victims in the parting. Mick supportively attended the West End first night of *The Graduate* in 2000, in which Jerry was briefly required to strip naked on stage in the role of the mature temptress Mrs Robinson. In December 2003 Mick was knighted for services to music, which led to mixed reactions; some die-hard fans thought a true anti-Establishment rebel would have refused the honour. The knighthood also caused friction between Mick and Keith, who was quoted as saying that he did not want to take the stage with someone wearing a coronet and sporting the old ermine, because it was not what the Stones was about.

In June 2004 Charlie Watts was diagnosed with throat cancer and underwent a course of radiotherapy treatment. Fortunately the cancer went into remission and he was able to work on the first Stones album for eight years, *A Bigger Bang*, which was released in September 2005. He also plays jazz regularly with his own group, The Charlie Watts Tentet, as well as with other, mostly jazz-related combos. He has appeared several times at the famous Ronnie Scott's jazz club in London. He and wife Shirley also own a thriving stud farm in Devon.

Unfortunately the 23-year marriage of Jo and Ronnie Wood hit the rocks in July 2008, when Ronnie became involved with a young Russian model whom he had met at a club. Jo was granted a divorce in November 2009, so even though Ronnie and his new girlfriend split up the following month, his marriage was beyond repair. Like the other Stones, Ronnie also has outside interests. In October 2009 he performed at a Faces reunion concert on behalf of charity, at which Bill Wyman played bass. He has his own regular radio show, on which he plays tracks by artists he has worked with as well as music he particularly likes.

Against all the odds, Keith Richards is still going strong, despite suffering a serious head injury after falling out of a tree while on holiday in Fiji in 2006. In 2007 actor Johnny Depp said he had based many of the mannerisms of Captain Jack Sparrow in *Pirates of the Caribbean* on Keith Richards, following which Keith was invited to appear as Sparrow's father in two of the following films in the series. In 2010 Keith published a book of his memoirs, *Life*, an entertaining romp through his career in which he spoke frankly of his personal life and of his often difficult relationship with Mick Jagger.

Ex-Stone Bill Wyman is still happily married to Suzanne and they have three daughters. He continues to play with his Rhythm Kings, but also has many other non-musical interests. A very keen photographer, he held an exhibition of his work in summer 2010, which featured many photographs of famous musicians taken throughout his career. He is also very interested in metal detecting and developed his own lightweight detector for children after his eldest daughter joined him in hunting for historic artefacts. And his Sticky Fingers restaurant is also still going strong. In April 2011 he recorded with the other Stones for the first time since leaving the band nearly 20 years earlier.

And the music has continued. It's in the blood and certainly the most enduring of any of The Rolling Stones' collective addictions. Now that Ronnie Wood has long been regarded as a fully fledged Stone, not as some cheerfully obliging stand-in, and with Mick and Keith friends again and still craving to rave when other commitments don't intrude – or perhaps even because of them – the Stones have somehow managed to stick together during the early years of the 21st century almost as never before.

In the end it is the Stones on tour that defines their enduring, ever-refreshed energy. Touring is exhausting but it always regenerates and pumps the blood back

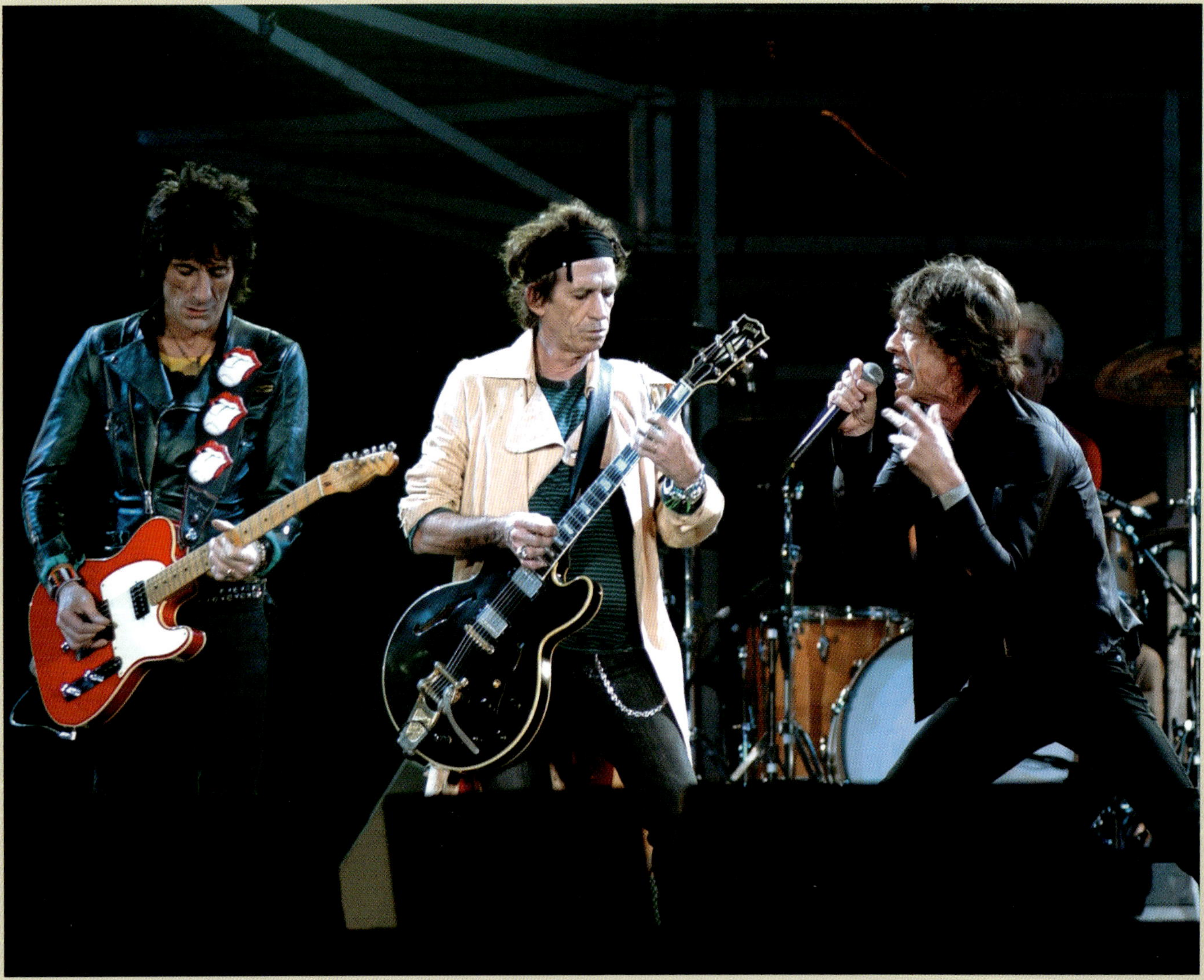

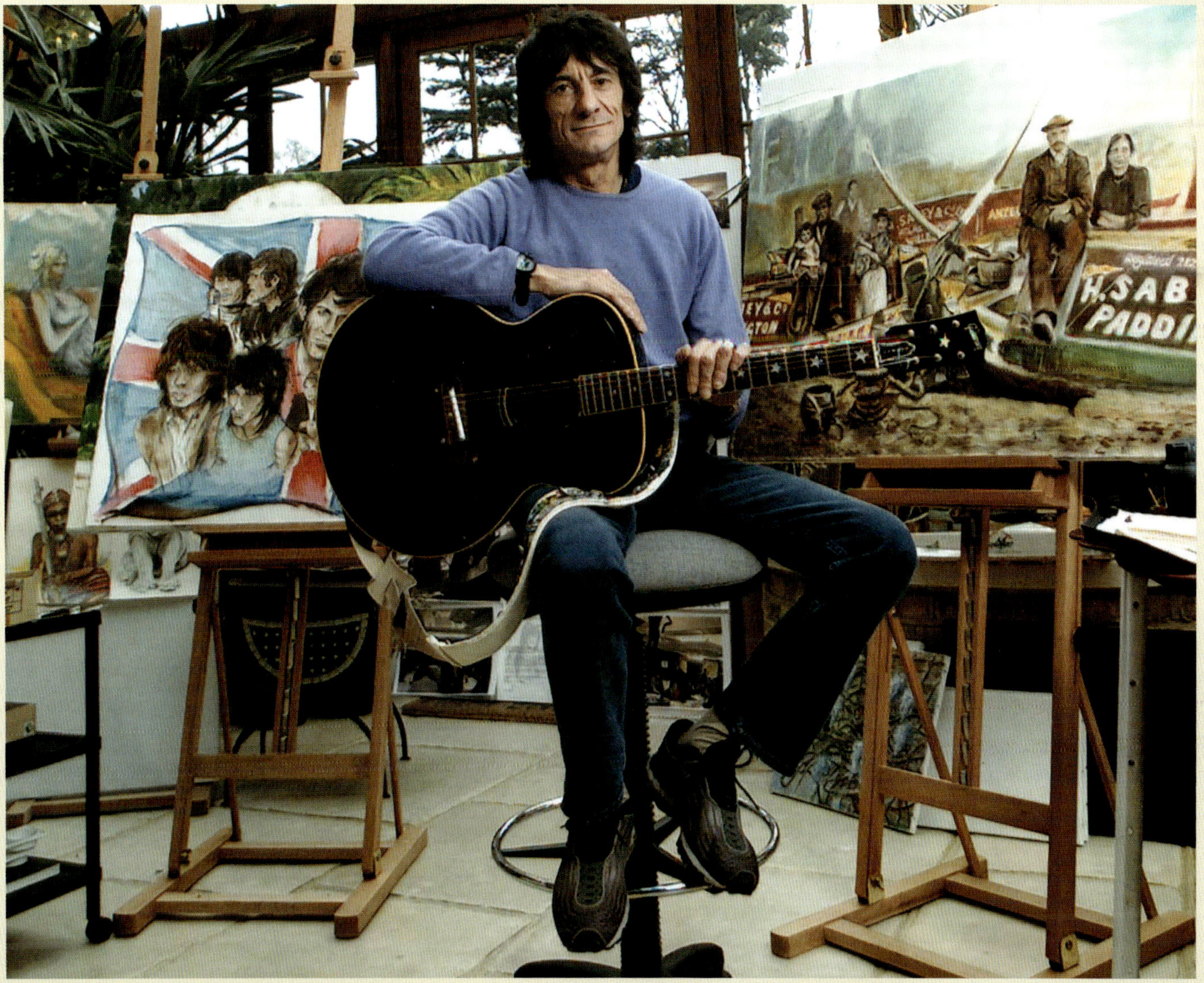

Previous page: Ronnie and Keith perform in Miami in 2005.

Opposite: Ronnie, Keith and Mick performing live onstage, with Charlie on drums just glimpsed in the background, during a concert on the American leg of the A Bigger Bang tour. The tour began in Toronto in August 2005 and covered North and South America, Australasia and Europe, before finishing in London in August 2007.

Above: Ronnie in his studio with some of his work. In the summer of 2000 he checked into the Priory Clinic to seek help in controlling his drinking. Ronnie still enjoys painting, even taking his art materials on tour.

into the unstoppable machine that The Rolling Stones has become. It is in their collective breath, guts and blood.

It may be that band members privately yearn for the intimacy of small clubs and a short set of pure blues, but there isn't much public sentimentality about the old days. The band still seem to relish the enormity of the productions, the stadiums, the ramps, spectacular lights and special effects that keep an entourage upwards of 100 people busy between shows, pre-show and back-stage. And the little luxuries of modern touring help to give the fans value for money over performances that can last hours and span 30 songs. As Charlie Watts has remarked, the days of staying in shabby bed-and-breakfast places were not much fun. Speaking of the band's ability to keep going, he says they couldn't have done it without the perks.

After an incredible 50 years of triumphs and tribulations the band rolls on and few would disagree with the claim that 'The Rolling Stones, now and forever, are the greatest rock and roll band in the world'.

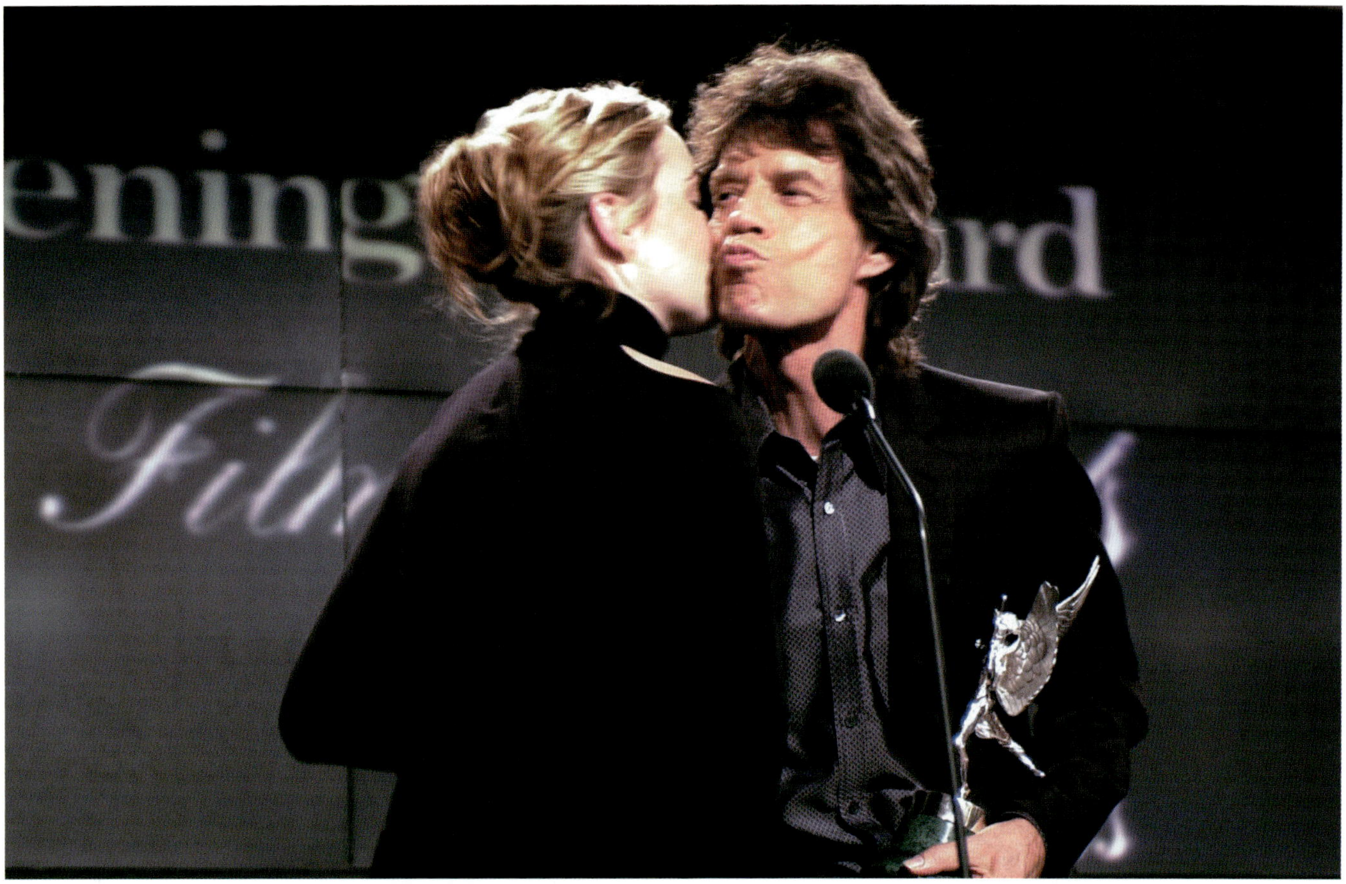

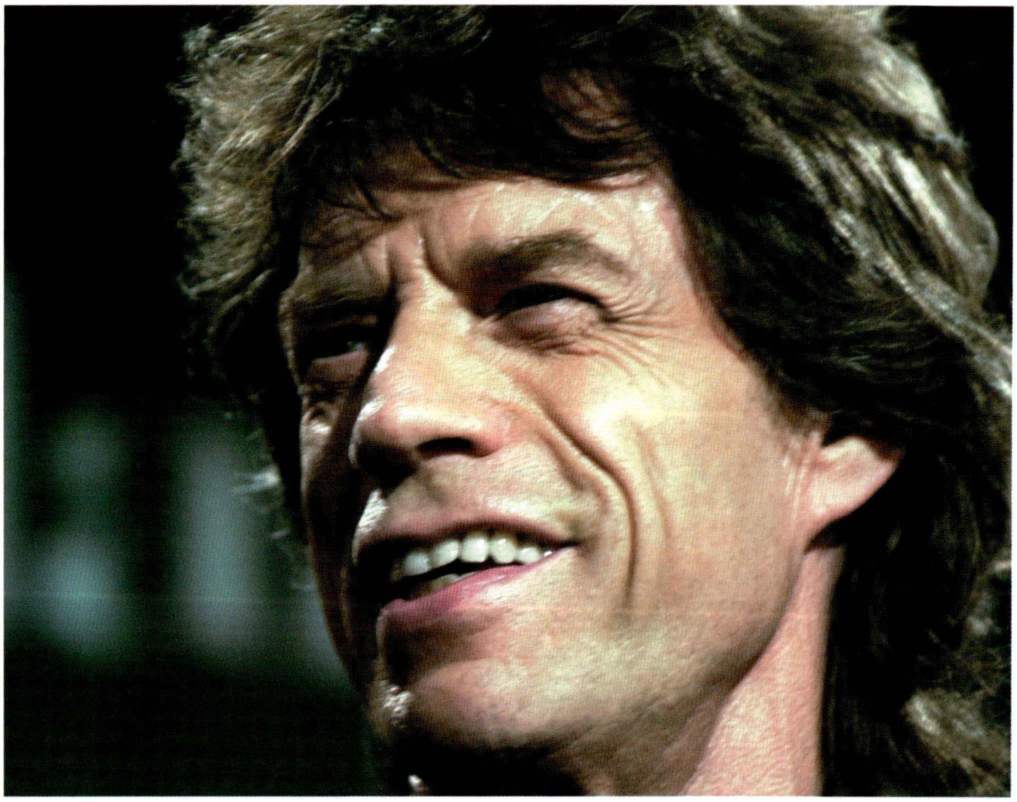

Above: Mick presents an award to Kate Winslet. Throughout his career he has displayed an interest in film, although he has not acted for a number of years. He now has a production company, Jagged Films, which was involved in the making of *Enigma*, in which Kate Winslet had a starring role.

Right: The Rolling Stones have travelled a long way since 1962, but no one then would have expected that Mick Jagger would be knighted for services to music in the Queen's Golden Jubilee Birthday Honours in 2002.

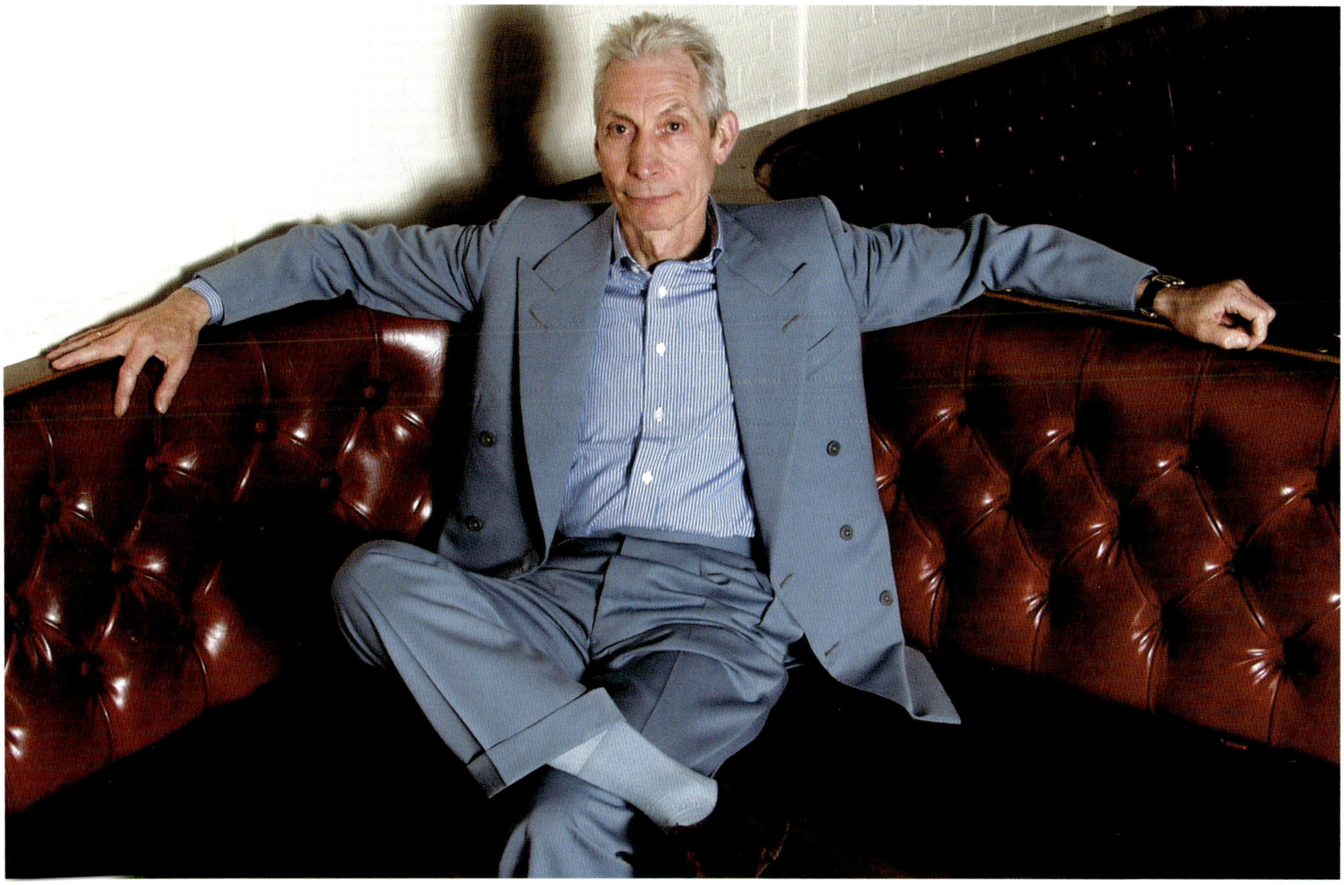

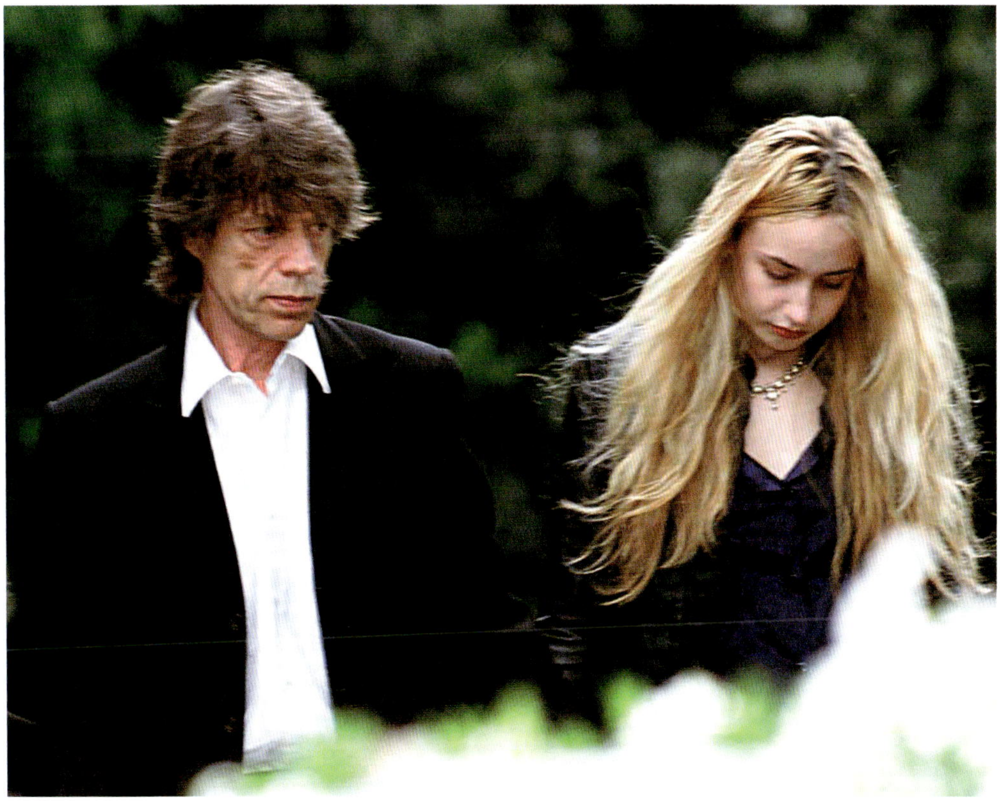

Long Ago And Far Away

Above: 2 June 2002: Charlie poses on his 60th birthday at Ronnie Scott's, where he will play later in the day. Although still committed to The Rolling Stones, Charlie continues to develop his private interest in jazz music. In 1996 the Charlie Watts Quintet issued an album of jazz and swing classics entitled *Long Ago And Far Away*.

Left: 27 May 2002: A sombre Mick Jagger draws on the support of his family and the band at the funeral of his mother Eva, who died aged 87. Sixteen-year-old Elizabeth stands by her father's side.

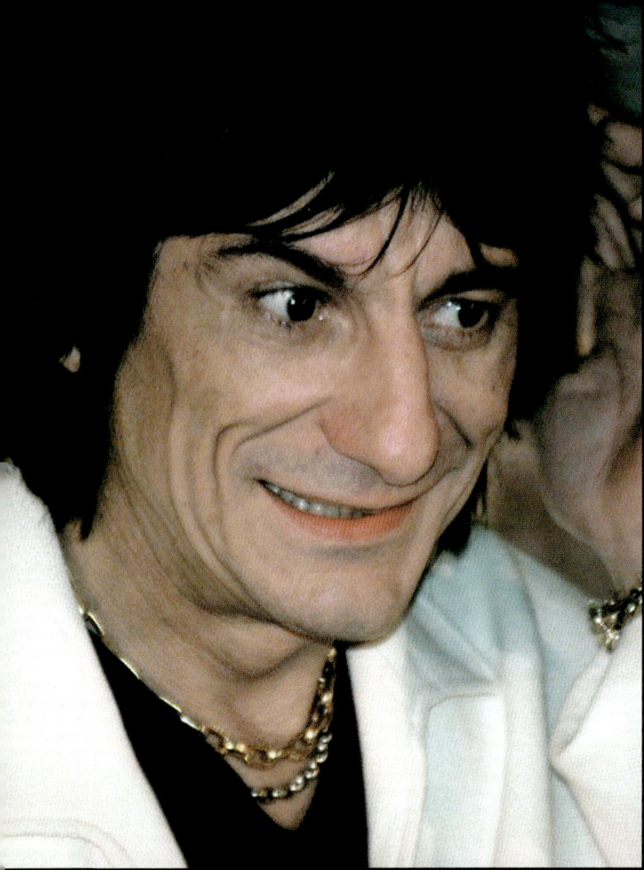

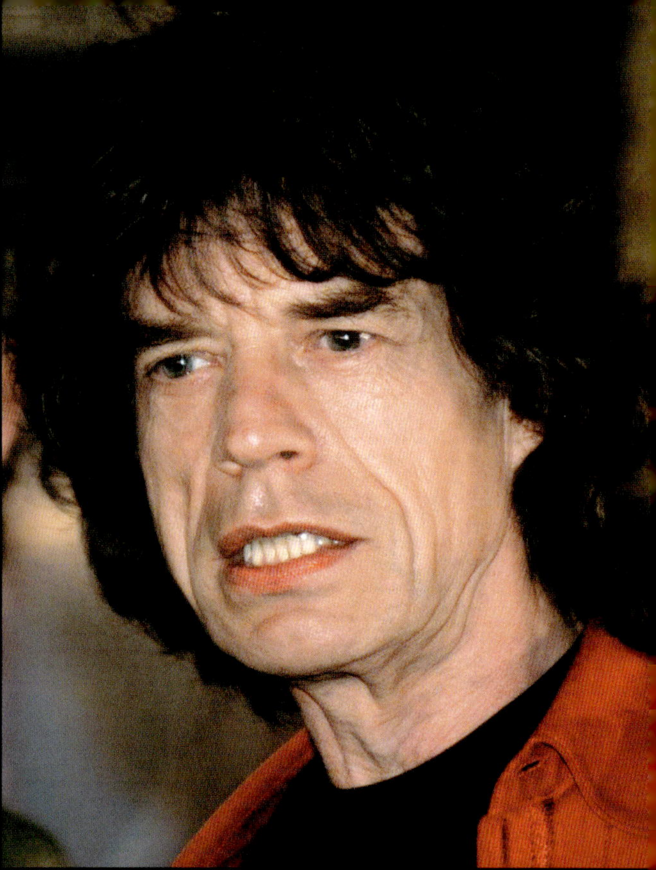

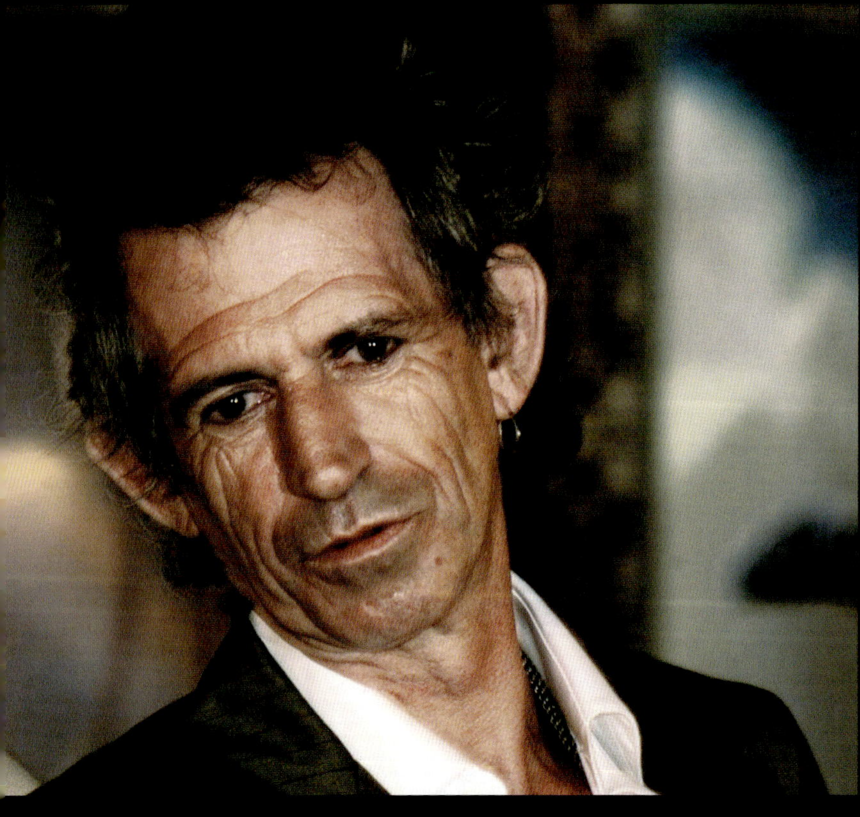

Stones go on …

And so after more than 40 years the band goes on. Each member is allowed to pursue personal interests but they will always be best known as part of the greatest rock 'n' roll band in the world. Despite their advancing years, they are still capable of drawing record breaking audiences. The 1997 Bridges To Babylon world tour grossed $87 million in the first three months in America, and the Stones are still finding new audiences, playing in Russia for the first time ever in 1998. The Licks tour began in August 2002 in Toronto and was virtually a sell-out three months before it opened. At the beginning of the millennium the Stones held the record for the three most-attended tours of all time: Steel Wheels, Voodoo Lounge and Bridges To Babylon. The new tour took this remarkable statistic to four

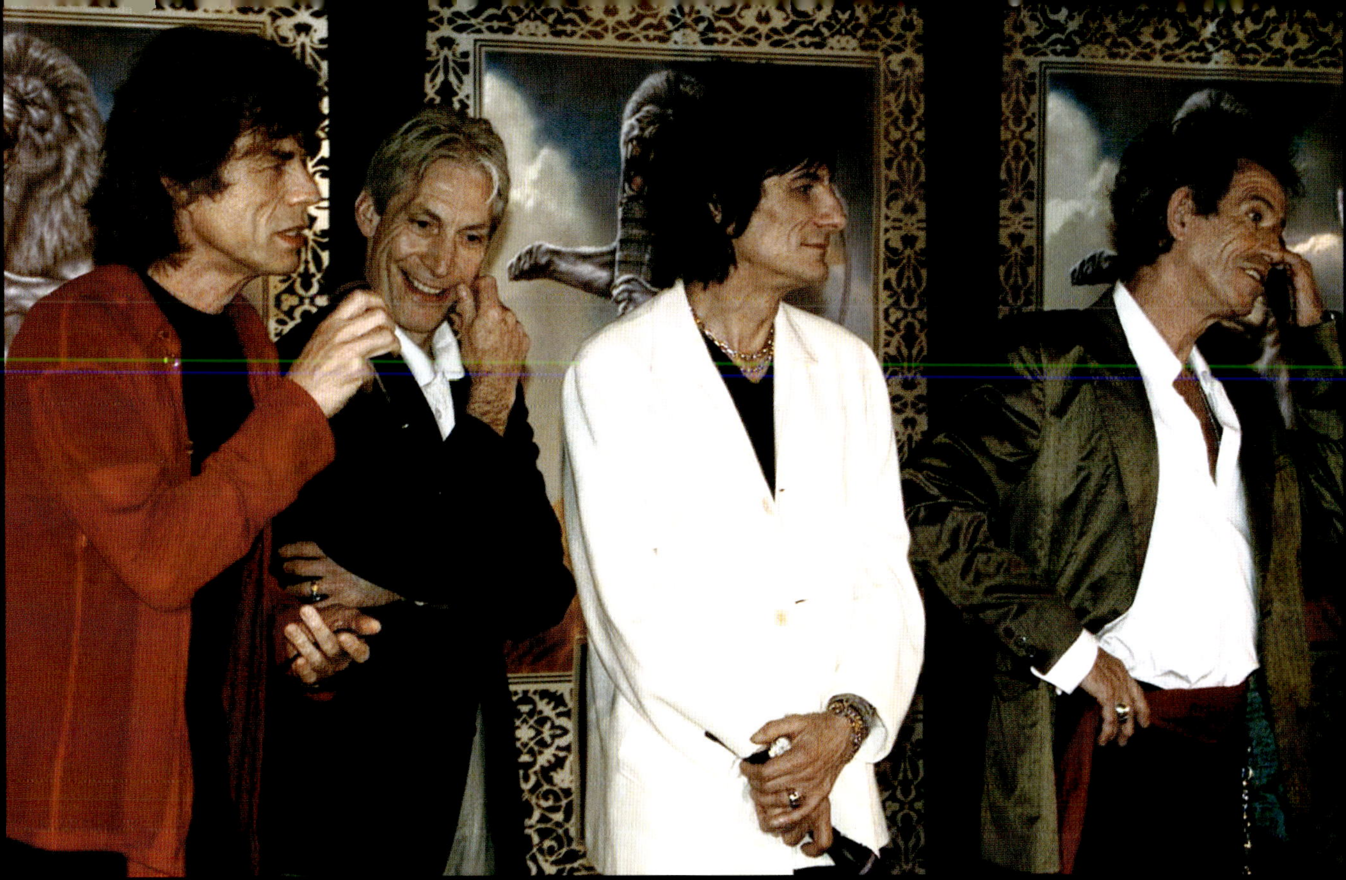

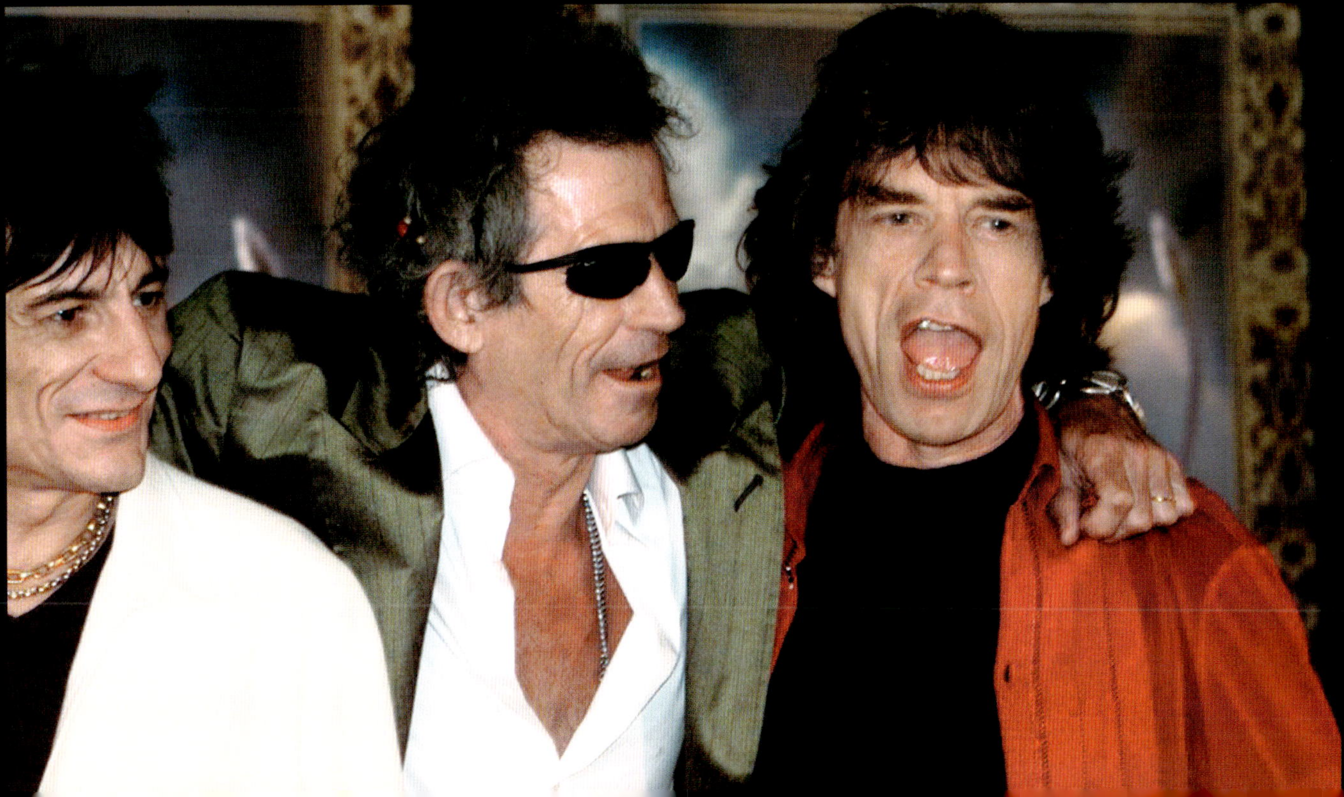

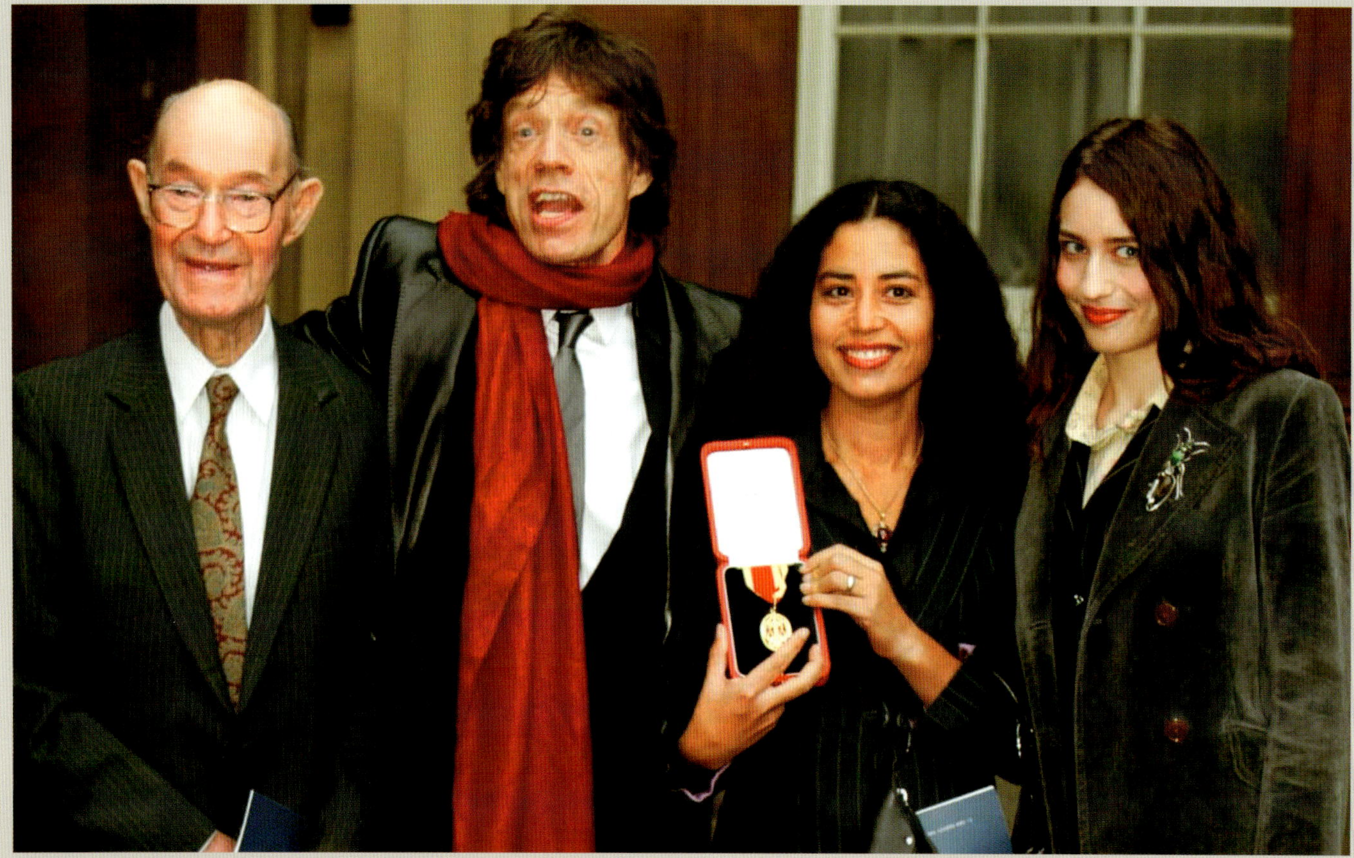

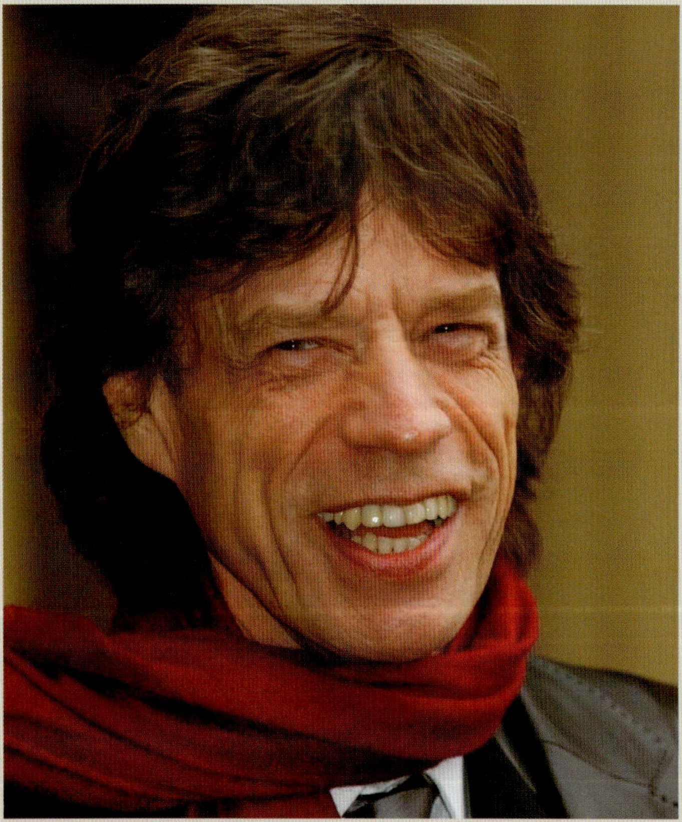

Sir Mick Jagger

Above and left: Mick attends Buckingham Palace in December 2003 to receive his knighthood for services to music from HRH Prince Charles, the Prince of Wales. He was accompanied by his father, Joe, and daughters Karis (*centre right*) and Elizabeth (*far right*). Mick's acceptance of the award caused some controversy, not only in the Establishment but also in the rock 'n' roll world.

Opposite: In June 2004, Charlie was diagnosed with throat cancer after noticing a lump in his neck, even though he had given up smoking 20 years earlier. After an operation he began a five-week course of radiotherapy, which soon put the cancer into remission. He was well enough to play on the new album, *A Bigger Bang*, which had begun recording in September 2004 and was released the following September. The Stones' first new studio album for eight years – the previous one having been *Bridges to Babylon* in 1997 – it was well received and quickly went to No.1 in several countries around the world.

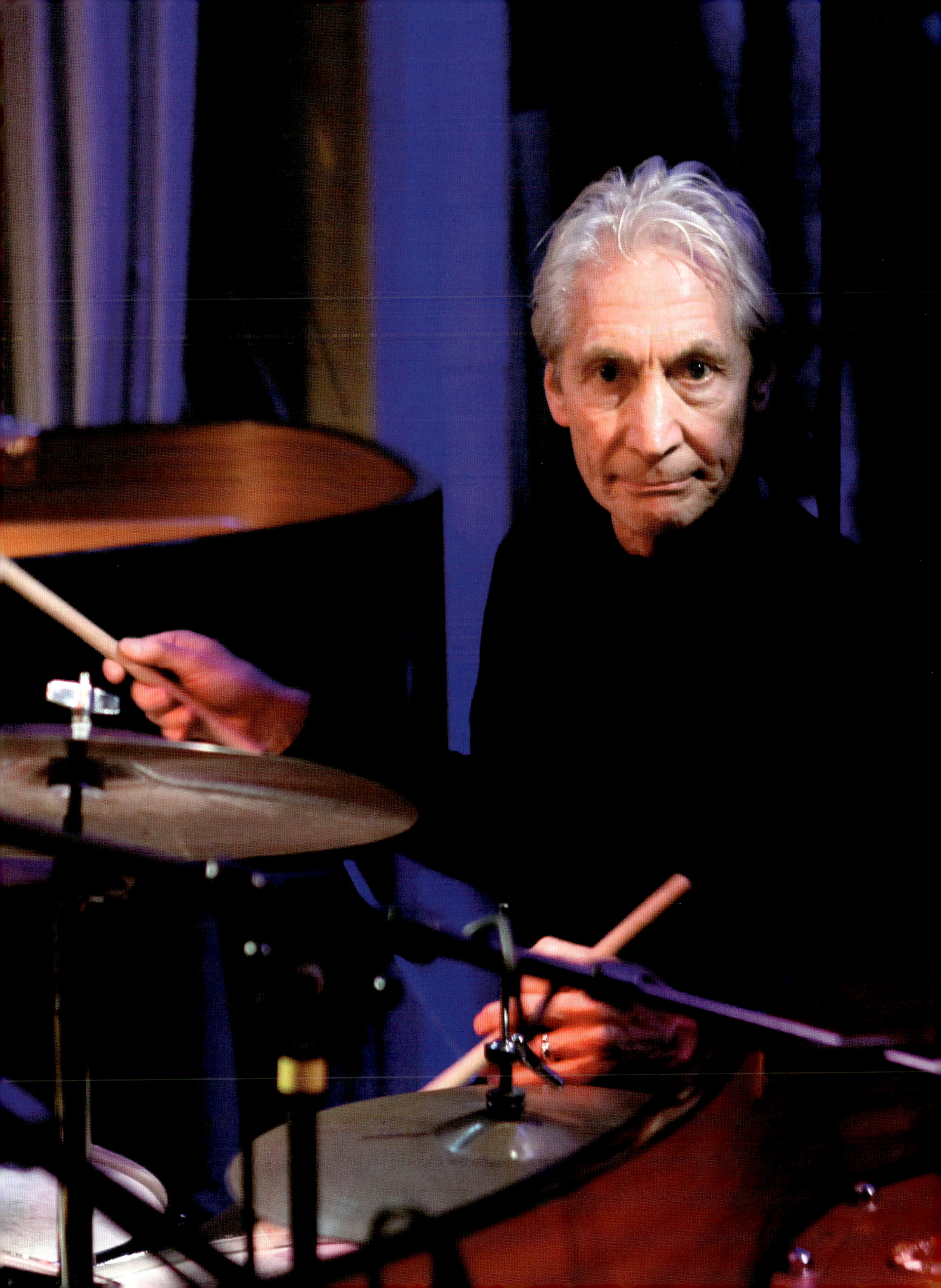

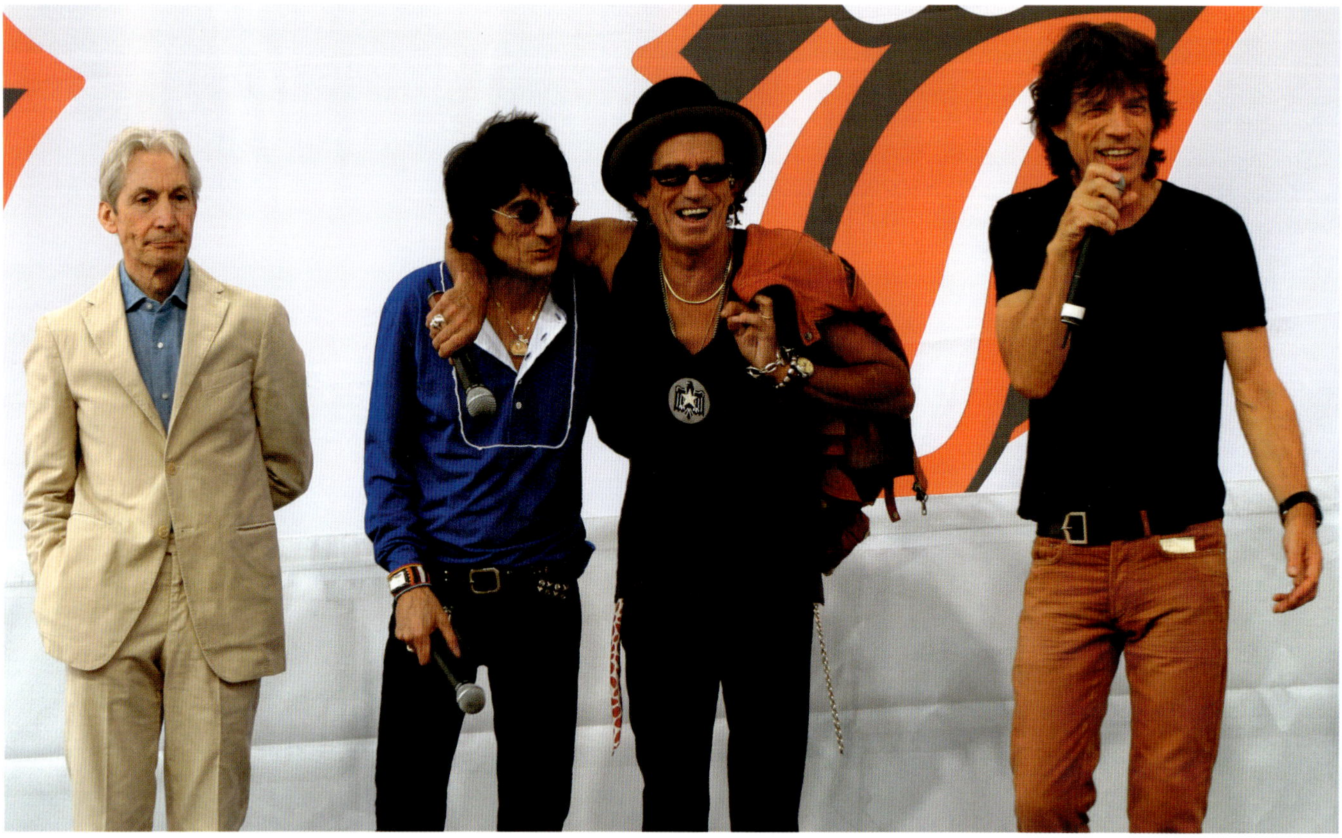

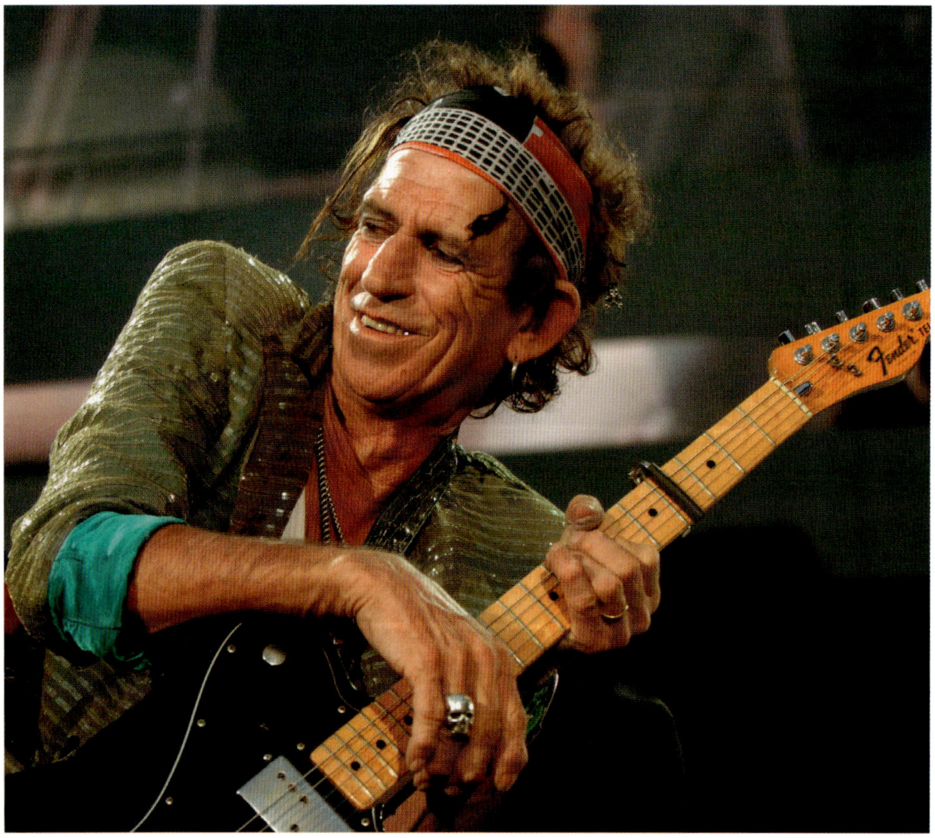

A Bigger Bang tour

Above: Charlie, Ronnie, Keith and Mick host a press conference at the Julliard School in New York to announce the forthcoming A Bigger Bang world tour, 10 May 2005.

Left: Keith Richards takes centre stage in Amsterdam on 31 July 2006.

Opposite: Mick performs at the Commerzbank Arena in Frankfurt during their first concert in Germany, on 13 June 2007. A Bigger Bang is said to have been the second highest grossing tour of all time, earning more than $500 million.

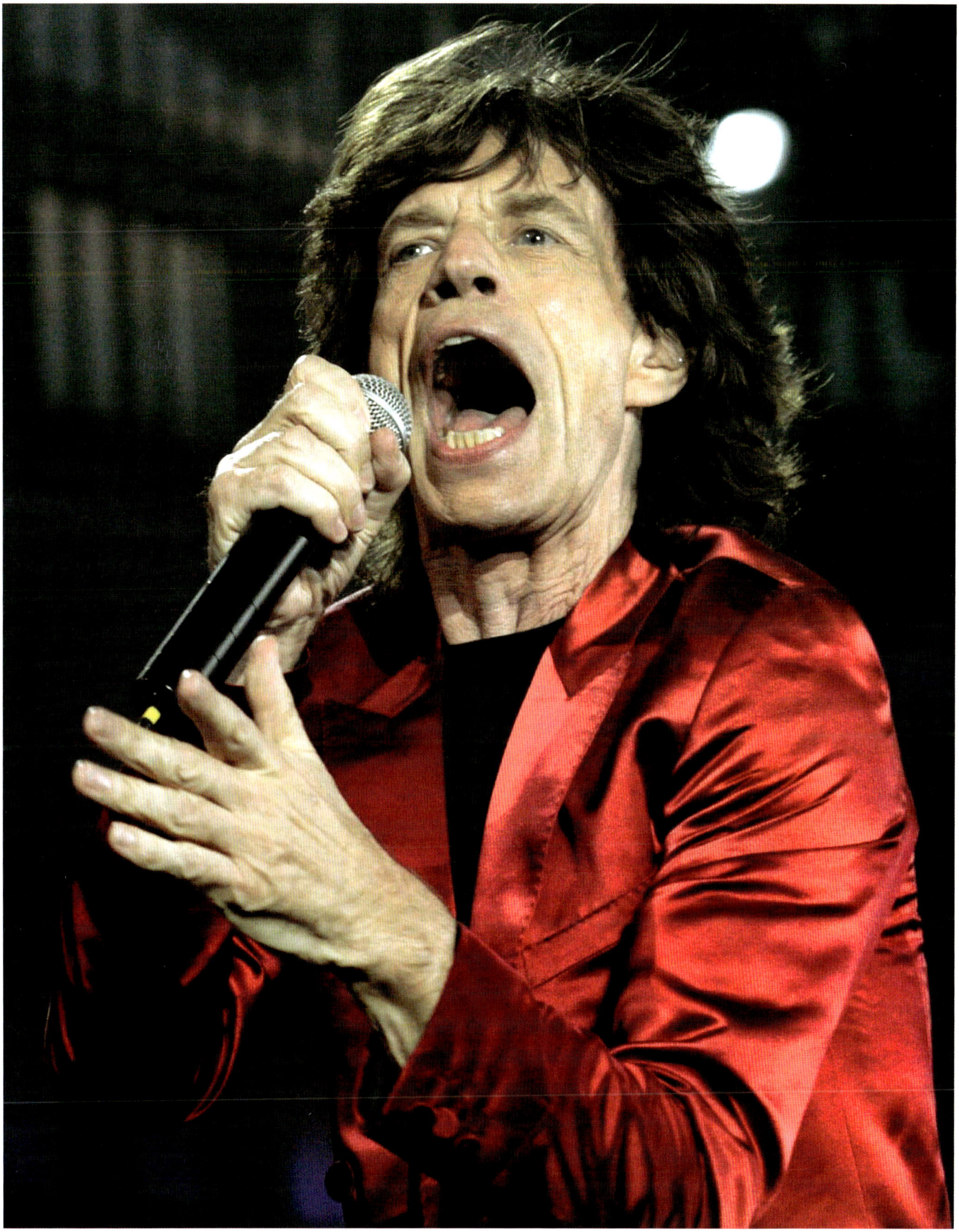

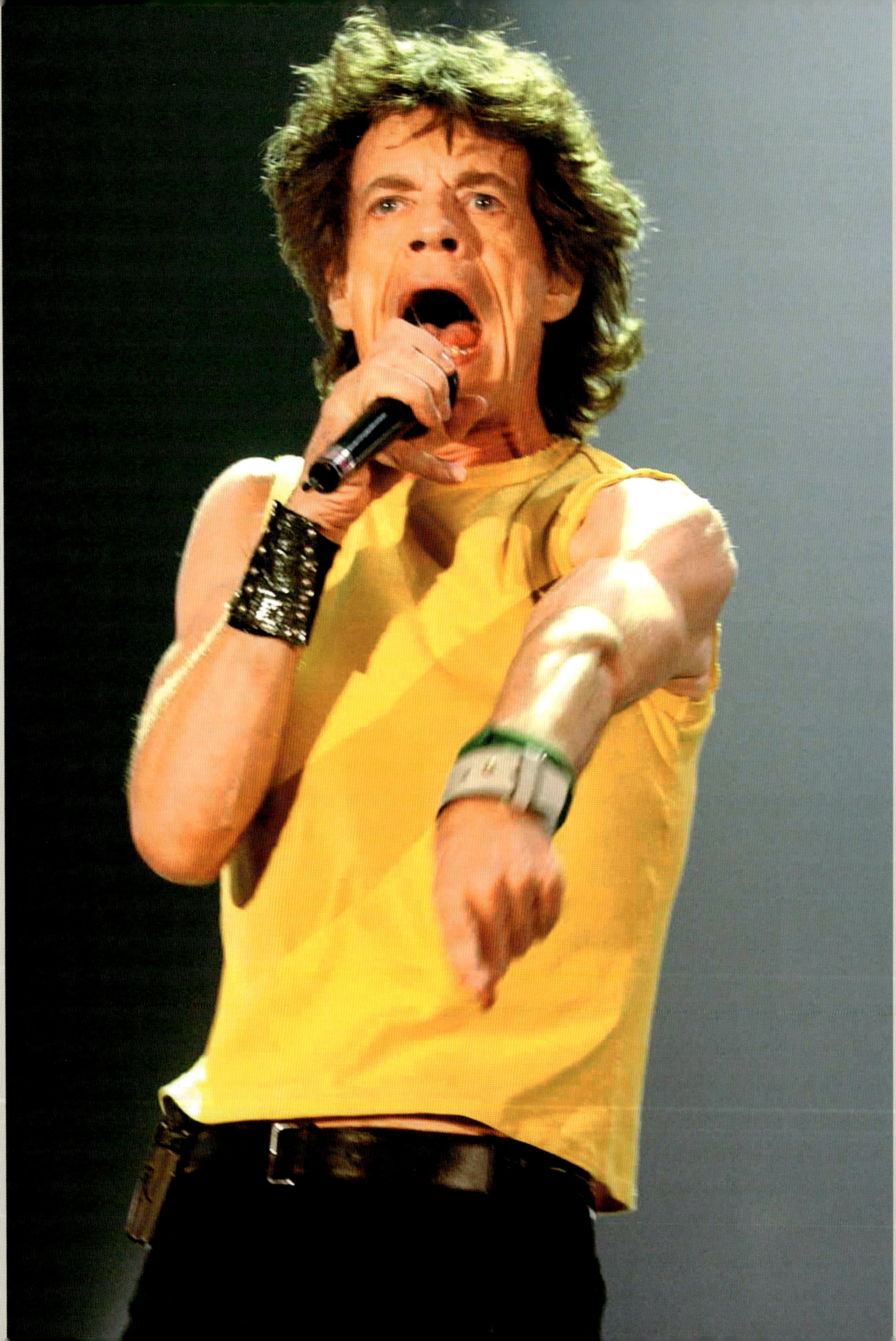

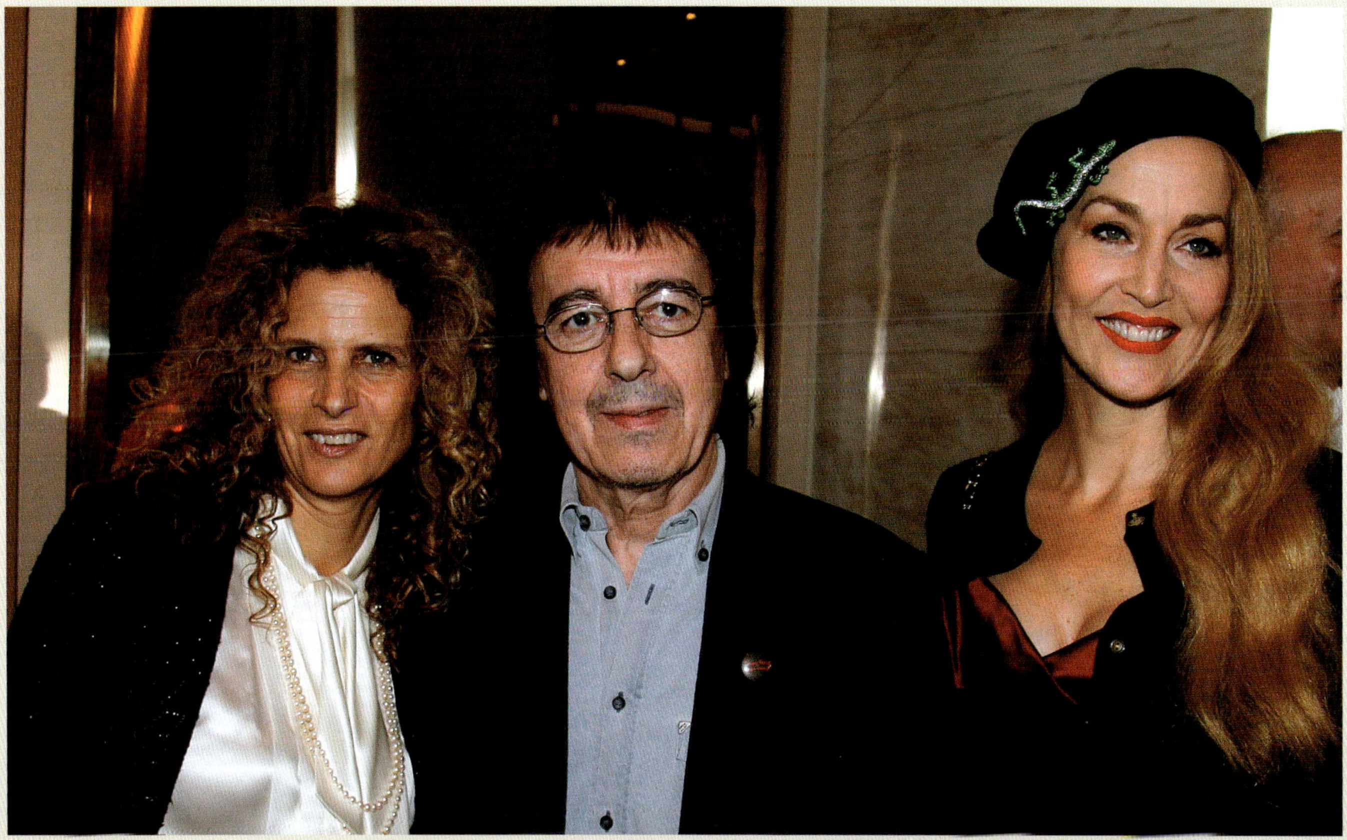

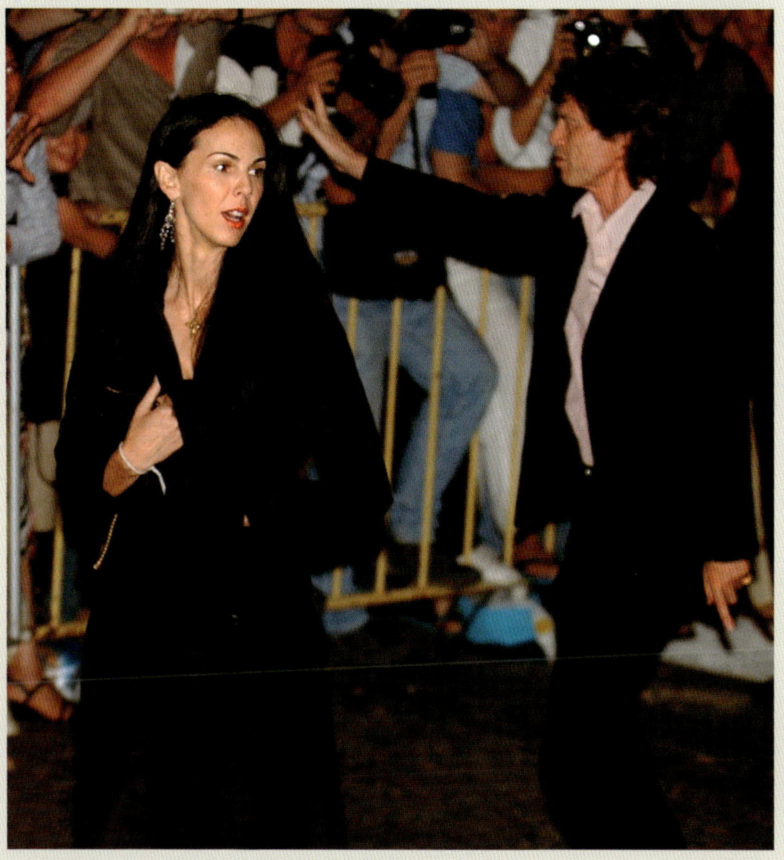

A Bigger Bang

Opposite: Mick in full flow on stage during a concert on the A Bigger Bang tour. After performing a concert in April 2006 in Auckland, the band members took time out for a short holiday. Ronnie and Keith went to Fiji for two weeks with their wives, during which time the two guitarists attempted to climb a coconut tree on the beach. Keith fell to the ground, hitting his head, which led to concussion and a blood clot on his brain. He was swiftly flown back to a private hospital in New Zealand, where a neurosurgeon performed an emergency operation.

Right: Mick with his girlfriend L'Wren Scott, an American fashion model and stylist, who he has been with for several years and describes as his 'main person of interest'.

Above: Jerry Hall, pictured with Suzanne and Bill Wyman in London. Jerry has also moved on to a new relationship, but she and Mick remain friends.

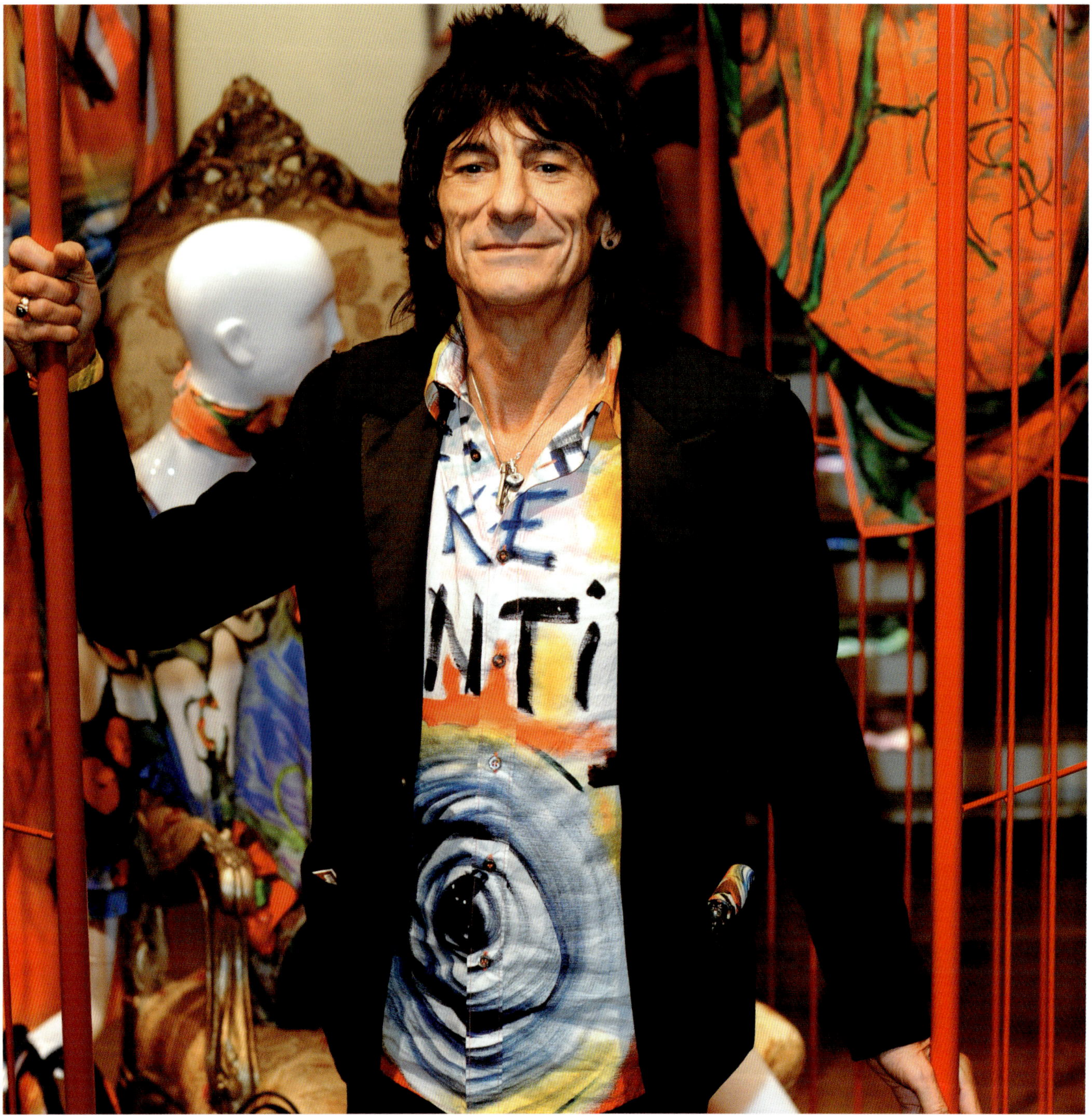

I Feel Like Painting

Above: Ronnie at the launch of his new fashion line, based on three of his paintings, in London in October 2009. He told reporters that one of the paintings, 'I Feel Like Painting', had been inspired by 'the day when I decided to turn my life around' after a six-week period in rehab the previous year for drink problems. The following month Ronnie was presented with an Outstanding Achievement award by Pete Townshend of The Who, at the Classic Rock Roll of Honour ceremony in London, although, in a less celebratory vein, the same month his divorce from Jo, his wife of 23 years, was finalized. However, the awards keep coming: in May 2011 he won the Sony Radio Personality of the Year award for *The Ronnie Wood Show*, which he has presented on Absolute Radio late on Saturday nights since April 2010.

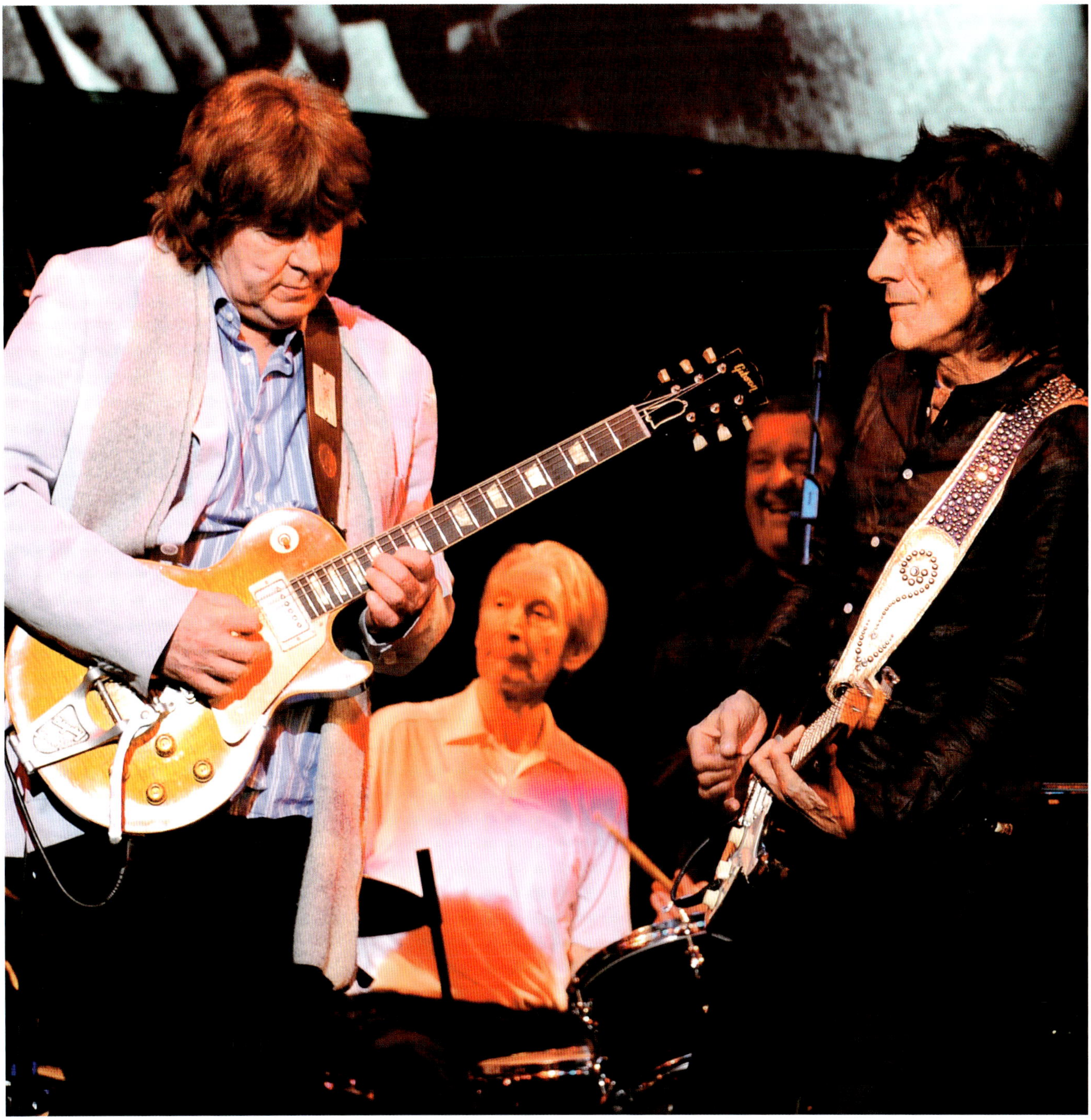

Not Fade Away

Above: Ex-Rolling Stone Mick Taylor performs with Charlie Watts and Ronnie Wood at Boogie for Stu: A Tribute to Ian Stewart, a charity concert in memory of Rolling Stones co-founder Ian Stewart. In support of the British Heart Foundation, the concert was held at the Ambassadors Theatre in March 2011. Ex-Stone Bill Wyman also appeared, the first time he had played with the others for 20 years. The concert led to a tribute album, also called *Boogie for Stu*, the highlight of which was a version of Bob Dylan's song 'Watchin' The River Flow' which featured Mick on vocals and harmonica, Keith on guitar, Charlie on drums, Ronnie on guitar and Bill on bass. In May 2011, during an interview on *USA Today*, Keith announced to the world that The Rolling Stones were planning to play a special 50th anniversary gig in London the following year and that none of the band members currently had any plans to retire ... so it seems that The Rolling Stones have no intention of fading away.

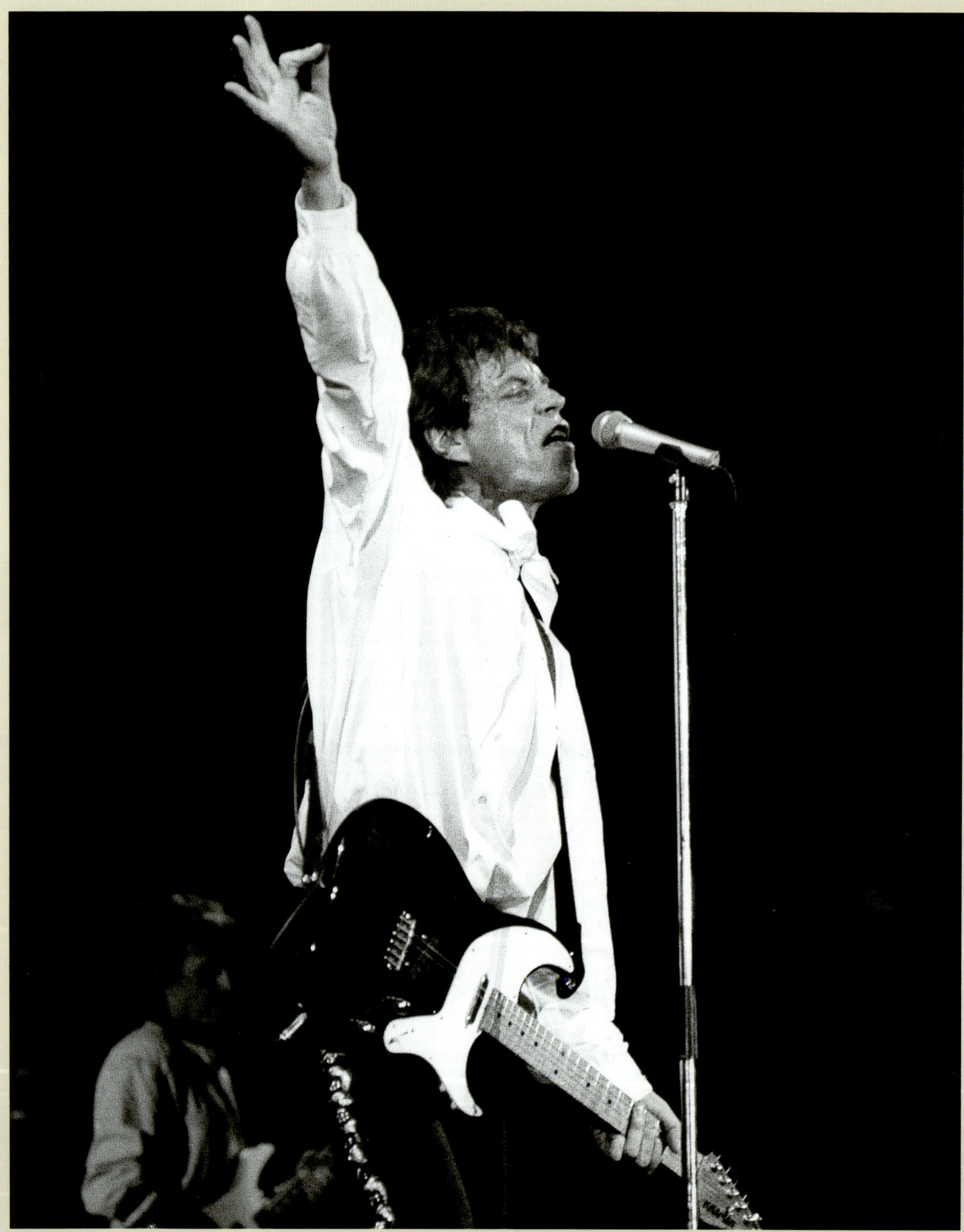

Chronology

1936

24 Oct Bill Wyman (William Perks) is born in Lewisham, south London.

1941

2 Jun Charlie Watts (Charles Robert Watts) is born in Islington, north London.

1942

28 Feb Brian Jones (Lewis Brian Hopkin Jones) is born in Cheltenham, Gloucestershire.

1943

26 Jul Mick Jagger (Michael Philip Jagger) is born in Dartford, Kent.

18 Dec Keith Richards is born in Dartford, Kent.

1947

1 Jun Ronnie Wood (Ronald Wood) is born in Hillingdon, Middlesex.

1948

17 Jan Mick Taylor (Michael Taylor) is born in Welwyn Garden City, Hertfordshire.

1962

Mar Alexis Korner's Blues Incorporated begin regular Saturday night gigs at the Ealing Jazz Club in west London. Mick Jagger and Keith Richards become friends after a chance meeting on a south London train.

Apr Mick and Keith meet Brian at the Ealing Club. Mick starts singing with Blues Incorporated, sometimes at the Marquee Club in Soho.

May The band is formed but is not named the Rollin' Stones until Jun.

12 Jul First gig as the Stones at the Marquee.

Dec Bill Wyman considers joining the band, by now called The Rolling Stones.

1963

Jan Charlie Watts' recruitment persuades Bill Wyman to enlist. First demo recordings are cut but no record label offers a contract.

Apr The Beatles see the band in a Richmond, Surrey, club and a friendship is forged while socializing in the Chelsea flat shared by Mick and Keith. Andrew Loog Oldham decides to manage the band.

10 May Oldham produces the first cut of 'Come On' – destined to become the Stones' first single.

18 May Journalist Norman Jopling files the first national rave review of the band.

7 Jun 'Come on/I Wanna Be Loved' is released on Decca, reaching No.20 in the British charts in Aug.

29 Sep The Rolling Stones' first tour begins at the Victoria Theatre in London, supporting Bo Diddley and The Everly Brothers.

1 Nov A second single, 'I Wanna Be Your Man', a Lennon/McCartney composition, is released. It enters the charts on 8 Nov and remains there for 13 weeks, reaching No.9.

28 Nov The Stones meet American singer Gene Pitney. Three weeks later his record 'That Girl Belongs to Yesterday', written by Jagger and Richards and produced by Loog Oldham, begins its UK chart ascent.

20 Dec The Rolling Stones are voted sixth best British small group in a *New Musical Express* poll.

1964

6 Jan The Rolling Stones' second British tour opens in Harrow, London.

17 Jan An EP is released, featuring five tracks. It spends 11 weeks in the singles charts, reaching No.15.

8 Feb Another UK tour begins, in London. It closes on 7 Mar, just as the band's new single 'Not Fade Away' is released in the UK and the US.

16 Apr Decca release the first album, *The Rolling Stones*. On 24 April it reaches No.1 in the UK album charts.

1 May A third UK tour begins, the day before 'Not Fade Away' enters the US charts; it remains there for 13 weeks but does not achieve a high placing.

12 May The band are refused lunch in a Bristol hotel because they are not wearing ties.

19 May Riots in Hamilton, Scotland, as police attempt to calm 4,000 fans – some with forged tickets – who storm a gig at a local hotel.

27 May A Coventry headmaster suspends 11 boys for wearing their hair like Jagger's.

1 Jun The band fly to New York for a first American tour. More than 5,000 fans greet them at Kennedy Airport.

5 Jun First US concert in San Bernardino, California. A few days later a stadium in San Antonio fails to fill – locals profess to prefer their high school band. However, in other cities over the next few weeks the Stones are greeted rapturously.

23 Jun British fans riot at Heathrow Airport as the band returns.

24 Jun Rolling Stones voted best British vocal band in a *Record Mirror* poll.

26 Jun 'It's All Over Now' is released and enters the British singles charts a week later at No.7, making No.1 soon afterwards.

24 Jul A new British tour opens in Blackpool. Thirty of the 7,000 fans and two policemen are injured in the crush.

31 Jul A Belfast concert is abandoned after 12 minutes as hysterical girls are lifted away in straitjackets.

6 Aug The Rolling Stones record an appearance for a networked American TV show. The next day they perform at the Richmond Jazz and Blues Festival, and then record for ITV's seminal *Ready, Steady, Go* television programme.

14 Aug The EP 'Five By Five' is released by Decca, recorded in Chicago in Jun. It is in Britain's singles chart within days. Marianne Faithfull's single 'As Tears Go By' is released.

5 Sept A British tour begins at Finsbury Park Astoria, London.

10 Sept The Rolling Stones are voted best British band in a *Melody Maker* poll. 'Not Fade Away' is voted best single.

13 Sep Thousands of fans are restrained by rugby players hired as a 'human shield' at a concert in Liverpool.

16 Sept Andrew Loog Oldham marries Sheila Klein in Glasgow. The next day police dogs are required to control fans at a concert in Carlisle. In Edinburgh some days later, armoured cars are on standby to protect band members from excited fans.

9 Oct The album *12 x 5* is released in the US, two days before the tour finishes in south London.

14 Oct Charlie Watts marries Shirley Ann Shephard in Bradford, Yorkshire.

17 Oct 'Time Is On My Side' enters the US charts at No.80. It remains there for thirteen weeks without becoming a major hit.

18 Oct The Stones are banned from appearing on Belgian TV after 5,000 fans greet them at the airport in Brussels. Two days later, French fans riot in Paris.

23 Oct The band fly to New York for their second US tour.

24 Oct Ed Sullivan promises his massive TV show audience that the Stones will never appear again. He professes to be shocked by them.

31 Oct After a further series of triumphant and controversial US dates and filming of their slot for the classic film *Gather No Moss*, the Stones greet loyal fans in San Bernardino.The tour ends in Nov.

20 Nov Back in Britain the new single 'Little Red Rooster' goes straight to the top spot in the UK charts. The band is simultaneously banned from a BBC radio programme for failing to honour an earlier booking.

12 Dec Brian denies rumours that he is leaving the group. The Stones have just been voted best R & B group in a British poll.

21 Dec Charlie Watts' book about Charlie Parker, *Ode to a High Flying Bird*, is published.

1965

15 Jan *Rolling Stones No.2*, the second album, is released.

21 Jan The group arrive in Sydney, Australia. 3,000 fans welcome them.

22 Jan The new album enters the UK charts at No.1.

31 Jan The Rolling Stones fly to New Zealand after nine sell-out gigs in Melbourne.

15 Feb The group fly to Singapore.

17 Feb After a final tour date in Hong Kong, the group fly to the US.

26 Feb 'The Last Time' is released. It enters the charts at No.8 and holds the No.1 position for four weeks.

5 Mar A two-week British tour begins.

18 Mar The tour ends in Romford, Essex; there are complaints when Mick Jagger, Brian Jones and Bill Wyman urinate against a garage forecourt wall.

24 Mar The Rolling Stones begin a short Scandinavian tour in Denmark, West Germany and Paris.

22 Apr Start of The Rolling Stones' third tour of North America.

26 Apr The group is forced to leave the stage in London, Ontario, after police turn off the power.

2 May The Rolling Stones appear again on *The Ed Sullivan show* in New York.

27 May 'Satisfaction' is released in the US.

30 May Final date of the tour, in New York. Shortly afterwards, The Rolling

Stones beat The Beatles into second place in an American pop poll.

11 Jun The EP 'Got Live If You Want It' is released amid rumours of Mick Jagger's plans to marry Chrissie Shrimpton.

15 Jun Beginning of a short tour of Scotland.

23 Jun Start of a Scandinavian tour, opening in Norway.

1 Jul Summonses are issued against Wyman, Jones and Jagger for their alleged 'insulting behaviour' in Essex on 18 March.

10 Jul In a Radio Luxembourg poll The Rolling Stones are voted more popular than The Beatles. The third album, *Out Of Our Heads*, is about to be released.

1 Aug Launch of Andrew Loog Oldham's Immediate record label.

20 Aug 'Satisfaction' is released in the UK, entering the charts at No.3 a week later. It spends three weeks at No.1.

2 Sept Brian Jones, who has recently bought a house in Los Angeles, counters rumours that the group is planning to decamp to the US, where they have been recording.

3 Sep The first of several shows in Dublin, Belfast and the Isle of Man, followed by a new tour of West Germany and Austria.

15 Sep Fans demolish 50 rows of seats in West Berlin and vandalize a train. Four hundred riot police do battle; 32 fans and six policemen need hospital treatment.

24 Sep Start of a 22-date UK tour which coincides with the release of *Out Of Our Heads*.

3 Oct Keith Richard and Mick Jagger are both injured by over-enthusiastic fans at a concert in Manchester.

22 Oct 'Get Off Of My Cloud' is released.

29 Oct A fourth North American tour opens in Montreal.

5 Nov 'Get Off Of My Cloud' is No.1 in both the UK and US.

14 Nov An American magazine, *Blast*, suggests that Mick Jagger is leaving the band, just as a new LP, *Dec's Children*, is released in the US.

5 Dec The tour finishes in San Diego. Anita Pallenberg flies from London to join Brian, who had denied their impending marriage the previous day.

10 Dec 'Satisfaction' is voted single of the year in a British music press poll and the band is named best R & B group and second best vocal group in the world.

1966

1 Jan The band appear on *Ready, Steady, Go*.

4 Feb Release of '19th Nervous Breakdown'.

12 Feb The group flies to New York for TV appearances, going on to tour Australia and New Zealand.

1 Mar Final tour date in Auckland. Later this month Cliff Richard releases 'Blue Turns to Grey', written by Jagger and Richard.

12 Mar The last of 21 new tracks are recorded at the RCA Studios in Hollywood. Many will be included on the forthcoming album, *Aftermath*.

25 Mar Beginning of a two-week European tour.

30 Mar Fans in Marseille take on the police as hysteria mounts during a concert. The group's first anthology album, *Big Hits (High Tide and Green Grass)*, has been released.

15 Apr Release of the classic album *Aftermath*. One track 'Goin' Home' runs for nearly 12 minutes – unprecedented in pop music. The album spends seven weeks at No.1 in the British charts. 'Paint It Black' is released in the US this month.

13 May 'Paint It Black' is released in the UK. It charts for six weeks, reaching No.1. Keith Richard has bought Redlands, a moated house in Sussex.

15 Jun Despite a nervous collapse the previous day, Mick Jagger appears on a BBC chat show.

17 Jun Chris Farlowe's single 'Out Of Time', written by Jagger and Richard, is released on Immediate Records.

23 Jun The Stones arrive in New York for their sell-out fifth North American tour, staying on a chartered yacht in the harbour as so many hotels have declined to take their booking.

28 Jul The tour closes in Hawaii; the band record in Hollywood and make TV appearances before taking holidays and returning to Britain.

27 Aug Having hurt his hand on holiday in north Africa, it is rumoured that Brian Jones will be unable to play for at least two months.

23 Sept 'Have You Seen Your Mother Baby, Standing In The Shadow' is released as The Rolling Stones' new single. Its picture sleeve (a novelty) depicts band members in drag and the record is banned by the BBC. Nonetheless it enters the charts a week later, peaking at No.5.

24 Sept Start of a new UK tour.

4 Nov 'Got Live If You Want It' is released in the US, reaching No.6 and remaining in the charts for a total of 48 weeks. This month Brian Jones poses in Nazi regalia with Anita Pallenberg. Rumours of their forthcoming marriage persist as the band cut material for a new album in a Paris studio.

10 Dec The band are voted second best in the world in two British polls. Later that month Mick Jagger and Chrissie Shrimpton part. He is involved with Marianne Faithfull; Shrimpton attempts suicide.

1967

13 Jan 'Let's Spend The Night Together' is released. The B side is the elegiac 'Ruby Tuesday'. Several US radio stations ban the record and Jagger has to sing 'Let's Spend Some Time Together' on a US TV show.

20 Jan Release of *Between The Buttons* – all written by Jagger and Richard.

22 Jan The group appear on the family-orientated British TV variety show, *Sunday Night At The London Palladium* but refuse to join other stars waving on the revolving stage that traditionally closes the show.

4 Feb Jagger attends the annual music business award ceremonies in Cannes with Marianne Faithfull. The Rolling Stones are nominated best British act.

15 Feb Fifteen police officers raid Keith Richard's Sussex home armed with a warrant issued under the Dangerous Drugs Act. Afterwards Jagger, Jones, Richard and various women friends head for Morocco, hoping to relax after the 'bust'. On the way, asthmatic Brian Jones is admitted to a French hospital with respiratory problems.

10 Mar Brian flies from Nice to hospital in London. By the time he is well enough to join the party in Marrakech, Anita Pallenberg and Keith Richard have become lovers. While Brian is out recording ethnic music the others fly home from Tangier via Madrid, leaving no note.

18 Mar Brian returns to London. Jagger and Richard are issued with court summonses.

25 Mar A three-week European tour opens in Sweden; there are concerts in West Germany, Austria, Italy, France, Switzerland, Holland and Poland. There are tensions between the band and police and customs officials since the Stones have increasingly become associated with crowd violence and alleged drug-related offences.

10 May After the first of a series of court appearances relating to the raid at Keith's Sussex home, Keith Richard – and Mick Jagger – are remanded on bail. The same day Brian Jones is arrested at home in Kensington for separate drug-related offences. He is also given bail.

15 Jun Jagger and Richard supply backing vocals for The Beatles' song 'All You Need Is Love'. A compilation album, *Flowers*, is released in June.

27/28 Jun Jagger and Richard's cases are heard at a court in Chichester, West Sussex. They are both given prison sentences.

30 Jun Jagger and Richard are awarded bail and the right of appeal.

1 Jul A leader in *The Times* reflects surprising public outrage at the severity of their sentences.

7 Jul Without Brian, who is in hospital with nervous strain, the other Rolling Stones record. Jones is well enough to join them on 12 Jul.

31 Jul In the court of appeal Mick is given a conditional discharge and Keith's sentence is quashed.

18 Aug 'We Love You' is released.

26 Aug Mick Jagger and Marianne Faithfull join The Beatles at the Maharishi Mahesh Yogi's seminar in Wales.

14 Sept Band members arrive in New York from London and Paris and are questioned by immigration officials about their drugs trials in England.

29 Sept The Rolling Stones part company with Andrew Loog Oldham.

15 Oct Bill Wyman applies for membership of the Royal Horticultural Society.

30 Oct Brian Jones is sentenced to nine months' imprisonment for drug offences. He is released on bail from Wormwood Scrubs the next day; on 12 Dec his sentence is commuted to three years' probation.

27 Nov *Their Satanic Majesties Request* is released in the US. It is weeks before it is available in Britain.

12 Dec The Rolling Stones are voted best British R & B group and second best vocal group in an *NME* poll.

14 Dec *Their Satanic Majesties Request* enters the British album charts and remains there for nine weeks, reaching No.3. Brian Jones collapses and is rushed to a London hospital suffering from strain and exhaustion.

1968

13 Mar The band begin cutting a new album in the Olympic Studios in London; work continues until 18 Apr.

11 May It is announced that Mick Jagger is to star in a film called *The Performance*.

21 May Brian Jones is arrested for possession of cannabis at home in Chelsea. He denies the charge.

25 May The classic single 'Jumpin' Jack Flash' is released. It reaches No.1 in both the UK and the US.

26 Jul 'Street Fighting Man', taken from the forthcoming album, is released in the US.

17 Aug There is speculation that Eric Clapton will join The Rolling Stones now that the 'supergroup' Cream have disbanded.

24 Aug Disputes about the 'lavatorial' sleeve of *Beggars' Banquet* delay its release.

12 Sept As Mick Jagger begins work on his film, now called *Performance*, Marianne Faithfull's film *Girl on a Motorcycle*, co-starring Alain Delon, premieres in London.

26 Sept In a London court Brian Jones is fined for possession of cannabis.

4 Oct Marianne Faithfull happily announces her pregnancy. Six weeks later and nearly six months pregnant, she is taken to a maternity home and loses her baby the next day. Mick reports that they are both very upset.

21 Nov Brian Jones buys Cotchford Farm in Sussex, formerly the home of A. A. Milne, creator of Winnie the Pooh.

27 Nov Fears that The Rolling Stones are to split gather even as the new album is released in North America.

5 Dec *Beggars' Banquet* is at last released in Britain, with an ironic sleeve spoofing an invitation to a formal party. It enters the charts days later at No.3 and remains for 12 weeks without going higher.

1969

4 Jan Brian Jones is reported to be 'furious' when hotels in Sri Lanka bar him in the belief that he is a drifter.

Mar The band return to Olympic Studios in London to cut a new album. Jagger and Richard work together on new songs, spending time writing in Italy in April.

24 May It is announced that Mick Jagger and Marianne Faithfull will star in an Australian film, *Ned Kelly*.

28 May After a police raid at Mick Jagger's Chelsea home, he and Marianne are arrested for possession of cannabis. They are remanded and released on bail.

8 Jun Band members collect at Cotchford Farm and an amicable split is agreed with Brian Jones. Musical differences are cited.

10 Jun Mick Taylor is appointed as Jones' replacement.

1 Jul Drug charges against Mick Jagger and Marianne Faithfull are adjourned until 29 Sept.

2/3 Jul The body of Brian Jones is lifted from the bottom of his swimming pool at Cotchford Farm. A coroner later reports that he drowned under the influence of alcohol and drugs.

5 Jul A free Rolling Stones concert in London's Hyde Park goes ahead as planned. Thousands of white butterflies are released as Mick Jagger reads from Shelley in Brian's honour.

8 Jul Marianne Faithfull overdoses and falls into a long coma in Australia. Another actor takes over her part in *Ned Kelly*. 'Honky Tonk Women' enters the US and UK charts. Two weeks later it will be No.1 in Britain.

9 Jul The divorce of Bill and Diane Wyman is announced.

10 Jul Brian Jones is buried in Cheltenham.

13 Jul Mick Jagger starts work on *Ned Kelly*. Filming ends in Sept.

12 Sept Another compilation, *Through The Past Darkly (Big Hits Volume 2)*, is released. It reaches No.1 and stays in the UK charts for 16 weeks.

17 Oct The Rolling Stones fly to Los Angeles to prepare for their first American tour in three years and to mix the next album, *Let It Bleed*. It will be released in Britain in December.

7 Nov This sixth American tour is a sell-out and opens in Colorado.

13 Nov Warner Bros waver about the US release of *Performance* because they find the English actors' accents 'unintelligible'.

28 Nov *Let It Bleed* goes on sale in the US and The Rolling Stones are triumphant at a filmed Madison Square Gardens concert. Jimi Hendrix is backstage.

6 Dec At Altamont, California, the final concert of the tour descends into tragedy. Three fans die and many more are seriously injured.

7 Dec The Rolling Stones are voted best British R & B band in the *NME* poll.

8 Dec Anita Pallenberg is informed that she must marry or leave England.

11 Dec Marianne Faithfull, who was in Italy with her son and a new friend during the recent tour, reunites with Mick Jagger.

19 Dec At a London court Mick Jagger is fined for possession of cannabis. Marianne is acquitted.

21 Dec The band give two Christmas shows at a ballroom off the Strand, London.

1970

14 Mar It is announced that The Rolling Stones' first European tour for three years will open in Holland in May and finish in Helsinki in early Jun. In fact the tour is postponed for four months.

May Reports in the British press suggest that Brian Jones' debts were over five times greater than his assets. His estate may be due royalties from songwriting earnings.

24 Jun *Ned Kelly* is premiered in London.

28 Jun Mick Jagger is said to be dating American actress Patti D'Arbanville.

31 Jul The Rolling Stones' contract with Decca expires. The band are set to launch their own record label.

6 Sept Release of *Get Yer Ya-Ya's Out!*, which reaches No.1 and remains in the charts for 13 weeks.

10 Oct The day before the European tour ends in Munich Mick visits London with a new girlfriend, the Nicaraguan Bianca Perez Morena de Macia.

20 Oct Mick Jagger, cited as co-respondent, is ordered to pay costs in John Dunbar's divorce from Marianne Faithfull.

6 Dec A documentary film, *Gimme Shelter*, covering the Stones' last US tour

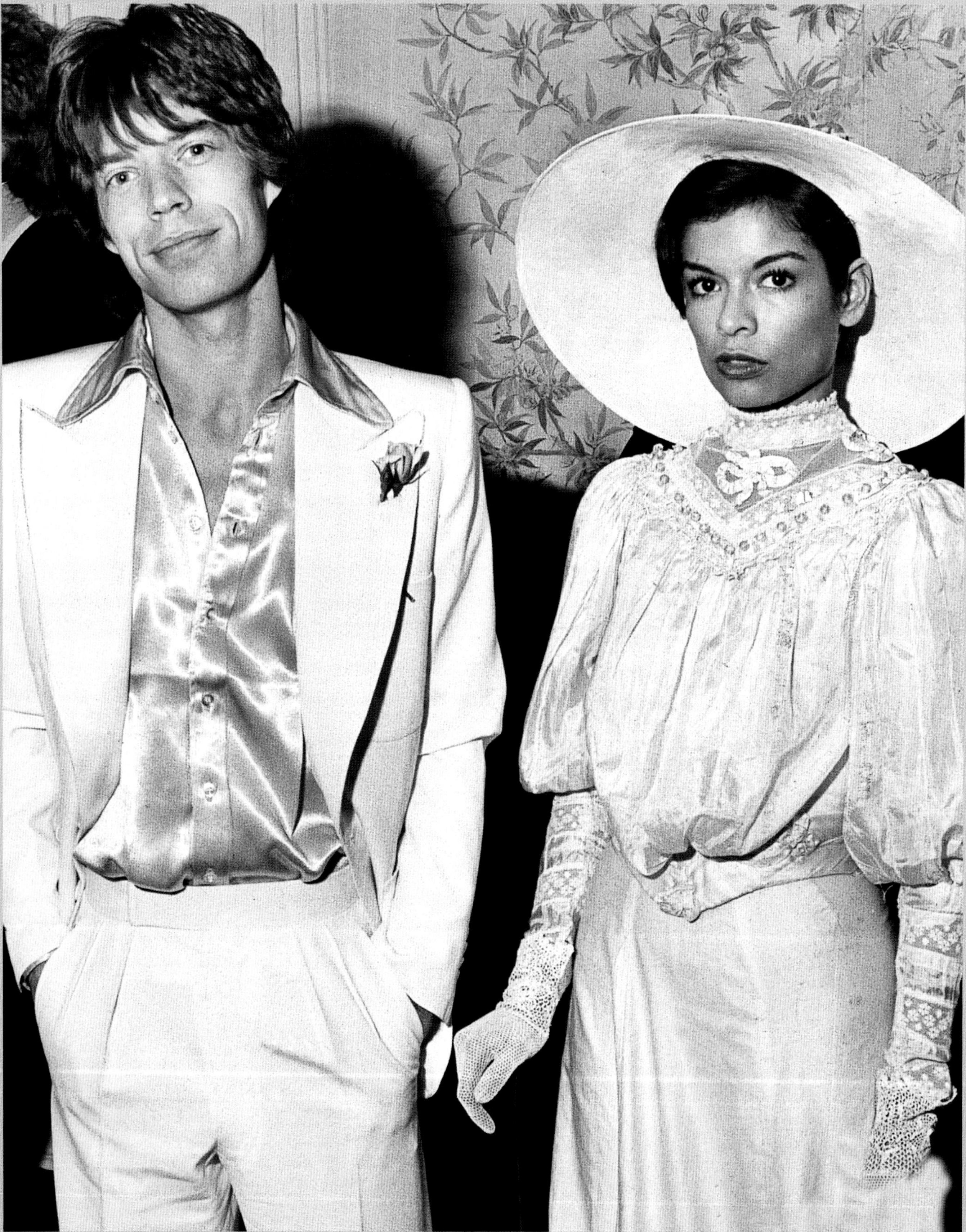

and featuring scenes from Altamont, is premiered in New York.

1971

4 Jan British premiere of *Performance*.

6 Feb A farewell tour is announced amid expectations that the band will become tax exiles in France. It opens in Newcastle and ends at the Roundhouse in north London.

26 Mar The Rolling Stones are filmed in performance for TV at the Marquee Club.

1 Apr The band gives a farewell party in Maidenhead before leaving for France. Band members take up residence in neighbouring houses.

15 Apr 'Brown Sugar', the Stones' next single, is featured on the BBC's *Top of the Pops*. It enters the charts a week later and will reach No.1.

23 Apr Release of *Sticky Fingers*.

12 May Mick Jagger marries Bianca in a civil ceremony in St Tropez. Both wear white suits. The bride is already several months pregnant.

28 May Keith Richard has a road accident and will appear in court on subsequent assault charges. *Gimme Shelter* is screened in Cannes.

1 Jun The Rolling Stones top the UK singles and album charts with 'Brown Sugar' and *Sticky Fingers*.

31 Jul British premiere of *Gimme Shelter*.

31 Aug The four surviving original Stones and Brian Jones's father launch a complex lawsuit against Andrew Loog Oldham about alleged irregularities relating to earnings derived through their original recording contract with Decca and other rights.

Oct Mixing of 20 new recorded songs continues and the band plans a new album to coincide with next spring's American tour.

Dec The band work on the new album at the Sunset Sound studios in Los Angeles. Mick and Bianca house-hunt in California.

3 Dec French magistrates accept Keith Richard's defence of self-defence after the 'assault' that followed his road accident in May. Charges are dismissed.

15 Dec Decca release a double compilation album, *Hot Rocks 1964–1971*.

1972

20 Feb Decca release another anthology, *Milestones*.

14 Apr Release of 'Tumbling Dice' a track from the forthcoming *Exile On Main Street*. It will reach No.5 in the UK charts.

26 May *Exile On Main Street*, a double album, is released by Rolling Stones Records.

3 Jun The seventh North American tour opens in Vancouver. Thirty policemen are injured as 2,000 fans attempt to gatecrash.

31 Jul The marathon tour finishes in New York on Mick Jagger's birthday.

9 Aug Keith, Anita and their children move to Montreux, Switzerland.

20 Nov Mick Jagger sings back-up on Carly Simon's single 'You're So Vain'.

25 Nov Band members convene in Kingston, Jamaica, for four weeks' recording.

23 Dec An earthquake devastates Nicaragua. After Christmas Mick and Bianca Jagger fly there to search for her family and bring medicines. A benefit concert for victims of the earthquake will be announced in the new year. Various fundraising activities eventually raise £350,000.

1973

4 Jan Confirmation of their safety in Managua averts fears that misadventure has befallen Mick and Bianca Jagger.

8 Jan Mick's hopes to play in Japan are dashed as an old drugs conviction prevents his entry. A tour has to be cancelled despite record-breaking ticket sales.

21/22 Jan The Rolling Stones preview their Australasian tour with two concerts in Honolulu.

Mar The new album is mixed in Los Angeles.

9 Jun Mick Jagger denies rumours that Keith is leaving the band. The denial is echoed by Keith two days later.

15 Jun While mixing *Goats Head Soup* at Island Studios in London, Keith Richard – now domiciled in Jamaica – speaks of plans to record with a Rastafarian band.

18 Jun Marsha Hunt files an application at a London court, claiming Mick Jagger is her daughter Karis's father. The court orders that blood tests are taken.

26 Jun Keith Richard and two others are arrested for possession of cannabis. Keith is also charged with possessing a firearm and ammunition without a licence. He is remanded on bail.

31 Jul A fire causes serious damage to Keith and Anita's Sussex home.

6 Aug Tickets for the forthcoming UK tour go on sale and are an almost instant sell-out. Further venues and dates are arranged.

20 Aug 'Angie', recorded in Jamaica, is released and charts at No.2. Both the single and the album it was cut from will be No.1 in the US in Oct.

31 Aug *Goats Head Soup* is released; it holds the No.1 position for two weeks.

1 Sept The European tour opens in Mannheim, West Germany.

7 Sept First British leg of the tour at Wembley – one of four dates there.

17 Sept Final UK show in Birmingham. The tour continues with concerts in Germany, Holland, Belgium and Scandinavia, closing in Berlin on 19 Oct.

24 Oct Keith Richard is fined £205 for possession of various drugs, firearms and ammunition. For her possession of Mandrax, Anita Pallenberg is conditionally discharged.

13 Nov The Rolling Stones begin new recording sessions in Munich.

1974

5 Jan Bill Wyman is in Los Angeles recording a solo album. *Monkey Grip* will be released in May on The Rolling Stones' own label.

10 Feb Mick Jagger once again denies his marriage is on the rocks.

1 Mar A film about the US tour, *Ladies and Gentlemen, The Rolling Stones,* is previewed in New York.

9 Jul The Rolling Stones preview 'It's Only Rock 'n' Roll (But I like It)' on BBC TV's *Old Grey Whistle Test*. The single hits the charts on 30 July, making No.10.

27 Jul Mick answers a Brian Jones fan who expressed sorrow at the Stones' apparent indifference to the anniversaries of Brian's death, explaining via a public letter that rather than send flowers to Brian's grave, band members sent donations to a United Nations children's charity that Brian had supported.

7 Dec The band embark on new recording in Munich.

12 Dec It is announced that Mick Taylor is leaving the band; he will work with former Cream bassist Jack Bruce. Massive speculation about his replacement centres on Ronnie Wood of The Faces.

1975

9 Feb After recording in Rotterdam Mick Jagger flies to New York while Keith Richard returns to London and works with Ronnie Wood at the latter's home studio in Richmond.

22 Mar Recording sessions continue in Munich, where the band is soon joined by Ronnie Wood.

14 Apr It is announced that Ronnie Wood will join the Stones for part of their new American tour, but merely 'guesting' and on loan from The Faces.

1 May Central New York is brought to a standstill as The Rolling Stones perform 'Brown Sugar' from the back of a truck. The tour as planned will be the band's longest ever.

13 May Ronnie Wood departs to join The Faces for their overlapping tour.

13 Jun Mid-tour the band release a compilation album, *Made In The Shade*, on their own label.

5 Jul Keith and Ronnie are arrested on the highway in Fordyce, Arkansas, charged with possession of an offensive weapon – a can opener with a blade attachment. Both are released on bail.

Aug The South American shows having been postponed, the tour closes in Buffalo.

13 Oct The Rolling Stones and Ronnie Wood begin recording new album material at studios in Montreux. Sessions finish on 15 Nov.

3 Dec Further recording continues in Munich until 16 Dec.

18 Dec Rod Stewart quits The Faces, apparently unhappy about Ronnie Wood's frequent guesting with the Stones; rumours strengthen that Ronnie will become an official Stone.

26 Dec American magazines name The Rolling Stones best live band, best R & B band, and best band of the year. Ronnie Wood is most valuable player and *Made In The Shade* is best reissue album.

1976

26 Feb Release of *Stone Alone*, Bill Wyman's solo album.

28 Feb It is unofficially announced that Ronnie Wood will join the band.

10 Apr Rehearsals for a new European tour begin in France.

20 Apr Release of *Black And Blue*. It enters the British charts a week later and reaches No.2.

28 Apr The tour opens in Frankfurt.

8 May 'Fool To Cry' enters the British singles charts. It will reach No.4.

10 May The British tour begins with a show in Glasgow.

19 May After crashing his Bentley in Buckinghamshire, Keith, Anita and Marlon are unhurt but the car is a write-off. Police find 'substances' in the wreckage and he is arrested but released as they must be identified before any charge is brought. Keith is astonished to learn later that the substances were LSD and cocaine; some newspapers speculate that a Rolling Stone could be used as an unwitting drugs courier.

4 Jun First of three concerts at Les Abattoirs in Paris. Before going on stage, on 6 June Keith Richard learns that his ten-week-old son Tara has died of a mysterious virus. White and stricken, he plays on, and insists that the tragedy remains secret and that tour plans should not be disrupted.

23 Aug The band performs before 200,000 fans, headlining the Knebworth Festival. New rumours of tension in the Jagger marriage circulate when they go their separate ways after Mick meets Bianca at Heathrow Airport.

Sept Mick and Ronnie have whittled down 150 hours of live concert tapes for a new live LP.

6 Oct Before a magistrate Keith Richard chooses to go to a higher court for his recent charges to be heard. Bail is renewed at £5,000.

1977

12 Jan At Aylesbury Crown Court, after a three-day trial with Mick lending a supportive presence, Keith is found guilty of possessing cocaine. He is fined £750 and ordered to pay £250 costs. The following month he is fined a further £25 for driving without tax on the night of the accident the previous May.

Feb At Toronto Airport Keith and Anita's luggage is searched and Anita is arrested, then released. Days later both are charged with possession of heroin but released, Keith on bail. A court hearing is eventually set for March 14; Anita is fined $400, and for his alleged crimes Keith is remanded on bail.

4 Mar Margaret Trudeau, glamorous wife of Canada's premier Pierre Trudeau, throws a party for the band after their opening gig at a small club. As the tour progresses and she parties with them elsewhere, rumours of inappropriate behaviour are dismissed as mischievous gossip. Mrs Trudeau's husband is staunchly supportive of her.

15 May Touring in Britain, Nils Lofgren dedicates his song 'Keith Don't Go (To Toronto)' to Richard, whose voluntary treatment for drug addiction renders him unable to attend a Toronto court appearance. It is rescheduled for 19 July when he is once again unable to appear. The case is adjourned to Dec.

13 Sept The live album that will reach No.3 in the British charts, *Love You Live*, is launched at the Marquee Club in London.

23 Sept The film of the band in concert, *Ladies And Gentlemen, The Rolling Stones*, is premiered at the Rainbow Theatre in London. The band will soon begin to record a new album in Paris, resuming work on 5 Dec after a break.

19 Nov A compilation album, *Get Stoned*, is released and sells well.

26 Nov Mick Jagger goes to Morocco with Jerry Hall; they fly to Barbados after Christmas in London together.

2 Dec In a Toronto court Keith hears his trial is postponed. Further delays mean he has to wait until Oct 1978.

11 Dec As Bianca Jagger leaves London, rumours of a divorce become louder.

1978

3 Mar Recording for the new Stones' album concludes.

19 Mar Krissie Wood files for divorce, citing model Jo Howard in her petition.

14 May Bianca Jagger files for divorce in London.

19 May 'Miss You' is released. It reaches No.2 in the UK charts.

9 Jun *Some Girls* is released the day before the American tour opens in Florida. Fifty-five thousand tickets for the 10 July gig at Anaheim, California, sell out within two hours. More than $1,000,000 is taken in advance sales for the 80,000-capacity auditorium in New Orleans.

26 Jul The tour ends at Oakland, California.

20 Oct As of now, Keith changes his name back to Keith Richards.

23 Oct Keith's trial in Toronto starts. He is given a one-year suspended prison sentence and ordered to give a charity concert. People incensed by the judge's leniency begin an appeal for a harsher sentence the next month.

3 Dec Keith's first solo single, 'Run Rudolph Run', is released in the US (Feb in the UK).

15 Dec Japan relents after six years and lifts its ban on The Rolling Stones.

28 Dec The band are voted artists of the year and *Some Girls* album of the year in a *Rolling Stone* magazine poll.

1979

18 Jan The band convenes in Nassau to cut new album material.

5 Apr Bianca's lawyers serve divorce papers on Mick in New York.

21 Apr The Rolling Stones give their only live performance of the year in Toronto, arranged by Keith Richards to meet his recent sentencing stipulation.

4 May Mick Jagger's divorce proceedings begin with a High Court hearing in London. Later that month, in Los Angeles, Mick's lawyers state the marriage had been over in any true sense since 1973. As an interim measure the LA judge orders Mick to maintain his wife in the 'sumptuous' style she is used to.

18 Jun The band gather in Paris to cut a new album. Work will continue intermittently for some months.

27 Jun Keith Richards' appeal case is heard in Toronto but no decision is made as to whether he should, after all, be jailed.

20 Jul A teenage boy dies after shooting himself whil visiting Anita at Keith's New York State home. She is cleared of any part in his death when the case is heard in Nov, although she is indicted on charges of illegal possession of firearms.

17 Sept A Canadian court finally rejects the appeal against Keith Richards' light sentence.

19 Oct Paris recordings finish. The planned release date of the new album is in Jan.

2 Nov Bianca is granted a decree nisi and custody of daughter Jade.

18 Dec At his birthday party in New York Keith Richards meets American model Patti Hansen, whom he will eventually marry.

1980

18 Feb Bill Wyman tells the *Daily Express* that he plans to leave the band in two years' time – their 20th anniversary.

20 Jun 'Emotional Rescue', taken from the forthcoming album of the same name, is released. It will reach No.1 and stay there for four weeks. The next single, 'She's So Cold', is released in Sept but is less successful.

18 Sept Mick Jagger buys a chateau in the Loire Valley.

11 Oct Recording for a new album begins in Paris.

2 Nov At a private hearing at the High Court in London, Bianca Jagger's divorce settlement is adjudged. It is thought to be in the region of £1,000,000.

1981

Jan Mick Jagger flies to Peru with Jerry Hall. He is to star in the Werner Herzog film *Fitzcarraldo* but leaves the project the following month. The entire enterprise is troubled – not least by Amazonian Indians. Eventually the film is completed and is widely regarded as a masterpiece.

4 Mar The anthology *Sucking In The Seventies* is produced by Mick and Keith and released on The Rolling Stones label. It has mixed fortunes: many American shops refuse to stock it because of the title, and it only charts for a few weeks, peaking at No.17. The UK release is 13 April.

Jun Bill Wyman sues the *Daily Star* for claiming he is quitting the Stones. The following month his solo single 'Je Suis Un Rock Star' is released and reaches No.11 in the UK charts.

14 Aug Rehearsals for a new tour begin in Massachusetts.

17 Aug 'Start Me Up', produced by Mick and Keith, is released, taken from the forthcoming *Tattoo You*. It sells a million copies in the US in the week of its early Sept release.

25 Sept The tour opens before a 90,000-strong crowd in Philadelphia.

19 Dec The tour finishes in Virginia. It is estimated that the has band grossed $50 million in ticket sales and earned almost half as much again via merchandising, record sales and sponsorship. A film of the 50-date tour has been shot by Hal Ashby for release in 1982.

1982

11 Jan 'Hang Fire' is released in the US.

4 Mar The Rolling Stones collect a slew of awards in *Rolling Stone* magazine's annual prize-giving. They are voted band of the year and Jagger best vocalist. *Tattoo You* is judged best album and 'Start Me Up' best single. Jagger and Richards are best songwriters and Keith is best instrumentalist. Later this month Jagger and Richards start editing Hal Ashby's tapes of the recent US tour.

26 Apr The band's first British concert for six years, in Aberdeen. European tour dates in England, Ireland, France, Spain, Holland, Germany, Austria, Belgium, Sweden, Switzerland, Denmark and Italy are arranged.

Jun Sell-out concerts in London and Bristol. The tour finishes at Leeds.

1 Jun Release of live album *Still Life*.

24 Jun On behalf of the band Bill Wyman collects the British Music Industry's award for outstanding achievement. Keith Richards is interviewed for BBC 2's *Newsnight*.

1 Sept Sixty-five firemen extinguish another fire at Redlands, Keith Richards' Sussex home. Later in the month another single from *Still Life*, 'Time Is On My Side', is released in the US. In Britain it is issued as part of a 12-inch single featuring two other songs. British publisher Weidenfeld & Nicolson sign Mick Jagger for his memoirs. A *Sunday Times* journalist, John Ryles, is engaged to help with the writing. Towards the end of the month rumours abound that Jerry Hall has embarked on a romance with millionaire racehorse owner Robert Sangster. They met in June at Royal Ascot.

7 Nov Recording sessions resume at the Paris studios.

12 Nov Keith Richards confirms reports in the *Sun* that he and Patti Hansen are to marry. Jerry Hall flies from New York to Paris. The following day Venezuelan model Victoria Vicuna joins Mick in Paris. A double anthology album, *The Best Of The Rolling Stones*, is released this month on a budget label.

1983

14 Jan Mick Jagger plays the Chinese Emperor in a US TV production of *The Nightingale* by Hans Christian Andersen.

25 Jan In a *Sun* interview Mick Jagger talks about the possibility of the Stones breaking up. He tells John Blake that it will disintegrate very slowly and that he doesn't know what goals are left.

25/26 Apr To celebrate the 25th anniversary of the Marquee in London, Charlie Watts and Bill Wyman join Alexis Korner on stage.

4 May Editing and mixing of the Paris sessions begin, in New York. Keith joins Mick and Ronnie there.

4 Jul Mick Jagger tells the *Daily Star* he has moderated his earlier drink and drugs lifestyle now he has to retain peak fitness for touring; he will turn 40 on 26 July.

25 Aug The Rolling Stones sign with CBS in a $28,000,000 deal said to make music business history. Later in Aug it is announced Jerry Hall is pregnant and that Bill Wyman is splitting from Astrid Lundstrom, his girlfriend for 14 years.

20 Sept At a Royal Albert Hall concert in London fundraising for ARMS, the multiple sclerosis charity, Charlie Watts,

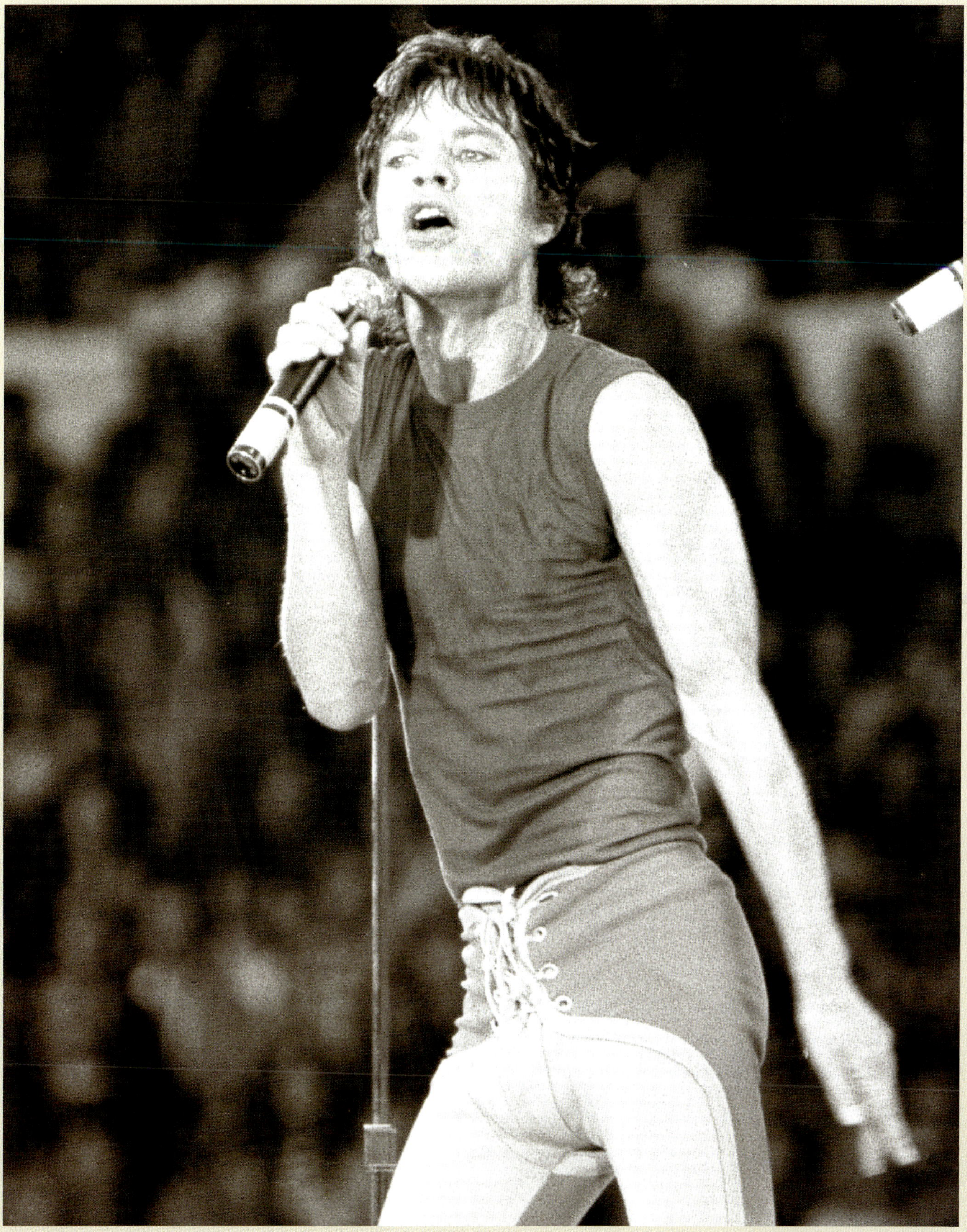

Eric Clapton, Steve Winwood, Jeff Beck and Jimmy Page join ex-Face and MS sufferer Ronnie Lane on stage. Ten months later a live album, *The Ronnie Lane Appeal to ARMS*, is released.

18 Oct Shooting for a video to accompany the next single, 'Undercover Of The Night', begins. It continues in Mexico City.

30 Oct 'Undercover Of The Night' is released. A week later *Undercover* is released on Rolling Stones Records. Three days later the BBC bans the video and the next day Mick Jagger defends it on a Channel 4 youth programme, *The Tube*. The single will reach No.12 in the UK charts and the album No.1.

9 Dec Final date of a short US tour to raise cash for ARMS, in New York.

18 Dec On his 40th birthday Keith Richards marries Patti Hansen in Mexico.

1984

23 Jan 'She Was Hot' is released. It dips into the UK charts at No.40 and only makes No.44 in the US, possibly hindered by the banning of a raunchy video with the trouser flies of band members popping open.

27 Mar Critical remarks made by Bill Wyman about band members are published in the *Sun*. A week later he denies having made them.

6 May Mick Jagger begins working on 'State Of Shock' with Michael Jackson in New York. It is released in Jun, reaching No.3 in the US charts and No.14 in the UK in July.

29 Jun *Rewind*, a compilation LP, is released and reaches No.12 in the UK.

23 Jul News of Mick Jagger's forthcoming solo album causes speculation about fractures within the band. He offers assurances that the Stones are still very much together and planning a new tour.

Aug Decca release *Beggar's Banquet*, remastered with its original sleeve.

Sept Tour plans are postponed due to Mick Jagger's solo schedules. Bill Wyman produces an LP by Willie and the Poor Boys, featuring Charlie Watts and other musicians.

Oct Mick Jagger declines £1,000,000 to appear on TV in *Dallas*.

Nov Band members meet in Amsterdam to discuss their future. Mick, Jerry and film/video producer Julian Temple fly to Rio de Janeiro to shoot a promo video for Jagger's new album.

28 Nov An exhibition of Ronnie Wood's portraits of musicians and friends opens in Dallas. The show runs well into the new year.

1985

3 Jan Ronnie Wood and Jo Howard marry in Denham, Buckinghamshire. All the other Stones, except Mick Jagger, attend. Later that month Mick and Keith begin work on a new Stones album at the Pathé Marconi Studios in Paris.

4 Feb Mick Jagger's first solo single, 'Just Another Night', is released in the UK and US. It is taken from his forthcoming album, *She's The Boss*, and reaches No.27 in the UK charts.

11 Apr Just after Mick Jagger begins work on the video for his next single, 'Lucky In Love' (to be released 19 April), the band resume work in Paris on their next album. Thirty tracks are recorded by the end of June. Release has been delayed to Sept.

13 Jul The Live Aid concerts take place in London and Philadelphia, broadcast to a global audience of 1.6 billion. The Rolling Stones as such do not take part but Mick, Keith and Ronnie all separately play their parts.

19 Aug Charlie Watts breaks his leg in three places after a fall at home in Devon.

23 Aug 'Dancing In The Street', the Mick Jagger/David Bowie duet, is released worldwide and becomes a disco classic, thanks partly to an inspired video. It is immediately No.1 in the UK charts. There are rumours of Jagger and Bowie reprising the Tony Curtis/Jack Lemmon roles in a remake of *Some Like It Hot*.

18 Nov Charlie Watts opens for a week at Ronnie Scott's jazz club in London with his 29-piece Big Band. Musicians include Jack Bruce and Stan Tracey. Performances are attended by Keith, Mick and Bill.

25 Nov Work on the new album resumes in New York. A few days later Mick Jagger sings 'Honky Tonk Women' with Tina Turner in Carolina.

12 Dec Ian Stewart, friend, colleague, some-time back-up musician and management stalwart, dies of a heart attack in London, aged 47. His funeral on 20 Dec is attended by all The Rolling Stones. On 23 Feb 1986 the band plays at an invitation-only memorial gig for Ian Stewart at the 100 Club in London.

1986

25 Feb The Rolling Stones are given a lifetime achievement award at the Grammys in Los Angeles, presented to them by Eric Clapton.

3 Mar 'Harlem Shuffle' is released. It will reach No.7 in the UK charts and No.5 in the US.

24 Mar *Dirty Work* is released, it enters UK charts in April and reaches No.3.

19 Apr The Charlie Watts Orchestra begins a week's engagement at Ronnie Scott's club.

1 May The band convenes at Elstree Studios, north of London, to shoot a video for 'One Hit To The Body'. The single is released on 19 May.

20 Jun Before the Prince and Princess of Wales, Mick Jagger – along with David Bowie, Elton John, Paul McCartney, Phil Collins, Eric Clapton and Tina Turner – takes part in a fundraiser for the Prince's Trust. Earlier in the month Ronnie Wood and Keith Richards have been busy with separate musical commitments in the US.

5 Jul Ronnie Wood and Bill Wyman join Rod Stewart on stage for a Faces reunion concert at Wembley.

12 Jul Keith discusses a possible film project with Chuck Berry in St Louis.

15–17 Jul Keith Richards joins Bob Dylan for concerts at Madison Square Garden, New York.

31 Jul Mick Jagger's single 'Ruthless People', theme song for a Disney film of the same name, is released.

3 Aug Sixteen-year-old Mandy Smith speaks to a British newspaper about her relationship with Bill Wyman. It has lasted for over two years and now she is tiring of it.

29 Aug A version of 'Jumpin' Jack Flash', recorded by Aretha Franklin and produced by Ronnie and Keith, is released. It reaches No.21 in the US charts in September.

15 Sept Mick discusses plans for his next album with Dave Stewart of Eurythmics in Los Angeles. Recording will begin in Holland in November.

Nov Charlie Watts and his 33-piece orchestra arrive in New York for a short East Coast tour.

1987

21 Jan Jerry Hall is arrested at the airport in Barbados, charged with importing marijuana. Some hours later she is released on bail.

20 Feb After two adjournments Jerry Hall is finally found not guilty. She and Mick fly to New York where work on his solo album continues. Both Keith Richards and Ronnie Wood concurrently work on their albums.

13 Apr Bill Wyman launches his AIMS project in London.

13 Jun Charlie and his orchestra play at the Playboy Jazz festival in Hollywood.

13 Jul Keith discusses a Virgin solo deal with Richard Branson. It is signed on 17 July.

31 Aug Release of Mick Jagger's 'Let's Work'; it reaches No.35 in the UK.

14 Sept Release of Mick *Primitive Cool*; it reaches No.18 in the UK charts.

27 Sept A British newspaper suggests some tracks on Mick's album contain critical messages about Keith.

29 Oct An exhibition of Ronnie Wood's paintings of legendary musicians opens in London. Two days later he flies to Miami, checking progress on his nightclub and restaurant.

4 Nov Ronnie Wood opens a North American tour in Columbus, Ohio.

14 Nov The entire Stones back catalogue is rereleased by CBS.

19 Dec Ronnie Wood and Bo Diddley play at the opening of Woody's on the Beach in Miami.

1988

7/8 Jan Mick Taylor joins Ronnie on stage at the Miami club.

20 Jan At the annual Rock 'n' Roll Hall of Fame in New York, Mick Jagger jams with Bruce Springsteen and George Harrison, and also with both Bob Dylan and Jeff Beck. He sings 'Satisfaction' solo.

20 Feb Bill Wyman and Ronnie Wood join Phil Collins, Eddy Grant, Ian Dury, Kenney Jones, Elvis Costello and Chris Rea at a Royal Albert Hall benefit that Bill has arranged for Great Ormond Street Children's Hospital.

12 Mar Mick Jagger and Ronnie Wood, in Japan on separate tours, meet at the former's hotel in Osaka. Mick is reputed to receive £1,000,000 for each of his sell-out shows.

25 Mar By the time the Jagger tour closes in Nagoya, over a quarter of a million tickets have been sold. Before leaving Japan he guests with Tina Turner at her own concert in Osaka.

26 Apr Mick Jagger is cleared of copyright infringement charges regarding 'Just Another Night' on his *She's The Boss* album.

18 May All five members of The Rolling Stones meet for the first time in two years, at a London hotel. Plans for working together again are discussed.

22 Jul Bill Wyman's book deal with Viking/Penguin is announced.

26 Jul Mick Jagger celebrates his 45th birthday and Jerry's first night in *Bus Stop* at a theatre in New Jersey.

22 Aug Mick Jagger announces the Stones will record and tour together the following year. 'Satisfaction' is voted best single of the last 25 years by *Rolling Stone* magazine.

24 Aug Upon arrival in Australia for his solo tour Mick Jagger says he will stop touring when he hits 50.

4 Oct Virgin release *Talk Is Cheap*, Keith Richards' first solo album.

16 Oct Keith Richards, whose home has been damaged in the recent hurricane, plays at the fundraising Smile Jamaica concert in London.

16 Nov Ronnie Wood receives undisclosed libel damages after an erroneous newspaper report that he had been unfaithful to his wife.

24 Nov Keith Richards and his band The X-Pensive Winos open their US tour in Atlanta.

1989

Jan Mick Jagger and Keith Richards plan a new Stones album in Barbados.

18 Jan At the New York Hall of Fame awards the band is inducted. Bill and Charlie are absent but Mick Taylor joins the others.

19 Jan Charlie Watts joins Mick, Keith and Ronnie in New York to make plans.

18 Feb The Stones' financial, legal and business advisers join Jagger and

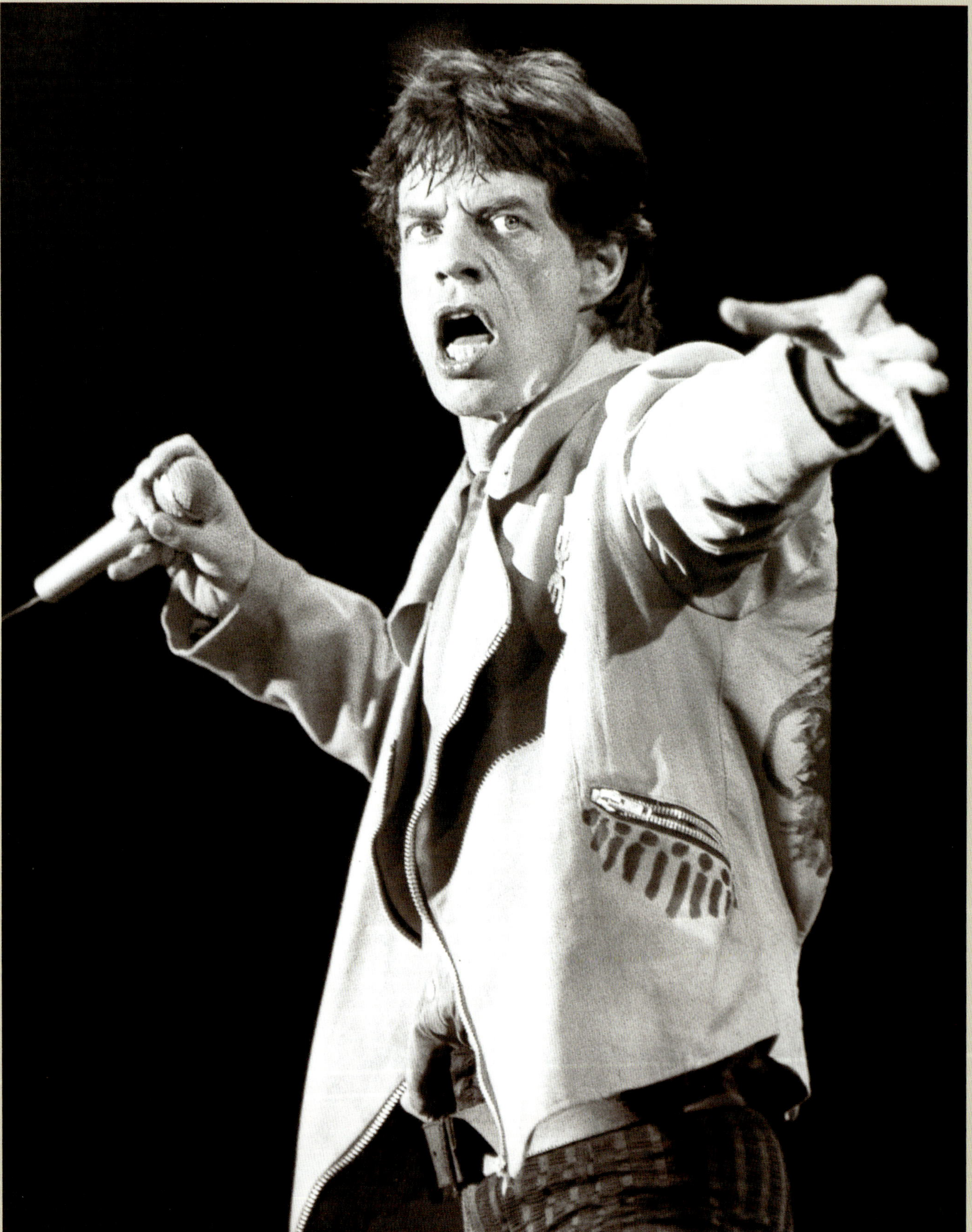

Richards in Barbados. Charlie Watts arrives two days later. Bill Wyman is giving a charity concert in Britain but he and Ronnie Wood join the others in early March.

15 Mar The band sign a multi-million dollar contract – the biggest in rock 'n' roll history – relating to promotion and merchandising of their next tour, for which over 50 dates are proposed.

28 Mar Recording a new album begins in Montserrat.

31 Mar Mandy Smith announces her engagement to Bill Wyman.

9 May Party to launch the opening of Bill Wyman's restaurant, Sticky Fingers, in Kensington. Montserrat recordings completed, this month sees the mixing of the new album in London.

11 May Bill Wyman captains the team he has assembled for a show business charity cricket match in aid of terminally ill children.

17 May A newspaper reports an altercation between Charlie Watts and Mick Jagger in Amsterdam, where the band have gathered for group discussion.

2 Jun Bill Wyman marries Mandy Smith in Bury St Edmunds. Three days later a reception is held at the Grosvenor House Hotel. Mick Jagger gives the couple a £200,000 Picasso etching.

11 Jul The Stones announce the Steel Wheels tour at a press conference at Grand Central Station, New York. There will be an album of the same name. Advance ticket sales for the tour break all records. The band and their entourage set up elaborate camp in Washington, Connecticut.

17 Aug 'Mixed Emotions' is released. It reaches No.5 in the US.

31 Aug Steel Wheels opens in Philadelphia. Black market tickets sell at up to 40 times the original price.

9 Sept 'Mixed Emotions' enters the UK charts, reaching No.33.

19 Dec Final North American date of the tour, in Atlantic City.

1990

Feb The Stones tour Japan for the first time.

14 Feb Steel Wheels opens in Tokyo.

8 Mar *Rolling Stone* magazine nominates the Stones as best band and artists of the year for 1989, *Steel Wheels* best album and 'Mixed Emotions' best single. Mick Jagger is nominated best male singer, Bill Wyman best bassist and Charlie Watts best drummer.

22 Mar Mick Jagger announces the Urban Jungle European tour in London. It will feature a new stage set and lighting and a different playing order from the Steel Wheels shows. By the following day 120,000 tickets for the Wembley concerts have sold out.

18 May The tour opens in Rotterdam and moves through France, Germany, Portugal, Spain, Ireland, Italy, Austria, Sweden, Norway and Denmark.

Jul Release of *Voodoo Lounge*.

4 Jul British concerts open at Wembley.

9 Aug The European leg of the tour closes in Copenhagen.

Sept/Oct The tour moves to Australia.

1991

1 Mar Julian Temple directs the 'Highwire' video in New York.

2 Apr The Stones' fifth live album, *Flashpoint*, is released.

2 May The Stones are honoured at the Ivor Novello awards in London for an outstanding contribution to British music.

19 Nov The Rolling Stones sign to Virgin Records.

10 Dec Keith Richards and The X-Pensive Winos' live album is released on CD and video.

1992

The Rolling Stones do not tour or release an album this year.

Aug Ronnie Wood's solo album, *Slide On This*, is released.

20 Oct Keith Richards' second solo album, *Main Offender*, is released.

27 Nov Keith and the Winos begin a short European tour.

31 Dec Keith and his band play at a small New York venue.

1993

Bill Wyman and Mandy Smith divorce.

Jan Bill Wyman leaves The Rolling Stones. Bassist Darryl Jones replaces Bill for the 1994/5 Voodoo Lounge tour.

10 Jan Ronnie Wood gives the first of four solo concerts in Japan.

17 Jan Keith Richards' Main Offender tour opens in Seattle.

9 Feb Mick Jagger's third solo album, *Wandering Spirit*, is released.

16 Feb Bill Wyman stands in for ailing bassist Ronnie Lane at a Faces reunion performance at London's Brit Awards.

Apr Mick and Keith fly to Barbados to begin writing songs for a new album, shortly joined by Charlie Watts.

9 Jul Recording begins in Ireland.

12 Oct The Charlie Watts Quintet release *Warm & Tender*.

28 Nov Virgin release *Jump Back*, an 18-track greatest hits CD compilation.

1994

Jan The Rolling Stones win an MTV lifetime achievement award and a *Billboard* Award for Artistic Excellence.

Aug The two-year Voodoo Lounge tour opens in the US.

10 Nov The Rolling Stones are the first rock 'n' roll band to broadcast live on the Internet.

1995

Jan The South American leg of the tour opens with concerts in Mexico and Argentina. Shows in South Africa, Japan and Australasia follow.

30 Aug The tour closes in Rotterdam. Live recordings during the tour are released as *Stripped* in November.

1996

Oct *Rock 'n' Roll Circus* is released. Charlie Watts' quintet release *Long Ago And Far Away*, an album of jazz and swing classics. Keith Richards works on a solo album.

1997

23 Sept The Bridges To Babylon tour opens in Chicago. Young Leah Wood, Ronnie's daughter, guests with the band at Wembley.

Oct Bill Wyman announces the formation of his new band, The Rhythm Kings. A first album, *Struttin' Our Stuff*, features guest musicians Eric Clapton, Albert Lee, Georgie Fame and Peter Frampton.

16 Oct Bill Wyman's first live performance since leaving The Rolling Stones, at the Forum, London.

18 Dec It is announced that so far the *Bridges To Babylon* tour of North America has grossed nearly $87 million – a box office record.

1998

23 Apr The tour closes in Chicago – where it had started months earlier.

11 Aug The Rolling Stones play in Moscow for the first time.

2 Nov *No Security*, recorded live at an Amsterdam concert, is released.

1999

Jan Jerry Hall files for divorce from Mick Jagger but wins an annulment; the court did not recognize the Bali marriage. Afterwards she said Mick's settlement was 'very generous'.

10 Jun The Rolling Stones play slightly longer than agreed at a small venue in west London and are fined £50,000 for breaching regulations.

9 Jul In *Death Of A Rolling Stone* author Anna Wohlin (Brian Jones' girlfriend at the time of his death) asserts that he was murdered.

27 Jul DNA tests confirm Mick Jagger is the father of Luciana Morad's baby.

Oct Mick Jagger resumes residence in his former 'marital' home with Jerry Hall. The couple live amicably in separate parts of the house.

13 Nov A remix of 'It's Only Rock 'N' Roll' is released as a Christmas single, with proceeds going to charity.

26 Nov A landlord defeats Mick Jagger and Keith Richards in the High Court after the Stones attempt to sue him for exploitation because he named his pub 'Rolling Stone'.

2000

3 Jan '(I Can't Get No) Satisfaction' tops a US poll of the 100 greatest rock songs of all time.

16 Jan A spokesman denies that Downing Street had vetoed a knighthood for Mick Jagger in the Queen's New Year's honours, in which both Elton John and Paul McCartney were knighted.

28 Mar Mick Jagger returns to his old school, Dartford Grammar, to open a new arts centre named after him.

May Mick, Ronnie, Charlie and Keith play at a private pub gig in south London – a wake for the band's long-term employee Joe Seabrook who died shortly before, aged 58.

27 May Band members convene at the funeral of Eva Jagger, Mick's 87-year-old mother.

30 Jun Ronnie Wood checks into the Priory Clinic in London. He calls 'time' at his private pub in the grounds of his house in Ireland.

3 Jul Mick Jagger and Marsha Hunt attend the wedding of their daughter Karis, in San Francisco.

2 Dec Jade Jagger and her two children survive a car crash near their home in Ibiza. Mick and Bianca Jagger charter a jet to take them to Britain for treatment.

Andrew Loog Oldham's memoirs, *Stoned*, are published, with cheerfully unrepentant insights into the early years. Its author, now a Scientologist and living in Bogotá, expresses no regret about his parting of the ways with the band he helped to create.

Jerry Hall appears as Mrs Robinson in *The Graduate* in London's West End.

2001

Mar UK newspaper the *Sun* reports a rift between Mick and Keith – the latter apparently worried that Mick is more interested in film projects than getting back on the road.

Aug Bono, Pete Townsend and Missy Elliott, among others, join Mick Jagger as he records his next solo album, *Goddess In The Doorway*.

23 Oct Mick Jagger announces that the Stones will tour again after he has promoted *Goddess In The Doorway*.

2002

May A new Rolling Stones tour is announced in New York.

31 May *The Rolling Stones Remastered* series is announced. Twenty-two classic albums, various compilations and singles will be reformatted for modern home music technology.

16 Aug The Live Licks tour opens in Toronto. The first leg finishes in Las Vegas in February 2003.

2003

Feb/Mar Australian leg of the Live Licks tour. It moves to Asia in March, crosses Europe, and finishes with two concerts in Hong Kong in November.

Dec Michael Phillip Jagger is knighted for services to music.

2004

Jun Charlie Watts is diagnosed with throat cancer. Radiotherapy treatment puts it into remission.

1 Nov *Live Licks*, a double live album of the tour, is released.

2005

26 Jul The band announce plans for their first new album for eight years.

Aug 'Streets of Love' is released as a double A with 'Rough Justice', both from the forthcoming album.

10 Aug A Bigger Bang tour kicks off in Toronto. It covers North and South America, Australasia and Europe, finishing in August 2007.

5 Sept *A Bigger Bang* is released.

2006

27 Apr Keith Richards suffers a head injury after falling out of a tree on holiday in Fiji, and later undergoes cranial surgey in New Zealand.

Oct/Nov Martin Scorsese films concerts at New York's Beacon Theater. The resulting film, *Shine A Light*, is released in 2008.

2007

May Premiere of *Pirates of the Caribbean: At World's End*, in which Keith Richards has a cameo role as Captain Jack Sparrow's father.

10 Jun The Stones appear at the Isle of Wight Festival – their first festival performance for 30 years.

26 Aug Final date of the A Bigger Bang tour at the O2 Arena in London.

2 Oct Mick Jagger releases a compilation of his solo work, *The Very Best of Mick Jagger*.

2008

1 Apr *Shine a Light*, the soundtrack to the Scorsese film, is released and debuts at No.2 in the UK charts.

Jul Ronnie Wood leaves his wife of 23 years for a young Russian model.

2009

25 Oct Bill Wyman fills in for the late Ronnie Lane at a Faces reunion concert, performing alongside Ronnie Wood.

Nov The divorce of Jo and Ronnie Wood is finalized. The following month, Ronnie and the Russian model part company.

2010

17 Apr 'Plundered My Soul' is released as a limited edition single in honour of Record Store Day.

23 May *Exile On Main Street* is reissued and goes straight to No.1 again in the UK charts.

Sept Ronnie Wood releases his seventh solo album, *I Feel Like Playing*.

11 Oct *Ladies and Gentlemen: The Rolling Stones* is released in cinemas and later on to DVD. A digitally remastered version of the film was shown in select theatres across the US.

26 Oct Publication of Keith Richards' memoirs, *Life*.

2011

19 Apr An Ian Stewart tribute album, *Boogie 4 Stu*, features The Rolling Stones with Bill Wyman for the first time in 20 years, performing Bob Dylan's 'Watchin' the River Flow'.

May Premiere of *Pirates of the Caribbean: On Stranger Tides*, in which Keith Richards appears again as Captain Jack Sparrow's father.

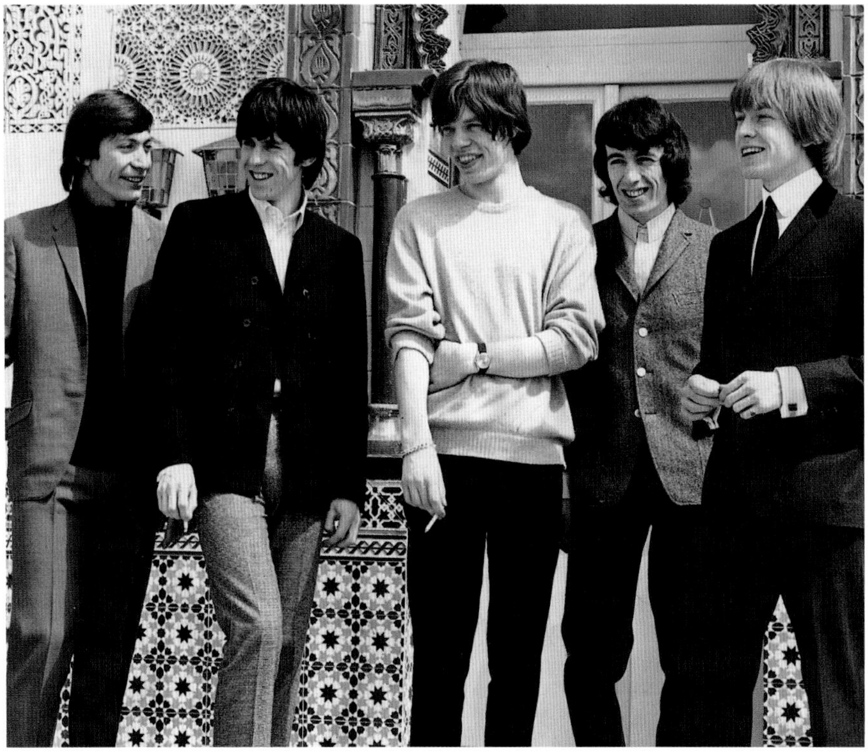

Bibliography

Days in the Life, Jonathon Green, Pimlico, London, 1998

The Stones, Philip Norman, Sidgwick and Jackson, London, 2001

A Life on the Road, ed. Jools Holland and Dora Lowenstein, Virgin, London, 1998

The Rolling Stones, Robert Palmer, Sphere, London, 1984

Up and Down with the Rolling Stones, Tony Sanchez and John Blake, Blake, London, 1991

The Rolling Stones Chronicle, Massimo Bonanno, Plexus, London, 1990

The Rolling Stones Rip This Joint, Steve Appleford, Thunder's Mouth Press, New York, 2000

Complete Guide to the Music of the Rolling Stones, James Hector, Omnibus Press, London, 1995

Acknowledgements

The photographs in this book are from the archives of the *Daily Mail*. They have been carefully maintained by the dedicated staff in the Picture Library, without whose help this book would not have been possible.

Particular thanks to Steve Torrington, Dave Sheppard, Brian Jackson, Alan Pinnock, Paul Rossiter, Richard Jones and all the staff.

Thanks also to Karen Beaulah, Trevor Bunting, Julie Crane, John Dunne, Anthony Linden, Tim Newton, Nicki Pendleton Wood, Cliff Salter, Sandra Stafford and Peter Wright.